WORDS, NAMES AND HISTORY

Selected Writings of Cecily Clark

Cecily Clark (1926–1992) is familiar to medievalists in the United Kingdom and abroad as the editor of the *Peterborough Chronicle*; others will know her work in Anglo-Saxon, Anglo-Norman and Middle English studies, in particular her extensive researches in medieval English onomastics. She lectured at the universities of London, Edinburgh and Aberdeen before settling in Cambridge as a Research Fellow of, successively, Newnham College and Clare Hall. She was a past joint editor of *Nomina*, a Council member of the English Place-Name Society, and a member of the International Committee of Onomastic Sciences.

This volume contains a series of Cecily Clark's masterly and innovative essays on personal-naming patterns in post-Conquest England, ranging from case studies of towns in which contact between settler and native was especially close (Canterbury, Battle, King's Lynn) to a series of fundamental discussions of the linguistic situation in late eleventh- and twelfth-century England as a whole, in particular of the role of women as name-bearers, and of the unexpected persistence of Old English as the dominant language of everyday speech long after the Conquest.

Other items reprinted include articles on the principles and methodology of onomastic research; a small but important group of studies of the *Liber Vitae* of Thorney Abbey; and four essays that show her using linguistic tools to illuminate such apparently familiar texts as *The Battle of Maldon* and *Sir Gawain and the Green Knight*.

Cecily Clark in Vienne in 1981
By courtesy of Gordon Anderson

WORDS, NAMES
AND
HISTORY

Selected Writings of
Cecily Clark

EDITED BY   Peter Jackson

D. S. BREWER

First published 1995
D. S. Brewer, Cambridge

ISBN 0 85991 402 X

D. S. Brewer is an imprint of Boydell & Brewer Ltd
PO Box 9, Woodbridge, Suffolk IP12 3DF, UK
and of Boydell & Brewer Inc.
PO Box 41026, Rochester, NY 14604–4126, USA

British Library Cataloguing-in-Publication Data
Clark, Cecily
    Words, Names and History:Selected
    Writings of Cecily Clark
    I. Title   II. Jackson, Peter
    412
    ISBN 0–85991–402–X

Library of Congress Cataloging-in-Publication Data
Clark, Cecily.
    Words, names, and history : selected writings of Cecily Clark /
edited by Peter Jackson.
        p.   cm.
    Includes bibliographical references and index.
    ISBN 0–85991–402–X
    1. English language – Middle English, 1100–1500 – Etymology –
Names. 2. English language – Old English, ca. 450–1100 – Etymology
– Names.   3. Great Britain – History – Medieval period, 1066–1485.
4. Names, Geographical – England.   5. Names, Personal – England.
6. Names, English. I. Jackson, Peter, 1960– . II. Title.
PE262.C57   1995
427'.02–dc20   94–17927

The paper used in this publication meets the minimum requirements
of American National Standard for Information Sciences –
Permanence of Paper for Printed Library Materials, ANSI Z39.48–1984

Printed in Great Britain by
St Edmundsbury Press Ltd, Bury St Edmunds, Suffolk

Contents

STUDIES IN HISTORY, LITERATURE AND LANGUAGE

ESSAYS IN ONOMASTICS

— PRINCIPLES AND METHODOLOGY

— POST-CONQUEST ENGLAND: GENERAL STUDIES

Introduction

When Cecily Clark died in Cambridge in March 1992 at the age of 65, the desire was soon expressed by those colleagues and friends closest to her to see collected some of the most characteristic and original examples of her academic writing. This need, often felt when researchers as energetic and vigorously productive as Cecily have passed away, was particularly urgent in her case, for the specialized nature of her interests meant that much of her work was widely scattered and not easily accessible; moreover, the scholarly article was a form in which, with her flair for lucid, precisely-directed argument, thoroughly researched and scrupulously documented, she felt most readily at home. This volume is the outcome. This is not the place to attempt an assessment of the permanent value of Cecily's achievement in her chosen provinces, and Professor Peter Clemoes' appreciation that follows this note will give a sensitive and uniquely informed impression of her memorable personality.* But it may not be amiss to add here a few words by way of introduction to give the barest outline of her life, to summarize her principal concerns and preoccupations, and to suggest what may be seen as the unifying themes and characteristics of her work.

Cecily Clark was born in London in 1926, the only child of a civil servant and a former lady's companion, and like many of her generation, her earliest education was interrupted by the War. For seven years she was a pupil at Dame Alice Owen's School (then still in Islington), but the Pitman College in Southampton Row was the only institution in the heart of wartime London where she could prepare for Oxford entrance. Thereafter, however, her progress was rapid. Entering St Hugh's College in 1945 as its Jubilee Scholar, in 1948 she graduated with First Class Honours in English, and after a period of graduate research she embarked on an academic career that took her from assistant lectureships to lectureships at King's College, London, Edinburgh University and latterly Aberdeen. It was in this city in 1959 that she married Gordon Anderson, a university administrator and himself a native Aberdonian, whom she had met when they were contemporaries at Oxford; and it was when her husband's profession took him south to Cambridge in 1965 that the decisive break in her life occurred, when she gave up her own career and for the next quarter-century worked very largely as an independent scholar.

It is tempting – but as I shall suggest later, I think partly illusory – to see this break reflected in her published writing. Differences in size of output, and perhaps also in range, there certainly were. The earlier years of her scholarly life, from 1952 to about 1970, culminate in the book by which she is probably best known to British

---

* Obituaries of Cecily have been published in *Journal of the English Place-Name Society*, 24 (1991–92), 51–52 (Margaret Gelling); *Newnham College Roll Letter*, 1993, 93–95 (Liesbeth van Houts), *Nomina*, 15 (1991–92), 130–33 (O.J. P[adel]), *Onoma*, 31 (1992–93), 42–43 (Margaret Gelling) and *St Hugh's College Chronicle*, 65 (1991–92), 87–89 (Helen Wallis and Gordon Anderson), and one is forthcoming in *Medieval English Studies Newsletter* (Alexander Rumble); shorter notices or reports have appeared in *Annual Bibliography of English Language and Literature*, 64 (1990), v (E[lizabeth] E[rskine]), *Clare Hall Newsletter*, 1991–92, 57 and in *England in the Eleventh Century: Proceedings of the 1990 Harlaxton Symposium*, edited by Carola Hicks (Stamford, 1992), p. xii (Lisbeth van Houts).

medievalists, her superb edition of the 1070–1154 annals of *The Peterborough Chronicle*, originally prepared as an Oxford thesis under the supervision of C.L. Wrenn and subsequently published by OUP in 1958, with a second, and thoroughly revised, edition in 1970. But if her bibliography in those years was dominated by several articles on historical and linguistic aspects of the *Chronicle*, whose content was later, and rightly, to be absorbed into her edition, they had never represented her only interest. Gifted with naturally wide intellectual sympathies, she had responded eagerly to a thorough training in the Oxford English school of the 1940s, with its characteristic emphasis on literary history and criticism as much as on philology, and some of these broader interests found expression in print – that they were not more is largely owing to the heavy burden of teaching and administration that she bore throughout that time. *Sir Gawain and the Green Knight* in particular was an early and continuing love. It provided the inspiration for her only published foray into verse, and her last academic contribution to the study of the poem (a review) appeared as late as 1985; while a 1966 paper on 'characterisation by syntax' in the romance (reprinted here) showed her at her distinctive, precise and keenly sensitive best in employing linguistic tools for a literary-critical end: it is significant that it appeared in *Essays in Criticism*, which at that time, under the editorship of F.W. Bateson, was a flagship for the Oxford ideal of the scholar-critic. Similar work on the bilingual poetry of Charles d'Orléans, only a little of which appeared in print, gave her the opportunity to extend her range still further, into medieval French; while at the end of this first period her attention was drawn to the stylistic analysis of a text whose qualities as literature are sometimes overlooked, when she contributed to the *Festschrift* of her friend and mentor Professor Dorothy Whitelock a notable essay on 'The Narrative Mode of *The Anglo-Saxon Chronicle* Before the Conquest'.

Cecily's earliest work, concentrating as it did on an historical work that also has much to say to those interested in the fortunes of the English language in the post-Conquest period, already showed her peculiar genius for blending historical with philological scholarship; and the period in which she had chosen to specialize of course required an informed awareness of the historical and linguistic situation in contemporary Normandy and the surrounding territories. But it was only compara-tively late in life, after her move to Cambridge and her withdrawal from full-time teaching, that the second phase of her career began, when, under the initial guidance of Professor Giles Constable, she at last found a field in which all her gifts could be used to the full: onomastics, and in particular the study of personal naming patterns in England in the two centuries after the Conquest. The wealth of surviving material, the uniqueness, by definition, of each scrap of primary evidence, and the possibility thus raised of a *pointilliste* re-creation of the population of a medieval community, all fascinated her. But personal names were of more than antiquarian interest, for their persistence made them channels of cultural survival, even when their language of origin was changing or dead, and, perhaps most importantly for her, they raised questions of etymology, distribution and transmission that required both historical and linguistic tools for their answer.

Once launched on this new topic, she soared. Beginning in 1976 with a paper in the *Journal of Medieval History* on 'People and Languages in Post-Conquest Canterbury', she went on to publish over the next fifteen years a series of masterly, innovative essays ranging from analyses of naming-evidence in centres where language contact between English and French was especially close (Canterbury, Battle, King's Lynn) to entirely original reassessments of the linguistic situation in late eleventh- and twelfth-century

England as a whole. Central to her concerns throughout were the role of women in the century after the Conquest (not least as name-bearers) and the interaction of the English and French languages at that time, especially the persistence of Old English as the dominant language of everyday speech, even among the invaders or settlers. To everything she wrote she brought a rare fusion of historical awareness, philological expertise, shrewd common sense and a lucid and vigorous prose style, so that a subject that in other hands can sometimes be obscure was never less than exciting and thought-provoking in hers. Moreover, her work, if anything, gained in confidence and distinction with the passing years: some of her most daring and iconoclastic articles, such as a fundamental reassessment of Zachrisson's eighty-year-old monograph on *Anglo-Norman Influence on English Place-Names* and two closely associated papers on 'The Myth of "the Anglo-Norman scribe" ' and 'Domesday Book – a Great Red-Herring: Thoughts on Some Late-Eleventh-Century Orthographies' (all reprinted here) were produced in the last two or three years of her life. Nor, except perhaps towards the end, did this absorption in things onomastic lead to any narrowing of focus in her intellectual interests. Papers written for *Nottingham Medieval Studies* in 1983, and for an Amiens *colloque* in 1979, saw her once more using linguistic evidence (by now onomastic) to shed fresh light on literary texts, in one case as well-known a poem as *The Battle of Maldon*, and in the other the still partly unexplored terrain of twelfth-century Anglo-Latin hagiography. She was keenly responsive to the explosion of interest in women's history in the 1980s, contributing to a collaborative volume published in 1984 a chapter on women in post-Conquest England that showed such thorough mastery of primary and secondary material (among which her own onomastic work, though she was too modest to acknowledge it in the bibliography, found an informative but unobtrusive place), and such a gift for clear and forcible exposition for an intelligent if unspecialized audience, that it is a pity she did not write more in that vein. Her undiminished output at the end of her life gives ample evidence that she died still at the height of her powers.

One's admiration for this achievement grows when it is remembered how much of it was carried out with little formal recognition. For over twenty-five years she had no academic position, other than short-term research fellowships (one of them non-stipendiary) at two Cambridge colleges and a looser association, in the form of a Directorship of Studies, with a third. The extent of this marginalization should not, however, be exaggerated. She was able to supervise undergraduates, to attend and address seminars, and occasionally to lecture; she had the resources of a great university library within easy reach; she had almost no administrative responsibilities; and her home life was secure in every way. It ought to be remembered, too, that much of her best work was produced when she was already over fifty – an age at which any scholar would find a return to full-time employment difficult. But these years of comparative isolation took their toll nonetheless. She had no opportunity to build up a research school, nor had she the stimulus of daily contact with equal minds that a lectureship or a permanent fellowship would have brought her, and there were times when she felt this deprivation keenly.

Undoubtedly, too, this anomaly was in part responsible for the neglect of much of her work in this country, even by professional medievalists, but there were other reasons also; for instance, one of her preferred forums, the journal *Nomina* (of which she was an editor and a leading spirit) was not widely read outside the small company of English onomasts. More significantly, however, she was perhaps the victim of her own great virtue of a lack of insularity, for in some ways her work was more akin to that of continental than of English scholars. She was a regular attender and speaker at French academic conferences, and her research on monastic confraternity lists had more in common with that of French or German colleagues than with anything being done at that time in this country, though here too she had her own distinctive contribution to make, for the thrust of her work (unlike, for example, that of Karl Schmid and Joachim Wollasch's school at Freiburg and Münster) was as much onomastic as prosopographical. Some wider recognition, it is true, came at the very end of her life, when she was given the opportunity to distil much of her learning in two long essays on 'Onomastics' contributed to the first two volumes of the *Cambridge History of the English Language* (1992); it is thought that both of these (perhaps in particular the second, on the period 1066–1476) will become the classic discussion of their subject. Yet there is still an urgent need for the earlier studies that preceded these articles to be made available here in a more easily accessible form, for three reasons. First, because in the longer essays the detailed evidence that she had previously so skilfully marshalled in several invaluable case-studies had to be fragmented rather than discussed in its proper informative context; secondly, and conversely, because it was not possible in the longer studies to do more than summarize the fundamental reconsideration of the linguistic situation in post-Conquest England which she was engaged on at the time of her death; and thirdly, and fundamentally, because all her essays are models of how historical and linguistic scholarship can be mutually illuminating.

Yet this does not exhaust the scope and interest of Cecily's work. Unable (as she said herself) ever to resist an intellectual challenge, she was forever conscious of the need to place her research on a firm methodological base, and a few short papers reprinted here show her articulating what she saw as the characteristic principles of onomastic research in a way that was not possible in her more specialized writings; one of these in particular ('Certains éléments français de l'anthroponymie anglaise du Moyen Age: essai méthodologique') also includes a charming fragment of autobiography. Here too a place has been found for a small group of articles on the *Liber Vitae*, or confraternity book, of Thorney Abbey – which is, however, only a fragment of a much longer study of that document, taking its inspiration from the work of the late Olof von Feilitzen, that she had planned but was never able to finish: the material is now in the hands of Dr John Insley. Finally, I have added one or two specimens of her detailed and forthright reviews (which were themselves often real contributions to scholarship) and of her short articles on topics in what might be called 'popular onomastics', such as the paper on the evidence for nicknaming practice to be gleaned from 'naive' memoirs. These last selections reveal in their ripest form Cecily's forthrightness, her down-to-earth, practical common sense and her humour – but these were characteristics that were never wholly absent from her writing, for she had no embarrassment in drawing on the rest of her life and experience even in her most serious work when the insights they gave could be genuinely illuminating. A good example of this is to be found in some of her earliest onomastic work, when she speculated whether the emergent Anglo-Norman gentry 'disdain[ed] employing local maids for their children' – for her parents had met in India, and though Cecily herself never lived there, her perception of the English nurse or servant as a conduit of the native vernacular in a Norman, or partly Norman, household surely owed much to that mainstay of Anglo-Indian life, the *ayah*. Few scholars, however, would have admitted that an interpretation of a problematic Middle English term was inspired by 'the legend . . . observed on cartons in the chill-cabinet and subsequently on the family table' during a holiday in France; and less seriously, perhaps – though she might not have recognized the distinction – she was prepared to characterize a list of citations from earlier scholars with whom she wished to take issue as a '*hortus siccus*' (she was a keen gardener), and once observed that variation in current English speech-styles was exemplified by what could be heard 'around the paddock on any racecourse' (she loved horses and was a devoted attender at Newmarket).

This unity of style and character that I have tried to indicate extends also to the larger themes of her research. I said earlier that her work divided into two parts, with the break occurring about 1970, and a glance at the distribution of the items in her bibliography will show in what an obvious sense that is true. But surveying all her publications (and even the present generous selection includes only part of her writings), one is struck far more by the continuities than by the contrasts that they present. Throughout her life she was impatient of conventional academic distinctions and boundaries. Her early work on *The Peterborough Chronicle*, no less than her later onomastic researches, is historical as much as linguistic; the same fusion of literary andlinguistic concerns informed her discussions of *Sir Gawain and the Green Knight* in 1966 and of *The Battle of Maldon* in 1983; her interest in the 1960s in the English poetry of a French exile, Charles d'Orléans, was of the same order as her pre-occupation in the 1970s and after with the bilingualism of children and townspeople in the century after the Conquest. Under everything she wrote lay one abiding fascination, however far from it she sometimes appeared to have travelled: with the lost reality of the spoken languages of medieval England. It was the same interest that inspired her essays on colloquialism in *Sir Gawain* and *Ancrene Wisse* that finally found expression in her study of personal names, with their stamp of everyday speech (whether English or French) and their vivid particularity. In her own written style, too, for all its meticulous literacy, the tones of a speaking voice – alert, assured, but with a delight in its very crispness and concision – are clearly audible. Yet the exemplary strength of the best of Cecily Clark's work lies in her ability to transcend the sometimes narrow categories of material she had chosen to exploit, and to speak to those outside her immediate area of expertise: to historians; to philologists; and indeed to any medi-evalists who practise interdisciplinary, boundary-crossing scholarship of the kind that pervaded everything she wrote. There can be few scholars whose achievement, for all its apparent diversity, yet forms so coherent a whole.

In reprinting these articles and reviews, I have corrected obvious misprints and a few minor inconsistencies (some of which Cecily Clark had noted on her own copies), and have occasionally supplied publication details for work which she had referred to only as 'forthcoming'. I have also, where appropriate, replaced references in the originals to other publications by the writer with cross-references to the pagination in the present volume. In two cases ('People and Languages in Post-Conquest Canterbury' and 'Some Early Canterbury Surnames') Cecily had left heavily annotated working copies of her articles, perhaps in anticipation of eventual reprinting, and I have tried wherever possible to incorporate these revisions here. It has not seemed necessary to draw attention in the text to most of these corrections and emendations (though a list of places of first publication is supplied at pp. xiii–xiv below for any reader who wishes to check the wording of the originals), but in a few cases slightly larger editorial interventions are supplied within double square brackets, thus: [[ ]]. It must be emphas-ized, however, that no systematic checking, revision or standardization of the originals has been undertaken, and in particular, that there has been no attempt to impose consistency on the references in over a thousand footnotes; with the exceptions just mentioned, these writings are reprinted here substantially as they first appeared.

Several people have helped bring this book about. Margaret Gelling, John Insley, Alexander Rumble and Elisabeth van Houts helped me choose articles and reviews to reprint, or spoke to me about Cecily's work and personality. Peter Clemoes generously allowed me to publish here the address he gave at Cecily's memorial service in Cambridge. Paul Cavill (Survey of English Place-Names), and Mrs A.T. Williamson and Mr W.J. Hamilton-Hinds (Dame Alice Owen's School) and Helen Pandeli advised me on specific problems. Treve Brown twice came to my rescue at critical points in the preparation of the onomastic index. Derek Brewer first suggested that I should edit the book, and Richard Barber and Pru Harrison of Boydell and Brewer bore with me while I finished it. My greatest debt, however, is to Gordon Anderson, Cecily's husband, first for entrusting this work to one who at the time was virtually a stranger, but more especially for his patience and good humour, endless practical assistance and untiring hospitality. Needless to say, none of these scholars and friends are responsible for any errors or misunderstandings which remain.

Peter Jackson
October 1995

Places of First Publication

The articles and reviews reprinted here first appeared in the following places and are reprinted by kind permission of the original publishers or copyright holders.

1   *England Before the Conquest: Studies in Primary Sources Presented to Dorothy Whitelock*, edited by Peter Clemoes and Kathleen Hughes (Cambridge: CUP, 1971), 215–35

2   *Nottingham Medieval Studies*, 27 (1983), 1–22

3   *Le récit bref au Moyen Age: Université de Picardie, Centre d'études médiévales: Actes du Colloque des 27, 28 et 29 avril 1979*, edited by Danielle Buschinger (Paris: Champion, 1980), 287–311

4   *Essays in Criticism*, 16 (1966), 361–74

5   Christine Fell, Cecily Clark and Elizabeth Williams, *Women in Anglo-Saxon England and the Impact of 1066* (London: British Museum Publications, 1984), 148–71

6   *Nomina*, 3 (1979), 13–19

7   *L'Onomastique, témoin de l'activité humaine (Actes du Colloque du Creusot, 31 mai–2 juin 1984)*, edited by Gérard Taverdet (Fontaine-lès-Dijon: Association bourguignonne de dialectologie et d'onomastique, 1985), 259–67

8   *Papers from the 5th International Conference on English Historical Linguistics*, edited by Sylvia Adamson *et al.*, Current Issues in Linguistic Theory, 65 (Amsterdam and Philadelphia: Benjamins, 1990), 55–68

9   *Naming, Society and Regional Identity*, edited by David Postles (Oxford: Leopard's Head Press, forthcoming)

10   *Speculum*, 53 (1978), 223–51

11   *Language Contact in the British Isles: Proceedings of the Eighth International Symposium on Language Contact in Europe, Douglas, Isle of Man, 1988*, edited by P. Sture Ureland and George Broderick (Tübingen: Niemeyer, 1991), 275–95

12   *England in the Eleventh Century: Proceedings of the 1990 Harlaxton Symposium*, edited by Carola Hicks, Harlaxton Medieval Studies, 2 (Stamford: Paul Watkins, 1992), 317–31

13   *History of Englishes: New Methods and Interpretations in Historical Linguistics*, edited by Matti Rissanen *et al.*, Topics in English Linguistics, 10 (Berlin and New York: Mouton de Gruyter, 1992), 117–29

14   *Journal of Medieval History*, 2 (1976), 1–33

15   *English Studies*, 57 (1976), 294–309

16   *Proceedings of the Battle Conference on Anglo-Norman Studies*, 2 (1980 for 1979), 21–41 and 168–72

17   *Nomina*, 6 (1982), 51–71 *and* 7 (1983), 65–89

18   *Nomina*, 11 (1987), 7–33

19   *Anglo-Norman Studies*, 7 (1985) (=*Proceedings of the Battle Conference 1984*), 50–65 (with an appendix by Elisabeth M.C. van Houts, 66–68)

20   *Nomina*, 9 (1985), 53–72

21   *Studies in Honour of René Derolez*, edited by A.M. Simon-Vandenbergen (Gent: Seminarie voor Engelse en Oud-Germaanse Taalkunde RUG, 1987), 73–85

22   *Nomina*, 5 (1981), 83–94

23   *Studies in Honour of Kenneth Cameron*, edited by Thorlac Turville-Petre and Margaret Gelling (=*Leeds Studies in English*, NS 18 [1987]), 101–10

24   *Nomina*, 4 (1980), 88–90

25   *Nomina*, 6 (1982), 101–05

26   *Nomina*, 10 (1986), 180–83

27   *Nomina*, 14 (1990–91), 127–30

Cecily Clark: An Appreciation

Gonville and Caius College Chapel, Cambridge, 17 October 1992

I daresay most of us present today will have known Cecily as the life and soul of many a conference. The directness and exacting standards of her papers invariably made their mark on such gatherings, while her lively, pertinent, conversation, her irrepressible sense of humour, her forthright wit, her gaiety, her sheer sense of fun, never failed to leave an indelible impression. Here, one immediately felt, was a vivid, rare sort of person, sharing joyously with others like-minded the academic pursuits which she had made especially her own. No wonder that one of the many who wrote marvellously appreciative letters to Gordon, when shocked to hear of her untimely death, paid this simple tribute: 'the "Battle" Conferences, which Cecily attended every year, will never be the same without her.'

A considerable number, only some of whom can be here today, have been privileged to count her as a loyal friend, too, perhaps of long-standing, as my wife and I came to know her and Gordon living next door for some twenty-five years. Over time, and with close connections such as ours, her unstinted warmth and affection came to the fore, and also, not unrelated to a sense of her own insecurity, her sweetness and sympathy for others when afflicted or sad. And so did her clearcut enthusiasms and disapprovals, among the former her fondness for dogs, birds, horses, especially the last; her love of gardening, bringing out the peasant in her, she used to say; her engagement with the imprint of history on her surroundings; her pleasure in visits abroad, particularly in France; her ceaseless attention to the puzzlements of language and her ever-ready comic perception of incongruity of any sort, to say nothing of her raciness in expressing it. Our social parties she used to regard as definitely too staid. Gordon and she have indeed formed a special couple for their many friends. As letters to Gordon have made abundantly clear, I know I speak for all in offering to him our heartfelt sympathy for his premature loss of such a many-faceted partner.

Today, however, on this occasion, we hold in honour, perhaps more than anything else, Cecily's unique contribution to professional scholarship. Following her First in English Honours in Oxford, she initially made her reputation by her critical edition of *The Peterborough Chronicle 1070–1154* for the degree of BLitt, which Professor C.L. Wrenn adjudged 'one of the best editions of a text ever examined here'. In 1958 this elegant piece of work was published in the Oxford English Monographs series, to be reissued in a revised second edition in 1970 and to remain the standard edition to this day. From this auspicious start Cecily never looked back. A stream of lucid, pointed, articles on Old and Middle English language and literature came steadily from her pen in the late 50s, 60s and early 70s, especially in the field of stylistics, as exemplified by her 1966 essay, '*Sir Gawain and the Green Knight*: characterisation by syntax', later to be included, in part, in a collection of *Twentieth-Century Interpretations* of that poem. Most notable, from my point of view, was her brilliant, innovative, analysis of 'The Narrative Mode of *The Anglo-Saxon Chronicle* Before the Conquest' in Dorothy Whitelock's 1971 *Festschrift*. Also exhibited in these relatively early days was a growing cross-disciplinary interest in history, for instance in her *English Historical Review* article of 1969, entitled ' "This Ecclesiastical Adventurer": Henry of Saint-Jean d'Angély'.

But it was in the early 1970s that Cecily really came into her own when she began to focus her many talents on personal naming in Anglo-Norman England, for in that tricky, understudied, field her rigorous historical training in the English language and its continental origins, and her sound knowledge of the other early medieval languages concerned and of the modern languages of later scholarship (including fluent French), backed up by her palaeographic and diplomatic skills, could all join forces effectively with her innate ability for shrewd, close, critical analysis and logical deduction. Moreover, her grasp of the need to correlate assessment of linguistic patterns with patterns of settlement, politics, society and culture quickly made her, in the words of an historian writing to Gordon, 'one of the few philologists who really spoke to historians'. In short, her formidable combination of breadth of outlook, acute analytic faculties and mastery of strict scholarly procedures was invaluable in this difficult, neglected, area of study usually left wide open to speculation.

The source materials which Cecily confronted present the anthroponymist with peculiar difficulties, consisting, as they do, of such disparate, specialized and unevenly distributed survivals. But such limitations held no terrors for her. Here was the challenge she had been looking for. In workmanlike fashion she set about replacing the broad, loosely based, rather vague, impressions then current, by systematically exposing the ambiguities and errors to which any particular body of evidence was prone and by only advancing whatever provisional, cautious, generalizations her findings justified. Her strictness administered douches of new realism. Typically in the 1970s, as witnessed by the title of her article in *Nomina*, 3 (1979), 'Clark's First Three Laws of Applied Anthroponymics', she was thinking out the underlying principles of what she was about. In the 1980s she was characteristically tackling various substantial units of material, an early example being her two-part 'The Early Personal Names of King's Lynn: an Essay in Socio-Cultural History' in *Nomina*, 6 and 7 (1982–3). In the last 80s and the first 90s she was increasingly questioning prevailing concepts, as two posthumously published articles testify, 'The Myth of "the Anglo-Norman Scribe" ' and 'Domesday Book – a Great Red-Herring: Thoughts on Some Late-Eleventh-Century Orthographies', as well as a third article, published before she died, disarmingly entitled 'Towards a reassessment of "Anglo-Norman Influence on English Place-Names" ', which a leading toponymist has characterized as 'a devastating attack on one of the most venerable shibboleths of English place-name study, making it now incumbent upon scholars in that discipline to address themselves to the significance of the points she has raised'.

Deep satisfaction can be felt that Cecily contributed to volumes 1 and 2 of the new *Cambridge History of the English Language*, published this year, two superb state-of-the-art summaries of onomastic study of the Old and Middle English periods. And there is much else to be grateful for, which I have not yet mentioned: her devoted service as an editor of *Nomina*; her frequent and perceptive reviews; her highly successful English adaptation of Georges Bourcier's *Histoire de la langue anglaise* in 1981, subsequently readapted for the Japanese market by Akio Oizumi; her directness and clarity as a teacher (mostly at Aberdeen); her generous help and encouragement to other scholars. Regret there has to be that she has been cut off in full stream while she still had so much to offer; but thankfully this fades in the knowledge that the core of her achievement, her almost single-handed transformation of the study of English personal names in the early, especially Anglo-Norman, period, will be lastingly inherited by future scholars in a volume of collected papers to be edited by Peter Jackson and published by Boydell and Brewer, as soon as may be.

Cecily, as a scholar and as a person, has occupied a position in Old and Middle English name studies which will never be refilled. Few in her time in any discipline have been able to report the complex results of meticulous scholarship with such clarity unpolluted by jargon. And surely no-one else would be expected to write thus in the august pages of *The Cambridge History of the English Language* (about the disadvantages of Domesday Book returns for modern onomastics):

> At the orthographical level, basic to onomastic study, [the extant DB texts] are notoriously unreliable. . . . working conditions were unpropitious: name-material, unlike common vocabulary, cannot be predicted from context, and so the DB clerks, interpreting utterances of witnesses from varied linguistic backgrounds, sometimes perhaps toothless ancients, and editing drafts that bristled with unfamiliarities, were liable to mishear, misread, misunderstand, miscopy or otherwise mangle the forms.

Point taken. Cecily has left her distinctive mark on scholarship right enough, and with it a firm reputation abroad as well as in this country as someone who in any lecture or publication invariably made points which were new, reliable and important.

Peter Clemoes

Cecily Clark: *curriculum vitae*

1926   24 November. Born in London, only child of Thomas Clark (d. 1950), customs watcher, and Mary Beatrice Emily, *née* Milton (d. 1977), formerly a lady's companion

1932–45 Attended Dame Alice Owen's Girls' School, Islington, and Pitman Central College, Southampton Row, London

1945   Entered St Hugh's College, Oxford, as its Jubilee Scholar

1948   First Class Honours, Final Honours School of English, University of Oxford

1952   BLitt, University of Oxford, with a thesis on the 1070–1154 annals of *The Peterborough Chronicle*; first academic publication ('Caxton's "Tullius of Olde Age" ', *Times Literary Supplement*, 22 August)

1952   Temporary Assistant Lecturer in English Language, University College of Hull

1952–55 Assistant Lecturer in English Language, King's College, London

1955–57 Assistant Lecturer in English Language, University of Edinburgh

1957–65 Lecturer in English Language, University of Aberdeen

1958   (ed.) *The Peterborough Chronicle 1070–1154*, Oxford English Monographs 5 (Oxford: OUP)

1959   2 April: married in Aberdeen, Gordon Rae Anderson, university administrator

1966   Moved to Cambridge, after her husband was appointed in 1965 an Assistant Registrary (from 1970 Senior Assistant Registrary) in the General Board Office at the University

1966–69 Mary Bateson Research Fellow, Newnham College, Cambridge

1966–85 Director of Studies in Anglo-Saxon, Norse, and Celtic, Gonville and Caius College, Cambridge

1970   (ed.) *The Peterborough Chronicle 1070–1154*, second edition (Oxford: Clarendon Press)

1976   First publications on onomastic subjects ('People and Languages in Post-Conquest Canterbury', *Journal of Medieval History*, 2 and 'Some Early Canterbury Surnames', *English Studies*, 57)

1977–92 Member, Council for Name Studies in Great Britain and Ireland

1978   First publication in *Nomina* ('Thoughts on the French Connections of Middle English Nicknames')

1978–81 Research Fellow, Clare Hall, Cambridge

1981   English adaptation of *An Introduction to the History of the English Language* by Georges Bourcier (Cheltenham: Stanley Thornes)

1985–92 Joint Editor, *Nomina*

1986–89 Ordinary Member, Council of the English Place-Name Society

1990–92 Member, International Committee of Onomastic Sciences

1991   *An Introduction to the History of the English Language*, further adapted and edited with notes by Akio Oizumi (Tokyo: Nan'un-do)

1992   26 March: died in Cambridge

The Published Writings of Cecily Clark

compiled by Peter Jackson

The present bibliography has for the most part been compiled from a list of her writings kept by Cecily Clark herself, with the addition of a few items (particularly from later years) found among her papers and elsewhere; articles and reviews included in the present selection are indicated with an asterisk (*). An attempt has also been made to list forthcoming papers that had been accepted for publication at the time of Miss Clark's death, even where it is not possible to supply full details at present. Other than these, unpublished writings have not been included, with the (partial) exception of the first item on the list, Miss Clark's Oxford BLitt thesis, for, though not all of this has appeared in print, there is a copy available for consultation in the Bodleian Library (MS B.Litt.d.486–487). The only intentional omissions are of editorials and conference reports in *Nomina*, vols 11 (1987) – 14 (1990–91), and of anonymous contributions to the MHRA *Annual Bibliography of English Language and Literature*, vols 59 (1984) – 65 (1990).

I am indebted to Gordon Anderson, Cecily Clark's husband, for giving me access to his wife's papers. Any remaining errors are, of course, my responsibility alone.

1952

'An Edition of the Annals, 1070 to 1154, of the Peterborough Chronicle, with Introduction, Grammar, Commentary and Glossary', 2 vols (BLitt thesis, University of Oxford). v.1: ccxxxv pp.; v.2: [vi]+192+xciii+xix pp. v.2 includes an 'index verborum' (pp. xvii–xciii) omitted from the published version (for which see 1958 and 1970, below).

'Caxton's "Tullius of Olde Age" ' (letter), *Times Literary Supplement*, 22 August, 549.

'Studies in the Vocabulary of the *Peterborough Chronicle*, 1070–1154', *English and Germanic Studies*, 5 (1952–53), 67–89.

1953

'Gawain in London' (verses), *Oxford Magazine*, 72 (1953–54), 280.

1954

'Appendix: The Anglo-Norman Chronicle', in *The Peterborough Chronicle (The Bodleian MS. Laud Misc. 636)*, Early English Manuscripts in Facsimile, 4, edited by Dorothy Whitelock (Copenhagen: Rosenkilde and Bagger), 39–43.

'A Mediæval Proverb', *English Studies*, 35, 11–15.

'Notes on MS. Laud Misc. 636', *Medium Ævum*, 23, 71–75 and two plates.

' "Sawles Warde" and Herefordshire', *Notes and Queries*, 199, 140.

1955

'The Green Knight Shoeless: A Reconsideration', *Review of English Studies*, NS 6, 174–77.

'Natural Love in *The Parlement of Foules*' (contribution to a discussion), *Essays in Criticism*, 5, 405–07.

1957

'Assistants' Apotheosis?', *University of Edinburgh Gazette*, no. 15 (February), 40–46.
'Gender in "The Peterborough Chronicle" 1070–1154', *English Studies*, 38, 109–15, and
'Corrigenda', 174.

1958

(ed.) *The Peterborough Chronicle 1070–1154*, Oxford English Monographs (Oxford:
Clarendon Press). pp. lxx+120. (See also 1952, above and 1970, below.)

1962

[as Cecily Anderson] 'Confessions of a Rock-Less Gardener', *Journal of the Scottish Rock
Garden Club*, 8 (1962–63), 25–29.

1965

[as Cecily Anderson, with Gordon Anderson] 'The Old Tannery: No. 33 High Street, Old
Aberdeen', *Aberdeen University Review*, 41 (1965–66), 161–73.
(with Henry Hargreaves) 'An Unpublished Old English Psalter-Gloss Fragment', *Notes
and Queries*, 210, 443–46 and plate.

1966

'*Ancrene Wisse* and *Katherine Group*: A Lexical Divergence', *Neophilologus*, 50, 117–24.
*'*Sir Gawain and the Green Knight*: Characterisation by Syntax', *Essays in Criticism*, 16,
361–74 (extract reprinted in *Twentieth-Century Interpretations of Sir Gawain and the
Green Knight*, compiled by Denton Fox [Englewood Cliffs, NJ: Prentice-Hall, 1968],
105–06).

1967

'Byrhtnoth and Roland: A Contrast', *Neophilologus*, 51, 288–93.

1968

'Ælfric and Abbo', *English Studies*, 49, 30–36.
'Early Middle English Prose: Three Essays in Stylistics', *Essays in Criticism*, 18, 361–82.

1969

' "France" and "French" in the *Anglo-Saxon Chronicle*', *Leeds Studies in English*, NS 3,
35–45.
' "This Ecclesiastical Adventurer": Henry of Saint-Jean d'Angély', *English Historical
Review*, 84, 548–60.

1970

(ed.) *The Peterborough Chronicle 1070-1154*, second edition (Oxford: Clarendon Press).
pp. lxxxvii+136. (See also 1952 and 1958, above.)
'A Select Bibliography 1945–1969', addendum to *The English Poems of Charles of Or-
leans*, edited by Robert Steele and Mabel Day, EETS OS 215 and 220, reprint (London:
OUP), pp. 257–60.

1971

'Charles d'Orléans: Some English Perspectives', *Medium Ævum*, 40, 254–61. (See also 'Postscript', 1976, below.)

*'The Narrative Mode of *The Anglo-Saxon Chronicle* Before the Conquest', in *England Before the Conquest: Studies in Primary Sources Presented to Dorothy Whitelock*, edited by Peter Clemoes and Kathleen Hughes (Cambridge: CUP), 215–35.

'*Sir Gawain and the Green Knight*: Its Artistry and its Audience', *Medium Ævum*, 40, 10–30.

1974

'Early Middle English Period' (part of the article 'Literature, Western'), *Encyclopædia Britannica*, 15th edition, 30 vols (Chicago, etc.: Encyclopædia Britannica, Inc.), Macropædia, 10, pp. 1108–09.

'The Middle-English Period (1100–1500). – 1. Introduction' and 'Middle English Literature to 1400. – (3) Travel', in *The New Cambridge Bibliography of English Literature*, edited by George Watson, 1: *600–1600* (Cambridge: CUP), cols 357–84 and 467–74.

1976

*'People and Languages in Post-Conquest Canterbury', *Journal of Medieval History*, 2, 1–33.

'Postscript', *Medium Ævum*, 45, 230–31 (to 'Charles d'Orléans: Some English Perspectives', 1971, above).

*'Some Early Canterbury Surnames', *English Studies*, 57, 294–309.

1977

'As Seint Austin Seith . . .', *Medium Ævum*, 46, 212–18.

'Winchester in the Early Middle Ages' (review article), *Archives*, 13 (1977–78), 84–89.

1978

(with Dorothy Owen) 'Lexicographical Notes From King's Lynn', *Norfolk Archaeology*, 38 (1978–80), 56–69.

'Thoughts on the French Connections of Middle-English Nicknames', *Nomina*, 2, 38–44.

' "Wið scharpe sneteres": Some Aspects of Colloquialism in "Ancrene Wisse" ', *Neuphilologische Mitteilungen*, 79, 341–53.

*'Women's Names in Post-Conquest England: Observations and Speculations', *Speculum*, 53, 223–51.

1979

*'Clark's First Three Laws of Applied Anthroponymics', *Nomina*, 3, 13–19.

'Notes on a *Life* of Three Thorney Saints: Thancred, Torhtred and Tova', *Proceedings of the Cambridge Antiquarian Society*, 69, 45–52.

'Some Early-Twentieth-Century Aberdeen Nicknames', *Aberdeen University Review*, 48 (1979–80), 195–99.

1980

*'Battle c. 1110: An Anthroponymist Looks at an Anglo-Norman New Town', in *Proceedings of the Battle Conference on Anglo-Norman Studies*, 2 (1980 for 1979), 21–41 and 168–72.

*'Certains aspects de l'hagiographie anglo-latine de l'Angleterre anglo-normande', in *Le récit bref au Moyen Age: Université de Picardie, Centre d'études médiévales: Actes du Colloque des 27, 28 et 29 avril 1979*, edited by Danielle Buschinger (Paris: Champion), 287–311.

[as 'Souris'] 'Nugae anthroponymicae', *Nomina*, 4, 14–17.

1981

An Introduction to the History of the English Language (an English adaptation of Georges Bourcier, *Histoire de la langue anglaise* ... . [Paris, 1978]) (Cheltenham: Thornes). viii+230pp. (See also 1979, above and 1991, below.)

'Another Late-Fourteenth-Century Case of Dialect-Awareness', *English Studies*, 62 (1981), 504–05.

'The Middle English Nickname *Kepeharm*', *Nomina*, 5 (1981), 94.

*'Nickname-Creation: Some Sources of Evidence, "Naive" Memoirs Especially', *Nomina*, 5 (1981), 83–94.

[as 'Souris'] 'Nugae anthroponymicae II', *Nomina*, 5 (1981), 77–80.

1982

'Dorothy Whitelock' (obituary), *Nomina*, 6, 2.

*'The Early Personal Names of King's Lynn: An Essay in Socio-Cultural History. Part I – Baptismal Names', *Nomina*, 6, 51–71.

[as 'Souris'] 'Nugae anthroponymicae III', *Nomina*, 6, 43–50.

1983

*'The Early Personal Names of King's Lynn: An Essay in Socio-Cultural History. Part II – By-Names', *Nomina*, 7, 65–89.

*'On Dating *The Battle of Maldon*: Certain Evidence Reviewed', *Nottingham Medieval Studies*, 27, 1–22.

'Starting from *Youlthorpe* (East Riding of Yorkshire): An Onomastic Circular Tour', *Journal of the English Place-Name Society*, 16 (1983–84), 25–37.

[as 'Souris'] 'Nugae anthroponymicae IV', *Nomina*, 7 (1983), 103–16.

1984

*'After 1066: The Factual Evidence', in Christine Fell, Cecily Clark and Elizabeth Williams, *Women in Anglo-Saxon England and the Impact of 1066* (London: British Museum Publications), 148–71; 'Select Bibliography', 197–99.

'L'Angleterre anglo-normande et des ambivalences socio-culturelles. Un coup d'oeil de philologue', in *Les mutations socio-culturelles au tournant des XIe–XIIe siècles: Actes du Colloque international du Centre National de la Recherche Scientifique – Études anselmiennes (IVe session)*, edited by Raymonde Foreville, Spicilegium Beccense, 2 (Paris: Éditions du CNRS), 99–110 (cf. pp. 192, 194, 409).

'L'Anthroponymie cantorbérienne du XIIe siècle: quelques exemples de l'influence normanno-picarde', *Nouvelle revue d'onomastique*, 3/4, 157–66.

'La réalité du mariage aristocratique au XIIe siècle: quelques documents anglais et anglo-normands', in *Amour, mariage et transgressions au Moyen Age: Université de Picardie,*

Centre d'Études médiévales: Actes du Colloque des 24, 25, 26 et 27 mars 1983, edited by Danielle Buschinger and André Crépin, Göppinger Arbeiten zur Germanistik, 420 (Göppingen: Kümmerle), 17–24.

(with M. Bateson) 'Bibliography' and 'Work in Progress', *Nomina*, 8, 121–33 and 134–35.

[As 'Souris'] 'Nugae onomasticae', *Nomina*, 8, 85–95.

1985

*'British Library Additional MS. 40,000, ff. 1v–12r', in *Anglo-Norman Studies*, 7 (= *Proceedings of the Battle Conference 1984*), 50–65 (with an appendix by Elisabeth M.C. van Houts, 66–68).

*'Certains éléments français de l'anthroponymie anglaise du Moyen Age: essai méthodologique', in *L'Onomastique, témoin de l'activité humaine (Actes du Colloque du Creusot, 31 mai–2 juin 1984)*, edited by Gérard Taverdet (Fontaine-lès-Dijon: Association bourguignonne de dialectologie et d'onomastique), 259–67.

*'The *Liber Vitae* of Thorney Abbey and its "Catchment Area" ', *Nomina*, 9, 53–72.

(with M. Bateson) 'Bibliography', 'Work in Progress' and 'Notabilia and Personalia', *Nomina*, 9, 141–52, 153 and 154–57.

[as 'Souris'] 'Nugae onomasticae II', *Nomina*, 9, 129–39.

1986

'English in Schools' (letter), *The Times*, 1 December, p. 17.

'La vie féminine en Angleterre au temps d'Aliénor d'Aquitaine', in *Y a-t-il une civilisation du monde Plantagenêt? Actes du Colloque d'histoire médiévale, Fontevraud, 26–28 avril 1984* (= *Cahiers de civilisation médiévale*, 29), 49–51.

(with M. Bateson) 'Bibliography' and 'Work in Progress', *Nomina*, 10, 186–203 and 204.

[as 'Souris'] 'Nugae onomasticae III', *Nomina*, 10, 149–61.

1987

'Appendix 2: Oggerus', in *The Book of St Gilbert*, edited and translated by Raymonde Foreville and Gillian Keir, Oxford Medieval Texts (Oxford: Clarendon Press), 338–40.

*'The *codretum* (Whatever That May Be) at Little Roborough', in *Studies in Honour of Kenneth Cameron*, edited by Thorlac Turville-Petre and Margaret Gelling (= *Leeds Studies in English*, NS 18), 101–10.

'English Personal Names ca. 650–1300: Some Prosopographical Bearings', *Medieval Prosopography*, 8, no. 1 (Spring), 31–60.

'Spelling and Grammaticality in the *Vespasian Homilies*: A Reassessment', *Manuscripta*, 31, 7–10.

*'*Willelmus rex? vel alius Willelmus?*', *Nomina*, 11, 7–33.

*'A Witness to Post-Conquest English Cultural Patterns: The *Liber Vitae* of Thorney Abbey', in *Studies in Honour of René Derolez*, edited by A.M. Simon-Vandenbergen (Gent: Seminarie voor Engelse en Oud-Germaanse Taalkunde RUG), 73–85.

(with M. Bateson) 'Bibliography', 'Work in Progress' and 'Notabilia and Personalia', *Nomina*, 11, 186–203, 204–05 and 206–11.

[as 'Souris'] 'Nugae onomasticae IV', *Nomina*, 11, 155–65.

1988

(with M. Bateson) 'Bibliography', *Nomina*, 12 (1988–89), 192–220.

[as 'Souris'] 'Nugae de nominibus eligendis', *Nomina*, 12 (1988–89), 179–85.

1989

'The Harvard System' (letters), *Times Literary Supplement*, 2–8 June, p. 611 and 14–20 July, p. 773.
(with M. Bateson) 'Bibliography' and 'Work in Progress', *Nomina*, 13 (1989–90), 150–86 and 187–88.
[as 'Souris'] 'Nugae de dignitatibus honoribusque; Or, Our Classless Society', *Nomina*, 13 (1989–90), 122–30.

1990

*'Historical Linguistics – Linguistic Archaeology', in *Papers From the 5th International Conference on English Historical Linguistics*, edited by Sylvia Adamson *et al.*, Current Issues in Linguistic Theory, 65 (Amsterdam and Philadelphia: Benjamins), 55–68.
'Scottish, Welsh, Cornish, Manx' (in the 'Onomastic Bibliography'), *Onoma*, 30 (1990–91), 86–87.
(with Peter Jackson) 'Bibliography', *Nomina*, 14 (1990–91), 135–69.
(with M. Bateson, K.B. Harder and L.A. Möller), 'English' (in the 'Onomastic Bibliography'), *Onoma*, 30 (1990–91), 97–110.

1991

'Preface' (pp. iii–iv) to Georges Bourcier and Cecily Clark, *An Introduction to the History of the English Language*, edited by Akio Oizumi (Tokyo: Nan'un-do). xii+188pp. (See also 1979 and 1981, above.)
'Nincom's Bunkum' (letter), *Spectator*, 24 August, p. 21.
'Personal-Name Studies: Bringing Them to a Wider Audience', *Nomina*, 15 (1991–92), 21–34.
*'Towards a reassessment of "Anglo-Norman Influence on English Place-Names" ', in *Language Contact in the British Isles: Proceedings of the Eighth International Symposium on Language Contact in Europe, Douglas, Isle of Man, 1988*, edited by P. Sture Ureland and George Broderick (Tübingen: Niemeyer), 275–95.

1992

*'Domesday Book – A Great Red-Herring: Thoughts on Some Late-Eleventh-Century Orthographies', in *England in the Eleventh Century: Proceedings of the 1990 Harlaxton Symposium*, edited by Carola Hicks, Harlaxton Medieval Studies, 2 (Stamford: Paul Watkins), 317–31.
'The English Place-Name Society', *Medieval English Studies Newsletter*, no. 26 (June 1992), 1–3.
*'The Myth of "the Anglo-Norman Scribe" ', in *History of Englishes: New Methods and Interpretations in Historical Linguistics*, edited by Matti Rissanen *et al.*, Topics in English Linguistics, 10 (Berlin and New York: Mouton de Gruyter), 117–29.
'Onomastics', in *The Cambridge History of the English Language*, 1: *The Beginnings to 1066*, edited by R.M. Hogg (Cambridge: CUP), 452–89.
'Onomastics', in *The Cambridge History of the English Language*, 2: *1066–1476*, edited by Norman Blake (Cambridge: CUP), 542–606.
'Pets, Pests and Pronouns: Aspects of Current English Pronominal Usage in Reference to Non-Human Animates', in *Language and Civilization: a Concerted Profusion of Essays and Studies in Honour of Otto Hietsch*, edited with the assistance of Teresa Kirschner, Donald Gutch and Judith Gilbert by Claudia Blank, 2 vols (Frankfurt am Main, etc.: Peter Lang), II, 634–44.

forthcoming

'*Alfordruncen, Brenebrec, Cattesnese*: Some Early-Twelfth-Century Suffolk Bynames', in *Names, Time and Place: Studies Presented to Richard McKinley*, edited by David Postles (Oxford: Leopard's Head Press).

'Names: Personal' and 'Names: Place', in *Medieval England: An Encyclopedia*, general editor: Paul Szarmach (New York and London: Garland Press).

*'Socio-Economic Status and Individual Identity: Essential Factors in the Analysis of Middle English Personal-Naming', in *Naming, Society and Regional Identity*, edited by David Postles (Oxford: Leopard's Head Press).

REVIEWS

Journal of Ecclesiastical History, 4 (1953), 103–05: *The Peterborough Chronicle*, translated by Harry A. Rositzke (New York and London, 1951).

Cambridge Review, 87 (1965-66), 64: *The Mediaeval Age: Specimens of European Poetry from the Ninth to the Fifteenth Century*, edited by Angel Flores (London, 1965).

Cambridge Review, 87 (1965–66), 336–37: *Medieval and Linguistic Studies in Honour of Francis Peabody Magoun, Jr*, edited by Jess B. Bessinger, Jr, and Robert Creed (New York, 1965).

Cambridge Review, 87 (1965–66), 427–29: Peter Dronke, *Medieval Latin and the Rise of the European Love-Lyric*, vols 1 and 2 (Oxford, 1965–66).

Neophilologus, 50 (1966), 396–98: Julians Barnes, *Boke of Huntyng*, edited by Gunnar Tilander (Karlshamn, 1964)

Neophilologus, 50 (1966), 477–80: Arne Zettersten, *Studies in the Dialect and Vocabulary of the Ancrene Riwle* (Lund, 1965).

Medium Ævum, 36 (1967), 89–92: Larry D. Benson, *Art and Tradition in Sir Gawain and the Green Knight* (New Brunswick, NJ, 1965).

Medium Ævum, 36 (1967), 285–87: *The Complete Works of the Gawain-Poet*, translated by John Gardner (Chicago, 1965).

English Studies, 51 (1970), 247–49: J.E. Cross, *Ælfric and the Mediæval Homiliary – Objection and Contribution* (Lund, 1963).

English Studies, 51 (1970), 545–46: *Homilies of Ælfric: A Supplementary Collection*, edited by John C. Pope, 2 vols (London, 1967–68).

Neophilologus, 54 (1970), 335–36: *Floris and Blauncheflur*, edited by Franciscus Catharina de Vries (Groningen, 1966).

English Studies, 54 (1973), 378–81: *Anglo-Saxon England*, 1 (1972).

English Studies, 54 (1973), 403–04: (short notice) Betty S. Cox, *Cruces of* Beowulf (The Hague and Paris, 1971).

English Studies, 55 (1974), 64–65: R.I. Page, *Life in Anglo-Saxon England* (London, 1970).

English Studies, 55 (1974), 463–64: William A. Chaney, *The Cult of Kingship in Anglo-Saxon England: The Transition from Paganism to Christianity* (Manchester, 1970).

Medium Ævum, 43 (1974), 47–50: David L. Shores, *A Descriptive Syntax of the Peterborough Chronicle from 1122 to 1154* (The Hague and Paris, 1971).

Medium Ævum, 43 (1974), 201–02: *Charles d'Orléans: Choix de poésies*, edited by John Fox (Exeter, 1973).

English Studies, 56 (1975), 545–46: *Anglo-Saxon England*, 3 (1974).

Archives, 12 (1975–76), 91: *Wynkyn de Worde's Gesta Romanorum* (Exeter, 1974).

English Studies, 57 (1976), 70–71: Michael D. Cherniss, *Ingeld and Christ: Heroic Concepts and Values in Old English Christian Poetry* (The Hague, 1972).

English Studies, 57 (1976), 366–67: *Anglo-Saxon England*, 4 (1975).

Medium Ævum, 45 (1976), 229–30: Shigemi Sasaki, *Sur le thème de Nonchaloir dans la poésie de Charles d'Orléans* (Paris, 1974).
Medium Ævum, 45 (1976), 336–38: Ralph W.V. Elliott, *Chaucer's English* (London, 1974).
English Studies, 58 (1977), 266–67: *The Study of the Personal Names of the British Isles: Proceedings of a Working Conference at Erlangen, 21–24 September 1975*, edited by Herbert Voitl with the assistance of Klaus Forster and John Insley (Erlangen, 1976).
English Studies, 58 (1977), 349–50: *Anglo-Saxon England*, 5 (1976).
Medium Ævum, 46 (1977), 350–52: Alice Planche, *Charles d'Orléans, ou, la recherche d'un langage* (Paris, 1975).
Review of English Studies, NS 28 (1977), 201–02: *English Hawking and Hunting in* The Boke of St. Albans*: A Facsimile Edition of sigs. a2–f8 of* The Boke of St. Albans *(1486)*, edited by Rachel Hands (Oxford, 1975).
English Studies, 59 (1978), 257–60: Bo Seltén, *The Anglo-Saxon Heritage in Middle English Personal Names: East Anglia 1100–1399*, 1 (Lund, 1972) and *Early East-Anglian Nicknames: Bahuvrihi Names* (Lund, 1975).
Medium Ævum, 47 (1978), 367–69: Norman Blake, *The English Language in Medieval Literature* (London, 1977).
Nomina, 2 (1978), 64–65: Marianne Mulon, *L'Onomastique française: bibliographie des travaux publiés jusqu'en 1960* (Paris, 1977).
Études anglaises, 32 (1979), 212–14: Georges Bourcier, *Histoire de la langue anglaise du Moyen Age à nos jours* (Paris, 1978).
Études anglaises, 32 (1979), 461–62: André Crépin, *Problèmes de grammaire historique: de l'indo-européen au vieil-anglais* (Paris, 1978).
Journal of Ecclesiastical History, 30 (1979), 97–98: Milton McC. Gatch, *Preaching and Theology in Anglo-Saxon England* (Toronto, 1977).
Nomina, 3 (1979), 113–14: Richard McKinley, *The Surnames of Oxfordshire* (London, 1977).
Archives, 14 (1979–80), 55: (short notice) Robert A. Kelham, *A Dictionary of the Norman or Old French Language* . . . (facsimile reprint of the 1779 edition, Wakefield, 1978).
English Studies, 61 (1980), 456–57: *Anglo-Saxon England*, 6 (1977).
* *Nomina*, 4 (1980), 88–90: P.H. Reaney, *The Origin of English Surnames* (London, repr. 1980).
Nomina, 4 (1980), 91: *Dialectologie et onomastique: actes d'un Colloque tenu à Loches (mai 1978)*, ed. M. Mulon *et al.* (Dijon, 1980).
English Studies, 62 (1981), 473: Bo Seltén, *The Anglo-Saxon Heritage in Middle English Personal Names: East Anglia 1100–1399*, 2 (Lund, 1979).
English Studies, 63 (1982), 168–70: Jan Jönsjö, *Studies on Middle English Nicknames. – I. Compounds* (Lund, [1979]).
Nomina, 6 (1982), 99–100: *L'Onomastique, témoin des langues disparues: Actes du Colloque d'onomastique romane de Dijon (27–30 mai 1981)*, edited by Gérard Taverdet (Dijon, 1982).
Nomina, 6 (1982), 101–05: Adrian Room, *Naming Names: Stories of Pseudonyms and Name Changes, With a Who's Who* (London, 1981) and *idem*, *Dictionary of Trade Name Origins* (London, 1982).
English Studies, 64 (1983), 92–93: (short notice) Traugott Lawler, *The One and the Many in the Canterbury Tales* (Hamden, CT, 1980).
English Studies, 64 (1983), 93: (short notice) *The Chester Mystery Cycle: A Reduced Facsimile of Huntington Library MS. 2*, edited by R.M. Lumiansky and David Mills (Leeds, 1980).
English Studies, 64 (1983), 189: (short notice) F. Anne Payne, *Chaucer and Menippean Satire* (Madison and London, 1981).

English Studies, 64 (1983), 189–90: (short notice) Anna P. Baldwin, *The Theme of Government in Piers Plowman* (Cambridge, 1981).

English Studies, 64 (1983), 274–75: Margaret E. Goldsmith, *The Figure of Piers Plowman: The Image on the Coin* (Cambridge, 1981).

English Studies, 64 (1983), 275: *The Alliterative Morte Arthure: A Reassessment of the Poem*, edited by Karl-Heinz Göller (Cambridge, 1981).

English Studies, 64 (1983), 281–82: *Arthurian Literature*, 1 (1981).

English Studies, 64 (1983), 570–71: *Signs and Symbols in Chaucer's Poetry*, edited by John P. Hermann and John J. Burke, Jr (University, AL, 1981).

Nomina, 7 (1983), 125–27: Basil Cottle, *Names* (London, 1983).

Nomina, 7 (1983), 137–38: Rosie Boycott, *Batty, Bloomers and Boycott: A Little Etymology of Anonymous Words* (London, 1982).

English Studies, 65 (1984), 370–71: Herbert Grabès, *The Mutable Glass: Mirror-Imagery in Titles and Texts of the Middle Ages and English Renaissance*, translated by Gordon Collier (Cambridge, 1982).

English Studies, 65 (1984), 466–67: *Hali Meiðhad*, edited by Bella Millett (London, 1982).

English Studies, 65 (1984), 467–68: *English Wycliffite Sermons*, 1, edited by Anne Hudson (Oxford, 1983).

English Studies, 65 (1984), 570–71: Mary Flowers Braswell, *The Medieval Sinner: Characterization and Confession in the Literature of the English Middle Ages* (Rutherford, NJ and London, 1983).

Nomina, 8 (1984), 114–15: Charles de Beaurepaire, *Dictionnaire topographique du département de Seine-Maritime comprenant les noms de lieux*, edited by Jean Laporte *et al.* (Paris, 1982).

Nomina, 8 (1984), 116–17: Mary Lassiter, *Our Names, Our Selves: The Meaning of Names in Everyday Life* (London, 1983).

English Studies, 66 (1985), 359–60: *Arthurian Literature*, 3 (1983).

English Studies, 66 (1985), 360–61: Robert J. Blanch, *Sir Gawain and the Green Knight: A Reference Guide* (New York, 1983).

English Studies, 66 (1985), 361–62: *Middle English Alliterative Poetry and its Literary Background: Seven Essays*, edited by David Lawton (Cambridge, 1982).

English Studies, 66 (1985), 362–63: *The Prophetia Merlini of Geoffrey of Monmouth: A Fifteenth-Century English Commentary*, edited by Caroline D. Eckhardt (Cambridge, MA, 1982).

Journal of Theological Studies, NS 37 (1986), 635: *Les documents nécrologiques de l'abbaye Saint-Pierre de Solignac*, edited by Jean-Loup Lemaître (Paris, 1984).

Nomina, 10 (1986), 180–83: G.W. Lasker *et al.*, *Surnames and Genetic Structure* (Cambridge, 1985).

English Studies, 68 (1987), 98–99: *Arthurian Literature*, 4 and 5 (1984 and 1985).

Nomina, 11 (1987), 185: (short notice) *Huguenot and Walloon Gazette*, 1, no. 3 (Spring, 1987).

Nomina, 11 (1987), 185: (short notice) *Nouvelle revue d'onomastique*, 1/2 (1983) – 7/8 (1986).

Journal of Theological Studies, NS 39 (1988), 368: (short notice) Jean-Loup Lemaître, *Les Heures de Peyre de Bonetos* (Ussel, 1987).

Nomina, 12 (1988–89), 172: (unsigned short notice) Rudiger Fuchs, *Das Domesday Book und sein Umfeld: zur ethnischen und sozialen Aussgekraft einer Landesbeschreibung im England des 11. Jahrhunderts* 13 (Stuttgart, 1987).

Nomina, 12 (1988–89), 172: (unsigned short notice) Jan Gerchow, *Die Gedenküberlieferung des Angelsachsen, mit einem Katalog der libri vitae und Necrologien* (Berlin, 1988).

Journal of Theological Studies, NS 40 (1989), 286–87: *Répertoire des documents nécrologiques français: supplément* (Paris, 1987), *L'Obituaire du chapitre collégial Saint-Honoré de Paris* (Paris, 1987), and *Prieurs et prieurés dans l'Occident médiéval: Actes du Colloque organisé à Paris le 12 novembre 1984 par la IVe section de l'École pratique des hautes études et l'Institut de recherche et d'histoire des textes* (Geneva, 1987), all edited by Jean-Loup Lemaître.

Nomina, 13 (1989–90), 132–35: C. Marynissen, *Hypokoristische Suffixen in oudnederlandse Persoonsnamen, inz. de -z- en -l-Suffixen* (Gent, 1986).

Nomina, 13 (1989–90), 143–45: Ingrid Hjertstedt, *Middle English Nicknames in the Lay Subsidy Rolls for Warwickshire* (Uppsala, 1987).

Nomina, 13 (1989–90), 147–48: Edwin D. Lawson, *Personal Names and Naming: An Annotated Bibliography* (New York and London, 1987).

Nomina, 13 (1989–90), 148–49: Marianne Mulon, *L'Onomastique française: bibliographie des travaux publiés de 1960 à 1985* (Paris, 1985).

*Nomina, 14 (1990–91), 127–30: Richard McKinley, *The Surnames of Sussex* (Oxford, 1988).

Nomina, 14 (1990–91), 132–33: J. Douglas Porteous, *The Mells: Surname Geography, Family History* (Saturna Island, BC, 1988).

Nomina, 14 (1990–91), 133: Oakham Survey Research Group, *The Oakham Survey of 1305: A Translation with Commentaries* (Oakham, 1988).

Nomina, 14 (1990–91), 133–34: (short notice) L. van Durme, *Toponymie van Velzeke-Ruddershove en Bochoute*, 2 vols (Gent, 1986–91).

STUDIES IN
HISTORY, LITERATURE AND LANGUAGE

1

The Narrative Mode of *The Anglo-Saxon Chronicle* before the Conquest

With a few exceptions,[1] scholars have paid more attention to the syntax of *The Anglo-Saxon Chronicle*[2] than to its style. True, stylistic observation has at least once thrown light upon its compilation, by identifying the author of the additional entries at 959DE and 975D as the homilist Wulfstan.[3] In general, however, the *Chronicle's* standing as an anthology of three centuries' prose writing has gone unacknowledged.[4] Yet stylistic study of the *Chronicle* is rewarding, for it reveals not only how prose style developed within a single genre and a single tradition but also how the very concept of annal writing shifted between the ninth century and the twelfth.

The Initial Alfredian Compilation

Shifts of style in the *Chronicle* must be related to stages in its compilation, some of which are revealed by changes of hand and ink in surviving copies. The earliest such change in any extant text occurs between the recto and the verso of fol. 16 of the Parker manuscript (A, Cambridge, Corpus Christi College 173), and involves also a change of layout, with annal-numbers assigned to a column of their own up to 16r but from there onwards being variously placed. This change, then, which occurs at the annal-number 892, may mark the end of a compilation in some respects unified by common principle. Does the unifying principle embrace style as well as layout?

As a rule, *Chronicle* entries up to this point (common, broadly speaking, to all the main versions) are terse: hence the high relief in which the more expansive entry at 755 stands out. A typical early-ninth-century annal reads:

---

[1] These exceptions include G.C. Donald, *Zur Entwicklung des Prosastils in der Sachsenchronik* (Diss. Marburg, 1914) and F. Viglione, *Studio critico-filologico su l''Anglo-Saxon Chronicle', con saggi di traduzioni* (Pavia, 1922); see also *English and Norse Documents Relating to the Reign of Ethelred the Unready*, ed. and trans. M. Ashdown (Cambridge, 1930), pp. 13–16 and D. Whitelock, 'The Prose of Alfred's Reign', *Continuations and Beginnings: Studies in Old English Literature*, ed. E.G. Stanley (London, 1966), pp. 97–9.

[2] Editions consulted include *The Anglo-Saxon Chronicle*, ed. B. Thorpe, Rolls Series, vol. 1 (1861); *Two of the Saxon Chronicles Parallel . . .*, ed. C. Plummer on the basis of an ed. by J. Earle (Oxford, 1892; repr. 1952 with contr. by D. Whitelock); Ashdown, *Documents*, pp. 38–70, for 978–1017C; and *The Parker Chronicle (832–900)*, ed. A.H. Smith (London, 1935). The customary sigla are used to indicate the different versions. In quotations I supply my own punctuation, both for the sake of consistency and to bring out the points under discussion.

[3] K. Jost, 'Wulfstan und die angelsächsische Chronik', *Anglia* XLVII (1923), 105–23; see also *The Homilies of Wulfstan*, ed. D. Bethurum (Oxford, 1957), p. 47 and *Sermo Lupi ad Anglos*, ed. D. Whitelock, 3rd rev. ed. (London, 1963), pp. 27–8.

[4] Viglione did make this point (*op. cit.* pp. 3 and 64–5), but his study is superficial.

833. Her gefeaht Ecgbryht cyning wiþ xxxv sciphlæsta æt Carrum, 7 þær wearþ micel wæl geslægen, 7 þa Denescan ahton wælstowe gewald. 7 Hereferþ 7 Wigþen, tuegen biscepas, forþferdon; 7 Dudda 7 Osmod, tuegen aldormen, forþferdon.

Adjectives are sparse, and adverbs rare or (as happens here) absent; nor is there any complexity of syntax, just a chain of simple sentences rendering a series of simple propositions. Furthermore, with the events noted all falling within a narrow range, vocabulary and phrasing are correspondingly restricted, annal after annal using the same semi-formulaic language. Compare, for instance, the entry for 837:

Her Wulfheard aldormon gefeaht æt Hamtune wiþ xxxiii sciphlæsta, 7 þær micel wæl geslog 7 sige nom. 7 þy geare forþferde Wulfheard. 7 þy ilcan geare gefeaht Æþel- helm dux wiþ Deniscne here on Port mid Dornsætum, 7 gode hwile þone here gefliemde, 7 þa Deniscan ahton wælstowe gewald 7 þone aldormon ofslogon.

Except for the use of the descriptive adverbial phrase, *gode hwile*, that annal hardly varies in vocabulary or phrasing from that at 833; and those at 838, 839, 840 and 845, for instance, observe the same conventions. Nor do longer entries necessarily show any greater range either of subject-matter or of style: thus the annal for 851 lists several campaigns all in the same standard, factual terms, departing from these only with a closing flourish of pride: '7 þær þæt mæte wæl geslogon on hæþnum herige þe we secgan hierdon oþ þisne ondweardan dæg, 7 þær sige namon'; and in the annal for 871 the account of the Battle of Ashdown and of the related campaign, although fuller than usual, likewise keeps to the conventional chain of simple sentences.

Now this restricted prose style was by no means the only one current in ninth-century English. Although no early literary prose is extant, there survive from the early ninth century, and before, vernacular charters, wills and laws,[5] and these show as much and as varied subordination and qualification as the matter requires, laws being rich in conditional clauses and jussive subjunctives, 'Gif hit oðrum his eage oðdo, selle his agen fore',[6] and charters likewise: 'Gif hit ðonne festendæg sie, selle mon uuege cæsa, ond fisces, ond butran, ond aegera ðaet mon begeotan maege, ond xxx ombra godes Uuelesces aloð ðet limpeð to xv mittum, ond mittan fulne huniges, oðða tuegen uuines, sue hwaeder suae mon ðonne begeotan maege.'[7] Nor is this, from a Kentish charter of the first decade of the ninth century, exceptional for the date.[8] The early *Chronicle* style, then, shows limitations peculiar to itself.[9]

Closer definition of this style may be reached through comparison with that of the Old English Orosius, which, as well as being comparable with this part of the *Chronicle* both in date and as historical narrative, also happens to be the only Old

---

5   Although surviving law-codes date back to the early seventh century, none, unfortunately, has been preserved in a pre-Alfredian text; for this reason I prefer not to explore the stylistic detail of the earlier codes.

6   *Gesetze der Angelsachsen*, ed. F. Liebermann (Halle, 1903–16; repr. Aalen, 1960), 1, 32.

7   *Sweet's Anglo-Saxon Reader*, rev. D. Whitelock (Oxford, 1967), p. 198.

8   See *The Oldest English Texts*, ed. H. Sweet, EETS o.s. 83 (London, 1885), pp. 441–2, 443–4, 445, 447–9 and 449–50, for several comparable documents all dated before 840.

9   This has sometimes been insufficiently recognized by investigators concerned with the *Chronicle* as evidence for chronological development of syntax; see, e.g., G. Rübens, *Parataxe und Hypotaxe in dem ältesten Teil der Sachsenchronik (Parker HS. bis zum Jahre 891)* (Diss. Göttingen, 1915), pp. 51–3 and A. Rynell, *Parataxis and Hypotaxis as a Criterion of Syntax and Style*, Lunds Universitets Årsskrift n.f. avd. 1. bd 48. nr. 3 (1952), p. 26.

English work still extant which the compiler of the early *Chronicle* certainly knew.[10] The style of the Old English Orosius is simple, admittedly, with little subordination other than temporal and relative clauses; but, instead of being terse as that of the early *Chronicle* is, it ranges freely both into description and into explanations of motive, thus, for instance:

> Swa egefull wæs Alexander þa þa he wæs on Indeum, on easteweardum þissum middangearde, þætte þa from him ondredan þe wæron on westeweardum. Eac him coman ærendracan ge of monegum þeodum, þe nan mon Alexandres geferscipes ne wende þæt man his naman wiste, 7 him firþes to him wilnedon. Þagiet þa Alexander ham com to Babylonia, þagiet wæs on him se mæsta þurst monnes blodes. Ac þa þa his geferan ongeatan þæt he ðæs gewinnes þagiet geswican nolde, ac he sæde þæt he on African faran wolde, þa geleornedon his byrelas him betweonum hu hie him mehten þæt lif oþþringan . . .[11]

The ampler narration derives, of course, from the Latin original; but it is noteworthy that the translator, although rendering his original loosely, makes no attempt to reduce this amplitude to a *Chronicle*-like simplicity. Indeed, his additions from contemporary vernacular sources, such as the narratives of Ohthere and of Wulfstan, admit not only circumstantial description: '7 þær is mid Estum ðeaw, þonne þær bið man dead, þæt he lið inne unforbærned mid his magum 7 freondum monað, ge hwilum twegen; 7 þa kyningas, 7 þa oðre heahðungene men, swa micle lencg swa hi maran speda habbað, hwilum healf gear, þæt hi beoð unforbærned 7 licgað bufan eorðan on hyra husum';[12] but also hypothesis: 'Þyder he cwæð þæt man ne mihte geseglian on anum monðe, gyf man on niht wicode, 7 ælce dæge hæfde ambyrne wind.'[13] Clearly, the Old English Orosius and the *Chronicle* are obeying different stylistic principles.

The origins of the *Chronicle*'s special stylistic principles are not, at first sight, obvious. The arts of rhetoric current in the early Middle Ages, being mainly concerned with oratory (or preaching) or with letter-writing, do not, as far as I know, specify styles for the various genres of historiography. Such hints as they give imply that for most narrative purposes some form of *stilus humilis* should be used: thus *Rhetorica ad Herennium* illustrates *oratio adtenuata* (i.e. *stilus humilis*) by a specimen of *narratio*,[14] and in *De Doctrina Christiana* Augustine prescribes *stilus humilis* for instructional use, that is, for factual, non-emotive writing.[15] Indeed, as Auerbach pointed out, plain Latin prose is best exemplified during the Dark Ages in the narrative parts of the bible, in the early saints' lives, and in the *Historia Francorum* of Gregory of Tours.[16] But the terse formulas of the early *Chronicle* are not simply *stilus humilis* in English, not 'the humblest sort of everyday speech',[17] but, as the contrast both with the charters and with

---

[10] See D. Whitelock, *Continuations and Beginnings*, pp. 73–4. The entry at 81, 'Titus . . . se þe sæde þæt he þone dæg forlure þe he noht to gode on ne gedyde', is derived from the Old English Orosius: *King Alfred's Orosius*, ed. H. Sweet 1, EETS o.s. 79 (London, 1883), p. 264, line 2.

[11] *Ibid.* p. 136.

[12] *Ibid.* p. 20.

[13] *Ibid.* p. 19.

[14] Ed. and trans. H. Caplan (Loeb, 1954), pp. 260–3.

[15] *On Christian Doctrine*, trans. D.W. Robertson (New York, 1958), pp. 145–7, 153–4, 159 and 162.

[16] E. Auerbach, *Literary Language and its Public in Late Latin Antiquity and in the Middle Ages* (London, 1965), pp. 52, 53, 60 ff., 87–8 and 103–11.

[17] *Infimum et cotidianum sermonem* (*Rhetorica ad Herennium*, p. 260).

the Old English Orosius shows, constitute in their own way a highly artificial manner, especially in their avoidance of descriptive elements of all kinds.

The origins of this manner may lie in the *Chronicle*'s origins. Annals evolved from notes in the margins of Easter tables.[18] Necessarily brief, such notes, being adjuncts to the calendar rather than contributions to literature, were also factual and objective, remaining so as long as they continued to be made: witness, for instance, this sequence from a twelfth-century Peterborough table, '1087 *Obiit* Wille*lmus* rex. 1089 *Obiit* Landfranc*us* archie*piscopus*. 1096 Iter incepit ierosolimitanum. etc.'[19] The objective manner of the primitive annals abstracted from such tables (although not their extreme brevity) was imitated in annals independently composed: Dr C.W. Jones has remarked how Bede's specimen chronicles, in contrast with his work in other historical genres, are 'mundane and factual', eschewing all miraculous elements.[20] Similarly with the vernacular. What the sources of the *Chronicle* to 891 may have been is matter for conjecture, as no surviving text contains annals antedating it; analysis has suggested that as far as the early part of Æthelwulf's reign the compiler was drawing upon, amongst other things, various earlier sets of annals, but that from the latter part of that reign onwards he composed the annals himself.[21] At all events, many of the seventh- and eighth-century annals consisting of only one line (see, for instance, 7v of the Parker manuscript) could have been derived from Easter table notes; and there must have been some written record to preserve for over two centuries such entries as *671. Her wæs þæt micle fugla wæl.*

In spite of variations in origin, however, stylistic continuity is (with exceptions such as the entry at 755) well maintained: with the annals for 833 and 837 already quoted compare these across the centuries:

> 568. Her Ceaulin 7 Cuþa gefuhton wiþ Æþelbryht, 7 hine in Cent gefliemdon, 7 tuegen aldormen on Wibbandune ofslogon, Oslaf 7 Cnebban.

> 675. Her Wulfhere Pending 7 Æscwine gefuhton æt Biedanheafde; 7 þy ilcan geare Wulfhere forþferde, 7 Æþelræd feng to rice.

> 845. Her Eanulf aldorman gefeaht mid Sumursætum, 7 Ealchstan biscep 7 Osric aldorman mid Dornsætum gefuhton æt Pedridan muþan wiþ Deniscne here, 7 þær micel wæl geslogon 7 sige namon.

Although the compiler evidently knew Bede's *History*, he set down under 627, as the equivalent of six of Bede's chapters,[22] the single simple sentence, 'Her Edwine kyning wæs gefulwad mid his þeode on Eastron.' Contemporary events too he transmuted into his terse, timeless formulas, thus:

---

[18] R.L. Poole, *Chronicles and Annals: a Brief Outline of their Origin and Growth* (Oxford, 1926), pp. 26, 42 and 58 ff.; C.W. Jones, *Saints' Lives and Chronicles in Early England* (Cornell, 1947), pp. 7 ff. and 16 ff.

[19] *Ungedruckte Anglo-Normannische Geschichtsquellen*, ed. F. Liebermann (Strasbourg, 1879), p. 13; cf. *MÆ* XXIII (1954), pl. facing p. 71.

[20] Jones, *op. cit.* pp. 20, 22 and 27.

[21] See A.J. Thorogood, 'The Anglo-Saxon Chronicle in the Reign of Ecgberht', *EHR* XLVIII (1933), 353–63, and also *The Anglo-Saxon Chronicle*, ed. and trans. D. Whitelock with D.C. Douglas and S.I. Tucker (London, 1961), pp. xxi–xxiii.

[22] *HE* II. 9–14.

886. Her for se here eft west þe ær east gelende, 7 þa up on Sigene, 7 þær wintersetl namon. Þy ilcan geare gesette Ælfred cyning Lundenburg, 7 him all Angelcyn to cirde, þæt buton Deniscra monna hæftniede was, 7 he þa befæste þa burg Æþerede aldormen to haldonne.

His sense of continuity is a living one which allows creation of fresh conventions: that opening, *Her for se here*, appears in the entries for 867, 869, 872–5, 879–84 and 886–7, and is the basis for variants in 868, 870–1, 876–8 and 885.

Study thus suggests that, whether or not the distinction were as yet consciously formulated, 'annals' were felt to be a separate genre requiring a style of their own. Practice speaks for itself. For theory – and even then confined to the formal, superficial level – we have, however, to wait until the late twelfth century, when Gervase of Canterbury described the differences observable between chroniclers and historians:

> Historici autem et cronici secundum aliquid una est intentio et materia, sed diversus tractandi modus est et forma varia. Utriusque una est intentio, quia uterque veritati intendit. Forma tractandi varia, quia historicus diffuse et eleganter incedit, cronicus vero simpliciter graditur et breviter. 'Proicit' historicus 'ampullas et sesquipedalia verba;' cronicus vero 'silvestrem musam tenui meditatur avena.' Sedet historicus 'inter magniloquos et grandia verba serentes,' at cronicus sub pauperis Amiclæ pausat tugurio ne sit pugna pro paupere tecto. Proprium est historici veritati intendere, audientes vel legentes dulci sermone et eleganti demulcere, actus, mores vitamque ipsius quam describit veraciter edocere, nichilque aliud comprehendere nisi quod historiæ de ratione videtur competere. Cronicus autem annos Incarnationis Domini annorumque menses computat et kalendas, actus etiam regum et principum quæ in ipsis eveniunt breviter edocet, eventus etiam, portenta vel miracula commemorat. Sunt autem plurimi qui, cronicas vel annales scribentes, limites suos excedunt, nam philacteria sua dilatare et fimbrias magnificare delectant. Dum enim cronicam compilare cupiunt, historici more incedunt, et quod breviter sermoneque humili de modo scribendi dicere debuerant, verbis ampullosis aggravare conantur.[23]

Broadly understood, that could apply to the differences between the Old English Orosius and the *Chronicle*: as a history, the Old English Orosius uses some amplitude of narration (although to describe its style as *ampullas et sesquipedalia verba* would be exaggeration), whereas the *Chronicle*, in its different genre, *simpliciter graditur et breviter*, intent on chronology and on fact, rather than on personality or on verbal ornament.

Gervase, however, deals only with the surface. In a deeper sense, the difference between annalists and historians is not that the latter discard chronological frameworks and indulge in rhetorical flourishes, 'making broad their phylacteries and enlarging the borders of their garments'; nor that they deal with the *mores vitamque* of their personages as well as with their *actus*, using for this purpose physical description, direct speech, even anecdote; nor even that, as medieval writers maintained, they described good men's good deeds so as to excite emulation but evil men's evil deeds so as to inspire revulsion;[24] but much more that on both personal and national levels they relate motive, causation, and consequence. Annalists, on the other hand, simply record events as they occur.

---

[23] *The Historical Works of Gervase of Canterbury*, ed. W. Stubbs, 2 vols., Rolls Series (1879–80) 1, 87–8; cf. Poole, *op. cit.* pp. 7–8.

[24] See, e.g., *HE Praefatio*.

For this function of plain record the early *Chronicle* style is well adapted, enabling events to be set forth with minimum interference from any author's personality. The absence of adjectives and adverbs allows the record to stand clear, unclouded by subjective impressions; the absence of subordination keeps it uncontaminated by conditions, concessions or speculations. To speak of 'meditating with a scrawny oatstalk a rustic muse' misses the mark: on its own level this unadorned, unqualified record is as near absolute fact as history can get; and, aesthetically, it has the dignity of utter plainness.

But objectivity is hard to sustain: feelings and opinions will break in. Even in early annals an adjective or an adverb sometimes betrays the annalist's point of view, as when Æthelhun is called *þone ofermedan aldormonn* (750), or when it is noted, not without pride, how, faced by Hengest's forces, *þa Brettas . . . mid micle ege flugon to Lundenbyrg* (457) and how *þa Walas flugon þa Englan swa fyr* (473); and, dealing with matters of living memory, the annalist calls Ceolwulf II of Mercia *anum unwisum cyninges þegne* (874) and notes that when Æthelwulf returned home with his Frankish bride his people *þæs gefægene wærun* (855) and that his son Æthelberht reigned *on godre geþuærnessse 7 on micelre sibsumnesse* (860). More elaborately, a relative clause or a causal one may lend character or motive to a personage of the record, as with the borrowing from the Old English Orosius, 'Titus . . . se þe sæde þæt he þone dæg forlure þe he noht to gode on ne gedyde' (81),[25] or with such notes as 'Hæfde hine Penda adrifenne 7 rices benumenne, forþon he his swostor anforlet' (658), 'se gerefa þærto rad 7 hie wolde drifan to þæs cyninges tune, þy he nyste hwæt hie wæron' (787), and 'Þy fultomode Beorhtric Offan, þy he hæfde his dohtor him to cuene' (836). Such touches bring both gain and loss: gain in that they put events into a contemporary, human perspective; loss in that they adulterate fact with impression, hearsay, and opinion.

The Later Alfredian Annals

At the top of 16v, beginning with what seems to be (in spite of the annal-number 892 entered at the foot of the recto) an addition to the annal for 891, a new hand takes over in the Parker manuscript, continuing probably, although not with perfect regularity, to 924.[26]

The opening entries in the new hand, those from 892 to 896 especially,[27] contrast markedly with those of the early Alfredian compilation.[28] Not only are they longer and fuller of detail, but their syntax, in contrast with the scarcely varied co-ordination of the preceding entries, shows free use of subordination: for instance, compare with the entries previously quoted this sentence from 893: 'Ond þa gegaderade Ælfred cyning his fierd, 7 for þæt he gewicode betwuh þæm twan hergum, þær þær he niehst rymet hæfde for wudufæstenne ond for wæterfæstenne, swa þæt he mehte ægþerne geræcan

---

25 See above, p. 5, n. 10.

26 N.R. Ker, *Catalogue of Manuscripts containing Anglo-Saxon* (Oxford, 1957), pp. 57–9.

27 Stylistically the break is not sharp: syntax is complex and description ample in 891A, both in the section by the first scribe and in that by the second, but the subject-matter there is unrelated to that of the following group of annals, 892–6, which form a unit because of their narrative continuity. A simple style relying on co-ordination reappears in 897. Note further that, although the entries for 891 and for 893–9 are common to A, B, C and D, E is blank for these years.

28 See Whitelock, *Continuations and Beginnings*, pp. 97 and 99.

gif hie ænigne feld secan wolden.' The novelty of style must not be exaggerated; for, on the one hand, these annals still show many passages of purely co-ordinate structure – thus, for instance, 'Þa forrad sio fierd hie foran, 7 him wið gefeaht æt Fearnhamme, 7 þone here gefliemde, 7 þa herehyþa ahreddon' (893) – and, on the other, as we have seen, there had appeared from time to time throughout the earlier annals clauses of condition (755), of result (716 and 867), of purpose (2, 48, 430, 853 and 867), of comparison (734, 797, 874, 877 and 885) and of reason (658, 661, 680, 694, 787, 823, 836 and 887). But, compared with previous entries, these later Alfredian annals do offer both a wider range of connectives for types of clause already used, for instance, *þa hwile þe* and *swa oft swa* for temporal clauses, and also some new types of clause, notably the concessive, *þeh ic ða geðungnestan nemde* (896); and, above all, they show subordination used in far greater density.

This new annalist does indeed wear his phylacteries a thought broader. His more complex syntax is accompanied, although to nothing like the same degree as in homiletic style, by rhetorical patterning. Doublets and triplets occur: *ægþer ge of East Englum, ge of Norþhymbrum* (893); *ægðer ge þæs ceapes, ge þæs cornes* (894); *ge on feo, ge on wifum, ge eac on bearnum* (893); and *ægðer ge swiftran, ge unwealtran, ge eac hieran* (896). The doublets are often antithetical, usually only in the simplest way – *oþþe on dæg, oþþe on niht* (CD); *ge of þære fierde, ge eac of þæm burgum*; *healfe æt ham, healfe ute*; *þiderweardes . . . hamweardes*; and *suð ymbutan . . . norþ ymbutan* (all from 893) – but sometimes more elaborately, as in 'tuwwa: oþre siþe þa hie ærest to londe comon, ær sio fierd gesamnod wære, oþre siþe þa hie of þæm setum faran woldon' (893), where the balanced clauses have similar structure and almost the same number of syllables (*isocolon*). Patterns so simple, often seemingly dictated by the material itself, would be unremarkable, were it not that in the earliest entries they had been very rare and had remained uncommon even in those from the 860s, 870s and 880s (*Ær wærun Romanisce biscepas, siþþan wærun Englisce* [690]; *oþer heold Daniel, oþer Aldhelm* [709]; *ge þa Walas, ge þa Deniscan* [835]; *sume binnan, sume butan* [867]; *on twæm gefylcum: on oþrum wæs . . . 7 on oþrum wæron . . .* [871]; and *oþer dæl east, oþer dæl to Hrofesceastre* [885]: these are almost the only examples of such patterning in the earlier annals).[29] Feeling for rhetoric comes out more strongly in the phrase, *manige eac him, þeh ic ða geðungnestan nemde* (896), with its touch of *occultatio*, and especially in the antithesis, combined with progression from positive to superlative: 'Næfde se here, Godes þonces, Angelcyn ealles forswiðe gebrocod, ac hie wæron micle swiþor gebrocede on þæm þrim gearum mid ceapes cwilde 7 monna, ealles swiþost mid þæm þæt manige þara selestena cynges þena . . . forðferdon' (896).

As that phrase, *Godes þonces*, shows, what has changed here is not simply syntax, or taste for word patterns, but the view of chronicling: objectivity is partly discarded. Whereas the earliest annals recorded facts, excluding condition, concession, comparison and causality, these late Alfredian annals go some way towards interpreting the facts they record: that is what the more complex syntax and the rhetoric are there for. Subordination gives insight, if only of an elementary kind, into purpose and motivation, usually those of King Alfred himself: 'Hæfde se cyning his fierd on tu tonumen,

---

[29] Rhetorical description being so all-embracing, it is often hard to decide whether an apparent 'trope' may not be accidental, e.g. *his tungon forcurfon 7 his eagan astungon* (797: ? *isocolon* and *similiter cadens*) or *þa he þæt hierde 7 mid fierde ferde* (835: ? *similiter cadens*).

swa þæt hie wæron simle healfe æt ham, healfe ute' (893); 'Þa wicode se cyng on neaweste þære byrig, þa hwile þe hie hira corn gerypon, þæt þa Deniscan him ne mehton þæs ripes forwiernan' (895); 'Rad se cyng up bi þære eæ 7 gehawade hwær mon mehte þa ea forwyrcan, þæt hie ne mehton þa scipu ut brengan' (895); and 'Næron nawðer ne on Fresisc gescæpene ne on Denisc, bute swa him selfum ðuhte þæt hie nytwyrðoste beon meahten' (896). Indeed, for such effects subordination is essential: compare 'For þæt he gewicode betwuh þæm twam hergum, þær þær he niehst rymet hæfde for wudufæstenne ond for wæterfæstenne, swa þæt he mehte ægþerne geræcan gif hie ænigne feld secan wolden' (893) with this version in which the same points are expressed through co-ordination plus one temporal clause, with the result that all sense of purpose is lost: '*Þa for he 7 gewicode betwuh þæm twan hergum. Þær hæfde he niehst rymet for wudufæstenne 7 for wæterfæstenne, 7 mehte ægþerne geræcan, þa hie ænigne feld secan woldon.' So, syntax is here being used to give an illusion of insight into the motives underlying King Alfred's various acts, a touch of 'historical' interpretation.

Another sign of 'historical' technique is the deliberate linkage between the annals. Whereas the earlier annals each stood alone, linked at most by an occasional cross-reference such as *Her for se ilca here* (868), here cross-reference is systematic. The entry for 892 describes how *se micla here, þe we gefyrn ymbe spræcon* (note how the annalist, instead of effacing himself, now presents himself as *we* or *ic*) landed *on Limene muþan*; that for 893, after referring to some other events, goes on to speak of *se micla here . . . þe ær on Limene muþan sæt*; that for 894, which begins *Ond þa sona æfter þæm*, referring back to the destruction of corn and cattle described at the end of 893, closes with 'Þæt wæs ymb twa ger þæs þe hie hider ofer sæ comon'; and the entry for 895, which opens by referring to *se foresprecena here*, ends with 'Þæt wæs ymb þreo ger þæs þe hie on Limene muðan comon hider ofer sæ.' Apart from this formal linkage, this block of annals from 892 to 896 is also united by some common themes, especially interest in tactics, expressed in concern with topography, with conditions of military service and availability of supplies, and also with the king's own ideas and methods. Thus, the campaign, occupying several years, is recorded as a single whole.

But the 'historical' virtues of this group of annals must not be exaggerated. To begin with, as there is no reason to suppose King Alfred himself their author, the insights into his motives cannot be more than conjectural. Further, although his mind is suggested behind many individual developments, there is little sense of any control of events as a whole, nor is the formal continuity controlled by any real plan of exposition; indeed, at times the mere sequence of events is unclear. The movement away from 'annals' towards 'history' is only relative. This is reflected by the use of adjectives and adverbs: the latter remain rare, and the former are still almost confined to definition, thus, *se micla here, anre westre ceastre, þara niwena scipa* and so on, with only an occasional phrase, such as *þara selestena cynges þena*, carrying even a hint of subjective evaluation. The chief virtue here remains the annalistic one of objectivity.

The Annals for the Reign of Æthelred II

During the tenth century greater divergences appear between the surviving versions of the *Chronicle*, divergences which are by no means closely related to the make-up of the extant manuscripts. A shows three hands at work between the entry for 925 and that for 1001; but its version is no longer the primary one. The other manuscripts show no significant changes of hand in this period: B breaks off at 977; C is in a single hand from the entry for 491 to that for 1045 or 1048; none of the several hands of D is to be dated before the mid eleventh century;[30] E is in one hand to 1121. As for the character of the entries, this ranges from the objective brevity of, for instance, those for 909, 912, 944 and 955, to the setting down under 937 of the whole poem on *The Battle of Brunnanburh.*

What divergences there can now be between the manners of the main versions of the *Chronicle* is well illustrated by the notices of Æthelred's accession in 978. A shows a laconicism worthy of an Easter table: 'Her wearð Eadweard cyning ofslegen. On þis ilcan geare feng Æðelred æðeling his broðor to rice.' C also uses the classic manner, departing from objectivity only with the one word, *gemartyrad*, to describe Edward's end, and is no less restrained in the following entry, where a fearful portent, *blodig wolcen . . . on fyres gelicnesse*, is noted but not explicitly linked with Æthelred's consecration as king, the only other event recorded there. D and E, by contrast, although they give no details of the horrid deed,[31] add an impassioned commentary, heavy with antitheses:

> Ne wearð Angelcynne nan wyrse dead gedon þonne þeos wæs, syþþan hi ærest Britenland gesohton. Menn hine ofmyrþredon, ac God hine mærsode. He wæs on life eorðlic cyning: he is nu æfter deaðe heofonlic sanct. Hyne noldon his eorðlican magas wrecan, ac hine hafað his heofonlic Fæder swyþe gewrecan. Þa eorðlican banan woldon his gemynd on eorðan adilgian, ac se uplica Wrecend hafað his gemynd on heofonum 7 on eorþan tobræd. Þa ðe noldon ær to his libbendan lichaman onbugan, þa nu eadmodlice on cneowum gebugað to his deadum banum. Nu we magan ongytan þæt manna wisdom 7 heora smeagunga 7 heora rædas syndon nahtlice ongean Godes geþeaht.

As is clear, both from the references to Edward's established sainthood and to the accomplishment of divine vengeance and also from the incongruous description immediately following of Æthelred's consecration *mid micclum gefean*, this must be a later interpolation in the annal. But, even as a later interpolation, it remains a remarkable sign of how far the *Chronicle* is coming to admit elements foreign to its original terse objectivity.

Indeed, the tone of the main record itself is shifting. Throughout the 980s, in spite of the fierce Viking raids recorded, the impersonal manner persists; but, from about 991, the annalist, enlarging the borders of his garments, begins to offer explanations of the events he records, and also comments on them. Thus he ascribes the decision taken after Maldon, to pay the Danes £10,000, to *ðam miclan brogan þe hi worhton be ðam særiman* (991). Further, as well as imputing motives to his personages, he allows himself to be far more openly partisan than the Alfredian annalists ever were: 'Ac hi (*sc.* the Danes) þær geferdon maran hearm 7 yfel þonne hi æfre wendon þæt him ænig buruhwaru gedon sceolde. Ac seo hlige Godes modor on þam dæge hire mildheortnesse þære buruhware gecydde, 7 hi ahredde wið heora feondum' (994C). From the mid-nineties until the end of the reign, this tone, imaginative and personal, dominates the entries.

In contrast with the earliest annals, where the personages are only names and ranks, and even with the later Alfredian ones, where only the king himself is presented from

---

[30] Ker, *Catalogue*, pp. 57–9, 252–3 and 254.

[31] For the various stories current about Edward's murder, see C.E. Wright, *The Cultivation of Saga in Anglo-Saxon England* (Edinburgh and London, 1939), pp. 162–71.

inside, these annals show much interest in personalities, their *mores* as well as their *actus*, and also some readiness to pass judgment on them, as when they tell of Ealdorman Ælfric of Hampshire, one of the generals, who 'sende . . . 7 het warnian ðone here; 7 þa on ðære nihte þe hy on ðone dæig togædere fon sceoldan, þa sceoc he on niht fram þære fyrde, him sylfum to myclum bysmore' (992). Another general, Ulfcytel, is both prudent and brave, first advising (unlike the dead hero of Maldon) 'þæt hit betere wære þæt mon wið þone here friðes ceapode, ær hi to mycelne hearm on ðam earde gedydon, forðæm hi unwæres comon 7 he fyrst næfde þæt he his fyrde gegaderede', yet, in the event, impressing the Danes by his prowess (1004). Byrhtric is vain: 'ðohte þæt he him micles wordes wyrcan sceolde þæt he Wulfnoð cucone oþþe deadne begytan sceolde' (1009). The Danes, though arrogant, 'wendon him þa andlang Æscesdune to Cwicelmeshlæwe, 7 þær onbidedon beotra gylpa' (1006), yet acknowledge the valour of Ulfcytel and his men, 'sædon þæt hi næfre wyrsan handplegan on Angelcynne ne gemitton' (1004) – not so much character drawing, perhaps, as a neat way to emphasize English merit. Lively as these portraits are, they are necessarily impressionistic and so diminish rather than enhance the absolute veracity of the recital. By contrast with the later Alfredian annals, the king himself is left undefined, with the massacre on St Brice's Day explained detachedly, 'forðam þam cyninge wæs gecyd þæt hi woldan hine besyrwan æt his life . . . 7 habban siþþan þis rice' (1002), and with his epitaph understated, 'he geheold his rice mid myclum geswince 7 earfoðnessum þa hwile ðe his lif wæs' (1016).

Circumstantial descriptions likewise enliven the narrative. The times and scenes of Ealdorman Ælfric's treacheries are indicated with economical brush-strokes, making moral points as well as visual ones, 'þa on ðære nihte þe hy on ðone dæig togædre fon sceoldan, þa sceoc he on niht . . .' (992) and 'sona swa hi wæon swa gehende þæt ægðer here on oþerne hawede . . .' (1003). The mastery of the Danes and the helplessness of the English, of the very citizens of the West Saxon capital, who see no confident army other than a Danish one, are ironically pictured: 'Ac þær mihton geseon Wincesterleode rancne here 7 unearhne, ða hi be hiora gate to sæ eodon, 7 mete 7 madmas ofer .l. mila him fram sæ fetton' (1006). In the account of Ælfheah's murder one phrase indicates not only the condition of the Canterbury Vikings but also the trade routes they dominated: *swyþe druncene, forðam þær wæs broht win suðan* (1012).

In association with these shifts in tone, style in the narrower sense has also evolved. Although grammatical resources are only a little richer than those of the later Alfredian annals, use of them is suppler, the range of clause-types wider. Hypothetical conditions, quite alien to the factual early annals, now add an extra dimension to the narrative: 'oft man cwæð, gif hi Cwicelmeshlæw gesohton, þæt hi næfre to sæ gan ne scoldon' (1006); 'ða buruh raðe geeodon, gif hi ðe hraðor to him friðes ne gyrndon' (1009); and, combined with supposed quotation of enemy testimony, 'Ac, gif þæt fulle mægen ðær wære, ne eodon hi næfre eft to scipon: swa hi sylfe sædon þæt hi næfre wyrsan handplegan on Angelcynne ne gemitton, þonne Ulfcytel him to brohte' (1004). This speculative turn gives the narrative new depth, partly because events are no longer seen as absolute and, as it were, predestined, partly because contemporary opinion and reaction are involved; but at the same time it reduces its factual value.

Diction too has become richer and suppler, giving a coloured and shaded effect that contrasts with the line-drawing of the earliest annals. Adjectives and adverbs, although still sparse, are more emotive, helping to set events against the background of contemporary reaction: the Danes, *se ungemætlica unfriðhere*, now do *unasecgendlice yfel, þæt mæste yfel þæt ænig here don mihte*, taking *unasecgendlice herehyðe*; betrayed seamen are *þæt earme folc* (999), the army marching past Winchester is *ranc 7 unearh* (1006) and the famine of 1005, *se micla hungor*, is *swylce nan man ær ne gemunde swa grimne*; the Danes murder Ælfheah *bysmorlice* and Eadric Streona slays Sigeferth and Morcar *ungerisenlice*; and in 'forleton þa scipu ðus leohtlice, . . . 7 leton ealles þeodscypes geswinc ðus leohtlice forwurðan' (1009) the reiterated *ðus leohtlice* stresses the magnates' frivolity in sacrificing the new fleet to a private quarrel. Vocabulary now comes from a wider range of registers. Colloquialism brings out the black comedy of Ealdorman Ælfric's second treachery: 'Þa sceolde se ealdorman Ælfric lædan þa fyrde, ac he teah ða forð his ealdan wrencas: sona swa hi wæron swa gehende þæt ægðer here an oþerne hawede, þa gebræd he hine seocne 7 ongan hine brecan to spiwenne, 7 cwæð þæt he gesicled wære . . .' (1003). *To spiwenne* conveys Ælfric's loss of dignity as well as of honour, while *ealdan wrencas* implies a complicity between the annalist and his audience, whom he assumes not only to know what he knows but also to share his view of it. Elsewhere it is poetic language which extends the emotional range. The kennings in *þær he wiste his yðhengestas* (1003) and in *næfre wyrsan handplegan . . . ne gemitton* (1004)[32] momentarily raise the war to an heroic plane; and in 1016 the doom overhanging Edmund Ironside's accession is implicit in the phrase '7 he his rice heardlice werode, þa hwile þe his tima wæs'.

These poetic snatches, with the further dimension of feeling they bring into the *Chronicle*, could be reminiscences of current lays; but, even if they are, they have nonetheless a stylistic function. Apart from the heightened emotion they convey, most of them form rhetorical codas to the entries they occur in. This is so with *þær he wiste his yðhengestas*, and also with the two most elaborate passages of this kind: 'Þonne æt ðam ende ne beheold hit nan þing, seo scipfyrding ne seo landfyrding, buton folces geswinc, 7 feos spylling, 7 heora feonda forðbylding' (999); and '7 hi þær togædere fæstlice fengon, 7 micel wæl ðær on ægðre hand gefeol. Ðær wearð East-Engla folces seo yld ofslagen. Ac, gif þæt fulle mægen ðær wære, ne eodon hi næfre eft to scipon: swa hi sylfe sædon þæt hi næfre wyrsan handplegan on Angelcynne ne gemitton, þonne Ulfcytel him to brohte' (1004). The rhyme and alliteration used here belong no less to rhetorical prose than to verse. Elsewhere alliteration may add emphasis, or perhaps echo a legal formula: 'mete 7 madmas ofer .l. [fiftig] mila him fram sæ fetton' (1006) and 'man þa fulne freondscipe gefæstnode mid worde 7 mid wedde on ægþre healfe, 7 æfre ælcne Deniscne cyng utlah of Englalande gecwædon' (1014); in 'ge fyrðon on þa wildan fennas hi ferdon' (1010) alliteration is combined with emphatic word-order, and in 'seo fyrding dyde þære landleode ælcne hearm, þæt him naðer ne dohte, ne innhere ne uthere' (1006), the unexpected *innhere*[33] instead of *fyrd* is stressed by the vocalic alliteration as well as by the antithesis; doublets are thrown into relief by rhyme and alliteration: 'þæt scyp genaman eall gewæpnod 7 gewædod' (992) and 'þa scypo ða ealle tobeot 7 toþærsc 7 on land awearp' (1009); and an exclamation, itself unusual enough in annalistic style, is reinforced by rhyme (*similiter cadens*): 'Ac wala þæt hi to raðe bugon 7 flugon!' (999).

Other rhetorical devices also occur, for this annalist's passionate feelings could not be expressed without *verbis ampullosis*. In 'Þonne wearð þær æfre ðuruh sum þing fleam astiht, 7 æfre hi æt ende sige ahton' (998) and in '7 á swa hit forðwerdre beon sceolde, swa wæs hit læbre fram anre tide to oþre, 7 á hi leton heora feonda werod

---

[32] Cf., e.g., 'Næfre he on aldordagum, ær ne siþðan, / heardran hæle healðegnas fand' (*Beowulf*, 718–19).

[33] The DE reading; C *inghere*.

wexan, 7 *á* man rymde fram þære sæ' (999), the repetition (*traductio*) of *æfre* and that (*repetitio*) of 7 *á*, the latter coupled with the antithesis *forðwerdre/lætre*, stress the permanence of the situation. The same point is later made by a series of antitheses, ending in a balanced pair: '7 þonne hi to scipon ferdon, þonne sccolde fyrd ut eft, ongean þæt hi up woldan: þonne ferde seo fyrd ham. 7 þonne hi wæron be easton, þonne heold man fyrde be westan, 7 þonne hi wæron be suðan, þonne wæs ure fyrd be norðan' (1010). Another chain of antitheses reflects on the capture of Ælfheah: 'Wæs ða ræpling, se ðe ær wæs heafod Angelkynnes 7 Cristendomes; þær man mihte ða geseon yrmðe, þær man oft ær geseah blisse, on þære earman byrig, þanon us com ærest Cristendom 7 blis for Gode 7 for worolde' (1011); and a combination of antithesis and *isocolon* describes his murder: 'sloh hine . . . þæt mid þam dynte he nyþer asah, 7 his halige blod on þa eorðan feol, 7 his haligan sawle go Godes rice asende' (1012). With the style of the *Chronicle* developing in this direction, the impassioned interpolation in 979 DE, so loaded with antitheses, can now be given its due place in the tradition.

Literary craft appropriate to history rather than annals appears not only in this emotive rhetoric but also in the devices used to weld the whole group of annals into a single narrative. These include forward glances, as when 1011 closes with a reference to Ælfheah's martyrdom the next year, and 1013 (which, exceptionally, opens not with *Her* but with *On ðam æftran geare þe se arcebiscop wæs gemartyrod*) with one to Swein's death, likewise in the next year. Sometimes the interval, although vague, seems longer: '7 him þa Anlaf behet, *swa he hit eac gelæste*, þæt he næfre eft to Angelcynne mid unfriðe cuman nolde' (994: one of the few examples here of a man of honour); and 'hine bebyrigdon on Scē Paules mynstre, 7 *þær nu God sutelað þæs halgan martires mihta*' (1012). Under 991 the repeated *ærest* in 'on þam geare man gerædde þæt man geald *ærest* gafol Denescum mannum . . . þæt wæs *ærest* .x. ðusend pund' implies all the further, larger, tributes to come, by 1017 reaching £72,000.[34] Even more, continuity appears in phrases which recur like refrains, each tied to its own theme, with an effect wholly unlike that of the earlier formulaic repetitions. In 999 the new fleet 'æt ðam ende ne beheold . . . nan þing, . . . buton folces geswinc 7 feos spylling . . .'; in 1006 the summoning of the fyrd 'naht ne beheold þe ma ðe hit oftor ær dide'; again in 1009 'we ða gyt næfdon þa gesælða ne þone wyrðscype þæt seo scypfyrd nyt wære þissum earde, þe ma ðe heo oftor ær wæs'. The measure of English demoralization is given by the frequency of the keywords *fleam, fleah, flugon*: *Þa onstealdan þa heretogan ærest þone fleam* (993), *Þonne wearð þær æfre ðuruh sum þing fleam astiht* (998), *Ac wala þæt hi to raðe bugon 7 flugon!* (999), *sona þæt wered on fleame gebrohton* (1006) and 'Þa sona flugon East-Engle. . . . Þone fleam ærest astealde Þurcytel Myranheafod. . . . Æt nextan næs nan heafodman þæt fyrde gaderian wolde, ac ælc fleah swa he mæst mihte; ne furðon nan scir nolde oþre gelæstan æt nextan' (1010). Complementary to English incapacity are the mastery and barbarity of the Danes. Time and again they overrun the country *swa swa hi sylf woldan* (1001; compare 994, 998, 999, 1006, 1009 and 1010), staying *swa lange swa hi woldon* (1011) and burning *swa mycel swa hi sylfe woldon* (1010). They observe what customs they please: *hi á dydon heora ealdan gewunan, atendon hiora herebeacen* (1006); *dydan eal swa hi bewuna wæron, slogon 7 bærndon* (1001); *dydon eal swa hi ær gewuna wæron, heregodon 7 bærndon 7 slogon* (1006); and *heregodon 7 bærndon, swa hiora gewuna is* (1009). Harrying, burning and

---

[34] 994, £16,000; 1002, £24,000; 1007, £36,000; 1009, £3000 (East Kent only); 1012, £48,000; 1014, £21,000; and 1017, £72,000.

slaying form, indeed, the most constant refrain: *on bærnette 7 heregunge 7 on manslyh-tum* (994); *on bærnette 7 on mannslihtum, bærndon 7 slogon* (997); *mid bryne 7 mid heregunge* (1006); and *geheregodon 7 forbærndon* (1003; compare 1004 and 1010). In 1013 a new turn of events is reflected by new keywords: *beah, gislas, bugon, gisludon* and *beah 7 gislude*; with the old refrains nevertheless returning, 'for eallon þam, hi heregodon swa oft swa hi woldon.' The next entry completes the pattern: Æthelred it was (for once) who 'hergode 7 bærnde 7 sloh eal þæt mancynn þæt man ræcan mihte', and Cnut saw to it that the English *gislas* paid the price. In 1016 all the strands are finally woven together: 'Com Cnut mid his here . . . 7 heregodon 7 bærndon 7 slogon eal þæt hi to comon. . . . Þa hi (*sc.* the fyrd) ealle tosomne comon, þa ne beheold hit nan ðinc, þe ma ðe hit oftor ær dyde. . . . Slogon 7 bærndon (*sc.* the Danes) swa hwæt swa hi oferforan, swa hira gewuna is . . . Þa dyde Eadric ealdorman swa swa he ær oftor dyde, astealde þæne fleam . . .' In spite of the momentary shift when Edmund Ironside *geflymde* the Danish *here*, events followed the old patterns until Edmund's death left the way open for Cnut to take peaceful possession of England.

For all the attempts at characterization and at continuity, and the free rhetorical comment, these annals cannot be called 'history' in the full sense. There is no sense of perspective or of causation; events may be commented on, moralized on even, but they are not explained even at the personal level. When the annalist says 'Man ne mihta geþencan 7 ne asmeagan hu man hi of earde adrifan sceolde, oþþe ðisne eard wið hi gehealdan' (1006), he does not transcend the helplessness he records but shares it. His diagnosis of the country's ills is pragmatic, and, for one who was probably a monk, oddly indifferent to metaphysical possibilities: 'Ealle þas ungesælða us gelumpon þuruh unrædas, þæt man nolde him a timan gafol beodan . . . ac þonne hi mæst to yfele gedon hæfdon, þonne nam mon frið 7 grið wið hi' (1011).[35] Whereas the value of the early annals had lain in objectivity, that of these annals lies in rendering, with literary skill, but without intellectual sophistication, the feelings of an ordinary observer of the events recorded.

The Annals for the Confessor's Reign

For most of Cnut's reign the *Chronicle* reverts to classic terseness, the several versions showing a general agreement. With the reigns of Cnut's two sons, Harold Harefoot and Harthacnut, the annalists not only begin again to expand their material and to comment on it, but also show some independence of one another, C and D being regularly more outspoken than E. Thus, in the entries for the year 1035, while E (*s.a.* 1036) remarks how 'Sume men sædon be Harolde, þet he wære Cnutes sunu cynges 7 Ælfgiue Ælfelmes dohtor ealdormannes, ac hit þuhte swiðe ungeleaflic manegum mannum', C and D impute the claim to Harold himself, adding roundly *þeh hit na soð nære*. E remains blank while C and D, under 1036, relate the shocking murder of *Ælfred se unsceððiga æþeling*, in a quasi-Laȝamonic verse which could be that of a popular lay.[36] Under 1037, although all three versions note how the ageing, widowed Emma was

---

[35] Compare not only the diagnosis in the contemporary *Sermo Lupi*, 'Nis eac nan wundor þeah us mislimpe, forþam we witan ful georne þæt nu fela geara mænn na ne rohtan foroft hwæt hy worhtan wordes oððe dæde' (ed. Whitelock, p. 60), but also 1087E, 'Ac swylce þing gewurðaþ for folces synna, þet hi nellað lufian God 7 rihtwisnesse.'

[36] F. Holthausen, 'Zu dem ae. Gedichte von Ælfreds Tode (1036)', *Beiblatt zur Anglia* L (1939), 157 has shown that behind the *Chronicle* versions there probably stood one with better rhymes.

expelled, only C and D add *butan ælcere mildheortnesse ongean þone weallendan winter*. Under 1040 and 1041 (= 1039 and 1040E) only C and D condemn the king, for doing *naht cynelices*, as *wedloga*, and for throwing his predecessor's body *on fenn*; and under 1042 (= 1041E) only they record the exact manner of his death in such terms as to make of this an implicit judgment: 'Her gefor Harðacnut swa þæt he æt his drince stod, 7 he færinga feoll to þære eorðan mid egeslicum anginne.'

How great a change has come over the *Chronicle* appears both in this free criticism of the kings and, at least equally, in the discrepancies between the various versions. Discrepancies there had always been, in plenty, but earlier ones seemed due to varying access to information, not to varying party allegiance. Now, however, although access to information still varies (whereas, for instance, 1046*E [= true date 1049] lists several bishops attending the synod of Rheims, the corresponding entry in D [dated 1050] complains that it is *earfoð to witane þara biscopa þe þærto comon*), what determines the differences between the versions of the *Chronicle* is party allegiance. Thus E's silence about Alfred's murder, in which C (but not D) implicates Earl Godwine, seems due not so much to lack of information as to the Godwinist sympathies which later become patent in E's account of Godwine's banishment in 1051 (*s.a.* 1048E).[37] Godwine's banishment is, indeed, a touchstone for the party allegiances of the chroniclers. C records it briefly, without explanation. D (*s.a.* 1052) depicts a hotheaded and arrogant man first challenging established authority, then fleeing from confrontation by it. E, in contrast, shows a good man first misunderstood in his endeavours to protect his own earldom and avenge *þæs cynges bismer . . . 7 ealles þeodscipes* and at the last denied a fair hearing. Indeed, forgetting that respect for plain fact which had dignified the early *Chronicle*, D and E make assertions so irreconcilable that Sir Frank Stenton considered the story to be garbled beyond reconstruction.[38]

Stylistically, the means by which these partisan impressions are conveyed differ from any previously noted. Among earlier styles, the one which those of both D and E here most resemble is that of the later Alfredian annals: modestly complex and without obvious rhetorical ornament. But, with the earlier annals impartial and these eleventh-century ones tendentious, the resemblance is not only superficial but misleading. Whereas, for instance, the later Alfredian annals eschewed descriptive elements, especially adverbial ones, these annals exploit such elements to impart bias to their narratives. This is partly how the E annalist gives his picture of Eustace of Boulogne and his men its hostile colouring. Some underhandedness in Eustace's original mission seems implied in the phrase, *spæc wið hine þet þet he þa wolde*, and then in the Dover episode all the adverbial phrases have a moral ring: *þa woldon hi innian hi þær heom sylfan gelicode*; *wolde wician æt anes bundan huse his unðances*; *ofslogon hine binnan his agenan heorðæ*; and *cydde be dæle hu hi gefaren hæfdon*. D, on the other hand, shows Eustace's men starting the affray stupidly, *dyslice*, rather than viciously, and notes Godwine's flight in a phrase like the one that the earlier annalist had used of

[37] See Earle and Plummer, *Chronicles* II, 211–15; cf. below, p. 18, n. 42. Independent accounts of this murder, both insisting on Godwine's complicity, occur in *Encomium Emmae Reginae*, ed. A. Campbell, Camden Third Series 72 (1949), 40–6 (cf. pp. lxiv–lxvii) and in *Guillaume de Poitiers: Histoire de Guillaume le Conquérant*, ed. and trans. R. Foreville (Paris, 1952), pp. 6–12.

[38] *Anglo-Saxon England*, 2nd ed. (Oxford, 1947), p. 553; see also B. Wilkinson, 'Freeman and the Crisis of 1051', *Bulletin of the John Rylands Library* XXII (1938), 368–87.

Ealdorman Ælfric: *For ða on niht awæg.* This shows the danger inherent in the *Chronicle*'s shift away from plainness and impartiality: once comment on motive and character was acceptable, indeed, once subjective description was admitted, the way was open for biased interpretation.

Yet, biased as it is, interpretation here shows an enhanced sense of causation. Events are not happening willynilly, as in the annals for Æthelred's reign, but are determined by previous acts. In E, everything hinges on that phrase, *cydde be dæle,* for from Eustace's one-sided report arises all the king's anger and misunderstanding of God-wine; and the same motif reappears when the French 'castlemen' of Herefordshire 'wæron ... ætforan mid þam cynge 7 forwregdon ða eorlas, þet hi ne moston cuman on his eagon gesihðe': consistently, if not always clearly, Godwine is being shown as a victim of duplicity and of calumny. With the Frenchmen at his ear, the king continues to refuse his earl a fair hearing and so comes to banish him out of hand. D, too, traces events back to individual actions and so to personal character, but to Godwine's own irascible arrogance rather than to Eustace's mendacity: 'Þa undernam Godwine eorl swyðe þæt on his eorldome sceolde swilc geweorðan; ongan þa gadrian folc . . .' D indeed displays its chain of causation better than E does, better perhaps than any previous annals had done. Whereas E, perhaps advisedly, skips some of the steps in the narrative, D offers a tale apparently complete (although not for that necessarily truer to the facts).[39] Godwine assembles forces *ealle gearwe to wige ongean þone cyng.* That said, it needs no further explanation why the king summons his loyal earls to bring their forces to his aid or why Godwine is summoned to answer for his deeds before the court.

In both narratives this sense of human causation is underlined by reference to the thoughts and feelings of the protagonists. In E it is Godwine's heart which is laid bare: he finds it *lað to amyrrene his agenne folgað,* and *lað . . . þet hi ongean heora cynehlaford standan sceoldan.* In D insight is shown rather into the minds of the loyal earls. Having come to the king with token forces, they appraise the situation, and 'siððan hy wiston hu hit þær be suðan wæs, þa . . . leton beodan myccle fyrde heora hlaforde to helpe.' But, unlike the hotheaded Godwine, these earls think before acting:

Wurdan þa ealle swa anræde mid þam cynge, þæt hy woldon Godwines fyrde gese-can, gif se cyng þæt wolde. Þa leton hy sume þæt þæt mycel unræd wære, þæt hy togedere comon, forþam þær wæs mæst þæt rotoste þæt wæs on Ænglalande on þam twam gefylcum, 7 leton þæt hi urum feondum rymdon to lande 7 betwyx us sylfum to mycclum forwyrde.

Such an explanation why *no* battle took place shows how the concept of annal writing has shifted since those strictly factual records of two centuries earlier, 'Her gefeaht se cyning, 7 micel wæl geslog 7 sige nam.'

For all that, causation is not yet seen in any but short and personal perspectives. Some naïveté of outlook is indeed betrayed by D's comment on Godwine's fall: 'Þæt wolde ðyncan wundorlic ælcum men þe on Englalande wæs, gif ænig man ærþam sæde þæt hit swa gewurþan sceolde, forðam þe he wæs ær to þam swyðe upahafen, swylce he weolde þæs cynges 7 ealles Englalandes.' Neither D nor E offers the wider view of events that history in the modern sense requires. Indeed the Eustace-Godwine

---

[39] Wilkinson, *ibid.* p. 385 describes D as the best of the extant accounts of the crisis; but see below, p. 18, n. 42, for some omission from it.

clash, which personified the clash at the Confessor's court between Norman and Anglo-Danish interests and which 'through its results became one of the ultimate causes of the Norman invasion of 1066',[40] gets little more attention than episodes with few repercussions such as Swein Godwinsson's murder of his cousin Beorn.[41] True, the 'Frenchmen' are seen as a party: '. . . 7 geutlagedon ealle þa Frenciscean þe ær unlagon rærdon 7 undom demdon 7 unræd ræddan into ðissum earde' (1052CD) and '. . . 7 cweð man utlaga Rotberd arcebiscop fullice, 7 ealle þa Frencisce menn, forðan þe hi macodon mæst þet unseht betweonan Godwine eorle 7 þam cynge' (1052E). But there is no sign that either motives or consequences were understood in political rather than in personal terms; and, even on the personal level, the rôle of Robert of Jumièges is left obscure.[42] Not even the E annalist, partisan as he is, has expressed what issues his partisanship involves.

Yet, although these annals thus show objectivity replaced by rather short-sighted partisanship, the change is not all loss. To know how differently events were seen by chroniclers apparently based respectively at York (D) and at Canterbury (E) is itself a gain.

The Conquest

7 þa hwile com Willelm eorl up æt Hestingan on Sancte Michaeles mæssedæg; 7 Harold com norðan, 7 him wið gefeaht ear þan þe his here come eall; 7 þær he feoll, 7 his twægen gebroðra, Gyrð 7 Leofwine. And Willelm þis land geeode, 7 com to Westmynstre, 7 Ealdred arcebiscop hine to cynge gehalgode, 7 menn guldon him gyld 7 gislas sealdon 7 syððan heora land bohtan.

In defeat E recaptures the lapidary dignity of the earliest annals, refraining from either lament or recrimination. Behind all the passion and partisanship of the preceding century, the old tradition of objective recording still flowed strong.

The D annalist, in contrast, uses a voice not unlike that of his predecessor in Æthelred's reign, not hiding his scorn, whether for the supporters of Edgar the Ætheling as laggards alike in war and in peace: 'Ac swa hit æfre forðlicor beon sceolde, swa wearð hit fram dæge to dæge lætre 7 wyrre[43] . . . Bugon þa for neode, þa mæst wæs to hearme gedon; 7 þæt wæs micel unræd þæt man æror swa ne dyde, þa hit God betan nolde for urum synnum', or for the Conqueror as a hypocrite: '7 he heom behet þæt he wolde heom hold hlaford beon – 7, þeah, onmang þisan, hi hergedan eall þæt hi oferforon . . . 7 he sealde him on hand mid Cristes bec, 7 eac swor . . . þæt he wolde þisne þeodscype swa wel haldan swa ænig kyngc ætforan him betst dyde, gif hi him holde beon woldon – swa þeah, leide gyld on mannum swiðe stið . . .'

Nevertheless, it is D, not E, which to express the outcomes of the two battles, Stamford Bridge and Hastings, reverts to the ninth-century formula:[44] 'Engle ahton

---

40 Stenton, *loc. cit.*

41 1049C, 1050D and 1046*E.

42 Neither version mentions the story that Robert of Jumièges had helped to bring about Godwine's fall by accusing him of Alfred's murder; see *The Life of King Edward*, ed. F. Barlow (London, 1962), pp. 18–23 and cf. Wilkinson, *loc. cit.* pp. 371 and 379–82.

43 Compare especially the extract from 999 quoted above, p. 14.

44 First used in the *Chronicle* in the annal for 833 quoted above, p. 4. Note that 1066C says of the Battle of Fulford 7 *Normen ahton wælstowe gewald.*

wælstowe geweald . . . 7 þa Frencyscan ahton wælstowe geweald.' This formula, so characteristic of the *Chronicle* although not peculiar to it,[45] is not recorded again in any of the extant texts, as though, once used of the Conquest, it could never again be used of any punier victory.

Thus the narrative mode of the *Chronicle* sways continually between the austere objectivity of the original Easter table entries and a more emotive utterance, sometimes as of the pulpit, sometimes as of every day. This oscillation will continue to the very end; for the Final Continuation, best known for its moving account of the Anarchy, can also be classically objective: '7 te eorl of Angæu wærd ded, 7 his sune Henri toc to þe rice. 7 te cuen of France todælde fra þe king; 7 scæ com to þe iunge eorl Henri, 7 he toc hire to wiue, 7 al Peitou mid hire. Þa ferde he mid micel færd into Engleland, 7 wan castles' (1140E). For all the occasions when rhetoric – not to mention human nature – breaks in, there remains nevertheless an underlying sense of annals as a genre of their own, requiring a special diction and a special attitude of mind: the feeling which Gervase of Canterbury tried to express when he warned chroniclers against 'making broad their phylacteries'. But what Gervase failed to see was that the modest style, the 'scrawny oatstalk', expressed a respect for absolute truth in the record.[46]

---

[45] See BT, *s.v. wælstow*.
[46] I am deeply grateful to Professor Clemoes for having read this article several times in draft and having suggested many improvements in my argument.

2

On Dating *The Battle of Maldon*:
Certain Evidence Reviewed[1]

For the Old-English poem known as *The Battle of Maldon* there was recently proposed, instead of the traditional dating to the early 990s, a new one 'about or after 1020'.[2] This was based on the use there of the term *eorl* supposedly in the technical sense 'ealdor-mann', on the grounds that such a usage, involving as it does semantic borrowing from Scandinavian *jarl*, must necessarily have post-dated Cnut's accession. Among critics welcoming this new dating at least one has gone further, reinterpreting it as 'no . . . earlier than *c.*1030' and alleging as further proof of the poem's lateness various other probable and possible Scandinavianisms.[3] Because this seemingly precise dating has thus been partly accepted – although not by the poem's most recent editor[4] – and also used as a foundation on which to build further hypotheses, perhaps the evidence put forward ought to be reassessed before conjecture hardens unchecked into dogma.

The argument rests on two premises: that on the poem's place of origin any Scandinavian impact had been 'minimal';[5] and that official Old-English usage, as preserved in writs and charters, accurately represents the irrecoverable everyday one, the 'real language of men' drawn upon by poets for revivifying antique conventions. These basic assumptions, which bear upon issues wider and deeper than the date of one fragment of verse, in themselves merit our close scrutiny.

*   *   *

[1] I am grateful both to the British Academy and to the Judith E. Wilson Fund (administered by the Cambridge University English Faculty) for research grants which assisted with my working expenses during the compilation of this paper. I must also thank most warmly the several friends who have encouraged me, and most of all Christine Fell, who has done her best to mitigate my unfamiliarity with matters Scandinavian. For whatsoever inadequacies remain I alone am to blame.

[2] J. McKinnell, 'On the date of *The Battle of Maldon*', *Medium Ævum*, xliv (1975), 121–36, esp. 132.

[3] N.F. Blake, 'The genesis of *The Battle of Maldon*', *Anglo-Saxon England*, vii (1978), 119–29, esp. 120, 124, 125 n. 1, 126, 128. Another enthusiastic acceptance has come from George Clark, 'The hero of *Maldon: vir pius et strunuus*', *Speculum*, liv (1979), 257–82, esp. 265 n. 33, 281–2 and n. 65.

[4] See *The Battle of Maldon*, ed. D.G. Scragg (Manchester, 1981), pp. 26–7. This appeared in mid-February 1982, when the present article was already in its penultimate draft; I was delighted to find the editor's views, although not identical with my own, inclining partly the same way. A sceptical attitude has been taken also by H. Gneuss, *Die 'Battle of Maldon' als historisches und literarisches Zeugnis* (Sitzungsberichte der Bayerische Akademie der Wissenschaften: philosophisch-historische Klasse, 1976/v, Munich, 1976), p. 12 n. 22, cf. p. 7.

[5] See McKinnell, 'Date', pp. 121–2.

First of all, the meaning of *eorl* at issue may not be so much 'ealdormann' as 'commander, leader', which fits all the contexts involved (an individual's possession of an official title by no means compels all references to him to confirm to that style). Not even the combination *Æþelredes eorl* (line 203), where some have thought 'ealdormann' especially apposite, in fact excludes a wider sense, as is clear from analogous phrases such as *ðone æþelan Æþelredes þegen* (151).

Translating *eorl* as 'commander, leader' still, however, leaves a problem to be resolved, because this sense too had at first a restricted field of reference. With *eorl* as an official title it is common ground that, although often applied during the tenth century to leading men from the Northern Danelaw, it was not until Cnut's time given to provincial governors in general.[6] With the wider sense chronology is less clear. Certainly, from the later ninth century on a new prose sense of 'Viking leader' began developing alongside the older, poetic one of 'noble warrior'.[7] Already in the Alfredian West-Saxon of the Parker annal for 871 (of which the extant text dates from *c*.892) the new meaning is well established.[8] But, although soon becoming common, the new sense seems to have kept for a fair time its original nationally-restricted application: throughout the tenth-century annals, for instance, it is used only of Viking or Danelaw leaders; and the same seems true of the generic use in law-codes, such as *III Æthelred*, with its specific reference to the Five Boroughs, and likewise the so-called *Laws of Edward and Guthrum* now attributed to the homilist Wulfstan.[9] On the other hand, Wulfstan himself in the opening decade of the eleventh century more than once used *eorlas & heretogan* in an entirely general sense.[10]

So the relevant question must be how soon the term *eorl* might have acquired, in any area where the *Maldon* poem is likely to have been composed, the meaning 'leader' *tout court* – not 'theirs', but 'ours': whether, that is, this semantic shift is, in any such area, likely to have pre-dated Cnut's accession.

Where the poem was composed can still be only conjectured. As a provenance for the largely-burnt British Library Cotton MS. Otho A XII, of which the *Maldon* fragment in the seventeenth century formed part, Barking abbey has recently been

---

6 See McKinnell, 'Date', pp. 122–7; cf. also, for instance, F.M. Stenton, *Anglo-Saxon England* (3rd edn, Oxford, 1971), pp. 414–16.

7 For the poetic sense, see, for instance, P. Wormald, 'Bede, *Beowulf* and the conversion of the Anglo-Saxon aristocracy', in *Bede and Anglo-Saxon England*, ed. R.T. Farrell (British Archaeological Reports, xlvi, Oxford, 1978), pp. 32–95, esp. 36 – a reference which I owe to Christine Fell. For the possible relevance of this sense here, see D. Hofmann, *Nordisch-englische Lehnbeziehungen der Wikingerzeit* (Bibliotheca Arnamagnæana, xiv, Copenhagen, 1955), pp. 197–8, and also *Maldon*, ed. Scragg, p. 27.

8 See *The Anglo-Saxon Chronicle*, ed. B. Thorpe (Rolls Series, 1861, 2 vols), i. 136–40.

9 See *Die Gesetze der Angelsachsen*, ed. F. Liebermann (Halle, 1903–16, 3 vols), i. 228–32, esp. para. 9.12, and i. 128–34, esp. 134 (for Wulfstan's authorship of *Edward and Guthrum*, see D. Whitelock in *English Historical Review*, lvi (1941), 1–21); the twelfth-century *Quadripartitus* each time translates *eorl* as *comes*. For discussion of the term *eorl*, see also *Gesetze*, ii. 388–9. The Scandinavian influence on the legal terminology and practice of *III Æthelred* has been noted by, amongst others, S. Keynes, *The Diplomas of King Æthelred 'the Unready' 978–1016* (Cambridge, 1980), pp. 196–7. For the usage in *ASC*, see, for instance, the passages cited below pp. 24–5 and also McKinnell, 'Date', pp. 122–3.

10 See *Die 'Institutes of Polity, Civil and Ecclesiastical': ein Werk Erzbischoff Wulfstans von York*, ed. K. Jost (Swiss Studies in English, xlvii, Bern, 1959), pp. 62, 78 – examples which McKinnell, 'Date', seems to have missed. See further below pp. 34–5.

suggested.[11] But, as the poem's latest editor points out, no pre-Cottonian evidence links the *Maldon* folios with the Barking hagiography with which they were then bound up; rather the reverse, for if, as seems the case, the fragment consisted of the inner three bifolia of a quire whose outer one had been lost, it must have spent some time unbound.[12] In any event, the lost manuscript's provenance, from wheresoever it may have been, has little bearing on the poem's place of origin (and *a priori* no nunnery would seem the likeliest home for a battle-poem, no matter how conventionalized in diction or symbolic in intention). The poem's linguistic forms are, as preserved, predominantly those of the late West-Saxon *Schriftsprache*, variegated not only by Anglian forms such as were traditional in poetic use but also by a few scattered South-Eastern ones.[13] Provisionally, therefore, *Maldon* may reasonably, and vaguely, be presumed to have been composed somewhere – perhaps in south-eastern England, but not necessarily in the battlefield's immediate vicinity – where Byrhtnoth's memory was kept especially green.

That leaves a field inconveniently wide. For what such evidence may be worth, *Domesday Book* shows forms of *Beorhtnoð* as favoured among the late-eleventh-century gentry mainly in Suffolk.[14] As for Ealdormann Byrhtnoth's own connections, these were widespread.[15] Although his ealdormanry was seemingly that of 'Essex' (not, of course, confined within that county's modern boundaries),[16] his family estates, and therefore his influence and his fame, extended north well into East Anglia proper as well as west across Cambridgeshire and Huntingdonshire into the central Midlands and beyond. His widow's will shows property at her disposal concentrated in Essex, Suffolk and Cambridgeshire.[17] Although his own will has not survived, Ely records make clear that he had himself held estates in plenty in that abbey's vicinity.[18] His tomb was, and is, at Ely, where he was revered as a major benefactor and his *obit*, together with those of several relatives of his, was celebrated at least until the twelfth century.[19] His widow had marked the funeral by donating to the abbey several nearby estates, a torque, and a hanging which depicted her late husband's deeds.[20]

Because of these links, Ely abbey has sometimes been suggested as a possible home for the *Maldon* poem.[21] Certainly the *Liber Eliensis*, which took its extant form in the mid twelfth century, not only includes a romanticized account of Byrhtnoth's heroic death but also alludes to tales of him preserved *Anglicè*.[22] On the other hand, the oldest

---

11 See Gneuss, *Zeugnis*, pp. 62–4; cf. *idem*, 'Die Handschrift Cotton Otho A. XII', *Anglia*, xciv (1976), 289–318.
12 See, for instance, *Maldon*, ed. Scragg, pp. 1–4.
13 See *Maldon*, ed. Scragg, pp. 22–8; also Gneuss, *Zeugnis*, pp. 55–8.
14 See O. von Feilitzen, *The Pre-Conquest Personal Names of Domesday Book* (Nomina Germanica, iii, Uppsala, 1937) [*PNDB*], p. 196.
15 See, for instance, *Maldon*, ed. Scragg, pp. 15–20; cf. map facing p. 17.
16 See, for instance, *Maldon*, ed. Scragg, pp. 17–18, and references p. 48 n. 74.
17 See *Anglo-Saxon Wills*, ed. and tr. D. Whitelock (Cambridge, 1930), pp. 38–43, with commentary pp. 141–6.
18 See *Liber Eliensis*, ed. E.O. Blake (Camden third series, xcii, 1962), pp. 133–6, 422–3. Cf. E. Miller, *The Abbey and Bishopric of Ely* (Cambridge, 1951), pp. 22–3.
19 See B. Dickins, 'The day of Byrhtnoth's death and other obits from a twelfth-century Ely kalendar', *Leeds Studies in English*, vi (1937), 14–24.
20 See *Liber Eliensis*, p. 136.
21 See, for instance, *The Battle of Maldon, etc.*, ed. W.J. Sedgefield (London, 1904), p. viii.
22 *Liber Eliensis*, pp. 133–6.

datable account of the fatal battle – other, that is, than the various Anglo-Saxon annals[23] – is preserved in the *Vita Oswaldi* composed before 1005 and attributed by modern scholars to Byrhtferth of Ramsey.[24] Partly for this reason, Ramsey abbey, which had enjoyed minor benefactions from Byrhtnoth,[25] has likewise been proposed as a possible home for the poem;[26] but, concentrating as it did on reverence for its principal lay founder, Ealdormann Æthelwine (admittedly a kinsman and associate of Byrhtnoth's), it perhaps seems a less promising candidate than Ely. In any event, Ely, Ramsey and Barking were not the only religious houses enjoying the bounty of Byrhtnoth and his kin: other beneficiaries included Bury St Edmunds, Stoke-by-Nayland, and Christ Church, Canterbury.[27] Nor indeed was the poem necessarily monastic in origin: a household chaplain or even a layman might equally well have been its author. All in all, its exact provenance may never be definitively established; but perhaps a modest confirmation that it did originate somewhere in those Eastern counties where Byrhtnoth's main connections lay may be afforded by the fact that the only place named in its surviving text is Sturmer (line 249), near where the modern boundaries of Essex, Suffolk and Cambridgeshire converge.

On such a reckoning, the areas relevant to the poem's composition would mostly fall within the 'Southern Danelaw' – according as that district can be demarcated not only on the (perhaps dubious) evidence of the early-twelfth-century so-called *Laws of Edward the Confessor* but more cogently on that of the Alfredian *Treaty of Wedmore*, which had set the western boundary of Guthrum's territory at Watling Street (*i.e.*, on a line roughly from Chester through Bedford and Hertford to London).[28] For nearly two generations, that is, from Guthrum's settlement to Edward the Elder's reconquest,[29] these areas had experienced not only Viking rule but also, and more importantly, whatever cultural influences that rule had entailed. The next question is, therefore, not

---

[23] The CDE annal for 991 seems part of the late-Æthelredian block composed at the earliest in 1116: see C. Clark, 'The narrative modes of *The Anglo-Saxon Chronicle* before the Conquest', above pp. 3–19, esp. pp. 10–15, and S. Keynes, 'The declining reputation of King Æthelred the Unready', in *Ethelred the Unready: Papers from the Millenary Conference*, ed. D. Hill (BAR, British Series, lix, Oxford, 1978), pp. 227–53, esp. pp. 229–31, 233. As for the A annal, the layout of the Parker manuscript is here confused: see, for instance, *Maldon*, ed. Scragg, pp. 9–10 and nn. on pp. 43–4. The latest attempt to unravel it has been made by A. Lutz, in *Die Version G der angelsächsischen Chronik* (Munich, 1981), pp. 232–5: working from her reconstruction of G, a close copy of the Parker annals as they stood *c.*1005, she takes the 'Maldon annal' as inserted in A after 994 but before c.1005, noting that a *signe de renvoi* links it to the annal-number 991.

[24] Printed in *The Historians of the Church of York and its Archbishops*, ed. J. Raine (Rolls Series, 1879–94, 3 vols), i. 399–475, esp. 456. For Byrhtferth's authorship see M. Lapidge, 'The hermeneutic style in tenth-century Anglo-Latin literature', *Anglo-Saxon England*, iv (1975), 67–111, esp. 90–5; cf. S.J. Crawford, 'Byrhtferth of Ramsey and the anonymous Life of St Oswald', in *Speculum Religionis: Studies presented to C.G. Montefiore* (Oxford, 1929), pp. 99–111. Blake, 'Genesis', pp. 122, 128, claims that this *Life* was the *Maldon* poem's sole source.

[25] See *Chronicon Abbatiae Rameseiensis*, ed. W.D. Macray (Rolls Series, 1886), pp. 116–17.

[26] See, for instance, E. John, 'War and society in the tenth century: the Maldon campaign', *Transactions of the Royal Historical Society*, 5th series, xxvii (1979), 173–91, esp. 187 (no real argument is put forward here).

[27] See, for instance, *Wills*, ed. Whitelock, pp. 38–41, also pp. 105–7, 142–5.

[28] See *Gesetze*, i. 126–8, 660; also the discussion of *Denalagu* at ii. 347–8.

[29] Cf. below pp. 24–5.

how dense Viking settlement had been in the Southern Danelaw but how tenaciously its cultural influences had survived the West-Saxon reconquest.

Because pre-Conquest vernacular texts from Eastern England hardly exist,[30] the cultural and linguistic patterns prevailing there can be studied only indirectly. One traditional source for information about the Viking settlements in England consists of place-names. For Essex, and even more for Cambridgeshire and Huntingdonshire, these reveal clear though sparse signs of Scandinavian influence.[31] But, because few extant records antedate the Norman Conquest, let alone the Cnutian one, little of this place-name evidence is admissible in the present context. For Cambridgeshire, however, two names, from opposite sides of the county, show Scandinavian influence recorded before the end of the tenth century: these are *Carlton*, identifiable with a *Carletun* mentioned in a will of *c.*990, and *Conington*, likewise found, as *Cunning-tun(e)*, in a late-tenth-century will and explained by Reaney as attributable to Scandinavianization of an earlier **Cyning-tūn*[32] (the Huntingdonshire *Conington* probably had a like origin, but its early records are less clear[33]). As for field- and other minor names, these, although indeed offering evidence for fair Scandinavian influence in this area,[34] are never recorded early enough to be admissible in a pre-Cnutian context (in fact, their variations do seem related to the original ninth-century settlement patterns rather than to the Cnutian hegemony, which probably affected the whole country more evenly[35]).

Whether or not 'minimal' correctly describes the degree of Scandinavian influence so far detected in the Eastern counties, the harvest looks meagre enough, considering how firmly under Danish domination the whole area had at one time been. So much is clear from the *Anglo-Saxon Chronicle* alone, and especially from its accounts of Edward the Elder's reconquests. The Parker annal for 913 (true date, 912) tells how, after Edward had established forts at Hertford and also at Witham near Maldon, there

---

30 See A. Campbell, *Old English Grammar* (Oxford, 1959), pp. 4–11, also pp. 362–3; and cf. my own remarks in *The Peterborough Chronicle 1070–1154* (2nd edn, Oxford, 1970), pp. xxxviii–xxxix.

31 See: P.H. Reaney, *The Place-Names of Essex* (English Place-Name Society [EPNS], xii, Cambridge, 1935), pp. xxviii–xxix; *idem*, *The Place-Names of Cambridgeshire and the Isle of Ely* (EPNS, xix, Cambridge, 1943), pp. xix–xxii; A. Mawer and F.M. Stenton, *The Place-Names of Bedfordshire and Huntingdonshire* (EPNS, iii, Cambridge, 1926), pp. xix–xx. Cf. O.K. Schram, 'Fenland place-names' in *The Early Cultures of North-West-Europe (H.M. Chadwick Memorial Volume)*, ed. Sir C. Fox and B. Dickins (Cambridge, 1950), pp. 429–41, esp. pp. 438–41.

32 See *PNCambs*, pp. 116–17, 165–6; *Wills*, ed. Whitelock, pp. 32–3, cf. p. 136.

33 See *PNBeds and Hunts*, p. 182; *Wills*, ed. Whitelock, pp. 66–7, cf. p. 178, also p. 130.

34 See G. Fellows Jensen, 'English field-names and the Danish settlement', in *Festskrift til Kristian Hald* (Copenhagen, 1974), pp. 46–55, esp. p. 50, and *eadem*, 'The Vikings in England', *Anglo-Saxon England*, iv (1975), 181–206, esp. pp. 196–7; K.I. Sandred, 'Ortnamns- och ordstudier i Englands fenland', *Ortnamnssällskapets i Uppsala Årsskrift*, 1972, 41–52 (English summary, 51–2), and *idem*, 'Scandinavian place-names and appellatives in Norfolk: a study of the medieval field-names of Flitcham', *Namn och Bygd*, lxvii (1979), 98–122; J. Insley, 'Addenda to the Survey of English Place-Names: personal names in field- and minor names', *Journal of the English Place-Name Society*, x (1977–78), 41–72, esp. 43–4 (Essex), 55 (Herts) and 69 (Cambs).

35 See, for instance, H.R. Loyn, *Anglo-Saxon England and the Norman Conquest* (London, 1962), pp. 50, 62; cf. Stenton, *Anglo-Saxon England*, pp. 413–14. Veronica Smart's partly unpublished studies of pre-Conquest moneyers' names (cf. below n. 42) show no shifts of naming-patterns during the reigns of Cnut and of his two sons – I am grateful to Dr Smart for permission to refer to her 1981 Nottingham PhD thesis. [[See now V.J. Smart, 'Moneyers of the late Anglo-Saxon coinage: the Danish dynasty 1017–42', *Anglo-Saxon England*, xvi (1987), 233–308.]]

submitted to him a great host of people 'þe ær under Deniscra manna anwalde wæron'.[36] The annal for 918 [914] shows Edward having a fort built at Buckingham, where subsequently 'Þurcytel eorl hine gesohte to hlaforde, & þa holdas ealle, & þa ieldstan men ealle mæste þe to Bedanforda hierdon, & eac monige þara þe to Hamtune hierdon'[37] – note here the use not only of *eorl* in its Scandinavian sense but also of the loanword *hold(as)* representing the Scandinavian *hǫldr*. Next, Edward recaptured Bedford itself. Among districts involved in the many campaigns recorded in the annal for 921 [917] there were again several especially relevant to the present study.[38] A *here* representing the Danes of Huntingdonshire and of East Anglia established a base at Tempsford in Bedfordshire and then, hoping to extend their territory, marched on Bedford itself, but there met their match; Edward's men then drove them from the advance base at Tempsford, killing several *eorlas* and forcing the rest to submit. That autumn the king's forces retook Colchester. Then a fresh *here*, mobilized in East Anglia not only from the *landhere* but also from Vikings they summoned to their aid, marched on Maldon but was there put to flight. Edward's men then retook Huntingdon itself. And in late autumn the king received at Colchester the submission of a multitude, from East Anglia as well as from Essex, 'þe ær under Dena anwalde wæs'.[39] Likewise, the Cambridgeshire *here* submitted and swore him oaths of fealty.

For all that they left so little mark on major place-names, some forty years of Danish rule, ended mainly by submission rather than by expulsion, must have left some cultural legacy. Later law-codes imply distinctive customs in most countries east of Watling Street, and certainly in Suffolk and in Cambridgeshire.[40] Another domain potentially susceptible to, and thus revelatory of, Scandinavian influences consists of personal names. But, again, as with place-names, few records from this area can be dated to the tenth century, one notable exception being the list of Peterborough abbey sureties so frequently cited for its high proportion of Scandinavian forms.[41] Another name-sample so datable consists of the Æthelredian moneyers' names collected by Veronica Smart: this corpus, although too specialized to permit of safe conclusions about the population at large, shows Scandinavian names occurring, albeit sporadically, at the small mints serving Northampton, Huntingdon, Cambridge, Bedford, Ipswich and Colchester, and

---

[36] 'Who had previously been under the domination of the Danes': *Chronicle*, i. 186. For the chronology of this part of *ASC*, see *English Historical Documents c.500–1042*, ed. and tr. D. Whitelock (2nd edn, London, 1979), pp. 211–16; cf. W.S. Angus, 'The chronology of the reign of Edward the Elder', *English Historical Review*, liii (1938), 194–210, and R. Vaughan, 'The chronology of the Parker Chronicle, 890–970', *ibid.*, lxix (1954), 59–66, esp. 63. For a general view of the Reconquest, see Stenton, *Anglo-Saxon England*, pp. 319–29.

[37] 'Earl Thurcytel and all the leaders submitted to him as lord, and so too did all the chief men based on Bedford and likewise many of those based on Northampton': *Chronicle*, i. 190.

[38] *Chronicle*, i. 194–5.

[39] 'Who had previously been under the domination of the Danes': *Chronicle*, i. 195.

[40] The question remains delicate: see, for instance, D.M. Stenton, *English Justice between the Norman Conquest and the Great Charter, 1066–1215* (London, 1965), pp. 16–17, 'The strength of the Scandinavian influence in England is one of the great imponderables'. Cf. above n. 28.

[41] Printed in, for instance, *Anglo-Saxon Charters*, ed. and tr. A.J. Robertson (Cambridge, 1939), pp. 74–82. See especially E. Ekwall, 'The Scandinavian element', *Introduction to the Survey of English Place-Names*, ed. A. Mawer and F.M. Stenton (EPNS, i, part I, Cambridge, 1924), pp. 55–92, esp. pp. 72–4, and similar later references, including *idem*, 'The proportion of Scandinavian settlers in the Danelaw', *Saga-Book of the Viking Society*, xii (1937–45), 19–34, esp. 20–6.

rather more often at those of Norwich and of Thetford – in clear and probably significant contrast with their complete absence from the coins of many southern and south-
western mints.[42] Both these samples suggest for the Eastern counties a Scandinavian
cultural influence more pervasive and more tenacious than the major place-names
implied; but neither, the second especially not, can be claimed as wholly representative
of the population there.

As it happens, a further, and perhaps more typical, sample of personal names can be
collected from the late-tenth-century sections of *Liber Eliensis*, already cited for its
romanticized account of Byrhtnoth's death;[43] and, ill omen though that might seem,
this compilation is in general deemed to represent reliably the pre-Conquest vernacular
materials on which it drew.[44] The tale of the abbey's fortunes from its refoundation in
970 until Cnut's accession names many laypeople, mostly local landowners belonging
to what may be termed its 'catchment area' – that is, the area within which its principal
estates lay and from which it drew much of its lay patronage and probably most of its
monks. Far from being confined to the two hundreds composing the 'Isle' of Ely, the
abbey's interests embraced estates and dependent landholders in Suffolk, Norfolk and
Essex, and, to a lesser degree, in Huntingdonshire and in Hertfordshire.[45] Thus,
whether or not Ely abbey had played any part in either the composition or the preservation of the *Maldon* poem, its 'catchment area' happens, most conveniently, to cover a
fair part of those Eastern districts with which the work can provisionally be linked.

The names found in this section of *Liber Eliensis* are predominantly native Old-
English ones, and commonplace enough. But, as Dorothy Whitelock pointed out, they
also include a fair leavening of Scandinavian forms, all masculine.[46] Indeed, the
name-stock represented here partly coincides with that of the Peterborough list just
cited for its notable proportion of such forms. Estimating what relation these Scandinavian names in *Liber Eliensis* bear to the whole corpus is tricky – not least because
often it is unclear whether a subsequent instance of a name previously mentioned did
or did not denote the same individual. What can most readily be compared are therefore the name-stocks; but, with a certain number of forms etymologically ambiguous,
even these present problems.[47] Altogether, after forms obviously not referring to local
men have been subtracted, the stock of masculine names here amounts to nearly 100, of
which just over 60 are unremarkable Old-English ones.[48] Forms clearly Scandinavian
amount to just under a quarter of the total stock:

---

[42] See V.J. Smart, 'Moneyers of the late Anglo-Saxon coinage, 973–1016', in *Commentationes de
Nummis Saeculorum ix–xi in Suecia Repertis*, ii (Kungl. Vitterhets Historie och Antikvitets
Akademiens Handlingar: Antikvariska Serien, xix, Stockholm, 1968), pp. 191–276, esp. pp.
242–50.

[43] See above n. 18. The section analyzed here is *Liber Eliensis*, pp. 72–142.

[44] See Dorothy Whitelock's Foreword, in *Liber Eliensis*, pp. ix–xvii.

[45] See Miller, *Ely*, pp. 16–25 (the map facing p. 76 shows the abbey's thirteenth-century holdings).

[46] See *Liber Eliensis*, p. xi.

[47] For general discussion of name-study problems, see C. Clark, 'Battle c.1110: an anthroponymist
looks at an Anglo-Norman New Town', below pp. 221–40, esp. pp. 222–7.

[48] Given by *Liber Eliensis* in twelfth-century spellings, these names can be listed in normalized
West-Saxon forms as follows: *Ælfgār, Ælfhelm, Ælfmǣr, Ælfnōð, Ælfrīc, Ælfsige, Ælfstān,
Ælfw(e)ald, Ælfweard, Ælfwīg, Ælfwine, Æðelfrið, Æðelmǣr, Æðelnōð, Æðelrīc, Æðelstān,
Æðelweard, Æðelwine, Æðelwulf (Æðulf), Bēahmund, Beorhtfrið, Beorhthelm, Beorhtlāf,
Beorhtnōð, Beorhtsige, Brūnstān, Burghelm, Cenw(e)ald, Cynehelm, Ēadfrið, Ēading, Ēadnōð,*

Appe[n][49] (p. 92; infl. gen.)   Omundus[58] (107)
Bondo[50] (88, etc.)   One[59] (108; gen.)
Clac[51] (of Fulbourn; 108)   Oscitelus[60] (108)
Grim[52] (88, etc.)   Othulf[61] (of Exning; 89)
Gunulfus[53] (96)   Scule[62] (comes; 111)
Hawardus[54] (95)   Steapa[63] (115)
probably Hugo[55] (108)   Sumerlede[64] (91)
Ingulfus[56] (110)   Thorð[65] (son of Oslacus comes; 106)
Ogga[57] (of Mildenhall; 94)   Thurverthus[66] (114)

Ēadrīc, Ēadwine, Ealdstān, Eama, Gōdhere, Gōding, Gōdwine, Hererīc, Lēofing, Lēofrīc, Lēof-
sige, Lēofstān, Lēofwine, Ordhelm, Ordmær, Ōswīg, Seaxfrið, Wīggār, Wihtgār, Wine, Wulfgār,
Wulfhēah, Wulfhelm, Wulfnōð, Wulfrīc, Wulfsige, Wulfstān, Wulfwine, Wynsige. For some ambiguous forms, see below nn. 75–85. Wedwine, although looking native, does not occur in PNDB
and is the only instance in Wed- listed in W. G. Searle, Onomasticon Anglo-Saxonicum (Cambridge, 1897).

[49] ON Ap(p)i: see PNDB, p. 162, and G. Fellows Jensen, Scandinavian Personal Names in Lincolnshire and Yorkshire (Copenhagen, 1968) [SPLY], p. 11. I am deeply grateful to Dr Fellows-Jensen
for private comments on certain forms discussed here; for any misuse I may have made of her
information she is in no way to blame.

[50] ON Bóndi: see PNDB, p. 206, and SPLY, pp. 60–1.

[51] ON Klakkr: see PNDB, p. 305, and SPLY, pp. 172–3.

[52] ON Grímr: see PNDB, p. 276, and SPLY, pp. 105–7.

[53] ON Gúnnulfr: see PNDB, p. 278.

[54] ON Hávarðr: see PNDB, p. 278, and SPLY, pp. 136–7.

[55] Although later normally representing Continental-Germanic Hugo (cf., for instance, PNDB, p.
294), here, just as Bondo represents ON Bóndi, this form probably represents Latinization of ON
Hughi; cf. O. von Feilitzen, 'Notes on some Scandinavian personal names in English twelfth-
century records', in Personnamnstudier 1964 tillägnade minnet av Ivar Modéer (1904–1960)
(Anthroponymica Suecana, vi, Stockholm, 1965), pp. 52–68, esp. p. 57, and also SPLY, p. 143;
and for other similar Latinizations, see PNDB, p. 128, and SPLY, pp. c–ci.

[56] ON Ingólfr: see PNDB, p. 298, and SPLY, pp. 152–3.

[57] ON Oggi (probably a hypocoristic of Auðgrímr or of Oddgeirr): see von Feilitzen, Personnamnstudier, p. 65 (but cf. PNDB, p. 335, and O. von Feilitzen and C. Blunt, 'Personal names on the
coinage of Edgar', in England before the Conquest, pp. 183–214, esp. p. 202 n. 5).

[58] Suggested by John Insley to represent ON Auðmundr (for forms like Aumund, etc., see SPLY, p.
40, also p. xciv); alternatively, perhaps ON Ámundr, for which see SPLY, p. 10.

[59] Probably ON Auni: see PNDB, p. 169 (but cf. p. 161, s.n. Áni).

[60] ON Ásketill: see PNDB, pp. 167–8, s.n. Áskell, and SPLY, pp. 25–32.

[61] ON Auðulfr: see PNDB, p. 170, and SPLY, pp. 40–1.

[62] ON Skúli: see PNDB, p. 366, and SPLY, p. 254.

[63] ON Stjúpi: see PNDB, p. 375, and SPLY, p. 266.

[64] ON Sumarliði: see PNDB, pp. 377–8, and SPLY, pp. 270–1.

[65] ON Þórðr < Þor(f)røðr: see PNDB, pp. 396–7, and SPLY, p. 302, and cf. below n. 66. The
individual here concerned, a son of Oslac comes, may have been the Þorede eorl of ASC 992
(Chronicle, i. 238–9): see D. Whitelock, 'The dealings of the kings of England with Northumbria
in the tenth and eleventh centuries', in The Anglo-Saxons: Studies in some Aspects of their
History and Culture presented to Bruce Dickins, ed. P. Clemoes (London, 1959), pp. 70–88, esp.
pp. 78–80.

[66] ON Þorfrøðr: see PNDB, p. 392, and SPLY, pp. 303–4, and cf. above n. 65.

Toli[67] (*comes*; 98)   Ulf[70] (89)
Tope[68] (98)   Uvi[71] (84)
Tucca[69] (89)

These Scandinavian names prove notable not only for their number but also for their almost regular Anglicization: for instance, the element Ás- is replaced by its cognate Ōs-,[72] the unfamiliar *au*-diphthong (as in *Auð*-) by the phonetic approximation *o*,[73] and the Scandinavian weak-masculine *i*-ending by the corresponding Old-English *-a*, as in *Steapa* for **Stepi* (the earlier form of *Stjúpi*) and *Tucca* for *Tóki*. Such Anglicizations – all common, together with various others, in English renderings of Scandinavian names[74] – have a double importance: as evidence of cultural integration; and as a guide for interpreting ambivalent forms.

And, owing to the basic similarity of the two languages, a good few forms here do indeed seem ambivalent, among them *Glor* (p. 89), *Herulfus* (106), *Manne* (92), *Osebernus* (of Soham; 89), *Oslacus* (92, etc.), *Osmundus* (90, etc.), *Osulfus* (84, etc.), *Osuuoldus* (87), *Ringulfus* (115), *Simundus* (89, etc.), *Siverthus* (84, etc.), *Sprouue* (105), and *Wacher* (of Swaffham; 88). Given the regular replacement of Ás- by Ōs, coupled with the close similarity of many cognate second-elements, plus substitution of English equivalents for the less familiar ones, nearly all names in Ōs- prove ambivalent;[75] and the same goes for those in *Si*-, which could represent either Old-English *Sige*- or Scandinavian *Síg*-. But in some cases the contexts suggest what the name-bearers' cultural affinities may have been: one *Osulf*[76] was the father of a *Grim*, and of the several instances of *Oslac*, one refers to the *comes* (*eorl*) of Northumbria, another to a son of *Appe* and a third to a kinsman of *Hawardus*;[77] likewise, one *Simundus*[78] here had a *nepos* called *Tucca*, and one *Siverthus*[79] was brother to *Ingulfus*. *Herulfus*[80] and *Ringulfus*[81] are likewise linguistically ambivalent. As for the single-element names, always the most obscure, the form *Manne* could represent either Old-English *Manna*,

---

[67] ON *Tóli*: see *PNDB*, p. 386, and *SPLY*, pp. 289–90. The individual here concerned is the *Toglos eorl* (*Toglauss*) slain, along with his son *Manna eorl*, at Tempsford: see *Chronicle* i. 194–5 (921 [917]).

[68] ON *Topi*: see *PNDB*, p. 386, and *SPLY*, p. 291.

[69] ON *Tóki*: see *PNDB*, pp. 385–6, and *SPLY*, pp. 287–8.

[70] ON *Ulfr*: see *PNDB*, pp. 400–1, and *SPLY*, pp. 321–4.

[71] ON *Úfi*: see E.H. Lind, *Norsk-isländska Dopnamn ock Fingerade Namn från Medeltiden* (Uppsala, 1905–15), cols 1047–8.

[72] Cf. *PNDB*, pp. 164–5, also p. 338, and von Feilitzen and Blunt, 'Edgar', p. 202; also *SPLY*, pp. lxx–lxxi. See also below nn. 75, 76, 77.

[73] Cf. *PNDB*, p. 68, and *SPLY*, pp. lxxviii–lxxix.

[74] For Anglicization in general, see further *PNDB*, p. 126, cf. pp. 66–9, and *SPLY*, pp. xcix–c; also J. Insley, 'Regional variation in Scandinavian personal nomenclature in England', *Nomina*, iii (1979), 52–60, esp. 53, 55–7.

[75] Cf. above n. 72. In particular, for ON *Ásbjǫrn*/OE *Ōsbeorn*, see *PNDB*, pp. 165, 338–9, and *SPLY*, pp. 18–19; for ON *Ásmundr*/OE *Ōsmund*, see *PNDB*, pp. 169, 340, and *SPLY*, pp. 34–5; and for ON *Ásvaldr*/OE *Ōsw(e)ald*, see *PNDB*, p. 340.

[76] ON *Ásulfr*/OE *Ōswulf*: see *PNDB*, pp. 169, 341, and *SPLY*, p. 35.

[77] ON *Áslákr* (variant *Ásleikr*)/OE *Ōslāc*: see *PNDB*, pp. 168, 340, and *SPLY*, pp. 33–4. Cf. above n. 65.

[78] ON *Sigmundr*/OE *Sigemund*: see *PNDB*, p. 363, and *SPLY*, p. 233.

[79] ON *Sigfrøðr*/OE *Sigefrið* (-ferð): see *PNDB*, p. 360, and *SPLY*, p. 231.

[80] ON *Her(i)olfr*/OE either *Herewulf* or *Heoruwulf*: see von Feilitzen and Blunt, 'Edgar', p. 198, and cf. *PNDB*, p. 289.

[81] ON *Ringolfr*/OE *Hringwulf*: see *PNDB*, p. 293, and *SPLY*, p. 219.

with twelfth-century *-e* for earlier unstressed *-a*, or else Scandinavian *Manni* Anglicized and showing similar treatment,[82] and *Wacher* too seems uncertain;[83] but *Glor*[84] and *Sprouue*,[85] the most difficult of the names here, may on balance best be taken as both native. In all ambivalent cases, plumping for one etymology rather than the other may be pointless; for, if medieval people of mixed 'race' behaved at all like many present-day bilinguals, they may expressly have sought names acceptable to both cultures. Among the most celebrated examples of what looks like such choice were Archbishop Oda of Canterbury (941–958), his nephew (St) Oswald, archbishop of York (972–992), and their kinsman Oscytel, bishop of Dorchester (c.950–971) and then briefly archbishop of York; for, of these three men, all descended from Danish settlers, two bore the ambivalent names *Oda* and *Oswald*, and the third the fully Anglicized Scandinavian *Oscytel*.[86] And, as tenth-century men of the Danelaw, they and their cultural affinities are no less relevant here than the local landowners and others figuring in *Liber Eliensis*.

One or two names look Continental-Germanic: that is, *Folcardus*,[87] *Henricus*, and perhaps also *Boga* and *Waldgist*. But again, if it is true, as various evidence suggests, that Vikings reaching England by way of the German North-Sea coast brought with them Frisian and Flemish names,[88] then culturally these forms too ought perhaps to be classed with the Scandinavian ones. At all events, the uncle through whom the sons of

---

[82] See *PNDB*, p. 324, and *SPLY*, pp. 194–5. For the *Manna eorl* who was son of *Toglos eorl*, see above n. 67.

[83] ON *Vakr(i)*/(OE)*Wacor*: see *PNDB*, p. 407.

[84] Native parallels found in early-recorded place-names are cited by O. von Feilitzen, 'Some Old English uncompounded personal names and bynames', *Studia Neophilologica*, xl (1968), 5–16, esp. 8; but cf. also the (admittedly rare) ON *Glóra*, for which see E.H. Lind, *Norsk-isländska Personbinamn från Medeltiden* (Uppsala, 1920–1), col. 112.

[85] Possibly connected with *Sprouuintune*, which has been tentatively identified with Sproughton, Suffolk: see *Liber Eliensis*, p. 101 n. 2. Although English forms of ON *Sprógr* have been identified in Danelaw place-names – see *SPLY*, p. 261, and G. Fellows Jensen, *Scandinavian Settlement Names in the East Midlands* (Copenhagen, 1978), pp. 186–7 – the present form seems unlikely to represent this because of the *uu* (*w*), which is not normally found for an older voiced guttural spirant as early as the late twelfth century (let alone the late tenth!). For suggestions of an OE *Sprow*, see J.McN. Dodgson, *The Place-Names of Cheshire: Part II* (EPNS, xlv, Cambridge, 1970), p. 254, and also W.F.H. Nicolaisen, *Scottish Place-Names: their Study and Significance* (London, 1976), pp. 36, 38.

[86] See *Historians*, ed. Raine, i. 404, where Oda's father is said to have come over with *Huba* and *Hinwar*, also pp. 401, 420, and *Chronicon Abbatiae Rameseiensis*, pp. 21, 24, 25. Cf. D. Whitelock, 'The conversion of the Eastern Danelaw', *Saga-Book of the Viking Society*, xii (1937–45), 159–76, esp. 169–71, 174–5, and *eadem*, 'Dealings', 73, 75–6. For ON *Oddi*/OE *Od(d)a*, see *PNDB*, p. 333, and *SPLY*, p. 202; for *Oswald*, see above n. 75, and for *Oscytel*, above n. 60.

[87] Found also, as are likewise *Boga* and *Waldgist*, as a moneyer's name: see V.J. Smart, *Sylloge of Coins of the British Isles: Cumulative Index of Volumes 1–20* (SCBI, xxviii, London, 1981), p. 36, also von Feilitzen and Blunt, 'Edgar', p. 196 n. 1.

[88] For the association of Frankish-named moneyers with the so-called 'St Edmund' coinage of East Anglia, see V.J. Smart, 'Moneyers' names on the Anglo-Saxon coinage', *Nomina*, iii (1979), 20–8, esp. 22, and also M. Dolley, in *Mediaeval Scandinavia*, ii (1969), 181, 182; cf. above n. 87. For Frisians in East Anglia, see also G.C. Homans, 'The Frisians in East Anglia', *Economic History Review*, second ser., x (1957–8), 189–206, and R.J. Faith, 'Peasant families and inheritance customs in medieval England', *Agricultural History Review*, xiv (1966), 77–95, esp. 77–81. More generally, cf. K. Hald, 'Danes and Frisians in Lincolnshire', *IIIe Congrès international de toponymie et d'anthroponymie* (Louvain, 1951, 3 vols continuously paginated), pp. 627–32.

Boga of Hemingford – one of the most vexed of personal names[89] – laid claim to certain Huntingdonshire estates had not only borne the Scandinavian name *Tope* (*Topi*), but had also had a grandmother who in 917 had been among the host making submission to Edward the Elder at Cambridge.[90] *Waldgist*, borne here by a man who had forfeited certain Norfolk estates *tempore Ædmundi regis* (p. 115) and found also, in the form *Wælgist*, as the name of a Thetford moneyer of Æthelred II's time, recalls not only the West-Germanic *Waltgis(us)* but also the *Wal(æ)gæst* noted in Denmark.[91]

Thus far, evidence from the tenth-century names in *Liber Eliensis* has confirmed the impression given by the other two personal-name samples of fair Scandinavian influence in the Southern Danelaw. Purely linguistic analysis shows that among the landholding classes roughly a quarter of the men's names in use reflected such influence; and in formally ambivalent names family background often amplifies the Scandinavian resonances present. Even so, the case may still remain understated. For a good few men whose own names look purely English prove to have near-relatives with Scandinavian ones, as with *Æfnopus* son of *One* (p. 108), *Ælfstanus* and *Æthestanus* the brothers of *Bondo* (108), *Osuui* brother of *Ulf* (93) and *Oswi* brother of *Uvi* (108), *Saxferð* father of *Oscitelus* (108), and *Wine* father of *Grim* (93); one *Ædricus* is surnamed *Dacus* (116).

To dwell on these various sorts of naming-pattern is not, of course, to claim that all men with names of Scandinavian types had Viking blood running in their veins (that some of them in fact had is, however, likely). Evidence of this sort bears solely on cultural influences; and those are for the present purpose all that matters. At all events, such levels of Scandinavian influence as can here be discerned among the pre-Cnutian gentry of the Southern Danelaw surely deserve to be classed as more than 'minimal', especially as some of the individuals concerned seem to have been locally prominent and thus capable of setting the fashion.

So, with their free Anglicization and the constant interchange within families of names from both categories, naming-patterns imply that by the late tenth century the descendants of the Danish settlers in Eastern England had become fully integrated with the native English[92] – incidentally raising again the grisly question of how 'Danes' were supposed to be defined for the purposes of the St Brice's Day massacre. Throughout the Danelaw such integration seems to have been normal. In the ecclesiastical sphere archbishops Oda, Oscytel and Oswald have just been cited. In the military and

---

[89] See von Feilitzen and Blunt, 'Edgar', pp. 189–91, and cf. *PNDB*, p. 205, and *Studia Neophilologica*, xl.7.

[90] *Liber Eliensis*, pp. 98–9, cf. comments p. xi.

[91] *Liber Eliensis*, pp. 114–15. Cf. Smart, *Index*, p. 75. For *Waltgis(us)*, see, for instance, M.-Th. Morlet, *Les noms de personne sur le territoire de l'ancienne Gaule du vi^e au xiie siècle* (Paris, 1968–72, 2 vols), i. 213a; and for *Wal(æ)gæst* in Denmark, see K. Hald, *Personnavne i Danmark: I – Oldtiden* (Copenhagen, 1971), p. 23.

[92] On a wider geographical basis, similar findings about a cultural *modus vivendi* between the Danelaw English and their Scandinavian rulers have been reached by N. Jacobs, 'Anglo-Danish relations, poetic archaism and the date of *Beowulf*: a reconsideration of the evidence', *Poetica* [Tokyo], viii (1978), 24–43, esp. 35–40 (an essay by P. Poussa in *Neuphilologische Mitteilungen*, lxxxii (1981), 276–88, puts a like point of view in an amateurish way); a similar theme had been more tentatively treated by M. Ashdown, 'The attitude of the Anglo-Saxons to their Scandinavian invaders', *Saga-Book of the Viking Society*, x (1928–9), 75–99. Cf. also Keynes, *Diplomas*, pp. 202–5.

political spheres too the descendants of the Viking settlers seem often, understandably, to have thrown in their lot with their English neighbours rather than with the fresh bands of marauders. True, little weight can be attached to the 'Five Boroughs' verses forming the Parker annal for 942 and their picture of the Danes settled in that district as gratefully liberated from the Northmen's heathen clutches.[93] Unambiguously, however, the CDE annals name among the commanders whom Æthelred appointed in 992 *Þorede eorl*, that is, Thored of Northumbria (perhaps the *Thorð* of *Liber Eliensis*)[94] – with the annalist, it may be noted, accepting that title as appropriate for a Northern representative of the West-Saxon administration. In 993, not only were two of the English commanders taking flight called *Frœna* and *Friðegist* but they were accompanied by a *Godwine* and had also, it seems, been set an example by Ealdormann Ælfric of Hampshire's treachery in the previous year.[95] And in 1004 an English commander in Norfolk bearing the unambiguously Scandinavian name of *Ulfcytel* led his incompletely-assembled *fyrd* so resolutely against the Vikings attacking Thetford that he surprised them into admiration – 'never', the *Chronicle* reports them as saying, 'had they met in England *wyrsan handplegan* than Ulfcytel offered them.'[96] Nor were such men as Thored, Fræna, Frithegist and Ulfcytel mere unofficial leaders in their provinces: together with other *ministri* with Scandinavian names they appear as witnesses to several of Æthelred's diplomas,[97] as well as to Edgar's main 'privilege' to Ely.[98]

On the basis of this, necessarily sketchy, survey of tenth-century cultural patterns in the former Southern Danelaw, a fresh attempt may now be made to relate the *Maldon* poem to its putative milieu. Apart from the supposedly crucial meaning of *eorl*, various other Scandinavianisms can, as already remarked, be noted here, although about their number no less than about their bearing critics differ.[99]

One such element sporadically noted in earlier studies consists of personal names:[100] the very kind of cultural evidence whose value has just been urged. When one loyal hero is named as *Wistan, Þurstanes sunu* (lines 297–8), not only is the father's name unmistakably Scandinavian, with its second element Anglicized in the typical way,[101]

---

93 *Chronicle*, i. 208–11 (another of the many altered dates in A is involved here, see Lutz, *Die Version G*, 226). Cf. A. Mawer, 'The Redemption of the Five Boroughs', *English Historical Review*, xxxviii (1923), 551–7.

94 *Chronicle*, i. 238–9. Cf. above n. 65.

95 *Chronicle*, i. 240–1. Keynes, *Diplomas*, p. 206, questions the degree of their culpability. For their names, see *PNDB*, pp. 252, 255.

96 *Chronicle*, i. 254. For the name, see *PNDB*, pp. 399–400, *s.n. Ulfkell*, and *SPLY*, pp. 325–7.

97 See Keynes, *Diplomas*, pp. 161–2, and Tables 7 and 8.

98 *Liber Eliensis*, p. 78 n. If it is true that minor attestations of royal diplomas may have a local flavour (see Keynes, *Diplomas*, pp. 161–2), the occurrence here of the names *Frena*, *Frithegist* and *Ulfcytel* is interesting.

99 See, for instance: Hofmann, *Lehnbeziehungen*, pp. 193–9, and Gneuss, *Zeugnis*, p. 58, both of whom prefer geographical explanations; F.C. Robinson, 'Some aspects of the *Maldon* poet's artistry', *Journal of English and Germanic Philology*, lxxv (1976), 25–40, esp. 26–8, for a literary one; and Blake, 'Genesis', pp. 124, 125 n. 1, 126, for a chronological one.

100 The fullest notes previously available on the personal names in the poem are to be found in *Byrhtnoth and Maldon*, ed. E.D. Laborde (London, 1936), pp. 37, 38, 73–4, and in E.V. Gordon's edition (London, 1937; reissued, with supplement by D.G. Scragg, Manchester, 1976), pp. 83–6. The article by H.B. Woolf, in *Modern Language Notes*, liii (1938), 109–12, is unhelpful.

101 ON *Þorsteinn*: see *PNDB*, p. 396, and *SPLY*, pp. 313–17. On Anglicization in general, see above nn. 72–5.

but the son's is ambivalent, representing either Old-English *Wīgstān* or else an Anglicization of Scandinavian *Vésteinn* or *Vígsteinn*.[102] Another probably Scandinavian form occurs in *Gaddes mæg* (287); for, whereas no clearly native English instance of *Gadd* seems so far noted, a Scandinavian *Gaddr* is recorded and probably forms the first element in Danelaw place-names like *Gadsby*.[103] Again, the name *Maccus* given to one of the three defenders of the causeway (80) is now recognized as common among Irish Vikings; already in the mid tenth century, it was – in addition to its occurrences in Cornwall and as a moneyer's name from an unspecified mint – quite certainly current in Eastern England, because records show it as the first element of the Northamptonshire place-name *Macuseige* (*Maxey*).[104] Less clear but, given the popularity of ambivalent names in the Southern Danelaw, no less interesting is the description of the fugitive Godric as *earh Oddan bearn* (238), for – as with the tenth-century archbishop of Canterbury's name – the form *Od(d)a* could represent either a native name or an Anglicization of Scandinavian *Oddi*;[105] but, even though it did here represent the latter, there would still be no call to see the Scandinavian connection as necessarily explaining Godric's treachery,[106] because (to look no further) the *Þurstanes sunu* of the poem is a model of loyalty. Admittedly, the proportion of Scandinavian forms among the personal names is far lower here than in, say, *Liber Eliensis*. On the other hand, in a poem celebrating an almost single-hearted resistance against Viking attackers, for any of Byrhtnoth's men to be given names which, although partly Anglicized, still carried a Scandinavian flavour might seem paradoxical. That it was done suggests the poet either to have been intent on accurately depicting the hybrid culture of the Southern Danelaw, where Scandinavian influence underlay well over a quarter of the current masculine name-stock, or else – and more probably – to have been himself so steeped in that culture as to bring in Scandinavianisms in spite of himself.

Such a view of the poem as reflecting a mixed culture – predominantly English, but with a Scandinavian tincture well blended in – squares with the sporadic use here of other Scandinavian words and phrases. True, several such items, like *selfra dom* and *grið*, are so clustered in the Viking messenger's speech as to suggest to some critics

---

[102] Cf. *PNDB*, p. 412, 'The native compounds in *Wīg-* cannot as a rule be distinguished from the OSc equivalents in *Víg-* and the ESc names in *Vi-* (OE *Wīoh-, Wēoh-*; ON *Vé-*)'; on p. 413, *s.n.* *Wīgstān*, a single instance of *Wistan* is cited, from Norfolk, and compared with the Scandinavian *Visten* and *Vígsteinn*, for which see G. Knudsen *et alii, Danmarks gamle Personnavne: I – Fornavne* (Copenhagen, 1936–48, 2 vols continuously numbered), col. 1592, *s.n. Wisten*, and also Lind, *Dopmamn*, cols 1086, 1105. Cf. *Maldon*, ed. Gordon, p. 85, and Hofmann, *Lehnbeziehungen*, p. 194.

[103] For ON *Gaddr*, see Lind, *Personbinamn*, col. 96, and Knudsen, I – *Fornavne*, col. 335, also *idem, ibidem*, II – *Tinavne* (1949–64), col. 313. Cf. Hofmann, *Lehnbeziehungen*, p. 194.

[104] See Smart, *Index*, p. 57, and Insley, 'Regional variation', p. 53. For *Maxey*, see J.E.B. Gover *et alii, The Place-Names of Northamptonshire* (EPNS, x, Cambridge, 1933), pp. 236–7, also p. xxv, and also Fellows Jensen, *Scandinavian Settlement Names*, p. 219, also p. 265, cf. *SPLY*, pp. 192–3 (hence A.H. Smith, 'Some aspects of Irish influence in Yorkshire', *Revue celtique*, xliv (1927), 34–58, esp. 44–5, now needs modifying). Blake's assertion, 'Genesis', p. 126, that in *Maldon* this name is anachronistic is thus quite unfounded (I am grateful to Kenneth Cameron and John Insley for pointing this out).

[105] See above n. 86.

[106] Cf., for instance, Gneuss, *Zeugnis*, p. 36 n. 98.

'the first literary use of dialect';[107] and others, such as *æsc(here)* and *dreng*,[108] refer to specifically Scandinavian things and people. Even more debatable is the Scandinavian influence which some have seen behind forms like *upgangan* (87) and *forwegen* (228).[109] As for *ceallian*, its once-supposed Scandinavian origins have been impugned;[110] and whether a metaphorical sense of *cald* (which can scarcely be taken literally when applied to a shallow creek in early August) is Scandinavian or simply poetic remains unresolved.[111] The point is not, however, that Scandinavian influence is especially strong here; rather that, once a Southern-Danelaw provenance is accepted for the poem and its implications understood, such influence loses all chronological bearing.

There may well be here a deeper level of Scandinavian influence, hard to specify, let alone to quantify, but for all that pervasive. In 1976 the late Rosemary Woolf, pointing out how alien many aspects of the 'heroic ideal' celebrated here were to real tenth-century England, revived Bertha Phillpotts's suggestion that certain motifs might have been imitated from an Old-Danish poem such as *Bjarkamál*, possibly made known in England by the ninth-century settlers.[112] And in the same year Helmut Gneuss assembled evidence of different sorts for the *comitatus*-motif as here a purely literary device.[113] Interestingly, a further instance of tenth-century English warriors choosing to die beside their lord occurs in the Ramsey *Vita Oswaldi*, in the episode immediately preceding that of Byrhtnoth's death.[114]

In general, therefore, the *Maldon* poem, provisionally localizable somewhere in the Southern Danelaw, exhibits in spirit and in language just such diluted and naturalized Scandinavian influences as might be expected in that district. This brings into sharper focus the use of *eorl* to mean 'our own (English) leader'. Of course that sense ultimately stemmed from Scandinavian *jarl*; but now its appearance in *Maldon*, far from seeming to imply post-Cnutian composition, begins to look simply like a piece of Southern-Danelaw dialect.

Such a view is confirmed by the likely relationship of poetic usage to the 'chancery' one on which the contested argument turns. Poetic diction is often revivified by transfusing ancient conventions with current usages; but the latter, although they might on occasion include legal terms, as with *gafol* (lines 32, 46, 61) and *heregeatu* (48), were assuredly never restricted to terms or senses consecrated by official use; for this, being more often archaistic than innovatory, offers little guide to colloquial language. As for late-tenth-century 'chancery' usages in particular, a recent mapping of the places where royal councils met has shown how peripheral the eastern counties were to

---

107 Robinson, 'Artistry', p. 26.
108 Cf. R.I. Page, ' "The proper toil of artless industry": Toronto's plan for an Old English Dictionary', *Notes & Queries*, April 1975, pp. 146–55, esp. p. 154.
109 See Hofmann, *Lehnbeziehungen*, pp. 194–5, 195–6; cf. *Maldon*, ed. Scragg, pp. 73–4.
110 See E.G. Stanley, 'Old English -*calla*, *ceallian*', in *Medieval Literature and Civilization: Studies in Memory of G.N. Garmonsway*, ed. D.A. Pearsall and R.A. Waldron (London, 1969), pp. 94–9; cf. Hofmann, *Lehnbeziehungen*, pp. 195–7.
111 Cf. *Maldon*, ed. Scragg, p. 74.
112 See R. Woolf, 'The ideal of men dying with their lord in the *Germania* and *The Battle of Maldon*', *Anglo-Saxon England*, v (1976), 63–81, esp. 78–80; cf. B. Phillpotts, '*The Battle of Maldon*: some Danish affinities', *Modern Language Review*, xxiv (1929), 172–90. Blake, 'Genesis', p. 128, concurs, but again sees this motif solely as proof of post-Cnutian date.
113 Gneuss, *Zeugnis*, pp. 15–45.
114 *Historians*, ed. Raine, i. 456.

this governmental circuit; and, likewise, although Danelaw representatives did attend these gatherings, they seem rarely to have been prominent there.[115] Danelaw language could therefore hardly be expected to dominate the documents drafted. So the superficial precision of the semantic evidence adduced from 'chancery' usages masks its essential irrelevance to the present case. Recourse must therefore be had to lines of thought whose lesser precision may be counterbalanced by common sense.

By the time of the Norman Conquest *eorl* was firmly and widely enough established as a term of rank (rendered in Latin by *comes*) to become at once the English equivalent of Old-French *quens/conte*: as well established, that is, as terms like *cniht, hlaford* and *hlæfdige* which had until then enjoyed purely native semantic developments. Now, the view that, outside the Northern Danelaw, *eorl* could not until after Cnut's accession have acquired the senses 'our own (English) commander' and 'provincial governor' would allow these meanings just one bare generation, from Cnut's accession to the Confessor's, to spread from Anglo-Danish official usage into general currency. Investigation of what really happened is partly blocked not only by the already-noted dearth of pre-Conquest vernacular materials from Eastern England but even more by the inaccessibility of all Old-English colloquial usages whatsoever. So, with little authenticated pre-Cnutian record from outside the Northern Danelaw of *eorl* meaning 'our own (English) commander', the likelihood of its wider currency will be assessed mainly by analogy.

Certainly, by Æthelred II's time certain Scandinavian terms had become such a familiar part of the English language as no longer to be restricted, even in West-Saxon, to designating peculiarly Scandinavian persons or things. Thus, the homilist Ælfric came to adopt – apparently in imitation of Wulfstan's usage – the loanword *lagu* for general and theological senses he had earlier rendered by the native *æ*, and he used for it a declensional pattern perhaps reflecting its Scandinavian etymology.[116] And both in his homily *De falsis deis* and in his *Life of St Martin* he found that it suited his purpose to use as equivalents of the classical Mercury, Jove and Venus, not the native forms of the pagan gods' names but the Scandinavian *Oðon, Þor* and *Fricg*.[117]

Wulfstan's usage presents a more complex picture. In also using the Scandinavian names for the gods he seems simply to have been copying Ælfric.[118] His general vocabulary, on the other hand, shows, when compared with Ælfric's, a far more marked Scandinavian element: as well as *lagu* and its compounds *folclagu* and *unlagu*, he also favoured *grið*, with its compounds *griðleas* and *griðian*, and also several less common loanwords like *þræl, bonda*, and the verb *fesan*, plus several apparent translation-loans such as *þegengyld* and various compounds in *nyd-* (cf. Scandinavian *nauð-*) including *nydgyld* and *nydmage*.[119] Above all, he 'uses *ealdormann* only in quotations; his own

---

[115] See Keynes, *Diplomas*, pp. 161–2, 204, and map on p. 36.

[116] See *Homilies of Ælfric*, ed. J.C. Pope (Early English Text Society: Original Series [EETS OS], cclix and cclx, Oxford, 1967–68, 2 vols continuously paginated), 661; also M. Godden, 'Ælfric's changing vocabulary', *English Studies*, lxi (1980), 206–23, esp. 214–17.

[117] See *Homilies*, [ii.] 683–4, 686, also notes on 715–16, and *Ælfric's Metrical Lives of Saints*, ed. W.W. Skeat (EETS, OS, lxxvi, lxxxii, xciv and cxiv, Oxford, 1881–1900, paginated as 2 vols), ii. 265. Cf. C.E. Fell, 'Gods and heroes of the northern world', in *The Northern World: the History and Heritage of Northern Europe, A.D. 400–1100*, ed. D.M. Wilson (London, 1980), pp. 33–46, esp. pp. 36–7.

[118] See *The Homilies of Wulfstan*, ed. D. Bethurum (Oxford, 1957), pp. 221–4, and notes on pp. 333–9.

[119] See especially *Sermo Lupi ad Anglos*, ed. D. Whitelock (3rd edn, London, 1963), pp. 45 and

word, in homilies, *Polity* and laws, is *eorl*'[120] – examples of this usage of his have already been cited above,[121] and they seem especially relevant to the present context. Indeed, Donald Scragg as well as Dorothy Whitelock has briefly suggested analogies between Wulfstan's usage and that of the *Maldon* poem.[122] Gross differences of topics and of genres may forbid full systematic comprison between the two vocabularies; but those very differences make all the more telling their undeniable similarities, not just in the sharing of such common loanwords as *grið* but especially in the ways both show assimilated Scandinavian influences running just beneath an apparently 'standard' West-Saxon surface. Exactly how pertinent these similarities may be judged will depend on which biographical explanation is preferred for Wulfstan's Scandinavian-isms. If these are attributed mainly to his 'sojourns in the north',[123] then their interest here will be limited. On the other hand, what little is known of Wulfstan's life suggests some early connections with the Fenlands, and in particular with Ely abbey; certainly he had close enough links with that abbey to be taken there for burial – alongside Ealdormann Byrhtnoth, as it happened.[124] Had Wulfstan indeed been by origin a man of the Southern Danelaw, then the lexical resemblances between his usage and that of the *Maldon* poem, and in particular the like applications of the term *eorl*, would at the least afford a curious coincidence. For the present such speculation cannot, however, be taken further.

At all events, if – whether through family background or through later pastoral contacts with the Northern Danelaw – Scandinavian influences could colour so strongly the usage of a prominent representative of West-Saxon officialdom, *a fortiori* it might well have tinged that of a poem celebrating a hero linked with what had not long before been the Southern Danelaw. The districts concerned had known nearly two generations of Viking hegemony; and descendants of Viking overlords – or, rather, men whose cultural patterns were consonant with such origins – were still prominent there. The signs are plain: among the upper-class men of the Ely 'catchment area' over a quarter of late-tenth-century personal names were of Scandinavian types; and, through-out the Southern Danelaw, place-names, major and minor, were also affected, although in ways less quantifiable. Then too the *Maldon* poem itself exhibits motifs as well as diction attributable to Scandinavian influences, at levels seemingly compatible with localization in this area.

Thus, a clearer perspective is now being established in which to assess disputable usages in the poem, such as that of *eorl* to mean 'our own (English) leader'. Even into Ælfric's 'pure' West-Saxon *lagu* had made its way, while Wulfstan's more eclectic

---

n. 1, 48 n. 14, 50 n. 40, 55 nn. 108, 109, 115 and 118. Cf. *Homilies of Wulfstan*, ed. Bethurum, p. 54, and Hofmann, *Lehnbeziehungen*, pp. 188–93.

[120] D. Whitelock, 'Wulfstan at York', in *Medieval and Linguistic Studies in Honor of Francis Peabody Magoun*, ed. J.B. Bessinger and R.P. Creed (London and New York, 1965), pp. 214–31, esp. p. 226.

[121] See above nn. 9 and 10.

[122] See *Maldon*, ed. Scragg, p. 27, and Whitelock, 'Wulfstan at York', p. 226.

[123] So Whitelock, 'Wulfstan at York', p. 226.

[124] See D. Whitelock, 'Archbishop Wulfstan, homilist and statesman' [originally 1941, but re-printed with revisions], in *Essays in Medieval History*, ed. R.W. Southern (London, 1968), pp. 42–60, esp. p. 55, also *Sermo*, pp. 7–8; and D. Bethurum, 'Wulfstan', in *Continuations and Beginnings*, ed. E.G. Stanley (London, 1966), pp. 210–46, esp. p. 211. The main source is *Liber Eliensis*, p. 156.

diction embraced a far wider range of Scandinavian loans and translation-loans, including that very sense of 'leader' for *eorl*. Now, even more than *lagu, grið* and *þræl*, *eorl/jarl* might be thought exactly the kind of term likely to have been imposed by a ruling élite on to its subjects. And, seeing that even the pre-Alfredian annals had regularly used *eorl* to mean 'Viking leader', no great semantic leap would have been needed to establish 'leader' *tout court* as one of the word's normal meanings in those areas where, as the *Chronicle* itself shows, effective leaders had for nearly two generations all been Vikings, and been called *eorlas* even by strictly West-Saxon writers. For the official title, admittedly, *Liber Eliensis* consistently used *alderman(nus)*;[125] but in doing so probably reflected the official usage of its sources rather than the everyday language of their time (besides, when the *Liber* was compiled in the later twelfth century *eorl* had acquired a new and incompatible official meaning). With authentic records of pre-Conquest Eastern dialect so scarce, little can be proved; but the chances that throughout the old Southern Danelaw, in the South-East Midlands and in East Anglia alike, 'our own leader' had during the tenth century been a current colloquial meaning of *eorl* are surely too great to allow of taking this usage as proof of post-Cnutian composition.

*   *   *

With that king-pin knocked out of the argument, the whole question of dating *The Battle of Maldon* is reopened. Of course those still attracted by a post-Cnutian date may continue seeking evidence – but of a different kind – to support their view. But meanwhile the others who, with Helmut Gneuss and Barbara Raw,[126] continue to prefer the traditional early date are not debarred from that preference. Others again may, with James Cross (and the present writer), see *Maldon* as one panel of a triptych completed by *Sermo Lupi* and the late-Æthelredian annals, and date its composition accordingly.[127]

Furthermore, now that the cultural patterns of the Southern Danelaw are being brought into a better focus, perhaps some of its other literary products might gain from being analyzed from a like point of view: *Gesta Herwardi*, for instance, with the folk-tale spae-wife prophesying from on high.

---

[125] *E.g.*, *Liber Eliensis*, p. 134 (of Byrhtnoth himself), 'Anglica lingua *alderman*, id est, "senior" vel "dux", ab omnibus cognominabatur' [my own punctuation]; cf. p. 157, 'Brithnoði cognomento alderman'.

[126] See Gneuss, *Zeugnis*, p. 7, and B. Raw, *The Art and Background of Old English Poetry* (London, 1978), p. 30; the latter's bibliography omits McKinnell's article, although including several items published later.

[127] See J.E. Cross, 'Mainly on philology and the interpretative criticism of *Maldon*', in *Old English Studies in Honour of J.C. Pope*, ed. R.B. Burlin and E.B. Irving (Toronto, 1974), pp. 235–53, esp. pp. 247–8; cf. Robinson, 'Artistry', pp. 28–32.

3

Certains aspects de l'hagiographie anglo-latine de l'Angleterre anglo-normande

Avant d'aborder nos documents, posons le problème qui sous-tend notre étude. Dès le milieu du XIIᵉ siècle se manifesta, chez certains du moins parmi les Normands venus s'établir en Angleterre, une velléité de s'enraciner dans le passé anglo-saxon, voire de se créer comme une identité anglaise. C'était le cas des patrons pour lesquels Geoffroi Gaimar rédigea son *Histoire des Anglais*; de la famille qui adopta comme ancêtre cet insoumis notoire, Hereward 'the Wake'; et encore de ceux qui transformèrent Waltheof, noble anglo-scandinave, mari d'une nièce du Conquérant, et enfin traître mis à mort – qui transformèrent ce personnage ambigu non seulement en saint martyr mais même en héros d'un immense roman fantaisiste en vers français.[1] A qui ne considérerait les Anglais de cette époque que comme les vaincus de Hastings, cette velléité, cette recherche d'une identité anglaise paraîtrait on ne peut plus bizarre. Pour que l'identité anglaise pût exercer un tel attrait sur des Normands, encore que ce ne fût que sur certains d'entre eux, il lui a fallu se maintenir quelque part intact et fière. Mon thème sera donc de découvrir l'un – certainement pas le seul – mais l'un d'entre les véhicules de la survie, pendant le siècle qui suivit la Conquête normande de l'Angleterre, d'une identité anglaise assez séduisante pour captiver les nouveaux venus.

Passons maintenant à notre premier texte: modeste, bref à souhait, et plus ou moins délaissé non seulement par nous autres érudits modernes mais aussi, paraît-il, par ses propres contemporains. Il s'agit d'une *vita sanctorum* qui n'a survécu, à ce que je sache, que dans une copie unique.[2] Dans un recueil hagiographique de la première

---

Je tiens à exprimer une très vive reconnaissance envers M. André Crépin, qui m'a très gentiment aidée à corriger mon texte; pour les fautes de français qui s'y seraient malgré tout glissées je suis seule responsable.

1 Voir: M.D. Legge, *Anglo-Norman Literature and its Background* (Oxford, 1963), pp. 4, 32 (pour Gaimar), 140–1, 143–56 (pour *Le roman de Waldef*); R.W. Southern, 'England's first entry into Europe', pp. 135–57 de son recueil, *Medieval Humanism and Other Studies* (Oxford, 1970), en particulier, pp. 137 (pour Waltheof), 154–5; et, surtout, R.H.C. Davis, *The Normans and their Myth* (Londres, 1976), pp. 122–32. Aussi: A. Bell, *L'Estoire des Engleis*, Anglo-Norman Text Society XIV–XVI (Oxford, 1960); *The Complete Peerage*, XII/ii, 295 *et seq.*, et E. King, 'The origins of the Wake family: the early history of the barony of Bourne in Lincolnshire', *Northamptonshire Past and Present*, V (1975), 167–76 (à l'origine le sobriquet 'Wake', dont la signification reste obscure, appartenait à la famille normande); B.J. Levy, 'Waltheof "Earl" de Huntingdon et de Northampton; la naissance d'un héros anglo-normand', *Cahiers de civilisation médiévale*, XVIII (1975), 183–96.

2 Aux ff. 64v–65v du ms. Harley 3097 de la Bibliothèque Britannique (l'ensemble hagiographique dont fait partie cet opuscule commence au f. 61v); ce morceau fut publié par W. de Gray Birch comme appendice (pp. 284–6) au *Liber Vitae: Register and Martyrology of New Minster and Hyde Abbey, Winchester*, Hampshire Record Society (Londres et Winchester, 1892). Voir aussi

moitié du XIIe siècle, une courte préface, que nous examinerons plus loin, se voit suivie en premier lieu d'une *Vie de saint Botulf* plutôt bien connue, et ensuite d'un morceau plus obscur placé sous la rubrique, 'De sanctis Thancredo et Torhtredo' (je m'excuse de prononcer, avec mon accent d'Outre-Manche, ces vocables qui, au XIIe siècle déjà, offusquèrent notre élégant anglo-latiniste, Guillaume de Malmesbury[3]). Ce morceau prend comme sujet trois ermites anglais du IXe siècle: deux frères, Thancred et Torhtred, qui, avec leur soeur Tova, habitèrent l'îlot où devait, un siècle plus tard, être fondée l'abbaye de Thorney, au fin fond de cette région marécageuse que nous appelons toujours 'the Fens'. Cette petite *Vita* est suivie, à son tour, d'une *Translatio*,[4] qui complète ce qu'à mon avis nous devrions considérer comme un ensemble hagiographique, et qui s'occupe en premier lieu de saint Botulf, passe ensuite à un saint anglo-saxon encore moins connu que nos trois ermites et qui s'appelait Herefrith,[5] et se termine en parlant du petit oratoire bâti au Xe siècle sur l'ancien emplacement de la cellule de la sainte Tova.

A première vue, la *Vita* de ces trois ermites paraîtrait n'offrir qu'un intérêt minime. Très brève, elle n'ajoute rien aux maigres renseignements incorporés dans la charte de fondation de l'abbaye,[6] et que l'hagiographe, pour en faire une lecture pieuse, étoffa, mais modestement, de théologie morale plutôt banale. Pourquoi, alors, prendre comme point de départ un récit si peu important?

Par paradoxe, ce manque même d'intérêt apparent devrait nous alerter. Car celui auquel on aurait droit d'attribuer cet ensemble hagiographique n'était point un antiquaire anglais. C'était Fulcard, Flamand et ancien moine de Saint-Bertin, envoyé à Thorney pendant les années qui suivirent la Conquête normande pour gouverner la maison alors acéphale.[7] Pourquoi ce Flamand choisit-il de rédiger ce petit ensemble 'thorneyois' (si l'on me passe l'adjectif), de célébrer ces saints presque perdus dans les brumes montées des marécages entourant l'îlot de Thorney? D'abord, parce qu'il avait des instincts d'historien, comme il l'explique lui-même dans la préface où il présente son oeuvre à l'évêque de Winchester: 'En m'apercevant qu'aucun écrivain n'avait jamais célébré les saints qui reposent dans cette église, je me suis indigné contre nos prédécesseurs' – et il énumère les sources où il est allé puiser, y comprise la charte de

---

mon article, 'Notes on a *Life* of three Thorney saints: Thancred, Torhtred and Tova', *Proceedings of the Cambridge Antiquarian Society*, LXIX (1979), 45–52.

3 Voir N.E.S.A. Hamilton, *Willelmi Malmesbiriensis monachi de gestis pontificum Anglorum libri quinque*, Rolls Series (Londres, 1870), pp. 327–8. Cf. le futur saint Barthélemy de Farne (né peut-être vers 1130), dont des camarades moqueurs remplacèrent par *Willelm* le nom anglo-scandinave et démodé de *Tosti* (*Vita Bartholomæi Farnensis*, imprimée comme appendice (I, 295–325) par T. Arnold, *Symeonis monachi opera omnia*, 2 tomes, Rolls Series (Londres, 1882–85), p. 296) – exemple que je dois à la gentilesse de M. Martin Brett, de Robinson College, Cambridge.

4 Publiée par Birch, *Liber Vitae*, pp. 286–90.

5 On espère voir paraître prochainement une étude où M. Arthur Owen, de la Bibliothèque Universitaire de Cambridge, proposera une identification de ce personnage obscur [[A.E.B. Owen, 'Herefrith of Louth, saint and bishop: a problem of identities', *Lincolnshire History and Archaeology*, XV (1980), 15–19]].

6 Voir C.R. Hart, *The Early Charters of Eastern England* (Leicester, 1966), pp. 165–72; aussi Sir William Dugdale, *Monasticon Anglicanum*, revu par J. Caley *et alii*, 6 tomes en 8 (Londres, 1817–30; réimprimé en 1970), II, 598–9.

7 Pour sa carrière et ses oeuvres, voir F. Barlow, *The Life of King Edward who Rests at Westminster* (Londres, 1962), pp. li–lviii.

fondation de l'abbaye.[8] Voilà una motivation d'historien: motivation qui n'est point étrangère à nous autres érudits du XXe siècle. Ce n'est pas là, cependant, que je voudrais m'arrêter. Fulcard avoua aussi une motivation sur le plan humain, en disant qu'en grande partie c'était l'amour pour son abbaye adoptive qui l'avait poussé à ses recherches: 'Saisi par la grâce de cette abbaye célèbre, ... je m'y suis vite attaché, un âne ou un boeuf à la crèche du Seigneur . . .'[9] Peut-être renchérissait-il un peu sur la réalité; car, s'il aimait, lui, son abbaye plantée au milieu des marais, ses moines ne paraissent guère avoir partagé son sentiment . . .[10] Quoi qu'il en soit, l'important, c'est que ce Flamand se mit à rédiger des *Vitae* de très modestes saints on ne peut plus anglo-saxons, de saints dont le souvenir s'était presque éteint même dans leur propre pays.

Mais vous me direz que ce n'est point là chose remarquable. Au Moyen Age ni l'idée de 'nationalité' ni, par conséquent, celle de 'patriotisme' n'avaient atteint leur importance moderne. En plus, il peut sembler normal qu'un Flamand ait éprouvé pour la culture anglaise une sympathie plus vive et plus profonde qu'aucun Normand n'aurait su éprouver. N'y a-t-il pas le cas tout analogue de Goscelin, lui aussi ancien moine de Saint-Bertin et hagiographe encore plus prolifique?[11] Goscelin, qui vécut en Angleterre un demi-siècle entier, rédigea lui aussi des *Vitae* de saints dont les noms sonnaient, résonnaient, d'un timbre incontestablement anglo-saxon: sainte Ætheldræd, sainte Eadgyth, et d'autres. Quand même, n'est-ce point remarquable de voir ces deux Flamands se mettre à célébrer des saints enracinés dans le passé anglo-saxon? Cela ne nous apprend-il pas quelque chose d'important quant au prestige dont jouissait la sainteté anglo-saxonne dans la société cosmopolite de l'Angleterre anglo-normande?

De l'histoire ancienne, passons aux cas contemporains. Certes, des personnages dignes de célébration hagiographique ne manquaient point à l'époque. Par exemple, cet ermite Wulfsige qui, quelques années avant la Conquête, décida le futur saint Wulfstan à accepter le siège épiscopal de Worcester; un peu recordman dans son genre, il fut censé avoir passé 'au désert' soixante-quinze années . . .[12] Malheureusement,

---

8 Ms. Harley 3097, ff. 61v–62r; imprimé dans une note infrapaginale par T.D. Hardy, *Descriptive Catalogue of Materials relating to the History of Great Britain and Ireland*, 3 tomes en 4, Rolls Series (Londres, 1862–71), I/i, 373–4.

9 *Loc. cit.*

10 Dans une chronique abbatiale insérée dans le grand cartulaire de l'abbaye de Thorney (les mss. additionnels 3020 et 3021 de la Bibliothèque Universitaire de Cambridge – le 'Red Book' de Thorney; toujours inédit), on lit: 'Primo Siwardus, de genere Danorum, et postmodum Fulcardus, natione Flandrensis, dictam abbatiam invaserunt, set neuter eorum vel muner episcopalis benedictionis vel professionem a monachis perceperunt; set . . . Fulcardus, vice-abbas Thornensis, a Lanfranco, Cantuariensi archiepiscopo, degradatus est' (ff. 415v–416r); cf. la note plus brève inscrite au f. 11r du ms. additionnel 40000 de la Bibliothèque Britannique (le *Liber vitae* de Thorney).

11 Voir Barlow, *King Edward*, pp. 91–111 (pour une liste de ses oeuvres), et xlv–li; aussi A. Wilmart, 'Eve et Goscelin', *Revue Bénédictine*, XLVI (1934), 414–38, et L (1938), 42–83; et C.H. Talbot, 'The *Liber confortatorius* of Goscelin of Saint-Bertin', *Studia Anselmiana*, XXXVII (1955), 1–117.

12 Voir B. Thorpe, *Florentii Wigorniensis monachi chronicon ex chronicis*, &c., 2 tomes (Londres, 1848–49), I, 220, et W.D. Macray, *Chronicon abbatiæ de Evesham*, &c., Rolls Series (Londres, 1863), pp. 83, 322–3, 394; aussi H. Dauphin, 'L'érémitisme en Angleterre aux XIe et XIIe siècles', pp. 271–303 du Colloque sur *L'Eremitismo in Occidente nei secoli XI et XII*, Miscellanea del Centro di Studi Medioevali dell'Università del Sacro Cuore (Milan, 1965), p. 276. Wulfsige, paraît-il, ne battit que de trois ans son confrère Basing.

cette vie si longue ne fut célébrée que de façon plutôt sommaire. Performance impress-
ionnante, quand même!

Puisque c'est l'hagiographie qui nous concerne plutôt que la sainteté tout court,
prenons un autre recueil hagiographique, dont le contenu paraîtrait choisi exprès pour
illustrer mon thème: le ms. additionnel 3037 de la Bibliothèque Universitaire de
Cambridge.[13] Quoique la structure de ce volume ne soit pas exempte de problèmes,
dont je m'abstiens de vous fatiguer les oreilles, je me crois en droit de le traiter comme
un recueil uni conçu à la fin du XIIᵉ siècle. Qu'est-ce qu'il nous offre? En premier lieu,
la copie unique des *Vita et Miracula* du petit saint Guillaume de Norwich, 'martyrisé'
en 1144.[14] Ensuite on y trouve une des quatre copies qui nous sont parvenues de la *Vita*
de saint Wulfric de Haselbury[15] et un texte de la rédaction courte de celle de saint
Godric,[16] tous deux ermites anglais de la première moitié du XIIᵉ siècle. Vu l'hétérogé-
néité qui caractérise tant de recueils hagiographiques, où des saints anglo-saxons
s'entremêlent à ceux du premier temps de la chrétienté, cette unité sur les plans
chronologique et géographique ne peut guère manquer de nous frapper.

Résumons ce que leurs *Vitae* nous apprennent des milieux où vécurent ces trois
saints. Il sera utile de nous reporter en premier lieu aux noms de personnes, qui, du
moins dans une certaine mesure, reflètent toujours à cette époque certaines affinités
culturelles.[17] Le petit saint Guillaume de Norwich, seul d'entre les trois à ne pas porter
un nom de type anglo-saxon, n'en était pas moins un Anglais des plus anglais: ses père
et mère s'appelaient *Wenstan* [*Wynstan*] et *Elvive* [*Ælfȝifu*]; son grand-père maternel,
c'était le curé *Wulfward*, et son oncle maternel, curé lui aussi, s'appelait *Godwine Stert*
et avait pour épouse une *Livive* [*Leofȝifu*]; à Norwich c'était chez un autre *Wulfward*
que logeait le jeune apprenti.[18] Quant à saint Godric, né comme Guillaume en Norfolk
(mais quelque cinquante ans plus tôt), il avait eu pour père et mère *Æilward*
[*Æþelweard*] et *Aedwen* [*Eadwynn*], qui donnèrent à leur fille aussi, tout comme à leur
fils aîné, un nom des plus traditionnels, *Burcwen* [*Burgwynn*]. A l'âge mûr, frère et
soeur se firent ermites tous les deux; et quand la soeur, morte la première, fit chez son
frère apparition posthume, ce fut, tout naturellement, en anglais, 'verbis Anglicis',
qu'elle entonna quelques vers. Ce fut également dans cette même langue, 'verbis

[13] Je tiens à exprimer ici ma grande reconnaissance envers mon amie Mme Jayne Cook, de la
Bibliothèque Universitaire de Cambridge, qui a bien voulu me communiquer les fiches inédites
qu'elle dresse pour le nouveau catalogue des manuscrits médiévaux qui appartiennent à cette
Bibliothèque. Le problème majeur consiste en ce que le volume se compose de deux tranches
distinctes; mais l'examen à la fois des écritures et de la reliure très ancienne paraît nous autoriser
à le considérer comme dès l'abord un recueil uni. Quant à la datation, le *terminus post quem*
dépend de la date assignée à la *Vie de sainte Wulfric* (voir Dom M. Bell, *Wulfric of Haselbury, by
John of Ford*, Somerset Record Society XLVII (Frome et Londres, 1933), pp. xiv, xvi–xviii; et,
pour notre manuscrit, p. lxxviii).

[14] A. Jessopp et M.R. James, *The Life and Miracles of St William of Norwich* (Cambridge, 1896).

[15] Voir *supra* n. 13. Cf. H. Mayr-Harting, 'Functions of a twelfth-century recluse', *History*, LX
(1975), 337–52.

[16] [J. Stevenson], *Libellus de vita et miraculis S. Godrici, heremitæ de Finchale, auctore Reginaldo
monacho Dunelmensi*, Surtees Society XX (Londres et Edimbourg, 1845); notre manuscrit, qui
n'entra à la Bibliothèque de Cambridge qu'en 1889, n'y figure pas.

[17] Cf. *supra* n. 3. Pour l'anthroponymie anglo-saxonne, se référer à W.G. Searle, *Onomasticon
Anglo-Saxonicum* (Cambridge, 1897) [périmé, pourtant], et à O. von Feilitzen, *The Pre-
Conquest Personal Names of Domesday Book*, Nomina Germanica III (Uppsala, 1937); pour une
bibliographie un peu moins sommaire, voir *infra* p. 126 n. 53, aussi nn. 52 et 55.

[18] *St William*, pp. 10, 16, 40.

Anglicæ linguæ', que la Sainte Vierge dicta des vers. L'hagiographe lui-même, en racontant les miracles attribués à Godric, insiste au moins une fois sur les mérites de cet Anglais, par contraste avec l'inefficacité des médecins français . . .[19] Quant à Wulfric de Haselbury, plus ou moins contemporain de Godric, son cas était presque semblable. Lui aussi portait un nom typiquement anglo-saxon. Son ami le plus proche, c'était le curé de village *Brihtric* [*Beorhtric*], dont nous aurons à reparler tout-à-l'heure; curé marié lui aussi, Brihtric avait une femme appelée *Godida* [*Godʒyð*], et pour leur fils, qui succéda à la cure familiale, ils choisirent le nom d'*Osbern*, à cheval entre les traditions anglo-scandinave et normande. Un autre curé marié à nom anglo-saxon se comptait parmi les associés de Wulfric, *Segar* [*Sægar*], dont les quatre fils se firent tous moines.[20]

Quelle floraison d'anthroponymes anglo-saxons! Puis, eu égard à l'aspect géographique de ce recueil, on s'aperçoit qu'il représente à peu près chaque coin de l'Angleterre: pour le sud-ouest, voilà Wulfric, qui habitait en Somerset; pour l'est, voici le petit saint Guillaume de Norwich; et, pour le nord, il y a Godric, qui, bien que né lui aussi en Norfolk, choisit pour s'établir comme ermite les environs de Durham. Ce manuscrit ne paraît-il pas rassembler des cas représentatifs de la sainteté anglaise du XIIe siècle?

Voilà pour un seul recueil; mais ce ne furent point là les seuls saints anglais à se faire reconnaître pendant le siècle qui suivit la Conquête normande. Cas frappant: celui de sainte Christine de Markyate, née elle aussi vers la fin du XIe siècle et recluse dès avant 1120. A plusieurs reprises, les commentateurs modernes ont insisté sur la forte saveur anglaise qui émane des milieux où elle passa sa jeunesse.[21] Née d'une famille de la bourgeoisie aisée de Huntingdon, elle avait pour père *Auti*, porteur d'un nom de type anglo-scandinave, et se vit fiancée, bien contre son propre gré, à un certain *Burhred*, porteur d'un non purement anglo-saxon; sa tante maternelle, ancienne maîtresse de Ranoul Flambard, s'appelait *Alveva* [*Ælfʒifu*] (notons qu'un fils de Flambard, peut-être aussi fils d'Alveva, fut parmi ceux qui aidèrent Godric à s'installer dans son ermitage[22]). S'étant enfuie de la maison paternelle, Christine se réfugia d'abord chez une recluse appelée *Alfwen* [*Ælfwynn*]. Ensuite elle vécut comme disciple d'un certain Roger, qui, malgré son nom de type continental, n'en était pas moins anglais à la fois par ses attaches familiales et par sa langue habituelle: son cousin s'appelait *Eadwine*,

19 *Godric*, pp. 22, 23 (cf. 140–1), 119, 144, 454 ('Magis itaque illi virtus et misericordia Godrici simplicis Anglorum idiotæ sub festinatione præstitit quam omnis peritia et prudentia omnium medicorum Francorum . . .'). Pour les vers anglais, voir aussi C. Brown et R.H. Robbins, *Index of Middle English Verse* (New York, 1943) et *Supplement* (Lexington, 1965), nos 589, 2988, et 3031.

20 *Wulfric*, pp. 29, 38, 52, 83, 109. Pour le nom *Osbern*, voir G. Fellows Jensen, *Scandinavian Personal Names in Lincolnshire and Yorkshire* (Copenhague, 1968), pp. 18–19, et J. Adigard des Gautries, *Les Noms de personnes scandinaves en Normandie de 911 à 1066*, Nomina Germanica XI (Lund, 1954), pp. 78–81.

21 Voir C.H. Talbot, *The Life of Christina of Markyate, &c.* (Oxford, 1959), pp. 12–13, et C.J. Holdsworth, 'Christina of Markyate', dans D. Baker, *Medieval Women*, Studies in Church History: Subsidia I (Oxford, 1978), pp. 185–204, et, en particulier, 202–3; cf. Mayr-Harting, 'Functions', pp. 337–8.

22 *Godric*, p. 66. Pour Flambard lui-même, voir R.W. Southern, 'Ranulf Flambard', pp. 183–205 de *Medieval Humanism*, et, en particulier, pp. 186, 201–2.

et Roger lui-même, de façon bien révélatrice, exprimait son affection envers sa disciple en l'appelant *'myn sunendaege dohter*, quod latine dicitur, mea dominica dies filia'.[23]

Autre cas marquant de la sainteté de souche anglaise: celui d'Ailred de Rievaulx. Nous venons de remarquer, dans les entourages de nos saints, plusieurs de ces familles cléricales si caractéristiques de l'époque, et c'est encore ce milieu qui donna naissance à Ailred, fils et petit-fils de curés 'héréditaires' de Hexham. Son père était *Eilaf fils d'Eilaf*, donc porteur d'un nom doublement anglo-scandinave, et un parent aussi portait un patronyme anglo-scandinave, Guillaume fils de *Toli*. Si j'insiste tant sur les noms de personne, ce n'est pas seulement parce que je suis à mes heures quelque peu anthroponymiste; mais je suis fortement persuadée que pour les Anglais du siècle qui suivit la Conquête normande les anthroponymes fournissent en effet l'un des meilleurs indicateurs culturels. D'indicateurs culturels, il y en a pourtant d'autres. Le saint patron auquel se vouait Ailred, c'était saint Cuthbert de Durham, et il affectionnait aussi les saints anglo-saxons dont se vantait son Hexham natal.[24] Au moins une fois il rendit visite à l'ermite Godric, dont nous venons de noter le caractère anglais; et encore ce fut lui qui suggéra à l'hagiographe Réginald de Durham de rédiger la *Vita* de cet ermite.[25] Au plan politique aussi Ailred exprima plus d'une fois sa fidélité aux traditions anglaises. Sur son lit de mort il invoquait Dieu en anglais – 'car en anglais', commente l'hagiographe, 'le nom du Christ, n'ayant qu'une seule syllabe, se prononce plus facilement et se fait comme plus doux à entendre' – et, en priant d'être délivré de ses souffrances, il entrecoupait d'anglais ses intercessions, en disant, 'Festinate, *for Crist luve!*' ('Dépêchez-vous, pour l'amour du Christ!').[26]

Malheureusement, je ne peux pas me vanter d'avoir flairé la première cette saveur anglaise, cette 'Englishness', qui émane des saints de l'Angleterre anglo-normande; nous sommes en effet plusieurs à l'avoir remarquée.[27] Néanmoins, je crois y être parvenue indépendamment; et, si nous sommes plusieurs à remarquer, de façon indépendante, ce phénomène, notre pluralité ne fait que renforcer notre conclusion commune.

Sans aucun doute, la sainteté constituait une sphère où la conscience anglaise, l'identité anglaise, la fierté anglaise, sut non seulement se maintenir intacte mais encore s'épanouir. Pour être vaincu et assujetti à des envahisseurs étrangers, on ne renonce pas pour autant aux aspirations spirituelles; celles-ci ne s'en trouvent peut-être qu'accrues. Par exemple, on recopiait toujours, en plein XIIᵉ siècle, des homélies anglo-saxonnes.[28] Hagiographie anglo-saxonne et sainteté contemporaine: voici des refuges jumeaux pour la conscience anglaise refoulée par le défaite et l'occupation.

---

[23] *Christina*, pp. 34 &c., 62 &c., 40, 86 et 92 &c., 80 et 82 &c., 106; cf. H.T. Riley, *Gesta abbatum Sancti Albani*, 3 tomes, Rolls Series (Londres, 1867–69), I, 97–105, et, en particulier, 99. Pour le nom *Auti*, voir Fellows Jensen, *Scandinavian Personal Name*, pp. 43–4; il paraît ne pas être attesté en Normandie (voir Adigard des Gautries, *Les Noms de personnes scandinaves*, index).

[24] Voir F.M. Powicke, *The Life of Ailred of Rievaulx by Walter Daniel* (Londres, 1950), pp. xxxiii–xxxvi, xxxvii–xxxix. Pour *Eilaf* et *Toli*, encore des noms scandinaves qui paraissent ne pas être attestés en Normandie, voir Fellows Jensen, *Scandinavian Personal Names*, pp. 74–5, 289–90 (mais cf. Adigard des Gautries, *Les Noms de personnes scandinaves*, p. 150).

[25] *Godric*, pp. 173, 176–7, et xxxii.

[26] *Ailred*, pp. xxxix, xlii–xlviii, 60 ('. . . et Anglice quidem, quia nomen Christi hac lingua una sillaba continetur et facilius profertur, et dulcius quoddammodo auditor').

[27] Voir *supra* n. 21.

[28] Pour des copies faites au XIIᵉ siècle des homélies d'Ælfric, voir J.C. Pope, *Homilies of Ælfric,*

Cependant, je ne voudrais pas en rester là; car il s'agit de montrer comme cette identité refoulée put se redresser, prendre conscience du monde plus large, et s'en faire accepter. A y regarder de plus près, on s'aperçoit que l'hostilité entre Normands et Anglais ne s'avéra point intransigeante. Déjà pendant les années 1070 les deux 'nations' co-opérèrent pour restaurer les abbayes northumbriennes: en quittant la Worcestershire, Aldwine emmena non seulement son compatriote Ælfwig mais aussi Reinfrid, ancien chevalier; et, arrivés dans le Nord, ils se firent aider par le vicomte normand, Hugues fitz Baudry, par l'évêque Walcher, d'origine flamande ou lorraine, par le comte Waltheof, notable anglo-scandinave dont des traditions postérieures feraient un 'martyr' anglais, et par la famille normande de Percy.[29]

Revenons, maintenant, à l'opuscule avec lequel nous avons commencé notre exposé, oeuvre d'un Flamand quelque peu épris du passé anglo-saxon. Ce dont il témoigne, c'est surtout que la sainteté constitue un valeur universelle . . . ou presque. On remarque, néanmoins, chez certains esprits cosmopolites, comme l'ombre d'une antipathie contre les traditions anglaises. A Lanfranc il arriva même de douter des mérites de l'archevêque Ælfheah; mais, en se confiant à Anselme (lui-même futur canonisé), il se vit bientôt rassuré, et au point de commander au moine Osbern une cantique en l'honneur de l'archevêque martyr.[30] Anselme non plus ne se borna pas à reconnaître la sainteté véritable des saints anglo-saxons, mais également encouragea Eadmer à s'occuper d'hagiographie anglo-saxonne[31] – entreprise analogue à celles auxquelles s'étaient adonnés notre Fulcard et son compatriote Goscelin. Est-ce alors sur ce plan-là, de la spiritualité et de l'hagiographie, que prirent place les premiers rapprochements intellectuels et culturels entre vainqueurs et vaincus? Les saints anglais y ont-ils contribué eux-mêmes?

Revenons donc sur quelques-uns de nos 'héros'. D'abord, sur saint Godric, si anglais que, pour qu'il pût s'exprimer tant soit peu en français, il lui fallut un miracle de Pentecôte.[32] Réfléchissons-y: un miracle, c'est ce qui comble, au-delà de tout espoir humain, un désir ardent; ce qui guérit une plaie inguérissable. Alors, si ce fut *par miracle* que Godric prit (ou, était censé avoir pris) connaissance de la langue française, n'est-ce pas que pour lui (ou, du moins, pour son hagiographe, qui se présente comme témoin) parler français, c'était trouver la clé d'un monde plus large et où la sainteté pût mieux s'épanouir?

Pendant que nous sommes aux miracles linguistiques, revenons au Bienheureux

&c., 2 tomes, Early English Text Society O.S. 259 et 260 (Oxford, 1967–68), I 14, 18, 24, 35, 48, 67.

[29] Voir Dom David Knowles, *The Monastic Order in England*, 2ᵉ édition (Cambridge, 1963), pp. 166–71; aussi, *Symeonis monachi opera omnia*, I, 108–9. Pour Waltheof, cf. *supra* n. 1.

[30] Voir R.W. Southern, *The Life of St Anselm*, 2ᵉ édition (Oxford, 1972), pp. 51–4; cf. *idem, Saint Anselm and his Biographer* (Cambridge, 1963), pp. 217, 248–52, et M. Gibson, *Lanfranc of Bec* (Oxford, 1978), pp. 170–2.

[31] Voir Southern, *Biographer*, pp. 277–87.

[32] *Godric*, pp. 203–4 ('Haec omnia lingua Romana peroptime disseruit, nosque admirando stupore perfudit; erat enim quondam hujus linguæ penitus ignarus, utpote simpliciter lingua materna edoctus. . . . Quærente me si aliquando in seculo hanc loquelam didicisset, dixit quod ejus notitiam non habuisset, sed Spiritus Sanctus, qui linguas disertas facit, ipse hoc tempore Apostolis suis omnium notitiam linguarum atque sermonum tradidit. Tunc in me conversus, statim adverti quia Spiritus Sanctus per os ejus loquebatur, cujus festivitas tunc in Pentecoste exstitit, in qua mecum primum hac lingua loqui coepit'), et 206; cf. p. 352, où l'on raconte qu'un abbé 'Francigena' eut besoin d'un interprète pour s'entretenir avec Godric.

Wulfric. Cette fois il s'agit d'un sourd-muet guéri et encore devenu bilingue – ce qui valut à Wulfric un commentaire aigri de la part de son ami le curé Brihtric: 'A cet étranger, auquel ç'aurait été bien assez que de donner la parole tout court, tu lui as conféré un parler double; tandis qu'à moi, obligé que je suis, quand je comparais devant l'évêque et l'archidiacre, de me taire comme si j'étais vraiment muet, tu ne m'as point donné la connaissance du français.'[33] Certes, il ne manquait pas d'amertume à cette plainte attribuée au vieux curé monoglotte; mais, plutôt qu'une amertume de quelqu'un qui déteste les oppresseurs auxquels il désespère de jamais échapper, ne serait-elle point celle d'un homme dont les moyens n'égalent pas les ambitions légitimes? Quant à notre bon, notre Bienheureux Wulfric lui-même, il entretenait des relations des plus amicales avec son patron anglo-normand, Guillaume fitz Gautier, et avec tout le clan de ce dernier; en plus, on le représente comme recevant dans sa cellule les rois Henri Ier et Etienne, sans aucune mention d'interprète.[34]

De tous les cas que nous avons examinés, le plus révélateur, c'est celui de Christine de Markyate. Tout en insistant sur son ascendance anglaise,[35] l'hagiographe ne donne aucun lieu de supposer chez cette famille le moindre irrédentisme anglais. Comme nous l'avons déjà remarqué, la tante maternelle, au nom bien anglais d'*Alveva*, eut une liaison avec Ranoul Flambard, originaire de Bayeux et futur évêque de Durham; et des relations fort amicales subsistaient non seulement entre l'évêque et son ancienne maîtresse, mais encore entre lui et toute cette famille 'huntingdonaise'. Vu que Flambard, normand lui-même, avait fait figure dans la région de représentant oppressif de l'administration anglo-normande, une telle amitié suggère chez le bourgeois Auti un certain manque d'irrédentisme. Enfin – petite question que je me suis souvent posée – en quelle langue ces amis se seraient-ils entretenus? En quelle langue, surtout, l'évêque débauché s'adressa-t-il à la chaste Christine le soir où il voulut la séduire?[36] Les témoignages directs nous font défaut. Un témoignage oblique, cependant, existe; témoignage un peu tardif et plutôt lointain, mais qui mérite de nous retenir. Il s'agit du fastueux Psautier, dit de Saint-Auban, mais qui maintenant repose à Hildesheim – s'y morfond, peut-être, si loin de sa patrie – et qui se rattache par des liens multiples à l'entourage de Christine.[37] Parmi les éléments rassemblés dans ce recueil – 'recueil', car le volume est plus qu'un Psautier – se trouve un texte, le meilleur des textes connus, de *La Vie de saint Alexis*.[38] Il est devenu normal de développer le parallélisme entre la carrière de Christine et celle de saint Alexis;[39] ici ce n'est point l'anecdote qui doit nous retenir, mais bien cette question de langue. Christine était de souche purement anglaise; et voilà que ce recueil, qu'il y a tout lieu de croire rassemblé à son intention, multiplie les textes de littérature française – non seulement l'*Alexis* mais encore une

[33] *Wulfric*, p. 29 (Dom Maurice Bell se trompa en attribuant ce miracle au moine Guillaume, pp. xxiii, xxv); cf. Mayr-Harting, 'Functions', p. 344.

[34] *Wulfric*, pp. 64–5, 108, 117.

[35] *Christina*, p. 82 ('. . . duxerat originem ex antiquis Anglis nobilibus et potentibus').

[36] *Christina*, pp. 40, 42.

[37] Voir O. Pächt, C.R. Dodwell et F. Wormald, *The St Albans Psalter*, Studies of the Warburg Institute XXV (Londres, 1960), pp. 5–6, 27–30 [Wormald]; cf. Talbot, *Christina*, pp. 22–7, et Holdsworth, 'Christina', pp. 189–95.

[38] Voir C. Storey, *La Vie de saint Alexis* (Genève, 1968); cf. M.D. Legge, 'La précocité de la littérature anglo-normande', *Cahiers de civilisation médiévale*, VIII (1965), 327–49, et, en particulier, 331–2.

[39] Voir: Pächt, *Psalter*, pp. 136–7, 140; Talbot, *Christina*, p. 26; et Holdsworth, 'Christina', p. 191.

traduction française d'un morceau latin.[40] C'est ici que je crois trouver une réponse – provisoire, je l'admets volontiers – à ma question concernant la langue employée dans les entretiens entre la famille bourgeoise de Huntingdon et leur ami épiscopal: en toute probabilité, c'était le français, langue prestigieuse que ces citadins aisés et ambitieux avaient dû, sans retard, apprendre. Conclusion qui ne se voit que renforcée quand on considère l'amitié qui marqua l'âge mûr de la sainte, d'anachorète devenue prieure d'une communauté féminine; car l'ami en question, c'était l'abbé Geoffroi de l'abbaye de Saint-Auban, moine d'origine mancelle.[41] D'après ce que nous venons de constater, on supposerait plus facilement que dans leurs longs entretiens (. . . des plus chastes, précise l'hagiographe) c'était Christine qui s'exprimait en français, plutôt que le moine manceau qui adoptait l'anglais . . . Toutefois, l'on ne sait rien de certain.

Où que nous regardions dans le XIIᵉ siècle anglais, le monde que nous révèle l'hagiographie évolue de façon semblable. Que la sainteté était reconnue comme valeur universelle, c'est encore ce que nous apprend le choix des langues hagiographiques.

Comme nos documents l'ont tous montré, à cette époque le latin était devenu la langue hagiographique presque sans rivale. Malgré le fort caractère anglais des saints, la langue anglaise ne s'employait presque plus pour les célébrer. Il y avait, pourtant, au moins une *Vie* anglaise dont le souvenir nous est parvenu, et dont on ne saurait jamais trop déplorer la perte: celle que rédigea, vers la fin du XIᵉ siècle, Coleman, ancien chapelain de saint Wulfstan de Worcester, ce dernier seul parmi les évêques anglo-saxons à garder son siège épiscopal pendant une période appréciable du règne du Conquérant. Mais, pour mieux faire connaître les mérites du saint, cette *Vie* fut bientôt traduite en latin par Guillaume de Malmesbury, et c'est seule cette version latine qui nous est connue.[42]

Et, dernier avatar de l'hagiographie anglo-saxonne, à partir des années 1160 environ, des *Vies* de certains saints d'avant la Conquête se virent traduites en vers français. Par exemple, celle de 'saint Edmond le roi', 'martyrisé' vers 870, et donc contemporain célèbre de nos trois petits ermites 'thorneyois'; car à deux reprises des moines se mirent à le célébrer en vers français, non seulement à l'abbaye de Saint-Edmond, où reposait son corps exempt de toute corruption, mais encore, semble-t-il, à Ramsey.[43] Cas plus complexe, celui du dernier roi anglo-saxon, Edouard le Confesseur, dont la *Vita* latine rédigée par Ailred de Rievaulx fut traduite en vers français par une religieuse de l'abbaye de Barking;[44] tout en témoignant du respect qu'inspirait aux Anglo-Normands la sainteté anglo-saxonne, cette *Vie* mit en valeur l'élément anglais dont voulait se réclamer le roi Henri II, soucieux d'être reconnu comme successeur légitime du Confesseur.

Dans une optique différente, on peut penser que cette universalité, cette internationalité, des saints ressortit également au culte populaire. Celui, par exemple, du

---

40 Wormald, *Psalter*, p. 4; cf. Pächt, pp. 137–8. Remarquons toutefois que l'on aurait de bonnes raisons de croire qu'en ce temps-là la communauté de Saint-Auban restait pour la plupart anglophone (voir *Gesta abbatum*, I, 88 – épisode où, faute de parler anglais, des convives namurois durent s'exprimer en latin).

41 Voir *Gesta abbatum*, I, 72 *et seq.*, et Talbot, *Christina*, pp. 134–56, 160–70, 172–4, 176–82, 192.

42 R.R. Darlington, *The Vita Wulfstani of William of Malmesbury, &c.*, Camden Third Series XL (Londres, 1928), p. 2.

43 Voir Legge, *Anglo-Norman Literature*, pp. 244–6.

44 Voir *ibidem*, pp. 246–7, et *eadem*, 'Précocité', pp. 342–3.

petit saint Guillaume de Norwich. Malgré l'ascendance purement anglaise du jeune martyr, le culte dont se vit bientôt entouré son tombeau ne revêtait aucun caractère nationaliste. Parmi les premiers à signaler la présence du nouveau saint fut une représentante de la petite noblesse de la région, la dame Liéjard, 'domina Legarda Willelmi Apuli quondam uxor', veuve adonnée à de bonnes oeuvres parmi les pauvres de la ville. Parmi les miraculés, aux paysans et aux mendiants se mêlaient des nobles; car le petit apprenti-pellissier ne refusait pas son aide aux rejetons des vainqueurs de Hastings, pas plus que ceux-ci ne dédaignaient de se vouer à lui. Par une touchante sympathie entre garçons d'à peu près le même âge, le petit martyr anglais guérit aussi le faucon dont un jeune noble pleurait la maladie apparemment mortelle.[45]

*   *   *

Pour revenir à la question que nous avons posée au début, concernant l'identité anglaise et l'attrait qu'elle exerça sur certains Anglo-Normands, il est évident que l'hagiographie y contribua beaucoup. Aux Anglais les saints anglais permettaient de se respecter eux-mêmes, et aux Normands ils inspiraient de l'admiration pour certains du moins d'entre leurs vaincus. Sans doute parviendrait-on à des conclusions similaires en parcourant les calendriers monastiques et les litanies du XIIe siècle, mais pour le moment c'est l'hagiographie seule qui nous retient. Bien sûr, les rapprochements entre vainqueurs et vaincus se voyaient facilités, encouragés même, par bien d'autres influences: un peu par le goût partagé des légendes héroïques du pays, peut-être par une sociabilité générale, et notamment par les mariages 'mixtes' entre les deux 'nations'.[46] Toutefois, la sainteté anglaise du XIIe siècle constituait un moyen de réconciliation entre les deux peuples, plutôt qu'un ébauche de mouvement nationaliste.

*   *   *

Cependant, mon exposé a pu paraître pécher par nationalisme, s'être trop attardé sur des saints à noms anglo-saxons, comme si en Angleterre anglo-normande il eût fallu être anglais pour devenir saint . . . Loin de là: à en juger par Hugues d'Avalon, évêque de Lincoln, il ne fallait même pas comprendre la langue anglaise![47] Les vocations ne font aucun cas des nationalités, 'l'Esprit souffle où il veut'; et parmi les nombreux ermites de l'époque se trouvait plus d'un ancien chevalier.[48] Pour être ermite, on n'en devient pas forcément saint; mais, à constater la présence normande dans les ermitages anglais, on se rend compte de l'universalité de la recherche d'une vie parfaite.

En effet, l'Angleterre anglo-normande vit bientôt fleurir des saints de souche étrangère (bien entendu, nous laisserons de côté les personnages internationaux tels saint Anselme). Par exemple, saint Gilbert de Sempringham, fils d'un seigneur anglo-normand et – détail peut-être significatif – d'une mère anglaise.[49] Contemporain

---

[45] *St William*, pp. 31–4, 258–60, et *passim*.
[46] Cf. mon article, 'Women's names in post-Conquest England: observations and speculations', *infra*, pp. 115–41.
[47] Voir D.L. Douie et H. Farmer, *The Life of St Hugh of Lincoln*, 2 tomes (Londres, 1961–62), II, 118, 127 (des épisodes où Hugues paraît avoir eu besoin d'un interprète pour communiquer avec des Anglais de condition modeste).
[48] Voir, par exemple, Dauphin, 'L'érémitisme', pp. 280, 282.
[49] *Vita S. Gileberti confessoris*, dans *Monasticon*, VI/ii, *v–*xxix, et, en particulier, *v ('. . . mater verò ortu Anglica, à parentibus fidelibus, non inferioris tamen conditionis originem trahens').

approximatif des saints Godric, Wulfric et Christine, et, comme Godric, censé être mort centenaire, Gilbert naquit vraisemblablement pendant les années 1080. Tout comme le petit Guillaume guérissait, sans aucune distinction, mendiants anglais et nobles anglo-normands, Gilbert, anglo-normand lui-même, ne refusait point son aide posthume aux paysans anglais: comme le note Raymonde Foreville, 'la principale clientèle du tombeau de Gilbert est celle des colons et vilains des villas voisines.'[50] Ici notre méthode anthroponymique trouve moins de prise, car, à l'époque des miracles posthumes attribués à Gilbert, les anthroponymes de type continental s'étaient déjà répandus partout dans la population anglaise. Citons, cependant, les miraculées *Brictiva* [*Beorht3ifu*] *de Sempingham* et, avec de légères rectifications orthographiques, *Elvi[v]a* [*Ælf3ifu*] *de Folkingham*, une certaine *Aili[v]a* [*Æþel3ifu*], et la *paupercula mulier Kenua*, c'est-à-dire, *Queniva* [*Cwen3ifu*] (remarquons que parmi les noms anglo-saxons les féminins résistèrent plus longtemps à la mode continentale que ne le firent les masculins);[51] et, ce qui à cette date ne laisse pas d'être significatif, parmi les témoins des miracles on trouve un *Herewardus* et un chanoine au nom anglo-scandinave de *Gamelus*.[52] Les paysans qui se vouent à ce noble devenu saint font diptyque avec la noblesse agenouillée devant le tombeau du petit apprenti de Norwich.

En l'an de grâce 1170 se perpétra le meurtre, le martyre, le plus célèbre de tous: celui de saint Thomas Becket. Bien que né mon concitoyen lointain, de Londres, saint Thomas était de souche purement normande, le père de Rouen, la mère de Caen.[53] Ici encore s'opéra le rapprochement culturel que nous prenons comme thème. Beaucoup d'Anglais, aux noms traditionnels, se trouvèrent parmi les premiers miraculés du martyr.[54] Et, parmi les nombreux hagiographes qui se mirent aussitôt à le célébrer, il y en eut un qui s'appelait *Edward Grim*, témoin oculaire de l'assassinat au crépuscule du 29 décembre, et lui-même grièvement blessé au bras.[55] Permettez-moi de me replonger une dernière fois dans l'anthroponymie. Les nom et surnom de cet *Edward Grim* – né, semble-t-il, à Cambridge – relèvent de la culture anglo-scandinave d'avant la Conquête: *Edward*, de par sa phonologie même, ne saurait être qu'anglais (l'équivalent continental en est *Odoard*); et le *Grim* patronymique appartient au stock de noms scandinaves apportés en Angleterre par les Vikings, dont l'influence en Cambridgeshire, pour être plutôt légère, n'en est pas moins claire.[56] A n'en pas douter, Edward Grim était issu d'un milieu anglo-scandinave des plus traditionalistes; mais ce fut un saint de souche normande dont il célébra, en latin, les mérites.

*　　　*　　　*

[50] R. Foreville, *Un Procès de canonisation à l'aube du XIIIe siècle (1201–1202): Le Livre de saint Gilbert de Sempringham* (Paris, 1943), p. xlvi.

[51] *Ibidem*, pp. 43, 56, 54, 62; cf. 'Women's names', *passim*.

[52] *Gilbert*, pp. 65 (cf. 7), 67. Pour *Gamelus*, voir Fellows Jensen, *Scandinavian Personal Names*, pp. 89–95.

[53] Voir J.C. Robertson et J.B. Sheppard, *Materials for the History of Thomas Becket, &c.*, 7 tomes, Rolls Series (Londres, 1875–85), III, 14, et IV, 3, 81; aussi R. Foreville, 'Les origines normandes de la famille Becket, &c.', *L'Année canonique*, XVIII (1973), 433–80, et, en particulier, 439–48.

[54] Voir, par exemple, 'People and languages in post-Conquest Canterbury', *infra*, p. 186 et n. 12.

[55] Voir *Thomas Becket*, II, 353–450, cf. xlv–xlvii.

[56] Voir Fellows Jensen, *Scandinavian Personal Names*, pp. 105–7. Pour l'influence scandinave sur cette région, voir P.H. Reaney, *The Place-Names of Cambridgeshire, &c.*, English Place-Name Society XIX (Cambridge, 1943), pp. xix–xxii; aussi J. Insley, 'Addenda to the survey of English place-names: personal names in field and minor names', *Journal of the English Place-Name Society*, X (1977–78), 41–72, et, en particulier, 69.

Je risque de paraître m'être éloignée de l'opuscule modeste dont je suis partie; mais, ce que j'ai voulu démontrer, c'est que même un document en apparence si peu important peut offrir de précieux renseignements à qui se donne la peine de l'intérroger avec soin. Cette petite *Vita* de très modestes saints contient en germe tous les rapprochements spirituels, intellectuels et sociaux qui vont se réaliser au siècle suivant. Fulcard, notre Flamand à la carrière de semi-raté, amoureux de son abbaye perdue au milieu des marécages, illustre peut-être mieux que le magnifique Becket l'union possible entre la culture continentale, voire internationale, et les traditions anglaises.

   Si aujourd'hui c'est ce récit brévissime que j'ai choisi comme point de départ, ce n'est pas (. . . ou pas tout à fait) qu'il soit seul de son espèce à être présent à mon esprit. C'est que les conclusions auxquelles il nous entraîne me paraissent convenir, et admirablement, au contexte. Réunis ici en milieu français, et francophone, nous représentons plusieurs pays distincts – l'Allemagne, l'Angleterre et l'Ecosse, la Belgique, et les Etats-Unis, en plus de la France. Pour nous, gens du XXe siècle, notre thème commun, notre valeur universelle, ne saurait plus guère être la sainteté; mais nous n'en avons pas moins une entreprise commune. Ce que l'Angleterre du XIIe siècle nous apprend, c'est que l'unité morale et intellectuelle dépasse toutes les frontières, linguistiques aussi bien que politiques.

4

Sir Gawain and the Green Knight: Characterisation by Syntax

In his recent book *Criticism and Medieval Poetry* (1964) A.C. Spearing has attempted what until now has too rarely been attempted: 'detailed analysis of literary texture' (p. 1) applied to medieval poetry. One of the works to which he applies this technique of 'close reading' is *Sir Gawain and the Green Knight*; and among the passages he deals with are certain speeches put into the mouths of Gawain, especially lines 343–61, and of the Green Knight. By studying these speeches Mr Spearing reaches the conclusion that 'in both cases, character is expressed through syntax rather than through imagery' (p. 45). It may not be amiss, especially as I shall later wish to refer back to some of them, to quote at length some of his observations (pp. 40–45). '[Gawain's] character', he says, 'is declared as soon as he appears in the poem, partly by what he says, but still more by the way in which he says it'; and how this is done he explains in some detail:

> Gawain's *cortaysye* is expressed most fully in the *way* in which he says what he says. . . . A number of peculiarly circumlocutory phrases . . . the length and complexity of [the] sentences . . . and each . . . is full of subordinate clauses. . . . The main point . . . is delayed until the very last line by a pair of conditional clauses, with a consecutive clause sandwiched between them. Similarly in the last sentence the crucial request is delayed by subordinate clauses, and immediately qualified by a further condition. The sense one has in moving through the passage is of the skirting of a series of obstacles, the overcoming or evading of one difficulty after another: the syntax seems to wind itself along, to move two steps sideways for every step forward. . . . The profusion of parenthetic phrases inserted before the main point of each clause is reached. . . . There are parentheses and subordinate clauses even within the subordinate clauses. . . . The extremely complex manner of expression, full of qualifications and delays, is typical of Gawain in the situations which most test his *cortaysye*. . . .
>
> The Green Knight's bluffness is expressed through a series of short sentences, usually linked by 'and' – by co-ordination as opposed to the elaborate subordination of Gawain's idiom. Where Gawain's speeches are full of conditional and subjunctive verbs, the verbs here are most often in the simple present or past indicative, or else, significantly, in the imperative. . . . Where Gawain is subtle, the Green Knight is brusque. . . .

To me this seems a most illuminating analysis, opening up as it does the way to a deeper understanding of the subtleties of medieval poetic technique. Unfortunately, however, Mr Spearing does not carry this analysis as far as he might, even in relation to this one romance. So, following the path he has indicated but has not chosen to explore further for himself, I have found my way to several new observations about the *Gawain*-poet's use of syntactic variation to indicate character and tone of voice. Such an analysis seems to me all the more worth while because of our present relative ignorance about the finer points of medieval literary technique.

The Green Knight and the Lord of the Castle

The Green Knight's habitual tone of voice has already been characterised by Mr Spearing: it is brusque and peremptory, and the syntactic features by which this tone is created are shortness of sentence, frequent use of the imperative and avoidance of conditional and qualifying clauses – an indication of the unconditional and unqualified assent the speaker demands to all his propositions. So far, syntax is indeed character. What Mr Spearing might have gone on to investigate (but did not) is how far there may be similarities between the Green Knight's syntax and that of his *alter ego*, the Lord of the Castle. Since the two figures are aspects of one personality it would, after all, be fitting for them to be made to speak the same language.

One obvious trick of speech they certainly share: over-ready *tutoiement*. The Green Knight *thou*'s everyone without distinction. The Lord begins conventionally by greeting Gawain with 'Ye ar welcum' (835), but soon he is from time to time dropping a 'thou' and a 'thee' (for instance, 1068, 1674 ff.); and in this his usage contrasts with Gawain's, who in all his talk with the Lord consistently keeps to the formal mode of address.

Does the Lord also share with the Green Knight those syntactical features observed by Mr Spearing, avoidance of subordination and repeated use of indicative and imperative verbs? To discover this it is fairest to examine some of the Lord's longer speeches, those in which subordination would *a priori* seem most likely to occur. (For typographical convenience, my quotations are taken from the slightly modernised text edited by A.C. Cawley, Everyman's Library 1962, though I have added the italics. For those unfamiliar with the dialect I offer literal translations of the more difficult passages.)

> Thenne laghande quoth the lorde: 'Now *leng the byhoves*,   (1068)
> For *I schal teche* yow to that terme bi the tymes ende.
> The grene chapayle upon grounde *greve yow* no more;
> Bot *ye schal be* in yowre bed, burne, at thyn ese,
> Quyle forth dayes, and ferk on the fyrst of the yere,
> And cum to that merk at mydmorn, to make quat yow likes in spenne.
>   *Dowelles* whyle New Yeres daye,
>   And *rys* and *raykes* thenne.
>   *Mon schal yow sette* in waye;
>   Hit is not two myle henne.'

> Then, laughing, the Lord said: 'Now stay you must, for at the due time I shall direct you to that appointed place. Do not let the Green Chapel and its location fret you any more; but, sir, until late in the day you shall lie at your ease in your bed, and then ride away on the first day of the year, and arrive at that landmark at mid-morning, to carry out there whatever you wish. Stay till New Year's Day, and then get up and ride off. Someone shall show you the road; it lies not two miles away.'

> 'For ye haf travayled', quoth the tulk, 'towen fro ferre,   (1093)
> And sythen waked me wyth, ye arn not wel waryst
> Nauther of sostnaunce ne of slepe, sothly I knowe.
> *Ye schal lenge* in your lofte and lyye in your ese
> To-morn quyle the messe-quyle, and to mete wende
> When ye wyl, wyth my wyf, that wyth yow *schal sitte*
> And comfort yow with compayny, til I to cort torne.

Ye lende,
And I schal erly ryse;
On hunting wyl I wende.'

'As you have been travelling', the Lord said, 'having journeyed from a distance, and have since been revelling the nights away with me, you are not well restored, either in food or in sleep, that I am sure. Tomorrow morning you shall stay in your room and take your ease until time for Mass, and then, when you wish, come down to dinner with my wife, who shall sit with you and entertain you with her company until I return home. You stay behind, and I shall rise early; I mean to go hunting.'

The predominance of imperatives found by Mr Spearing in the Green Knight's speech marks the Lord's also; thus, 'dowelles, rys, raykes, ye lende'. And, if we take 'imperative mood' in the psychological sense rather than in a purely grammatical one, a great deal more of these speeches is seen to consist of virtual commands; thus, 'leng the byhoves, the grene chapayle . . . greve yow no more, ye schal be in yowre bed, ye schal lenge in your lofte and lyye in your ese', and so on. Moreover by his liberal use of futures of obligation with 'schal' the Lord implies that not only his interlocutor but third parties also are subject to his command, thus, 'mon schal yow sette in waye, my wyf, that wyth yow schall sitte and comfort yow', and so on. The syntax of these apparently jocular speeches proposing the sporting covenant is not so far from that of the Green Knight's original 'forward', in which he laid on Gawain the duty

'that *thou schal siker me*, segge, bi thi trawthe,   (394)
That *thou schal seche me thiself*, where-so thou hopes
I may be funde upon folde, and foch the such wages
As thou deles me to-day bifore this douthe ryche . . .'

Nor is it only in this predominantly imperative tone that the Lord's speech resembles the Green Knight's: they share also that avoidance of subordination, and particularly of conditional and concessional clauses, which Mr Spearing has shown to distinguish the Green Knight's speech so markedly from Gawain's. In the two speeches I have quoted there are two relative clauses (one continuative, describing further development in action, and the other negligible), two short temporal clauses, two causal clauses introduced by 'for', and no conditional or concessive clauses at all. Even when two propositions are clearly connected in his mind, the Green Knight tends to prefer the briskly paratactic construction, thus, 'mon schal yow sette in waye; hit is not two myle henne', and 'and I schal erly ryse; on huntyng wyl I wende', where a different speaker might in each case have introduced the second clause with a causal conjunction.

It might be argued that the style and syntax of these speeches are due to context rather than to character; but I think not. There are other ways for inviting a guest to prolong his stay (and a subtle man such as Gawain would have found them) than seizing his lapel and beating him into submission with imperatives and peremptory *shall*'s while at the same time establishing a detailed and fixed programme for the rest of his visit.

By their syntax, then, the Lord and the Green Knight reveal themselves as only superficially different embodiments of the same personality. And not only in their syntax, for (as I hope to show elsewhere[1]) another linguistic trait that they share is use

---

[1] [['Sir Gawain and the Green Knight: its Artistry and its Audience', *Medium Ævum*, 40 (1971), 10–20, especially pp. 11–12.]]

of colloquial dialect terms much freer than that of any of the other characters in the romance. Nor is it surprising that they should have been given this linguistic resemblance, since in general aspect and manner they are represented as not unalike. Like the Green Knight, the Lord of the Castle is 'a hoge hathel', with a broad beard and a forthright manner. Both are bluff and boisterous, with overflowing physical energy: in Arthur's hall the Green Knight swaggers with insolent restlessness, and at the Green Chapel he comes 'whyrlande out of a wro' and vaults nimbly over the stream. As for the Lord, time and again he seizes hold of his guest, 'luflych aloft lepes ful ofte' and 'let for luf lotes so myry, as wyy that wolde of his wyte' (981, 1086). Allowance being made for the differing circumstances, there is nothing incompatible in the behaviour of the two characters, and so it is appropriate that both speak in the same voice and that a masterful one.

As we see, then, these two aspects of the same personage, the Green Knight and the Lord of the Castle, share certain habits of speech, habits which evidently reflect a certain cast of mind and attitude to the rest of the world. What that attitude is appears even more clearly when we observe who else in the poem adopts such a style: only one other speaker, King Arthur himself (that is, if we except the special case of the Guide, whose style I discuss in the next section). Altogether, Arthur speaks only about sixteen lines, but these are enough to show what his characteristic manner is: he too uses imperatives freely and rarely stoops to qualify any proposition – and from him this is what is to be expected, since a king is above condition and concession and has every right to command. This likeness between Arthur's usage and that of the Green Knight (in both his incarnations) underlines the latter's masterfulness: whether he is in his own hall or in Arthur's he speaks in the same lordly tone, and by this he shows himself to stand outside the ordinary conventions of Arthurian society.

The Guide

For years I have been puzzled by the figure of the Guide, who is no ordinary squire, but an active agent in the testing of Gawain. No very obvious clues to his standing and motivation have been given by the author, and so we may wonder whether there are any hidden ones to be detected in the language given to him.

Certain affinities do indeed come to light as soon as we look attentively at the Guide's two speeches (2091–2125, 2140–2151); as these speeches are long, I shall try to make my comments intelligible without quoting them in full. One trait the Guide certainly shares with the Green Knight is that over-ready *tutoiement* already noted: not only does he regularly *thou* Gawain after the latter has rejected his advice, but, even before this, in his first speech, he drops a 'thee' – 'Forthy I say the . . .' (2110). On looking further we see that he seems to share some of his master's other linguistic habits also: the predominant use of the indicative and of paratactic constructions, and the frequent use of the imperative; thus, 'trawe ye me that trwely (2112), let the gome one, and gos away (2118–9), cayres bi sum other kyth (2120; ride to some other region), haf here thi helme on thy hede (2143), ryde me doun this ilk rake (2144), loke a littel on the launde (2146)'. In the first of the two speeches there is, however, a fair amount of subordination: not only a number of causal clauses introduced by 'for' and 'sythen', as well as half a dozen defining relative clauses ('that note place that ye han spied and spuryed so specially after', 'the place that ye prece to', and so on), but also a fair sprinkling of conditional and concessive clauses. But, when we examine these conditional and concessive clauses, we at once observe that they function very differently from those which Mr Spearing noted as filling so many of Gawain's speeches with 'qualifications and delays'. Far from attenuating the force of the main proposition, these serve rather to emphasise it, thus,

'Forthly I say the, as sothe as ye in sadel sitte, (2110)
Com ye there, *ye be kylled*, may the knyght rede,
Trawe ye me that trwely, thagh ye had twenty lyves to spende.'

In this passage, there is no delaying of the main point, which is not made to follow the qualifying clauses but is sandwiched between them, and there is no muffling of the speaker's intention. In the second of the Guide's speeches the brusque tone is even more marked: 'thou' is used regularly, as a sign of the speaker's contempt for a man who refuses to heed the voice of reason; the imperatives are, with reference to the length of the two speeches, comparatively more frequent and might even be said to set the rough tone; and of the four subordinate clauses not one expresses even grammatical condition or concession.

For anyone inclining to Dr Mabel Day's view that it is the Green Knight himself who 'in the likeness of a servant . . . escorts Gawain to the Green Chapel' (p. xxxvi of Gollancz's edition, EETS 210 (1940)), these features of the Guide's speech might seem valuable evidence in favour of this identity. In the absence of other evidence it may, however, seem too hardy to suggest such an identification. What is certain is that, like the Green Knight, the Guide ignores the ordinary conventions of society; he speaks quite unlike the ordinary squire he is supposed to be. When he had wished to turn his uncle the King aside from his purpose of taking up the Challenge, Gawain had adopted a circumlocutory and therefore apologetic syntax: the Guide, in a not dissimilar situation vis-à-vis Gawain himself, soon passes from his circumstantial preamble to the far from oblique assertion,

'Wolde ye worch bi my wytte, ye worthed the better' (2096)

and couches his main advice not in conditionals but in imperatives,

'Forthy, goude sir Gawayn, *let the gome one*, (2118)
And *gos away* sum other gate, upon Goddes halve!
Cayres bi sum other kyth, ther Kryst mot yow spede . . .'

This style gives his warning some urgency, but at the same time it makes very clear just what he is tempting Gawain to do. Dramatically, therefore, it serves two purposes. First, it puts the situation facing Gawain into unambiguous terms and so enables him in his reply to express clear-sighted determination (this does, of course, ring a little false to those who remember that green girdle). Further, this blunt and barefaced expression of pusillanimity makes Gawain's refusal come the more appropriately: partly because the more openly shameful a temptation is the less enticing it appears; and partly because an idiom so different from Gawain's own fails to touch either his heart or his mind.

The Lady

Thus, the Guide's function as agent of the Green Knight may be hinted at in the brusque and unceremonious tone, so like that of his master and so unlike Gawain's own, in which he proffers his temptation to cowardice. This leads us to the further question: in what sort of voice the does the Green Knight's other agent, the Lady, proffer her (rather more successful) temptations?

There is one trait which the Lady shares with the Guide and also with her husband: that over-familiarity we have already noted. Already in her third speech in the romance (not, of course, her third speech to Gawain, for she had already had a number of unreported conversations with him, 'dere dalyaunce of her derne wordes' (1012)), she drops a couple of *thee*'s (1252). Does this mean that her tone of voice is in general like theirs?

If we wish to examine one of her longer speeches, that is, one in which syntactical peculiarities would find scope, a good choice might seem to be that in which on her second visit to Gawain the Lady tries to argue him into conformity with her interpretation of the courtly code (1508–1534). Here, the most obvious feature is anacoluthon. The speaker embarks on a question which looks as though it will be, 'Why are you so reluctant to make love to me?' But, in the middle of amplifying the personal reasons why Gawain's behaviour seems so incredible ('so yong and so yepe as ye at this tyme, so cortayse, so knyghtyly . . .'), she breaks off to develop in a parenthesis the major premiss on which her whole argument rests, the universal obligation on all true knights to be the servants of Love. This parenthesis is itself long and complex, lasting for eight lines of alliterative verse, and when it is over and the speaker returns from the general to the particular she still does not put the question but continues to refine on the circumstances that inspire her perplexity ('and ye ar knyght comlokest kyd of your elde . . .'). Finally she does put a question, in two parts:

> 'Why! ar ye lewed, that alle the los weldes,   (1528)
> Other elles ye demen me to dille your dalyaunce to herken?'

> 'What! are you, who possess such a high reputation, quite ignorant, or is it
> that you think me too stupid to listen to your courtship?'

This is not quite, however, the question which the beginning of the speech had implied; and, further, these questions, as well as being leading rather than open ones, function in fact not so much as interrogation as a reproach. There is no pause for an answer, but instead the interrogative is at once replaced by the imperative:

> 'Dos teches me of your wytte,   (1533)
> Whil my lorde is fro hame.'

Mr Spearing's comment on syntax that moves 'two steps sideways for every step forwards' seems even more appropriate for this than for any speech of Gawain's. Here, just as in some of Gawain's most typical speeches, the main point is held back until all the conditions and qualifications bearing on it have been rehearsed; but here, as is never the case with Gawain's speeches, the conclusion (if such it can be called) is not what the beginning implied and required. Here the anacoluthon is the distinguishing feature: it distinguishes the Lady's style in this speech very sharply from that of her husband, who comes so briskly to every point; and it distinguishes it also from Gawain's, for in all his complex courtesies he never loses track of his main argument. What such a style is meant to represent is not so far made clear: it could be simple eagerness; or the tumbling confusion of a lively mind devoid of training (as most women's minds must necessarily have been during the Middle Ages); or embarrassment, feigned or true; or a representation of the devious ways a mind has to work when it is not being altogether frank.

That the broken syntax in that speech is to be interpreted as a reflection of particular circumstances rather than of any constant trait of the Lady's mind is suggested when we examine other speeches given to her, as, for instance:

> 'Bi Mary,' quoth the menskful, 'me thynk hit another;   (1268)
> For were I worth al the wone of wymmen alyve,
> And al the wele of the worlde were in my honde,
> And I schulde chepen and chose to cheve me a lorde,
> For the costes that I haf knowen upon the, knyght, here,
> Of bewté and debonerté and blythe semblaunt,
> And that I haf er herkkened and halde hit here trwee,
> *Ther schulde no freke upon folde bifore yow be chosen.*'

> 'Indeed', said the noble lady, 'it seems to me quite the contrary; for, if my worth equalled that of all living women taken together and all the riches of the world were in my possession and if I were to be casting about and seeking to get myself a husband, then, for the qualities that I have recognised in you now, your handsomeness and courtesy and pleasant manners, and that I have heard tell of before and now know to be true, no knight alive should be preferred to you.'

Here there is no anacoluthon, no confusion at all in the train of thought: phrases and clauses are all clearly related, and the conclusion follows in a logical and expected way. Again, however, the conclusion is held back, almost artificially, until the multiple conditions and motives bearing upon it have first been stated at length. Structurally, indeed, this is very much in Gawain's own manner, but not in its total effect: in Gawain's usage such delaying of a conclusion usually serves to attenuate and muffle the main point, but here it serves rather to make of it an arresting and emphatic climax. Nevertheless, in spite of this distinction, one may begin to suspect that part at least of the Lady's appeal to Gawain lies in the way she speaks his own language, or at least one nearly related to his own. This is borne out if we examine her speeches during the final interview, the speeches by which Gawain's resolution is at last overcome, and especially the last one (my italics):

> 'Now forsake ye this silke,' sayde the burde thenne,   (1846)
> 'For hit is symple in hitself? And so hit wel semes.
> Lo! so hit is littel, and lasse hit is worthy.
> Bot *who-so knew* the costes that knit ar therinne,
> He wolde hit prayse at more prys, paraventure;
> For *quat gome so is gorde* with this grene lace,
> While he hit hade hemely halched aboute,
> *Ther is no hathel under heven tohewe hym that myght,*
> *For he myght not be slayn for slyght upon erthe.*'

> 'Now are you rejecting this silken girdle', the Lady then asked, 'because it is a plain thing? So indeed it looks. See, it is only so big, and so of even less value. But anyone who knew the properties that are woven into it would perhaps esteem it more highly; for whatsoever man is girt with this green girdle, as long as he has it properly fastened about him, there is no warrior alive can strike him down, for he cannot be slain by any stratagem there is.'

Here again complexity of idea is paralleled by complexity of syntax. Most notably, this speech, the crucial one for Gawain's resolution, shows delaying tactics used to especially good effect: the 'lace' is strongly but cryptically commended for the 'costes that knit ar therinne', but what these 'costes' may be is kept back until the last two lines of the speech, in such a way as to arouse the listener's curiosity to the full. Moreover, this crucial point, when it is reached, is put in an indirect way, in a universalised third person and the conditional mood: not 'if you knew, you would . . .' but 'who-so knew . . . he wolde . . .'; not 'if you wear this girdle, you cannot be slain' but 'quat gome so . . . he myght not be slayn . . .' The Lady gives no hint that she even guesses how relevant this property of the girdle is to her hearer's own present predicament. So, as in the earlier passage (1268 ff.), the conclusion here is delayed to the very end, partly at least by the interposition of conditional clauses; and, again as in the earlier speech, the Lady is here using a Gawain-like syntax for her special purpose of creating suspense and so throwing her main point into relief. The style is made appropriate to the occasion, and it is also made characteristic of the Lady: how characteristic we realise when we ask ourselves how her husband would have made the same offer (he would no doubt have urged, clapping his guest heartily on the shoulder as he said it: 'Lappe this lace the aboute, and so lach never harme At wyye of this worlde . . .').

The Lady, then, is given her own characteristic voice: a variable voice, admittedly, sometimes marked by breaks of syntax and shifts of tone, at others more disciplined, but always complex and nuanced and slyly building up suspense in the hearer's mind – though no more variable, certainly, than that of any real person. Apart from the minor point concerning pronouns of address, her style bears no resemblance to her husband's: whereas his speeches are almost devoid of conditional elements, these are just what hers abound in, being one of the chief means by which delay and suspense are achieved; and, although she may now and then throw out an imperative ('*Dos teches me of your wytte* . . .'), her normal address is much more indirect than his. This indirect and shifting manner is appropriate to the disingenuous rôle she is playing, and her use of suspense enhances her temptations.

Moreover, there is yet a more subtle way in which the Lady's style is adapted to the rôle she plays, for, as we have already observed, it is indeed Gawain's usage which hers most closely resembles. The two styles are not identical (it would be a considerable blemish in the poem if they were), but to serve their different ends they use much the same syntactical devices, 'qualifications and delays'. And this is dramatically satisfying. In analysing the Guide's temptation of Gawain we noted that the alien idiom in which this is expressed seems to make it easier and more natural for Gawain to reject it. With the Lady it is just the reverse: the speech-patterns (and therefore the thought-patterns) with which she assails Gawain are very like his own, so that at its most persuasive her voice must seem to him to be saying things he might have thought himself. It is natural and dramatically right therefore that this temptation proffered in his own complex idiom should be the one to which Gawain succumbs.

Even an analysis as brief and incomplete as this makes it clear how each of the characters in *Sir Gawain and the Green Knight* is given an individual voice and how the chief means of differentiating these voices is variation in syntax. This is particularly effective as a means of characterisation, since of all the elements of language syntax is the one which most readily creates the illusion of reflecting the inner workings of the mind. Not, of course, that the poet himself would have formulated his method in any such terms: he no doubt worked by intuition based on observation of how differences in linguistic habit often reflect differences in personality (do we not all know living speakers who combine the Green Knight's fondness for unqualified imperatives with his domineering attitude to his fellow-men?). In any event, for a poet working within the conventions of alliterative verse it was a brilliant stroke to choose syntax as the instrument of characterisation, for in this medium syntax is the linguistic feature most readily varied, vocabulary and phraseology being necessarily so much subject to the exigencies of the metre. And this is not all; for, not content with inventing distinctive voices for each main character, the poet has so tuned and modulated those voices as to make them echo, contrast and counterpoint one another in as it were an orchestration of character.

5

Women in England after 1066: The Factual Evidence

Post-Conquest England saw nearly all the native aristocracy and gentry dispossessed by 'Norman' settlers, who for a generation or two remained somewhat apart. In matters of family structure, land-tenure and inheritance the newcomers observed legal and social customs partly at variance with those prevailing in pre-Conquest days. To regulate these customs they established within little more than a century a formidable bureaucracy, of which many products survive. Yet, for all the documentation, women of the twelfth and thirteenth centuries are only intermittently visible to historians, because the matters with which extant records mostly deal are ones, like land-holding and politics, in which women had a limited share: a negative finding significant in itself.

When a medieval theorist divided society into three orders – those who fight, those who till the earth, and those who pray – he explicitly omitted women, noting their role simply as 'to marry and to serve' the fighters and the workers. Throughout the Middle Ages and beyond marriage was a central theme of women's lives, but no personal diaries survive to tell of it, nor any truly private, vernacular letters from earlier than the fifteenth century. Some shreds of personal testimony exist. The early fifteenth-century *Book of Margery Kempe* depicts, from her point of view and as an incident in her spiritual odyssey, a marriage which produced fourteen children. The church-court records of matrimonial causes, which begin in the early thirteenth century and are voluminous by the late fourteenth, sometimes seem, despite their Latinised form, to catch the voices of the parties and their witnesses; but for the most part these remain unpublished.

On the other hand, accessible evidence abounds for the place of marriage in socio-economic and moral-theological structures: civil and canon laws alike expound women's role in society, showing also what individuals could expect from life. Laws often encapsulate the ethos of the community whose conduct they regulate. For twelfth-century England the problem is that sometimes the codes conflicted (as they had in earlier times begun to do) with canon law prohibiting what civil and customary law allowed or even prescribed. As to which code more nearly reflected current attitudes, the best clue lies perhaps in the term 'customary': whereas canon law rested on ideal concepts of behaviour, twelfth-century Anglo-Norman civil law codified traditional customs. Certainly canon law was in the long run to influence social morality; but for the twelfth century civil law seems best to represent current attitudes to marriage and to women's role in society.

Post-Conquest society was based upon, indeed obsessed with, land-tenure. How this coloured the view taken of marriage by the twelfth-century Anglo-Norman or English aristocracy is clear from one administrative document: the *Rotuli de dominabus et pueris et puellis* compiled in 1185. Translating the title as 'A Register of Rich Widows and of Orphaned Heirs and Heiresses' gives an inkling of its content: it lists widows 'in the king's gift' and orphans 'in wardship', giving brief accounts of their family circumstances but detailed ones of their property, down to the last pig. Because all land belonged ultimately to the king, to be granted by him according to military or political expediency, familial inheritance – male primogeniture being the preferred Norman custom – suffered constraints, with heirs obliged to seek and to pay for royal approval of their succession. If a baron died before his heir was of age the lands reverted meanwhile to the Crown, the widow and under-age children being taken into the wardship of the king, who saw to the arranging of marriages for them: the position of the 'widows and orphans' in our *Register*. That was simply a special case of the regular royal control of nobles' marriages, including any that a baron might in his lifetime plan for a daughter or other kinswoman, because of the way that marriage affected land-holding. In this system based (at least theoretically) on 'military' tenure, a woman land-holder was an anomaly. Because military duties could (as when a male land-holder was aged or disabled) be vicariously performed or commuted for a money-payment, a female could, in the absence of a male heir, inherit her family's land, but her rights in respect of it remained circumscribed. When an heiress married (not 'if': no woman of property was likely to be left single) her husband acquired for as long as the marriage lasted full control of her properties and, if he fathered a live child, retained it all his life. A widow's remarriage likewise conveyed all her holdings, including the 'dower' due from her late husband's estate, to her new one. A union contracted without prior royal approval incurred a fine, and might entail forfeiture of the lands. A register of heiresses and of propertied widows could thus assist royal clerks charged with collecting the fees due either from would-be suitors or, alternatively, from ladies anxious to keep their freedom. That fees and fines were in fact exacted is proved by surviving account-rolls. The system gave widows of an age to assert themselves and with money to hand fair freedom of choice, for their orphaned children as well as for themselves. But the fees were substantial and accordingly resented; a main freedom laid down in Magna Carta was that thenceforth no widow wishing to remain single should have to suffer financial penalty.

Young girls' wishes were another matter. Children of both sexes, whether orphaned or not, were married off at the tenderest ages: the *Register* notes one 'widow' as aged ten and her brother's 'wife', aged five, as already living in her mother-in-law's house-hold. Rank and riches were no protection – rather the reverse. Heiresses' marriages, with their tenurial consequences, were saleable commodities, to be purchased by the highest bidder or granted by the king, as favour or reward, to a courtier or a captain. Thus, in the late 1180s Henry II rewarded William the Marshal, a landless younger son of minor nobility, with the hand of the orphan heiress of the great Clare family, such a match being what William needed to add wealth and rank (the earldom of Pembroke) to his personal distinction. Nowhere are the girl's feelings mentioned, even though it was she who, as a middle-aged widow, commissioned William's extant verse-biography; her acquiescence in a marriage to a man twice her age was seemingly taken for granted by all parties, herself included. Not all girls did manage to acquiesce in their arranged marriages. The future St Christina of Markyate (of burgess, not baronial, stock) refused, despite threats and thrashings, to accept the husband her parents had chosen; she ran away dressed as a boy, to take refuge with an anchoress; how her life unfolded we shall see later.

A twelfth-century girl's reactions to an arranged marriage may have been different from a modern one's. Hard though it is to interpret in human terms stories preserved only in quasi-official documents, some episodes seem significant. About 1162 the fifty-year-old Aubrey de Vere, earl of Oxford – still childless after two marriages (one swiftly annulled, the other ended by early death) – married a twelve-year-old bride called Agnes, only to repudiate her less than a year later on the pretext of her alleged previous betrothal to his brother Geoffrey; the true motive more probably lay in the disgrace recently incurred by her father, a former royal constable. Protesting that she had never known of any such betrothal, far less consented to it, Agnes appealed for validation of her marriage to the Bishop of London and then to the Pope. To hinder her prosecution of the case, the earl kept her in custody so close as to prevent her even from attending church. In 1172 the Pope pronounced the marriage valid and commanded the earl thenceforth to treat the countess as his wife before God, threatening eternal punishment of any dereliction. The couple had several offspring, including an heir to the earldom. Widowed in her forties, Agnes paid a large fee not to be obliged to remarry (*pro pace habenda de se maritanda*). Uncomfortable though the marriage seems, her anxiety to maintain it is understandable: committed since the age of three to the de Vere family and since humiliated by the disgrace of her own, she can have seen little future elsewhere. Most women of this time must have envisaged marriage as a job, a distasteful one possibly, but for all that essential to any tolerable way of life.

So far we have focused on the nobility, whose lives are reflected in the records most readily accessible. The middling strata of society observed like customs. Among the 'under-tenants' or 'knightly class' usages were similar to those of the nobility, with this difference, that the rights of wardship and of marriage control over under-tenants were exercised not by the Crown but by their immediate lords, the barons. As for the urban society, at this time beginning to develop, the more prosperous burgesses (those whose lives are most open to our scrutiny) evidently took much the same view of marriage as did nobles and gentry, arranging alliances for economic advantage. At all events, such urban 'patriciates' as have been studied – the London one, for instance – had their leading families linked in complex webs of intermarriage hardly likely to have resulted from a free play of fancy. In one respect burgesses were freer than nobility or gentry, being exempt from the 'incidents' (fees and fines) accompanying feudal tenure. Borough customs sometimes explicitly provide that citizens shall freely 'give their daughters in marriage'. The limitation of such 'freedom' is clear: so much was 'giving in marriage' deemed to be not the parents' prerogative but their duty that municipal charities, such as the London 'court of orphanage', were set up for freemen's orphans, not only to manage their business affairs but also to arrange marriages for them.

Given this regulation of marriage choice among the upper ranks of society, scant freedom might be expected among the peasantry. Rural society was divided by ranks and its customs, unlike those of nobility and gentry, varied from manor to manor. Free farmers enjoyed liberties analogous to those of burgesses: rights, that is, for parents to arrange their children's marriages without payment or need for outside approval. For villeins matters were different. The customs ruling their lives (hence the term, 'customary tenant'), although varying in detail, followed certain general principles. In the harshest view villeins formed part of a manor's livestock, and could be conveyed along with their land from one lord to another. For a villein girl to marry away from the lordship of her birth robbed the lord not only of her work but also of any villein children she might produce, and therefore she had to seek the lord's approval of any proposed marriage and pay for this a fee called 'merchet', liability for which was proof of servile status. This was not mere form: cases are recorded where women who had married without leave were taken back to their original homes. On widows, too, custom could bear hard. Sometimes a widow succeeded automatically to her late husband's holding. In other cases a lord, deeming only an adult male equal to working the land and performing adequately the labour services due from it, might force a widow lacking a grown son either to remarry or else to move out; the lord himself might choose the prospective husband, who was for his part liable to be fined if (as some did) he refused the match despite the land that went with it. When the dead man left an adult male heir then the widow was entitled to claim from him (often her own eldest son) her 'free bench', that is, a right to shelter and maintenance for as long as she continued in 'chaste widowhood'; for, unlike a noblewoman with her dower, on remarriage (or if detected in fornication) a peasant widow forfeited her rights. Another difference lay in average ages of marriage: unlike a daughter of the great and rich, who might be married off at twelve, a peasant girl had to wait, perhaps until well into her twenties, for a suitable holding to be available for the founding of a new household. Peasant customs thus varied in detail rather than principle from those of nobility, gentry and bourgeoisie. Women's own freedom of choice could hardly have been more circumscribed than among the nobles, for whom it was regularly subordinated to questions of land, money and rank. Comparative poverty did not necessarily mean – except in terms of material comfort – a more restricted life. By the time church-court records appear promises and vows were being freely exchanged between couples clearly obeying their own wishes, not those of parents or of lords. How often peasant girls took lovers is shown by the frequently recorded fines for birth of bastards; church-court records tell of couples seen lying, in unambiguous postures, under hedges. On those manors where custom prescribed that a female serf's bastard child should not follow her condition but be free, such births might occasionally have represented deliberate choice of a route to freedom.

Customs and civil laws regulating conduct on mainly economic principles had long been experiencing the rivalry of the differently orientated canon law, which, in contrast, neither varied from realm to realm nor was tailored to rank, but arrogated to itself a universality based upon divine sanction. Already in the pre-Conquest period influence from this system had begun to introduce new rigour to English legislation about marriage and sexual morality: a process now accelerated and intensified by the late eleventh-century Gregorian Reforms. All enforcement of marriage laws and of morals was in time to be taken over by the church courts; and, by dint of thus presiding over public behaviour, canon law eventually succeeded in modifying private expectations. During the twelfth century its relationships with civil custom were still being worked out.

The canon law of marriage rested on a particular concept of woman's basic nature. Despite Christian protestations that all human souls were equal, anti-feminist attitudes inherited from Graeco-Roman society had early come to dominate the Church. Excluded from every priestly office, women found themselves enjoined to public silence. These restrictions the churchmen justified by reference to the Bible, especially as interpreted by the Fathers of the Church. *Genesis* was held to show Eve, and all her daughters with her, as essentially inferior to Adam, having been created after him, from one of his ribs, and explicitly as a 'help' to him, not as an equal partner. It depicted her as readier than Adam to succumb to temptation and therefore, unless strictly disciplined, a moral danger to him; as instigator of the Fall, she had justly (it was claimed) been set under Adam's authority. Such a view of women, as inferior to men in morals and in intellect, underlay the Pauline pronouncements on marriage:

> Wives, submit yourselves unto your own husbands, as unto the Lord. For the husband is the head of the wife, even as Christ is the head of the church . . . Husbands, love your wives, even as Christ also loved the church . . . Let every one of you in particular so love his wife even as himself; and the wife, see that she reverence [*timeat*] her husband. (*Ephesians*, v. 22–33; cf. I *Corinthians* vi.)

During the twelfth-century renewal of theology and of canon law such notions – earlier elaborated by the Fathers, in particular Tertullian, Augustine, Ambrose and Jerome – were studied and commented on anew. In degrees of anti-feminist bias the reinterpretations varied marginally, with some venturing to suggest that Mary's part in the Incarnation counterbalanced the harm that Eve had wrought. The Fall none the less continued to dominate theological concepts of woman, and hence of marriage, while the horror of the flesh felt by so many male clerics inspired condemnations of sexuality and consequent restrictions upon the role of women.

Despite such unpromising premisses, twelfth-century canon law did somewhat temper Anglo-Norman marriage customs, and this, by a paradox, partly because of its theological basis. To the pragmatism of feudal custom canon law opposed an ideal, allegorised concept; the Pauline view of marriage as figuring Christ's relationship with His Church had generated an ideal of the spiritual love – to be as little as possible contaminated by fleshly passions – that ought to subsist between spouses. Hence the injunctions laid upon Aubrey de Vere to 'love his wife as his own self'. Canon lawyers came to demand as a precondition for a valid marriage full and free consent from both parties. Any contract made under duress or between children below years of discretion was void, whilst any freely made between competent parties was binding, even though clandestine and even though opposed by parent, guardian or overlord (the Church's authority did not, however, extend over related questions of property and inheritance). Some flexibility remained, so that child marriages, for instance, might still be countenanced if necessary 'for peace'. Safeguards for self-determination in any case remained imperfect: the age of valid consent was set for girls at twelve, and at this time when parents might freely thrash their adolescent children (as did the mother of the future St Christina) interpretations of 'duress' were not always generous to the victim. That apart, awareness of economic dependency must have dissuaded many a girl from questioning parental plans. In the long run, nevertheless, canonical insistence on freely given mutual consent did modify secular views of marriage.

For all that, canon law was not a liberalising force. Theology alleged women to be essentially inferior to men and in need of constant male tutelage (Gratian saw servitude as their proper condition). The tighter the grip of canon law grew on secular affairs, the further women's already limited rights were eroded, always under pretext of affording their weakness a necessary protection. Without her husband's consent no married woman could now – by contrast with pre-Conquest custom – make a valid will; in practice a husband would often allow his dying wife to make bequests of her personal chattels and even of such lands as might fall to her portion, but that in no way mitigated the code's essential harshness. A woman's own consent was needed before her husband could alienate matrimonial property acquired through her right, an act which might reduce provision for her widowhood; but how 'free' such consent sometimes was may be doubted (in other contexts the law regularly assumed a wife to be subject to 'duress').

Although the law-codes, canon and civil, combine to reveal not only the practical constraints within which women (and men) had to live their lives but also something of the social climate shaping expectations, what form average expectations took remains uncertain. Individual reactions varied: whereas the future St Christina, rather than accept the decent enough young man her parents proposed, fled to a hermitage, the young countess of Oxford strove to validate her union with the elderly, callous Aubrey de Vere. In all ranks of life, it may be surmised, many a girl saw her arranged marriage not as an exercise in parental tyranny, but as a means of social promotion, enabling her to become at very least mistress of her own household and probably in time a matriarch. Even child-betrothal might, for all the church's strictures against it, have had its good side, for children raised in the same nursery could have learnt mutual tolerance, comradeship even. An arranged marriage, besides, offers less scope for disappointment than one of inclination.

That remains surmise, for lack of private papers prevents access to personal feelings. As for literary treatments of love and marriage, fictional ones are reserved for the following chapter;[1] those not avowedly fictional need assessment by special criteria. The author of *Holy Maidenhood*, when depicting a wife as her husband's victim, tormented so cruelly she would rather be dead, was both propagandising for the virgin life and reworking commonplaces going back to antiquity. Even chronicles and biographies are not above suspicion, being almost all compiled by monks and clerics frankly intent on drawing from their materials the maximum of edification. When Orderic Vitalis pictures the wives whom the Conqueror's barons had left in Normandy as 'burning with lust' and summoning their husbands to return forthwith, else they would find themselves other mates, can his account be taken at face-value? Men who complied, he says, lost their chances of rich pickings in the newly conquered lands; so was he (himself a cloister-monk since boyhood) seizing a chance to animadvert on the temporal disadvantages of lust rather than recording a real episode? With the private behaviour, let alone sentiments, of their subjects inaccessible to them, chroniclers and biographers necessarily eked their material out with conventional motifs; and marriage had become tangled with theological idealisations. Bishop Turgot's *Life of St Margaret of Scotland* depicts the saint's husband, the warlike King Malcolm, as fondling and kissing for love of her the devotional books which he himself could not read. The monk Eadmer of Canterbury represents as a love-match the political marriage between Henry I and one of St Margaret's daughters, Edith, later known as Matilda: although Henry had, Eadmer says, 'fallen in love' with the Scottish princess, rumours of her having taken the veil 'set tongues wagging and held back the two from embracing one another as they desired'. Monastic chroniclers seemingly found a calculated contracting of marriage for worldly advantage even less admissible than fleshly lusts.

Yet, conventionalised and idealised though twelfth-century literature may have been, its currency was fact. Marie de France's *Lays* antedate the *Register of Widows and Heiresses*. Wives given in marriage as tokens of land-transfer and maidens knowing themselves destined for a like fate heard not only preachers commending a spiritual love like Christ's for His Church but also minstrels singing of earthlier loves between women like themselves and men (not quite) like their husbands. Did they listen with envy, or with an ironical twitch of an eyebrow? Illicit affairs were not unknown. Although royalty is never typical, its well-publicised adventures illustrate some possible freedoms. Henry I, for instance, acknowledged over a score of bastards, by a dozen or so mistresses; the offspring grew up to enjoy appropriate ranks and make advantageous marriages. Nor were the mothers social outcasts. One, another Edith, from a pre-Conquest line of Cumbrian magnates, married into the d'Oilly family of Oxford; another, a Welsh princess, married the Norman grandfather of Gerald of Wales; yet another, a Beaumont, married Gilbert de Clare, first earl of Pembroke. Similar freedoms appear also among people of modest to middling condition, such as

---

1 [[Elizabeth Williams, 'After 1066: The Literary Image', in Christine Fell, Cecily Clark and Elizabeth Williams, *Women in Anglo-Saxon England and the Impact of 1066* (London, 1984), 172–93.]]

the Londoners shown in a late thirteenth-century breach-of-promise case as frequent-ing, sometimes in couples, a public bath-house with beds, near the Tower.

One small, anomalous group of early twelfth-century women consisted of priests' 'wives'. Clerical marriage, often combined with heredity of benefice, had long been current throughout Western Europe; and so in the early twelfth century it partly remained. Records datable soon after 1100 show priests and their wives admitted jointly to confraternity with Thorney Abbey – a house famed for its austere morals. The hermit Wulfric of Haselbury numbered among his closest friends the married priest Brihtric, whose son succeeded to his benefice. A better-known inheritor of clerical office was the annalist Henry, nowadays surnamed 'of Huntingdon' from the archdea-conry which he held for some forty-five years, having in about 1110 succeeded his father Nicholas in this and in a Lincoln canonry; Henry in his turn fathered a son, Adam. Even the ascetic Cistercian abbot Ailred of Rievaulx was descended from a line of hereditary priests of Hexham. This very paragraph, having on the surface little to do with 'women', illustrates their near invisibility in many records; for instance, Henry of Huntingdon's family history implies, but never names, at least two respectable 'wives' of archdeacons (one of whom may have been the unnamed 'archdeacon's wife' ad-mitted to confraternity with Thorney Abbey in the 1120s).

Such women were, however, becoming less secure. The Gregorian Reforms streng-thened demands for clerical celibacy; council after council commanded clergy living in concubinage to repudiate their women forthwith or else surrender their benefices. Commentator after commentator noted, and usually deplored, widespread indifference to these exhortations. Such partnerships, perhaps contracted with less of an eye than most to worldly advantage, may have been closer than most. Rural priests like Brihtric lived much like the peasants they served and had at least as great a need of a second pair of hands about the small-holding. Obeying the directives would, besides, have left many women and children destitute. No woman's comments on the subject survive. Henry of Huntingdon's do: doubly involved, as family man and as archdeacon charged with enforcing church discipline, he took a line opposite to those of the monastic chroniclers. Prohibiting marriage would, he asserted, simply promote vice; and under 1125 he related, almost with glee, that the Papal legate inveighing against clerical marriage had himself been caught with a whore. Prelatical authority in these matters was often undermined by the bishops' own laxity. The first bishop whom Henry served, Robert Bloet of Lincoln, had a son who became dean in his father's diocese. Roger of Salisbury, chief minister of the realm as well as bishop, made little secret of his relationship with Matilda of Ramsbury; one of their sons, another Roger, became royal chancellor, and Matilda's own standing is clear from her being entrusted during the Anarchy with command of one of the Bishop's castles. As for Rannulf Flambard ('the Firebrand'), Bishop of Durham, he had several sons by an aunt of Christina of Markyate's.

Outside religion marriage was the normal state; for women especially a single life outside the cloister was little esteemed. Feudal and familial pressures towards marriage must have been further reinforced by economic ones, because staying even temporarily single required either property (a magnet to fortune-hunters) or else a livelihood, and for that opportunities were limited.

Widows enjoyed greatest freedom. With a marriage-portion of her own, plus a third of her late husband's property, a widowed noblewoman needed only to pay her overlord the requisite fee for self-determination (sometimes backed by a vow of chastity) – not even that after Magna Carta had taken effect. A widow whose husband had held on burgess-tenure might also be well placed: town surveys regularly mention widows holding large properties and assessed for tax at high rates. A merchant's widow might continue the trade on her own account, and even take her husband's place as member of his gild; the ordinances of the London weavers explicitly laid down that, provided she did not marry out of the craft, a member's widow could continue to work one of her husband's looms. As already noted, a peasant woman likewise had her 'free bench'.

Few girls – except perhaps those born to landless squatters – can in the long run have fallen outside the twin net of marriage / nunnery. For villein girls, however, the need to delay marriage until a holding became available sometimes impelled those whose families could not meanwhile support them to seek a living elsewhere. It was for women in this position that jobs were most plentiful. As manorial labour-services were more and more often commuted for money-rents, so demand grew, especially at harvest-times, for hired field-workers of both sexes (often footloose people who got a name for petty crime). A thirteenth-century treatise on farm-management points out that a woman can be engaged to look after poultry and such 'for less money than a man would ask'. Skill and a sense of responsibility could take a woman to be head dairy-maid: just as in the Old English text *Rectitudines* the cheesemaker is the only female specialist on the farm, so medieval treatises assume that the dairy, and the dairy only, will be overseen by a woman. Manorial records note licences given to villein girls to leave their villages to seek work. Among these must have been many of the servants that all households of any pretension, in town and country alike, employed. Especially important were nurses and nursemaids, among whose duties the encyclopaedist Bartholomew the Englishman includes that of thoroughly chewing the young child's food. At higher points on the social scale, living as underling in a superior's household must have been the main resort for an ill-provided woman. A girl of gentle birth might become a noblewoman's lady-in-waiting: in the mid-twelfth century the widowed Alice de Clermont, a tenant-in-chief, had in her train an under-tenant's daughter, Mabel of Coton, who witnessed some of her mistress's charters and was admitted with her to confraternity with Thorney Abbey. A more colourful figure is the matron – perhaps a promoted ex-wetnurse – attendant upon one of Henry I's mistresses, depicted by Gerald of Wales as rounding in pithy English on the priest whose intercessions had failed to bring about her lady's (illegitimate) pregnancy.

From the twelfth century onwards developing urban life offered women, married or single, more varied opportunities. Just what occupations they could follow is a tricky question. Occupational surnames must, for both sexes, be treated with reserve, because by 1200 (and for some families earlier) a father's surname might be (but was not invariably) transferred to children of either sex. For women the question is complicated by a tendency (but at this date little more) for them to be known under their husbands' surnames. Names plainly transferred to women from men, whether fathers or husbands, include those like *Edith the Chaplain*, *Margaret Bullman*, *Emma Shipman*, and so on. As time passes less and less weight can be placed on surnames: thus a London tax-roll of 1292 lists a *Leticia la aylere*, literally, 'the garlic-dealer', but parallel records not only show her as widow of Luke Garlicmonger but also reveal that Luke in fact dealt in cured fish. To a limited extent specifically feminine terms – seldom, it seems, turned into family-names – can be informative. True, by the Middle English period, and in Northern dialects especially, some of the old feminines in -*stere* had, as noted in an earlier chapter,[2] come to be applied to both sexes, and certain of them,

---

[2] [[Christine Fell, 'Daily Life', in Fell, Clark and Williams, *Women in Anglo-Saxon England*, 39–55, at 41, 49.]]

including *baxter* ('baker'), *brewster* and *maltster*, *dexter* and *litster* ('dyer'), and *webster*, were now mainly applied to men; and many of these do soon figure as family-names. Some of these forms did, however, keep mainly feminine connotations, among them *spinster* and the analogous *silkthrowster*, together with rarer forms like *quernster* ('one who uses a hand-mill'), *ropester*, *soapster*, *hopster* ('dancer') and *songster*. When suffixed to a woman's first name these probably did indicate her own trade, because in England there is little evidence for any conventional feminising of family-names. Less ambiguous are the compounds in *-wife / -woman* (far fewer than those in *-man*), such as *candlewife*, *featherwife*, *fishwife*, *flaxwife*, *silkwife / -woman*, *bower-woman* ('housemaid'), *chapwoman* ('trader'), *cheesewoman*, and the like. The best indications of all, mostly, for our purposes, very late, come from terms added after family-names, as with *Matilda Baker*, *girdlester* (1377), and those showing spouses as following different trades, as with *John Baron, tailor, and his wife Anneys, embroidress* (1425).

Many townswomen lived, often humbly, by their own hands, like the washerwomen noted in the Domesday description of Bury St Edmunds and the unnamed early twelfth-century one renting a property near Winchester's city ditch. A mid-century schedule of the royal household shows the washerwoman as the only female office-holder (hers is the only pay unspecified); in King John's time this functionary was called Florence. In many towns, though not in London, women so dominated the brewing trade – the one in which Margery Kempe made a commercial venture – that local ordinances regulating it were drafted, quite exceptionally, in the feminine; for offences against the assize of ale women were frequently brought to court. Urban life enhanced opportunities for saleswomanship (in London the retailing of bread, for instance, was mainly done by women known as breadmongsters or regratresses) and for trades, in catering as well as in cloth-working and needlecraft, that needed skill rather than strength. Spinning was, in town and country alike, so specifically and universally women's work that medieval knockabout farce allotted the distaff a role like that more recently given to the rolling-pin. The fifteenth century saw the London silk-trade wholly in women's dextrous hands. The currency of terms such as *hopster* and *songster* implies that some women worked as entertainers – dancers, acrobats, singers, and perhaps instrumentalists as well; a woman minstrel is recorded in Stratford-upon-Avon, and about 1200 a *saltatrix* or acrobatic dancer called Maud Makejoy performed several times before the royal court. Sometimes such performers are depicted in manuscript marginalia; but these vignettes may represent jest, fantasy or allegory rather than realistic record. As for prostitution, although presumably an ever-present possibility, in the ports and the greater market-towns especially, it barely seems to be mentioned in surviving records dating from before the fourteenth century. Casual references include that to the Papal legate of 1125 caught with a whore; the 'gorgeous girls' who earlier, 'with their back hair let down', entertained Bishop Rannulf Flambard and his monks must have belonged in a like category. A woman witness in a church-court case was deemed unreliable because 'a witch, a thief and a whore'. Whether or not the thirteenth-century girls who accompanied men to London bath-houses were necessarily prostitutes is unclear. At all events, bath-houses got a bad name, and by the later Middle Ages the municipality was frankly regulating the river-traffic to and from 'The Stews' in Southwark.

Some wives, as we have seen, followed trades distinct from those of their husbands. Despite legal restrictions attendant on her 'protected' status, a married woman could trade independently; often, it seems, this status inconvenienced husband more than wife, to judge by the bye-laws which all-male corporations often drew up to exempt men from sharing in debts or penalties that their wives might incur. Some merchant-gilds admitted women – mainly widows, but on occasion daughters inheriting their fathers' businesses – as members in their own right. In some crafts, and notably in the London silk-trade, women functioned *de facto* as 'masters', taking on girl apprentices; the indentures, although for form's sake joining in the husband's name, show the wife's skill as that to be taught. By the later Middle Ages women figured among the entrepreneurs of international trade.

For women disinclined for trade or service virtually the sole alternative to marriage was the cloister. Scope there was limited in comparison with men's. Women's sanctity, it has been observed, was everywhere less readily acknowledged than men's; for whatsoever reason religious houses for women attracted less generous patronage than did those for men. Despite the high esteem for female virginity practical provision was inadequate for the numbers of those anxious to preserve it. The monastic Rules were drafted specifically for men, not just in the grammatical sense but also in assuming male styles of dress, male dietetic needs and male capacities for heavy work. By the early twelfth century this lack of provision for women's religious vocations was acutely felt. The old Benedictine nunneries were not only smaller and fewer than the men's houses (amounting to about a dozen, beside the forty or more of the latter) but were confined to southern England, mainly to Wessex, and were aristocratic in their recruitment; in 1066 there was not one nunnery north of the Trent. So when at this time all of Europe was swept by a spiritual fervour in which women, Englishwomen included, fully shared, existing nunneries could not provide for all the new vocations. There were fundamental reasons why women's religious vocations were more likely than men's to be frustrated. Men's yearnings for a more austere religious life were in the early twelfth century being met by several new Orders, and by the Cistercian Order in particular; but because of their proud austerity these Orders for almost a century set their faces against admitting women (so-called 'Cistercian nunneries' of this period were unofficial, unrecognised by the Order). A main stumbling-block was the ban on female ordination, and even on women's playing the most subsidiary liturgical role: whereas men could form a self-sufficient community, women could never do so, because they were compelled by this ban to rely for all the sacraments, confession included, on male chaplains. Every nunnery, therefore, made demands on the same Order's male religious, who feared and often openly repudiated possible moral dangers to themselves.

Nevertheless, the most remarkable of all attempts to provide for women's vocations came from a man: St Gilbert of Sempringham, founder of the only purely English religious order in all history. Having set up a school for children of both sexes, he became distressed to observe among young women who had been his pupils vocations for which they could find no outlet. So he established beside his church at Sempringham a cloister where these women could live as nuns, with lay-sisters to carry out the mundane chores. To do the heavy work on the associated lands lay-brothers were recruited: so too were learned canons to serve as chaplains. In Lincolnshire and Yorkshire there were soon nine mixed houses, in which perilous contacts between the sexes were minimised by systems of walls and of hatches through which food, and also clothes for washing and mending, could be passed (the lay-sisters did everybody's chores, not only those of the choir-nuns).

Other initiatives came from women themselves, among them the already noted Christina of Markyate, born in the late 1090s into a prosperous family of burgesses at Huntingdon. Although some episodes in her extant *Life* – the prophetic dove's visit to the mother before Christina's birth, the child's precocious piety and vow of chastity, her flight from a forced marriage – smack of hagiographical commonplace, her achievement was real enough. Around her hermitage at Markyate there grew up a community of women which by 1145 had been recognised as a priory dependent on St Albans Abbey; it survived until the Dissolution. The magnificent manuscript known as the St Albans Psalter (now at Hildesheim) is believed to have been compiled for Christina before 1123. As told in the *Life*, her personal story turns on conflict between sexuality and asceticism. The chastity she had vowed was threatened first by lewd advances from Rannulf Flambard, who before becoming a bishop had fathered a family on one of her aunts, and then by the lawful ones of the husband chosen by her parents. For a time she found peace as a disciple of the fatherly hermit Roger; but after his death she became passionately involved with a priest appointed as her guardian. When prioress of Markyate, she formed a deep friendship with Abbot Geoffrey of St Albans, for whom on occasion she made warm underwear.

Many women had flocked to join Christina in what had originally been a hermitage at Markyate. Others preferred, as she herself had done at first, a more truly solitary life, among them some great ladies: Loretta, the widowed Countess of Leicester, lived for nearly fifty years as a recluse just outside Canterbury; her sister Annora also retired to a hermitage at Iffley. Another recluse was a sister of the Cistercian Abbot Ailred of Rievaulx, who wrote for her a Latin handbook. An even more famous manual of the kind, based partly upon Ailred's, was the English one known as *Ancrene Wisse* dating from about 1230 and now believed to have been compiled by an Austin canon of Wigmore for a neighbouring cell of anchoresses; possibly, but not certainly, the writer's own sisters. Be that as it may, the tone of this manual, as also of Ailred's, is that of an authoritative instructor, not of a brother or an equal.

Not every nun was fired by devotion. Some resorted to the cloister for lack of an earthly bridegroom, some because widowed, some (especially in the aftermath of the Conquest) to seek refuge from a war-torn countryside. The lax tone of some twelfth-century houses, women's and men's alike, can be inferred from repeated conciliar fulminations against rich attire and forbidden furs and, for women, against jewellery and elaborate coiffures. Some were as children placed in nunneries by their families. For, despite the new canonical prohibitions of committing to religion any child, boy or girl, too young to give an informed consent, during the twelfth century the old practice of oblation partly continued – as well it might in an age countenancing child-marriage. A signal instance of the problems that could arise occurred during the later twelfth century in the Gilbertine double house at Watton in Yorkshire. A girl's 'impudent' eye caught that of a brother. When their clandestine affair and her consequent pregnancy could no longer be concealed, the other nuns thrashed the girl and cast her, fettered, into a cell. The young man fled, but was decoyed and captured by his former brethren, then delivered to the nuns, who forced the girl to mutilate him with her own hands (in itself castration was then a conventional enough punishment for many offences). The guilty nun, now fully contrite, was reconciled with her sisters through a miracle by which angel-midwives spirited away her newborn child, struck off her fetters and restored her to virginity. Such a story, related with great rhetorical display by Ailred of Rievaulx, helps to explain the dread so many monks felt of any association with nuns.

In everyday social life women freely shared. The *Life of St Christina*, for instance, shows the future saint as often (albeit unwillingly) participating, together with her mother, in public as well as private feasts and drinking-parties; one episode depicts the maiden as ceremonially serving drink in the style of fictional heroines in Old English literature. Court records, as has been noted, reveal much freedom of morals as well as of manners, and a limited concern with premarital chastity.

In official life, by contrast, women figured little. Those in control of property had the same powers as men of making grants by charter, and had their personal seals. But, because a wife's property passed wholly into her husband's care, virtually the only women land-holders or taxpayers were widows, and records dealing with such matters usually show them as amounting to under 10 per cent of the total. A married woman could not act independently to sell, give away or bequeath her 'own' property. Although women could, and did, witness charters, their surviving attestations are rare, except for those of male grantors' wives and, less often, those of the attendants of female grantors. Even women of independent standing played little overt part in public affairs: female tenants-in-chief did not figure at royal councils, nor abbesses at ecclesiastical ones (by this time all nuns were subject to rules of enclosure far stricter than were ever imposed upon monks); 'sisters' of merchant- or craft-gilds did not become officials, still less have any voice in local government. It went without saying that no woman was eligible to serve as knight of the shire, or on a criminal or civil jury. In the twelfth century no woman could appear in a criminal court as plaintiff, let alone witness, except concerning her husband's murder or her own rape. In order to bring a charge of rape the victim had to raise an immediate hue and cry, exhibiting at once to a law-officer torn garments and bodily injuries; even so, such charges were commonly dismissed. Confraternity-lists – in theory admitting all on equal terms – named women more seldom than men, often specifying them simply in relation to male heads of family-groups. On the other hand, an English ecclesiastical court could and sometimes did, somewhat uncanonically, convoke a jury of seven 'honest matrons' to examine a man accused of impotence.

Women's marginal position in society was reflected and reinforced by limited access to schooling. Medieval education ranged among men from total illiteracy to subtle multilingual and philosophical accomplishment. Among women too accomplishment varied but normally, it seems, remained lower than that of corresponding men: thus, a canonisation-process of about 1300, in which witnesses used the most 'learned' language they knew, shows some male clerics testifying in Latin but not one woman and, among laypeople of each social rank, more men than women competent in French.

Debarred as they were from the developing universities, which catered mainly for aspiring clergy, medieval women can have had small chance of reaching the highest levels of literacy. For nuns, the strict enclosure now imposed upon them must have hindered access to learning; so too would the reluctance of the male religious, the chief scholars of the age, to meddle further than the liturgy demanded with their sisters' affairs. Evidence as to nuns' attainments is hard to come by, and harder to assess. A 'mortuary-roll' of 1122–3 circulated among Norman and English religious houses contains several sections representing English nunneries, with Wilton offering verses and Shaftesbury some fairly ornate lettering but other houses making only plain and conventional Latin entries. What this means is uncertain: by no means all men's houses displayed resplendent literacy or calligraphy and, besides, nunneries might sometimes have entrusted such duties to their chaplains (of whom the Wilton entry names several). As for books, nunneries, because in general poorer than the men's houses, might *a priori* be assumed to have had less lavish libraries. To attach great weight to comparison between the books surviving from their libraries and those from the men's might be unwise, in so far as conditions of survival might have differed. For what it is worth, such comparison strengthens impressions of women's lesser learning, for the nuns' books are not only fewer but consist mainly of psalters, together with a little hagiography in one or other vernacular. A few Latin texts survive, mainly of the twelfth century; and one Barking liturgical manual of about 1400 is almost wholly in Latin, with French translations given of one or two sections only. Often, however, and increasingly in the later Middle Ages, documents of whatever kind addressed to nuns were couched in one or other vernacular. The author of *Ancrene Wisse* assumed the anchoresses for whom he was writing, and whom he evidently knew well, to read regularly in French as well as in English, but when quoting in Latin he always offered an immediate translation. These women could write, but had to get their confessor's permission before doing so. Ailred of Rievaulx did use Latin – admittedly simpler in style than that of his other works – for the manual he wrote for his anchoress sister, but then she, like he, was a child of a clerical family. As to any literary activity of nuns themselves, little evidence survives (attempts have been made, unconvincingly some may think, to identify Marie de France with an abbess of Shaftesbury). One at least had enough confidence to embark on verse-hagiography in French, together with enough Latin to use works in that language as her sources: the late twelfth-century Clemence of Barking, author of a *Life of St Catherine* and probably also of an anonymous *Life of the Confessor*. Perhaps Barking, with its ancient tradition of learning, may have been better able than some houses to maintain literacy and intellectual activity.

As to laywomen's accomplishments, evidence is even less clear. Some cynics of the time asserted that teaching a girl to write merely enabled her to carry on clandestine correspondence. Against that view would have militated the convenience for merchants and others of having wives who could keep records and accounts. More women, it may be surmised, would have been able to read than could write: for one thing, reading was an aid to religious practice and, for another, until paper became a common commodity, writing-materials cannot have been ever-present. Queens and noblewomen often figure as patrons of literature but, given the custom of oral performance, this need not imply that they themselves could read fluently (at this date, after all, literacy was far from universal among men of such ranks). On the other hand, girls of good birth sent to be educated in nunneries, as many were, would presumably have had the chance to learn reading and perhaps writing as well as morals (then esteemed the most essential element in feminine education), deportment and fine needlework. The warnings given in *Ancrene Wisse* as well as in Ailred's handbook against an anchoress turning school-mistress imply that some did take pupils; the leave nevertheless given in the former for one of the handmaids to teach any girl 'who ought not to have to study among boys or men' further implies that some parish schools were, as St Gilbert's had been, open to both sexes. The late thirteenth-century manual compiled by Walter of Bibbesworth to help Lady Dionyse de Munchensy to teach her children French (rather broad 'Anglo-Norman', in fact) implies not only that she could read in two languages, but also that she would do the teaching herself. In the wider sense of education – moral, cultural and social – even illiterate women, nurses and maids as well as mothers, would have been responsible for training young children of both sexes. The expression 'mother-tongue' is no empty one, because mothers and their women helpers have always been instrumental in transmitting language from one generation to the next; the encyclopaedist Bartholomew explicitly includes among the nurse's duties that of teaching her charge to speak. The maintenance of the English language in the face of post-Conquest fashions for French probably depended on such women's unrecorded chatter to the children, including those of Anglo-Norman nobles, in their care.

Despite frequent pregnancies, few women can have had large families of children at home: infant mortality was high, in towns especially, and the survivors were early dispersed by marriage or else, according to rank, by apprenticeship or by enlistment as a handmaid or a squire. How large an ordinary medieval household might be is a vexed question. All but the humblest employed servants of both sexes; merchants and crafts-men had living-in apprentices. Most dwellings must have teemed with life; but, for the better-off, congestion would in summer have been eased by the omnipresence, even in towns, of gardens. Among humble folk, the chaotic interpenetration of farm and family is pictured in *Holy Maidenhood* (in one of its few passages so far untraced to any source): returning home, the woman finds her baby screaming, the cat gnawing the bacon and the dog worrying a hide, her loaf scorched, the calf suckling its mother, the cooking-pot boiling over – and her husband in a fury.

For everyone, of whatever rank or sex, who lived before the rise of modern medicine, illness and early death were ever-present spectres. Study of medieval cem-eteries has shown women as having had markedly shorter life-expectancies than men. This is, of course, an average, based on burials of humble folk, because the better-off sometimes, as the *Register of Widows* shows, attained ages of 'seventy and upwards'; but it implies widespread poor health. Medieval women's experience of medical care probably differed from men's. At first sight they might be thought lucky in being assured, for childbirth and related matters, of help from their own sex. About the ubiquitous midwives too little is now known. We may suspect a female freemasonry with private, unwritten traditions (the line between midwife and white witch seems uncertain), but suspecting is not enough. At all events, modern scholars who trace the history of contraception in Western Europe through twelfth-century Latin translations from the Arabic may be losing sight of some realities of village life (incidentally, surviving treatises, such as they are, often include recipes for male anaphrodisiacs). Whatever cosy complicities the midwife system may have allowed between practi-tioner and client, it had shortcomings. One late medieval author of a general medical treatise remarked that, because childbirth was exclusively women's province, he need not dwell upon its management; the brief advice he then gave to midwives contrasted with his lengthy disquisitions upon specifically male afflictions. Other treatises ignored obstetrics and gynaecology altogether. The flaw was that such medical training as then existed was, like all higher education, virtually barred to women, who were thus thrown back upon whatever private traditions they may have had. For other reasons, too, medical advances might have benefited female sufferers less than male ones: for, gynaecological problems apart, some women might have been shy of exhibit-ing their sick bodies to male practitioners. In the early period especially, when a good few physicians were clerks or monks, the reluctance might have been mutual. Public attitudes may be guessed from the coarse crack made in 1114 by Bishops Roger of Salisbury and Robert Bloet (worldly family-men both, not neurotic celibates), when the king proposed for the See of Canterbury Abbot Faritius of Abingdon, a noted physician who had attended the queen, Edith-Matilda of Scotland, in her first confine-ment: such preferment, they said, would be unseemly for a man who had examined a woman's urine.

A sidelight on female health comes from the records kept at supposedly curative shrines. When listing schools of therapeutic thought, the late medieval author just quoted referred to 'women and fools, who entrust merely to the saints sufferers from ailments of all kinds'. Whether or not women sought professional advice as often as they should have done, they did not, it seems, predominate among the clientele of shrines. Indeed, some shrines, notably St Cuthbert's, excluded female pilgrims. Even where all were admitted on equal terms, analysis of miracles officially recorded shows men as benefiting oftener than women. Discrepancies go further: the women reported as miraculously cured seem to have been, on average, of lower rank than the men and to have come from less far afield (a difference that can hardly, as has been suggested, simply reflect men's greater mobility, which illness would have cancelled out). Social attitudes and usages must have varied between the sexes in ways as yet not understood.

Neither the near invisibility of women in the surviving records nor their various socio-legal handicaps must mislead us into picturing them as personally meek and helpless. Perhaps we should discount the literary and iconographic stereotype of the shrewish wife belabouring her husband, sometimes with a distaff; but purportedly factual sources furnish ample instances of self-assertiveness, even of violence. Women and men shared the same world. We have noted the Watton nuns' ferocity towards their frail sister and how Christina of Markyate's mother thrashed the girl in hopes of extorting a consent to the projected marriage. Thirteenth- and fourteenth-century court records show peasant women as often dishonest, and sometimes bold and violent, with the ratio of female criminality to male supposedly similar to that nowadays taken as 'normal'. As well as women aiding and abetting the crimes of husbands or lovers (receiving stolen goods from relatives was the typical female offence), there were others who with their own hands wielded to effect whatever weapons they found. One Bedfordshire woman slit her sleeping husband's throat with a pruning-knife and then stove his skull in with a spade 'so that his brains flowed forth'; he had, she said, been seized with a fit of dangerous madness.

Great ladies played their parts in war. One Norman matron, from the Montfort family, was famed for riding armed – for all the world like a Viking 'warrior-maiden' reincarnated – among the knights. At need women commanded castles. In 1075, during the rebellion against the Conqueror led by the Norman earls of Hereford and of Norfolk, the latter's wife (also the former's sister, her marriage having sealed the alliance) captained Norwich castle and held out until granted safe-conduct to Normandy. When Stephen imprisoned Bishop Roger of Salisbury, Roger's mistress, Matilda of Ramsbury, held his castle at Devizes, surrendering it only to save their son Roger, the king's chancellor, from being hanged before its gates. During a rebellion against King John, the elderly Nicola de la Haye, by her own hereditary right castellan of Lincoln, was effective commander there.

Royal women often displayed generalship, among them the two Mauds, grand-daughters of St Margaret of Scotland and King Malcolm, whom the Anarchy found on opposite sides. One, Stephen's queen, exhibited when her husband was made prisoner 'a manly steadfastness', sending her forces first to ravage London and then success-fully to besiege Winchester. Meanwhile, her cousin and namesake, 'the Empress', daughter of Henry I and of his queen Edith-Matilda, was campaigning against her vigorously. The Empress, despite (perhaps because of) two marriages arranged to further her father's politics – the first, before she was nine, to the German Emperor Henry V; the second, as a widow in her mid-twenties, to Geoffrey of Anjou, some ten years her junior – was wax in no-one's hands. After her father's death her cousin Stephen stole a march and secured for himself the crown which Henry I had intended for her, his only surviving legitimate child. Maud, loyally seconded by her elder (but illegitimate) brother, came to England to claim her rights, and for several years waged war against the usurper; although never herself accepted as queen, she secured the succession for her son, later Henry II. Never is there a hint of her having been self-effacing; rather was it the chroniclers' constant complaint that she was, in contrast with her easy-going cousin Stephen, too high-handed. Perhaps the commentators were measuring her against some stereotype of the 'ideal lady', not against that of the rightful sovereign she was. In Empress Maud the warrior blood of Norman dukes and Scottish kings pulsed no less strongly than in the males of her race.

FURTHER READING

This chapter has been based on central and local administrative records, together with chronicles and biographies. The principal sources are: *Rotuli de Dominabus et Pueris et Puellis*, ed. Round; *Councils and Synods*, ed. Whitelock et alii; *The Laws and Customs of England*, ed. and tr. Hall; *Select Cases from the Ecclesiastical Courts*, ed. Adams and Donahue; *Borough Customs*, ed. Bateson; *The Peterborough Chronicle*, ed. Clark; *The Ecclesiastical History of Orderic Vitalis*, ed. and tr. Chibnall; *Henrici Huntendunensis Historia Anglorum*, ed. Arnold; *Eadmeri Historia Novorum in Anglia*, ed. Rule (also tr. Bosanquet); *Willelmi Malmesbiriensis Monachi de Gestis Pontificum Anglorum Libri Quinque*, ed. Hamilton; *The Historia Novella of William of Malmesbury*, ed. and tr. Potter; *Gesta Stephani*, ed. and tr. Potter and Davis; *The Life of St Margaret of Scotland*, in *Pinkerton's Lives of the Scottish Saints*, ed. Metcalfe (also tr. Metcalfe); *The Life of Christina of Markyate*, ed. and tr. Talbot; *Aelred de Rievaulx: la vie de recluse*, ed. and tr. Dumont; *Ancrene Wisse*, ed. Tolkien (also tr. Salu); *Hali Meiðhad*, ed. Millett.

Secondary sources extensively used include: *Complete Peerage*, ed. C[okayne] et alii; *La femme dans les civilisations des xe–xiiie siècles*; *La femme* (Recueils Jean Bodin 12); *Il matrimonio nella società altomedievale*; *Medieval Women*, ed. Baker; *Women in Medieval Society*, ed. Stuard; Holt, *Magna Carta*; Helmholz, *Marriage Litigation*; Sheehan, *The Will in Medieval England*; Williams, *Medieval London*; Thrupp, *The Merchant Class of Medieval London*; Gross, *The Gild Merchant*; Hallam, *Rural England 1066–1348*; Homans, *English Villagers of the Thirteenth Century*; Raftis, *Warboys* and *Tenure and Mobility*; Graham, *St Gilbert of Sempringham*; Legge, *Anglo-Norman in the Cloisters*; Labarge, *A Baronial Household of the Thirteenth Century*; Rowland, *Medieval Woman's Guide to Health*.

ESSAYS IN ONOMASTICS

PRINCIPLES AND METHODOLOGY

6

Clark's First Three Laws of Applied Anthroponymics*

From the outset my study of Personal Names – both baptismal names and by-names – has been 'Applied', that is, expressly directed at throwing light on social and cultural patterns: originally those of Anglo-Norman England; more recently those of the Dane-law too.[1]

My techniques of analysis have evolved in the course of the various projects under-taken. They are mainly comparative, with a range of samples representing specific localities or dates being used to establish geographical or chronological patterns of agreement or contrast. For this, working principles are needed. Mine I should like to put forward as Clark's First, Second, and Third Laws of Applied Anthroponymics. Although to me these 'Laws' seem wholly consonant with the findings from my studies so far, I shall scarcely be surprised if they are called into question or even comprehens-ively refuted.

The First Law is fundamental:

In any homogeneous community, naming-behaviour will remain constant, except when disturbed by outside influence.

That, I recognise, is a double tautology, since a 'homogeneous' community might be defined, either as one where naming-behaviour is both uniform and constant, or else as one free of outside influences. This Law's usefulness lies in alerting us to the likelihood that, if in some way a sample fails to agree with what might have been taken as the majority of analogous cases, then we must investigate the disagreement. In this context 'agreement' refers only to naming-*behaviour* in the widest sense, not to the details of name-*vocabulary*. Without doubt the bearings of the finer variations in name-choice will in time be made clear;[2] but at the moment I am concerned with no more than choices between the broadest categories. And the 'agreement' itself is envisaged in the broadest terms: in order to discount both the investigator's inaccuracies and the random elements present in all surviving records, variations of less than 5% are disregarded. The terms are thus of the crudest, but for that very reason, I hope, safe.

That First Law, tautologous as it is, may perhaps be allowed to pass. For practical application, however, one needs its more controversial riders. With the Second Law

I have to acknowledge the help towards presenting this paper and preparing it for publication given by a British Academy Research Grant awarded in Spring 1979.

* A paper given at the eleventh conference of the Council for Name Studies at Nottingham, 6 April 1979.

[1] For details, see *Nomina*, I (1977), 4–5, 9–10, and *ibid.*, II (1978), 4.

[2] Cf., for instance, the paper delivered by John Insley at the same Conference ('Regional Variation in Scandinavian Personal Nomenclature in England', *Nomina*, III (1979), 52–60).

tautology gives way to a principle at once more original and by the same token more questionable:

In any community previously characterised by uniform naming-behaviour, reactions to a uniform outside influence will likewise be uniform.

That is, if a single foreign name-influence produces differential reactions, then we must ask whether it was in the influence itself or in the host communities that the springs of discrepancy arose.

As a specimen of a discrepant sample we may take the well-known list of citizens of (King's) Lynn entered in the Pipe Roll for 1166.[3] Analysis shows here a percentage of surviving pre-Conquest names unexpectedly high for the date – unexpectedly high, not only in comparison with cosmopolitan cities like Winchester and Canterbury, but also with places like Newark, and, most tellingly, even with other records from Norfolk.[4] Before concluding that each district of twelfth-century England had its own independent rate of development, we may do well to see whether any other explanation fits this discrepancy. Now, to suggest that Lynn might have been less acquainted than the rest of Norfolk with the new continental name-fashions would hardly square with what we know of lively ports. So, if the outside influences could hardly have differed from those operating in other comparable English boroughs, perhaps we should ask whether the cause of the discrepancy lay either in the community at Lynn, or else in the particular sample. To suggest that the burgesses of Lynn were somehow, as a body, more attached than others to the old ways is hardly plausible, for at this time the town was little more than three generations old and so unlikely to have been a repository of unbroken traditions. What then of the sample? Certainly low social class would at this date explain old-fashioned names; but such an explanation would clash with the likelihood that burgesses taken cognisance of in Pipe Rolls must have been among the more prominent and prosperous of their kind. Perhaps the discrepancy in naming-patterns observable between these burgesses and other samples of the post-Conquest population of Norfolk may be due to a basic difference: a higher average age for the Lynn group. For, whereas most of our name-sources, such as rent-rolls, manorial extents and Feet of Fines, offer cross-sections of the male population ranging from those only just of age

---

3 *The Great Roll of the Pipe for 12 Henry II, A.D. 1165–1166*, Pipe Roll Society IX (London, 1888), 21–9.

4 Materials used for comparison include: O. von Feilitzen, 'The Personal Names and Bynames of the Winton Domesday', in M. Biddle (ed.) *et alii*, *Winchester in the Early Middle Ages: an Edition and Discussion of the Winton Domesday*, Winchester Studies I (Oxford, 1976), pp. 145–91; W. Urry, *Canterbury under the Angevin Kings* (London, 1967); M.W. Barley *et alii* (eds), *Documents relating to the Manor and Soke of Newark-on-Trent*, Thoroton Society Record Series XVI (Nottingham, 1956), pp. 1–15, and the discussion by Kenneth Cameron on pp. xi–xv; H.W. Saunders (ed. and tr.), *The First Register of Norwich Cathedral Priory*, Norfolk Record Society XI (1939); B. Dodwell (ed.), *The Charters of Norwich Cathedral Priory*, pt 1, Pipe Roll Society n.s. XL (London, 1974); J.R. West (ed.), *St Benet of Holme 1020–1210*, 2 vols, Norfolk Record Society II and III (1932); B. Dodwell (ed.), *Feet of Fines for the County of Norfolk for 10 Richard I, 1198–1199, and for 1–4 John, 1199–1202, &c.*, Pipe Roll Society n.s. XXVII (London, 1952); *eadem* (ed.), *Feet of Fines for the County of Norfolk for the Reign of King John, 1201–1215; for the County of Suffolk for the Reign of King John, 1199–1214, &c.*, Pipe Roll Society n.s. XXXII (London, 1958); also A. Jessopp and M.R. James (eds and trs), *The Life and Miracles of St William of Norwich* (Cambridge, 1896).

for holding land to those in extreme old age, burgesses substantial enough to be listed in a Pipe Roll might well all be men of maturity and weight – City Fathers, men of patriarchal experience and authority.

But some may feel refinements such as this to be altogether misplaced, seeing that the basic premiss of an original uniformity in Old-English naming-behaviour has not yet been proved, nor, *a fortiori*, the rider alleging uniform response to a uniform Norman influence. I can only say that, so far, my surveys of twelfth-century English name-materials have been leading me to the same general conclusion; from being, first, relieved to find the evidence all tending the same way, and, next, gratified, I then came to see how striking the agreements were, especially for a period when communications were poor and when many people of the humbler sort might never in their whole lives have stirred more than a few miles from their birthplace. Perhaps we should bear in mind that communications were better than might seem at first sight: gentry and higher clergy travelled constantly about, and with considerable trains, bringing glimpses and whispers of new fashions to the peasantry; pilgrims set off, and sometimes returned, while others passed through on their way to or from distant shrines; townspeople saw and heard foreign traders of all sorts, and many of them went on trading voyages of their own; peasants often had carrying-services to perform, so that a man from Ramsey, for instance, might be sent to Cambridge, to Bury, or even to Colchester, no doubt returning full of the novelities seen and heard on the way. Thus, townspeople would have been well up-to-date with fashions, and not even the humblest villagers need have been quite unaware of the great world and of its ways of thinking and behaving. Yet direct and indirect contacts of such kinds explain only how knowledge of current fashions might have seeped even into the remotest hamlets: they by no means explain the similar alacrity and enthusiasm shown throughout the country in the adopting of the new name-fashions, whether in Canterbury or in Newark, on the Glastonbury estates or on those of Ramsey or of Bury St Edmunds.[5] Admittedly, the new fashions did spread a thought faster among townspeople than among peasants; but, by the early thirteenth century, forms originally continental seem universally to have been accounting for between 90% and 95% of the names in current use.

Supposing, however, that the effects of an outside influence show widespread variations, rather than just isolated discrepancies, then the Third Law comes into operation, and this is the really questionable one:

In any community originally homogeneous, any variations in the effects of an outside influence on naming-behaviour will be proportional to variations in the strength of that influence.

This 'Law' is especially relevant to the question of the varying strengths of the Scandinavian influence in different areas of the Danelaw.[6] For, if pre-Viking England

---

5 To the materials listed in n. 4 should be added: J.E. Jackson (ed.), *Liber Henrici de Soliaco, &c.*, Roxburghe Club (London, 1882); W.H. Hart and P.A. Lyons (eds), *Cartularium Monasterii de Rameseia*, 3 vols, Rolls Series (London, 1884–1893), esp. III, 218–315; R.H.C. Davis (ed.), *The Kalendar of Abbot Samson of Bury St Edmunds*, Camden Third Series LXXXIV (London, 1954).

6 Here I must acknowledge my great debt to Mrs Dorothy Owen, Keeper of the Archives to Cambridge University, who, by inviting me to contribute a chapter to the edition which she is preparing for the British Academy of the early records of King's Lynn, drew my attention to the unsettled questions about Scandinavian settlement in East Anglia and encouraged me to explore

had been basically homogeneous in its name-choices (in respect, that is, of the basic categories of name, not of individual items belonging to the same category), then variations in the incidence of Scandinavian names might more plausibly be attributed to varying densities of settlement, that is, to varying availability of Scandinavian name-models, than to varying responses among the different indigenous communities. Indeed, Mrs Smart's work on Anglo-Saxon moneyers' names has already shown that, for this category at least, the ratio of Scandinavian forms to Old-English ones not only varies immensely, from some 75% at York down to zero at many southern mints, but that it does so in ways apparently corresponding to the original settlement pattern.[7] Thus far, then, the third Law seems well founded.

A yawning pit, however, confronts anyone seeking larger and less specialised samples of name-distribution in post-Viking, pre-Conquest England; for records ample enough for statistical analysis hardly survive for any periods less than two or even three centuries later than the original settlement of the Danelaw. Is it unjustifiably rash to try to argue back from the residual fashions of the twelfth century to the demographic patterns of the early tenth and even late ninth centuries? Rash in some degree it must be, because by the twelfth century the original distribution of Scandinavian names in England had been disturbed, indeed distorted, not simply by the passing centuries, but much more by two specific events: first, the Cnutian hegemony of the 1020s, with its influx of Danish magnates; and, next, by the Norman settlement, with its confusing contribution of Franco-Scandinavian names. Nevertheless, it might be argued that these two events, unlike the ninth-century settlement of the Danelaw, would have affected most parts of the country fairly uniformly, increasing the currency of Scandinavian names evenly, and not, therefore, deforming too drastically the comparative distributions. Whether such a point of view is tenable may best be determined by cautious experimentation.

Mrs Smart's findings imply that pre-Cnutian name-distributions reflected fairly closely the Viking settlement-patterns. Whether or not twelfth-century distributions still reflected the varying densities of settlement may be roughly determined by testing some samples against the known variations of settlement. Should these pilot tests prove reassuring, then samples may be taken from areas where the Scandinavian presence has been less precisely assessed with the aim of finding out how far personal names can usefully supplement demographic evidence of other kinds.

My findings are so far merely those of a pilot study, and by no means to be taken as definitive. Provisionally, it may be said that, although my figures differ from Mrs Smart's, our distribution-profiles are nonetheless compatible one with the other. South of the Thames, we know, pre-Cnutian Viking settlement would hardly have existed; and, correspondingly, pre-Conquest Winchester shows hardly any names identifiable as Anglo-Scandinavian. In Lincolnshire, on the other hand, settlement is known to have been dense, and there Anglo-Scandinavian names are correspondingly common: a section of the *Registrum Antiquissimum* dealing with the south of the county shows

---

the possible evidence to be derived from personal names. [[This chapter, which was in fact published in two parts in *Nomina*, VI (1982), and VII (1983), is reprinted below pp. 241–79.]] In my detailed work on this topic I have relied heavily upon Gillian Fellows Jensen, *Scandinavian Personal Names in Lincolnshire and Yorkshire* (Copenhagen, 1968).

[7] V.J. Smart, 'Moneyers of the late Anglo-Saxon Coinage, 973–1016', *Commentationes de nummis sæculorum ix–xi in Suecia repertis*, pt 2, Kungl. Vitterhets Historie och Antikvitets Akademiens Handlingar: Antikvariska Serien XIX (Stockholm, 1968), 191–276.

Scandinavian forms accounting for 70% or more of the insular names for men still current;[8] and from the early thirteenth century the Lincolnshire Feet of Fines and Assize Rolls similarly show Scandinavian forms running at between 60% and 70%.[9] At Newark, not far from the Lincolnshire border, and in the heart of the territory once owing allegiance to the Five Boroughs, Scandinavian forms account for some 60% of the insular men's names recorded in the 1170s. Those figures concern frequencies of occurrence; name-stocks tell a similar story, with the insular names current at Newark, for instance, including some 60% of Scandinavian forms. The 'southern Danelaw' (Northamptonshire, Huntingdonshire, Cambridgeshire, Bedfordshire and Hertfordshire) was less densely settled than Lincolnshire and Nottinghamshire, and also spent less long under Viking rule. A document which may, with some licence, be taken to represent the more northerly part of this district is the late-twelfth-century manorial survey from Ramsey (not ideal for the purpose, as it includes estates in Norfolk along with those lying close around the abbey itself, and I have not yet found time to assess the groups separately); this shows only some 30% of the insular names for men as Anglo-Scandinavian – about half the proportion at Newark, and under half that in south Lincolnshire. The Northamptonshire and Huntingdonshire materials in Sir Frank Stenton's *Northamptonshire Charters*[10] show Scandinavian forms as apparently amounting to some 35% of the insular names current for men – a figure perhaps on the high side owing to the difficulty of distinguishing between Anglo- and Franco-Scandinavian forms. For the more southerly part of the district there is the so-called 'Northamptonshire' Assize Roll of the early thirteenth century, covering not only the titular county but also much of the southern Danelaw and beyond:[11] this shows the Anglo-Scandinavian element among the insular names for men as amounting to no more than 25% at the most. These figures, although no more than the roughest samplings, seem to bear out the hope that even the twelfth- and early-thirteenth-century records of Anglo-Scandinavian names may still bear some relationship to the varying densities of the original Viking settlement, as asserted in my Third Law.

Emboldened by such provisional reassurance, we may attempt a further pilot survey, this time for an area for which evidence about Viking densities is less readily available: East Anglia. For Norfolk, most twelfth-century materials so far examined show the percentage of apparently Anglo-Scandinavian forms among the insular names for men as running at a fairly consistent 35% to 40% – a shade higher, that is, than the consolidated figure for the Ramsey survey including Norfolk manors alongside those in Huntingdonshire and Cambridgeshire. In itself the consistency of the figures seems to confirm the view that variations do not occur at random but as a reflection of cultural influences at work on the population concerned; even the *Miracula* of St William show a similar pattern – so perhaps *miraculés* do form valid cross-sections of

---

8 K. Major (ed.), *The Registrum Antiquissimum of the Cathedral Church of Lincoln*, VII (Hereford, 1953), dealing with Parts of Holland and Parts of Kesteven.

9 M.S. Walker (ed.), *Feet of Fines for the County of Lincoln for the Reign of John, 1199–1216*, Pipe Roll Society n.s. XXIX (London, 1954); D.M. Stenton (ed.), *The Earliest Lincolnshire Assize Rolls, A.D. 1202–1209*, Lincoln Record Society XXII (1926).

10 F.M. Stenton (ed.), *Facsimiles of Early Charters from Northamptonshire Collections*, Northamptonshire Record Society IV (Lincoln and London, 1930).

11 D.M. Stenton (ed.), *The Earliest Northamptonshire Assize Rolls, A.D. 1202 and 1203*, Northamptonshire Record Society V (Lincoln and London, 1930).

local people.[12] Of course, between believing figures to be significant and devising a formula for their precise interpretation, a great gulf yawns; but it seems tenable to suggest that in Norfolk Viking settlement was much lighter than in Lincolnshire, but in its turn denser than in the South-East Midlands. For Suffolk, the Feet of Fines corresponding to the Norfolk ones already quoted show a lower proportion of Anglo-Scandinavian forms among the current insular names for men: some 25%, as against Norfolk's 35% to 40%; and the figure is confirmed by the late-twelfth-century survey form Bury St Edmunds, which shows among the peasants an average of some 20% to 25%. And for Essex, the Domesday list of some 270 'king's burgesses' at Colchester shows Scandinavian forms accounting for no more than some 10% of the insular names for men.[13]

Provisional as these findings are, a pattern has emerged from them such as seems (unless the samples have all been wildly unrepresentative) to confirm the hypothesis that, even in twelfth- and early-thirteenth-century records, and in spite of intervening centuries and social upheavals, the percentages of Anglo-Scandinavian names bear some relationship to the original strength of Viking influence in the districts represented, so continuing to bear out my Third Law. It may be wise to speak only of 'influence', rather than of 'density of settlement', for, closely related as these two phenomena must be, the relationship between them is not easy to calibrate arithmetically. A vast amount remains to be done in this field, first in surveying and analysing the major records, and then in checking what small-scale variations there may have been in Scandinavian influence on medieval English personal names. What I hope may result from these studies is that soon historians seeking evidence of demographic and cultural movements will accept the evidence of personal names as ranking with – or even above – that of field- and other minor place-names.

As a coda, I should like to bring together two major topics, one linguistic, the other cultural: Scandinavian influence in England; and the rôle of women in early medieval society. The findings previously quoted all referred exclusively to men's names: not because these tell the whole story, but precisely because they do not. In 1978 I published a paper demonstrating that in Anglo-Norman England women's names were approximately a generation slower than men's to show the influence of the continental fashions brought by the invaders;[14] and with the Viking settlement too there seems to have been a differential effect on the naming-patterns of the sexes. Repeatedly one finds that among women's names Scandinavian forms are markedly less frequent than among the men's names in the same documents – and that in spite of the generally better preservation of insular names for women: in the Norfolk Feet of Fines, for instance, Scandinavian forms account for well under 10% of the surviving insular names for women, as against some 40% of those for men. The distribution is not going to be easy to plot, for in all medieval records women's names are scarce, and, if only names of insular types are counted, many samples prove tiny, probably too tiny to be valid. If, nevertheless, investigations do confirm this apparent discrepancy between women's names and men's, then it may be justifiable to claim, as I did concerning the

---

[12] Cf. 'the risk that beneficiaries of miracles may not make a representative sample', C. Clark, 'People and languages in post-Conquest Canterbury', below p. 186.

[13] *Domesday Book seu Liber Censualis Willelmi Primi Regis Angliae, &c.*, 4 vols (London, 1783– 1816), II, ff. 104r–106r.

[14] C. Clark, 'Women's names in post-Conquest England: observations and speculations', below pp. 117–43.

differential effects of post-Conquest influences, that the imbalance in the name-patterns may reflect one in the settlement-patterns, with many Viking men having arrived unaccompanied and married into the English population. This would constitute a further application of my Third Law. The conclusion would seem, *a priori*, far from unlikely. The Vikings were notoriously polygamous – so much so that 'more Danico' is the accepted term for a certain semi-official sort of concubinage; some, it was said, used to bath and change their linen expressly in order to pursue more successful careers of seduction.[15] They hardly sound likely to have been such devoted husbands as to have insisted on bringing their original Danish wives over to join them on their newly-acquired English estates. An *a priori* supposition is not, however, a fact, but needs as much confirmation as the surviving evidence will allow. In default of more direct evidence, it may be that differential frequencies of Anglo-Scandinavian names for women and for men may, in due course, afford at least an oblique confirmation of the guess that the Viking settlement in England was partly accomplished by men who arrived on their own and then took English wives.

[15] See J. Brøndsted (tr. K. Skov), *The Vikings*, Penguin Books (Harmondsworth, 1965), p. 254.

7

Certains éléments français de l'anthroponymie anglaise du Moyen Age: essai méthodologique[1]

A la suite de la conquête normande de l'Angleterre, le pays se vit bientôt muni – comme chacun sait – d'une nouvelle aristocratie de souche 'normande' (terme qui, dans le contexte présent, englobe aussi les Picards, les Angevins, les Flamands, les Bretons, et d'autres encore, qui participèrent à la colonisation ainsi qu'à la conquête). Cette aristocratie comportait beaucoup d'individus, voire quelques familles, à surnom français, que ce fût sobriquet ou nom d'origine. Pour banale que paraisse la constatation, ce thème, loin d'être épuisé, offre toujours un champ d'études fructueux.[2] Il intéresse pourtant plutôt les historiens que les philologues, anglicistes ou romanistes, et en tout cas ne fournira pas mon sujet aujourd'hui.

Je vise une matière moins élevée. Il s'agit de certains surnoms à forme française attribués pendant les XIIe et XIIIe siècles, non pas à l'aristocratie féodale, mais à des bourgeois des villes anglaises. Pour qui s'occupe moins de la langue et de la culture courtoises que de celles de tout le monde et de tous les jours, la bourgeoisie du Moyen Age revêt une importance particulière. D'ailleurs, moins connus que les nobles, plus difficiles à étudier, les marchands et les artisans excitent davantage la curiosité. Or, parmi les surnoms attribués aux bourgeois anglais dans les documents de cette époque, des formes en apparence françaises foisonnent; que ce soit un rôle de comptes royaux que l'on dépouille ou bien un registre de tenanciers urbains, on y remarque constamment des sobriquets à forme française aussi bien que des noms d'origine continentale. Pour le moment, j'écarte ceux-ci; malgré leur intérêt, leur importance certaine, ils n'offrent guère de mystère, de défi méthodologique.

C'est par la méthodologie que je voudrais aborder cette matière. Il faut commencer par se méfier des textes et s'interroger quant au statut des formes attestées. Nous nous trouvons, nous autres médiévistes anglicistes, confrontés à des problèmes que je nous crois propres, dus aux conditions socio-linguistiques qui régnaient en Angleterre. Les documents administratifs anglais du Moyen Age présentent des complications particulières, une couche complémentaire d'artifice. Comme partout dans l'Occident médiéval, en Angleterre aussi, on préférait rédiger en latin tout document public et, pour accroître la cohérence linguistique, on latinisait souvent, tant bien que mal, les éléments anthroponymiques: les prénoms régulièrement, et parfois aussi les surnoms –

---

[1] Je tiens à exprimer ma reconnaissance envers M. André Crépin (Sorbonne), qui m'a très aimablement aidée à corriger mon texte; des anglicismes qui s'y seraient néanmoins glissés, je suis seule responsable.

[2] Voir, par exemple, J.C. Holt, *What's in a Name? – Family Nomenclature and the Norman Conquest* (Stenton Lecture; Reading, 1982); aussi, D. Bates, *Normandy before 1066* (Londres, 1982), 113–14, 127.

noms d'origine, noms de métier, et encore sobriquets – qui possédaient, ou étaient censés posséder, une signification évidente. Ce n'est pas là le nœud du problème: quoique l'on ne soit pas toujours certain du terme-source vernaculaire précis, on ne risque guère de prendre de telles latinisations pour des formes courantes. Le problème réside dans un phénomène annexe et parallèle. Il n'y avait pas en Angleterre une seule et unique langue de prestige: le français (si l'on préfère, 'l'anglo-normand') jouissait, de par son association avec la nouvelle aristocratie, d'un prestige de second ordre, inférieur à celui du latin, supérieur à celui de l'anglais, langue de tout le monde, donc de n'importe qui.[3] Dans un contexte officiel ou public, celui qui ne se sentait pas maître du latin avait la possibilité de soulager son amour-propre en étalant une connaissance du français, comme le montre très clairement un procès de canonisation des années 1300, où chaque témoin choisit la langue la plus distinguée dont il (ou elle) se trouvait capable.[4] Pareillement, les textes moins soignés trahissent parfois des glissements du latin vers le français: par exemple, dans des documents latins qui proviennent de Cantorbéry au XIIe siècle, on trouve *unum pleinpein* à côté de *duos planos panes*, et d'autres cas semblables.[5] De telles constatations suggèrent que certains au moins d'entre les surnoms à forme française attribués à des bourgeois anglais représenteraient des gallicisations employées, de même que l'étaient les latinisations, pour ajouter à l'élégance de la rédaction. Pour renforcer cette hypothèse de traduction scribale, on trouve ici et là des surnoms – sobriquets aussi bien que noms de métier – à double forme, anglaise et française.[6] Voilà la source principale d'incertitude.

Une complication additionnelle résulte des nombreux emprunts moyen-anglais de termes courants vieux-français. Comment classer un sobriquet fondé sur un terme qui était devenu aussi courant en moyen-anglais qu'en vieux-français? La chronologie, comme on le verra, vient encore embrouiller la question: ainsi, parmi les attestations moyen-anglaises de *c(o)urteis* (fr. *courtois*, anglais modern *courteous*), celles du surnom – attesté, par exemple, à Cantorbéry pendant les années 1160 – précèdent d'environ un siècle et demi celles qui ont été relevées dans des textes littéraires, mettant en cause la priorité d'emploi.[7] J'y reviendrai plus loin.

Pour chaque surnom à forme française attesté dans un contexte anglais, il faut donc se demander si, loin d'être authentiquement français, il résultait simplement d'un emprunt lexical ou bien d'une intervention scribale. Qu'un scribe anglais écrivant en latin connaissait un peu de français ne serait pas pour nous apprendre grand-chose. Un emprunt précoce intéresserait surtout les lexicographes.[8] On doit donc chercher une méthode pratique pour trier les formes, pour contrôler l'authenticité des surnoms en apparence français attestés en Angleterre. Il y a deux champs comparatifs à fouiller: les

3 Voir M.D. Legge, 'Anglo-Norman and the historian', *History* 24 (1941–42), 163–75, et M.T. Clanchy, *From Memory to Written Record* (Londres, 1979), 160–3, 168–74, aussi 150, 157.

4 Voir M. Richter, *Sprache und Gesellschaft im Mittelalter* (Stuttgart, 1979), 173–97, 205–17.

5 W. Urry, *Canterbury under the Angevin Kings* (Londres, 1967) (*Canterbury*), Nos XXV, XLVII; cf. 'People and languages in post-Conquest Canterbury', plus bas 179–206 ('Canterbury'), 200.

6 Voir, par exemple, 'Canterbury', 191, 192, 193.

7 Voir H. Kurath *et alii*, *Middle English Dictionary* (Ann Arbor, 1954–) (*MED*), *s.v. courteis*, et P.H. Reaney, *A Dictionary of British Surnames* (2ème édition; Londres, 1976) (*DBS*), *s.n. Curtis*; cf. 'Canterbury', 190.

8 Voir 'Some early Canterbury surnames', plus bas 207–20 surtout les renvois 207 n. 1 et (en collaboration avec Dorothy Owen) 'Lexicographical notes from King's Lynn', *Norfolk Archaeology* 37 (1978), 56–69.

surnoms français du Moyen Age, et les noms de famille anglais de la période moderne. En établissant une comparaison double, on espère arriver à une appréciation plus précise des possibilités. Au cas où quelques-uns d'entre les surnoms en question se trouveraient authentifiés, la question éventuelle serait d'en déterminer la signification socio-culturelle.

Pour avoir de bonnes chances d'être authentiquement français, un surnom à forme française attesté en Angleterre devrait trouver un analogue exact attesté en territoire francophone. Cette règle ne saurait être absolue: vu les pertes catastrophiques de documents médiévaux, un surnom véritablement français pourrait bien ne plus être attesté que dans des contextes anglais (on verra plus loin quelques cas peut-être pertinents, en particulier celui de *Francenfant*).[9] Certains sobriquets bien attestés de nobles anglo-normands restent jusqu'ici inexplicables parce que privés d'analogues, autant parmi le vocabulaire courant vieux-français connu que parmi les surnoms relevés en France.[10] Cela dit, les spéculations invérifiables ne servent qu'à peu de chose, et il vaut mieux s'adresser à une comparaison systématique des formes existantes des deux côtés de la Manche. Pour faciliter la tâche, d'excellents recueils anthroponymiques vieux-français sont à notre disposition. Notre reconnaissance va surtout à Mademoiselle Morlet, dont les nombreux travaux apportent une aide indispensable. Ce qui ajoute à la précision des recherches, c'est que la plupart des répertoires français publiés reposent sur des bases localisées.

Par coïncidence, c'est à partir de documents localisés qu'ont commencé mes propres études anthroponymiques. Vous me pardonnerez, je l'espère, d'intercaler parmi mes considérations méthodologiques un bout d'autobiographie – en l'occurrence, pas tellement hors de propos. Il y a une dizaine d'années, au cours d'une tentative d'investigation socio-linguistique moyen-anglaise, mon regard s'est arrêté sur certaines listes qui provenaient de Cantorbéry au XIIe siècle et où se trouvaient enregistrés les tenanciers bourgeois qui dépendaient du prieuré de la Cathédrale. En m'efforçant de démêler les témoignages linguistiques et culturels à demi cachés dans ces listes, j'y ai remarqué beaucoup de sobriquets à forme française: anthroponymiste débutante, je me suis demandé s'il s'agissait de traductions scribales ou, au contraire, d'un bilinguisme communautaire. Provisoirement, et à cause de l'orientation de mon enquête originale, je me suis pendant un certain temps laissé entraîner vers la seconde solution, jusqu'au moment où mon regard s'est trouvé attiré Outre-Manche. J'ai le bonheur d'avoir à ma disposition une grande bibliothèque où l'on a le droit de flâner dans beaucoup de rayons – droit dont on profite. Un peu au hasard, j'ai fait de cette façon la connaissance de la *Revue Internationale d'Onomastique*. Ensuite, de renvoi en renvoi, j'ai fait mon chemin jusqu'à l'*Etude d'Anthroponymie picarde* de Mademoiselle Morlet ainsi qu'au *Nécrologe* arrageois publié par M. Roger Berger. En feuilletant de tels répertoires et d'autres encore – normands, picards, franco-flamands – j'ai reconnu, non sans un battement de cœur, d'étroites ressemblances entre certains surnoms cantorbériens et d'autres attestés dans le nord-est de la France: découverte qui m'a amenée à nuancer mon interprétation antérieure.[11]

---

9 Voir plus bas n. 16; cf. 'Lexicographical notes', 58, 67 n. 21.

10 Par exemple, *Meilleme*, surnom d'un tenancier féodal en Huntingdonshire au milieu du XIIe siècle (*Cartularium Monasterii de Rameseia*, éd. W.H. Hart et P.A. Lyons (3 tomes; Londres, 1884–93), I, 156–7).

11 Cf. 'Thoughts on the French connections of Middle-English nicknames', *Nomina* 2 (1978), 38–44 (39–40); aussi, 'Lexicographical notes', 57.

Puisque j'espère bientôt publier une étude détaillée des ressemblances anglo-françaises ainsi repérées, je ne ferai ici que proposer quelques exemples comme typiques du stock et des problèmes qu'il suscite. Un des surnoms les plus souvent attestés dans les documents cantorbériens du XIIe siècle est *Basset*, surnom bien connu en Angleterre dès la première génération anglo-normande. D'abord, les problèmes peuvent sembler minimes, puisque du point de vue étymologique cette forme est sans conteste française et qu'en l'occurrence aucun mot d'emprunt moyen-anglais n'y correspond. Tout n'est cependant pas clair: en effet, de nombreux analogues s'offrent parmi les surnoms français du Moyen Age, mais ceux-ci ne paraissent être attestés – du moins selon les répertoires disponibles – qu'à des dates plus tardives.[12] Des décalages chronologiques pareils, et pires, se manifestent partout. Comme sobriquet, *Gargate* 'gosier' est attesté en Angleterre à partir de 1130, tandis que le mot d'emprunt corre-spondant ne paraît guère avant le XIVe siècle finissant. Pour nous rassurer quant à la provenance de ce sobriquet, une forme identique était largement répandue en France; mais, pour nous rejeter sur les spéculations peu vérifiables, elle n'y paraît être attestée – c'est-à-dire, selon les répertoires disponibles – qu'environ un siècle plus tard.[13] Avec le surnom *Calderun* ou *Kaudrun*, si fréquent dans les documents cantorbériens du XIIe siècle, la question se fait encore plus délicate: comme d'habitude, les nombreuses attestations du sobriquet français sont, à ce qu'il paraît, postérieures aux premières relevées en Angleterre; et, d'autre part, le mot d'emprunt correspondant existait bel et bien en moyen-anglais, encore qu'aucune attestation antérieure à 1300 n'en ait jusqu'ici été relevée.[14] On a l'impression de se trouver en face d'un chassé-croisé onomastico-lexical franco-anglais. Pour comble de confusion, jusqu'ici certains sobri-quets à forme française relevés dans les listes cantorbériennes ne paraissent trouver – du moins dans les répertoires consultés – aucun analogue français contemporain: par exemple, *Bonechose, Butor, Caitevel, Pertrich, Timpan*.[15] Je reconnais volontiers à mon exposé un certain manque de rigueur; mais il faut se faire à la réalité. En grande partie, les difficultés sont dues à l'attestation tardive des analogues français – retard à son tour attribuable aux accidents de survie documentaire. Essayons donc de trancher ces difficultés par l'exercice du sens commun. Quand la forme dont il s'agit est typiquement française, encore qu'attestée plus tôt en Angleterre que dans les docu-ments continentaux existants, quoi de plus raisonnable que d'attribuer sa présence en Angleterre à un transfert spécifiquement onomastique, véhiculé par un déplacement humain? Vu la situation géographique de la ville de Cantorbéry, sans insister sur la célébrité qu'elle acquit après 1170 comme haut-lieu de pélerinage, quoi de plus simple que d'y envisager un groupe d'immigrés francophones, normands, picards et

---

12 *Canterbury*, Nos B167, XI, XXVIII, XXXI, XXXVI. Cf. *DBS, s.n. Basset*, et A. Dauzat, *Dictionnaire étymologique des noms de famille et prénoms de France* (revu Morlet; Paris, 1969) (*NFF*), *s.n. Bas*; aussi M.-Th. Morlet, *Etude d'anthroponymie picarde* (Amiens, 1967), 184, 286, et R. Berger, *Le nécrologe de la confrérie des jongleurs et des bourgeois d'Arras* (2 tomes; Arras, 1963–70), *s.a.* 1307.

13 *Canterbury*, Nos B71, C52, XX. Cf. *DBS*, 140, *s.n. Gargate*, et *MED, s.v. gargat(e*; aussi, *NFF, s.n. Gargaud, Anthroponymie picarde*, 195, 369, et *Nécrologe, s.a.* 1255.

14 *Canterbury*, Nos B7, D161, D257, D268, E33, E44, XIV, XLVII. Cf. *DBS*, 62, *s.n. Calderon*, et *MED, s.v. caudroun*; aussi, *NFF, s.n. Chaudron, Anthroponymie picarde*, 162, 300, et *Nécrologe, s.a.* 1220.

15 *Canterbury*, Nos LI, B1, B2, B3; A32, B210, D127, F91, F188, F416; D213; pour *Butor*, voir *Spicilegium Beccense* I (Le Bec-Hellouin, 1959), 585.

franco-flamands, immigrés qui maintenaient toujours le style anthroponymique natal? Mais je risque de devance mes propres conclusions.

Plus gravement, en fondant sur un seul échantillon des conclusions générales, on risquerait de s'égarer, surtout quand cet échantillon provient d'une ville particulière-ment ouverte – comme l'était Cantorbéry – aux influences étrangères en question. Heureusement, pour d'autres lieux en Angleterre des documents comparables ne font pas défaut; au contraire, ils sont assez nombreux pour inspirer au chercheur qui ne peut en dépouiller qu'un seul ensemble à la fois un sentiment d'incapacité coupable . . . Jusqu'ici j'ai réussi à étudier seulement deux autres communautés – choisies, il faut l'avouer, un peu au hasard des circonstances: la petite ville de Battle, en Sussex (aujourd'hui siège d'un congrès annuel d'études anglo-normandes), et le grand port commercial de King's Lynn, en Norfolk.[16] Chaque fois, même résultat: on retrouve beaucoup de sobriquets à forme française qui ne paraissent représenter ni des mots d'emprunt moyen-anglais ni des traductions scribales, mais qui correspondent exacte-ment à des surnoms amplement attestés en France. Le cas de Battle est surtout intéres-sant, parce que la liste dépouillée date de la première décennie du XIIe siècle; on y repère des attestations précoces de sobriquets français, tels *Barate*, *Cocard*, *Pechet*, et *Pinel*, et, en plus, la forme *Francenfant*, pour laquelle aucun analogue complet n'existe dans les répertoires français disponibles, mais qui possède assez de parallélismes partiels pour rendre vraisemblable son existence dans le système anthroponymique français du Moyen Age. Quant à King's Lynn, les résultats nouvellement publiés de mon enquête générale offrent des indications convergentes; puisque je compte procéder à une analyse plus détaillée des sobriquets à forme française, pour le moment je n'en dirai rien de plus. Trois villes, dont une minuscule, ne suffisent pas pour représenter l'Angleterre entière et, afin d'arriver à des conclusions valables, il faudrait une série nombreuse d'études semblables (ce qui nécessiterait une vie de Mathusalem ou, de préférence, un travail d'équipe). En attendant, l'accord remarquable offert par les études déjà entreprises nous rassure quant à la validité des premières conclusions. Il paraît donc justifiable d'affirmer que beaucoup d'entre les sobriquets à forme française attestés en Angleterre représenteraient des transferts onomastiques plutôt que des traductions scribales ou encore des emprunts lexicaux.

On se permet de supposer que ces surnoms français ont été introduits en Angleterre par des immigrés, marchands et artisans, qui les portaient: supposition qui demande à être confirmée par des témoignages indépendants. On se demande, en outre, pendant combien de temps un tel style continental a pu survivre en Angleterre. C'est cette seconde question qui m'occupera d'abord.

Au XIIe siècle la mode anglaise n'était pas encore aux noms de famille fixes et héréditaires: un individu changeait facilement d'appellation, des frères portaient par-fois des surnoms différents. Si, dans ces circonstances, les formes étrangères étaient vite disparues, ce ne serait pour étonner personne. Or, cela ne se produisit pas. Veuillez me pardonner cette affirmation mal étayée, au lieu d'être fondée – comme elle le serait dans un monde idéal – sur des rigoureuses études généalogiques. Espérons qu'un jour ce procédé-ci deviendra normal. Pour le moment, on est obligé de se contenter d'argu-ments approximatifs; primo, parce qu'entre généalogistes et anthroponymistes la colla-boration est rare; secundo, parce que les anthroponymistes anglicistes sont eux-mêmes

---

[16] Voir 'Battle c.1110: an anthroponymist looks at an Anglo-Norman new town', plus bas 221–40 (*Francenfant*, 238), et 'The early personal names of King's Lynn: an essay in socio-cultural history. Part II – by-names', plus bas 258–79.

trop peu nombreux pour permettre des travaux d'équipe. En attendant ce jour heureux mais, hélas!, lointain, où seront normales les recherches collectives et exhaustives, on ne peut qu'ébaucher des hypothèses. Par l'établissement de parallélismes entre, d'une part, les surnoms à forme française attestés dans l'Angleterre médiévale et, de l'autre, les noms de famille anglais modernes, on arrive – encore que sans parvenir à la certitude parfaite – à des conclusions significatives et utiles. Prenons comme exemple un surnom fréquent dans les documents anglais du Moyen Age: (*le*) *Rus*, comparable, à ce qu'il paraît, au nom de famille français *Leroux*. Malgré ce parallélisme, on se doit de considérer toutes les possibilités. S'agit-il ici d'une traduction scribale du terme moyen-anglais pour désigner cette couleur des cheveux, c'est-à-dire *rede*, adjectif qui fournit un sobriquet courant au Moyen Age et qui constitue par conséquent une source principale des noms de famille modernes, *Read(e)* et la variante écossaise *Reid*? De toute apparence, ce n'était pas – ou, du moins, pas toujours – le cas, parce que parmi les noms de famille modernes se repère aussi la forme *Rouse*, avec la prononciation qu'aurait acquise un emprunt médiéval du sobriquet français (*le*) *Roux*. Encore une fois, l'emprunt serait spécifiquement onomastique, puisque ce terme ne figurait pas, à ce que je sache, dans le vocabulaire courant moyen-anglais.[17] Quant au cas déjà cité du surnom *Curteis*, il correspond aussi bien à un sobriquet médiéval fréquent en France qu'au nom de famille anglais *Curtis*, et il a donc des chances de représenter un transfert onomastique plutôt qu'un emploi précoce, comme sobriquet 'moyen-anglais', du mot d'emprunt attesté un siècle et demi plus tard.[18]

Ayant ébauché, tant bien que mal, une méthode qui, pour grossière qu'elle demeure, permet de contrôler, certes de façon approximative, l'authenticité d'un surnom à forme française attesté en Angleterre, il faut se demander par quelles voies des surnoms authentiquement français seraient arrivés dans les villes anglaises. Avec ceux de la noblesse féodale, aucun problème: les barons et les chevaliers porteurs de ces surnoms étaient eux-mêmes de souche continentale, comme l'affirment à la fois les chartes et les chroniques. Qu'en était-il des bourgeois? Je me suis déjà permis, en passant, de supposer une immigration semblable de marchands et d'artisans de souche continentale: supposition qui demande à son tour d'être contrôlée. Pour des bourgeois, les renseignements biographiques existent seulement dans les cas exceptionnels. On note, par exemple, que les parents de saint Thomas Becket – domiciliés, quand leur fils nacquit, à Londres – étaient pourtant tous les deux d'origine normande: cas des plus rares, puisqu'il n'arrive pas à tout le monde de donner naissance à un saint de grande renommée. Mais, dans un autre sens, le cas était-il si rare? Combien y avait-il, parmi les marchands et les artisans de l'Angleterre d'après la conquête, d'individus venus d'Outre-Manche? Au dire d'Orderic Vital, des commerçants normands s'empressèrent d'affluer en Angleterre pour profiter des occasions offertes par le pays nouvellement conquis.[19] Comment confirmer, de façon détaillée, une hypothèse d'immigration bourgeoise? Pour essayer de résoudre de telles questions, un matériel traditionnel consiste en noms d'origine. Dans le contexte présent, cette méthode manque de rigueur, parce qu'on ne trouve que rarement un seul et même individu porteur de deux surnoms, c'est-à-dire, avec un nom d'origine relayant le sobriquet. Pour la plupart, les

---

[17] Voir *DBS*, 299, *s.n. Rous*, et 292, *s.n. Read*; cf. *NFF*, *s.n. Roux*.

[18] Voir plus haut n. 7; cf. *NFF*, *s.n. Courtois*.

[19] *Materials for the History of Thomas Becket*, éd. J.C. Robertson *et alii* (7 tomes; Londres, 1875–85), III, 81; *The Ecclesiastical History of Orderic Vitalis*, éd. M. Chibnall (6 tomes; Oxford, 1969–80), II, 256.

témoignages ne pourront être qu'indirects: si l'on constate, dans un groupe de bourgeois anglais, plusieurs individus à nom d'origine continentale, on se permettre d'en
conclure, par analogie, que ceux d'entre leurs voisins qui s'affublaient de sobriquets
français auraient été, eux aussi, d'origine continentale. En l'occurrence, des noms
d'origine française ne manquent pas parmi les bourgeois médiévaux des villes anglaises. A King's Lynn une dynastie marchande des plus en vue s'appelait 'de
Beauvais' (*de Belvaco*), et l'on y trouve des mentions de plusieurs autres villes du nord
et du nord-est de la France, tels Amiens, Bavent, Bernay, Crécy, Hauville, Roubaix,
Saint-Lô, Saint-Omer, parmi d'autres. D'ailleurs, des archives de douane font foi que
le commerce de guède amena dans cette région des commerçants picards.[20] Pour
Battle, la documentation est autre: la ville étant nouvellement fondée, comme dépend-
ance de l'abbaye érigée pour commémorer la 'bataille' décisive, on invita pour la
peupler, selon la chronique abbatiale, des colons tant d'Outre-Manche que des régions
anglaises avoisinantes (*nonnulli etiam ex transmarinis partibus*).[21] Dans une large
mesure, ces témoignages justifient, pour les villes en question, la supposition que les
porteurs de sobriquet français comprenaient beaucoup d'individus d'origine (person-
nelle ou familiale) continentale. Pour permettre de généraliser ces conclusions, il
faudrait – comme je l'ai déjà souligné – une enquête globale portant sur toutes les
villes importantes de l'Angleterre médiévale, enquête que je ne saurais, seule, mener à
bien.

Je résume: à la suite des recherches que je viens de décrire, on se trouve en droit
d'affirmer que la bourgeoisie anglaise des XIIe et XIIIe siècles comportait une proportion significative d'individus porteurs de sobriquets authentiquement français, et
d'ajouter en plus qu'entre les personnes ainsi signalées quelques-unes au moins de-
vaient être de souche continentale. Evidemment, je ne vais pas jusqu'à suggérer que
l'Angleterre d'après la conquête fût peuplée d'immigrés; loin de là. Mais si, dans
plusieurs villes anglaises, des Français figuraient parmi les citoyens les plus en vue,
cela contribuerait à expliquer certains phénomènes culturels, notamment les emprunts
lexicaux ayant rapport plutôt au commerce qu'à la vie courtoise. D'autre part, cette
enquête a confirmé l'importance du témoignage socio-historique des surnoms médiévaux.

Il reste cependant encore des obscurités à dissiper. La question des surnoms
étrangers attestés dans l'Angleterre du Moyen Age s'avère en réalité plus compliquée
que je ne l'ai laissé entendre jusqu'ici. De par leur forme et de par l'existence d'analogues attestés en France, certains sobriquets ont été considérés comme 'français';
mais l'étaient-ils tous par la provenance immédiate, étaient-ils tous vraiment 'français
de France'? Reconnaissons d'emblée que cela dépend en partie des définitions,
puisqu'au Moyen Age les frontières nationales n'avaient ni le même emplacement ni la
même valeur que de nos jours; mais je ne veux pas couper les cheveux en quatre.
Définissons 'la France' comme le territoire francophone (même s'il est difficile en
l'occurrence de préciser celui-ci). Ensuite, quittons ce territoire francophone pour
examiner les styles anthroponymiques des régions voisines, des Pays-Bas, et aussi des
pays rhénans. On ne tarde pas à voir qu'aux XIIe et XIIIe siècles l'Angleterre était loin
d'être le seul pays non francophone où certains bourgeois arboraient des sobriquets à
forme française: à Ypres, à Gand, à Cologne, apparaissent de temps à autre des formes

---

[20] Voir 'King's Lynn', plus bas 271–2; cf. E.M. Carus-Wilson, 'La guède française en Angleterre',
      Revue du Nord 35 (1953), 89–105 (98–9).
[21] *The Chronicle of Battle Abbey*, éd. E. Searle (Oxford, 1980), 50, 76.

tout à fait pareilles aussi bien aux formes attestées en Angleterre qu'aux formes normales en territoire francophone.[22] Ce phénomène nous plonge dans l'embarras: puisque l'Angleterre du Moyen Age entretenait des liens commerciaux aussi bien avec les Pays-Bas et avec les pays rhénans qu'avec le nord de la France, et puisque, en outre, un nom d'origine de bourgeois anglais affiche, ici et là, une provenance flamande ou rhénane,[23] comment être sûr de la source immédiate d'un sobriquet à forme française, mais à circulation internationale? S'il y a une solution, peut-être viendra-t-elle à la longue d'études prosopographiques plus approfondies des populations urbaines anglaises du Moyen Age. Aujourd'hui je me borne à soulever le problème, tout en réaffirmant qu'il ne concerne en tout cas qu'une proportion mineure des sobriquets français attestés en Angleterre.

[22] Voir: W. Beele, *Studie van de ieperse persoonsnamen uit de stadsen baljuwsrekeningen 1250–1400* (2 tomes; Handzame, 1975), *s.nn. Bataille, Blankaard, Cousin, Ioie,* etc.; C. Tavernier-Vereecken, *Gentse Naamkunde van ca.1000 tot 1253* (Tongres, 1968), *s.nn. Baiard, Blancart, Caudron, Ioie,* etc.; S. Hagström, *Kölner Beinamen des 12. und 13. Jahrhunderts* (Upsal, 1949), 478–81; aussi, O. Leys, 'Romaanse leenwoorden in de Westvlaamse naamgeving tot 1225', *Mededelingen van de Vereniging voor Naamkunde te Leuven en de Commissie voor naamgeving te Amsterdam* 30 (1954), 149–69.

[23] Voir, par exemple, 'King's Lynn', plus bas 272.

8

Historical Linguistics – Linguistic Archaeology

The history of language is part of 'history' in the wider sense, and can therefore be tapped for evidence of past socio-cultural patterns. The resultant discipline – already well-established – might be called 'Applied Historical Socio-Linguistics' or, as the title more succinctly puts it, 'Linguistic Archaeology', this latter formulation having the merit of indicating that linguistic phenomena can be to socio-cultural historians much as artefacts are to archaeologists. Linguistic 'finds' vary in context much as do those of artefacts: some items are scattered on the present-day surface, whereas others lie buried at varying depths; and, in both categories, some occur in quasi-isolation, but most of them amid complexes of interrelated material.

Relevant finds upon the present-day surface of the language are infinitely numerous, because any linguistic feature, from the orthographical to the syntactic, may have socio-cultural bearings that prove explicable only in historical terms. For vocabulary, and especially for the loanwords that have over the centuries been adopted into any language, this is a cliché. Thus, a well-ordered thesaurus reveals the world-view adopted by the users of the language in question. The common Indo-European roots deducible by means of comparative philology can be scanned for clues as to likely habitat and cultural patterns of the original Indo-European tribes. Especially rich testimony to the socio-cultural history of any people is offered by its heritage of name-material.

Taking name-material as historical evidence is nothing new. The English Place-Name Society, for instance, was founded – now well over sixty years ago – partly by historians and principally for historical ends; and, although it has over the years perforce numbered many philologists among its county editors, philosophically it continues to the present day serving those same hisorical ends. Its work illustrates admirably what 'linguistic archaeology' involves. Place-names form part of the present-day surface of the language and are constantly before our eyes and in our mouths; yet few, other than professional toponymists, give them much thought. As soon as one does reflect upon current place-names, one finds oneself ranging them into two categories: on the one hand, there are occasional forms which, like *Ashford*, *Black-heath* and *Eastfield*, are seemingly transparent in present-day terms; on the other, there looms a host of ones that are to greater or lesser degrees opaque, including many which, like *London* and like *York*, are wholly unintelligible. Being unintelligible does not, of course, disable a name: freedom from 'sense' has indeed been deemed essential to perfect fulfilment of the onomastic function. But no name ever began as a simple pointer: no-one ever gazed upon, for instance, a nascent settlement at the confluence of the Ouse and the Foss and then, fired with mystic inspiration, cried out, 'York!' Names of all kinds are created out of elements taken from ordinary language: a place-name, that is to say, normally begins as a description of the place originally concerned. The capacity of names to long outlive their intelligibility is indeed what enables them to rank as archaeological finds, and in some cases as prehistoric fossils. So, whether or not a present-day name-form may look intelligible, the linguistic archaeologist's duty is always to excavate deeper and deeper around it until a definitive interpretation be unearthed. 'Excavation' means burrowing back as far as may be possible through the successive strata of archive material (the palaeographical and diplomatic dating of which is the linguist's equivalent of dendrochronology and radio-carbon analysis), and then interpreting the findings in terms of the languages current at the places and times to which the records relate. This is what the county surveys published by the English Place-Name Society illustrate so well. Under each present-day place-name there is ranged, in chronological order, a selection of corresponding forms from ancient records, sometimes going back as far as Romano-British times. Then, on the basis of these early forms and in the light of all available topographical and tenurial information, an interpretation is suggested or, if none be possible, the obscurities are indicated. Some obscurity has in the end to be accepted: no-one has yet, I think, established any certain interpretation of the name *London* and that of *York* is also, as we shall see, in part somewhat speculative.

Establishing an etymology is, in any case, only the first stage in a linguistic archaeo-logist's work. With any sequence of early place-name forms, the aim is to use it – irregularities, obscurities, and all – much as one might a sequence of artefacts excavated from a site: that is, for throwing light upon the successive inhabitants of the locality and upon their linguistic and cultural affiliations. The Romans it was who transmitted to us the earliest known forms corresponding to the place-name *York*: *Eburācum* or *Eborācum* (transmitted by them also to the geographer Ptolemy). That name is not, however, of true Roman or Latin origin, but represents either a Celtic possessive formed upon a personal name *Eburos* or else upon a Celtic adjective derived from a plant-name whose meanings apparently varied from dialect to dialect, ranging from 'yew-tree' to 'hogweed'. The exact etymology may, luckily, be beside the point: what counts is that an undoubtedly Celtic name had been adopted by the occupying Romans from the usage of the local inhabitants. After the Romans had left, the English settlers made this district their own; and they did something at once strange and yet commonplace in the transmission of names. Their name for this place was *Eoforwīc*. Had no earlier form survived, that would have passed as an ordinary enough Old English place-name; for its second element represents the frequent Old English generic -*wīc*, adapted from the Latin *vicus* and carrying various meanings, such as 'settlement associated with a Roman camp' and 'landing-place, port', potentially applicable to Dark-Age York, and its first – the specific or qualifier – looks like Old English *eofor* 'boar', a term found several times elsewhere in a similar role (the boar, being a symbolic beast, might have been found apt either as eponymous patron for a settlement or else as source of a personal nickname for its founder or overlord). But, when compared with the Romano-British name, *Eoforwīc* looks less like an Old English creation than like a rendering into Old English terms of what the Germanic-speaking newcomers thought they heard the Celtic-speaking natives say. Such remodellings – usually called 'folk-etymology' – are not uncommon in place-name history, and imply that our remote ancestors, whose own place-naming was still at an early and therefore literally descriptive stage, were less at ease than we are with unintelligible onomastic pointers. Such a process implies communication of some kind between the two groups of people, yet at the same time little appreciation by the newcomers of the existing inhabitants' language. The next strangers to make York their own were the Vikings, and they too adapted its name to suit them. For the Old English first element *Eofor*- they substituted their own similar-sounding and cognate term *jǫfurr*, which had through metaphor acquired the connotation 'princely warrior'; and, as often, they also imposed upon the form as a whole their own articulatory habits, to wit, their tendencies to prefer rising diphthongs to falling ones, to elide medial [v] in certain contexts and not to assibilate palatal consonants. Old English *Eoforwīc* therefore gave place to Anglo-Scandinavian *Jǫfurvík > *Jórvík* > *York*. The place's whole history is thus summarily exhibited in this sequence of the forms successively given to its name. For the political shifts behind this thousand-year series of linguistic dislocations we do, of course, possess other sources of information; but, none the less for that, the linguistic evidence is invaluable for fleshing out the social and cultural concomitants of war and politics, for suggesting what sorts of everyday compromise may have been entailed by the invasions and the shifts of hegemony.

Linguistic finds usually form part of interrelated complexes of material. The name *York*, as well as carrying individual significance, also belongs to two of the major strata formed by 'English' place-names: the Romano-British one, and the Anglo-Scandinavian. Over the last quarter-century, the evidential value of such complexes has come to be more and more appreciated and exploited. Often, study of place-name strata has been combined with that of artefact archaeology, as in the many, still-continuing endeavours to identify more accurately the earliest types of truly English place-names and to plot their distributions as an aid towards tracing the course of the earliest settlements. Scandinavian-influenced place-names too have been, and are still being, intensively surveyed on archaeological lines. All over the former Danelaw – everywhere, that is, north and east of Watling Street – the Viking settlers imposed their stamp, in varying styles and to varying degrees, upon the nomenclature of the districts where they settled. The place-names that they created, or adapted, are classified by scholars according to modes of formation (*Jórvík*, for instance, represents Scandin-avianization of a pre-existing form), and then analyzed geographically and chronologi-cally, again with the aim of throwing light on patterns of settlement. Such modes of research are now the principal tools of place-name study, in which linguistic analysis constitutes a preliminary stage, not an end in itself.

There are other ways too in which place-names throw light upon the settlements and migrations that have shaped English history. For seven or more centuries such names have been serving not only to denote localities but also as bases for personal by-names (or surnames) helping to identify individual people and individual families. Among present-day family-names, there abound forms that coincide with those of current place-names, typical examples being *Appleby, Barton, Bolton, Burton, Crossland, Lancaster, London, Satterthwaite, Spofforth, Stow(e), Warwick, York(e)*, and so on by the thousand. Toponymic family-names like these mainly reflect the internal migra-tions underlying our present population-structure; and study of them on these lines has indeed become the most popular branch of personal-name research. One of its attrac-tions to would-be practitioners may sometimes be suspected to be a seemingly minimal need for philological competence; but matters are far from being as simple as they may appear to the uninitiated. A basic problem is exemplified by several forms in the token list just given: *Barton, Burton*, and *Stow(e)*, for instance. Early English place-naming was a pragmatic business, where wit and originality were at a discount, and many names simply specified in standard terms the type of settlement concerned. Certain such standard forms, of which *Barton* is typical, therefore recur over and over again throughout the country, so that a family-name representing one of these can give little clue to the original family home. In the end, only a minority of place-name forms prove to be of unique occurrence, and this restricts the usefulness of toponymic family-names as raw material for studies in migration. Furthermore, a family-name may – because of a predominantly oral transmission – represent a line of development different from that behind the current form of the place-name from which it is derived: thus, the family-name *Coxall* represents the directly developed form of the Essex place-name spelt <Coggeshall> and now commonly given the spelling-pronunciation ['kɒgɪʃɔːl]. Yet a further dimension of difficulty arises from the facts that there never had been a time when the English population was stable and that the 'surname-creating period' – running approximately from the twelfth to the fifteenth centuries – was also one of especially rapid urban development, with all the shifts of population that this involved. Using family-names as a basis for studies in migration is thus no business for the amateur (however enthusiastic) but demands a trained name-archaeologist, accomplished in socio-economic history as well as in philology and in archive-work. The possibilities that such studies can, when rightly exploited, bring to realization are well illustrated in the county surveys that have since the early 1970s been appearing in the English Surnames Series.

Analysis of toponymic family-names is, however, only one branch of personal-name archaeology. The general socio-onomastic bearings of personal-naming are, of course, familiar even to laypeople: if someone is called, say, 'Moira McLaren', one straightaway assumes that either she possesses family connections with the Scottish Highlands or else she, or her parents, have for some reason chosen to give that impression. That particular deduction involves, admittedly, not 'Anthroponymical Archaeology', merely the synchronic level of 'Applied Socio-Anthroponymics'; but, the historical dimension apart, the two disciplines differ little. In an historical context, too, personal identity may be encapsulated in a name; and assessing how far the etymology or the associations of a particular form may throw light upon its bearer's background and status can often assist the genealogist and the prosopographer. Archaeologically and methodologically, on the other hand, such individual exercises are of less moment than studies of whole communities. Every name-corpus encapsulates – if at times hermetically – the cultural influences that have over the centuries converged upon the community to which it belongs; and this should enable a name-archaeologist to deduce from any such corpus the cultural allegiances of the local or social group in question.

The archaeological potentialities of personal names are virtually the converse of those associated with place-names. People are – self-evidently – vastly more numerous than named places, so that, even if we reckon up under 'place-names' all the so-called 'minor' forms (such as names of landmarks, fields and streets), personal names will still be for any given time vastly more numerous than place-names. Moreover, whereas a place-name corpus, once established, is significantly increased or modified only in exceptional circumstances (such as those of the Viking settlement in the Danelaw), every personal-name one is inherently unstable, changing day by day as individuals die and others are born and baptized, and thus being entirely renewed in under a century. People, besides, move freely about the world, taking their own names on their backs and their former community's traditional name-stock in their heads. For all these reasons, personal names constitute a far fuller and more sensitive guide to socio-cultural history than place-names could ever be.

These great potentialities entail, unfortunately, problems no less great. For a voluminous personal-name corpus (amounting perhaps to tens of thousands of items), statistical analysis may offer the only means of imposing order upon the material and drawing conclusions from it; such analysis is in any event likely to be more and more often undertaken as computers become more and more widely used. Need for statistics faces us not simply with controversy but with fundamental difficulties. The trouble is not that 'statistics' as understood by mathematicians is a domain inaccessible to most scholars in the humanities: that could in the long run to remedied by different policies for recruiting and training onomasticians and, in particular, by assembling – as has already upon occasion been done, most notably at Münster and at Freiburg – teams in which philologists, historians and statisticians would work side by side. The true problems reside in the material itself. Even a comprehensive census of the modern kind involves some arbitrariness, in that even one day later the population, and with it the name-corpus, would have been modified by deaths and by births. Medieval records were, in any case, never meant to be comprehensive, but only to specify which individuals were responsible for certain duties, rents or taxes, or which of them had fallen foul of the law, and so on. These varying types of selectivity, as well as increasing the essential arbitrariness of the sample, also put at some risk any comparison between records of different types: setting, for instance, a gaol-delivery roll alongside a guild-roll of identical provenance and date might prove profitable, so too might comparing two guild-rolls either from the same town but of different dates or else of the same date but from different towns; but what significance to read into contrasts or agreements between unlike records from different places and/or dates must always remain problematic. Nor is that all: anyone who has ever tried to classify medieval names knows that always there remain a good few ambivalent forms, such as might with equal plausibility be assigned to any of several origins. Given these multiple uncertainties, it is not surprising that some anthroponymists should have counselled against any reliance at all upon statistics. Others, however, no less scrupulous and no less learned, have displayed personal-name distributions in percentages refined to two decimal places. What is then best to do? Common sense suggests a compromise: whether or not the difference between 52.37% and 54.13% ought, in the sort of contexts with which we are concerned, to be allowed any great statistical weight, that between 10% and 90% is likely to mean something; and so it may be safe even for non-mathematicians to allow themselves some 'coarse statistics', such as lend weight only to discrepancies of at least 5% and preferably 10% between samples and then only when the types of material seem adequately comparable. A fail-safe methodology has, in its unheroic way, something to commend it.

There remain questions of how to base any calculation. Personal names can be reckoned up in at least two ways: in terms either of the number of individuals named or of the number of distinct forms current in the stock represented. The latter method is by far the easier, because determining how many separate individuals are mentioned in a set of medieval records can in itself constitute a substantial research project. Choice is not, however, a matter just of diligence versus sloth, for the two techniques are not interchangeable: a point well illustrated by baptismal names current in twelfth-century England. Many records show a mixture of several types of name: some of native Old English origin, others introduced by the Viking settlers, and others again by the more recent post-Conquest ones. The two foreign influences are not on the same footing, and do not therefore lend themselves to identical modes of analysis. The so-called 'Norman' one was fresh and still increasing in popularity, and may thus be most effectively assessed in terms of the number of individuals named, in so far as ten different peasants all called *William* have more significance than a solitary one. By contrast, the Viking influence was at this time spent and indeed recessive, and so can best be assessed by the number of forms it had contributed to the name-stock rather than by the number of individuals currently bearing such names. Both techniques can, of course, be applied to each category in turn, because each has its own contribution to make to the whole analysis; but to attempt direct comparison between two such disparate influences would be pointless.

Etymologizing and counting the specimens is again only a preliminary procedure, because the personal-name archaeologist's aim is to assess the socio-cultural implications of the corpus as a whole. Now, trying to work out *in vacuo* the implications of a name-corpus is – to employ a simile that I have used before – rather like trying to deduce the familial, social and commercial relationships of any household solely from the stamps on its incoming letters: one observes a frequent connection with, say, Germany and sporadic ones with France and with Denmark, but whether such connections are recent or ancestral ones, whether they are based upon ties of kindred or affection or upon business relationships, one cannot tell. Similarly, the motivations and the implications behind the adoption and the perpetuation of particular personal names can be determined only by taking into account the whole context, in so far as it may be knowable; that is, by discovering as much as possible about the conquests, settlements, trade-patterns, religious movements and literary fashions that may have impinged upon the community concerned. Linguistic archaeology is indeed a branch of history rather than of linguistics.

Such a classification, indeed, such an affinity is already partly acknowledged in some quarters: for instance, by those bibliographers and librarians who place Onomastics under 'History: Auxiliary Sciences'. There was, however, a deliberate intent behind my choice of 'Linguistic', rather than 'Onomastic', 'Archaeology' as the title of this paper, because I regard the approach outlined as potentially extensible to all aspects of language. The historical bearings of vocabulary have already been mentioned in the passing. For orthography, I have myself elsewhere endeavoured to exhibit some socio-linguistic bearings, with special reference to the half-century following the Norman Conquest; and I have lately attempted to extend this study to include scribal choices between alternative letter-forms. As for pronunciation and for morpho-syntax, present-day experience constantly reveals both as sensitive indicators of social disarray. If one sees life as a continuum, synchronically as well as diachronically, as a seamless fabric in which language is woven together with politics, religion, economic developments and socio-cultural relationships, then all linguistic manifestations are – if rightly understood – capable of illuminating these other spheres, in the same measure as language is enriched, impoverished, reshaped by the contexts in which it is used. In order to reveal these cross-illuminations, all that is needed is appropriate technique.

WORKS CONSULTED

Benveniste, Emile. 1969. *Le Vocabulaire des institutions indo-européennes.* 2 vols. Paris: Les Editions de Minuit.

Brattö, O. 1956. *Notes d'anthroponymie messine.* (= Göteborgs Universitets Årsskrift, 62, part 4.)

Cameron, Kenneth. 1976. 'The Significance of English Place-Names'. *Proceedings of the British Academy* 62. 135–55.

Cameron, Kenneth, ed. 1977. *Place-name Evidence for the Anglo-Saxon Invasion and Scandinavian Settlements: Eight studies collected by K.C.* Nottingham: English Place-Name Society.

Clark, Cecily. 1978. 'Women's Names in Post-Conquest England: Observations and Speculations'. Below 117–43.

Clark, Cecily. 1979. 'Clark's First Three Laws of Applied Anthroponymics'. Above 77–83.

Clark, Cecily. 1980. 'Battle c.1110: An Anthroponymist Looks at an Anglo-Norman New
Town'. Below 221–40.

Clark, Cecily. 1982–3. 'The Early Personal Names of King's Lynn: An Essay in Socio-
Cultural History'. Below 241–79.

Clark, Cecily. 1983. 'On Dating *The Battle of Maldon*: Certain Evidence Reviewed'.
Above 20–36.

Clark, Cecily. 1984. 'L'Angleterre anglo-normande et ses ambivalences socio-culturelles'.
*Les Mutations socio-culturelles au tournant des XIe–XIIe siècles: Actes du Colloque
international du CNRS – Etudes anselmiennes (IVe session)* ed. Raymonde Foreville,
99–110. (= Spicilegium Beccense, 2.) Paris: Editions du CNRS.

Clark, Cecily. 1985. 'Certains éléments français de l'anthroponymie anglaise du Moyen
Age: Essai méthodologique'. Above 84–91.

Clark, Cecily. 1986. Review of *Surnames and Genetic Structure*. By G.W. Lasker *et al.*
(Cambridge: CUP, 1985). Below 377–80.

Clark, Cecily. 1987a. 'English Personal Names *ca.*650–1300: Some Prosopographical
Bearings'. *Medieval Prosopography* 8, part 1: 31–60.

Clark, Cecily. 1987b. 'Spelling and Grammaticality in the *Vespasian Homilies*: A
Reassessment'. *Manuscripta* 31, part 1: 7–10.

Clark, Cecily. 1987c. 'A Witness to Post-Conquest English Cultural Patterns: The *Liber
Vitae* of Thorney Abbey'. Below 339–47.

Clark, Cecily. 1987d. *'Willelmus rex? vel alius Willelmus?'* Below 280–98.

Ekwall, Eilert. 1956. *Studies on the Population of Medieval London*. (= Kungl. Vitterhets
Historie och Antikvitets Akademiens Handlingar: Filologisk-Filosofiska Serien, 2.)
Stockholm: Almqvist & Wiksell.

Ekwall, Eilert. 1964. *Old English wīc in Place-Names*. (= Nomina Germanica, 13.)
Uppsala: A.-B. Lundequistska Bokhandeln.

Ellegård, Alvar. 1958. 'Notes on the Use of Statistical Methods in the Study of Name
Vocabularies'. *Studia Neophilologica* 30. 214–31.

Fellows Jensen, Gillian. 1975. 'The Vikings in England: A Review'. *Anglo-Saxon England*
4. 181–206.

Fellows Jensen, Gillian. 1976. 'Place-Names and Settlement History: A Review'. *Northern
History* 13. 1–26.

Fellows-Jensen, Gillian, 1987. 'York'. *Leeds Studies in English*, new ser. 18. 141–55.

Gardiner, Alan H. 1940. *The Theory of Proper Names: A controversial essay*. London:
Oxford University Press.

Gelling, Margaret. 1973–76. *The Place-Names of Berkshire*. 3 vols. (= English Place-
Name Society, 49–51.) Cambridge: Cambridge University Press.

Gelling, Margaret. 1977. 'Latin Loan-Words in Old English Place-Names'. *Anglo-Saxon
England* 6. 1–13.

Gelling, Margaret. 1978. *Signposts to the Past*. London: J.M. Dent & Sons Ltd.

Jackson, Kenneth. 1953. *Language and History in Early Britain*. Edinburgh: Edinburgh
University Press.

McClure, Peter. 1979. 'Patterns of Migration in the Late Middle Ages: The Evidence of
English Place-Name Surnames'. *Economic History Review*, 2nd Ser. 32. 167–82.

McKinley, Richard. 1975. *Norfolk and Suffolk Surnames in the Middle Ages*. (= English
Surnames Series, 2.) London and Chichester: Phillimore & Co. Ltd.

McKinley, Richard. 1977. *The Surnames of Oxfordshire*. (= English Surnames Series, 3.)
London: Leopard's Head Press Ltd.

McKinley, Richard. 1981. *The Surnames of Lancashire.* (= English Surnames Series, 4.) London: Leopard's Head Press Ltd.

Martinet, André. 1986. *Des Steppes aux océans: l'indo-européen et les 'Indo-Européens'.* Paris: Payot.

Mawer, Allen, & Stenton, Frank Merry, eds. 1924. *Introduction to the Survey of English Place-Names.* (= English Place-Name Society, 1, part 1.) Cambridge: Cambridge University Press.

Michaëlsson, Karl. 1947. 'Questions de méthode anthroponymique'. *Onomastica* 1. 190–204.

Michaëlsson, Karl. 1954. 'L'Anthroponymie et la statistique'. *IVe Congrès international de Sciences onomastiques.* ed. Jöran Sallgren *et al.*, 380–94. Uppsala: A.-B. Lundequistska Bokhandeln.

Nicolaisen, W.F.H., ed. 1970. *The Names of Towns and Cities in Britain,* compiled by Margaret Gelling, W.F.H. Nicolaisen and Melville Richards. London: B.T. Batsford Ltd.

Reaney, P.H. 1935. *The Place-Names of Essex.* (= English Place-Name Society, 12.) Cambridge: Cambridge University Press.

Reaney, P.H. 1967. *The Origin of English Surnames.* London: Routledge and Kegan Paul.

Reaney, P.H. 1976. *A Dictionary of British Surnames.* 2nd edn. Revised by R.M. Wilson. London: Routledge and Kegan Paul.

Redmonds, George. 1973. *Yorkshire: West Riding.* (= English Surnames Series, 1.) London & Chichester: Phillimore & Co. Ltd.

Rivet, A.L.F., and Smith, Colin. 1979. *The Place-Names of Roman Britain.* London: B.T. Batsford Ltd.

Smith, Albert Hugh. 1937. *The Place-Names of the East Riding of Yorkshire and York.* (= English Place-Name Society, 14.) Cambridge: Cambridge University Press.

Smith, Albert Hugh. 1956. *English Place-Name Elements.* 2 vols. (= English Place-Name Society, 25 & 26.) Cambridge: Cambridge University Press.

9

Socio-Economic Status and Individual Identity: Essential Factors in the Analysis of Middle English Personal-Naming

Not long ago a mainstream scholar of English language and literature, venturing in search of linguistic, preferably Chaucerian, titbits into the *terra* (to him) *incognita* of late fourteenth-century legal records, remarked on the absence, from among the by-names[1] of professional lawyers, of formations of the *atte bridge* type: 'the aristocratic Serjeants and Justices, it seems, never have the surnames that are formed with "atte" and a common place-name, such as "atte Putte" '.[2] Naive though his air of slight surprise (never mind his terminology) might seem to those in the trade, the observation was just: Middle English by-name styles were to some extent socially stratified,[3] and at the time in question some continuing lack of fixity probably contributed to keeping them so,[4] in so far as a man on the make might have swapped a name of rustic or plebeian ring for one of more urbane style – a toponymic, say.[5]

The same reference exemplifies also a point of different order, to wit, the way that personal-name studies tend, to a far greater degree than do place-name ones, to be pursued by scholars whose training and dominant interests have previously lain, and

---

[1] This term, denoting an identificatory phrase of any type collocated with (normally, postposed to) a baptismal name, is used in order not to beg the question as to when hereditary family-naming, or 'surnaming', became the rule (cf. n. 19 below).

[2] W.F. Bolton, 'Middle English in the law reports and records of 11–13 Richard III', *English Language Notes*, 24, 1986–7, 1–8, esp. 6–7.

[3] For the preponderance, among persons bearing topographical by-names, of serfs and smallholders, see Richard McKinley, *A History of British Surnames*, London, 1990, 202; also *idem*, *The Surnames of Oxfordshire*, English Surnames Series, 3, London, 1977, 41–44 ('predominantly borne by the unfree section of the population'), 199–200; and *The Surnames of Sussex*, English Surnames Series, 5, Oxford, 1988, 11–13. (This aspect of the matter is never addressed by Stig Carlsson in his *Studies in Middle English Local Bynames in East Anglia*, Lund Studies in English, 79, Lund, 1989.) As with most onomastic patterns, the contrast is relative rather than absolute; and in this context I wish to thank David Postles for letting me see an unpublished study of his in which, whilst confirming the general infrequency of topographical by-names amongst burgesses, he points out the currency of certain specifically urban formations such as *atte barre*.

[4] See, e.g., E. Ekwall, 'Variations in surnames in medieval London', *Kungl. Humanistiska Vetenskapssamfundet i Lund Årsberättelse 1944–45*, 207–62.

[5] For the high frequencies of topographical by-names amongst burgesses as well as nobility and gentry, see, e.g., R. McKinley, *History*, 201; also *idem, Norfolk and Suffolk Surnames in the Middle Ages*, English Surnames Series, 2, Chichester, 1975, 82–83, 141–42; *Oxon.*, 65, 68; *The Surnames of Lancashire*, English Surnames Series, 4, London, 1981, 442–43; and *Sussex*, 13–14. Conversely, such forms were rare amongst serfs: see, e.g., *Oxon.*, 203–04; and *Sussex*, 105–07. Again distinctions are relative rather than absolute.

sometimes continue to lie, in other fields, such as prosopography, dialectology, lexicography, socio-linguistics, psychology, settlement geography, socio-economic history, medical genetics, and so on. This customary rôle of personal-name studies as an adjunct, an auxiliary, to some primary interest elsewhere means that, far as yet from crystallizing into a single discipline with standardized aims and approaches, they are still being pursued *ad hoc*, on bases governed by each individual scholar's underlying purpose. There is, in particular, a rift between the aims and methods of investigators who are primarily historians and those of the ones who are primarily linguists: a matter to which we shall return. This flexibility – if one prefers, this amorphousness – may prove, according to circumstances, a weakness or a strength. It means that anyone embarking on a personal-name project must reflect upon what the central purpose may be, and then upon what materials and what methods may best serve that purpose. It also means that students of the existing secondary works need unremittingly to attend to the varying purposes and approaches embodied therein. What it does not mean is that all approaches and all methodologies are equally valid; suggesting some criteria of validity will be a main aim of this paper.

In any branch of study, the first need is to recognize the nature of the material. This is especially true of onomastics, because names work differently from items of common vocabulary.[6] The denotation of a 'name' has by definition become divorced from its etymological meaning and focused upon some extra-linguistic entity. This is so whether or not a name-form remains lexically transparent: no one expects to find cattle wading the river at Oxford or Mr Smith toiling over an anvil. It is so even for seemingly transparent personal nicknames: in context, *Ginger*, for instance, denotes a particular man, not just anyone with hair of the relevant colour, and divorce from lexical origins is emphasized by the possibility of shortening the name, but never the common noun, to *Ginge*. The meaning of a name is always extra-linguistic, that of a personal name being primarily a social one.

Such understanding of the naming-process, grounded as it is in philosophy of language, has long been general among toponymists: no one would nowadays (I hope) dare to analyse any place-name system in isolation from the topography, the settlement history and the land use of the area concerned (for a treatment in the light of settlement history one may refer to a forthcoming paper by Dr Gillian Fellows-Jensen in *Naming, Society and Regional Identity*, edited by David Postles). With personal-naming too, this truth might seem self-evident. We all know, albeit without necessarily codifying such knowledge, that in our own society name-patterns replicate those of social groupings. Geographically, this is plain both for first-names and for family-names: a woman called 'Moira McLennan' could hardly not have Highland connections, and a man

---

6 See, e.g., A. Gardiner, *The Theory of Proper Names: A Controversial Essay*, Oxford, 1940; and recently, W.F.H. Nicolaisen, 'Onomastic onomastics', in J.-C. Boulanger, ed., *Actes du XVIᵉ Congrès international des sciences onomastiques*, Quebec, 1990, 3–14, esp. bibliography, 13–14. Cerebral separation of 'names' from 'words' has lately been demonstrated by psychiatrists examining a brain-damaged patient: see C. Semenza and M. Zettin, 'Evidence from aphasia for the role of proper names as pure referring expressions', *Nature*, 343, issue 6250 (7.xii.89), 678–79. Rules of linguistic development are now understood to apply to names less strictly than to common vocabulary: see, e.g., R. Lass's review of P.H. Reaney, *The Origin of English Surnames*, London, 1967, in *Foundations of Language*, 9, 1973, 392–402; F. Colman, 'Neutralization: on characterizing distinctions between Old English proper names and common nouns', *Leeds Studies in English*, new series 20, 1989, 249–67; and C. Clark, 'Towards a reassessment of "Anglo-Norman influence on English place-names" ', below 144–55.

called 'Owein Arwel Hughes' could be nothing but Welsh. Naming thus respects the 'national' or, rather, the linguistic and cultural divisions within the larger realm. Socially, demarcations are nowadays reflected mainly in first-naming, a sensitivity about surnames evinced by our Victorian forebears having seemingly gone by the board: Gary and Sharon are unlikely to live next door to Piers and Lucinda, and even less likely are the two couples to spend their holidays together. Twentieth-century first-naming shows chronological patterns too: Albert and Ethel may confidently be assumed to be at least two, more probably three, generations older than Gary and Sharon.

How far did similar patternings characterize the personal-naming of earlier times? *A priori*, all such contrast might be expected to have been even more marked in the Middle English period than at the present day. Travel was more difficult and dangerous, therefore less often undertaken; and other forms of communication too were scarcer and more expensive – by no means, however, so much so that travel and other modes of cultural interchange, literature included, can be discounted as vehicles of international onomastic influence. Medieval communities were, besides, more sharply stratified than our own, maintaining and reinforcing this stratification by arranged marriage. Tendencies to name children after relatives or after godparents chosen from within the parents' familial and social circle might further have restricted patterns of choice.[7] So, for regional and socio-economic distinctions to have been replicated by anthroponymical ones would not be unexpected. A socio-onomastic approach has always in fact governed the Leicester tradition of surname-history, developed as this has been under the aegis of the Department of English Local History. As yet, however, such approaches, commonsensed as well as academically justifiable though they are, are far from universal in historical anthroponymics. A main aim of this paper is to urge their wider adoption.

The Multiple Dimensions of Middle English Personal-Naming

Of the various dimensions of personal-naming that are accessible to historical analysis, locality is the most straightforward. Both in baptismal-naming and in family-naming, medieval English usages show contrasts so marked that, when pursued from this angle, socio-anthroponymics becomes virtually a branch of dialectology, offering evidence for the mapping of morphological procedures as well as of vocabulary, lexical as well as onomastic. For baptismal-naming, the geographical approach has recently been exemplified by, for instance, John Insley's study of some contrasts between Cumbrian name-fashions during the late eleventh and early twelfth centuries and contemporaneous ones in Colchester.[8] Much scope exists for further work: not only for noting local preferences (e.g., the currency in twelfth-century Canterbury of reflexes of Old English *Ælfhēah* and *Dunstān* and also of particular Continental forms such as *Hamon*)[9] but also for then endeavouring to explain these in prosopographical terms, as

---

7   See, e.g., P. Niles, 'Baptism and the naming of children in late medieval England', *Medieval Prosopography*, 3, i, Spring 1982, 95–107; and L. Haas, 'Social connections between parents and godparents in late medieval Yorkshire', *ibidem*, 10, i, Spring 1989, 1–21; also the paper by Dr Jeremy Boulton in Dr Postles' forthcoming volume.

8   J. Insley, 'Some aspects of regional variation in Early Middle English personal nomenclature', *Leeds Studies in English*, new series, 18, 1987, 183–92.

9   See, e.g., W. Urry, ed., *Canterbury under the Angevin Kings*, London, 1967: Index to Documents, s.nn. *Elfegus*, 459; *Dunstanus*, 457; *Hamo*, 464.

Insley has done for the Cumbrian 'comital' names like *Gospatric, Waltheof,* and so on.[10] Often, findings from regional surveys bear upon settlement history: for instance, the regional variations in the ratio of Middle English personal names of Anglo-Scandinavian etymology can hardly not reflect varying densities of Viking influence.[11] There is scope too for investigating the impact, upon east coast ports especially, of the Low-German trading contacts frequent during the later Middle Ages.[12] As for the incidence and the implications of Welsh personal-naming in the Marches and of Celtic naming in Cumbria, these remain largely unexplored.[13] Necessarily, analogous regional differences appear also in patronymic and metronymic by-naming, and so in the family-names thence derived.[14] In general, these aspects of by-naming and family-naming have so far been better served than those of baptismal-naming, in so far as the English Surnames Series has over the last two decades been publishing regional investigations carried out on a larger scale than any baptismal-name survey so far made and also in greater detail. Many regional differences have become clear, among them the southern preference for asyndetic patronyms and for ones formed in *-s*, by contrast with the typical northern use of *-son*.[15] Differing occupational and topographical by-name vocabularies throw light on general dialect variation. Analysis of toponymical by-names helps to document the migration patterns underlying the growth of major towns.[16] As the range of examples cited shows, a geographically based study need not adopt any set format or follow any preordained mode of approach, the sole requirement being for the locality – or, perhaps preferably, localities – to be so chosen that any contrasts or affinities detected may reasonably be invested with historical, cultural or social significance. Materials and methodology must, besides, be equal to setting in a true perspective whatever distinctive features may be found. Sadly, these requirements are at present not always met: thus the focusing of a recent thesis upon a single county, to the virtual exclusion even of comparison with all contiguous ones, precluded recognition of the full regional range of the *-en* form of patronymic and metronymic suffix.[17]

At first glance, the chronological dimension of personal-naming might be supposed

[10] See J. Insley, 'Aspects', 183–90; cf. C. Clark, '*Willemus rex? vel alius Willelmus?*', below 280–98.

[11] See, e.g., J. Insley, 'Regional variation in Scandinavian personal nomenclature in England', *Nomina*, 3, 1979, 52–60; C. Clark, 'Early personal names of King's Lynn, I', below 241–57, esp. 245–50 and notes thereto, and *eadem*, 'English personal names ca.650–1300', *Medieval Prosopography*, 8, i, Spring 1987, 31–60, with references in notes thereto.

[12] For some tentative suggestions on these lines, see C. Clark, 'King's Lynn, I', below 250–55 and 'King's Lynn, II', below 258–79, esp. 272, 274–75, 277–79.

[13] See, however, J. Insley, 'Aspects'; and also G. Fellows Jensen, *Scandinavian Settlement Names in the North-West*, Copenhagen, 1985, 305–06, 319–21.

[14] See, e.g., C. Clark, 'English personal names', 45 and n. 78; and, more particularly, R. McKinley, *Oxon.*, 238–46, *Lancs.*, 334–37, and *Sussex*, 306–12.

[15] See R. McKinley, *History*, 102–05, 111–14, 118–19, and *idem, Sussex*, 318–23, 325–34.

[16] Amongst the many studies in this field, the methodological critique by Peter McClure may be singled out: 'Patterns of migration in the late Middle Ages: the evidence of English place-name surnames', *Economic History Review*, 32, 1979, 167–82.

[17] I. Hjertstedt, *Middle English Nicknames in the Lay Subsidy Rolls for Warwickshire*, Acta Universitatis Upsaliensis: Studia Anglistica Upsaliensia 63, Uppsala, 1987, 28–31; cf. R. McKinley, *Oxon.* [not listed in Hjertstedt's bibliography], 219–20.

equally straightforward. It has long been recognized that between the late eleventh and the mid-thirteenth centuries English baptismal-naming styles were revolutionized[18] and, equally, that between the twelfth and the mid-seventeenth centuries what had begun as sporadic *ad hoc* by-naming evolved into universal fixed family-naming.[19] As soon, however, as either of these developments is scrutinized, what becomes – inconveniently or excitingly, according to taste – clear is that its genesis and unfolding were inextricably entwined, indeed entangled, with social circumstances, so much so that upon consideration the social dimension must be acknowledged to precede the chronological one.

Unfortunately, this social dimension, acknowledged though it has been in some quarters for sixty years and more,[20] is still sometimes slighted. Nor is the concept a simple one; for it involves not only familial and genealogical relationships but socioeconomic stratification, with all the latter's multifarious subdivisions into, for instance, occupational and educational groupings and, as Dr Boulton points out in his contribution to Dr Postles' forthcoming volume, after the Reformation into religious ones as well. Then there is the major category of gender.

In name-study, gender involves contrasts that may be perceived either as banal or else as subtle, complex and revelatory. All our West-European traditions use baptismal-name vocabularies that distinguish the sexes: 'cross-naming' is felt as hardly less bizarre than cross-dressing. Comparison between women's names and men's can thus focus only on general types of name, not on individual items; but this is in practice no great handicap, in so far as baptismal-name analysis often in any case proceeds in terms of name-type rather than of particular item. The medievalist contemplating such a topic is, on the other hand, faced with a true problem, that of seldom finding extant records of any sort at all in which women's names amount to even so much as a tenth of the total, let alone to the half that they constituted in everyday life.[21] This makes comparing women's names with men's, even in terms of name-type, a tricky business and no less so because most of the women recorded were widows and so might have been, on average, older than the men listed alongside them. Various generalizations have nevertheless been ventured: medieval naming of women is, for instance, often asserted to have been more varied than that of men, and sometimes the evidence put forward for this looks persuasive, as with Alexander Rumble's list of names current in medieval Winchester, showing items not just seemingly rare (a point which the paucity of record makes it hard to check) but oddly formed, in styles finding no counterparts among masculine forms.[22] Sometimes, too, there seems to be a higher incidence of

---

[18] See, e.g., C. Clark, 'English personal names', 40–43 with references thereto, and '*Willelmus*', *passim*.

[19] See R. McKinley, *History*, 25–39, 47–49, together with the relevant chapters in the individual volumes of the English Surnames Series.

[20] See, e.g., A.H. Smith, 'Early northern nicknames and surnames', *Saga-Book of the Viking Society for Northern Research*, 11, 1928–36, 30–60.

[21] Even where statistical manipulation of the asymmetrical evidence might be feasible, its application would at present be limited by the inexperience in such matters not only of the investigators but also of the readership envisaged.

[22] A.R. Rumble, 'The personal-name material', in D. Keane *et al.*, eds., *Survey of Medieval Winchester*, Winchester Studies, 2, Oxford, 1985, (ii), 1405–11, esp. 1406–07; cf. J.A. Raftis, *A Small Town in Late Medieval England: Godmanchester 1278–1400*, Toronto, 1982, 153–54.

saints' names among those borne by women.[23] In so far as not illusory,[24] such findings imply in the medieval mind a concept of feminity as at once more devout and more frivolous than masculinity. Unquestionably, the ways in which family-naming gradually took shape reflect patriarchal views of society.

Matters of gender also encompass topics more specific, yet at the same time wider, such as how far analysing name-stocks on these lines might serve to illuminate settlement history. Some dozen years ago I myself published a study (in which I had been greatly encouraged by an historian friend) that was aimed at discovering how far such analysis might help with determining whether or not the Norman settlement had involved equal numbers of men and of women – a question of some pertinence for linguistic history.[25] Findings suggested that, even with allowance for the possibly higher average age of the women named, there appeared to have been a time lag of roughly a generation between the rate at which Continental-style baptismal names for women were adopted among the native population and the more rapid spread of ones for men: a time lag which it seems not unreasonable to ascribe, at least provisionally, to a low proportion of women, and so of feminine name-models, among the first and major wave of settlers arriving in the aftermath of the Conquest. Attempts at a companion-piece that would use similar evidence as an indirect clue to the likely proportion of women among the Viking settlers of two centuries earlier have so far remained inconclusive, partly because of the general inadequacy of the records and, in particular, because all so grossly postdate the events concerned; but the name-patterns observed, for what they are worth, seem to suggest that the Scandinavian feminine forms adopted into the English name-stock were far fewer than the masculine ones.[26]

Attempts at investigating the socio-economic stratification of early medieval name-fashions tend likewise to founder on inadequacy of evidence. For the whole pre-Conquest period, names not only of peasants but of townspeople too are so sparsely preserved as to put their general character beyond investigation.[27] In the twelfth century, however, a marked increase in survival of relevant records happens to coincide with the already mentioned revolution in styles of English baptismal-naming. This revolution began from a clear and new socio-economic contrast, with the immigrant nobles and gentry all bearing baptismal names of Continental type, commonly supplemented by by-names (often toponymics referring either to Continental domains or to newly acquired English ones), whereas the peasants and the humbler townsfolk continued for a time to use traditional English and Anglo-Scandinavian forms and to supplement these only sporadically by by-names, such of the latter as do appear being mostly occupational or patronymic, seldom toponymical. In by-naming, these social contrasts did, as we have noted, persist into the later Middle Ages. With baptismal-naming, on the other hand, the original contrast soon blurred and faded, as more and more English people of the humbler sorts came to give their children names originally associated with immigrant gentry; by the mid-thirteenth century hardly any baptismal

---

[23] See, e.g., C. Clark, 'King's Lynn I', below 255 with references in the notes thereto.

[24] See, however, the paper contributed to Dr Postles' forthcoming volume by Dr Richard Smith.

[25] C. Clark, 'Women's names in post-Conquest England: observations and speculations', below 117–43.

[26] See, e.g., C. Clark, 'Clark's First Three Laws of Applied Anthroponymics', above 77–83, esp. 82–83, and 'King's Lynn I', below 256–57.

[27] See, e.g., D.A.E. Pelteret, 'Two Old English lists of serfs', *Mediaeval Studies*, 48, 1986, 470–513.

names of pre-Conquest type remained current.[28] That need not, of course, mean that no social variation in baptismal naming any longer obtained; simply that newer and subtler forms of it may wait to be uncovered.

Socially-Stratified Name-Analysis: An Experimental Essay

Even for the later medieval period, from which records survive in profusion, imbalance of sample sizes continues to bedevil analysis, as regards not only gender but social status too. In the latter context, problems arise not simply from the notorious under-recording of the humbler people[29] but from the population structure itself. Society consisted of a socio-economic pyramid with a few rich and powerful people at its apex and each descending layer larger than the one above. This is no theoretical construct, but a straightforward description of, for instance, the socio-economic distribution seen in records such as lay subsidy rolls, where – as Ekwall explained in his exemplary edition of two London rolls datable respectively c.1292 and 1319 – each main stage of decrease in liability corresponds with an increase in the number of those liable (and that is without taking account of the proletarian mass exempt through poverty).[30] There are admittedly flaws in the reasoning; for, as Ekwall pointed out, some men known from other sources to have been leading merchants figure in the rolls with unexpectedly low liabilities, perhaps because the day of assessment had happened to catch them with stock sold out but payment not yet received.[31] For all that, the tax assessments recorded might be hoped by and large to correlate with relative levels of prosperity and so to offer scope for onomastic comparison between burgesses of contrasting economic status.

For the London of c.1292, the most convenient contrast seems to be that between the men assessed at the bottom rate of 2s. (some 145 individuals, once the few women taxpayers have been eliminated) and the whole body of those assessed at £2 and over (nearly 70, all men). The justification for setting the latter cut-off point at £2 is that, as Ekwall noted, down to that level almost all those listed are known from other records as major merchants, whereas from there downwards the occupational range broadens, with the group on the bottom rate comprising mainly small craftsmen and traders such as bakers, cooks, hatters, and so on.[32] The economic contrast between the groups chosen seems substantial: in present-day terms (for what these may be worth) perhaps the equivalent to that between possessing, say, £5,000 worth of household goods,

---

[28] See, e.g., C. Clark, 'English personal names', 40–43, and *'Willelmus', passim*, with references there given, esp. n. 10.

[29] See comments by D. Postles and others elsewhere in Dr Postles' forthcoming volume.

[30] E. Ekwall, ed., *Two Early London Lay Subsidy Rolls*, Acta Regiae Societatis Humaniorum Litterarum Lundensis 48, Lund, 1951, 98–111. The taxes known as 'lay subsidies' were levied on moveable property (see J.F. Willard, *Parliamentary Taxes of Personal Property 1290–1334*, Cambridge, Mass., 1934), and the rolls list only heads of households. The 1319 roll edited by Ekwall represents, it should be noted, an original return, not an Exchequer copy (E. Ekwall, *Subsidy Rolls*, 8); for dangers attendant on use of the latter, see P. McClure, 'Lay subsidy rolls and dialect phonology', in F. Sandgren, ed., *Otium et Negotium: Studies in Onomatology and Library Science presented to Olof von Feilitzen* [Acta Bibliothecae Regiae Stockholmiensis 16, Stockholm 1973], 188–94; also R. McKinley, *Sussex*, 22, 59, 92–93.

[31] For an attempted evasion, see E. Ekwall, *Subsidy Rolls*, 91–92, 239, 313.

[32] *Op. cit.*, 99–102.

stock-in-trade and cash-in-hand and having £100,000 or more. By medieval standards, families so disparately endowed would scarcely have been intermarriageable; and intermarriage, as well as being a classic indicator of shared social status, bears crucially on naming-patterns. On the other hand, the social structure of medieval London was unstable: not only is a mercantile career necessarily one open to enterprise, with consequent rises and falls of individuals, but the city was a magnet to immigrants, who flocked in not only from almost all the English provinces but even from as far afield as north Italy.[33] *A priori*, then, some onomastic contrast between samples is predictable but, at the same time, it may be predicted to be relative rather than absolute. For 1319, the two extreme groups have likewise been chosen, though in awareness that they equate only imperfectly with those representing the earlier roll: *viz.*, the approximately 70 men assessed at £2 and over (the ceiling being this time, however, not £8 but £40) and the 116 on the two bottom rates of 6½d. and 6¾d. What makes correlation with the earlier samples even less exact is that in 1319 the value of moveable goods represented by the lowest assessment was only half a mark (6s. 8d.) instead of the three-quarters deduced for c.1292.[34] Fixing the cut-off point at 6¾d. and thereby eliminating those assessed marginally more highly at 7d. and upwards is arbitrary and due mainly to desire to limit the size of the sample.

To begin with by-naming: in the roll for 1319 – that for which the samples show the wider economic contrast – all the main types of by-name (patronymic; occupational; toponymical, *viz.*, phrases in *atte*; and characteristic, *viz.*, nicknames) are represented in both samples, but in differing proportions.[35] The key contrast seems to lie in frequency of occupational forms (at this date not necessarily referring to the trade actually followed[36]): among the men lowest assessed, these account for some 40 per cent of by-names found; but, among those highest assessed, for under ten per cent. The other contrasts look relatively minor: 40 per cent of toponymical forms among the lowest assessed as against 50 per cent among the highest (no attempt has been made to ascertain whether there might be any difference in average distance of, possibly ancestral, migration), 16 per cent as against 25 per cent for apparent 'nickname' forms of various types and origins, and four per cent as against eight per cent for patronymics. In keeping with the generalization voiced at the outset concerning urban name-fashions, phrases in *atte* are rare, although occasionally found in both samples; and so likewise are they in the roll of c.1292. For toponymical forms too, both rolls show roughly similar patterns, although in the earlier samples, where the economic contrast is seemingly less, the onomastic one is somewhat more marked, with 38 per cent among the lowest assessed group and 54 per cent among the highest. With patronyms too, the onomastic contrast is greater in the earlier roll, with seven per cent among the lowest assessed but 21 per cent among the highest, as against the mere four per cent difference in 1319. With 'nickname' forms, on the other hand, the roll of c.1292 has virtually no contrast between the samples, showing roughly 20 per cent all round, as against the nine per cent difference of a generation later. For what was taken as the key

---

[33] *Op. cit.*, 43–71; also E. Ekwall, *Studies on the Population of Medieval London*, Stockholm, 1956, *passim*.

[34] E. Ekwall, *Subsidy Rolls*, 92, 102–04, cf. 98–99 and 104–05.

[35] The figures to be offered do not always 'add up': this is because it seemed wise to round them off so as to present a clear outline rather than a fuzz of detail; cf. the apologia for such procedure made in my paper, 'Historical linguistics – linguistic archaeology', above 92–99, esp. 95–96.

[36] E. Ekwall, *Subsidy Rolls*, 38.

distribution, that of occupational forms, the earlier roll, with 36 per cent among the lowest assessed compared with three per cent among the highest, again follows a pattern similar to that in the later one. The overall impression looks fairly compatible with what was expected *a priori*, that is, a basically homogeneous system but one with some variations of emphasis. If there is any chronological trend, it would seem to be towards flattening of contrasts; but, unless similar comparison could be made over a longer time-scale, no firm assertion of any kind would be permissible.

Baptismal-naming patterns prove subtler. For both levels of prosperity at both dates, the name-stock represented remains almost constant, despite a few shifts in relative frequency over time.[37] How far, then, might it be tenable to interpret in socio-economic terms such minor variations as do appear between each pair of contemporaneous samples? Given the exiguity of these samples, no name borne by fewer than one to two per cent of the population concerned could be expected to figure there otherwise than at random; and some names in the stocks concerned, not always ones unusual in themselves, in fact appear only once in nearly 800 instances (c.1292) or even in over 1,700 (1319), and about the social distributions of these nothing can therefore be said. A further complication is that, because the larger strata of the population were the less affluent ones, a rare name that was in truth evenly favoured might happen to enjoy extant record only among humbler folk, and thus misleadingly appear to be plebeian. Worse than that: investigation reveals that not even positive recording only in the smaller sample of each pair, *viz.*, the higher assessed one, need be socially conclusive; for, although the pilot survey shows *Hamon*, for instance, as seemingly peculiar to the highest strata, with one instance there in c.1292 and three in 1319, a check through the full record produces for the latter date four additional bearers of the name, one assessed at 5s., one at 3s. 4d. and two at only 10d. So, to determine how far, if at all, distributions of the rare names might have correlated with socio-economic stratification would require, not a sampling like the present one, not even complete analysis of one extensive source, but a survey as wide as extant records of all kinds would allow: a sort of exercise for which the lay subsidy rolls, despite their notoriously incomplete socio-economic coverage and even despite the no less notorious textual and therefore also dialectal and onomastic unreliability of the Exchequer copies, might, because of the systematic (if occasionally misleading) indications that they give of relative prosperity, afford a handy basic framework. Indeed, given the widespread use made of this type of record, it seems odd that so little attempt has yet been made to exploit the socio-economic information built into it.[38]

As for the most frequent baptismal names, their distribution may be more accessible but are none the less for that puzzling in some details. For both dates, the most frequent names are, with some slight shifts of frequency and consequent minor ones of order: *John*, *William*, *Robert*, *Richard*, *Thomas* and *Walter*. As wholes, the two corpora show *John* (which in c.1292 represents one instance in five and a half and in 1319 has risen to one in four), *Richard* (one in 14 rising to one in 11), and *Thomas* (one in 18 rising to one in 16) as apparently gaining popularity, while *William* (roughly one in seven) and *Walter* (one in 21 or 22) remained stable, and *Robert* (one in 12½ falling to one in 14) lost a little ground. These consolidated figures do, however, mask internal variations. For c.1292 the samples show the group lowest assessed – perhaps on average younger –

---

[37] *Op. cit.*, 34–37, the lists not being broken down on either etymological or socio-onomastic principles.

[38] For surnames, McKinley has begun analysis on these lines in, e.g., *Sussex*, 13–14.

as in some ways more representative of long-term trends, with *John* having already ousted *William* from the top place that it still held amongst those highest assessed. In 1319, *John*, by then the leading name among both groups, again appeared as more strongly favoured among the lowest assessed, among whom the decline of *Robert* was also more marked. This might seem to call in question the supposed general principle that name-fashions start among the great and then get taken up by humbler folk a generation or two later,[39] for here the less well-off seem to be leading the way. With *Walter*, despite the appearance of stability given by the overall statistics, the detail is harder to interpret: in c.1292 this name, sixth overall, was among the highest assessed a poor sixth, at one in 34 way below *Thomas* (one in 14), whereas among the lowest assessed it stood fifth (at one in 16) and so ahead of *Thomas*; by 1319, both trends had accentuated, with *Walter* declining among the highest assessed to an even poorer sixth (one in 74), while rising among the lowest assessed to fourth (one in 14½) and so displacing *Robert* (one in 16½) – a pattern wholly unlike that shown by *John*. Perhaps some of the inconclusiveness, indeed seeming contradiction, derives from the choice of too narrow a basis that excludes, on the one hand, the feudal nobility and, on the other, the urban poor as well as the peasantry. To determine whether the middling and the upper ranks of urban society did or did not constitute a cultural unity and, if not, what the likely basis of sub-grouping might have been would make a valuable contribution to social as well as to onomastic history.

Personal Identity and its Bearing on Name-Studies

In order to make socio-economic sense of medieval personal-name records, it is – happily – unnecessary to become embroiled in statistics. The essential thing about any and every personal name, at whatsoever date and in whatsoever society current, is that, within its own proper context, it signifies one unique individual. Names are in practice often duplicated; but such accidents in no way impugn the principle that each instance is necessarily intended to specify one, and only one, individual. That name-forms preserved in medieval administrative documents did, in context, perform this function we must assume, for rent collectors and tax gatherers were no less exigent then than now.

'Social' definition applies no less pertinently to individuals than to groups; and, even for the medieval period, information about individuals can often be found, at least as far as occupation and socio-economic standing are concerned and often for family connections as well. A main reason why Ekwall's edition of the two London subsidy rolls remains, almost 40 years on, so splendid an achievement is that, within the means at his disposal, Ekwall strove to document as fully as possible as many as possible of the taxpayers listed; for such identifications – familial, occupational, residential, and socio-economic – form the essential background to any personal-name study. With occupational by-names, as Ekwall showed, identifying the trades actually followed enables some estimate to be made as to how far such names had become hereditary.[40] With nickname-forms, identification of their bearers may throw light upon such as might perhaps have been occupational: in a piece of work composed *pari passu* with

---

[39] See, e.g., C. Clark, '*Willelmus*', *passim* and references there given.
[40] See n. 36 above.

this paper, noting the generally low economic status of some early bearers of 'Shake-speare' or 'pickpocket' names has seemed to help elucidate the aetiology as well as the meaning of such forms.[41]

Sadly, some studies ostensibly dealing with medieval England personal-naming, and in particular some recent theses emanating from departments of English language and literature, still fail to follow Ekwall's example. Some students have disregarded the possible, and essential, identification of the individuals whose names are treated; and, through disregarding that, have at least partly failed in their professed aim. Such obtuseness often seems linked with a conjoint focus upon some non-onomastic topic, such as dialectology or etymology, that distracts attention from the nature of the source material. As Peter McClure put it ten years ago, in one of the most perceptive pieces ever written about the study of medieval personal names:

> 'If one dimension of information is chiefly lacking in the comparative methods used in [these] studies of ME bynames, it is that of local and biographical history. The name is treated as "word" rather than "person", as a manifestation of linguistic form rather than of social life.'[42]

Unhappily, that lesson has not yet been taken universally to heart, and theses continue to appear in which, from a lexical point of view, names are exhaustively annotated yet next to no account is taken of social, let alone prosopographical, background.[43]

Yet, to study in purely lexical and etymological terms a form recorded as a name, and sometimes solely so, may be to study something that never, and certainly not in the given context, existed at all. We all know – provided that we give the matter a moment's thought – that our own usage often involves specifically onomastic forms and meanings: *Baldy* and *Shorty*, for instance, exist only as nicknames; *Lofty*, although current also as a common adjective, has in that rôle a different range of applications, for, although a tower or a mountain can in a literal sense be 'lofty', a man cannot (his manner might, it is true, be so described, but as far as nickname-usage is concerned that is beside the point). Moreover, the 'meaning' of any name soon ceases to be either etymological or lexical, so that, for instance, the message carried by a medieval by-name of the *atte bridge* type came, as already observed, less and less to concern its bearer's address and more and more to imply origin with little claim to distinctiveness other than that of possessing a settled home (humble people, but still a good cut above squatters and landless labourers). The consequent illegitimacy, indeed futility, of anno-tating name-material in predominantly lexical terms is sometimes underlined by an obvious though barely acknowledged presence in the corpora under scrutiny of forms – such as, for instance, *Corbet* or *Peverel* – identical with names that ever since the Conquest had been associated with particular dynasties of the Anglo-Norman

---

[41] '*Alfordruncen, Brenebrec, Cattesnese*: studies on some early twelfth-century bynames', to appear in D. Postles, ed., *Names, Time and Place*.

[42] P. McClure, 'The interpretation of Middle English nicknames' [review article of J. Jönsjö, *Studies on Middle English Nicknames: I – Compounds*, Lund, 1979], *Nomina*, 5, 1981, 95–104, esp. 101; cf. G. Fellows Jensen's corresponding review article, 'On the study of Middle English by-names', *Namn och Bygd*, 68, 1980, 102–15, esp. 114–15; and the present writer's review in *English Studies*, 63, 1982, 168–70.

[43] E.g., the bibliography in I. Hjertstedt, *Nicknames* (cf. n. 17 above), omits this seminal article of McClure's, along with all other reviews of Jönsjö's work; cf. the comment on S. Carlsson, *Local Bynames*, in n. 3 above.

nobility.[44] Treating a name as though it were a 'word' becomes especially risky when the form happens to be one long handed down among descendants of foreign immigrants.

The name *Peverel* may serve as text. It is all very well to gloss this as a diminutive of Old North French *peivre* 'pepper', and to cite Tengvik's and Reaney's speculations as to what metaphor might have underlain its nickname use; but it gets no one very far. The form *Peverel* needs to be recognized as difficult in itself. True, the standard Latinization as *Piperellus* seems to prove contemporary interpretation of the name-form as a diminutive of the word for 'pepper', as Latinized *piper*, in a Norman form *peivre*.[45] Otherwise than as a personal by-name, however, the diminutive *pev(e)rel* and its reflexes are barely recorded, with the principal Old French dictionaries mustering between them only a single citation and that in a culinary context where the sense seems to be 'spicy sauce'.[46] By what transference of sense the same form came to figure as a personal nickname we may never know. It is not, of course, unknown for a gourmet or a glutton to be labelled by the name of his or her favourite dainty;[47] but, in default of evidence, such a motivation cannot just be assumed. We well know what sort of character *peppery* denotes in Modern English, and Reaney suggested a similar sense here.[48] We also know what *spicy* means when applied to discourse. Modern French – perhaps relevant, perhaps not – offers a further range of senses: in slang uses recorded from the eighteenth century on diminutives of *poivre* such as *poivret* and *poivrot*, mean 'drunkard' and the quasi-participial *poivré* means 'dissolute' more generally.[49] I am far

---

44 I. Hjertstedt, *Nicknames*, 91 (where the many potential connotations of a 'raven' metaphor are barely touched on: frequent failure to appreciate metaphor is noted by Insley in his review in *Studia Neophilologica*, 62, 1990, 115–19, esp. 117–18), 155. Fellows-Jensen has already re-marked how much the 'niggardly' treatment accorded here to the development of family-naming has hindered, in particular, the interpretation of forms of Old French origin: see her review in *Namn och Bygd*, 76, 1988, 220–23, esp. 221. For the Corbet family, see, e.g., I.J. Sanders, *English Baronies: A Study of their Origins and Descent*, Oxford, 1960, 29, 85, 90; and, for the group of families associated with the name *Peverel*, ibid., 19–20, 120, 151.

45 See e.g., O. von Feilitzen, 'The personal names and bynames of the Winton Domesday', in M. Biddle *et al.*, *Winchester in the Early Middle Ages*, Winchester Studies 1, Oxford, 1976, 143–229, esp. 215; cf. E. Ekwall, *Subsidy Rolls*, 162.

46 F. Godefroy, *Dictionnaire de l'ancienne langue française et de tous ses dialectes du IXᵉ au XVᵉ siècle*, 5 Paris, 1889, s.vv. *pevree*, *pevrel* 'poivrade' (in a culinary sense); A. Tobler and E. Lommatzsch, *Altfranzösisches Wörterbuch*, 7, Wiesbaden, 1969, refers back to Godefroy, trans-lating as 'Pfefferbrühe'; L.W. Stone *et al.*, *Anglo-Norman Dictionary*, 5, London, 1988, lists *peivere* and *pevree* but not *pevrel*.

47 See, e.g., C. Clark, 'Nickname-creation: some sources of evidence, "naive" memoirs especially', below 351–61, esp. 360.

48 P.H. Reaney, *A Dictionary of British Surnames*, 2nd edn rev. R.M. Wilson, London, 1976, 271, s.n. *Peverall*.

49 For some potentially relevant senses (all, of course, secondary ones, mostly current only in low slang), see, e.g., *Le Grand Larousse de la langue française*, 5 Paris, 1976, s.vv. *poivrade* 'beuverie', *poivre* 'obscénité; maladie vénérienne', *poivré* 'licencieux, atteint d'une maladie vénérienne', *poivrer* 'rendre licencieux; communiquer une maladie vénérienne (à quelqu'un)', *se poivrer* 'attraper une maladie vénérienne', *poivrot* 'ivrogne', *se poivroter* 'se soûler'. See also, under the same lemmata: *Le Grand Robert de la langue française*, 2nd edn, 7, Paris, 1985; *Trésor de la langue française: dictionnaire de la langue du XIXᵉ et du XXᵉ siècle (1789–1960)*, 13, Paris, 1988, which adds 'syphilis' s.v. *poivrade*, and also lists *poivrier* 'ivrogne' and *poivrière* 'prostituée'; M. Leitner and J.R. Lanen, *Dictionary of French and English Slang*, London, 1965; and J. Cellard and A. Rey, *Dictionnaire du français non conventionnel*, Paris, 1980.

indeed from suggesting any such senses to have been current six or seven centuries before their earliest extant record, but cite them purely as indications of what such a term might imply. If pressed, I might side with Reaney in suspecting behind the nickname *Peverel* moral connotations of some kind (whether of quick temper, of drunkenness, or of something not yet remarked) rather than the physical and visual ones proposed by Tengvik.

All that is, however, by the way: a self-indulgent excursus into entertaining but inconclusive speculations. *Peverel* is not an 'English' nickname: it was coined in a French-speaking milieu and probably on French soil. Its etymology and its meaning (whatever the latter may have been) have nothing in the world to do with the English language.[50] Exploring the semantic possibilities has nevertheless been salutary, not least because it has issued a warning (if warning still be needed) against pinning one's faith on Tengvik (his monograph is, as von Feilitzen pointed out in detail half a century ago,[51] so inadequate that it is hard to know to what to ascribe the authority that it seemingly continues to hold in anthroponymical mythology).

The present interest of the by-name *Peverel*, irrelevant though it is to English nicknaming, is that its occurrences bear upon social stratification in Middle English name-patterns. Instances found in fourteenth-century tax rolls raise questions as to the identity and status of the persons concerned. Were any, or all, of them descended from the post-Conquest nobles of that name? Or were some, or all, from families of lower degree that happened to share the same by-name? If the latter, were the families concerned purely English ones that had, for some reason as yet undetermined, become known by a name originally proper to immigrant nobles?[52] Or had they perhaps stemmed from immigrant merchants?[53] Records such as lay subsidy rolls unfortunately offer next to no background information about those listed; but, as already noted, one piece of information they must give about each and every individual: his or her tax assessment. That assessment, in so far as indicating whether the name-bearer were seriously rich or just barely taxable, might well suggest where to start looking for possible family connections; but, unaccountably, the sorts of study in question systematically omit this information, so that the reader has no means (short of seeking out the original documents) of knowing to what strata of society the Peverels listed, or any other bearers of possibly aristocratic names, should be assigned.

Personal-name studies ought properly to be conducted, not just in terms of socio-economic stratification, which, fundamental though it is, makes a fairly blunt instrument of dissection, but as far as possible in those of prosopography, with its sharper cutting edge. It is no accident that over the last two decades some of the most valuable work on medieval personal-naming has been carried out by interdisciplinary teams led by scholars who are primarily historians, not linguists.[54] For it is often the historian

---

[50] A similar point was made in 1980 by Klaus Foster in his review (*Nomina*, 4, 100–01) of P. Erlebach, *Die zusammengesetzten englischen Zunamen französischer Herkunft*, Heidelberg, 1979: a work that fails not only to take account of social and familial context but also to cite any primary source whatsoever.

[51] O. von Feilitzen, 'Notes on Old English bynames', *Namn och Bygd*, 27, 1939, 116–30.

[52] McKinley has noted the occasional bearing by bondmen and by others humble in station of by-names otherwise associated with families of nobility or gentry (*Oxon.*, 204–06; cf. *Sussex*, 92–93); by what process of transference this came about remains to be determined.

[53] See, e.g., C. Clark, 'Certains éléments français de l'anthroponymie anglaise du Moyen Age', above 84–91.

[54] A chief instance of this approach involves the Münster-Freiburg teams of prosopographical and

who suspects, indeed hopes, that acquiring onomastic information about some enigmatic personage may throw light upon his or her geographical origins or family background.[55] It is therefore by working within that sort of framework that we, as anthroponymists, can be most effective as members of the wider scholarly community. More than that: unless we do take heed, as far as evidence permits, of the human attachments of each personal name that we study, we cannot ply even our own trade adequately.

The traffic between prosopography and anthroponymics is a two-way one, because identifying a name-bearer sometimes resolves at a stroke ambiguities previously thought to envelop the name. One recent name repertory offers under the heading *Louote* (referred to OFr *louet* 'wolf-cub') a reference to an early fourteenth-century 'John de Bermyngeham, Earl of Loueth'.[56] The compiler, although noting that this example 'seems to suggest local origin', never takes the next step in investigating any individual given a title of nobility, that of consulting Cokayne's *Complete Peerage*: an unfortunate oversight, because this would in a twinkling have revealed the man in question as the first and only holder of the Irish earldom of Louth and thus irrelevant, even as a footnote, to the thesis concerned.[57] This problem could be thus instantaneously resolved because the man involved was a noble, and therefore Cokayne *et alii* had already done the work. With someone of lower degree, identification might be not only time-consuming but daunting in its archival complexity. The conclusion to draw from that is not, however, that such problems should be glossed over but rather that personal-name projects must be designed on a scale permitting of full, multidimensional exploration of the material.

onomastic researchers: see, e.g., Karl Schmid, 'Überlieferung und Eigenart mittelalterlicher Personenbezeichnung', in *Prosopographie als Sozialgeschichte? Methoden personengeschichtlicher Erforschung des Mittelalters*, Munich, 1978, 5–13; for an account in English, see J. Gerchow, 'Societas et fraternitas', *Nomina*, 12, 1988–89, 153–71, and especially the bibliography on 167–71.

55 See e.g., Schmid's paper cited in n. 54, esp. 7 ('Grundlage aller Prosopographie ist daher die Namenforschung'); cf. C. Clark, 'English personal names', *passim*.

56 I. Hjertstedt, *Nicknames*, 137; the reference was, moreover, taken not from the original text but from the anglicized calendar, E. Stokes and L. Drucker, eds, *Warwickshire Feet of Fines*, 2, Publications of the Dugdale Society, 15, 1939, 104, item 1518.

57 G.E. C[okayne] *et al.*, *The Complete Peerage of England, &c.*, 13 vols in 14, London, 1910–59, viii, 171.

ESSAYS IN ONOMASTICS

_____

POST-CONQUEST ENGLAND:
GENERAL STUDIES

10

Women's Names in Post-Conquest England:
Observations and Speculations

'Sed unus homo Wihenoc amauit quandam feminam in illa terra & duxit eam & postea tenuit ille istam terram . . .': so, with a rare romantic touch, Domesday Book on a tenant at South Pickenham in Norfolk.[1] There is, however, nothing at all romantic in a modern wish to know more about the Norman settlers' marriages, on which must have hung so much of the transmission of language and of culture in the post-Conquest period. By the mid-twelfth century not only did many of the aristocracy know some English,[2] but a few of them were even beginning to identify with the Anglo-Saxon past.[3] So far, however, the background and the mechanism of this cultural shift remain little known: was it connected with the settlers' patterns of marriage?

Mixed marriages certainly took place. For instance, several of the twelfth-century Anglo-Latin chroniclers – to name one group involved in recording culture if not in transmitting it – evidently sprang from such unions. William of Malmesbury makes his origins clear when he protests that in matters of national rivalry he is impartial, 'quia

It is a pleasure to record how much this paper owes to Professor Giles Constable, who not only offered the hypothesis on which it is based but also gave great help with the marshalling of the evidence. Without his prompting it would never have been begun, and only his own generosity prevents his name from appearing at its head.

1 *Domesday Book seu Liber Censualis Willelmi Primi Regis Angliae, &c.*, 4 vols. (London, 1783–1816), 2: fol. 232. Cf. the conflicting interpretations in *VCH Norfolk*, 2: 3, 16: as 'unus homo Wihenoc' can hardly denote Wihenoc himself, a major landholder in the district before the Breton forfeiture, it seems best to take *Wihenoc* as an uninflected genitive and translate 'a certain man of Wihenoc's'. The estate is assessed at three shillings.

2 See especially William Rothwell, 'The Role of French in Thirteenth-Century England', *Bulletin of the John Rylands Library* 58 (1975–76), 445–66, esp. 448–9, 455, and the still-valuable paper by G.E. Woodbine, 'The Language of English Law', *Speculum* 18 (1943), 395–436. See also Albert C. Baugh, *A History of the English Language*, 2nd ed. (London, 1959), chapters 5 and 6, esp. pp. 133–5, 141–6; and for some specialist points of view: Percy van Dyke Shelly, *English and French in England 1066–1100* (Philadelphia, 1921); M.D. Legge, 'Anglo-Norman and the Historian', *History*, n.s. 26 (1941), 163–75; eadem, *The Significance of Anglo-Norman*, Inaugural Lecture (Edinburgh, 1968); R.M. Wilson, 'English and French in England 1100–1300', *History*, n.s. 28 (1943), 37–60. The contribution by R. Berndt, 'The Linguistic Situation in England from the Norman Conquest to the Loss of Normandy', *Philologica Pragensia* 8 (1965), 145–63, is thin and unilluminating.

3 See Ralph Davis, *The Normans and their Myth* (London, 1976), pp. 122–32, and also Richard Southern, 'England's First Entry into Europe', in *Medieval Humanism and Other Studies* (Oxford, 1970), pp. 154–5. Both point to Gaimar's *L'Estorie des Engles*, written in French for Anglo-Norman patrons but based on the *Anglo-Saxon Chronicle* and telling of the Conquest from an English point of view.

utriusque gentis sanguinem traho'.[4] So, too, Henry of Huntingdon's father, a clerk at Lincoln called Nicholas, was probably an immigrant.[5] Most interesting of all is Orderic Vitalis. Born in 1075 in Shropshire as the eldest son of Odelerius of Orléans, a clerk to the Montgomerys, and of an unidentified mother, not only was he, unlike his two brothers, baptized with an Anglo-Saxon name, that of the officiating priest – a name which, 'quod Normannis absonum censebatur', was later replaced by *Vitalis* – but also he seems to have reached the age of ten without learning his father's tongue, for when sent at that age to Saint-Evroul 'exul in Normanniam veni', he tells us, '. . . Linguam, ut Joseph in Ægypto, quod non noveram audivi', and that unknown language can hardly have been Latin as for the last five years he had been studying 'letters, psalms, and hymns' with Siward, an English priest in Shrewsbury. Throughout his life he remained aware that Normandy was not his first home, repeatedly calling himself 'Angligena', 'advena', 'barbarus et ignotus advena'.[6] Everything, and especially young Orderic's evident ignorance of French, implies that the unknown wife of Odelerius of Orléans was English. Later in the twelfth century descent from a mixed marriage – perhaps even from a tradition of mixed marriages – may underlie the way the satirist Nigel ('Wireker', 'Wetekre', or 'Longchamp'), probably a son of a knightly family settled in Kent, distinguishes between two languages. Warning a 'parvus libellus' of his to mind its manners when greeting the bishop of Ely (probably his kinsman), he commands it to speak as with the 'paternal tongue':

> Lingua tamen caveas ne sit materna, sed illa
> Quam dedit et docuit lingua paterna tibi.[7]

As the bishop, William Longchamp, was notoriously a monoglot Frenchman,[8] choice between the vernaculars would matter; but it is interesting that Nigel should fear an uncouth lapse into the 'mother tongue', presumably the English which the bishop did not know (conceivably, the 'mother tongue' might be French and the second language 'learnt from the father' Latin; but that seems less likely than that the two vernaculars are in question).

Both William of Malmesbury and Orderic assure us that intermarriage was common. William puts it generally, as one aspect of the Normans' characteristic affability

---

4 *Willelmi Malmesbiriensis Monachi de Gestis Regum Anglorum Libri Quinque*, ed. W. Stubbs, 2 vols, Rolls Series (London, 1887–89), 2: 283.

5 *Henrici Archidiaconi Huntendunensis Historia Anglorum*, ed. T. Arnold, Rolls Series (London, 1879), pp. 237–8 (recording Nicholas's death *s.a.* 1110), cf. pp. xxxi–xxxiii.

6 *The Ecclesiastical History of Orderic Vitalis*, ed. and trans. Marjorie Chibnall, 6 vols (Oxford, 1969–80), 2: xii–xiv, 262, and 3: 6–8, 142–50; *Orderici Vitalis Ecclesiasticae Historiae Libri Tredecim*, ed. A. le Prévost, 5 vols, Société de l'Histoire de France (Paris, 1838–55), 5: 133–5. For Odelerius, see also Chibnall, 'Ecclesiastical Patronage and the Growth of Feudal Estates at the Time of the Norman Conquest', *Annales de Normandie* 8 (1958), 103–18, esp. 114, and J.F.A. Mason, 'The Officers and Clerks of the Norman Earls of Shropshire', *Transactions of the Shropshire Archaeological Society* 56 (1957–60), 244–57, esp. 253.

7 *Satirical Poets and Epigrammatists of the Twelfth Century*, ed. Thomas Wright, 2 vols, Rolls Series (London, 1872), 1: 151. For further information about Nigel, see: J.H. Mozley, 'Nigel Wireker or Wetekre?', *Modern Language Review* 27 (1932), 314–17; Nigel de Longchamps, *Speculum Stultorum*, ed. J.H. Mozley and R.H. Raymo (Berkeley, California, 1960), pp. 1–2, 123–5; William Urry, *Canterbury under the Angevin Kings* (London, 1967), pp. 153–4.

8 See *Chronica Magistri Rogeri de Houedene*, ed. W. Stubbs, 4 vols, Rolls Series (London, 1860–71), 3: 146, also 142–3; the tale is perhaps a shade highly coloured.

and lack of prejudice: 'matrimonia quoque cum subditis jungunt'. Orderic is more specific: 'Ciuiliter Angli cum Normannis cohabitabant . . ., conubiis alteri alteros sibi coniungentes'.[9] So common would it seem to have been that by the late 1170s *Dialogus de Scaccario* could declare the two 'nations' to have merged, at least above peasant level: 'Iam cohabitantibus Anglicis et Normannis et alterutrum uxores ducentibus uel nubentibus, sic permixte sunt nationes ut uix decerni possit hodie, de liberis loquor, quis Anglicus quis Normannus sit genere'.[10] This assertion occurs, however, in a complex context, that of the *murdrum* fine exacted from the local community whenever a victim of a secret slaying could not be proved to be English 'ex parte patris'.[11] This fine, the text explains, was now payable for all victims of unsolved murder 'exceptis hiis de quibus certa sunt . . . seruilis conditionis indicia', which on the face of it implies that all free-born English people had come to be esteemed 'honorary Normans'. Perhaps, since the *murdrum* fine was not abolished until 1340 and as 'Presentment of Englishry' meanwhile continued as a device for avoiding the corporate fine for unsolved murder, the situation might best be interpreted, as sometimes it was by contemporaries, in fiscal rather than in racial terms.[12] Be that as it may, the general statement may remain valid, that widespread intermarriage had blurred awareness of national origins.

Writers so far quoted do not distinguish between marriages of immigrant men with English women, such as were contracted by 'Wihenoc's man' and evidently by Odelerius of Orléans, and those of English men with women of continental origin. Undoubtedly alliances of the latter sort took place (although the 'turba' of female relatives whom William Longchamp was in the late twelfth century accused of importing were destined for 'noble' bridegrooms, not for specifically 'English' ones).[13] After all, quite apart from diplomatic and dynastic unions, occasional marriages of such kind had taken place even in pre-Conquest times, one probable case being the mid-eleventh-century marriage between the thane 'Ælfgeardus' and 'Edgithe venerande regine camerariam, Mahtildam nomine'.[14] After the Conquest such families of insular descent

---

9 *De Gestis Regum*, 2: 306; *Orderic Vitalis*, ed. Chibnall, 2: 256.

10 *Dialogus de Scaccario*, ed. and trans. Charles Johnson, Nelson's Medieval Texts (London, 1950), p. 53.

11 See *Leges Henrici Primi*, ed. Leslie John Downer (Oxford, 1972), pp. 284–92, also 234–6, 332, 417–22. See also: F.C. Hamil, 'Presentment of Englishry and the Murder Fine', *Speculum* 12 (1937), 285–98; N. Hurnard, 'The Jury of Presentment and the Assize of Clarendon', *English Historical Review* 56 (1941), 374–410, esp. 385–90; Florence Harmer, ed., *Anglo-Saxon Writs* (Manchester, 1952), p. 85.

12 See *The Life and Miracles of St William of Norwich*, ed. and trans. Augustus Jessopp and Montague Rhodes James (Cambridge, 1896), p. 25: 'Cumque murdri sermo circumcirca percrebuerit, non dubium est quin regie justicie exactores ad lucrandum voluntarii ambiciosas aures falso facile adhibeant rumore'.

13 See *Chronicles of the Reigns of Stephen, Henry II, and Richard II*, ed. Richard Howlett, 1, Rolls Series (London, 1884), 335.

14 *Hemingi Chartularium Ecclesiae Wigorniensis*, ed. Thomas Hearne, 2 vols (Oxford, 1723), 1: 253. See also: R.L.G. Ritchie, *The Normans in England before Edward the Confessor*, Inaugural Lecture (Exeter, 1948), pp. 15, 20, n. 5, and Henry Loyn, *The Norman Conquest*, 2nd ed. (London, 1967), p. 50 (both taking the queen to be, not the Confessor's Eadgýð, but Emma-Ælfgifu); Frank Barlow, *Edward the Confessor* (London, 1970), pp. 166, 192. The name *Ælfgeard*, although rare (see William George Searle, *Onomasticon Anglo-Saxonicum* [Cambridge, 1897], p. 9), is acceptably English (see Olof von Feilitzen, *The Pre-Conquest Personal Names of Domesday Book*, Nomina Germanica 3 [Uppsala, 1937], pp. 146, 259); *Mahtilda (-dis)* is a

as contrived to retain some standing naturally allied themselves with the new rulers. In the late eleventh century the London magnate Deorman named one of his sons 'Tierry' (a specifically French form of *Theodric*) and had him married to a Maud connected, perhaps illegitimately, with the FitzGilbert ('Clare') family.[15] In the 1150s the second FitzHarding lord of Berkeley, of Anglo-Saxon descent as the patronymic implies, married a daughter of the Norman family just dispossessed of that lordship.[16] From the north, where the insular aristocracy survived most strongly, several such marriages are noted: thus, the founder of the 'Birkin' family, the Domesday Book tenant Assolf (an Anglo-Norse name), married his son Peter to Emma de Lascelles, and Peter's son Adam was in turn married to the Norman Maud de Caux;[17] in the first half of the twelfth century Peter son of Gamel son of Ketel son of Norman, founder of the junior branch of the 'Meaux' family, married Beatrix daughter of Robert son of Radbod, and in the next generation his nephew Robert, from the senior line, married Maud daughter of Hugh Camin, each of them acquiring further estates thereby;[18] in the mid-twelfth century an heiress with Lacy connections was the bride of the William son of Godric who founded the FitzWilliams 'of Emley and Sprotborough';[19] and in the 1220s Robert son of Meldred of Raby, himself probably the offspring of an alliance with an Estoute-ville lady, married an Anglo-Norman heiress whose surname he adopted, thus founding the Nevilles 'of Raby'.[20]

A priori, however, we might expect the commoner case to be, as at South

---

Continental-Germanic form (see Thorvald Forssner, *Continental-Germanic Personal Names in England in Old and Middle English Times* [Uppsala, 1916], pp. 181–2, and von Feilitzen, op. cit., p. 323).

[15] David Douglas, ed., *The Domesday Monachorum of Christ Church, Canterbury* (London, 1944), pp. 62–3. The Pipe Roll for 31 Henry I lists 'Tierrico fil. Dermanni' under London (*Magnum Rotulum Scaccarii . . . de anno trecesimo-primo Regni Henrici Primi*, ed. J. Hunter [London, 1833; re-iss. Pipe Roll Society, 1929], p. 148). See also Christopher Brooke and Gillian Keir, *London 800–1216: The Shaping of a City* (London, 1975), pp. 218–9, 344, 372.

For the change from *Theodric* to *Tierri*, see Mildred Pope, *From Latin to Modern French, &c.*, (Manchester, 1934), p. 140. No firm evidence in any event exists for *Theodric* as a native English name: see Forssner, *Continental-Germanic Personal Names*, pp. 231–3, and von Feilit-zen, *Pre-Conquest Personal Names*, p. 323 (but cf. Eilert Ekwall, *Early London Personal Names*, Acta Regiae Societatis Humaniorum Litterarum Lundensis 43 [Lund, 1947], pp. 2, 66, 115).

[16] *Complete Peerage*, 2: 124–6; the family is probably descended from the Eadnoth the Staller of the Confessor's time.

[17] *Early Yorkshire Charters*, ed. William Farrer and Charles Clay, 12 vols (Edinburgh, later Wakefield, 1914–65), 3: 357–61, 365–7, 371; also *The Registrum Antiquissimum of the Cathedral Church of Lincoln*, ed. C.W. Foster and Kathleen Major, Lincoln Record Society (Hereford, 1931–53), 7: 209–17. For the name *Assolf* see von Feilitzen, *Pre-Conquest Personal Names*, p. 169, and Gillian Fellows Jensen, *Scandinavian Personal Names in Lincolnshire and Yorkshire* (Copenhagen, 1968), p. 35; the Gallo-Norse equivalent was *Osulf*: see Jean Adigard des Gautries, *Les Noms de personnes scandinaves en Normandie de 911 à 1066*, Nomina Germanica 11 (Lund, 1954), pp. 302–3.

[18] *Early Yorkshire Charters*, 9: 140 and 11: 261–4, 345 et seq.; Sir Charles Clay, 'The Family of Meaux', *Yorkshire Archaeological Journal* 43 (1971), 99–111. For the typically Anglo-Norse names *Gamel* and *Ketel*, see Fellows Jensen, *Scandinavian Personal Names*, pp. 89–95, 166–70; for *Norðmann*, see von Feilitzen, *Pre-Conquest Personal Names*, pp. 331–2 (but cf. below n. 79).

[19] *Early Yorkshire Charters*, 3: 335–6.

[20] *Complete Peerage*, 9: 491–4; John Horace Round, 'The Origin of the Nevilles', in *Feudal England* (London, 1895; repr. 1964), pp. 370–2; *Early Yorkshire Charters*, 9: 24, 26, and 10: xii; C.T. Clay, 'A Note on a Neville Ancestry', *Antiquaries' Journal* 31 (1951), 201–4; also Lewis Loyd et alii, *The Origins of some Anglo-Norman Families* (Leeds, 1951), pp. 72–3. See also F.M.

Pickenham, that of the English heiress married for her lands, or perhaps her father's (or late husband's) business connections, by a foreign adventurer (had a pre-Conquest match of such kind provided the apparently mixed parentage of the first William Malet?).[21] Unattached English girls may not have been far to seek, for, apart from the men killed not only in the three battles of 1066 but also in the various later rebellions, many others had emigrated to Malcolm of Scotland's court or to Byzantium, presumably leaving their sisters behind.[22] So Geoffrey 'de Wirce', 'de Wirchia' (probably from La Guerche near Rennes), may have got some of his wide estates through his wife 'Alveva' (that is, *Ælfgifu*), named in his charter to the priory of Monks Kirby, which he founded in 1077.[23] William Pecche, a minor magnate in the eastern counties, had a first wife, still living in 1088, called 'Alffwen' (that is, *Ælfwynn* or *Ælfwēn*).[24] In London Otho 'aurifaber', ancestor of the hereditary diesinkers to the Mint, who although his name may look German certainly had Norman connections, not only got lands through his marriage with a rich citizen's widow but also frustrated the late husband's intention of ultimately bequeathing those lands to St Paul's.[25] 'There was at least a medieval tradition', Sir Frank Stenton tells us, 'that Robert d'Oilly, the first castellan of Oxford, married a daughter of King Edward's kinsman Wigot of Wallingford'; and, as for the second Robert d'Oilly (nephew of the first), about 1130 a charter of his is attested by his wife, 'ipsa domina Edit' (that is, *Eadgyð*), who can be shown to have been a former

Stenton, 'English Families and the Norman Conquest', repr. in *Preparatory to Anglo-Saxon England, Being the Collected Papers of Frank Merry Stenton*, ed. Doris Mary Stenton (Oxford, 1970), pp. 325–34, esp. 333, and idem, *The First Century of English Feudalism, 1066–1166*, 2nd ed. (Oxford, 1961), p. 110, n. 3.

[21] See Edward Freeman, *The History of the Norman Conquest of England*, 2nd ed., 4 vols (Oxford, 1870–76), 3: 776–81 (note PP); also *The Carmen de Hastingae Proelio of Guy Bishop of Amiens*, ed. Catherine Morton and Hope Muntz, Oxford Medieval Texts (Oxford, 1972), p. 38, lines 587–8 and n.

[22] For noble maidens and widows unprotected, see *Orderic Vitalis*, ed. Chibnall, 2: 268; also *Eadmeri Historia Novorum in Anglia*, ed. Martin Rule, Rolls Series (London, 1884), p. 57.

[23] Sir William Dugdale, *Monasticon Anglicanum*, ed. J. Caley et alii, 6 vols in 8 (London, 1817–30; repr. 1970), vol. 6, pt 2, p. 996. See also: A.S. Ellis, 'Biographical Notes on the Yorkshire Tenants named in Domesday Book: XVIII Goisfridus de la Wirce', *Yorkshire Archæological and Topographical Journal* 4 (1877), 223–6; *VCH Northants.*, 1: 292; F.M. Stenton, 'English Families', p. 329, and idem, *English Feudalism*, p. 10, n. 2.

[24] *Cartularium Monasterii de Rameseia*, ed. William Henry Hart and Ponsonby A. Lyons, 3 vols, Rolls Series (London, 1884–93), 1: 121; *Complete Peerage*, 10: 331.

[25] See J.H. Round, 'An Early Reference to Domesday', in *Domesday Studies*, ed. Patrick Edward Dove, 2 vols (London, 1888–91), 2: 539–59, esp. 555–7. Some records call the wife 'Leveva' (*Leofgifu*; e.g., *Feudal Documents from the Abbey of Bury St Edmunds*, ed. David Douglas [London, 1932], pp. cxxxix–cxli, 61–2, 109, 127–8), others 'Eideva', 'Eadgiva' (*Eadgifu*; e.g., *Early Charters of the Cathedral Church of St Paul, London*, ed. Marion Gibbs, Camden Third Series 58 (London, 1939), pp. 136, n. 1, and 280). Otho was a minor tenant-in-chief in several counties, mainly Essex and Suffolk; for him and his descendants as moneyers, see George Cyril Brooke, *A Catalogue of English Coins in the British Museum: The Norman Kings*, 2 vols (London, 1916), 1: cxxxiii et seq., and Derek Fortrose Allen, *A Catalogue of English Coins in the British Museum: The Cross-and-Crosslets ('Tealby') Type of Henry II* (London, 1951), pp. cxii–cxiii. He certainly had Norman connections (either he or a son of the same name made the Conqueror's jewelled shrine at Caen, see *Orderic Vitalis*, ed. Chibnall, 4: 110–11), although his name suggests that, like others engaged in the London jewellery trade at this time, he may have been of German origin (see Forssner, *Continental-Germanic Personal Names*, pp. 198–9, and cf. Brooke and Keir, *London 800–1216*, pp. 266–8).

mistress of Henry I.[26] By the early twelfth century Muriel, a daughter of the post-Conquest Lincoln magnate Colsuein, usually believed to have been an Anglo-Norse quisling, had been married to the Norman Robert de la Haye ('de Haia'), constable of Lincoln castle.[27] The first lay steward of the abbey of Bury St Edmunds, Ralph, installed in Abbot Baldwin's time (that is, before 1098), had a wife 'Editha';[28] his successor Maurice of Windsor (from the family later to produce Gerald of Wales), installed before 1119, also had a wife variously called 'Edit(ha)' or 'Edgidia'.[29] In the mid-twelfth century Reginald, one of Henry I's illegitimate children by the Anglo-Norman Sybil Corbet, married a Cornish heiress related to a family of English descent which had furnished two of his father's scribes, and was then created earl of Cornwall.[30] Towards the end of the century Christiana, granddaughter of Swan Magnusson, a landholder in Lincolnshire, became the bride of Roger de Neville.[31] Nor, as mentioning Henry I has reminded us, must we forget the less regular alliances, any children of which might have been especially likely to follow their mother's traditions.

---

[26] (i) See Stenton, 'English Families', p. 329; if the spurious foundation charters of St George's, Oxford, are to be trusted, the wife's name was 'Alditha' (*Ealdgyð*; *Cartulary of Oseney Abbey*, ed. Herbert Edward Salter, 6 vols, Oxford Historical Society 89, 90, 91, 97, 98 and 101 [Oxford, 1929–36], 4: 1, 2, 4). For the supposed link with Wigot, see Freeman, *Norman Conquest*, 4: 728–34 (note C), and Ivor Sanders, *English Baronies: a Study of their Origin and Descent 1086–1327* (Oxford, 1960), p. 93, n. 2; and for Wigot as the Confessor's 'dear kinsman', see *Anglo-Saxon Writs*, ed. Harmer, no. 104 – with Wigot's ancestry unknown and with his name among the Norse forms current in Normandy as well as in England (see Adigard des Gautries, *Les Noms de personnes scandinaves en Normandie*, pp. 238–9, and cf. Fellows Jensen, *Scandinavian Personal Names*, pp. 335–6), it is in any case not clear how 'English' the family was. (ii) *Cartulary of Oseney Abbey*, 4: 11, 19, 266, and 5: 61, 206, 207, 208, 209; see also *Complete Peerage*, 9: 708–9, and Stenton, *English Feudalism*, p. 281, cf. p. 189; also below p. 124.

    Traditions more dubious surround 'Lucy', wife of Ivo Taillebois, *dapifer* to Rufus and a sheriff of Lincoln (either she herself or a daughter of the same name later married, first, Roger FitzGerold, so becoming the mother of William of Roumare, and, then, Rannulf le Meschin of Chester, so becoming the mother of Rannulf II of Chester: see *Complete Peerage*, 3: 166–7, and 7: 677–80, 743–6). Although some C14 sources call her a daughter of Earl Ælfgar of Mercia (*Monasticon*, 3: 215), more probably she was a daughter of Turold, a post-Conquest sheriff of Lincoln, himself probably Norman (*Turold*, although possibly Anglo-Norse, is among the commonest of all Gallo-Norse names: see Adigard des Gautries, op. cit., pp. 171–3, 342–7), and of a woman of the Malet family. See H.A. Cronne, 'Ranulf de Gernons, earl of Chester, 1129–53', *Transactions of the Royal Historical Society*, 4th ser. 20 (1937), 103–34, esp. 104–6, and James W.F. [Sir Francis] Hill, *Medieval Lincoln* (Cambridge, 1948), pp. 91–8.

[27] See Hill, *Medieval Lincoln*, pp. 48–50, 87–8, 95, 133 et seq., and John Le Patourel, *Normandy and England 1066–1144*, Stenton Lecture 1970 (Reading, 1971), pp. 34–5; and for the de la Haye family, Loyd, *Origins*, p. 51. The Norse name *Colsuein* was current in England (see Fellows Jensen, *Scandinavian Personal Names*, pp. 179–80) but not, apparently, in Normandy (see Adigard des Gautries, *Les Noms de personnes scandinaves en Normandie*).

[28] See B. Dodwell, 'Some Charters relating to the Honour of Bacton', in *A Medieval Miscellany for Doris Mary Stenton*, ed. P.M. Barnes and C.F. Slade, Pipe Roll Society, n.s. 36 (London, 1962), pp. 147–65, esp. 149, 160; also Douglas, *Feudal Documents*, pp. cxxxviii, n. 5, and 60.

[29] See Dodwell, 'Bacton', pp. 149, n. 5, and 161–2, 165; for tenurial reasons Miss Dodwell suggests identifying the two Ediths and, further, that despite the apparent difference of name Maurice's wife is the 'Eadiva' (that is, *Eadgifu*, not *Eadgyð*) whose brothers were the minor Essex landholders Walter Maskerel and Alexander of Wix (see ibid., pp. 150, 152, 154–5, n. 3, and 164; also L. Landon, 'The Barony of Little Easton and the Family of Hastings', *Transactions of the Essex Archæological Society*, n.s. 19 [1930], 174–9).

[30] Southern, *Medieval Humanism*, pp. 229, also 225 et seq.

[31] F.M. Stenton, *The Free Peasantry of the Northern Danelaw* (Oxford, 1969), p. 55.

Rannulf Flambard, later bishop of Durham, had a large family by Alveva, an aunt of Christina of Markyate's and from a respectable English bourgeois line (subsequently she was married off to a burgess of Huntingdon).[32] In the mid-twelfth century one scion of the gentry, Thomas son of Richard, lord of Cuckney in Nottinghamshire, can be seen providing for a mistress from the villein class when he grants 'to Ailiua [that is, *Æðelgifu*] and her younger daughter by me the land of her father which he held for the service of one bovate, and Reginald, her own brother, with his land which he also held for the service of one bovate'.[33] In general, however, the only alliances well documented are those of high politics, such as that of Earl Waltheof with the Conqueror's niece Judith and that of Henry I with Edith-Matilda of Scotland.[34] Even among 'the upper ranks of feudal society, the barons and their mesne tenants', Professor Painter complains, '. . . one cannot regularly discover who men's wives were and hence it is impossible to know all family connections'.[35] For settlers of more modest condition, those most perhaps involved in passing on languages and traditions, information is even more sparse and sporadic: it survives for the tenant of South Pickenham only because luckily (for us as well as for him) his love alighted where land was, and because the Norfolk survey is preserved in the 'Little' Domesday Book which was less drastically sub-edited than the main volume. How many of the Norman men who settled in England did arrive alone and then marry English women?[36]

Nor is it only wives and mistresses that are in question. We began from the premiss that it is usually women who are instrumental in transmitting language, and other traditions, from generation to generation; and that process does not involve mothers only, nor indeed, except in the humblest families, mothers principally. If indeed the Norman settlers brought with them comparatively few women of their own kind, then not only would some of the men have married English women but also, *a fortiori*, many children, some of purely continental parentage as well as those of mixed blood, would have been cared for by English nurses, maids, and other servants. Not many references to children's nurses in post-Conquest England come readily to mind. A girl called 'Brichtiva' (that is, *Beorhtgifu*) was employed by a priest Odo to look after his children, apparently in the late eleventh century, when a name like 'Odo' might well indicate continental origin.[37] And a story told by Gerald of Wales (whether or not it is

---

[32] *The Life of Christina of Markyate*, ed. and trans. Charles Holwell Talbot (Oxford, 1959), p. 40; see also Southern, 'Ranulf Flambard', in *Medieval Humanism*, pp. 183–205.

[33] Doris Mary Stenton, *The English Woman in History* (London, 1957), pp. 47–8, citing an unpublished charter.

[34] A projected alliance which, had it taken place and produced offspring, might also have come in this category was to have been between Gunnilda, Harold Godwinesson's daughter, and Count Alan the Red of Richmond, who abducted her from Wilton but died before he could marry her, as did his brother, Count Alan the Black, after him; see *S. Anselmi Cantuariensis Opera Omnia*, ed. F.S. Schmitt, 6 vols (Edinburgh, 1946–61), 4: 45–50 (Epp. 168, 169), and Richard Southern, *St Anselm and his Biographer* (Cambridge, 1963), pp. 185 et seq.

[35] S. Painter, 'The Family and the Feudal System in Twelfth-Century England', *Speculum* 35 (1960), 1–16, esp. 2.

[36] Cf. Shelly, *English and French in England*, pp. 62 et seq., and F. Barlow, 'The Effects of the Norman Conquest', in Dorothy Whitelock et alii, *The Norman Conquest: Its Setting and Impact* (London, 1966), pp. 123–61, esp. 137.

[37] *Memorials of St Edmund's Abbey*, ed. Thomas Arnold, 3 vols, Rolls Series (London, 1890–6), 3: 164, although no date is specified, the context suggests Baldwin's abbacy, that is, ante 1098. For *Odo*, see Forssner, *Continental-Germanic Personal Names*, pp. 198–9, and von Feilitzen, *Pre-Conquest Personal Names*, p. 334.

literally true hardly matters) may imply that waiting-women in general, even those of the highest nobility, were expected to be English-speaking. One of Henry I's mistresses, a 'puella nobilis', had a devoted 'matrona magistra', who, when a prayer on the lady's behalf – 'Rorate celi desuper' – went unanswered, rounded in English on the priest responsible – 'lingua materna, anglice scilicet, . . . "Rorie se þe rorie, ne wrthe nan!" ' ('Roar who will, it's useless!').[38] Admittedly, two of Henry I's recorded mistresses were English: that is, the Edith afterwards married to Robert II d'Oilly, a daughter of the Cumbrian magnate Forne of Greystoke,[39] and another Edith, the mother of the Countess of Perche;[40] and these might naturally have had maids of their own nation.[41] Gerald does not, however, put forward any such explanation, apparently assuming that any waiting-woman of any Anglo-Norman 'puella nobilis' might speak like that. Now, although the role of such 'matronae', waiting-women and nurses, in educating the children of the Norman settlers may be hidden from us, nevertheless they may well have been the agency by which, in little more than a century, the language of the conquered people became familiar to some at least of the ruling class.[42]

Is there, then, any evidence for a small proportion of women – as wives, and, *a fortiori*, as waiting-women and nursemaids – among the Norman settlers? Orderic's evidence is inconsistent, ranging from, on the one hand, the well-known comedy of the Norman wives afraid not only of warfare but even more of the Channel crossing – 'Non enim ad maritos suos propter inusitatam sibi adhuc nauigationem transfretare audebant . . .' – to the arrival in England of the Conqueror's Matilda with a train of 'noble ladies'.[43] Women are far from easy to trace in most kinds of early record, and after the Conquest they become even less so than before. Except for the greatest ladies, they rarely witness charters, not even those recording grants in favour of nunneries.[44]

---

[38] *Giraldi Cambrensis Opera*, ed. John Sherren Brewer, et alii, 8 vols, Rolls Series (London, 1861–91), 2: 128 (the printed text has been checked with a photograph supplied by the courtesy of the Lambeth Palace Librarian, Mr. E.G.W. Bill). Although the unique manuscript of *Gemma Ecclesiastica*, the C13 Lambeth MS 236, is described as a careful copy (see E.A. Williams, 'A Bibliography of Giraldus Cambrensis, c.1147–c.1223', *National Library of Wales Journal* 12 [1961–62], 97–140, esp. 116), the English phrase is patently garbled (I am deeply grateful to Professor Dorothy Whitelock for discussing with me some of the grammatical problems it raises); Gerald's own translation is free: 'In uanum cotidie roras tantum, oras et ploras, nosque ieiunandi tam male afficis et affligis, quia quod tantopere petis proculdubio non obtinebis'. Tentatively, one might reconstruct the Old English equivalent (that is, classical C10 forms, not C12 ones) as: **Rārige sē þe rārige, ne weorð[eð] nān þing* ('Let him roar who will, nothing happens').

[39] See *Complete Peerage*, 11: Appendix D, 105–21, esp. 108–9; cf. above p. 121. For the Anglo-Norse name *Forne*, see Fellows Jensen, *Scandinavian Personal Names*, pp. 84–5.

[40] See *Complete Peerage*, 11: Appendix D, 122.

[41] As the bilingual pun requires a southerly dialect in which OE $ā > ō$ by the early C12, the 'matrona' could hardly have been Cumbrian like Edith daughter of Forne; but perhaps one should not press any tale of Gerald's too far.

[42] Cf. above nn. 2 and 3. See also: Shelly, *English and French*, pp. 86–7; Legge, *Significance*, p. 3; Einar Haugen, *The Ecology of Language* (Stanford, 1972), p. 68; Frank Barlow, *The Feudal Kingdom of England 1042–1216*, 2nd ed. (London, 1961), p. 134.

[43] *Orderic Vitalis*, ed. Chibnall, 2: 218–20, 214.

[44] See, for instance, *Cartulary of St Mary, Clerkenwell*, ed. William Owen Hassall, Camden Third Series 71 (London, 1949). For some exceptional cases of charters witnessed by women other than the grantor's wife, all as it happens from the former Danelaw, see: *Documents Illustrative of the Social and Economic History of the Danelaw*, ed. F.M. Stenton (London, 1920), pp. 116, 121–2, 148, 285–6, 288; D.M. Stenton, *The English Woman*, pp. 36–7; and two both from the same Yorkshire milieu, (a) in Charles Frost, *Notices relative to the Early History of the Town and*

Even as party to a transaction a woman might be specified only as a man's nameless wife, widow, mother, sister, daughter, aunt, or niece. Moreover, by contrast with Anglo-Saxon custom the women of Anglo-Norman times had reduced rights to hold land or to make wills.[45] Tenancies by knight-service would not be initially granted to women and, if inherited, would normally be vested in a husband.[46] Customary tenancies were seldom in women's names, except for a few widows,[47] and those sometimes under pressure to remarry so as to have a man to drive the plough.[48] Consequently, source after source proves virtually silent about the women living in England in the late eleventh and early twelfth centuries.

Direct evidence will no doubt always elude us; but, as several examples already cited may have suggested, perhaps a faint sidelight on the proportions of men and of women involved in the post-Conquest settlement may be thrown by patterns of nomenclature.[49] Name patterns might hardly seem significant enough to support such an argument, were it not that some contemporaries did see meaning in choice of name. For instance, certain partisans of Robert Curthose, as William of Malmesbury reports, mocked Henry I for his political marriage with Edith of Scotland, 'Godricum eum, et comparem Godgivam, appellantes', with an insulting intent emphasised in the context.[50] Nor must we forget how the young Orderic's name was changed because

---

Port of Hull, &c. (London, 1827), pl. between pp. 8–9, cf. pp. 7–8, and (b) in *Early Yorkshire Charters*, 11: 348.

45 See D.M. Stenton, *The English Woman*, pp. 29–34, and, for a wider view, Eileen Power, *Medieval Women*, ed. M.M. Postan (Cambridge, 1975), pp. 38–40; for C13 and C14 statistics of women as landholders, see Josiah Russell, *British Medieval Population* (Albuquerque, 1948), pp. 62–3. For the more liberal Anglo-Saxon practice, cf. D.M. Stenton, op. cit., pp. 5–6, 9, 23, 25–7, and the fuller account by F.M. Stenton, 'The Historical Bearing of Place-Name Studies: The Place of Women in Anglo-Saxon Society', in *Collected Papers*, pp. 314–24. From the C12 on the common law increasingly limited the proprietary and testamentary rights of married women, see M.M. Sheehan, 'The Influence of Canon Law on the Property Rights of Married Women in England', *Mediaeval Studies* 25 (1963), 109–24. Some link the legal changes with general social climate, see B. Bandel, 'The English Chroniclers' Attitude toward Women', *Journal of the History of Ideas* 16 (1955), 113–18.

46 Exceptionally, an heiress or a widow might hold on such tenure in her own right: see, for instance, *Liber Henrici de Soliaco Abbatis Glaston.*, ed. John Edward Jackson, Roxburghe Club (London, 1882), p. 6, and *St Benet of Holme 1020–1210*, ed. James Rowland West, 2 vols, Norfolk Record Society 2 and 3 (Fakenham, 1932), 1: item 66, cf. 2: 243–4.

47 The only status allowing an Englishwoman of this date much independence, see: D.M. Stenton, *The English Woman*, pp. 34–5, 76 et seq., 84; James Ambrose Raftis, *Tenure and Mobility: Studies in the Social History of the Mediaeval English Village*, Pontifical Institute of Mediaeval Studies, Studies and Texts 8 (Toronto, 1964), pp. 36–42; Power, *Medieval Women*, pp. 38, 55–7; cf. above n. 45. Russell, *British Medieval Population*, pp. 64–5, suggested that often widows might be moved into landless cottages.

48 For at least one lord, the abbot of Ramsey, compelling widowed tenants to remarry, see D.M. Stenton, *The English Woman*, pp. 83–4.

49 The analogous question how many women took part in the Viking settlement of Normandy is discussed in an onomastic context by Adigard des Gautries, *Les Noms de personnes scandinaves en Normandie*, pp. 251–3 (cf. Davis, *The Normans and their Myth*, pp. 26–7, on the regular intermarriage between the ducal house and the Frankish aristocracy). As for Scandinavian women's names in England, I myself hope shortly to carry out a study comparable with this present one [[cf. 'The Early Personal Names of King's Lynn: An Essay in Socio-Cultural History. Part I – Baptismal Names', below pp. 241–57, esp. 246–50.]] (cf. F.M. Stenton, 'The Danes in England', in *Collected Papers*, pp. 136–65, esp. 154–5).

50 *De Gestis Regum*, 2: 471.

Norman ears found it 'inharmonious'.[51] So, with styles of name drastically altered in post-Conquest England,[52] perhaps the patterns which the innovations followed may justifiably be interpreted in social terms.

The Anglo-Saxons, sharing as they did a common Germanic tradition with Franks, Flemings, and other continental peoples, had mainly used names of the typical Germanic types, with dithematic forms, such as *Æþel-gifu* and *Wulf-stan*, predominating over monothematic ones, such as *Offa* and *Gode* (often hypocoristic). Common though the tradition was, each Germanic people had its own preferred range of names and name elements, and the Anglo-Saxons had theirs.[53] From time to time during the Anglo-Saxon period Continental-Germanic forms do appear in English records,[54] and throughout the Danelaw Norse names were from the tenth century onwards widely adopted alongside native ones;[55] but such additions only variegated the insular pattern

[51] See above p. 118.

[52] 'Post-Conquest' puts it too crudely, as, not only during the Confessor's reign but at least from the time of his mother's marriage to Æthelred II, military, ecclesiastical and courtly infiltration from the continent had been familiarizing many English milieux with foreign fashions. See: Round, 'The Normans under Edward the Confessor', in *Feudal England*, pp. 247–57; Ritchie, *The Normans in England before Edward the Confessor*; E.-J. Arnould, 'Deux siècles de contacts culturels franco-anglais (871–1066)', *Annales de Normandie* 8 (1958), 71–85 (over-reliant on secondary sources); Loyn, *The Norman Conquest*, pp. 50–9; M.W. Campbell, 'A Pre-Conquest Norman Occupation of England?' *Speculum* 46 (1971), 21–31. For the specifically onomastic consequences of these contacts, see: Forssner, *Continental-Germanic Personal Names in England*, esp. pp. lx–lxi; von Feilitzen, *Pre-Conquest Personal Names*, pp. 26–9, and idem, 'Some Continental-Germanic Personal Names in England', in *Early English and Norse Studies presented to Hugh Smith*, ed. A. Brown and P. Foote (London, 1963), pp. 46–61; also sporadic instances among moneyers' names collected by V.J. Smart, 'Moneyers of the late Anglo-Saxon coinage, 973–1016', in *Commentationes de nummis saeculorum ix–xi in Suecia repertis II*, Kungl. Vitterhets Historie och Antikvitets Akademiens Handlingar: Antikvariska Serien 19 (Stockholm, 1968), pp. 191–276, and by O. von Feilitzen and C. Blunt, 'Personal Names on the Coinage of Edgar', in *England before the Conquest: Studies in Primary Sources presented to Dorothy Whitelock*, ed. P. Clemoes and K. Hughes (Cambridge, 1971), pp. 183–214. The *TRE* landholders listed in the Winchester survey of c.1110 (see also below pp. 136–7) already show some 15% of 'continental' names: see O. von Feilitzen, 'Personal Names', in Martin Biddle et alii, eds, *Winchester in the Early Middle Ages: An Edition and Discussion of the Winton Domesday*, Winchester Studies 1 (Oxford, 1976), pp. 145–91, esp. 185 (I am deeply grateful to the late Dr von Feilitzen for allowing me to see this important study before its official publication).

[53] See: Searle, *Onomasticon Anglo-Saxonicum* (obsolescent); von Feilitzen, *Pre-Conquest Personal Names*; idem, 'Some Unrecorded Old and Middle English Personal Names', *Namn och Bygd* 33 (1945), 69–98; idem, 'Some Old English Uncompounded Personal Names and By-Names', *Studia Neophilologica* 40 (1968), 5–16; P.H. Reaney, 'Notes on the Survival of Old English Personal Names in Middle English', *Studier i Modern Språkvetenskap* 18 (1953), 84–112; Mats Redin, *Studies on Uncompounded Personal Names in Old English* (Uppsala, 1919). Owing to the nature of the sources available, many studies listed here and in later notes offer only scanty information about women's names, exceptions being von Feilitzen's paper in *NoB* 33 and Reaney's in *SMS* 18; see especially Maria Boehler, *Die altenglischen Frauennamen*, Germanische Studien 98 (Berlin, 1930), and also H.B. Woolf, 'The Naming of Women in Old English Times', *Modern Philology* 36 (1938–39), 113–20.

[54] See above n. 52.

[55] See: Erik Björkman, *Nordische Personennamen in England in alt- und frühmittelenglischer Zeit*, Studien zur englischen Philologie 37 (Halle, 1910), and idem, *Zur englischen Namenkunde*, Studien zur englischen Philologie 47 (Halle, 1912), cf. the review article by R.E. Zachrisson, 'Notes on Early English Personal Names', *Studier i Modern Språkvetenskap* 6 (1917), 269–98 (still interesting although now dated); D. Whitelock, 'Scandinavian Personal Names in the Liber

without superseding it. Then, between the Conquest and the end of the twelfth century, almost all the distinctively insular names were rapidly discarded, by peasants almost as fast as by burgesses, in favour of those current among the Norman settlers.[56] These 'continental' names were of several kinds. There were Continental-Germanic names, of the same general types as the insular ones, but permutating a different stock of name elements: these were now mainly adopted in gallicized form, thus *Raulf* for *Radulf*, *Gilbert* for *Giselber(h)t*, and so on (of course, the spoken forms are often partly disguised by scribal Latinizations).[57] There were Gallo-Norse names stemming from

Vitae of Thorney Abbey', *Saga-Book of the Viking Society* 12 (1937–45), 127–53; von Feilitzen, *Pre-Conquest Personal Names*, pp. 18–26, and idem, 'Notes on some Scandinavian Personal Names in English 12th-Century Records', in *Personnamnstudier 1964 tillägnade minnet av Ivar Modéer (1904–1960) = Anthroponymica Suecana* 6 (1965), 52–68; Fellows Jensen, *Scandinavian Personal Names*. For some complex international interactions, see O. von Friesen, 'Personal Names of the type Bótolfr', *Studia Neophilologica* 14 (1941–42), 357–65.

56 Thus, in the admissions lists of Hyde Abbey names of continental type begin to appear regularly, especially for 'pueri', from about the 1170s on (*Liber Vitae: Register and Martyrology of New Minster and Hyde Abbey, Winchester*, ed. Walter de Gray Birch, Hampshire Record Society [London, 1892], esp. pp. 36–7). See also: Ekwall, *Early London Personal Names*, pp. xii, 87, 90–6, 98–100; P.H. Reaney, 'Pedigrees of Villeins and Freemen', *Notes and Queries* (May 1952), 222–5, and idem, *The Origin of English Surnames* (London, 1967), pp. 129–52; G. Fellows Jensen, 'The Names of the Lincolnshire Tenants of the Bishop of Lincoln, c.1225', in *Otium et Negotium: Studies in Onomatology and Library Science presented to Olof von Feilitzen = Acta Bibliothecae Regiae Stockholmiensis* 16 (1973), 86–95 (Mrs Dorothy Owen points out to me that the true date of the document studied is 1258); von Feilitzen, 'Personal Names', in *The Winton Domesday*, esp. pp. 183–91.

Many studies have concentrated on the Anglo-Saxon elements surviving in post-Conquest nomenclature: as well as Ekwall's monograph on London names, see also Reaney, 'Survival', and Bo Seltén, *The Anglo-Saxon Heritage in Middle English Personal Names: East Anglia 1100–1399*, Lund Studies in English 45 (Lund, 1972).

57 For the present purpose the most useful compilation is: Marie-Thérèse Morlet, *Les Noms de personne sur le territoire de l'ancienne Gaule du VIe au XIIe siècle*, 2 vols (Paris, 1968–72), 1 (*Les Noms issus du germanique continental et les créations gallo-germaniques*); for some shortcomings of this see, however, the review by C. Wells in *Medium Ævum* 39 (1970), 358–64. Most studies of French names have been narrowly localized and concentrated on periods rather later than ours, thus: H. Jacobsson, *Études d'anthroponymie lorraine: Les Bans de tréfonds de Metz (1267–1298)* (Göteborg, 1955); M. le Pesant, 'Les Noms de personne à Evreux du XIIe au XIVe siècles', *Annales de Normandie* 6 (1956), 47–74; M.-Th. Morlet, 'Les Noms de personne à Eu du XIIIe au XVe siècle', *Revue internationale d'onomastique* 11 (1959), 131–48, 174–82, and ibid. 12 (1960), 62–70, 137–48, 205–19; *Le Nécrologe de la confrérie des jongleurs et des bourgeois d'Arras (1194–1361)*, ed. Roger Berger, 2 vols, Mémoires de la Commission départementale des Monuments Historiques du Pas-de-Calais 11 (pt 2) and 13 (pt 2) (Arras, 1963–70); Marie-Thérèse Morlet,, *Étude d'anthroponymie picarde: Les Noms de personne en Haute Picardie aux XIIIe, XIVe, XVe siècles*, Collection de la Société de linguistique picarde 6 (Amiens, 1967); G.T. Beech, 'Les Noms de personne poitevins du 9e au 12e siècles', *Revue internationale d'onomastique* 26 (1974), 81–100.

For West Germanic name traditions other than Frankish/French, see: Henry Bosley Woolf, *The Old Germanic Principles of Name-Giving* (Baltimore, 1939); Ernst Förstemann, *Altdeutsches Namenbuch*, 3 vols, rev. ed. (Bonn, 1900–16), 1 (*Personennamen*), and *Ergänzungsband*, ed. Henning Kaufmann (Munich, 1968); Wilhelm Schlaug, *Studien zu den altsächsischen Personennamen des 11. und 12. Jahrhunderts*, Lunder Germanistische Forschungen 30 (Lund, 1955); idem, *Die altsächsischen Personennamen vor dem Jahre 1000*, Lunder Germanistische Forschungen 34 (Lund, 1962); Joseph Mansion, *Oud-Gentsche Naamkunde: Bijdrage tot de kennis van het oud-nederlandsch* (The Hague, 1924); C. Tavernier-Vereecken, *Gentse Naamkunde van ca. 1000 tot 1253: Een Bijdrage tot de kennis van het oudste Middelnederlands*,

the Norse settlement of Normandy,[58] sometimes hard to tell from the corresponding Anglo-Norse forms,[59] and sometimes also open to confusion with Frankish forms.[60] And there was a comparatively new range of names which at this time was fast gaining ground on the continent, that is, the specifically 'Christian' names, the Hebrew, Greek, and Latin names of biblical characters and of saints.[61] For names of all these kinds there was also a great stock of hypocoristic forms, both shortenings and elaborate diminutives. By the end of the twelfth century nearly all Englishmen, in all districts and of all ranks, were bearing names drawn from this new 'continental' stock. Thus, although – as we have ventured to suggest in several instances already quoted – the 'nationality' of a name may for the first generation after the Conquest be a fair though not infallible guide to its bearer's origins, after that fashion comes to play a larger and larger part. With the trend as it was, use of the unfashionable insular names, in so far as it persisted, must have implied not only parentage at least partly insular – Norman settlers would have been unlikely to adopt forms which some at least of them mocked at for supposed uncouthness – but also some family attachment to English traditions.

Now, until the end of the twelfth century at least, the insular strain remains far commoner in women's names than in men's. This has several times been remarked: by Reaney, for instance, for the names of late-twelfth-century peasants,[62] and by Cameron for the 1177 survey from Newark;[63] but as yet no adequate investigation of the discrep-

Bouwstoffen en Studien voor de Geschiedenis en de Lexicografie van het Nederlands 11 (Brussels, 1968); O. Leys, 'De oudste Vrouwennamen in Zuid-Nederland', in *Onomastica Neerlandica: Anthroponymica* 10 (Louvain, 1959), 5–28.

[58] See Adigard des Gautries, *Les Noms de personnes scandinaves en Normandie*; also idem, 'Les Noms de personnes scandinaves dans les obituaires de Jumièges', in *Jumièges: congrès scientifique du xiiie centenaire* (Rouen, 1955), pp. 57–67.

[59] See Fellows Jensen, *Scandinavian Personal Names*, pp. lxi, lxiii, and passim; also Ekwall, *Early London Personal Names*, pp. 73–4, 87, 88, and Reaney, *Origin*, pp. 125–7. This is the most trying source of ambiguity in our material. Ritchie, *The Normans in England before Edward the Confessor*, suggested that the Scandinavian element in Norman culture may have been recognized and welcomed in the English Danelaw. Further complications arise from possible Anglo-Norse influence on the original settlement of Normandy; see L. Musset, 'Pour l'étude des relations entre les colonies scandinaves d'Angleterre et de Normandie', *Mélanges de linguistique et de philologie Fernand Mossé in memoriam* (Paris, 1959), pp. 330–9, and idem, 'Pour l'étude comparative de deux fondations politiques des Vikings: Le Royaume de York et le duché de Rouen', in *Essays in Honour of John Le Patourel* = *Northern History* 10 (1975), 40–54, esp. 47–51.

[60] See Adigard des Gautries, *Les Noms de personnes scandinaves en Normandie*, pp. 26–9; also Zachrisson, 'Notes on early English Personal Names', pp. 280–4.

[61] See: Morlet, *Les Noms de personne sur le territoire de l'ancienne Gaule*, 2 (*Les Noms latins ou transmis par le latin*); H. Carrez, 'Noms de personne féminins dans la région dijonnaise du XIIe au XVe siècle', *Annales de Bourgogne* 14 (1942), 85–129, esp. 109 et seq.; Jacobsson, *Etudes d'anthroponymie*, pp. 28–9; le Pesant, 'Les Noms de personne à Evreux', pp. 50–1; Morlet, 'Les Noms de personne à Eu', 11: 135; eadem, *Etude d'anthroponymie picarde*, pp. 17, 23; Berger, ed., *Le Nécrologe*, 2: 305–8; Beech, 'Les Noms de personne poitevins', passim. For Flemish Flanders, see O. Leys, 'La Substitution des noms chrétiens aux noms pré-chrétiens en Flandre occidentale avant 1225', in *Cinquième congrès international de toponymie et d'anthroponymie: Actes et mémoires* = *Acta Salmanticensia (Filosofia y Letras)* 11 (1958), 2 pts independently paginated, 1: 403–12.

[62] Reaney, 'Pedigrees', pp. 224–5; idem, *Origin*, p. 106.

[63] Kenneth Cameron in *Documents relating to the Manor and Soke of Newark-on-Trent*, ed. Maurice Willmore Barley et alii, Thoroton Society Record Series 16 (Nottingham, 1956), p. xii, cf. pp. xiii–xiv.

ancy seems to have been attempted.[64] And yet it is a very marked discrepancy: the late-twelfth-century pedigrees of near-villein families analyzed by Reaney show that, whereas by that time and in that class insular forms accounted for less than 30% of men's names, among women's they amounted to almost half (Thomas of Cuckney's Ailiva, we may recall, had a brother 'Reginald').

For this discrepancy the easiest explanation would be 'fashion'. Certainly fashion could work differentially on women's names and men's. In France itself, when between the tenth and the fifteenth centuries the specifically 'Christian' names, the biblical names and saints' names, came to displace the Germanic ones originally favoured, this change affected women's names faster than men's.[65] Yet this analogy is poor, as fashion was working in exactly opposite ways on the two sides of the Channel, with women's names leading the fashion in France but in England remaining Germanic, insular, and archaic. What makes this conservatism of English women's names all the more note-worthy is the narrowness of the insular name stock in common use. Some factor must have been at work other than simple modishness.

An hypothesis might be put forward. In some districts at least the continental names first to be adopted by the peasantry were identifiably those of the local gentry and magnates.[66] If, then, a fair number of the post-Conquest male immigrants had, like Geoffrey of La Guerche, like William Pecche, like that 'man of Wihenoc's', married English women instead of bringing wives of their own nation with them, then the early patterns of upper-class naming offered to fashion-conscious people of English stock would have included fewer women's names than men's. If, moreover, some of these hypothetical mixed couples had named more of their daughters than of their sons according to the maternal traditions, then imbalance in the name stock would have persisted (unhappily, the rarity of records naming entire families makes this last point unverifiable). Such practices would indeed explain the discrepancy between the rate at which continental men's names were being adopted by English families and that for women's; and they would have implications going far beyond mere name patterns.

Before indulging in interpretation, we must, however, be sure that the discrepancy is genuine and not a mere random quirk in the limited materials from which it has so far been reported. And, before further materials are analyzed, we must face several prob-lems. That some name forms are ambiguous we have already noted: with many Norse names scribal forms like *Turchetillus* and *Turmodus* conceal whether the spoken reality

---

It may or may not chime with these observations that when Gillian Fellows Jensen instances 'return to Scandinavian nomenclature after a break of one generation' the examples she cites involve a high proportion of women's names (*Scandinavian Personal Names*, p. lxiii).

[64] Thus, Seltén, *The Anglo-Saxon Heritage*, attempts no comparison between masculine and feminine name patterns.

[65] See: le Pesant, 'Les Noms de personne à Evreux', pp. 50–1, 63, and Morlet, *Etude d'anthropo-nymie picarde*, p. 23; likewise, Berger's statistics of the most popular names for both sexes seem to imply that in Arras also 'Christian' names were adopted faster for women than for men (*Le Nécrologe*, 2: 306). New fashions often affect women's names more drastically than men's (for an observation of this in a milieu very different from ours, northern Sweden in recent times, see *Anthroponymica Suecana* 6: 291). In Flanders development was complex, as there 'Christian' names seem to have been adopted later for women than for men but, once adopted, then to have spread faster; see Leys, 'La Substitution des noms chrétiens', p. 411, and idem, 'De oudste Vrouwennamen', p. 17 (his explanation by differences in male and female psychology is irrele-vant, as it assumes that individuals choose their own names).

[66] See below p. 132 and n. 80.

was Gallo- or Anglo-Norse;[67] and again, with name forms represented both in Anglo-Saxon and in Continental Germanic, scribal forms like *Osbertus*, *Wibertus*, even *Wlfricus*, might with equal plausibility be referred to either origin.[68] Common sense suggests that a theoretically ambiguous form may often be safely assigned to the same nationality as its bearer. Truly ambiguous forms are best left right out of the reckoning; luckily, they are seldom so numerous as gravely to affect the statistics. Other problems arise from the kinds of document available and their form. Often, when the same name recurs several times, it may be impossible to determine how many distinct individuals were involved. And, as we have already noted, documents concerned with property holding refer almost exclusively to adult males, and mainly to the upper classes. Such women as are named are often specified as widows, and so might well be a generation or more older than some of the men listed alongside them – an age gap which, unless compensated for, would falsify our whole analysis. For all these reasons, only gross discrepancies between the name patterns of the sexes will be relevant; citing percentages to several decimal places (easy though these are to calculate mechanically) would only lend a spurious precision to what can at best never be more than a shadow of the truth. Even the grossest discrepancies will not deserve much weight unless they occur consistently in a wide range of unrelated documents from many parts of the country. The imbalance between the totals of men's and women's names recorded does, moreover, make it impractical to apply one of the subtler measures of foreign influence by counting how many different foreign names were in use rather than how great a percentage of the recorded population bore them.

Indeed, the silence of so many records at times raises doubts whether any investigation at all will be possible. Domesday Book and its satellites deal with feudal tenancies of kinds only exceptionally held by women; so too the early-twelfth-century surveys from Abingdon, Lindsey, and Leicestershire.[69] The survey of the Peterborough estates made in the 1120s names few of the customary tenants and scarcely a woman at all, of any rank.[70] The cartulary of St Benet of Holme offers only a dozen women's names datable between 1066 and 1150.[71] The fascinating series of legal memoranda entered in the Exeter Book likewise offers too few women's names for any statistical comparison, especially as the men's names here represent no one social class but range from those

---

[67] See Adigard des Gautries, *Les Noms de personnes scandinaves en Normandie*, pp. 163–7, 322–6, 429–31, and Fellows Jensen, *Scandinavian Personal Names*, pp. 309–11; also von Feilitzen, *Pre-Conquest Personal Names*, pp. 394–5, idem, in *The Winton Domesday*, p. 174, and Ekwall, *Early London Personal Names*, p. 83. Pronunciation must, of course, have differed; cf. modern English surnames such as *Thurkell*, *Thurkettle*, with Norman place names such as *Torqueville*, *Tourmauville*. See also above nn. 59, 60.

[68] See: Forssner, *Continental-Germanic Personal Names*, p. 252; von Feilitzen, *Pre-Conquest Personal Names*, pp. 338, 413, 423–4; idem, in *The Winton Domesday*, pp. 167, 177, 178; Schlaug, *Die altsächsischen Personennamen des 11. und 12. Jahrhunderts*, pp. 160–1, 167; Tavernier-Vereecken, *Gentse Naamkunde*, pp. 78, 106; Morlet, *Les Noms . . . gallo-germaniques*, cols 46a, 223a, 231a.

[69] D.C. Douglas, 'Some early Surveys from the Abbey of Abingdon', *English Historical Review* 44 (1929), 618–25; *The Lincolnshire Domesday and the Lindsey Survey*, ed. Charles Wilmer Foster et alii, Lincoln Record Society 19 (Horncastle, 1924); *The Leicestershire Survey c.A.D. 1130*, ed. Cecil Frederick Slade, University of Leicester Department of English Local History: Occasional Papers 7 (Leicester, 1956).

[70] *Chronicon Petroburgense*, ed. Thomas Stapleton, Camden Society (London, 1849), pp. 157–82. The only woman named seems to be *Johanna* (Wake), p. 181.

[71] *St Benet of Holme*, ed. West.

of magnates to those of manumitted serfs.[72] The two Burton Abbey surveys, dating respectively from about 1115 and about 1126, offer only twenty-two women's names all told – too few to make effective evidence either way, at least these do not contradict our pattern, for, whereas the men's names here show 18% to 24% of continental forms, all the women's names look insular except for two instances of *Avelina*, both probably referring to the same individual.[73]

Several manorial surveys do, however, more amply illustrate the differential fashion we are studying, but only late in the twelfth century. The Glastonbury survey made by Henry of Sully in 1189 shows the contrast clearly: among men's names insular forms amount to under a quarter, but among women's to almost a half.[74] The other side of the country is represented by two documents. One of these is complex, a Ramsey survey usually dated in the 1160s and incorporating sporadic comparison with 'the time of the older King Henry', apparently the 1130s; it offers about a thousand names, mainly of peasants, less than a tenth being women's names.[75] Over 55% of such women's names as there are show insular forms, against an average of under 30% for the corresponding men's names. Predictably, most of the women named are widows, and fortunately the chronological complexity of the survey allows their names to be compared with those of the current men's fathers or other antecessors (in so far as these are given); even these earlier men's names show insular forms already amounting to much less than half the total. Rather later than the Ramsey survey is the one in the Kalendar of Abbot Samson of Bury St Edmunds, dating from between 1186 and 1191: not, unfortunately, the handiest document to use, for, as well as being highly repetitive, it does not consistently note the status of the various tenants.[76] Nevertheless, it emphatically exemplifies our patterns of name-giving: whereas only 25% of the names of the current male tenants show insular forms, about 60% of those of the current female tenants (amounting as usual to less than a tenth of the total and mainly widows) show such forms; and, whereas men of the preceding generations (fathers, former land-holders) show under 50% of insular names, women in the same categories show well over 70%. So women's names here – even more so than at Ramsey – are more conservative than those of the previous generation of men.

The famous Bury survey of about a century earlier, that in the Feudal Book of Abbot Baldwin,[77] does, however, prove frustrating from our point of view. Not surprisingly at

---

[72] *The Exeter Book of Old English Poetry* (facsimile), ed. Raymond Wilson Chambers et alii (London, 1933), fols 3v–7v; see also M. Förster, 'The Preliminary Matter', ibid., pp. 44–54.

[73] C.G.O. Bridgeman, ed., 'The Burton Abbey Twelfth-Century Surveys', *Collections for a History of Staffordshire edited by The William Salt Archaeological Society 1916* (London, 1918), pp. 209–310, esp. 212–47; see also J.H. Round, 'The Burton Abbey Surveys', ibid., n.s. 9 (London, 1906), 271–89. For *Avelina*, see Morlet, *Les Noms . . . gallo-germaniques*, col. 48a.

[74] *Liber Henrici de Soliaco*, ed. Jackson, pp. 21–142. Unfortunately, no comparably significant pattern seems discernible in the patronymics and metronymics, not in any case very common here.

[75] *Cartularium Monasterii de Rameseia*, ed. Hart and Lyons, 3: 218–315; see also James Ambrose Raftis, *The Estates of Ramsey Abbey*, Pontifical Institute of Mediaeval Studies, Studies and Texts 3 (Toronto, 1957), pp. 305–6. One section also refers to 'King John' (p. 292). The figures cited are averages, as the balance of insular names to continental ones varies markedly from section to section.

[76] *The Kalendar of Abbot Samson of Bury St Edmunds and Related Documents*, ed. Ralph Davis, Camden Third Series 84 (London, 1954), pp. 3–72.

[77] *Feudal Documents from the Abbey of Bury St Edmunds*, ed. Douglas, pp. 25–44; for the date, see

a date when most tenants must have been born before the Conquest, about 95% of men's names are still insular, with some Anglo-Norse cast. The women's names, much in the minority (less than forty out of some 700) and as usual mainly those of widows, show no certain continental forms at all.[78] We might have guessed as much about the peasantry of the 1090s; and where evidence would have been most welcome it fails entirely. The abbey's 'feudati homines', that is, those holding by knight-service, are duly listed, and their names (not one unambiguously insular)[79] neatly suggest how *Durandus, Fulcerius, Guarinus, Hubertus, Ricardus, Walterus*, and so on, were introduced into the local name stock for the English peasants to copy;[80] but of these enfeoffed knights' wives, not one word.

Yet one record about Bury does move the imagination. 'In uilla ubi quiescit humatus Scs Eadmundus' there were, Domesday Book tells us, 'xxxiiii milites in*ter* francos & anglicos'.[81] As the 'feudati homines' included several magnates far too grand to attend personally upon an abbot, these knights resident at the abbey gates were presumably stipendiaries who performed the actual military duties. Now, with such a mixed band of Frenchmen and Englishmen, there might have been little to hinder the incomers from marrying the sisters, or daughters, or widows, of their English comrades. Indeed, if the suggestion is true that small tenants by knight-service barely differed in financial or social standing from free farmers,[82] then throughout the country there might have been little barrier, other than language, to marriage between the humbler French 'knights' and the sisters, daughters, or widows, of the more prosperous of their peasant

---

ibid., p. xlix, but cf. V.H. Galbraith, 'The Making of Domesday Book', *English Historical Review* 57 (1942), 161–77, esp. 168, n. 1, where he suggests 'the early part of Henry I's reign'.

[78] Many of the names here have been discussed in the papers by von Feilitzen and by Reaney listed in nn. 52, 53 and 55 above. The feminine name *Æilgild*, for which a continental etymology has been proposed, is a ghost form, the true reading being *Æilgid* (that is *Æþelgȳð*); see Cambridge University Library MS Mm. iv. 19, fol. 138(2)v, and cf. *Feudal Documents*, p. 33.

[79] Two forms might be insular, that is, *Normannus* (*Feudal Documents*, p. 24) and *Wlwardus* (ibid., p. 17), but the equivalent continental forms were widespread: see Forssner, *Continental-Germanic Personal Names*, p. 260; von Feilitzen, *Pre-Conquest Personal Names*, pp. 31–2, and idem, in *The Winton Domesday*, p. 178; Ekwall, *Early London Personal Names*, pp. 55–6, 72; Schlaug, *Die altsächsischen Personennamen des 11. und 12. Jahrhunderts*, p. 166; Tavernier-Vereecken, *Gentse Naamkunde*, p. 35; Morlet, *Les Noms . . . gallo-germaniques*, cols 174a–b, 231a.

[80] I hope to publish a paper demonstrating this in more detail. [['*Willelmus rex? vel alius Willelmus?*', below pp. 280–98, and cf. 'Onomastics', *The Cambridge History of the English Language*, II: *1066–1476*, ed. Norman Blake (Cambridge, 1992), pp. 542–606, esp. 546, 559–61, 567–68, etc.]] For aping the upper classes as a general practice, see O. Leys, 'Socio-Linguistic Aspects of Name-Giving Patterns', *Onoma* 18 (1974), 448–55, esp. 452, cf. 453–4. In Normandy the names most popular were those associated with the ducal house and with local families of magnates (see le Pesant, 'Les Noms de personne à Evreux', p. 55, and Morlet, 'Les Noms de personne à Eu', 11: 138), and in Flanders the countesses' foreign names were widely copied (see J. Lindemans, 'Over de Invloed van enige Vorstinnennamen op de Naamgeving in de Middeleeuwen', *Verslagen en Mededelingen der Koninklijke Vlaamse Academie voor Taal- en Letterkunde* [1950], pp. 99–106).

[81] *Domesday Book*, 2: fol. 372r. See also Douglas, *Feudal Documents*, pp. cvi–cviii, and S. Harvey, 'The Knight and the Knight's Fee in England', *Past and Present* 49 (November, 1970), 3–43, esp. 12–13.

[82] See F.M. Stenton, *English Feudalism*, pp. 142–5, and Harvey, 'The Knight', passim; but cf. the literary evidence for strong class feeling in France itself adduced by P. Noble, 'Attitudes to Social Class as revealed by some of the older Chansons de Geste', *Romania* 94 (1973), 359–85.

neighbours. In this context we may think of the anonymous 'Francigenae' scattered in twos and threes, or even singly, across the manors belonging to the abbey of St Albans and across several counties in the Welsh Marches, regularly listed in Domesday Book alongside the villeins and bordars.[83] How often such intermarriages may in fact have taken place remains, unfortunately, mere speculation.

And consideration of those thirty-four knights living in the 'villa' of Bury opens a further line of thought. Perhaps clues to the merging of the two peoples might better be sought from town records than from rural ones. To begin with, women might well be more adequately represented in town records; for, whereas physical incapacity barred them from tenure (except by proxy) based either on military service or on driving a plough team, town life and trade afforded them more scope for independence and so for having their names recorded. At least this was so by the thirteenth century in such a town as Battle, where not only widows but also unmarried daughters often inherited property and held it in their own right.[84] For another thing, whereas in the country the two 'nations' often enjoyed different types of tenure and so to some extent occupied different social ranks, in many towns French burgesses were living alongside English ones on more or less equal terms. Some English towns encouraged French settlers by granting them specific fiscal privileges.[85] Apart from the mixed band of knights at Bury St Edmunds, Domesday Book notes sixty-five Frenchmen at Southampton, a hundred and forty-five at York, forty-three at Shrewsbury, twenty-four at Dunwich, twenty-two at Wallingford, four at Stanstead and four at St Albans, three at Cambridge, at Hereford a number unspecified but evidently considerable, and at Norwich forty-one 'in nouo Burgo' and apparently also eighty-three other 'burgenses franci'.[86] Even though some so-called 'burgenses' were absentee landlords, such towns may none-theless have had many French residents – Shrewsbury, for instance, where forty-three burgages out of some hundred and fifty were in French hands. Such an admixture must necessarily, one might think, have affected the language and the customs of the towns that experienced it; populous places full of the to-ing and fro-ing of trade ought, after all, to see languages and traditions more briskly and more thoroughly mixed than they would be in a sparsely peopled countryside. When Orderic spoke of the two nations living side by side and intermarrying, it was in such an urban context: 'Ciuiliter Angli cum Normannis cohabitabant, in burgis, castris et urbibus, conubiis alteri alteros mutuo sibi coniungentes . . .'.[87]

Matters were not, however, so simple, for the two groups did not always live in the closest harmony. At Norwich thirty-six Frenchmen at first shared their 'new town' with six English neighbours, but by 1086 the Englishmen had been ousted by five more Frenchmen; where the other eighty-three Frenchmen lived is not clear.[88] At Southampton some demarcation between the two groups is implied by a 'French street' running

[83] *Domesday Book*, 1: fols 135v–136v, 138r–138v, 139v, 173r–173v, 174v–177r, 179v–180r, 181r–183r, 252v–253r, 254v–255v, 256v, 258v–259r, 260r.
[84] See Eleanor Searle, *Lordship and Community: Battle Abbey and its Banlieu, 1066–1538*, Pontifical Institute of Mediaeval Studies, Studies and Texts 26 (Toronto, 1974), pp. 118–20; also Power, *Medieval Women*, pp. 10, 57 et seq.
[85] See, for instance, Loyn, *The Norman Conquest*, pp. 173, 177, 179.
[86] *Domesday Book*, 1: fols 52r, 56r, 179r, 189r, 252r, 298r, and 2: fol. 118r. Northampton and Nottingham also each comprise a 'novus burgus' as well as the old, but without any note on the origin of the residents (ibid., 1: fols 219r, 280r).
[87] *Orderic Vitalis*, ed. Chibnall, 2: 256.
[88] *Domesday Book*, 2: fol. 118r.

parallel to the main 'English street'.[89] At Shrewsbury the English burgesses openly resented the tax exemptions granted to the foreigners.[90] Were Englishmen so hostile or Frenchmen so aloof as to hinder the former from marrying their daughters to the more privileged incomers?

All too often the surviving documents again fail to reply. The earliest extensive burgess list extant, that of the king's burgesses in Colchester at the time of the Domesday survey, contains about two hundred and seventy names.[91] Not one of the few women's names here – less than thirty – seems continental.[92] Men's names include a few continental forms – not surprisingly, for the list includes tenants-in-chief (including our old friend William Pecche) who happened to hold burgages as well as rural estates. So all this shows is that in a town with only a tiny (and probably non-resident) foreign minority the independent widows flourishing one generation after the Conquest were all of unquestionably native stock.

One town whose residents certainly included some French people was Battle. Here, on a dry upland previously uninhabited, all were incomers and some specifically from overseas, 'ex transmarinis etiam partibus nonnulli'.[93] A rental of about 1110 incorporated in the late-twelfth-century *Chronicle* of the abbey lists well over a hundred burgage tenants, including nine women.[94] Unexpectedly, baptismal names show similar proportions of continental forms for both sexes: about 40%. A few of the men have by-names plainly indicating foreign origins, like 'Gilberti *extranei*' and 'Rotberti *de Cirisi*'.[95] Among the other bearers of 'continental' baptismal names[96] an unknowable

---

[89] Colin Platt, *Medieval Southampton: The Port and Trading Community, A.D. 1000–1600* (London, 1973), pp. 6–7.

[90] *Domesday Book*, 1: fol. 252r.

[91] *Domesday Book*, 2: fols 104r–106r. Not surprisingly for the date, the comments by J.H. Round in *The Antiquary* 6 (1882), 5–6, and in *VCH Essex*, 1: 414–24, cf. 574–6, are of little use for name study; some individual forms are discussed by von Feilitzen in *Namn och Bygd* 33. See also the next note.

   The other lists of citizens' names in *Domesday Book* – e.g., that for Oxford (1: fol. 154r), which shows insular forms as normal for both sexes – are all too brief to be representative.

[92] The gender of some names is uncertain, as final *-a* might mark either a continental feminine name or an OE feminine latinized or else an OE weak masculine; see von Feilitzen, *Pre-Conquest Personal Names*, pp. 127–8, and idem, in *The Winton Domesday*, pp. 224, 227. For *Berda* as masculine, see idem, *Namn och Bygd* 33: 74, and for *Dela* likewise, see Redin, *Studies on Uncompounded Personal Names*, p. 75.

[93] *Chronicon Monasterii de Bello*, [ed. J.S. Brewer], Anglia Christiana Society (London, 1846), pp. 12, 28.

[94] *Chronicon*, pp. 11–16; the text has been checked with the manuscript, British Library Cotton MS Domitian A II, fols 15v–18r. See also H.W.C. Davis, 'The Chronicle of Battle Abbey', *English Historical Review* 29 (1914), 426–34, and especially Searle, *Battle Abbey*, pp. 69–78 and App. 12, pp. 465–6, for comments on the distribution of population through the several districts of the town.

[95] Northern France offers several place names of possible form; see Auguste Longnon, *Les Noms de lieu de la France: Leur Origine, leur signification, leurs transformations* (Paris, 1920–29), p. 625, item 6949, and, with a different etymology proposed, Albert Dauzat and Charles Rostaing, *Dictionnaire étymologique des noms de lieux en France* (Paris, 1963), col. 162. For Cerisy-la-Forêt (*dép.* Manche), some early-C11 charters of the abbey show *Cirisiacus* as an alternative to the commoner *Cerisiacus* (e.g. *Recueil des actes des ducs de Normandie de 911 à 1066*, ed. Marie Fauroux, Mémoires de la Société des Antiquaires de Normandie 36 (Caen, 1961), p. 194; cf. *Monasticon Anglicanum* vol. 6, pt 2, p. 1073). (I am grateful to Mr Fairclough and the staff of the Map Room of Cambridge University Library for kind assistance with this problem.)

[96] The form *Herod'* (fol. 17r) is difficult, as the biblical name hardly seems acceptable (and is not,

number must, of course, have been of at least partly English stock, like 'Rotberti *filii Siflet*' (a metronymic formed with the English *Sigeflæd*). The women's names offer no notes of parentage, of origin, or even of widowhood. The pattern is unusual but, with numbers so small, random events might easily have affected the balance of the list. In any event, a new town like Battle, where wives as well as husbands had all to be incomers, might well have had an untypical structure of population.

One of the documents we noted earlier as already known to show a discrepancy between the name patterns of the sexes was the 1177 survey of Newark-on-Trent.[97] Here over 40% of the women's names remain insular, beside only some 20% of the men's. As usual, the women amount to only about an eighth of the total (some forty instances) and are mostly specified as widows, thus once again carrying the risk of an age gap between them and the men.

Fortunately, as was to some extent the case with the Ramsey and Bury surveys we have already examined, some sets of urban records do enable us to allow for any generation gap. The archives of Christ Church priory in Canterbury contain several substantial rentals, ranging in date from just after the middle of the twelfth century to the opening of the thirteenth.[98] Here too women's names are far fewer than men's and mainly those of widows. Within each rental the proportions of insular to continental names conform to the pattern already noted elsewhere. In Rental B, dating from the mid-1160s, insular forms still predominate among women's names, amounting to over 55% (some 51 individuals, with some 30 bearing insular names), whereas for men's names insular forms amount to less than 25%. The roughly contemporary list of 'brothers and sisters' of the Gild of St Anselm offers higher proportions of insular names but a similar balance between the sexes, with some 35% of men's names insular beside over 60% of women's (again a small sample, as many women members are nameless wives or daughters).[99] Perhaps the members of the Gild were on average older than the Christ Church tenants, or perhaps they belonged to more rural milieux. Around the turn of the century Rentals D, E, F, and G still show over 40% of women's names as insular (some 67 individuals, with some 28 bearing insular names), as against only 10% of all names taken together. Of these figures some corroboration comes from the cartulary of a minor religious house in Canterbury, St Gregory's priory; here, about a score of women's names datable in the last quarter of the twelfth century (some certainly from rural milieux) prove to be fairly equally divided between insular and

---

for instance, listed by Morlet in *Les Noms latins ou transmis par le latin*); it can, however, be paralleled elsewhere in C12 England (e.g., *Kalendar of Abbot Samson*, p. 37). Perhaps it was a 'pageant' nickname (for this category, see Reaney, *Origin*, pp. 170–1), or else it may represent a form of *Herold*, to be derived either from Continental-Germanic *Her(i)wald* or from Norse *Haraldr* (see: Förstemann, *Personennamen*, col. 780, cf. col. 813, also Kaufmann, *Ergänzungsbuch*, p. 183; von Feilitzen, *Pre-Conquest Personal Names*, pp. 284–6; Schlaug, *Die altsächsischen Personennamen des 11. und 12. Jahrhunderts*, p. 111; idem, *Die altsächsischen Personennamen vor dem Jahre 1000*, p. 106; Fellows Jensen, *Scandinavian Personal Names*, pp. 132–4; Morlet, *Les Noms . . . gallo-germaniques*, col. 127a).

[97] See above n. 63.

[98] Urry, *Canterbury under the Angevin Kings*, pp. 221–382 (I am deeply grateful to my friend, Mrs Dorothy Owen, for a very long-term loan of this basic text).

[99] W. Urry, 'Saint Anselm and his Cult at Canterbury', *Spicilegium Beccense* 1 (1959), 571–93, esp. 585.

continental forms.[100] If, then, the women's names recorded in the rentals from about the turn of the century are set beside men's of the mid-1160s – surely a more than generous allowance for any age-gap – there is still a discrepancy, with over 40% of the later women's names remaining insular beside less than 25% of the earlier men's. On the other hand, a list intermediate in date, Rental C, dated about 1180, shows only some 25% of women's names as insular; but the sample is tiny (less than a dozen names) and, as this rental lists not rents received but payments made to overlords, may in any case be weighted towards the gentry.

These Canterbury rentals, dating from a century to about a century and a half after the Conquest, presumably refer to individuals born and baptized from about 1110 to 1175; but where those individuals had been born or of what parentage they do not say, except for the few bearing foreign territorial surnames or specified as *Flandrensis* or *Mansel*.[101] What they illustrate so amply are twelfth-century fashions in names and the underlying cultural attitudes these imply. The names may indeed reflect some cultural groupings. In no list is the number of women whose fathers' names are given large enough for analysis; but (deceased) husbands' names conform to a clear pattern. Although in the 1160s insular forms generally amount to under 25% of men's names, over 40% of the husbands of women with insular names have insular names themselves (9 beside 12 continental): conversely, among husbands of women with continental names less than 15% bear insular names (2 beside 13 continental). Forty years later, in Rentals D and F, some 35% of the names of husbands of women with insular names still show insular forms (4 beside 7 continental), beside only 10% as the average for all names taken together, whereas for husbands of women with continental names the proportion is about average (1 insular beside 10 continental). Admittedly, the numbers are so small as hardly to make a scientific sample; but the regularity of the pattern is striking. It seems as though – in spite of the insistence in *Dialogus de Scaccario* that French and English had merged – some social or cultural division, not rigid or water-tight yet nonetheless real, must have been persisting between those families of Canter-bury townspeople by now using continental names almost exclusively and those others still keeping partly to insular forms, most markedly with women's names but to some extent with men's as well.

As for the cities *par excellence* of eleventh-century England, London and Winchester, these were, notoriously, omitted from Domesday Book.[102] For Winchester, which, although smaller not only than London but also than York, Lincoln or Norwich, was in many ways the premier city, the omission is more than made good by the successive surveys dating from about 1110 and again about 1148.[103] Even in the Confessor's reign

---

[100] *Cartulary of the Priory of St Gregory, Canterbury*, ed. Audrey Woodcock, Camden Third Series 88 (London, 1956).

[101] Possibly an adjective 'from Le Mans' (see Morlet, *Etude d'anthroponymie picarde*, p. 77; but Robert, *Dictionnaire alphabétique et analogique de la langue française*, 4: col. 406a, notes *manceau* as first recorded in C17, cf. Godefroy, *Dictionnaire de l'ancienne langue française*, 5: 154–5, where the medieval form is given as *mansois*, so also Tobler-Lommatzsch, *Altfranzös-isches Wörterbuch*); alternatively, from a diminutive of Continental-Germanic *Manzo* (cf. *Man-selinus* noted by von Feilitzen, in *Smith Festschrift*, p. 55; see also Förstemann, *Personennamen*, cols 1093–4, and Kaufmann, *Ergänzungsbuch*, p. 248).

[102] Brooke and Keir, *London 800–1216*, pp. 149, 156, suggest it was the very size and complexity of these two cities which defeated the Domesday clerks.

[103] Republished in *The Winton Domesday*, ed. Biddle et alii (see above n. 52); see also *Domesday Book*, 4 (*Additamenta*): 531–42, 542–62, and M. Biddle, 'The Winton Domesday: Two Surveys

continental influence had been at work here: some 15% of the names of property-holders *TRE* included in the 1110 survey already show continental forms. After the Conquest Norman magnates became familiar figures, if not all as residents, certainly as landlords; and they included some women, as witness, for instance, the names in both surveys of 'Emma de Perci' and of 'Adeliz soror Henrici de Port'.[104] With potential foreign influence thus at a maximum, the 'national' balance in personal names here ought to be significant. Rich though they are, these surveys are not, however, ideal for our study: all too often women property holders are specified only by a relationship or even more vaguely as 'quedam vidua', 'quedam lauandaria', so that the women's names mentioned, amounting to no more than some 5% of the totals, scarcely make a fair sample. For what such scanty samples may be worth, they do emphatically conform to our pattern.[105] Already in 1110 the men's names – including, admittedly, a good few belonging to Norman magnates – show insular forms reduced to under 30%: the corresponding women's names – also including some belonging to members of Norman families – show insular forms still amounting to some 65% (10 out of 15). These figures are remarkable, being almost as advanced as those we have noted fifty years later in Canterbury, a city by no means sheltered from foreign influences. In the survey of 1148 insular forms amount to less than 20% of the men's names recorded but still to 40% of the women's – a higher proportion than in the men's names of over a generation earlier. Coupled with the maintenance of native street names,[106] the comparative conservatism of the women's names recorded suggests that even here, in probably the most gallicized of all English towns, foreign influences may not have gone very deep. Certainly the men's names recorded in these surveys can scarcely have been typical of those of the local population as a whole.

A few names from these surveys appear also in the *Liber Vitae* of Hyde Abbey, Winchester.[107] At first glance, this looks promising for our study, as it offers women's names, not indeed in equal proportions with men's, but as about two-fifths of the total, and as it sometimes names both spouses (more rarely, whole families) together. Admittedly, those enjoying confraternity with an abbey do not reliably represent either a social class or a geographical location: not all need have lived in Hampshire, or even in England, let alone in Winchester itself. That a few did live there, and at dates relevant to our study, is guaranteed by the recurrence of their names in the surveys. But even more than most records this *Liber Vitae* needs careful interpretation, as from the

of an Early Capital', in *Die Stadt in der europäischen Geschichte: Festschrift Edith Ennen*, ed. Werner Besch et alii (Bonn, 1972), pp. 36–48.

[104] *The Winton Domesday*, pp. 45 &c., 63 &c., also pp. 40 (n. 39.2), 147, 155.

[105] Von Feilitzen gives very full statistics in *The Winton Domesday*, pp. 183–7, 190. Although for the present purpose these figures need some adjustment, in the event our estimates do not much differ from his; the main difficulty arises from the cultural ambiguity of names of Norse origin (see above nn. 59, 67, and von Feilitzen, op. cit., p. 191).

[106] See *The Winton Domesday*, pp. 231–9, and cf. the maintenance of English names for streets and other topographical features in C12 Canterbury (Clark, 'People and Languages in Post-Conquest Canterbury', below pp. 179–206, esp. 198–9).

[107] British Library MS Stowe 944; *Liber Vitae*, ed. Birch (see above n. 56). For description of the manuscript, see Birch, op. cit., pp. i–ii, lii–liv, and footnotes to the relevant pages of text, and also Neil Ker, *Catalogue of Manuscripts containing Anglo-Saxon* (Oxford, 1957), pp. 338–40.

A striking example of a name shared is *Godwine Greatseod* 'big purse', *Liber Vitae*, fol. 29r (p. 74), beside *Godwinus Gretsud*, in *The Winton Domesday*, p. 64 (*TRE*), see also ibid., p. 212.

mid-eleventh century on names are entered without apparent system, according as spaces presented themselves.[108] Therefore, to rely overmuch on the simplified printed versions of the name lists would be unwise. For what it may be worth, analysis of some of these, apparently ranging in date from the mid-eleventh century well into the twelfth and perhaps later,[109] suggests a name pattern not unlike that of the 1148 survey, with insular forms amounting to only some 20% to 25% of men's names but to some 40% or 45% or even more of women's. Especially relevant to our study – although not invariably supporting our hypothesis – are some of the names of married couples. In the later strata, dating from the mid-eleventh century on, a good few entries show couples one of whom bears an insular name and the other a continental one. Sometimes, as we have already observed at Canterbury, a man with an insular name might have a wife with a continental one (for one thing, 'national' origins and social class apart, men often choose wives younger than themselves, even by as much as a whole generation). Of such matches the Hyde *Liber Vitae* offers perhaps half a dozen clear examples: 'Eaduuinus' and 'Oriald', 'Eaduuardus' and 'Matildis', 'Godricus' and 'Sufficia', 'Æaduuinus uenator' and 'Odelma', and also 'Godwinus' the priest and 'Erenburch', who gave their son the culturally ambiguous Norse name 'Stigandus'.[110] In accordance with the general trend, the reverse pattern seems about twice as common, perhaps a dozen husbands with continental names having wives with insular ones: for instance, 'Hermannus' and 'Coleruna', 'Roðulf' and 'Ælfgyfu', 'Regnoldus' and his 'Gyðe' with her Anglo-Norse name, 'Odo' and 'Oreguen', 'Waerinus' and the Norse-named 'Ingrith', 'Gotselin' and 'Ealdgið', 'Egnulfus' and 'Æilíuu', 'Ansketillus' and 'Eadgyfu', and also 'Anscetillus' and 'Eadgiþa', 'Ricardus Palmarius' and 'Brihgiua'.[111] There is seldom any way of knowing which, if any, of the people with continental names may have been of foreign stock: 'Walter scot', husband of 'Leofyue', was evidently not;[112] for 'Teotselinus laicus', husband of 'Ealdgida', his father's name 'Folcuuinus' does suggest continental origins, at all events if this is the same 'Teotselinus' as attests a document of the 1080s.[113] Another possible clue is that spellings like *Ælfgyfu*, *Eadgyfu*, suggest early dates, perhaps before continental names had been much adopted by the English even for men.

As for London, this is far less well represented than Winchester by the extant

---

[108] The benefactors' names are entered on fols 20r, 24v, 25r, 25v, 28v, 29r, 54v and 55r. The complex stratification invites a study far more detailed than the present context allows; for an analogous case, see Giles Constable, 'The *Liber Memorialis* of Remiremont', *Speculum* 47 (1972), 261–77.

[109] Pp. 64–70 (top) and 123–47 of the printed text: over 1300 names.

[110] Fols 20r (p. 30), 24v (p. 51), 28v (p. 67). For the women's names, see Morlet, *Les Noms de personne sur le territoire de l'ancienne Gaule*, 1: cols 46b, 79b, 166b, 176b, and 2: cols 108b–109a; for *Stigandus*, see Adigard des Gautries, *Les Noms de personnes scandinaves en Normandie*, pp. 138–9, and Fellows Jensen, *Scandinavian Personal Names*, p. 266.

[111] Fols 20r (p. 30), 28v (p. 64), 29r (p. 71), 29r (p. 72), 29r (p. 73), 54v (p. 123), 54v (p. 125), 55r (p. 136), 55r (p. 138); a number of less clear examples have been omitted. For *Coleruna*, see von Feilitzen, in *The Winton Domesday*, p. 153, and for *Oreguen* (probably *Ordwynn*), see idem, in *Namn och Bygd* 33: 86; for *Gyðe* and *Ingrith*, see Fellows Jensen, *Scandinavian Personal Names*, pp. 119–20, 151.

[112] Fol. 29r (p. 72); cf. p. 164, where he appears as witness to a charter dated 1080–87.

[113] Fol. 29r (p. 74); cf. p. 164, where he appears as witness to a charter dated 1080–87. For *Folcwine*, see von Feilitzen, in *Smith Festschrift*, p. 52, and Morlet, *Les Noms . . . gallo-germaniques*, cols 95b–96a; for *Teotselinus*, see Forssner, *Continental-Germanic Personal Names*, p. 229, and Morlet, op. cit., col. 71b.

documents. No adequate survey exists; but then, if modern estimates of its eleventh-century population are anywhere near the mark,[114] to be adequate a survey of London would need to be many times larger than any extant for anywhere in post-Conquest England. Such material as does survive is in fact small in scale: for instance, a list of tenants holding from St Paul's about 1130 offers less than a hundred names all told[115] (whereas hardly more than 40% of men's names remain insular here, the grand total of eight women's names includes only one, *Eua*, that is certainly continental, plus one, *Ragenild*, that is ambiguous).[116] Information is excellent about a few special groups, such as the canons of St Paul's, 'the best documented chapter of the twelfth century in Christendom' (although even in the first decades of the century continental names predominate among them, some English element persists until a good deal later);[117] but these of their very nature contain no names of women. To tantalize us further, that vast population embodied a deep paradox: long since involved in trade with all northwestern Europe (laws of Æthelred II give special mention to merchants from the Low Countries and from Rouen),[118] London might well have become the most cosmopolitan of cities,[119] yet modern authority after modern authority, each concentrating on a different aspect of affairs, witnesses to the irreducible 'Englishness' not only of its populace but of its patriciate as well.[120] Plainly, no immigration, let alone the passing contacts of trade, could do more than season so vast a population.

Yet, 'English' though London remained, it saw immigrants enough in the upper ranks of society: men of property, traders and craftsmen such as had already so long

[114] Brooke and Keir, *London 800–1216*, pp. 70, n. 3, and 100, emphasize the unreliability of all such estimates, e.g., Russell's guess of over 17,000, based on an inflated notion of parish-size (*British Medieval Population*, pp. 51, 286–7, cf. Brooke and Keir, op. cit., pp. 122–48).

[115] H.W.C. Davis, 'London Lands and Liberties of St Paul's, 1066–1135', in *Essays in Medieval History presented to Thomas Frederick Tout*, ed. A.G. Little and F.M. Powicke (Manchester, 1925), pp. 45–59, esp. 55–9 (cf. Brooke and Keir, *London 800–1216*, pp. 86, 163, n. 2); see also Ekwall, *Early London Personal Names*, pp. 111–17.

[116] For *Eua*, see Morlet, *Les Noms latins . . .*, col. 49a; for *Ragenild*, either Norse or Continental-Germanic, see von Feilitzen, *Pre-Conquest Personal Names*, p. 347, Ekwall, *Early London Personal Names*, pp. 80, 104, 112, Morlet, *Les Noms . . . gallo-germaniques*, col. 185a, and Fellows Jensen, *Scandinavian Personal Names*, pp. 213–15 (Viking influence in London had been far from negligible; see Ekwall, op. cit., pp. 73–85, 86–7, and Brooke and Keir, *London 800–1216*, pp. 141–2, 178, 261–5). The other names are: *Alueva*, *Edild*, *Godid*, *Liuiua* (only in a metronymic), *Wakerild*, and *Bugia*. This last Ekwall, op. cit., p. 112, tentatively identified as a French nickname 'candle', but a better source seems to be *Bucge*, an OE hypocoristic form for names in *Burg-* or *-burg* (see Redin, *Studies in Uncompounded Names*, p. 115, Boehler, *Die altenglischen Frauennamen*, pp. 213–4, and also F.M. Stenton, in *Collected Papers*, p. 317).

[117] See C.N.L. Brooke, 'The Composition of the Chapter of St Paul's, 1086–1163', *Cambridge Historical Journal* 10 (1950–52), 111–32, esp. 121–2, and Brooke and Keir, *London 800–1216*, pp. 341–7; cf. Ekwall, *Early London Personal Names*, pp. 105–7 (too easily assuming, here and elsewhere, that even in the early C12 a continental name still means continental blood).

[118] *Die Gesetze der Angelsachsen*, ed. Felix Liebermann, 1 (Halle, 1903), 232. By the Confessor's time men from Ghent and from Rouen had each their own wharf: see F.M. Stenton, 'Norman London', in *Collected Papers*, pp. 23–47, esp. 41–2.

[119] See Brooke and Keir, *London 800–1216*, pp. 29, 178–9, 258–76.

[120] Thus: Ekwall, *Early London Personal Names*, pp. 1, 173; Stenton, 'Norman London', pp. 35–7; S. Reynolds, 'The Rulers of London in the Twelfth Century', *History* 57 (1972), 337–57, esp. 339; Brooke and Keir, *London 800–1216*, pp. 13–14, 29, 31–2, 86, 96 et seq., 142, 246–7. In the London section of the Pipe Roll for 31 Henry I insular names are not uncommon (ed. Hunter, pp. 143–50).

been frequenting the city, and senior churchmen (who, with the persistence of clerical marriage,[121] would by no means lie outside the scope of our study, but for the dearth of information about their wives).[122] Some of these incomers did, of course, bring wives with them, among these the father of St Thomas of Canterbury, Gilbert Becket, a merchant from Rouen with a wife from Caen, and in London prominent enough to become a sheriff.[123] What percentage of the settlers may thus have brought wives with them it would be idle to enquire, for the evidence is not there, having survived for the Becket couple only because their son became a saint. Other incomers certainly married in London. Otho the goldsmith we have already met, with his well-dowered widow and the estates she brought him.[124] Another well-known example, brought to light by Round over eighty years ago as illustrating 'the close amalgamation of the Normans and the English', is that of the 'Cornhill' family.[125] The titular founder of this family was Edward 'Upcornhille', 'de Cornhella',[126] who flourished in the early twelfth century; he and his wife 'Godeleva', daughter of another prominent citizen, Edward 'de Suthwerke',[127] gave their daughter the fashionable name 'Agnes' and married her

---

[121] See C.N.L. Brooke, 'Gregorian Reform in Action: Clerical Marriage in England, 1050–1200', *Cambridge Historical Journal* 12 (1956), 1–21, also 187–8. Among the early-C12 canons of St Paul's not only marriage but also inheritance of prebends were common; see idem, 'The Chapter of St Paul's', pp. 121, 125, and cf. Ekwall, *Early London Personal Names*, pp. 106–7.

[122] The name of one canon's wife has been preserved in the Durham *Liber Vitae*: 'Raulf filius Algoti . . . et Mahald socia eius . . . et mater Raulfi Leouerun' (*Liber Vitae Ecclesiae Dunelmensis: A Collotype Facsimile . . . &c.*, [ed. A.H. Thompson], Publications of the Surtees Society 136 [Durham, 1923], fol. 42 (+)r, and see also Brooke, 'The Chapter of St Paul's', p. 123, n. 66); although the couple both have French names of Continental-Germanic origin, the man's mother has an insular name (*Lēofrūn*; see von Feilitzen, *Pre-Conquest Personal Names*, p. 315) and his father an ambiguous one, probably Anglo-Norse but possibly Continental-Germanic (see von Feilitzen, op. cit., p. 146, Ekwall, *Early London Personal Names*, pp. 74–5, and Morlet, *Les Noms . . . gallo-germaniques*, col. 16a).

An earlier couple seems purely continental: Canon Ansger (from Bayeux) and his wife Popelina, the parents of Audouen bishop of Evreux and of Thurstan archbishop of York (see Brooke, 'The Chapter of St Paul's', p. 124 and n. 71, and Donald Nicholl, *Thurstan, Archbishop of York (1114–1140)* [York, 1964], pp. 5, 7–8).

[123] *Materials for the History of Thomas Becket, &c.*, ed. James Craigie Robertson and J.B. Sheppard, 7 vols, Rolls Series (London, 1875–85), 3: 14 'Mahalt', 4: 3 'Machildis' and 81 'Roesam, natione Cadomensem' (for this name, see Forssner, *Continental-Germanic Personal Names*, p. 220, also Morlet, *Les Noms . . . gallo-germaniques*, col. 138a). See also R. Foreville, 'Les Origines normandes de la famille Becket et le culte de saint Thomas en Normandie', in *Mélanges Andrieu-Guitrancourt = L'Année canonique* 18 (1973), 433–80, esp. 439–48. For Gilbert as sheriff, see Brooke and Keir, *London 800–1216*, pp. 33, 210, 212–3, 353, 372.

[124] See above p. 121 and n. 25.

[125] John Horace Round, *Geoffrey de Mandeville: A Study of the Anarchy* (London, 1892), App. K, pp. 304–12; see also idem, *The Commune of London, &c.* (London, 1899), p. 107, and Brooke and Keir, *London 800–1216*, pp. 206–11; also the Pipe Roll for 31 Henry I, ed. Hunter, pp. 147, 148.

[126] [H.C. Maxwell-Lyte], *Ninth Report of the Royal Commission on Historical Manuscripts* (London, 1883), Pt 1, pp. 1–72 (*Report on the Manuscripts of the Dean and Chapter of St Paul's*), esp. col. 61b; *Calendar of the Letter-Books . . . of the City of London . . .: Letter-Book C*, ed. Reginald Robinson Sharpe (London, 1901), p. 219. See also Ekwall, *Early London Personal Names*, p. 31.

[127] *Letter-Book C*, p. 220. For *Godeleva* (*Godleofu*; not included in von Feilitzen, *Pre-Conquest Personal Names*, or in *The Winton Domesday*), see Ekwall, *Early London Personal Names*, pp. 39–40.

to Gervase, son of the one-time sheriff of London, Roger Hubert's nephew, and of Ingenolda daughter of Herlewin – a sequence of names such as at this early date seems likely to mean a family whose male lines at least were continental.[128] This Gervase took his father-in-law's surname, 'of Cornhill', and throve exceedingly, becoming in his turn a City sheriff and surviving into the 1180s.[129] A probable uncle of Gervase's, Ralph son of Herlewin, also at one time a sheriff of London, married Mary, who was herself the child of a mixed marriage between a Baldwin of Arras and an unnamed daughter of Algar (probably, that is, *Ælfgar*) son of Cole, the hereditary incumbent of St Michael 'le Querne'; Algar's son Nicholas was in old age to make the church over to his great-nephew Robert, a son of Ralph and Mary.[130]

Confined as it has been to the tiny oligarchy of 'shrieval' families, our London material has so far been anything but representative. Moreover, such analysis as we can carry out rests to a dangerous degree on the name forms themselves, with all the uncertainties these inescapably entail once the post-Conquest generations enter the records. Thus, the 'Geroldus de Stratford' who around 1115 had a wife 'Godeva'[131] may or may not have been of immigrant stock. Yet sometimes patterns of naming do seem to imply mixed marriages in the background, even though the names of the wives and mothers themselves have not been recorded. A London goldsmith of the early twelfth century was called 'Leofstan son of Witso';[132] as he already at this time had a grown son, his own father 'Witso' can hardly have been born, at latest, much after 1055, a date at which such a name seems likely to mean continental birth, so that Leofstan's own English name may mean he had an English mother; in spite of the strong tendency for London patricians to adopt continental names, Leofstan himself kept up the bicultural tradition by naming his own sons 'Witso' and 'Edward'.[133] A more questionable case is that of the alderman in office about 1130, 'Eilwardus fil. Wizeli';[134] not only might his father 'Wizelo' (a diminutive of *Witso*) have been born

---

[128] Round, *Commune*, p. 107, notes an early-C13 tradition that this family hailed from Caen. Of their names only *Roger* and *Herlewin* are recorded by von Feilitzen, *Pre-Conquest Personal Names*, pp. 248, 350, both as rare and alien; see also Forssner, *Continental-Germanic Personal Names*, pp. 74, 79–80, 110–11, 156, 217–18, and Morlet, *Les Noms de personne sur le territoire de l'ancienne Gaule*, 1: cols 81b–82a, 136b, 140a, 146b, 2: col. 57a.

[129] See Reynolds, 'Rulers of London', pp. 346–7, also 354; and Brooke and Keir, *London 800–1216*, pp. 210–11.

[130] See *Report*, 1: col. 20a: 'Nicolaus sacerdos Sancti Micaelis filius Algari Colessune . . . Roberto filio Radulfi filii Herlewini filio nepte mee, scilicet Marie filie Baldewini de Araz'; see also Round, *Geoffrey de Mandeville*, pp. 309 et seq., and Ekwall, *Early London Personal Names*, p. 103. As a base for the English patronymic *Colessune*, Ekwall, op. cit., pp. 78–9, prefers Norse *Kolr* or *Koli* (see von Feilitzen, *Pre-Conquest Personal Names*, p. 307, and Fellows Jensen, *Scandinavian Personal Names*, pp. 176–7) to English *Cola* (see von Feilitzen, op. cit., pp. 217–18).

[131] *Report*, 1: col. 61b. For *Geroldus*, see Forssner, *Continental-Germanic Personal Names*, pp. 103–4, and Morlet, *Les Noms . . . gallo-germaniques*, col. 100b.

[132] 'Levestano filio Withsonis, Withsone filio ejus': *Chronicon Abbatiæ Rameseiensis, &c.*, ed. William Dunn Macray, Rolls Series (London, 1886), p. 245; also 'Witso fil. Leuestani' in the Pipe Roll for 31 Henry I, ed. Hunter, p. 145. For *Witso*, see Forssner, *Continental-Germanic Personal Names*, p. 259, and Morlet, *Les Noms . . . gallo-germaniques*, col. 222b.

[133] *Report*, 1: col. 63b; Pipe Roll for 31 Henry I, ed. Hunter, p. 145; see also preceding note. See Ekwall, *Early London Personal Names*, p. 97.

[134] E.g., Davis, 'London Lands and Liberties', p. 57. For *Wicelo*, see Morlet, *Les Noms . . . gallo-germaniques*, col. 222b.

and named after the Conquest but his own name 'Eilwardus', although most probably representing English *Æþelweard*, might possibly stand for the continental
Agilward.[135]

Clear records of mixed marriages are rare. Nor, in any event, was it invariably the
wife who was the English one. Tierry son of Deorman and his Clare bride we have
already met.[136] And early-twelfth-century London records offer some more speculative
possibilities of such marriages, such as the reference to 'Sinodus [that is, *Sigenoð*]
scutarius gener Radulfi (? aurifabri)'.[137] Records are, however, far too sparse to allow
even a guess at the relative frequency of the two kinds of intermarriage. And, as for
material allowing statistical analysis of naming patterns, nothing at all of such kind
seems to have survived from early post-Conquest London.

At the end of the day our picture remains ill-focused: the few identifiable individuals resist reduction to statistical trends, and what background we have of statistics
concerns fashion only, reflecting the origins of the names themselves rather than of the
people bearing them. Yet the view may have cleared a little. In twelfth-century England
women's names did lag oddly behind the fashion which was so drastically changing
those given to men. That time lag could be explained by a paucity of women, and so of
feminine name models, among the post-Conquest French settlers, and, if not so explained, would imply among twelfth-century English parents some otherwise unrecorded feeling that daughters were, in a way that sons were not, vessels of the native
tradition. A paucity of women among the incomers, although far from demonstrable
statistically, is at least compatible with such patterns of marriage as can be traced
among magnates and patricians. It is compatible also with the interpretation of the
satirist Nigel's distinction between 'mother's' and 'father's' tongues as referring respectively to English and to French;[138] but, quite apart from its uncertain interpretation, that
statement is too personal and individual to form any base for generalization. Yet, if our
guess is right, that Norman women did play but little part in the post-Conquest
settlement of England, it would have been no wonder that the Anglo-Norman gentry of
Nigel's sort, with some English mothers and many English maids and nurses, should
soon show some acquaintance with the English language, uncourtly though they felt it
to be.[139] Perhaps such considerations ought to move us, not necessarily to reject
entirely, but at all events somewhat to qualify certain recent pronouncements about
Norman attitudes in twelfth-century England: thus, 'The Normans were Normans
through all these years. Normandy was their home country . . .'.[140] Did those nameless,
humble 'Frenchmen' scattered in ones and twos across the Welsh Marches marry their
sons only to one another's daughters? Did the Cornhills of London wholly reject the
language and the traditions of the line of City burgesses from whom their ancestress

---

[135] See Ekwall, *Early London Personal Names*, p. 16 (but cf. pp. 97, 101), and Morlet, *Les Noms
    . . . gallo-germaniques*, col. 24a.
[136] See above p. 120 and n. 15.
[137] *Report*, 1: col. 61b; see also Ekwall, *Early London Personal Names*, p. 103 (for some even more
    speculative possibilities of similar matches, see ibid., p. 104).
[138] See above p. 118 and n. 7.
[139] See above p. 117 and nn. 2 and 3.
[140] Le Patourel, *Normandy and England 1066–1144*, p. 29. The argument here rests partly on
    literary evidence which a more recent study has adjudged to be politically inspired rhetoric
    (Davis, *The Normans and their Myth*, passim and esp. pp. 66–7).

Agnes was descended? Did 'Wihenoc's man' and his modest Norfolk heiress disdain employing local maids for their children? High politics tells one tale, and tells it in a clear and dominating voice; but the story being quietly lived out in towns and in manor houses had a different theme as well as a different style.

11

Towards a Reassessment of 'Anglo-Norman Influence on English Place-Names'

Introduction

As the force responsible for many apparently 'non-standard' phonological develop-ments found in English place-names, R.E. Zachrisson eighty years ago proposed a pervasive and often permanent 'Anglo-Norman influence' on their pronunciation (Zachrisson 1909 and also 1924). This hypothesis, reinforced by Johan Vising's views of socio-linguistic conditions in medieval England (Vising 1923: 8–27), has over the years so far hardened into dogma that, in the face of any difficult place-name form, some of the less critically minded workers have tended simply to invoke the name of Zachrisson.

Those same eighty years have meanwhile witnessed changes in all the many disci-plines that converge into English place-name studies or, rather, would in an ideal world so converge. Their documentary basis has been transformed by the foundation in the 1920s of the English Place-Name Society and the subsequent publication of (to date) over sixty volumes of its projected Survey. Their theoretical basis ought likewise to have been transformed by the vast changes taking place not only in phonetic observa-tion and phonological analysis and, consequently, in our notions of the Middle English and the Anglo-French soundsystems, but also in social history and in the philosophy of language. The time might thus seem more than ripe for reassessing Zachrisson's hypothesis and the conventional wisdom therefrom derived. That this seems so far hardly to have been attempted may in part be attributed to the necessarily limited overlap between the intellectual world of the English toponymists and that of the Anglo-Norman socio-linguists. Even what is here essayed is no point-by-point refuta-tion of Zachrisson's claims but simply a plea for an alternative approach, some sugges-tions for which are adumbrated.

1. The Socio-Linguistic Background

First, a word as to what is here of only marginal concern: medieval spelling. No-one denies that a great many place-name forms found in medieval English documents reflect non-English orthographical traditions; and, given that normally the contexts in which such forms are embedded are Latin ones, their alien aspect may seem explicable enough. For the present purpose, these seemingly 'non-English' spellings will be deemed relevant only in so far as they might be taken to show permanent phonological developments. There is a paper waiting to be written on 'The myth of the Anglo-Norman scribe' and indeed I myself hope before long to tackle the task elsewhere.[1]

---

[1] [[See below 168–76.]]

Meanwhile, the contention is that no medieval spelling should ever be interpreted as in a vacuum but that the whole orthographical context should always be considered.

There is, of course, a shared socio-linguistic assumption underlying both the Zachrissonian view of place-name development and the belief, still prevalent among some workers, in the widespread presence throughout medieval England of 'Anglo-Norman scribes'. That assumption may not unfairly be represented by Zachrisson's own formulation, as expressed in 1924, of 'the part played by French in a[n English] town of importance . . . in the late thirteenth century':

> All instruction in schools was given in French and as a rule by French teachers. The French element among the clergy was strong. Nearly all the highest dignitaries of Church and State – earls, bishops, abbots, judges and sheriffs, as well as a great many minor officials – were Frenchmen by birth or origin. In the town there resided many influential French burghers. There were also Frenchmen in humbler walks of life – soldiers, tradesmen and artisans (Zachrisson 1924: 96).

Thus, Zachrisson postulated a continuing presence in England, up to (it would seem) at least 1300 and perhaps beyond, of a substantial body of native French-speakers, not only nobles and prelates but also schoolmasters, scribes and craftsmen; and he assumed the speech-habits of these people to have been crucial for the development of many English place-names. Any reassessment of his hypothesis must therefore start by reconsidering the number and the social distribution of native-level French-speakers in medieval England.

Certainly, the England of the twelfth, thirteenth and fourteenth centuries did contain multitudes of people who, either as a professional necessity or as a social accomplishment, spoke and wrote (Anglo-) French with varying degrees of accuracy and fluency; but for the present purpose that is neither here nor there. The question is one not of fluency nor of idiomatic and stylistic command but of native articulatory setting. Acquisition of a second language in no way impairs the ability to pronounce one's cradle-tongue (years of exile might perhaps do so, but that is precisely not the point). The reverse effect is the normal one, with the articulatory setting characteristic of the cradle-tongue warping the pronunciation of any acquired one. Can anything be suggested as to the types of articulatory setting dominant in medieval England? That Anglo-French pronunciation was *sui generis* is generally agreed, and at least some Romanists ascribe its peculiarities specifically to influences from the Middle-English substratum. Over sixty years ago Prior claimed the 'phonetic evolution of Anglo-Norman', and its prosody in particular, to have been 'strongly influenced by English' (Prior 1924: ix–xxvii). Pope subsequently made the same point in far greater detail, summarizing her findings thus:

> The strongest factor in the growing instability of Anglo-Norman pronunciation was undoubtedly the influence of English speech habits. Displacement, together with contact with a foreign tongue, shook tradition, and the acquirement of French by people with a different organic basis induced gradually many modifications. The most disturbing factor in the English speech-habits was the heavy tonic stress. . . . Consonantal sounds that were unfamiliar to the English were early modified . . .; those that were moribund or rather ephemeral in French were sometimes retained longer than on the Continent if they had a place in the English sound-system (Pope 1952: 431–2, 432–50).

The phonological processes there envisaged would have been the very converse of the ones that Zachrisson asserted to have at much the same time been distorting the development of many English place-names. Both notions can hardly be right.

Various attempts at weighing up the likely balance in medieval England between native-level speaking of the two languages have already from time to time been made.[2] For the line of thought here to be pursued, the effective starting-points are two papers published in 1943, that is, Wilson's general survey and, more particularly, Woodbine's study of the language of medieval English law; but to some extent Shelly's thesis of 1921 had pointed the way. Over the last quarter-century various further studies on related lines have appeared, among them those by Berndt (1965, 1976, and 1982: 23–30),[3] by the present writer (1976, 1978, 1980 and 1987), by Richter (1979 and 1985), by Short (1979–80), and above all by Rothwell (1968, 1975–6, 1978 and 1985). The upshot is that many scholars, mainstream historians included, are now of the belief that, even among the nobility of Anglo-Norman England, native (as distinct from acquired) use of French must not only be deemed extinct shortly after the loss of Normandy in 1204 but also be suspected of having been far in decline by the latter part of the twelfth century (e.g., Clanchy 1979: 151–4, 156–9, 162–74, and 1983: 59–60, and likewise Lass 1987: 54–61).[4]

On this score, interesting albeit inconclusive testimony is given in his *Speculum Duorum* (datable *post* 1208) by Gerald of Wales, of the very social class in which native use of French would *a priori* be expected longest to persist. In castigating a nephew for neglecting his studies, Gerald used terms seeming, on the face of it, to imply that, at that date and in those circles, French had to be learnt in much the same way as had Latin; for he coupled the two languages together, saying 'nec linguam latinam, aut etiam gallicam, addidicistis' and condemning the young man's ignorance 'linguarum omnium precipueque duarum, latine scilicet et gallice, que pre ceteris apud nos prestant' (Lefèvre 1973 and 1974: 32, 132; Short 1979–80: 470–1; Richter 1979: 68, 159, and 1985: 47–8).[5] As model, he instanced a certain *magister Iohannes Blundus*, apparently of the same social class (a background with which the French-derived by-name would be consonant), who had for his part striven to perfect his command of French (*Francorum lingua, ydioma gallicum*) with the help of uncles who had, like Gerald himself, studied in France, indeed to such effect that he could speak it 'tanquam materna sibique nativa' (Lefèvre 1974: 56–7; Richter 1985: 53–4). There unfortunately remains here some ambiguity, for Gerald nowhere makes it clear, concerning either young man, whether the 'Anglo-French' stigmatized as 'rough and corrupt' (*rudique Anglorum . . . Gallico et feculento*) were in fact the imperfect French of a native English-speaker or simply a dialectal mother-tongue (Rothwell 1978: 1082; Short 1979–80: 470–1).

One thing clear, and accepted by even the stoutest proponents of Anglo-Norman as a

---

[2] In his oral presentation Dr H. Lüdtke also pointed this out. [[Dr Lüdtke's paper on 'Middle English-French' was not included in the published volume of conference proceedings.]]

[3] Berndt's articles, condensed from his Rostock Habilitationsschrift of 1962, present common-sense conclusions which unfortunately are seldom, as published, adequately supported by documentation.

[4] Barlow (1986: 17), for instance, took a similar point of view for granted when discussing Becket's likely command of languages.

[5] Between 1976 (68–9) and 1979 (159) Richter's views of Gerald's own linguistic background changed somewhat. The view that Gerald's 'mother tongue was French' is maintained, but without the adducing of any evidence, by Bartlett (1982: 13).

living vernacular, is that not only Gerald's nephew and Master John Blund but also many other descendants of the post-Conquest settlers were, within only a few generations, needing to strive assiduously to acquire and maintain, through continental contacts, a 'good' pronunciation of French (e.g., Legge 1980). Implications remain uncertain: the unacceptability of 'Anglo-French' might simply have lain in its being, by contrast with 'French of Paris', a provincial dialect, one among many such (Rothwell 1985). If, however, Pope was right in concluding, from her intensive comparison of the two phonologies, that the idiosyncrasies of unreconstructed Anglo-French pronunciation arose principally from its having soon become tainted by English speech-habits (Short 1979–80: 469), then there would have been particular reason for the insular self-consciousness about it and also for the frequent continental ridicule. A second thing that is clear is that by the mid-thirteenth century at the latest even the gentry were, as Walter of Bibbesworth's manual shows, thinking primarily in English terms; and it might not be unreasonable to suppose pronunciation likely to have become Anglicized earlier than semantic structures.

Pope's conclusions, if accepted, undercut Zachrisson's assumption of an enduring inability among the descendants of the post-Conquest settlers to get their tongues round English place-names. And, as well as being founded on comparative phonology, Pope's is also the commonsense view. Whatever difficulties the first generation of settlers might have had with English pronunciation, for anything of the kind to have persisted widely among their English-born descendants is unlikely. Not only is it impolitic, even downright dangerous, to cultivate ignorance of the language spoken by a potentially hostile majority, but doing so would demand highly artificial insulation of the young from the world around them. For such insulation there seems to be no evidence: the settlers, the knightly class especially, intermarried with the English gentry (Clark 1978: above 117–23; Chibnall 1986: 208–9), sometimes coming to take pride in the insular side of their ancestry; they would also have employed English attendants, including nurses and maidservants (Clark 1978: above 123–4).[6] Indeed, Zachrisson's insistence, as exemplified in the paragraph quoted, upon male settlers and functionaries, 'Frenchmen', betrays an unrealistic indifference to the rôles played by mothers and nurses in the transmission of language from generation to generation. If, as mainstream historians maintain, the settlers were for the most part quick to identify themselves in a socio-political sense with their new country, a concomitant willingness to acquire a working knowledge of its vernacular would hardly be surprising (e.g., Chibnall 1986: 208–14).

The fewer the speakers to whom English speech-habits were alien, the less likely might seem extensive foreign influence upon English phonology. The crucial point may, however, be not so much numbers of speakers as modes of transmission; for influence can operate only through bilingual contact. Whatever a speaker's cradle-tongue, in actual French discourse the pronunciation of English names of all kinds would have had to be partly modified, if only because of the incompatible stress patterns; and this would seem to open the way for linguistic snobbery. Gallicized pronunciations required by French contexts would have been familiar to any English attendants or officials who used French in the course of their work; such people might have affectedly imported such pronunciations – or, rather, re-Anglicized versions of

---

6 In a partly analogous situation, the young Kipling, cared for by Indian servants, had to make an effort in order to speak ' "English", haltingly translated out of the vernacular idiom that one thought and dreamed in' (Kipling 1937: 3).

them – into their native discourse with family and friends, who might in their turn have cultivated and propagated the affectations to such effect as to oust the native forms. Such a scenario cannot be ruled out *a priori*, because, as will shortly be explained in fuller detail, the special semantic character of names partly emancipates them from the rules governing the rest of the language and makes them vulnerable to unhistorical notions of 'correctness' (in present-day English manifested chiefly through spelling-pronunciations). How often is snobbish affectation likely thus to have intervened in the medieval development of English place-names? No direct assessment is possible, but with the most distinctively French variants such as *Nicol(e)* for ME *Lincolne*, there certainly seems little sign of their ever having been carried over into English contexts (Cameron 1985: 1–3).

Would it, in any case, have been likely for such affectation to have been limited, as seems supposed, to place-name forms?

2. *The Lexical and Phonological Background*

A sidelight is thrown on this whole problem by the few English place-names actually created out of French elements (Gelling 1978: 236–40). That these are few is in itself significant. Of the names borne by the 140-odd new towns founded between the late eleventh century and the early thirteenth, no more than a dozen were formed from French elements (Beresford 1967: 386–99, 414–526); and those that were so formed were almost all commonplace compounds like *Belveder* > *Belveir* 'fair prospect' (Ekwall 1960: 37), *Beaurepair* 'fair dwelling' (Cameron 1959: 525–6), and *Richmond* 'splendid hill' (Smith 1928: 287). A few manor-houses received French names, and so did a few newly-founded abbeys, such as Battle (Mawer *et alii* 1929–30: 495), *Dieu-lacres* or *Delencres* (Greenslade 1970: 230) and *Haltemprice* (Smith 1937: 208). There were also occasional renamings of pre-Conquest settlements. All told, however, such cases are so rare as to imply that French, for all its snob value, seldom prevailed over native styles and traditions of place-naming. Even street-naming, largely of post-Conquest growth though it was, shows scant French influence: medieval forms involve few French elements; such as do appear are mostly commonplace loanwords like *drapery* and *poultry* or current occupational terms like *butcher* and *mercer*. This is true of towns, like Southampton and York, for which Domesday Book records high numbers of French burgesses (Platt 1973: 47–8; Palliser 1978),[7] of those, like Canterbury and Winchester, constantly frequented by foreigners (Clark 1976, below 198–9; Biddle 1976: 233–5), and of those, like Cambridge, Exeter, Gloucester, Nottingham and Worcester, the present forms of whose own names have often been ascribed to 'Anglo-Norman influence' (Reaney 1943: 36–8, 44–50; Gover *et alii* 1931–2: 20–4; Smith 1964–5: ii, 123–34; Gover *et alii* 1940: 13–22; Mawer *et alii* 1927: 19–23). Ekwall's verdict on what was hardly the least cosmopolitan of cities sums the situation up: 'Practically all London street-names are purely English formations which presuppose

[7] For privately informing me that French influence on the street-names of two other towns in this category, *viz.* Norwich and Shrewsbury, is likewise of limited extent, I am grateful to Dr K.I. Sandred and Dr M. Gelling respectively. I also wish to thank Dr Gelling and Dr G. Fellows-Jensen for discussing with me the general presentation of this paper; neither of them is, however, to be held responsible for any unwise opinion expressed.

an English-speaking community' (Ekwall 1954: 19–23).[8] So marked a paucity of lexical influence might in itself be thought to call into question any extensive phonological influence in the same sphere; for, whereas lexical borrowing is commonplace and easy in all sorts of socio-linguistic contexts, phonological influence might seem to require at least a local supremacy of the articulatory setting characteristic of native speakers of the donor language (on both counts, French interaction with English toponymy might be held to contrast strongly with the heavy Scandinavianization seen in the Northern Danelaw). At all events, the subsequent developments of the few Anglo-French coinages show little sign of any lastingly Gallicized pronunciation: normally, their modern forms are consonant with an early shift to initial stress, with *Belveir* giving /'bi:və/ (spelt *Belvoir*), *Belrepair* giving /'belpə/ and so on.[9]

Further clues as to what was happening at the interface between the two languages are afforded by general vocabulary. In the very terminology of social rank, *lord*, *knight*, and *lady* became – one might almost say, remained – the accepted designations for members of the gentry; and that despite the presence in *knight* of at least one phonetic feature, initial /kn/, allegedly unpronounceable by people of Anglo-Norman background (Zachrisson 1924: 96). Above all, English loans from French imply phonological patterns somewhat different from those that the Zachrissonians have postulated. Among the effects of 'Anglo-Norman influence on English place-names' most often alleged is a sporadic substitution of /ts/ > /s/ for the /tʃ/ expected as reflex of OE palatalized <c> (Zachrisson 1924: 100–3). Cases in point include the modern forms of some, but by no means all, names formed with OE *-ceaster*, such as *Exeter*, *Gloucester*, *Leicester* (Ekwall 1960: 294), *Towcester* (Gover *et alii* 1933: 94–5) and *Worcester*, together with various miscellaneous ones like /sɜ:n/ *Cerne* < OE *Cerne(l)* of obscure origin, *Diss* supposedly < OE *dīc* 'ditch', and *Lancing* supposedly < OE **Wlencingas* 'followers of Wlenc' (Ekwall 1960: 93, 145; Mawer *et alii* 1929–30: 199–200, 24–5): the present forms of these and many other names have often been ascribed to 'Anglo-Norman sound-substitution'. Was inability to pronounce /tʃ/ and a tendency to replace it by /ts/ > /s/ in fact rife in medieval England? (For what it is worth we may note in passing that speakers of Modern French, who certainly do not possess /tʃ/ in their native lexical material, seem to encompass the sound quite adequately when it occurs in foreign place-names like *Tchad* or *Tchéchoslovaquie*.) Twelfth-century spellings, far from affording help, merely multiply confusions, owing to the uncertain values of the graphemes <c> and <ch> (for some French vernacular usages, see Waters 1928: 171–3 and Storey 1946: p. xiv).[10] The Romance philologists, in their considered opinions based upon the full spectrum of available evidence, represent /tʃ/ as current until the mid-thirteenth century at least both in Anglo-Norman and also, but with a contrasting distribution, in Francien (e.g., Pope 1952: 93–4, 450); and it should, moreover, be observed that in both dialects the later reflex of /tʃ/ was regularly /ʃ/, not /ts/ or /s/. That

---

8 On the varying currency of French in twelfth-century English towns, cf. the admittedly dramatic and tendentious speech inserted into his *Chronicle* by Richard of Devizes (Appleby 1963: 66).

9 Sometimes, indeed, unstressed generics of French origin were during the Middle English period itself replaced by English ones more or less similar in sound: instances include *Beadlow*, derived from Fr *beau lieu* but reformed as if with a reflex of OE *hlāw*, and *Rewley*, derived from Fr *real lieu* but reformed as if with a reflex of OE *-leah* (Mawer and Stenton 1926: 147; Gelling 1953–4: 22–3).

10 The Digby text of the *Chanson de Roland*, for instance, shows both spellings sometimes interchanging in the same word so that 'hot' appears as *calz* or *chald*, and so on.

a sound which speakers of Middle English identified with their own reflex of OE palatalized <c>, that is, with the antecedent of Modern English /tʃ/, did occur in whatever dialects were represented in Anglo-French is borne out by the multitudinous loanwords that contain this sound both in initial and in (originally) medial positions. So numerous are these that space forbids offering here more than a small selection (cited in modern spelling and with the date of the earliest *MED* citation):[11] *catch* 1225 and its doublet *chase* 1330, *chain* 1300, *chair* 1300, *challenge* 1230, *chamber* 1230 and *chamberlain* 1230, *champion* 1230, *chance* 1300, *chancellor* 1300 and *chancery* 1300, *change* 1230, *(en)chantment* 1300, *chapel* 1225, *chapter* 1230, *charge* 1300, *charity* 1225, *charter* 1250, *chaste* 1225, *cheer* 1225, *chequer* 1330 and *exchequer* 1300, *chess* 1312, *chief* 1300, *chimney* 1325, *chine* 1330, *approach* 1325, *arch* 1300, *archer* 1300, *blanch* 1398 (cf. *blanchet* 'cosmetic' 1225), *brooch* 1230, *couch* (vb) 1325, *haunch* 1230, *launch* 1330, *merchandise* 1300, *perch* 'rod' 1300, *pinch* 1325 (*ipinchunge* 1230), *porch* 1300, *pouch* 1325, *preach* 1230 and *preacher* 1230, and so on. The tally is at all events high enough to cast doubt on Zachrisson's attempted dismissal of this category of word (1924: 100–1). So, without venturing into any subtleties of pronunciation in either language, we seem justified in affirming the existence of similar sounds in both; and, if in lexical material, why not in names? If *blanch* and *launch*, why not *Launching* < **Wlencingas*, especially as this form does occur in thirteenth-century documents? At very least, ascribing the modern pronunciations of *Exeter, Gloucester, Worcester, Diss* and so on to Middle English imitation of a sporadic Anglo-French inability to pronounce the antecedent of Modern English /tʃ/ begins to look oversimplified.

3. *The Possibility of 'Onomastic Sound-Change'*

Yet, no matter how justified scepticism may be as to any wholesale impact of 'Anglo-Norman influence' on the pronunciation of English place-names, it cannot cancel out the need to explain the many instances of seemingly aberrant development. As a general basis for such explanation, what I propose is the already mentioned special semantic character of names. Names, that is to say, although ultimately derived from ordinary meaningful elements of language, have by definition ceased to carry any 'sense' as normally understood. This obviates maintenance of formal links or analogies with the related lexical items and so, as others have already noted, allows free rein to tendencies, elsewhere curbed, towards assimilation or dissimilation, elision and syncope, procliticization, folk-etymology (or 'analogical reformation', as some prefer to call it), and so on (cf. Lass 1973 and Coates 1987). Zachrisson (1924: 98) himself conceded the difficulty of distinguishing between what he saw as effects of 'Anglo-Norman influence' and those of non-standard native sound-changes.

The danger with invoking any principle as nebulous as 'non-standard sound-change' is that it could make all too easy the explaining away of any and every apparent deviation from the supposed norm. If the aim is to couch explanations in terms of native, but unbridled native, tendencies, then some care must be put into defining these

[11] For reasons already given, twelfth-century spellings are too unreliable to be cited. In the list provided here, many of the citations dated 1225 and 1230 come from the *Katherine*-Group or the *Ancrene Wisse*, in the orthography of which <ch> does regularly indicate reflexes of OE palatalized <c>.

tendencies. To attempt to do so in Middle English terms might risk complete circularity of argument. To do so in present-day ones might lead to anachronistic assumptions of affinities between modern modes of articulation (especially, perhaps, the investigator's own) and Middle English ones. The latter course is nevertheless the one that I shall provisionally adopt: the general principles of sound-change will be those of Samuels's *Linguistic Evolution* (1972), and the sorts of detailed observation those exemplified in Brown's *Listening to Spoken English* (1977) and in Lass's account of what he calls 'allegro speech', that is, 'communication with maximal ease in the least time possible' (1987: 118–21). Nothing at present put forward is meant as definitive, the aim being simply to try out one possible methodology alternative to the traditional Zachrissonian one and to see whether it is, in the long run, likely to yield any acceptable explanations of phenomena hitherto often attributed to 'Anglo-Norman influence'.

The name *Cambridge*, for instance, is one of those often taken to show the effects of 'strong Norman influence' (Zachrisson 1909: 136–8 and 1924: 105, 108, 114; Reaney 1943: 36–8). The earliest forms, dating back to c.900, are *Grantanbrycg*, *Grantebrycg* 'bridge over the river Granta'; for the present purpose, the river-name, which is obscure (Reaney 1943: 2–3, 6), may be taken just as a given name-element, and indeed its obscurity will not prove irrelevant. Although spellings with initial <gr-> continued to be used until the late thirteenth century at least, ones with <c-> were from the late eleventh century onwards appearing alongside them. Compatible though this chronology might on its own seem to be with 'Norman influence', on closer consideration such an explanation looks less convincing. There is nothing specifically French about the 'distant dissimilation' or 'regressive dissimilatory lightening' by which /r/ was elided from the first of two successive consonant-groups containing it so as to produce from *Grantebricge* a reflex *Cambridge* (Samuels 1972: 16); and in fact present-day colloquial English offers various parallels for it, as in the casual pronunciations /'febjʊri/ *February*, /'sekɪtri/ *secretary*, /'vetɪnri/ *veterinary*, and so on. Nor, in this context, is there any call to see substitution of <c-> for <g->, of /k/ for /g/, as necessarily French; for this can at least as acceptably be taken as generated by the spoken chain, that is, as an assimilation of the initial consonant of the name towards the final /-t/ of the frequently preceding *at* and, given the sporadic procliticization of such a /-t/ (Smith 1956: i, 5–7), such an assimilation would in no way be extraordinary. Elision and assimilation would have been facilitated by the long-standing 'meaninglessness' of the element affected, especially as not everyone referring to the town need have been aware of the original form of the river-name. As for the appearance of the first *Cante-* forms not long after the Conquest, this might reflect only the break in orthographic traditions and a consequent tendency to render colloquial pronunciations. There is, after all, little reason to suppose Cambridge, as a town, to have been more subject than most to French influences: among its medieval street-names, for instance, there is only one that might conceivably be invoked as evidence of such a thing, and that is *Petty Cury* (Reaney 1943: 44–50).

To return to the names in OE *-ceaster*: if the /k/ variants characteristic of the Danelaw are left aside, we find that, whereas forms of the generic range from /ˌtʃɪstə/ to /stə/ or /ɪtə/, those of simplex names and of the specific are virtually always /'tʃestə/;[12] and this might be thought to suggest the workings of some process

___

[12] I am unaware of any exceptions to this among simplex names. For the specific, there is at least one apparent exception involving the name *Seighford* (Staffs.), seemingly corresponding to a

associated with low stress, rather than any kind of outside influence. Geographically, the full and the reduced forms of the generic seem to show no significant distribution-pattern: *Chichester, Colchester*, the two *Dorchesters, Ilchester, Manchester, Porchester, Rochester, Silchester* and *Winchester* coexist with, for instance, /'bɪstə / *Bicester* (Gelling 1953: 198), /'glɔstə/ *Gloucester*, /'lestə / *Leicester*, /'təustə / *Towcester* (Gover *et alii* 1933: 94), /'wustə / *Worcester*, also /'eksɪtə / *Exeter* and /'rɒksɪtə/ *Wroxeter*. Socially, it is hardly obvious why Bicester or Towcester should seem to have been more of a hotbed of 'Anglo-Norman influence' than, of all places, Winchester. On the other hand, patterns of syllabification do seem to the point: loss of /tʃ/ leads to a contracted /stə / or /ɪtə /, not to */ˌsɪstə /.[13] This strengthens suspicions that we may have to do with development associated with reduced stress. Because any medial syllable of three may be liable to syncope, as in /'lemstə / < OE *Leomynster* (with a first element of uncertain origin: Ekwall 1960: 295), a generic *ceaster* might some-times have been contracted to */ˌtʃstə / and then, in rapid or casual speech especially, further simplification of the four successive dental or alveolar consonants would have been inevitable. The further simplification seen in *Exeter* < OE *Exanceaster* might have been due to a dissimilation provoked by the /ks/ in the initial syllable: no-one could pronounce */'ekstʃstə/, with its six successive consonants, otherwise than as a feat of phonetic athleticism. Again, the phonetic obscuration might have been facili-tated by some loss of meaning from the element involved: the latest *MED* records of a reflex of the OE common noun *ceaster* date from c.1200 and in the *Chronicle*, despite the availability of suitable contexts, the last is in the annal for 1095. An instructive contrast to these place-name developments is afforded by the genuinely French-derived term *exchequer*, ME *escheker* – a ruling-class word if ever there was one: /tʃ/ had occurred in the French etymon and, unlike the similar sound in the reflex of OE -*ceaster*, in Middle English it escaped obscuration because the syllable to which it was initial had become stressed. As for the variation of the place-name generic between /ˌtʃɪstə/ and /stə/, some names show parallel currency of both forms until late in the Middle English period, and this would be compatible with the suggested origin of the variation in the differences between what Lass calls 'allegro speech' and the more careful formal style. Survival of /tʃ/ seems to have been favoured, but not governed, by the presence of a preceding /l/, /n/ or /r/, that is, a consonant whose point of articulation was related to that of the affricate.

To sum up: what has been proposed is that a traditional explanation of certain phenomena in terms of the effects of 'language contact' should be discarded in favour of one invoking an unchecked operation of general native tendencies. The argument for this rests on two premises: first, that name-material may, of its very nature, develop more freely than common vocabulary; and, secondly, that the developments Zachrisson and others have sought to explain through 'Anglo-Norman influence' seem to have been peculiar to place-names. And, on this basis, it is urged that, whenever any apparently aberrant development is observed solely in name-material, explanation ought first of all to be sought within the language to which that material belongs, sought, that is, in an unrestrained operation of regular processes and, specifically, in standardization of variants originally generated in rapid and casual speech. It was only

---

Domesday Book form *Cesteforde*; but the whole development there is so aberrant as to constitute a special case.

[13] The modern /'saɪrnˌsestə/ *Cirencester* represents an artificially 'restored' spelling-pronunciation (Smith 1964–5: i, 60–2).

after having formulated this hypothesis of what might be called 'onomastic sound-change', involving developments related to the normal processes of the language in question but more drastic (and sometimes also more capricious) in their operation, that I discovered that a similar proposal had been made fifteen years ago, and in a different context, by Roger Lass. While not in the least wishing to shelter behind anyone else's phonological authority, I do venture to claim that the independent excogitation of this concept by two minds so differently stored and motivated may lend my hypothesis more weight than it might otherwise have carried.

REFERENCES

Appleby, J.T. (ed.) (1963): The Chronicle of Richard of Devizes of the Time of King Richard the First. London: Nelson.

Barlow, F. (1986): Thomas Becket. London: Weidenfeld and Nicolson.

Bartlett, R. (1982): Gerald of Wales, 1146–1223. Oxford: Clarendon Press.

Beresford, M.W. (1967): New Towns of the Middle Ages. London: Lutterworth Press.

Berndt, R. (1965): 'The linguistic situation in England from the Norman Conquest to the loss of Normandy (1066–1204)'. Philologica Pragensia 8: 145–63. Reprinted in Lass (ed.) (1969): 369–91.

—————— (1976): 'French and English in thirteenth-century England'. In: Aspekte der anglistischen Forschung in der DDR. Martin Lehnert zum 65. Geburtstag. Sitzungsberichte der Akademie der Wissenschaften der DDR, Gesellschaftswissenschaft pt 1: 129–50.

—————— (1982): A History of the English Language. Leipzig: Verlag Enzyklopädie.

Bestmann, F. (1938): Die lautliche Gestaltung englischer Ortsnamen im Altfranzösischen und Anglo-Normannischen. Romanica Helvetica 9. Zürich: M. Niehans.

Biddle, M., *et alii* (1976): Winchester in the Early Middle Ages. Winchester Studies 1. Oxford: Clarendon Press.

Brown, G. (1977): Listening to Spoken English. London: Longman.

Cameron, K. (1959): The Place-Names of Derbyshire, 3 pts. English Place-Name Society 27, 28, 29. Cambridge: Cambridge UP.

—————— (1985): The Place-Names of Lincolnshire, pt 1. English Place-Name Society 58. Nottingham: The Society.

Chibnall, M. (1986): Anglo-Norman England 1066–1166. Oxford: Blackwell.

Clanchy, M.T. (1979): From Memory to Written Record. London: Edward Arnold.

—————— (1983): England and its Rulers, 1066–1272: Foreign Lordship and National Identity. London: Fontana.

Clark, C. (1976): 'People and languages in Post-Conquest Canterbury'. Below 179–206.

—————— (1978): 'Women's names in post-Conquest England: observations and speculations'. Above 117–43.

—————— (1980): 'Certains aspects de l'hagiographie anglo-latine de l'Angleterre anglo-normande'. Above 84–91.

—————— (1987): 'Spelling and grammaticality in the Vespasian Homilies: a reassessment'. Manuscripta 31, pt 1: 7–10.

Coates, R. (1987): 'Pragmatic sources of analogical reformation'. Journal of Linguistics 23: 319–40.

Ekwall, E. (1954): Street-Names of the City of London. Oxford: Clarendon Press.

—————— (1960): Concise Oxford Dictionary of English Place-Names. 4th edn. Oxford: Clarendon Press.

Gelling, M. (1953–4): The Place-Names of Oxfordshire, 2 pts. English Place-Name Society 23, 24. Cambridge: Cambridge UP.
—— (1978): Signposts to the Past. London: Dent.
Gover, J.E.B., *et alii* (1931–2): The Place-Names of Devon, 2 pts. English Place-Name Society 8, 9. Cambridge: Cambridge UP.
—— (1933): The Place-Names of Northamptonshire. English Place-Name Society 10. Cambridge: Cambridge UP.
—— (1940): The Place-Names of Nottinghamshire. English Place-Name Society 17. Cambridge: Cambridge UP.
Greenslade, M.W. (ed.) (1970): A History of the County of Stafford, III. Victoria History of the Counties of England. Oxford, for the Institute of Historical Research.
Kipling, R. (1937): Something of Myself. London: Macmillan.
Lass, R. (ed.) (1969): Approaches to English Historical Linguistics: An Anthology. New York: Holt, Rinehart and Winston.
—— (1973): Review-article based on P.H. Reaney (1967): The Origins of English Surnames. Foundations of Language 9: 392–402.
—— (1987): The Shape of English: Structure and History. London: Dent.
Lefèvre, Y. (1973): 'De l'usage du français en Grande Bretagne à la fin du XIIe siècle'. In: Etudes de langue et de littérature du Moyen Age offertes à Félix Lecoy. Paris: Champion: 301–5.
—— *et alii* (eds) (1974): Giraldus Cambrensis: Speculum Duorum. Cardiff: University of Wales Press.
Legge, M.D. (1980): 'Anglo-Norman as a spoken language'. In: Proceedings of the Battle Conference on Anglo-Norman Studies 2: 109–17, 188–90. Woodbridge: Boydell and Brewer.
Mawer, A., *et alii* (1927): The Place-Names of Worcestershire. English Place-Name Society 4. Cambridge: Cambridge UP.
Mawer, A. and F.M. Stenton (1926): The Place-Names of Bedfordshire and Huntingdonshire. English Place-Name Society 3. Cambridge: Cambridge UP.
—— (1929–30): The Place-Names of Sussex, 2 pts. English Place-Name Society 6, 7. Cambridge: Cambridge UP.
Palliser, D.M. (1978): 'The medieval street-names of York'. York Historian 2: 2–16.
Platt, C. (1973): Medieval Southampton: The Port and Trading Community, A.D. 1000–1600. London: Routledge and Kegan Paul.
Pope, M.K. (1952): From Latin to Modern French, with Especial Consideration of Anglo-Norman. 2nd edn. Manchester: Manchester UP.
Prior, O.H. (ed.) (1924): Cambridge Anglo-Norman Texts. Cambridge: Cambridge UP.
Reaney, P.H. (1943): The Place-Names of Cambridgeshire and the Isle of Ely. English Place-Name Society 19. Cambridge: Cambridge UP.
Richter, M. (1976): Giraldus Cambrensis: The Growth of the Welsh Nation. 2nd edn. Aberystwyth: National Library of Wales.
—— (1978–9): 'Giraldiana'. Irish Historical Studies 21: 422–37.
—— (1979): Sprache und Gesellschaft: Untersuchungen zur mündlichen Kommunikation in England von der Mitte des elften bis zum Beginn des vierzehnten Jahrhunderts. Monographien zur Geschichte des Mittelalters 18. Stuttgart: Anton Hiersemann.
—— (1985): 'Towards a methodology of historical socio-linguistics'. Folia Linguistica Historica 6, pt 1: 41–61.
Rothwell, W. (1968): 'The teaching of French in medieval England'. Modern Language Review 63: 37–46.
—— (1975–6): 'The rôle of French in thirteenth-century England'. Bulletin of the John Rylands Library 58: 445–66.

—— (1978): 'A quelle époque a-t-on cessé de parler français en Angleterre?' In: Mélanges de philologie romane offerts à Charles Camproux. Montpellier: Université Paul-Valéry: 1075–89.

—— (1985): 'Stratford-atte-Bowe and Paris'. Modern Language Review 80: 39–54.

Short, L. (1979–80): 'On bilingualism in Anglo-Norman England'. Romance Philology 33: 467–79.

Shelly, P. van D. (1921): English and French in England 1066–1100. Philadelphia.

Smith, A.H. (1928): The Place-Names of the North Riding of Yorkshire. English Place-Name Society 5. Cambridge: Cambridge UP.

—— (1937): The Place-Names of the East Riding of Yorkshire. English Place-Name Society 14. Cambridge: Cambridge UP.

—— (1956): English Place-Name Elements, 2 pts. English Place-Name Society 25, 26. Cambridge: Cambridge UP.

—— (1964–5): The Place-Names of Gloucestershire, 4 pts. English Place-Name Society 38, 39, 40, 41. Cambridge: Cambridge UP.

Storey, C. (ed.) (1946): La Vie de saint Alexis. Oxford: Blackwell.

Vising, J. (1923): Anglo-Norman Language and Literature. Oxford: Clarendon Press.

Waters, E.G.R. (ed.) (1928): The Anglo-Norman Voyage of St Brendan. Oxford: Clarendon Press.

Wilson, R.M. (1943): 'English and French in England, 1100–1300'. History 23: 37–60.

Woodbine, G.E. (1943): 'The Language of English Law'. Speculum 18: 395–436.

Zachrisson, R.E. (1909): A Contribution to the Study of Anglo-Norman Influence on English Place-Names. Lunds Universitets Årsskrift, NF I, iv, 3. Lund.

—— (1924): 'The French element'. In: Mawer, A., and F.M. Stenton (eds.): Introduction to the Survey of English Place-Names. English Place-Name Society 1, i. Cambridge: Cambridge UP: 93–114.

—— (1925): 'Some English place-names in a French garb'. In: Mélanges de philologie offerts à M. Johan Vising. Gothenburg: N.J. Gumpert: 179–201.

12

Domesday Book – A Great Red-Herring: Thoughts on Some Late-Eleventh-Century Orthographies

Some dozen years ago an eminent English toponymist declared of Domesday Book that it enabled us 'to study the effects of Norman French pronunciation on English place-names'. Only two or three years ago a distinguished medieval historian expressed to me in conversation his surprise at discovering, in an English monastic obituary compiled about a century later than Domesday Book,[1] numerous spellings, of personal names and of place-names, markedly more traditional than those of the older document. For all the eminence of the scholars concerned, neither viewpoint is, I contend, a true one; if so, then the acceptance of both among scholars of distinction lends urgency to the task of their redressing.

I: *Defining the Domesday Texts*

Before anatomizing either misapprehension, we must first define, in linguistic terms, the corpus of Domesday texts and its place among source-materials bearing upon late-eleventh-century English socio-linguistic conditions.

It is unfortunate that it should be Domesday Book which happens to provide not only the earliest extant records of perhaps 40% of English place-names[2] but also the most extensive as well as the best-known corpus of eleventh-century English personal names; and doubly so that this mischance should, for personal names, have been compounded by Olof von Feilitzen's magisterial treatment of those recorded in the pre-1066 stratum of that document.[3] For it is to von Feilitzen's monograph that everyone concerned with eleventh-century English personal-naming inevitably – and rightly so – turns, only to absorb from it, along with the author's scholarship, an impression (often, it seems, a dangerously subliminal one) that the orthographical styles characteristic of the Domesday manuscripts were typical of that time. To deplore this is neither to impugn the information laid up in Domesday Book nor to decry the young von Feilitzen's remarkable and lasting achievement – all the less, since (as we shall shortly see) he himself was careful not to present Domesday orthography as typical of late-eleventh-century English usages. The present concern is solely with the matter – which some might perhaps regard as marginal – of spelling traditions; but to

---

[1] The obituary in question is published as no. 24 in *Die Gedenküberlieferung der Angelsachsen, mit einem Katalog der libri vitæ und Necrologien*, ed. J. Gerchow (Berlin, 1988), pp. 280–9 and 343–50. (References to the two misapprehensions cited are withheld.)

[2] See, e.g., P.H. Sawyer, 'The Place-Names of the Domesday Manuscripts', *Bull. John Rylands Library*, 38 (1955–56), 483–505, esp. p. 483.

[3] Olof von Feilitzen, *The Pre-Conquest Personal Names of Domesday Book*, Nomina Germanica 3 (Uppsala, 1937) (hereafter *PNDB*).

philologists orthography, far from being marginal, is the foundation of all their study, and it may further be considered a crucial, albeit subtle, indicator of cultural patterns, and even of cultural health.[4]

What is the charge now brought against Domesday Book and its orthography? Why ought not spellings from these records to be accepted as central source-material for the history of the English language and, in particular, for mainstream developments of English place-names? Simply because, from a linguistic point of view, the Domesday texts are not 'English' ones at all.

That assertion may not seem new. The young von Feilitzen, for instance, in his *Pre-Conquest Personal Names*, described the Domesday texts as 'the oldest extant A[nglo-]N[orman] record',[5] a definition on which he elaborated, making clear his adherence to the lines of orthographical interpretation laid down by his supervisor, R.E. Zachrisson:

> From the point of view of phonology D[omesday] B[ook] is essentially an A[nglo-]N[orman] record, and in attempting to elucidate the manifold phonetic and orthographic problems . . . one of our principal tasks will consequently be to ascertain the significance and the range of the A[nglo-]N[orman] influence.[6]

That point of view was questioned by Peter Sawyer thirty-five years ago;[7] nor has it since found many active defenders. To stress that is by no means to dismiss it as wholly false; for, as might *a priori* be expected, there are Anglo-Norman strains clearly represented in the Domesday complex, and the late John Dodgson, for one, several times made great play with the clashes between the English and the French orthographies manifest in the rendering of certain name-items.[8]

Such Anglo-Norman strains are not, however, the ruling element there, and so ought not to be made the methodological basis for a comprehensive analysis. Von Feilitzen himself, handicapped though he was by having as his mentor the main proponent of pervasive phonological as well as orthographical 'Anglo-Norman influence', had already acknowledged something of the true complexity of the situation:

> O[ld] E[nglish] documents were sometimes used in the compilation of the original D[omesday] B[ook] returns, and it is even possible that native scribes were occasionally employed on the clerical staff of the . . . commissioners and perhaps in the Anglo-Norman chancery.[9]

---

4 See, e.g., C. Clark, 'L'Angleterre anglo-normande et ses ambivalences socio-culturelles: un coup d'oeil de philologue', in *Les Mutations socio-culturelles au tournant des XIe–XIIe siècles*, ed. R. Foreville, Spicilegium Beccense, 2 (Paris, 1984), pp. 99–110.

5 *PNDB*, pp. 40–1, esp. 41, n. 1.; cf. pp. 3, 8, 34.

6 *PNDB*, p. 41. See R.E. Zachrisson, *A Contribution to the Study of Anglo-Norman Influence on English Place-Names*, Lunds Universitets Årsskrift I, iv, 3 (Lund, 1909) (hereafter *ANI*); also idem, 'The French Element', in *Introduction to the Survey of English Place-Names*, ed. A. Mawer and F.M. Stenton, English Place-Name Society 1, i (Cambridge, 1924), pp. 93–114.

7 Sawyer, 'Place-Names', pp. 497–8, also 495, 505–6.

8 John McNeal Dodgson, 'Some Domesday Personal Names, mainly Post-Conquest', *Nomina*, 9 (1985), 41–51; 'Domesday Book: Place-Names and Personal Names', in *Domesday Studies*, ed. J.C. Holt (Woodbridge, 1987), pp. 79–99; 'Notes on Some Bynames in Domesday Book', in *Le Nom propre au carrefour des sciences humaines et des sciences sociales: Actes du XVIe Congrès international des sciences onomastiques*, ed. J.-C. Boulanger (Quebec, 1990), pp. 221–8.

9 *PNDB*, p. 41, cf. pp. 6–8.

How accurate that suggestion was half a century of research has underlined, making it ever clearer how much allowance must be made for influence from lost sources, exemplars and drafts as well as for the varying palaeographical and orthographical practices visible in the extant texts, and at the same time bringing out the extent and the range of the native elements present. Sawyer, pointing to the correction in the principal Domesday texts of many place-name forms garbled or over-Gallicized in extant exemplars, confirmed von Feilitzen's suggestion that some at least of 'its scribes were familiar with O[ld] E[nglish] orthography and probably included Englishmen'.[10] More telling still, in so far as obviating risk of arguing from orthography to orthography, are the palaeographical findings. Several hands employed on the Domesday complex, including that of the principal scribe of Great Domesday Books, are reckoned by recent scholarship, as exemplified in several papers published over the last five years by Alexander Rumble and independently by Pierre Chaplais, to show English, perhaps pre-Conquest English, traits.[11] That is not, of course, true of all the hands contributing to the extant corpus (some texts, including *Liber Exoniensis*, have in any case not yet been fully analysed). In the main, however, recent work has pretty unanimously been discrediting old assumptions about the overridingly 'Anglo-Norman' character of the record.

Yet this exposition began with a denial that the Domesday corpus of records was an 'English' one: has there then been a volte-face? By no means. For all their weight, the palaeographical findings are not, for the present purpose, the nub of the matter. Nor yet are the 'nationalities' (if so anachronistic a term be permitted) of the individual scribes; nor even their backgrounds or training. The assertion that these are not 'English' documents is meant in the simplest sense: all were drawn up in Latin, not in English; and the Latin usages represented were, besides, not in the main those of pre-Conquest Anglo-Latin records but normally the Continental ones favoured by the Anglo-Norman administration.[12] The specifically Insular letters of the alphabet were eschewed, so making impossible traditional spelling of many names, whether of places or of people.[13] That must not be deemed a shortcoming, for (as will appear) there were principles involved that set other considerations above traditional, let alone 'phonetic', spelling of vernacular elements. Nor did traditional Old English spelling just go by default, for (as will even sooner appear) the England of the 1080s, and even that of over a generation later, was amply supplied with men who could readily, if but asked, have

---

[10] Sawyer, 'Place-Names', p. 495.

[11] A.R. Rumble, 'The Palaeography of the Domesday Manuscripts', in *Domesday Book: A Reassessment*, ed. P. Sawyer (London, 1985), pp. 28–49, esp. 41–9, and 'The Domesday Manuscripts: Scribes and Scriptoria', in *Domesday Studies*, ed. Holt, pp. 79–99, esp. 84, 97; P. Chaplais, 'William of Saint-Calais and the Domesday Survey', in *ibid.* pp. 65–77, esp. 69–70, 72–4; cf. *Regesta regum Anglo-Normannorum*, I, ed. H.W.C. Davis (Oxford, 1913), p. xvi.

[12] The orthographical affinities of Domesday Book may be appreciated by comparing the treatment there of names of all kinds, first, with that in Late Old English documents like those published as *Charters of Rochester*, ed. A. Campbell, *Anglo-Saxon Charters* I (London, 1973), nos 29 and 30, and as *Charters of Burton Abbey*, ed. P.H. Sawyer (London, 1979), nos 23, 27 and 32 (all those cited being preserved in contemporary single-sheet form), and, secondly, making due allowance for the difference in underlying vernacular, with that in Norman documents such as those published in *Recueil des actes des ducs de Normandie (911–1066)*, ed. M. Fauroux, Mém. Soc. Ant. Normandie, 36 (Caen, 1961).

[13] For the GDB alphabet, see Rumble, 'Scribes', pp. 82–91, esp. 84 ('not thorn, eth or wynn'). Cf. Clark, 'Ambivalences', pp. 101–3.

furnished impeccably Late-West-Saxon spellings. The aim of those responsible for the Domesday texts was not to observe vernacular traditions of any sort, English or Norman, but to Latinize as thoroughly as possible every item that could be Latinized; witness the frankly Latin forms used for specifying certain well-known places, e.g., *IN CIVITATE CANTVARIA, IN EBORACO CIVITATE,* and so on.[14] How thoroughly Latinate the ambience of the scriptorium might be is suggested by certain marginalia in *Liber Exoniensis.*[15]

If it is, then, tenable to interpret the name-spellings found in Domesday Book and its satellites, not as consciously representing current pronunciations used either by scribes or by informants, but rather as aimed at bringing vernacular intrusions into harmony with the orthographical as well as the grammatical norms of medieval Latin, then as a guide to the state of vernacular English orthography in the late 1080s these documents have little standing. That anyone should, even momentarily, have thought otherwise results from the compartmentalization that dominates academic life, discouraging linguists from getting to grips with administrative records and, conversely, historians from mastering philology.

II: *Post-Conquest English Spelling*

Assertions that the Domesday texts were, whether deliberately or not, distanced from vernacular usages and that they therefore carry, on a linguistic level, less weight than some other records from this period are not new. Twenty years ago Gillian Fellows-Jensen scrutinized the Lindsey Survey datable 1115 × 1118 – a good generation, that is, later than Domesday Book – and found it, not surprisingly perhaps, to be in some ways more traditional and truer to local usages than the corresponding sections of the central, governmental record.[16] From the point of view of English historical linguistics, those scholars stressing the 'Norman' affinities of the Domesday corpus might, even though arguing from what I consider a false premiss, be thought to have made an analogous point. The present aim is not, however, so much to elucidate Domesday Book for its own sake as to marginalize its linguistic testimony. For, once we glance up from this particular corpus of records and allow our gaze to rove across other survivors from early post-Conquest England, we cannot but perceive that it was Domesday Book that was anomalous, that was – evidently by design – out of step with the England all around.

There is a wealth of contemporary vernacular material extant, far more than some-times seems realized. What is extant probably, moreover, represents a mere fraction of the vernacular writing produced. David Pelteret's new *Catalogue* of administrative records happening to survive in English versions apparently (though not always unam-biguously) dating from the first century after the Conquest runs to some 140 items, about a third of them consisting of royal writs and charters;[17] and these documents

[14] *Domesday Book: Kent,* ed. P. Morgan (Chichester, 1983), C1; *Domesday Book: Yorkshire,* ed. M.L. Faull and M. Stinson (Chichester, 1986), 1a.

[15] See Chaplais, 'William of Saint-Calais', pp. 66–7.

[16] G. Fellows Jensen, 'The Scribe of the Lindsey Survey', *Namn och Bygd,* 57 (1969), 58–74; cf. *eadem,* 'The Domesday Account of the Bruce Fief', *Jnl English Place-Name Soc.,* 2 (1969–70), 8–17.

[17] D.A.E. Pelteret, *Catalogue of English Post-Conquest Vernacular Documents* (Woodbridge, 1990).

illustrate a variety of vernacular orthographies. That the English language was readily, and so much more widely than is sometimes appreciated, used as a post-Conquest medium of administrative record and communication is in itself important for socio-linguistic history; but, because so many of the items preserved are not only brief but fairly idiosyncratic, only limited use will be made of them here.

Recourse to miscellanea is indeed unnecessary, in so far as there is available at least one substantial piece of testimony as to the state of the English language, orthography included, from the time of the Conquest on into the 1120s – during, that is, the first half-century or, to put it more pertinently, the first two generations after Hastings: the only period when foreign-born scribes, or others, can have been at all thick on English ground. The text in question runs to some forty pages of modern print, being the Laud version of the *Anglo-Saxon Chronicle*, especially its annals up to and including that for 1121.[18] This is the section which it is not – except as shorthand, or code – accurate to call a 'Peterborough' chronicle. Its provenance remains obscure: certainly the extant text was recopied, with local interpolations, at Peterborough Abbey in 1121 × 1122, probably to replace a chronicle lost in the fire of 1116; but whence the abbey had obtained the exemplar is nowhere stated, nor (so far as I am aware) has modern scholarship had much to say on the matter, beyond recognizing that the range of reference implies a house, or series of houses, somewhere in the south-east.[19] Exact provenance may, luckily, be beside the point, because for the present purpose the importance of this text lies in the proof that by itself it gives that somewhere in south-east England there was at least one scriptorium, perhaps more than one, where the capacity as well as the will to write good Late West Saxon persisted through at least two generations following 1066. It is chiefly because the West Saxon used did remain so conventional that the exemplar's provenance is difficult to determine.[20]

It is not, however, the vernacular orthography that is most telling for the present argument. So far were the authors and scribes (the plurals are used because in over half a century changes of personnel surely occurred) of the late *Chronicle* from losing their grasp of native conventions that they uncompromisingly rendered in Insular terms all French personal names and place-names figuring in the narrative, freely deploying the Old English characters *æ, þ, ð*, and *wynn*. At first sight, this might seem a mirror-image of the sorts of sporadic Anglo-Normanism that John Dodgson and others have identi-fied in the Domesday texts;[21] but upon scrutiny the chroniclers' Anglicism proves to be more systematic, more competent as well as more confident, than the occasional Gallicisms of some Exchequer clerks. The chroniclers' procedure was, besides, for their particular purpose the only one appropriate: in any vernacular record, let alone an English one, the conventionalized Latin forms in which Norman names were set down in Norman records[22] would have been incongruous; and, as for French vernacular spellings, these were in the early twelfth century, and for some time to come, so far from being standardized as scarcely to afford any model at all.[23] Authentic French

18 *The Peterborough Chronicle 1070–1154*, ed. C. Clark, 2nd edn (Oxford, 1970) (hereafter *PC*), pp. 1–40.
19 *PC*, pp. xxi–xxiii.
20 *PC*, pp. xli–xlv.
21 See note 8 above.
22 See, e.g., Fauroux, *Recueil*.
23 For a general view, see, e.g., C.T. Gossen, 'Graphème et phonème: le problème central des langues écrites du Moyen Age', *Revue de linguistique romane*, 32 (1968), 1–16; for the areas in

spellings would, in any case, have clashed with the English alphabetical values underpinning the text as a whole: a general principle to which we shall return.

Because the Peterborough hand of c.1121 in which this part of the *Chronicle* survives is in the main a traditional Insular one,[24] there is no call to enumerate all the many times when Insular forms of <r> and of <s> figure in foreign names. Certain usages are, however, noteworthy (because the Peterborough scribe was an accurate copyist,[25] these may be presumed, even though not proved, to have been imitated from the lost exemplar, especially as the local usages of the 1120s partly differ from them):[26]

(i)   Where in Latin, and usually also in French vernacular spelling, an <e> would have been used, there sometimes appears an <æ> or a digraph <ea>, these various graphs being by this date partly interchangeable in English, both for long and for short vowels:[27] e.g., *Bæc* 'Bec' 1093 (<ON *bekkr*, *AN* IV, 49; Lat *Beccum*); *Bælesme*, *Bælæsme* 'Bellême' 1102–08 (Lat *Bellisma*, *Bellismum*); *Bærneʒe* 'Bernay' 1076 (*AN* IV, 50; Lat *Bernaicum*, *Berniacum*); *Ræins* 'Rheims' 1119 (Lat abl. pl. *Remis*, OFr *Reins*); *Ansealm* 1095–1115 (CG *ans/helm*, *NP* I, 39a; Lat *Anselmus*); *Heanriʒ(e)*, *Heanric*, *Heanri* 1087–1120 beside *Henri* from 1106 on (CG *haim/rik*, *NP* I, 122a; Lat *Henricus*); *Herbearde* 1094 (CG *here/berht*, *NP* I, 125a; Lat *Herbertus*); *Moræl* 1093, *Moreal* 1095 (Lat *Maurellus*, *Morellus*, *NP* II, 77a); *Rodbeard*, *Rotbeard* up to 1095 beside *Rotbert* from 1095 on (CG *hrod/berht*, *NP* I, 136a; Lat *Ro(d)bertus*); *Waltear* 1095 (CG *wald/here*, *NP* I, 213a–b; Lat *Walter(i)us*). Although use of <æ> instead of <e> might by itself be attributed to the interchangeability of those two graphs in medieval Latin, here the variation between <æ> and <ea> points rather to the contemporary English near-equivalence of these two graphs, as seen in the surrounding *Chronicle* text. In so far as any phonological deduction might be legitimate, we might surmise that to an English ear the vowels in question sounded noticeably open, that is, as [ɛ] rather than [e]: a surmise proving compatible with what Romance linguists believe about realizations at this time of OFr /e/ before /l/ and before /r/ as well as before nasals.[28]

question, see, e.g., *The Anglo-Norman Voyage of St Brendan by Benedeit*, ed. E.G.R. Waters (Oxford, 1928), pp. 143–74, and *La Vie de Saint Alexis*, ed. C. Storey (Geneva, 1968), pp. 32–51 ('ses graphies sont, pour la plupart, celles des textes anglo-normands de la bonne époque').

[24] See *The Peterborough Chronicle (The Bodleian Manuscript Laud Misc. 636)*, ed. D. Whitelock, Early English Manuscripts in Facsimile, 4 (Copenhagen 1954), p. 15. For the degree to which Insular styles of writing generally prevailed in early twelfth-century England, see N.R. Ker, *English Manuscripts in the Century after the Norman Conquest* (Oxford, 1960), pp. 32–4.

[25] See *PC*, pp. xli–xliii.

[26] Cf. Clark, 'Ambivalences', pp. 103–4. Space allows here no more than token illustration: the sample Normanno-Latin forms are taken mainly from Fauroux, *Recueil*, and from *The Ecclesiastical History of Orderic Vitalis*, ed. M. Chibnall, 6 vols (Oxford, 1969–80). Citation of reference works is likewise kept to a minimum: for personal names, M.-Th. Morlet, *Les Noms de personne sur le territoire de l'ancienne Gaule du VIᵉ au XIIᵉ siècle*, 2 vols (Paris, 1968–72) (hereafter *NP*) and C. Marynissen, *Hypokoristische Suffixen in oudnederlandse Persoonsnamen* (Ghent, 1986) (*HS*); for place-names, the articles published by J. Adigard des Gautries in *Annales de Normandie* I (1951) – IX (1959) (*AN*), and also C. de Beaurepaire, *Dictionnaire topographique du département de Seine-Maritime*, 2 pts (Paris, 1982–84) (*SM*).

[27] See, e.g., *PC*, pp. xliii–xliv (NB: I no longer support blanket ascription of these spellings to 'Latin and French influence'), cf. pp. xlvi–xlvii, xlix–li.

[28] See, e.g., M.K. Pope, *From Latin to Modern French*, 2nd edn (Manchester, 1952), §§ 447, 492, 493, 1089, 1098.

(ii)   The French medial and final dentals destined for early effacement[29] were often represented here by <p> or by <þ>: *Caþum* 'Caen' 1087, 1105 (*AN* II, 222; Lat *Cadomum, Cadon*); *Maðante* 'Mantes' 1087 (Lat *Metanta*, acc. *Metantem*); *Na-tiuiteð* 1102–16; *Aðelis* 1121 (CG *adal/haid*, *NP* I, 16b; 12th-c. OFr *Aelis* or *Aaliz*, Lat *Adelaidis, Adelicia*, etc.); *Gosfrið* 1088 (CG *gaut/frid*, *NP* I, 165a; 12th-c. OFr *Gefreid* or *Gefrei*, Lat *Gosfridus*); *Loðepis* 1108, 1116 (CG *hlud/wig*, *NP* I, 133b; 12th-c. OFr *Loewis*, Lat *Ludouicus*).

(iii) Because Caroline <g> was rare in this text,[30] the only significant cases of Insular <ʒ> are ones not corresponding to <g> in conventional Latin (or French) orthography, as in the *Bærneʒe* already cited. Most noteworthy are several names ending in stressed [i:] or [i:ə]: *Cluniʒ* 'Cluny' 1119 (Lat *Cluniacum*; cf. *Clunni* 1127–31); *Lumbardiʒe* 'Lombardy' 1117 (12th-c. OFr *Lumbardie*; Lat *Lombardia*); *Normandiʒ(e)* 'Normandy' passim (12th-c. OFr *Normendie*; Lat *Normannia*); also *Maniʒe* beside *Mannie* 'Maine'; *He(a)nriʒ*, etc., sporadically to 1120 beside *He(a)nri* from 1104 on, possibly by analogy with the traditional spellings of native names in *-siʒe* and *-wiʒ*.

(iv)   The Caroline form for <w> appears only for the capital,[31] the small letter being regularly represented by *wynn*. Capricious initial capitalization means that often this letter appears as initial of a foreign name: *sce paleri* 'Saint-Valery' 1090 (*AN* IX, 161–2; *SM* 939; Lat *Sanctum Walaricum*); *palcelin* 1098 (CG *walh* + dimin., *HS*, 231–2; Lat *Walc(h)elinus*); *palchere* 1080 (CG *walh/here*, *NP* I, 214b–215a; Lat *Walcherus*); and *pillelm* passim alongside forms in <W->. (On the other hand, <W-> sometimes appears in native names like *Walþeof* 1075 and *Wlstan* 1088.) Medial and final occurrences of *wynn* appear in: *Anʒeop* 1110–19 (12th-c. OFr *Anjou*, cf. Lat acc. *Andegauem*); *Puntip* 'Ponthieu' 1120 (cf. Lat *Pontiuum*); *Baldepine* 1070–1119 (CG *bald/wini*, *NP* I, 50b; Lat *Balduinus*), probably assimilated to native names in *-wine*; and *Loðepis* 1108, 1116 (see above).

Interpretation of such spellings as systematic Anglicization seems confirmed by some frank replacements, not only here but also in other records from this time, of continental personal names by English (or Anglo-Scandinavian) ones of similar form, sometimes but not necessarily cognate: e.g., occasional renderings of the name of Odo of Bayeux (CG *aud-*, *HS*, 196–200) as OE *Oda*, obl. *Odan*, 1082, 1088 3x, and, even more strikingly, the attribution to a notorious Norman abbot of Glastonbury, a former monk of Caen, of the Anglo-Scandinavian name *þurstane*, dat. 1083, not only spelt with small initial <þ> but also having as second element *-stan*, instead of Normanno-Scandinavian *-stein* or *-stin*.[32] Second elements of foreign place-names too seem sometimes to have been identified with native generics of similar form: e.g., the

---

29 *Ibid.*, §§ 346, 347, 1097, 1113, 1175–7.
30 See Whitelock, *MS Laud Misc. 636*, p. 15.
31 *Ibid.*, pp. 16–17.
32 J. Adigard des Gautries, *Les Noms de personnes scandinaves en Normandie de 911 à 1066*, Nomina Germanica, 11 (Lund, 1954), pp. 167–9, also 253, 326–40. For some instances on English soil, see, e.g., O. von Feilitzen, 'The Personal Names and Bynames of the Winton Domesday', in *Winchester in the Early Middle Ages*, ed. M. Biddle (Oxford, 1976), pp. 143–229, esp. 175. Cf. note 36 below.

Bærneʒe already cited looks as though remodelled on native place-names in -*eg*,[33] such as *Anʒleseʒe* 'Anglesey' 1098, *Ceortesæʒe/eʒe* 'Chertsey' 1084, 1110, and *Rumeseʒe* 'Romsey' 1086. Later in the Middle English period, similar adaptation of French place-names transferred to English soil was to be common enough.

On its own, therefore, this section of the *Chronicle* testifies to the tenacity of native orthographical traditions during the first two generations after the Conquest; but its testimony does not – and this must be emphasized – in fact stand alone. Related sorts of Anglicization are, to begin with, frequent in the first series of Peterborough Continuations: that is, the annals from 1122 to 1131, written up in six stints.[34] Despite being less accomplished in Late West Saxon (here an alien dialect), the scribe(s) of these annals continued confidently to Anglicize spellings of foreign names: <æ> appears in, e.g., *Sæis* 'Sées' 1130 (cf. Lat dat. pl. *Sagiis*), *Æðelic* 1127 (here probably assimilated to native names in *Æðel-*), *Martæl* 1127 (cf. Lat *Martellus*); in *Henri* the digraph <ea> varies with <e> and may even have been preferred, in so far as the annals for 1129 and 1130 show *Henri* fairly consistently corrected to *He`a´nri*; <ð> or <þ> figures in *Æðelic, Godefreið* 1123 (CG *god/frid*, NP I, 112a; Lat *Godefridus*), *Gosfreið* 1125, 1127, *Loðepis* (as before, spelt also with *wynn*), *Peccep* (Lat *Peccatum*) 1123, and *Roðem* 'Rouen' 1124 (*AN* IX, 153–4, *SM* 859; Lat *Rotomagus, Rodomum*). Apparent assimilation of a foreign place-name to native patterns appears in *Mun(d)ford*, as if with the native generic -*ford*,[35] for French *Montfort* (*AN* IV, 254–5). Again, too, *Þurstan* varies with *Turstein*, this time for the name of the Norman archbishop of York.[36]

In the later *Chronicle*, admittedly, such usages might be taken as imitation by the Peterborough scribe(s) of ones from the preceding copied text; might be so taken, were it not that, fortunately for the present argument, they can be paralleled from independent materials. Thus, the H-Fragment giving annals for 1113–14 shows two instances of *Caðum* 'Caen', one of *Goisfriðe*, one of *Henriʒ*, and one of *Turstane* for the name of the archbishop of York.[37] Analogous spellings appear in the *Liber Vitae* of Thorney Abbey, begun during the first decade of the twelfth century: <Æ> appears as initial capital in *Æmma* (CG *erm-, irm-*, HS, 108–10; Lat *Emma*), *Ærmentruða* (CG *ermin/trudis*, NP I, 83a; Lat *Ermentrudis*), *Ærnis* (CG *arn/gis*, cf. NP I, 41b; Lat *Ernisius*), *Ærnoldus* (CG *arn/wald*, cf. NP I, 41a; Lat *Arnoldus, Ernaldus*), *Ærnulfus* (CG *arn/wulf*, NP I, 41a; Lat *Arnulfus, Ernulfus*), *Æscelinus* (CG *ad(al)* + dimin., HS, 53–4; Lat *Azzelinus*), *Æþeliza, Æþelina* (CG *adal* + dimin., HS, 51; Lat *Adelina*) – as alternative, that is, sometimes to <A>, sometimes to <E> – and <æ> appears medially in *Bæta* (CG *berht*, HS, 74–7; Lat *Berta*), *Dræpe* (Lat *Drogo*, HS, 102–3; later OFr *Dreu*), *Roæis* (CG *hrod/haid*, NP I, 137a), and so on; <þ> and <ð> appear, more or less interchangeably, in *Albreþa/Albreðe* (CG *alb/rada*, NP I, 29b; Lat *Alberada*),

---

[33] See, e.g., M. Gelling, *Place-Names in the Landscape* (London, 1984), pp. 34–40.

[34] See Whitelock, *MS Laud Misc. 636*, p. 14, and Clark, *PC*, pp. xvi–xvii (both quoting Neil Ker).

[35] See, e.g., Gelling, *Landscape*, pp. 67–72.

[36] Note that *Hugh the Chanter: The History of the Church of York 1066–1127*, ed. and trans. C. Johnson, rev. M. Brett *et alii*, Oxford Medieval Texts (Oxford, 1990), regularly names the archbishop, who was of Norman parentage (*ibid.*, pp. xxvii–xxviii and references there given) as *Turstinus*, which the translator renders as *Thurstan*. Cf. note 32 above.

[37] The text used is that in *Two of the Saxon Chronicles Parallel*, I, ed. C. Plummer and J. Earle (Oxford, 1892), pp. 243–5; cf. J. Zupitza, 'Fragment einer englischen Chronik aus den Jahren 1113 und 1114', *Anglia*, I (1878), 195–7. For the predominantly Insular hand involved, see N.R. Ker, *Catalogue of Manuscripts containing Anglo-Saxon* (Oxford, 1957), p. 188.

Ærmentruða, Æðelic/Æþeliza, Freþesenda (CG *frid/sindis*, *NP* I, 93b), *Gosfriþ, Haðeuuis/Haþeuuis* (CG *had/widis*, *NP* I, 119b); <ʒ> appears in *Aʒnes, Ʒrantamaʒni* 'Grandmesnil' (*AN* III, 26; Lat *Grentemaisnilium*) where the second example renders a French preconsonantal <s>, *Huʒo* (CG *hug*, *NP* I, 140a, *HS*, 156–63), *Liʒarda/Liʒard* (CG *leud/gardis*, *NP* I, 159b; Lat *Ligardis*), *Roʒer* (CG *hrod/gair*, *NP* I, 136b) *le byʒod*, and so on; and <þ> in *Baldeþinus, Dræpe, Haþþis, Þalter*.[38] A few more such spellings can be gleaned from the documents calendared by Pelteret: *Hæimonem* (CG *haim*, *HS* 146–7), *Hugæn* (with OE obl. case), *Rodbært, Wælcælin, Willælm, Aðelicc, Ʒosfreʒð* and *Viðel* (Lat *Vitalis*, OFr *Viel*), also *Eorlawine* for *Herluin* (CG *erl/wini*, *NP* I, 81b–82a).[39] If an 'iceberg' principle of calculation be admissible, then from these stray sightings of Anglicized names it might be deduced that, for at least the first half-century after the Conquest, English cultural and linguistic attitudes had been marked by a robust self-assurance that unhesitatingly subjugated foreign items to native structures and usages – and that despite the ubiquity of immigrant abbots and bishops as well as of alien administrators.

Domesday Book spellings of English place-names and personal names are thus by no means to be taken as typical of current native usages. Vernacular spelling traditions not only remained in force for the English language itself but retained vigour and authority enough to subjugate any foreign items falling within their ambit. Nor ought English monastic houses and their scriptoria to be supposed as in the main either culturally or linguistically swamped by the Continental, mainly Norman-French, usages associated with the foreign prelates presiding over them.

III: *Questions of Phonetic Implication*

To return, now that the onomastic orthography of Domesday Book has been set in a wider and – it is to be hoped – truer perspective, to the first proposition cited: the one asserting that the spellings in question enable us to 'study the effects of Norman French pronunciation on English place-names'. This rests on a many-layered complex of assumptions.

On one level, it assumes 'Norman French' pronunciation to have had upon a fair number of English place-names effects permanent enough to merit more than passing attention. Over the past eighty years this Zachrissonian notion has become so entrenched as to pass in some quarters for 'fact' rather than hypothesis.[40] It has been urged elsewhere how shaky its foundations are.[41] Points telling against it include, first, the unlikelihood of a supposed snobbish affectation that, although widespread socially, confined itself linguistically to place-names, leaving personal names and common

---

[38] British Library Add. MS 40,000, ff. 1v–12r. See Clark, 'Ambivalences', pp. 104–5, also 'British Library Additional MS 40,000 ff. 1v–12r', below pp. 301–19, esp. 303, and 'A Witness to Post-Conquest English Cultural Patterns: The *Liber Vitae* of Thorney Abbey', below pp. 339–47, esp. 344–6.

[39] Pelteret, *Catalogue*, nos 8, 25, 31, 32, 33, 62, 96, 105; for the form *Ʒosfreʒð*, see *Facsimiles of English Royal Writs to A.D. 1100 presented to Vivian Hunter Galbraith*, ed. T.A.M. Bishop and P. Chaplais (Oxford, 1957), pl. XIV ('the work of a scribe thoroughly practised in the OE minuscule').

[40] For Zachrisson's work in this field, see note 6 above.

[41] See Clark, 'Towards a Reassessment of "Anglo-Norman Influence on English Place-Names" ', above pp. 144–55.

vocabulary untouched; and, even more, the existence of an alternative possibility, probability rather, that most of the modifications imputed to 'Anglo-Norman influence' could well have arisen spontaneously in rapid and casual speech. Such matters of long-term development are, however, tangential to the present theme.

A second, and more fundamental, set of assumptions is, first, that Domesday Book spellings of vernacular items were essentially intended to transcribe actual pronunciations, perhaps the scribe's own, perhaps an informant's; and, further, that such 'phonetic transcription' was precise and explicit enough to be accurately interpretable nine centuries later. Spelling must not, however, be confused with phonetic transcription: a point that should be self-evident to anyone conversant either with Modern English or with Modern French, let alone (as most medievalists are) with both. Spelling – at least as long understood in Western Europe – involves a system of conventionalized representation to which any alien elements must in some measure be adjusted (in modern usage, for instance, by italicization). In discussing eleventh-century English renderings of foreign proper names, emphasis has been given to the regular imposition upon these of specifically English spelling conventions and to occasional further assimilations towards native structure. Now, if English vernacular conventions were thus capable of subjugating alien intruders, then so *a fortiori* must have been those of Latin, at this date not only more prestigious but also more systematized than English ones, never mind such French vernacular ones as existed. When any vernacular item was adopted into Latin, some adjustment was inescapable, because Latin syntax relied upon inflections and so required any adopted item to be tricked out with a set of these. At alphabetical level, degrees of adjustment varied, with pre-Conquest Anglo-Latin charters and chronicles sometimes showing native names spelt with the appropriate Insular characters but Norman records, composed as they were with small background of vernacular literacy, showing more thorough-going Latinization.[42] That the latter tradition was the one governing the drafting of Domesday Book can be deduced not just from *a priori* notions about 'Anglo-Norman' administration but, more cogently, from the avoidance in its text of the Insular characters needed for traditional and precise representation of English material.

With this in mind, a fresh eye may be cast over the Domesday texts. One widely accepted line of interpretation begins by postulating a 'Norman inability to pronounce /þ/ and /ð/', goes on to suppose those sounds to have been replaced in speech by /t/ and /d/, and then invokes this supposed oral substitution in explanation of the <t> and <d> spellings found in Anglo-Latin documents for names containing the spirantal sounds.[43] We have, however, observed – as indeed did von Feilitzen – that the sorts of Old French with which late-eleventh-century writers of English and of Anglo-Latin were coming into contact did contain sounds that English-speakers identified with their own dental spirants;[44] and, if we look at French and Franco-Latin materials of this date, we find those Old French sounds regularly spelt with <t> and with <d>.[45] It is thus unwise to

---

[42] See references in note 12 above.

[43] *ANI*, pp. 39–49, 82–116. This tradition of interpretation was reviewed in my paper, 'The Myth of "the Anglo-Norman Scribe" ', below pp. 168–76, a principal contention being that its underlying socio-linguistic premisses (e.g. *ANI*, p. 11) are gravely flawed.

[44] See Pope, *From Latin to Modern French*, §§ 1175–7 (pronunciation), 1210, 1215 (spelling). Cf. *PNDB*, pp. 100–2, where it is recognized that [θ] and [ð] did occur in Anglo-Norman speech.

[45] Cf. Waters, *Brendan*, pp. clviii–clxii, and Storey, *Alexis*, pp. 47–8 (but this includes an unintelligible reference to 'la graphie anglo-saxonne *th*').

dogmatize about phonetic implications of spellings in <t> or <d> found in Domesday Book or, for that matter, elsewhere in medieval materials. Given that the Latin alphabet afforded no means of distinguishing between dental stops and dental spirants, orthographic approximation or compromise was inevitable. Given too what has lately been put forward as to the Englishness of several hands responsible for the Domesday record,[46] it makes better sense to take approximate spellings as conventional rather than as reflecting faulty pronunciation. So too with another frequent line of interpretation: the one assuming <c>, when found in names like *Cicestre* 'Chichester' or *Glouuecestre* 'Gloucester', to signify, not the [tʃ] expected as reflex of Old English palatalized <c>, but, instead, a Gallicized replacement of this by [ts] (soon to be simplified to [s]).[47] This assertion is, if anything, odder than the previous one, in so far as the traditional English spelling here always had been <c> and remained so well into the twelfth century[48] and in so far as [tʃ] would seem not to have been alien to eleventh-century Norman French.[49] What alternative graph the commentators in question envisage as available for [tʃ] is unclear, for at this time <ch> most often denoted [k].[50] To argue the case more closely would demand confident knowledge, such as few can now possess, of just how Exchequer clerks of the 1080s and English monastic scribes of the early twelfth century pronounced their Latin.

If, then, the name-spellings found in Domesday Book reflect in general a Procrustean attempt to accommodate English materials within an alien and, for this purpose, inadequate set of alphabetical conventions, it must follow that what these spellings reveal about anyone's pronunciation, whether a scribe's or an informant's, must be limited. As a present-day partial analogue, I propose the sort of 'imitated pronunciation', which 'should be read as if it were English', that is offered in the otherwise admirable Berlitz phrase-books. That the analogy is imperfect must be stressed; for the Berlitz versions are aimed at representing pronunciation, where the Domesday Book ones (it is argued) were precisely not so aimed; but for the discrepancy to go that way only makes the comparison more telling. The Berlitz procedure – intended, one supposed, to spare learners the trauma of encountering anything as logical and clear as the International Phonetic Alphabet – consists of transcribing foreign phrases into a sort of code based upon English alphabetical values:

Zher ner kawngprahng pah. Pooreeay voo pahrlay plew lahngtermahng? Pooreeay voo raypaytay, seel voo pleh? Mawngtray mwah lah frahz dahng ler leevr – ang nangstang, zher vay vwahr see zher lah troov dang ser leevr.[51]

[46] See note 11 above.

[47] *ANI*, pp. 18–32; *PNDB*, p. 110, likewise assumes partial substitution of [ts] for OE [tʃ].

[48] See, e.g., A. Campbell, *Old English Grammar* (Oxford, 1959), §§ 431–4, and cf. *Ciceastre, Cæstre, PC,* s.aa. 1130, 1140. R. Jordan, *Handbuch der mittelenglischen Grammatik,* i: *Lautlehre* (Heidelberg, 1934), §§ 177, 179, dates the appearance of ME <ch> spellings for [tʃ] to the second half of the 12th century; D.G. Scragg, *A History of English Spelling* (Manchester, 1974), pp. 44–5, cf. p. 28 n. 2, dates it 'about 1200'.

[49] For [tʃ] in Norman-French, see Pope, *From Latin to Modern French,* §§ 1092, 1181.

[50] For <ch> representing [k], *ibid.,* § 1029; Waters, *Brendan,* pp. 44–5, 172, cf. 173, and Storey, *Alexis,* p. 46 ('l'occlusive gutturale est donc représentée par *k, ch, qu* et *q*'); also *PNDB,* pp. 107–9.

[51] *French for your Trip,* Editions Berlitz (Lausanne, 1979), pp. 17–18 (the phrases excerpted having been minimally repunctuated), also p. 12.

The crucial question is this: can any transcription so approximate tell us anything about anyone's pronunciation of French? Nothing, surely, about that of the compilers, whom one would assume to be, if not native speakers, at all events accomplished linguists. And, if these transcriptions, aimed as they are at 'imitating' pronunciation, reveal so little, how much could anyone hope to discover from Domesday Book spellings, intended as these evidently were to cast a Latinate veil over the rugosities of the vernacular?

The end of the trail is, however, no dead end. Details have been added to the picture compositely painted over the last few decades of a post-Conquest England that was for the most part sturdily Anglophone. More than that: there now opens up before us a potential new field of study, in which orthographical analysis, palaeography and textual history would combine to complement and cross-fertilize each other. One might, for instance, ask how far (if at all) particular orthographical usages, especially perhaps ones found in Little Domesday Book and in *Liber Exoniensis*, might prove to correlate with individual hands identifiable there. Or one might consider how far orthographical styles correlate with textual history; with, for instance, apparent shifts between documentary and oral inputs, or with links between the Domesday texts themselves and their satellites. In considering this complex of records, we must always bear in mind that the nickname by which its central monument has been known from the late twelfth century on is an unimpeachably English one, which 'Anglo-Norman' administrators seem nevertheless soon to have made their own.[52]

---

[52] *Dialogus de Scaccario*, ed. C. Johnson (Edinburgh, 1950), p. 64. Cf. M.T. Clanchy, *From Memory to Written Record: England 1066–1307* (London, 1979), pp. 18, 110.

13

The Myth of 'the Anglo-Norman Scribe'

1. *Texts*

The following extracts are taken from secondary works, mostly either standard reference-books or approved doctoral theses (the boldface type is the commentator's device for highlighting significant phraseology).

1942   In many cases [viz. of topographical by-names recorded in French form in documents mostly dating from the late 13th c. onwards] we are concerned with mere translations made by scribes **who had perhaps more knowledge of French than English**.

1950   Some such names [viz. occupational by-names recorded in French form in documents dating from the 13th and 14th cc.] may be suspected of being translations of the corresponding English word made by a scribe of **Norman descent**.

1968   The majority of these men [viz. 12th-c. scribes conversant with Latin] must have been **of Norman descent** . . . It seems probable, then, that at any rate the vast majority of the scribes of the 12th- and 13th-century documents were **Norman or Anglo-Norman**.

1969   Their occurrence [viz. that of topographical terms of French origin] in surnames must not be taken as proof that they belonged to the Middle English vocabulary. Some such names may be translations made by **Norman scribes who had a better knowledge of French than English**.

1972   The variants <t> and <d> [viz. ones found in renderings used in 14th-c. records for reflexes of OE /þ/ and /ð/], both pronounced [t], are probably due to **AN influence**.

1987   In initial position OE θ appears as /t/ in [examples dated 1316–27]. The above forms are due to **AN influence**. . . . The following two forms [dated circa 1330] with loss of medial /ð/ are probably due to **AN influence**.

1987   OE þ, ð are sometimes [viz. in 13th- and 14th-c. tax-rolls] written *t*, *d*, owing to the **inability of the French scribes to pronounce these sounds**.

1988   The thirteenth-century forms in *Gelver-*, etc. [viz. for the place-name now *Yelver-toft*] are found in such documents as *Feet of Fines*, *Close Rolls*, *Assize Rolls*, etc., where the forms were generally taken down by **Norman copyists**. A **Norman scribe** was not familiar with /j/. His nearest equivalent was [dʒ], which he rendered by <g> or <j>. Such forms . . . may therefore be put down to **Anglo-Norman scribal influence**.

1989   The occurrence of a French name [viz. a topographical by-name of French origin] is by no means proof that the element(s) it contains were part of the spoken language. It may well be that such a word was translated by a scribe **of Norman descent**, or by one inclined to show off his knowledge of the language of the upper classes.

2. *The Myth*

Among certain workers on Middle English language, and certain onomasticians in particular, there has grown up over the last century or so a custom of ascribing all seemingly non-native or non-traditional usages, orthographical ones especially, to widespread scribal ignorance of the English language. Some expressions of this belief are illustrated in the small *florilegium*, or *hortus siccus*, set out above. Because the aim is to question the academic tradition, not to pillory any of its individual adherents, authors' names are omitted. The dates are, on the other hand, germane to the issue, because they reveal the custom concerned as continuing in full vigour into the late 1980s.[1] It is to emphasize this aspect of the matter that the anterior cut-off point has been set in the 1940s rather than, as it might more logically have been, in the 1890s (e.g., Skeat 1895–98: 403–16).

The term 'myth' figuring in the title was chosen advisedly, and is used with the primary meaning given in the *New English Dictionary* of 'a purely fictitious narrative usually . . . embodying some popular idea concerning . . . historical phenomena'. For in some quarters, it is plain, the intervention of a 'Norman' or 'Anglo-Norman' scribe, even of a 'French' one, has come to be ritually invoked whenever any seemingly unEnglish usage, whether orthographical or lexical, appears in a post-Conquest English document of any date up to and including the mid-fourteenth century. How ritualized such invocation has become is clear from the repetitive phrasing conspicuous in the texts cited; this leaves no room for supposing purely coincidental agreement between individuals happening to have hit on similar explanations. Small attempt seems to have been made either to think the situation through afresh or to take note of findings from neighbouring disciplines, still less to seek out contemporary evidence for or against the assumptions being made. Passive acceptance betrays itself most blatantly in the mentions of 'Norman descent', because 'descent', of whatsoever kind, is beside the point, which concerns not the scribes' genealogies but their cradle-tongues and, above all, their professional training.

Being customary, and even being unreflectingly parroted, does not in itself discredit any assertion. The question is how far the underlying assumptions may be valid. Here, the major one seems to be that, up to the mid-fourteenth century at least, English tax-rolls and the like were regularly and as a matter of course faircopied by 'Norman' or 'French' scribes possessing but a limited command of the English language. Given that by the mid-fourteenth century almost twelve generations had elapsed since the post-Conquest settlement and almost six since King John's loss of his Norman dominions, such an assumption might seem, even *a priori*, a large one. Is it to be supposed that there were still, after such lapses of time, bodies of people long-settled in England who nevertheless had 'more knowledge of French than English' and, furthermore, that it was normally from their ranks that taxers' clerks – the humblest servants of the bureaucracy – were recruited? So repugnant to commonsense are such suppositions that their verification demands rigorous proof.

---

[1] The approach embodied in this paper crystallized during the writing of two chapters for the forthcoming *Cambridge History of the English Language* [['Onomastics', vol. 1: *The Beginnings to 1066*, R.M. Hogg (ed.), Cambridge: Cambridge University Press, 1992, 452–89; vol. 2: *1066–1476*, N. Blake (ed.), Cambridge: Cambridge University Press, 1992, 542–606]]. The falsity of some arguments put forward as demonstrating intervention by an 'Anglo-Norman' scribe has already been indicated in Clark 1987a; and the present piece forms part of a trilogy, the other members of which are Clark 1991 and Clark 1992.

3. *Contemporary Evidence and its Implications*

A priori scepticism as to the socio-linguistic assumptions that underlie invocations of an 'Anglo-Norman scribe' is strengthened by the findings from the many investigations into post-Conquest developments that have been appearing from the 1920s on (e.g., Shelly 1921; Wilson 1943; Woodbine 1943; Rothwell 1968, 1975–76, 1978 and 1983; Lefèvre 1973; Clark 1978, 1987a and b, 1991 and 1992; Richter 1979 and 1985).[2] These findings have meanwhile been accepted by general historians of post-Conquest England and incorporated by them into the syntheses that they have made for under-graduates (e.g., Clanchy 1979: 151–74 and 1985: 56–61; Chibnall 1986: 212–14). Much contemporary evidence is, besides, readily available in print.

Admittedly, late-eleventh-century England did see a widespread, though by no means complete, replacement of the native aristocracy and gentry, also of the highest clergy, by new men (specifically 'men', not 'people'), followers of the Conqueror: some Norman, others Picard or Angevin, others again Flemish or Breton – and so not all even in the widest sense French-speaking. These incomers, concentrated as they were in the narrow social categories specified, were not numerically overwhelming. Exactly how numerous they were is probably unascertainable, because the extant records, being mostly concerned with landholding, seldom divulge whether a settler had brought a wife and family with him or had formed a new household on English soil with an English wife.

This question of the largely unrecorded women is central to the socio-linguistic issue. Thin though the documentation is, it reveals a certain amount of intermarriage between incoming men and English women (see, e.g., Shelly 1921: 62–5; Davis 1976: 123–4; Clark 1978: above 117–23; Chibnall 1984: 3, 8–12 and 1986: 208–9): some-thing only to be expected, given that men seeking their fortunes abroad were often young and single and that, by medieval standards, marrying an heiress was a highly acceptable way of securing title to land. Half-English families growing up in English manor-houses could hardly not have known the English language. Even families at first purely French by blood would have employed English domestics, nursemaids included, whose speech could not but have been familiar to the children. As for immigrant merchants, such as flocked to the major towns, all that is known of mercan-tile life forbids us to envisage them as keeping their children ignorant of the local language spoken by potential customers.[3] Even, therefore, among the mighty and among the rich, Francophone monolingualism must be deemed unlikely to have per-sisted for more than a generation or two.

At this point, one must be careful to avoid replacing one myth simply by another. The surmise concluding the previous paragraph is, fortunately, confirmed by such evidence as survives. By the mid-thirteenth century, at latest, the children of the gentry were needing formal instruction in French; and some textbooks compiled for their mothers or tutors to use started from an English basis, grouping French terms accord-ing to the English ones they translated (Rothwell 1975–76: 461–2). Such procedure

---

2 Berndt (1965 and 1976), although presenting acceptable conclusions, fail to cite the evidence upon which these are based and therefore afford little foundation for further work.

3 A similar view of the likely linguistic accomplishments of Thomas Becket, son of an identifiable immigrant merchant, is expressed – though not, unfortunately, supported by direct evidence – in Barlow (1986: 17).

presupposed that already for the instructors envisaged, born perhaps circa 1200, English would be the first, the dominant, language. Exactly when Anglo-French had begun to die out as a first language is uncertain; but by the 1170s *Dialogus de Scaccario* was asserting that, so far as free people were concerned, it had become scarcely possible to tell who was English and who Norman by race (Johnson 1983: 53). Such an assertion might seem to imply a common language; and, if common language there indeed were, then it could hardly have been other than English, not only because of the impending 'language-death' of Anglo-Norman but more essentially because there could have been little means by which families of purely English stock could in the mass have made their children into native-level, accent-free speakers of French. Even among the gentry, therefore, Francophone monolingualism may not have survived for more than three or so generations after the Conquest.

The gentry constitute, moreover, a limiting case; for, if by the mid-thirteenth century at latest children of unquestionably part-Norman descent no longer had French as their cradle-tongue and if, by the mid-twelfth, people from such families were – as *Dialogus de Scaccario* may be taken to imply – speaking an English indistinguishable from that of the natives, then for any members of the lower middle classes (if one may be permitted thus anachronistically to describe taxers' clerks) ever to have been monolingual French-speakers becomes improbable in the extreme. That English was beyond doubt the current language of all towns, even of the apparently cosmopolitan ones like London, Canterbury and Winchester, is plain from the paucity of French elements in their street-naming (see, e.g., Ekwall 1954: passim and esp. 19–20; Keene 1976, Clark 1976: below 198–9, and 1991).

Of other social groups open to scrutiny, the most relevant are monastic ones. Now, throughout the first two or more generations after the Conquest and the subsequent Norman settlement – that is, during the only period when native-born speakers of French were at all thick on English ground – many monastic scriptoria effectively maintained pre-Conquest literary and scribal traditions, orthographical ones included (see, e.g., Clark 1992). One well-known instance is the E-Text of the *Anglo-Saxon Chronicle*, of uncertain provenance up to the annal for 1121 (Clark 1970: 1–40, cf. xli–xlv); likewise the independent H-Fragment for 1113–14, also of uncertain provenance (Plummer – Earle 1892: 244–5). Various other monastic productions, such as the first part of the *Liber Vitae* of Thorney Abbey (Clark 1987b: below 343–5), also show pre-Conquest orthographical traditions being observed well into the second post-Conquest generation, and sometimes beyond. So, even while Continental influences were at their height, with foreign-born abbots and bishops everywhere at the head of affairs, native scribal traditions were far from being wholly disrupted.

Later in the twelfth century Francophone monolingualism, seemingly by then recessive even among the nobility, could hardly have been increasing its hold on any social group, monastic or other. Indeed, towards the end of the century a monk of Bury St Edmunds remarked, concerning a successful candidate for preferment, upon the man's special accomplishment in being *uolubilis lingue in Gallico idiomate, utpote Normannus nacione*, that is, 'fluent in the French language because of being Norman by birth' (Butler 1949: 129); had such fluency been general among the monks of Bury, there would have been no thought of singling this one out on that account. The abbot of that time moreover declared that edification might better be served by preaching to the community, not in Latin, but *Gallice uel pocius Anglice* 'in French or, preferably, in English' (Butler 1949: 128), again implying that, of the two supposed vernaculars, English was the one with which the monks were most at home.

As to scribes other than monks, information is sparse. That the immediate post-Conquest period did see some foreign-trained clerks working in England, in monastic scriptoria as well as in the royal Exchequer, no-one denies. This truth may have been a formative element in the 'myth' under scrutiny. On the other hand, even Great Domesday Book itself, the capital achievement of the Anglo-Norman bureaucracy, now appears not to have been so purely 'Norman' a production as was once supposed but rather to have had multiple strata of compilation as well as of input; within the last five years at least two scholars working independently have identified its principal scribe as English-trained and probably English-speaking (Rumble 1985: 49 and 1988: 84, 97; Chaplais 1988: 70–5; cf. Sawyer 1956: 497–8). That seems to square with what little we know of later members of the royal staff: thus, tenurial records concerning a Bernard who was a scribe of Henry I's make clear his at least partly, and perhaps wholly, English ancestry (Round 1899; Southern 1970: 225–8; cf. Davis 1913: xvi). It squares too with the already noted maintenance of English traditions in early-twelfth-century monastic scriptoria, and equally with the native characteristics seen in various administrative records of that date (see, e.g., Fellows Jensen 1969, cf. 1969–70).

All that has so far been brought to light reduces to nil the likelihood that any English taxers' clerk working in the thirteenth, let alone the fourteenth, century could have been a native speaker of French; for, not only was native speaking of French apparently recessive in England by circa 1200, but it cannot ever have been widespread outside the ranks of the landholding gentry. This is no fresh revelation, in so far as Ekwall said as much forty years ago: noting the intrusion of various English elements into the Latin of the London Lay Subsidy Roll for 1292, he commented that the 'clerks who wrote the rolls were doubtless English-speaking people, who sometimes left English occupational terms untranslated' (Ekwall 1951: 28–9). The point has not yet, alas, been universally taken.

4.   *An Alternative Explanation*

If, then, the scribes of the documents implicated in the texts assembled in my *hortus siccus* were not native speakers of French but Englishmen whose French had, like their Latin, been acquired as a professional accomplishment, then the orthographical and lexical phenomena for which 'the myth of "the Anglo-Norman scribe" ' purported to account will have to be otherwise explained.

That there are phenomena to be explained is not contested. Many sorts of medieval English administrative document regularly present spellings that not only look unEnglish but might on the face of it be supposed inadequate to represent the names or terms concerned. This is especially, though by no means solely, so when the vernacular items involve reflexes of Old English /þ/ or /ð/. The same sorts of document also offer occasional French words and phrases. If these various kinds of Gallicism, actual or supposed, can no longer be fathered onto 'scribes who had perhaps more knowledge of French than English', then an alternative aetiology must be sought. Relevant considerations include, first, the nature of spelling in general and, second, that of the sorts of document chiefly concerned.

Spelling, as anyone conversant with Modern English must already appreciate, rests not upon phonetic transcription but upon some system of conventionalized representation clear enough to allow the items in question to be recognized by anyone familiar with the language involved. So a 'spelling' need not – and often in Modern English (or Modern French) does not – correspond symbol by symbol with the equivalent sequence of phonemes; some languages have managed for centuries with ideograms unrelated to any vocal realization of the items represented. Literate people of the Middle Ages would have been attuned to the idea of conventionalized spelling through their training in Latin, which was everywhere set down in similar form, irrespective of local idiosyncrasies of pronunciation. Because of being thus conventionalized, spelling-systems must – as some other contributors to this symposium remarked in contexts far removed from the present one[4] – be assessed in their own cultural and chronological terms.

The nature of the documents underlying the texts originally cited is therefore central to any alternative explanation. All are administrative records. This is one reason why it is no accident that, as remarked at the outset, it is often onomasticians who tend to see everywhere the hands of 'Anglo-Norman scribes'; for onomasticians work mainly upon material excerpted, sometimes by others, from just such administrative records. Unless gifted with the perspicacity of an Ekwall, such workers sometimes fail to grasp that these records are not, in a linguistic sense, 'English' ones at all: *Feet of Fines* and *Assize Rolls*, for instance, consist of Latin prose requiring all names inserted in it to be at least inflexionally Latinized; tax-rolls are based on Latin frameworks (usually, it must be said, somewhat canine), and consequently show hit-or-miss Latinization or, failing that, Gallicization of names and other vernacular elements. The scribes are not, therefore, to be envisaged as aiming to write 'English', still less as striving to devise phonetic transcriptions of anyone's pronunciation, their own or an informant's. Rather were they endeavouring to accommodate English items, mainly names of persons and of places, within the obligatory Latin framework – to give, as it were, a quick lick of Latin paint to the rough vernacular.

With lexical items and with baptismal names, Latinization is unambiguous. It consistently affects not only baptismal names themselves but also expressions of relationship in which they figure: e.g., *Ricardus filius Roberti, Willelmo fratri suo* (dat.), and so on (Brooke – Postan 1960: 3, *et passim*).[5] It commonly affects occupational terms serving as descriptions or as personal by-names: e.g., *Radulphi carpentarii* (gen.) 'the carpenter' rather than 'Carpenter', *Nigellus cissor* 'the tailor', and so on (Brooke – Postan 1960: 3, 5, 7, *et passim*). Somewhat less regularly but fairly often nevertheless, it affects topographical terms used in personal by-names: e.g., *Agnetis* (gen.) *sub bosco* beside *Willemi* (gen.) *Underwode* (Brooke – Postan 1960: 6, 10). Occasionally, an English place-name may be replaced by a Latinized equivalent: e.g., *Willelmo* (abl.) *de Wyntonia* beside *Waltero* (abl.) *de Wynchestre* (Ekwall 1951: 295, 322). These latter examples emphasize how inaccurate it is to speak in such contexts, as is sometimes done, of 'the French preposition *de*' (e.g., Hjertstedt 1987: 17).

The above observations afford a background against which to assess the sporadic occurrences in similar documents of unambiguously French items, mostly occupational terms and an occasional Gallicized place-name form: e.g., *Denys le orfeure* parallels *Walt' Aurifaber*, so too *Thoma* (abl.) *de Loundres* beside *Johanne* (abl.) *de Londonia*, and *Rog' de Schorne pessoner* beside *henr' de f'nham aurifaber*, and so on (Ekwall 1951: 144, 148, 156, 323). There is no call to regard the Gallicization as any

---

4 [[See, for example, Anne King, 'Old English ABCs', in: M. Rissanen *et al.* (eds), *History of Englishes: new methods and interpretations in historical linguistics*. (Topics in English linguistics, 10.) Berlin and New York: Mouton de Gruyter, 1992, 130–43.]]

5 Brooke – Postan (1960), although admittedly chosen for citation here mainly because of ready availability, is in fact highly representative of usages in the class of document concerned.

more indicative than the Latinization of the scribe's native usages. Likewise, the occasional French relative clauses found in such documents, like *Rob' le clerc ky maint de coste ly* and *Sabine ke fu la femme phelippe le tailur* (Ekwall 1951: 182, 186), ought to be taken, not as lapses into a scribe's own vernacular, but rather as the best he could manage by way of distancing the record from that. Certainly, nothing in the examples quoted, and they are typical ones, implies a scribe with 'a better knowledge of French than English'; nor would such an inference be logical, for a translator needs adequate command of the source language as well as of the target one. What the Gallicizing scribes presumably had was a lesser knowledge of Latin than of French.

As for orthography, given the lexical and inflexional adjustments needed for harmonizing vernacular items – mainly names, that is – with bureaucratic convention, there seems no call at all to expect spellings used in Latin records to conform with vernacular usages; all the less so, when one bears in mind the limited degree of standardization as yet attained by the latter. Nor, given that the Latin alphabet provided no distinct symbol for /þ/ or for /ð/, is it either surprising or phonetically significant to find names containing these phonemes spelt with <t> or with <d>. Certainly, these spellings frequent in Anglo-Latin records did constitute a special type of 'scribal' usage; but that usage was based, not on any kind of (mis)pronunciation, 'Anglo-Norman' or other, simply upon the conventions and the limitations of the Latin alphabet.

So it is not any scribe's own speech that is at issue here, but the training of scribes in general and, above all, the nature of the documents upon which they were employed. In a Latin context, decorum required a Latinization as thorough as possible – not only grammatical but orthographical and sometimes lexical as well – of all alien and therefore intrusive elements; and there seems to have been a tacit proviso that, should a clerk's Latin fail, then French might serve the turn (cf. Legge 1941: 165, 'a sort of ignoble substitute for Latin'). In short, the trilingual interplay seen in the England of the thirteenth and fourteenth centuries involved, not two vernaculars and one learned language, but one vernacular and two learned ones. To bear that in mind should obviate the invention of false problems and consequently of myths for explaining them.

REFERENCES

Barlow, Frank, 1986. *Thomas Becket*. London: Weidenfeld and Nicolson.

Berndt, Rolf, 1965. 'The linguistic situation in England from the Norman Conquest to the loss of Normandy (1066–1204)', *Philologica Pragensia* 8: 145–63.

Berndt, Rolf, 1976. 'French and English in thirteenth-century England', in: *Aspekte der anglistischen Forschung in der DDR: Martin Lehnert zum 65. Geburtstag.* (Sitzungs-berichte der Akademie der Wissenschaften der DDR: Gesellschaftswissenschaft, part 1.). Berlin: Akademie-Verlag, 129–50.

Brooke, Christopher – M.M. Postan (eds), 1960. *Carte Nativorum: a Peterborough Abbey cartulary of the fourteenth century.* (Publications of the Northamptonshire Record Society 20.) Oxford: Northamptonshire Record Society.

Butler, H.E. (ed. and trans.), 1948. *The chronicle of Jocelin of Brakelond.* Oxford: Claren-don Press.

Chaplais, Pierre, 1988. 'William of Saint-Calais and the Domesday Survey', in: J.C. Holt (ed.), *Domesday studies*. Woodbridge: Boydell, 65–77.

Chibnall, Marjorie, 1984. *The world of Orderic Vitalis.* Oxford: Clarendon Press.

————, 1986. *Anglo-Norman England 1066–1166.* Oxford: Blackwell.

Clanchy, M.T., 1979. *From memory to written record: England 1066–1307.* London: Edward Arnold.

————, 1983. *England and its rulers 1066–1272: foreign lordship and national identity.* London: Fontana.

Clark, Cecily, 1976. 'People and languages in post-Conquest Canterbury', below 179–206.

————, 1978. 'Women's names in post-Conquest England: Observations and speculations', above 117–43.

————, 1987a. 'Spelling and grammaticality in the *Vespasian Homilies:* A reassessment', *Manuscripta* 31, 1: 7–10.

————, 1987b. 'A witness to post-Conquest English cultural patterns: The *Liber Vitae* of Thorney Abbey', below 339–47.

————, 1991. 'Towards a reassessment of "Anglo-Norman influence on English place-names" ', above 144–55.

————, 1992. 'Domesday Book – a great red-herring: Thoughts on some late-eleventh-century orthographies', above 156–67.

Clark, Cecily (ed.), 1970. *The Peterborough Chronicle 1070–1154.* (2nd edition.) Oxford: Clarendon Press.

Davis, H.W.C. (ed.), 1913. *Regesta regum Anglo-normannorum,* 1. Oxford: Clarendon Press.

Davis, R.H.C., 1976. *The Normans and their myth.* London: Thames and Hudson.

Ekwall, Eilert, 1954. *The street-names of London.* Oxford: Clarendon Press.

Ekwall, Eilert (ed.), 1951. *Two early London subsidy rolls.* (Acta Regiae Societatis Humaniorum Litterarum Lundensis 48.) Lund: Gleerup.

Fellows Jensen, Gillian, 1969. 'The scribe of the Lindsey Survey', *Namn och Bygd* 57: 58–74.

————, 1969–70. 'The Domesday Book account of the Bruce fief', *Journal of the English Place-Name Society* 2: 8–17.

Hjertstedt, Ingrid, 1987. *Middle English nicknames in the lay subsidy rolls for Warwickshire.* (Acta Universitatis Upsaliensis: Studia Anglistica Upsaliensia 63.) Uppsala: Almqvist and Wiksell.

Johnson, C. (ed. and trans.), 1983. *Dialogus de Scaccario.* (2nd edition.) Oxford: Clarendon Press.

Keene, Derek, 1976. 'The early place-names of Winchester', in: M. Biddle (ed.), *Winchester in the early Middle Ages.* (Winchester studies 1.) Oxford: Clarendon Press, 231–9.

Lefèvre, Yves, 1973. 'De l'usage du français en Grande Bretagne à la fin du XIIe siècle', in: *Etudes de langue et de littérature du Moyen Age offertes à Félix Lecoy.* Paris: Champion, 301–5.

Legge, M. Dominica, 1941–42. 'Anglo-Norman and the historian', *History* 26: 163–75.

————, 1980. 'Anglo-Norman as a spoken language', *Proceedings of the Battle Conference on Anglo-Norman Studies* 2: 109–17 and 188–90.

Plummer, Charles – John Earle (eds), 1892. *Two of the Saxon chronicles parallel,* 1. Oxford: Clarendon Press.

Richter, Michael, 1979. *Sprache und Gesellschaft: Untersuchungen zur mündlichen Kommunikation in England von der Mitte des elften bis zum Beginn des vierzehnten Jahrhunderts.* Stuttgart: Hiersemann.

————, 1985. 'Towards a methodology of historical socio-linguistics', *Folia Linguistica Historica* 6, 1: 41–61.

Rothwell, William, 1968. 'The teaching of French in medieval England', *Modern Language Review* 63: 37–46.

————, 1975–76. 'The rôle of French in thirteenth-century England', *Bulletin of the John Rylands Library* 58: 445–66.

————, 1978. 'A quelle époque a-t-on cessé de parler français en Angleterre?', in: *Mélanges du philologie romane offerts à Charles Camproux*. Montpellier: Centre d'Etudes Occitanes, 1975–89.

————, 1983. 'Language and government in medieval England', *Zeitschrift für französische Sprache und Literatur* 93: 258–70.

Round, J.H., 1899. 'Bernard the king's scribe', *English Historical Review* 14: 417–30.

Rumble, Alexander R., 1985. 'The palaeography of the Domesday manuscripts', in: Peter Sawyer (ed.), *Domesday Book: a reassessment*. London: Edward Arnold, 28–49.

————, 1988. 'The Domesday manuscripts: scribes and scriptoria', in: J.C. Holt (ed.), *Domesday studies*. Woodbridge: Boydell, 79–99.

Sawyer, Peter H., 1955–56. 'The place-names of the Domesday manuscripts', *Bulletin of the John Rylands Library* 38: 483–506.

Short, Ian, 1979–80. 'On bilingualism in Anglo-Norman England', *Romance Philology* 33: 467–79.

Shelly, Percy van Dyke, 1921. *English and French in England 1066–1100*. Philadelphia: University of Pennsylvania.

Skeat, Walter W., 1895–98. 'The Proverbs of Alfred', *Transactions of the Philological Society*: 399–418.

Southern, R.W., 1970. *Medieval humanism and other studies*. Oxford: Blackwell.

Wilson, Richard M., 1943. 'English and French in England 1100–1300', *History* 23: 37–60.

Woodbine, G.E., 1943. 'The language of English law', *Speculum* 18: 395–436.

ESSAYS IN ONOMASTICS

POST-CONQUEST ENGLAND:
CASE-STUDIES

14

People and Languages in Post-Conquest Canterbury*

Summary

The balance between French and English in post-Conquest England is still being discussed. One line of investigation not often followed hitherto is analysis of individual communities; and a start is made here with Canterbury, further subdivided into the cathedral priory of Christ Church, St Augustine's abbey, and the town.

Evidence is taken, first of all, from the hands and languages of manuscripts, from references by contemporary writers, and from literary work in general. The core of the argument, however, consists of onomastic evidence. From the second half of the twelfth century there survives a considerable corpus of citizens' nicknames; and these show that French forms, although in widespread use and even at times coupled with Anglo-Saxon personal names, were on the whole less original and less picturesque than English ones. The dominance of English is confirmed by its almost exclusive use for topographical names. The linguistic bias of some of the scribes is also investigated: although French is ever-present behind the Latin, Old English traditions are far from forgotten.

In conclusion, English, although subject to great and varied competition from French,

---

* The following abbreviations have been used:

A1, B1, XXI, AppA, etc.	References to documents printed in Urry 1967
BB	Turner and Salter 1915 and 1924 (continuously paginated), cited by page
Bosworth-Toller	Bosworth, Toller and Campbell 1898, 1921 and 1972
DB	Domesday Book
EDD	Wright 1898–1905
EETS OS	Early English Text Society, Original Series
EPNS	English Place-Name Society
ES	English Studies
Godefroy	Godefroy 1881–1902
LSE	Lund studies in English
ME	Middle English
MED	Kurath, Kuhn and others 1954– in progress
NED	Murray and others 1884–1928
NG	Nomina Germanica
OE	Old English
OFr	Old French
PR	Stenton 1932: 207–9
RIO	Revue internationale d'onomastique
RS	Rolls series
RSHLL	Regia Societas humaniorum litterarum Lundensis
SA	Urry 1959: 585
SG	Woodcock 1956, cited by document no
SMS	Studier i modern språkvetenskap
Tobler-Lommatzsch	Tobler and Lommatzsch 1925– in progress
VCH Kent	Page 1932

See also note 14 on page 187.

cannot be regarded as superseded for any function, or even much discouraged. Some of the apparent weaknesses in twelfth-century English material from Christ Church may be due not so much to French influence as to uncertainty resulting from the decline of the former standard literary language based on the West-Saxon dialect.[1]

'The confusion of vocabulary, phonology and inflexions . . . defies historical analysis . . . How such a gloss came to be written into a splendid manuscript at the scriptorium of Canterbury Cathedral in the twelfth century is a problem for historians of education' (Sisam 1959: 56–8). That sums it up. The Psalter preserved as Trinity College, Cambridge MS. R. 17. 1 (facsimile: James 1935), which goes by the name of Eadwine, its chief scribe, is one of the most splendid products of mid-twelfth-century Canterbury (Ker 1957: 135–6; Dodwell 1954: 36–7, 41–7, 48; Dufrenne 1964; A.P. Campbell 1968). Magnificently illuminated, it offers the three variant Latin versions of the Psalms in parallel, with *Gallicanum*, liturgically the most important of them, in pride of place and with *Romanum* and *Hebraicum* in slim ribbons of text alongside. An exegetical gloss accompanies *Gallicanum*. An English translation is interlined with *Romanum* (Harsley 1889),[2] and a French one with *Hebraicum* (Michel 1876; see also Woledge and Clive 1964: 14–15, 94–7), both probably added after the main texts were complete. Whereas, however, the French gloss, the earliest French version of the Psalms extant, is, in spite of some Latinisms, praised by competent judges (for instance, Legge 1963: 176), the English one, entered by several hands and only partially overseen by a corrector, is an uncritical copy of an original not only archaic but often inaccurate. Moreover, the later and closely related Psalter preserved as BN MS. lat. 8846, the third copy of the 'Utrecht' Psalter and, like Eadwine's, also from the cathedral priory of Christ Church (Dodwell 1954: 98, 122; Heimann 1975), shows only a few odd scraps of English gloss, by contrast with a full French one (Hargreaves and Clark 1965). What then was the relative standing of the two vernaculars at Christ Church priory in the twelfth century? Was English neglected or despised, or even, it might seem, half-forgotten by the literate?

In Middle English times the Kentish dialect in general – as distinct from the English of Christ Church scriptorium in particular – was, far more than any other dialect recorded, grammatically conservative and tenacious of Old English forms and usages. The five *Kentish Sermons*, preserved in a late thirteenth-century manuscript (Hall 1920: 214–22, 657–75; Bennett and Smithers 1966: 213–22, 390–8; see also Robson 1952: 63), are remarkably archaic for their date, retaining not only grammatical gender but also many other features by then discarded from most other dialects.[3] Even more archaic for its date – even allowing that the author, if he was the priest ordained in 1296 (Emden

---

[1] I should like to express my gratitude to several friends who have helped me during the preparation of this paper. Professor C.R. Cheney and Professor Dorothy Whitelock both gave their time and their skill to advising me on the first draft of it; and Professor Giles Constable, who generously offered to read the final version, made stimulating comments on many points. I am very grateful to them all not only for their expert advice but also for their kindness.

[2] The study by B. Hein has not been available to me; the various monographs by Wildhagen were all concerned with the history of psalter-glossing rather than with the special features of this gloss itself.

[3] For instance, *se* and *si* for nom. sing. masc. and nom. sing. fem. respectively of the definite article; likewise some distinction still surviving between the acc. and the dat. forms of the masc. and of the pl. of the personal pronoun.

1968: 14), was then an old man – is *The Ayenbite of Inwyt* (Morris 1876; Gradon 1979), written in 1340 by a monk of St Augustine's abbey, Dan Michael of Northgate, presumably hailing from the Canterbury ward of that name; this not only keeps some case and gender distinctions in the definite article but also shows purely native forms for the personal pronoun (Wallenberg 1923: 112–15, 249–50). Archaism so consistent implies strong and undisturbed tradition: incidentally, as both works just mentioned are translated from French, the district must have numbered many people ignorant of that language. This may seem to have little bearing on the Christ Church scriptorium in the mid-twelfth century; yet it does offer a perspective in which to view the usage there.

Twelfth-century Canterbury must have been as subject as any town in England – except perhaps for Winchester, the first seat of the Anglo-Norman treasury – to continental influences. Its nearness to ports such as Dover and Sandwich would by itself have ensured this: so regular a staging-post was Canterbury that the royal messengers had their own pasture there for their horses (Ballard 1920: 7; VCH Kent: 206). Religious houses, be it remembered, kept open house for travellers, with whom at least the guestmaster and his staff must have conversed. Then, after Becket's martyrdom and his canonisation in 1173 pilgrims streamed into Canterbury from all quarters, from France and the Low Countries no less than from the rest of England.

Such casual contacts apart, Christ Church priory could not but be a focus for continental influences. From the Norman Conquest until the later twelfth century the archbishops of Canterbury – Lanfranc, Anselm, Ralph d'Escures, William of Corbeil, Theobald of Bec – were all of continental birth and upbringing, and the London-born Thomas Becket too was Norman in interests as well as in blood. True, the archbishops by no means always had great day-to-day influence on the cathedral priory: Anselm, for instance, even when not in exile, resided little in Canterbury; Becket spent much longer in exile than at his see. Resident or not, however, they imposed their policies, which necessarily reflected their continental background. Thus, Lanfranc, questioning the authenticity of the local Canterbury saints, and especially of Ælfheah, was only just dissuaded by Anselm from discouraging their worship (Southern 1962: 50–4). Most importantly, these archbishops, moved not so much by racial bias as by desire to restore discipline in a house where before the Conquest it had become lax, brought from the Continent, mainly from Bec, monks whom they settled at Christ Church, amounting to a quarter or even a third of the community there (Southern 1963: 246); and some of these Norman monks were among those drafted to the other Canterbury house, the abbey of St Augustine, after the troubles of 1087 and of 1089 (see below, 184). From Lanfranc's accession until 1128 the continental contingent furnished all the priors of Christ Church, the effective day-to-day heads of the house; all destined for abbacies or bishoprics, they were no doubt men who set their own stamp on affairs (Southern 1963: 269–73).

The Norman influences quickly showed themselves. By the 1180s the former Anglo-Saxon script had been replaced at Christ Church, far earlier than in most English houses, by an angular hand like that of Bec (Dodwell 1954: 6–7; Ker 1960: 25ff). Studies in general took on a less insular cast: whereas before the Conquest Christ Church had been strong in vernacular learning but weakish in Latin (Southern 1963: 243),[4] under Lanfranc and Anselm Latin became its main literary medium, with the

---

[4] As well as the 'standard' Old English *Schriftsprache* based on the West-Saxon usage of

Englishmen Eadmer and Osbern the leading writers. Latin letters continued to flourish there throughout the twelfth century, with, for instance, the historian Gervase (Stubbs 1879 and 1880) and the satirical poet of *Speculum stultorum*, Nigel 'Wireker' or 'Wetekre' (Mozley 1932; Mozley and Raymo 1960: 1–2, 123–5; Urry 1967: 153–4),[5] as well as two biographers of Becket, William and Benedict (Robertson 1875 and 1876 respectively), Benedict later becoming abbot of Peterborough.

Necessarily, the incomers, as well as encouraging the literary movement towards Latin, also introduced their own vernacular into Christ Church. Eadmer tells a story of early post-Conquest days implying that at first neither incomers nor English monks normally understood the others' speech: a monk Ægelword, writhing in a speechless frenzy, was vouchsafed a sudden cure, proved to be miraculous when he not only understood his colleagues' comments *Francigena lingua* but even capped them with a pun in the same tongue, *dicens, 'Non ut catulus, sed ut catellus'* (Stubbs 1874: 234–7; Southern 1963: 247–8). In the following period the community is far from easy to analyse;[6] but evidently some French strain persisted. It might have been that which led the first hand of the *Domesday monachorum*, dated about 1100, even though regularly using insular characters, to make some gross mistakes over local place-names (Douglas 1944: 3, 9). Less ambiguous evidence is that of the new French gloss copied into *Eadwine's Psalter* in the mid-twelfth century. Towards the end of the century, several senior monks were bilingual – how far they were typical in this we cannot tell: Odo, prior from 1167 to 1175, would later, as abbot of Battle, expound the Scriptures *nunc Latine nunc Gallico sermone* but, for the common people, *lingua materna* (Brewer 1846: 148); the satirist Nigel admonishes a *parvus libellus* of his, presumably embodying his own talents, to address William Longchamps, bishop of Ely and at the same time chancellor, and possibly a kinsman of Nigel's, in the proper tongue, *paterna*, not *materna* (Wright 1872: 151). French culture was enjoyed: in the 1170s, in Odo's time as prior, the Frenchman Guernes de Pont-Sainte-Maxence spent a year as guest at Christ Church writing his *Vie de Saint Thomas*, which he often recited at the saint's tomb (Walberg 1936: lines 6156–65, Appendice, lines 16–19; see also Woledge and Clive 1964: 15) – perhaps, however, for foreign pilgrims rather than for local people. As in other English houses, such French culture was to be long maintained: the early fourteenth-century catalogue of the library shows many volumes containing items *Gallice*, not only psalters and devotional works but also medical tracts and *Bruts* (James 1903: 13–142; Blaess 1973: 329–31); several of these *Bruts* are among the French books surviving, together with at least three copies of Walter of Henley (Ker 1964: 29–40).

These continental influences and the consequent cultural shift towards Latin and French might seem to explain that English gloss in *Eadwine's Psalter*. Yet not quite. A strong English element continued to figure in the priory: witness the name of the *scriptorum princeps* himself and forms such as *Edieue*, *Egelnodus*, and *Lieuenoth* recorded as names of parents of late twelfth-century monks (Urry 1967: B126, B221, D67); for, as we shall see in more detail later (below 186–88), the drift away from

Winchester, there may also have been a southeastern variant based at Christ Church, see Campbell 1959: 11.

5 *Wetekre*, that is, 'wheat-acre', now *Whiteacre*, was enfeoffed to a Norman family in which the name Nigel was common (Douglas 1944: 51; SG 1; Urry 1967: 59).

6 The lists of monks printed in Searle 1902 are neither complete nor detailed enough for this purpose.

Anglo-Saxon names makes it unlikely that these were often given to people of purely continental ancestry. By the mid-twelfth century Englishmen were occupying senior ranks. The prior from 1128 to 1137 was *Elmerus*, that is, either *Ælfmær* or *Æþelmær* (Stubbs 1879: 98, 100; and 1880: 383; Southern 1963: 271–3; Leclercq 1953). Later, as we have seen, *lingua materna* evidently meant English both for Prior Odo and for the well-connected Nigel; and Odo's successor as prior, Alan – to be elected abbot of Tewkesbury in 1186 – is described by Gervase as *natione Anglus* (Stubbs 1879: 293). Even immediately after the Conquest there had been little attempt to suppress the native culture, for some of the incoming Norman churchmen supported English traditions, as when Anselm persuaded Lanfranc to acknowledge Ælfheah's sanctity, or when both archbishops in turn encouraged Osbern and Eadmer to write *Lives*, in Latin admittedly, of several English saints (Southern 1963: 248ff). The English language itself to some extent held its own against the encroachments of Latin as the formal medium, being used for at least one legal memorandum of Anselm's time (Urry 1967: 385; compare two bilingual documents mentioned by Ker 1957: xxvi–xxvii). As for the second Norman prior of Christ Church, Ernulf, a man universally loved: if as bishop of Rochester he encouraged compilation of the great *Textus Roffensis* (Sawyer 1957: 18), he cannot have been hostile to English tradition; he has indeed been credited with encouraging vernacular annal-writing at Christ Church (Southern 1963: 270). Be that as it may, such work did flourish there around the opening of the twelfth century. One scribe not only added to the Parker text of the *Anglo-Saxon Chronicle* but also compiled a bilingual (English/Latin) epitome of it based on a variant version; the interest taken in this work is shown by the various marginal additions, possibly by the original hand, dealing with Christ Church affairs (Whitelock 1961: xii, xvii; Ker 1957: 57–9, 187–8; Fernquist 1937) – surprisingly, perhaps, these are couched in a late West-Saxon which, although markedly 'late', is only sporadically tinged with Kenticism. A few much briefer English annals up to 1109, plus one last English addition of 1130, were entered in the margins of an Easter table, part of a volume also containing other English material (Ker 1957: 173–6; Liebermann 1879: 1–8; Southern 1963: 252–3). The 'West-Saxon' Gospels were copied here during the twelfth century, and a thirteenth-century marginal note in English shows that this text, now BL MS. Royal 1 A xiv, remained in use (Ker 1957: 315–6). *Eadwine's Psalter* itself shows on f. 10r a contemporary note giving a definition of 'comet' in tolerable late West-Saxon. William of Canterbury, in his Latin *Life of Becket*, quotes in full, with many southeastern forms, an English anthem chanted in a vision to a Norfolk priest (Robertson 1875: 151) – one of the earliest surviving pieces of English rhyming verse. Twelfth- and thirteenth-century English jottings appear in various Christ Church volumes, and these include not only glosses but also a snatch from *Poema morale* (Ker 1957: 22–3, 323–4, 413). Indeed, Oxford, Bodleian MS. Digby 4, which contains amongst other items a complete text of *Poema morale*, was a Christ Church book (Ker 1964: 38; Hill 1977: 109–10); and three leaves of an early thirteenth-century text of *The Proverbs of Alfred*, showing the insular characters þ, ð, and ƿ and ȝ, may once have formed part of the same volume (Ker 1936; but compare Arngart 1942: 8, 135–6; and 1955: 11–17).

Across at the abbey of St Augustine cultural change went at its own pace. In later medieval times, as the library catalogue shows, St Augustine's was to own even fewer English books than Christ Church, and far more French ones, including a host of romances such as *Ipomedon*, *Le chevalier au cygne*, and at least four copies of *Guy de Warewick* (James 1902: lxxxiv, 51, 371–4; Blaess 1973: 351–6; compare Emden 1968);

surviving books include several copies both of Wace and of *La chanson d'Aspremont* (Ker 1964: 40–7) and a twelfth-century copy of the earliest Anglo-Norman prose lapidary (Woledge and Clive 1964: 78–9). The fourteenth-century customary pre-scribes French for schoolroom, chapter, and cloister, banning not only English but also, except for sufficient cause, Latin (Thompson 1902: 210).

That, however, was yet to come: just after the Norman Conquest St Augustine's was slow to change. The script, unlike that of Christ Church, remained characteristically Anglo-Saxon until well into the twelfth century (Dodwell 1954: 24, 26–32; Ker 1960: 22, 26, 29). This house not only, like Christ Church, committed Anglo-Saxon hagi-ography to Latin record but even inspired the Fleming Goscelin and the Poitevin poet Reginald to undertake the task (Barlow 1962: 91–111). Perhaps attachment to native traditions underlay the monks' reaction to their second Norman abbot: details are not, however, wholly clear, partly for lack of an Eadmer here, partly owing to the destruc-tion of many muniments not only at the Dissolution but probably also in the fire of 1168. By 1070 the Anglo-Saxon abbot Æthelsige (Southern 1958: 194–8) had been replaced by Scotland (Scollandus), a learned monk of Mont-Saint-Michel brought here, according to Orderic, *ad emendationem morum* (Chibnall 1969: 248). On Scotland's death in 1087 Lanfranc chose as his successor Wido (Guy), a Christ Church monk evidently of continental origin,[7] and installed him regardless of the monks' unanimous rejection of him. Their contumacy Lanfranc then punished by transferring the prior Ælfwine and several others to Christ Church; rebellion persisting, he exiled some to distant abbeys and cast the most militant into Canterbury gaol, one called Columbanus being publicly flogged for openly wishing to kill the new abbot. After Lanfranc's death in 1089 monks and citizens joined in a murderous attack from which Wido barely escaped. Afterwards, the guilty monks were first chastised by two brothers from Christ Church and then dispersed to houses throughout England, their places at St Augustine's being taken by twenty-four monks drafted from Christ Church under a new prior, Anthony (Plummer and Earle 1892: 287–92). Motives remain unclear: Gervase of Canterbury implies a simple wish to hold a free abbatial election (Stubbs 1879: 71); some modern scholars allege 'racial feeling' (Knowles 1963: 115). Whatever the issues, Wido remained in possession until his death near the end of the century, to be succeeded by Hugo *de Flori*, a kinsman of William the Conqueror and a former knight with a late vocation (Knowles 1963: 420; 1972: 34–7). Not surprisingly, from this time on Christ Church influence – continental influence, that is – made itself manifest at St Augustine's, as, for instance, in the styles of script now adopted (Ker 1960: 26, 29).

Nonetheless, English did remain current at St Augustine's. Several of the abbey's manuscripts show twelfth-century English glosses (Ker 1957: 329–30; 350; Meritt 1945: 59); in particular, the great illustrated Hexateuch, now BL MS. Cotton Claudius B IV, contains extensive late twelfth-century English notes, in a hand using insular characters and in a language combining Kenticism with some West-Saxon influence (Ker 1957: 178–9; Crawford 1923; Dodwell and Clemoes 1974).

---

[7] An OE *Wida* would barely be possible (Forssner 1916: 254), and any abbot appointed in 1087 must have been born before 1066. This might be the Wido, probably to be identified with one professed at Bec in 1073, who was a friend of Lanfranc's nephew Lanfranc and whose virtue earned Anselm's praise (Clover 1962: 80–1, Letter 29, App. I, p. xi; Schmitt 1946: 139, 149–51). A monk *Guidonem* of an unspecified house attests the foundation charter of St Gregory's priory in 1086–7 (Woodcock 1956: 2).

Canterbury was, however, more than a monastic centre. Already before the Conquest a thriving town with, as Domesday Book shows, several hundred burgesses (VCH Kent: 198–9, 206–7), it may have numbered by the mid-twelfth century some eight hundred households (Urry 1967: 170). And, in so far as monks were recruited locally – and many were, for notes refer to relatives of theirs in the district and to holdings which some, including the chronicler Gervase, took with them to Christ Church[8] – the monasteries must have reflected the social and cultural textures of the town, all the more perhaps because some of the local recruits, like Lambert Garegate and the landholder William I of Eynsford, had taken the cowl late in life (Urry 1967: 156, 401; Douglas 1944: 45–7). Necessarily, most of the monastic servants, at least as numerous as the monks themselves (Urry 1967: 156–63, 173ff; compare Knowles 1963: 439–41), came from the town. And throughout town and countryside the monks had tenants, with whom they had at least business dealings.

Like the rest of England, the country around Canterbury had been taken under Norman overlordship. On the archiepiscopal estates over sixty 'knights' were enfeoffed, and not only their names, recorded both in the Exchequer Domesday Book and in the local *Domesday monachorum*, but also their verifiable origins are nearly all continental, among them being the Wadard and the Vitalis depicted on the Bayeux Tapestry (Douglas 1944: 17, 28, 36–58, 102; VCH Kent: 187, 209–18). Likewise, those lands of the abbey of St Augustine not kept in demesne were nearly all granted to Normans, apart from an unnamed *villanus* holding half a yoke at Rooting who was presumably of native stock (Ballard 1920: esp. 6; VCH Kent: 242–6). The rest of Kent, mainly under the overlordship of Odo of Bayeux, was also parcelled out among Norman 'knights', some of whom held of all three overlords (Douglas 1944: 29ff; VCH Kent: 187–94, 220–42). At first sight settlement may look overwhelmingly dense; but caution. Many 'knights' and other under-tenants were, like Richard 'of Tonbridge' alias 'FitzGilbert' alias 'de Clare', tenants-in-chief elsewhere and so unlikely to have become in any sense men of Kent. Lesser men might each have a dozen or even a score of scattered holdings. Even the few unambiguously insular names in the list of Christ Church 'knights' mostly prove to belong to London magnates (Douglas 1944: 58–63). For all these reasons some scholars would wholly omit both tenants-in-chief and under-tenants from any census of local populations 'because it is often difficult to locate the place of their residence' (Darby 1952: 51–4); but that may be too drastic. Medieval landholders were nomadic, moving from manor to manor as supplies dictated. Even by appearing in a neighbourhood only once in a while Norman lords and their households might encourage new fashions; by putting in stewards of their own nation lords might introduce foreigners with some prestige and so open the way for a shift of cultural attitudes. In any event, some lesser Normans did settle on Kentish estates firmly enough to take second surnames from them: the Shoford family, for instance, probably descended from the Vitalis on the Bayeux Tapestry (Urry 1958: 130–1), and the Crevequers, otherwise *de Blean* (Woodcock 1956: SG 80, 85–88, 201).

The townspeople are a little easier to know. True, not all who held Canterbury *mansurae* were residents: the tenant-in-chief Ralf *de Curbespina* (Courbépine, near Bernay), for instance, with his great rural estates as well as his fifteen burgages (VCH

---

[8] For monks' relatives in the district, see Urry 1967: A35, A36, B4, B126, B175, D126, D266 and E42 (Nigel's sister), D268 and E44, F392, IX and X, XI; for property given with monks, see B54, B55, B168, D26 and D28 (Gervase), B213 and D126, B216, B221, D67, D293, F55, F472, XX.

Kent: 206; Urry 1958: 123–5). The earliest post-Conquest list of urban landholders, not necessarily residents, names some expropriated when the castle was built; as the castle antedated Domesday Book, those dispossessed bear mainly Anglo-Saxon, or Anglo-Norse,[9] names: *Ælfred, Godwin, Leifsi, Osward, Wulfsi, Wulfred, Sired, Ketel, Wulford, Wulfric, Buct* (Urry 1967: 445, with the most traditional forms selected from the extant variants). A tiny but influential group consists of moneyers: until well into the twelfth century these bear insular names (Brooke 1916a: clxv, ccii–cciii, compare clvi–clix). Of sitting tenants listed in an English document of Anselm's time all except one *Willelm*[10] have unambiguously insular names: *Ælfric . . . Bruman . . . Siword Cutfert & Brihtric & Goldwine & Hereword & Willelm & Wulfgeue & Ælfwine* (Urry 1967: 385). The *portgerefa* witnessing the act is, however, *Calueal*, evidently the ancestor of the Cauvel family prominent here throughout the twelfth century and linked by marriage with the knightly Shofords; these links, coupled with the North-French name (*calvellus* 'small and bald'), imply that here, as in other great cities such as London, the premier position had been taken by a Norman.[11] That Norman settlement did in general affect town no less than countryside Orderic is our witness, speaking of neighbourliness, intermarriage, and international trade, and of how the English were in outward aspect soon 'completely transformed by foreign fashions' (Chibnall 1969: 256–7). How far cultural fashions may also have been transformed, especially in Canterbury, is our question.

The later twelfth century offers many references to Canterbury townspeople. Benedict's *Miracles of Becket*, for instance, mentions a poor woman called *Brithiva*, a guesthouse-keeper called *Wlviva, Geldewinus* son of *Godefridus* the baker, *Ansfreda* the daughter of *Hubertus*, and many others, almost evenly divided between those with insular names and those with continental ones;[12] but, apart from the risk that benefi-ciaries of miracles may not make a representative sample, etymology of baptismal names is by now, as we shall shortly see, little guide to ancestry. Similar cautions apply to the well over a hundred 'votaries of St Anselm' listed about 1166; here 'continental' names dominate by more than three to two, with some country gentry listed alongside citizens (Urry 1959: 585). Luckily, the best documented group of Canterbury citizens is also the largest: the tenants of Christ Church, which owned between a third and a half of the urban property. Rentals and surveys in the cathedral archives, together with some associated charters, have enabled large areas of Angevin Canterbury to be

---

9 Obviously, economy forbids annotating each form. My authorities for personal names and their provenance are: Adigard des Gautries 1954; Ekwall 1947; Feilitzen 1937, 1945, 1963 and 1968; Feilitzen and Blunt 1971; Forssner 1916; Morlet 1968 and 1972; Reaney 1952 and 1953; Redin 1919; Seltén 1972; Smart 1968; Whitelock 1940. For the slight Norse element in pre-Conquest Canterbury, see Smart 1968: 259–60.

10 Although a possible insular form, *Willelm* must owe its immense post-Conquest vogue to Norman influence (see Forssner 1916: 255–7; Feilitzen 1937: 415; and below 281–2).

11 For the Cauvel family, see Urry 1967: 62–4. The likeness of the name to the OE synonym *calu/se calewa* may have helped to establish it. For Geoffrey I de Mandeville as port-reeve of London by 1067, see Bishop and Chaplais 1957: plate xiv.

12 Brithiva, Wlviva, Atheldrida, Guillelmus, Matthæi uxor Goditha, Godefridi pistoris filius Geldewinus, Manwinus, Emelina, Edilda, another Wlviva, Eadmundus, Muriele, Ethelburga, Agnes, Godeliva, Ertinus, a Fleming, and his wife Matildis, Ansfreda Huberti filia, Aylwardus, Ailmerus, Johannes Viviani filius prepositus (Robertson 1876: 41, 49, 54, 56, 58, 59, 60, 61, 62, 63, 64, 68, 71, 81, 104, 118, 123, 138). For some forms, of course, either insular or continental origin is possible, so that precise statistics are out of the question.

mapped, with their streets lined with houses and shops and peopled with identifiable individuals, many known by trade and ancestry as well as by name (Urry 1967: the maps especially). Although not every holding was the named tenant's home, for some had several holdings and some rented property occupied by others, notes such as *domus ubi ipse manet* show that many were living on the priory lands they were renting (Urry 1967: 71–2). Some of the same names recur among the 'votaries', in the Pipe Roll for 1198 (Stenton 1932: 207–9), in the late thirteenth-century cartulary of St Gregory's priory (Woodcock 1956), and in the register of St Augustine's abbey, likewise of the late thirteenth century, known as the Black Book (Turner and Salter 1915 and 1924): although, unfortunately, neither cartulary is much concerned with urban Canterbury – and the Black Book in any case offers too many problems of dating, often aggravated by curtailed witness-lists, to make a convenient base for study – these parallel records do often supplement and illuminate the information from the Rentals.

Between Anselm's time and the opening of the thirteenth century fashion in names changed strikingly. In Rental F, dated about 1206, out of over five hundred names of current tenants only some fifty look distinctively insular. Even in Rentals A and B, compiled before 1167, some three quarters of the names look 'continental'[13] – that is, of continental-Germanic, Franco-Norse, Biblical, or classical origin: as with the 'votaries', however, some local gentry appear, perhaps slightly weighting the sample towards foreign fashions. Demonstrably fashion seems at work here, for families where at least one parent has an insular name may show children with 'continental' ones: thus,[14] *Warinus f. Siwardi* A35, *Walterus sacerdos f. Alwoldi fabri* B13, *Hugo f. Simeri sacerdotis* B94, *Mauricius f. Eadwardi* B98, *Edieue m. Jacobi* B126, *Henricus & Simon f. Ælfwini* F8, *Cristina f. Brictieue* F23, *Laurentius f. Ætelburge* F97, *Maria f. Ælueue* F107, *Cecilia f. Goduini Bradhefed* F139; likewise, *Andrea f. Godwini & Simone fr. suo* SG 42, *Lambertus f. Semeri* SG 46, *Johannes f. Eadmeri* SG 51, *Radulfus f. Lefwini* SG 52; and so on frequently throughout the country, not just in metropolitan centres such as Canterbury, London and Winchester (Forssner 1916: v–vi, xxxviii; Whitelock 1940: 130; Ekwall 1947: 91–6; Reaney 1952; and 1967: 101–7, 126ff), can be illustrated from almost any twelfth-century family: Eadmer the historian, for instance, had a nephew, his sister's son and a monk at Christ Church by 1113, who was called *Haimo*, his father's name and origin being unrecorded (Southern 1962: 159; compare Southern 1963: 231); towards the end of the century the *scriptor Cantuariensis* who wrote the three-volume Bible now in the Bibliothèque Sainte-Geneviève names himself as *Mainerus* and his sister and brothers as *Dionisia, Radulphus, Robertus, Giroldus* and *Johannes* but his parents as *Wimund* (probably insular) and *Livena* (read: *Liueua*) and his grandparents as *Ulgerus* (*Wulfgar*) and *Eluera* (*?Elueua*) (Wright 1839: 354–5; compare Dodwell 1954: 109–11 and Urry 1967: 174). Beginning before the end of the eleventh century – continental-Germanic names and a

---

13 With these proportions compare the 1130 survey of St Paul's tenants in London, with just over fifty 'French' names beside some thirty insular ones (Ekwall 1947: 111–17). Women's names throughout show higher percentages than men's of insular forms, a topic I hope to investigate further elsewhere [[see above, 117–43]].

14 My abbreviations: *f. – filius* etc.; *fr. – frater* etc.; *s. – soror* etc.; *m. – mater* etc.; *p. – pater* etc. Here and in later lists forms from SG and BB are normally taken only from material roughly contemporary with the Rentals and the associated charters, that is, dating before about 1225 (for BB date has to be deduced from the presence of known names), and dealing with Canterbury itself rather than with the surrounding countryside.

few Biblical ones do occur sporadically in English contexts well before the Conquest but then presumably mark actual immigrants (Forssner 1916: lxi; Feilitzen 1937: 26–9, 30–1; Feilitzen and Blunt 1971: 208–9; Smart 1968) – the new fashion was general by the end of the twelfth. There was, however, no more a clean sweep of insular names here than elsewhere (Ekwall 1947: xi–xii, 3–4; Reaney 1952 and 1953; Seltén 1972). Mid-twelfth-century ward aldermen, for instance, include *Wlnodus* (*Wulfnoð*) B213 and *Eadwardus* B125 etc. (he was, however, *filius Odboldi*, a continental form). Many families, even some where at least one parent has a 'continental' name, go on using both types: *Edwino fr. Martini* A35, *Maria & Wluiua s. eius* B132, *Eluiua s. Ernaldi* B152, *Godithe f. Helewis* C71, *Godelief f. Salomonis* F280, *Edith f. Johannis Swin* F141, *Liuieua f. Walteri presbiteri* F158, *Eadwinus f. Roberti sacerdotis* XVIII, *Alditha f. Henrici Coppe* XXXIV, *Wlfricus fr. Thome* SG 73, *Ethelstanus f. Mayneri diuitis* BB 581, and many other examples in all the sources.

Yet, although so often 'continental' names belong to people of English stock, some immigration had occurred, and this had no doubt encouraged the new fashions among the native English. Of course, when a mid-twelfth-century document speaks of *omnibus ciuibus Cant' Francis & Anglis* (Urry 1967: 390), such a formula was merely conventional. On the other hand, the currency around 1200 of such a nickname as *Galfrido Anglico* (LX and PR) has its implications. For some settlers evidence is clear because the documents label them as *Franceis, Bretun, Iudeus, Brabacun* 'Brabanter', *Flameng* or *Flandrensis* – be it said in passing that the sizeable contingent from the Low Countries, with their dialects close to yet contrasting with the native Kentish, cannot but have added another twist to any linguistic tangle here.[15] The Jews from France were important, for at Canterbury they formed a colony surpassed in size only by those of London and of Lincoln and by 1206 numbering perhaps a hundred; they apparently lived amicably beside the other citizens and indeed helped the Christ Church monks during the 'siege' of 1187 (Stubbs 1879: 405; Adler 1939: 47, 52, 55–6, 62; Richardson 1960: 1–4). For other kinds of settler matters are more speculative: builders, for instance, for whom in post-Conquest Canterbury there was work in plenty, with St Augustine's abbey being partly rebuilt in the late eleventh century and the cathedral twice having to be rebuilt after fires, once by Lanfranc and again after 1174. About the logistics of Lanfranc's work we know little, but of the second rebuilding Gervase has left a full account. The very stones were brought from across the sea (Stubbs 1879: 7), and the planning was international, with *artifices Franci et Angli* vying for the post of master mason; in the event William of Sens was appointed, but after being crippled in a fall he was replaced by another William, *Anglus natione* (Stubbs 1879: 6, 21). Architecturally both rebuildings show continental influences, not only Norman ones but others evidently Cluniac (Webb 1965: 26, 72–4). How and where the main work force was recruited we do not know, for Gervase speaks vaguely of *his qui convenerant sculptoribus* (Stubbs 1879: 7). In general, medieval masons were peripatetic, moving to wherever work was (Salzman 1952: 33ff; Knoop and Jones 1967: 7–8); and, for what it may be worth in the light of what has just been said about naming, the masons mentioned in our documents, unlike the carpenters, all happen to bear 'continental' names; so also the one *vitrearius* and at least four of the five *pictores*, the fifth being an ambiguous *Osmundus*.

---

[15] Flemish influence on Kentish was probably of long standing, see Samuels 1971 and Derolez 1974.

In any case, the core of the problem is not ancestry but cultural and linguistic allegiances. How far had French fashions, French culture, and the French language swamped native traditions either among the monks of Christ Church or among the townspeople from whom they were largely recruited?

No direct records may survive of the language of cloister or of street at this time. Hints, however, do survive. A faint one may be given by the persistence of some insular names. Much stronger ones are given by the nicknames distinguishing many individuals; for, unlike occupational terms, nicknames normally appear in one or other vernacular, at most only lightly Latinised – thus, *Beiuinus* B88 beside *Beiuin* B86 – and that only rarely,[16] being usually, therefore, indeclinable. These nicknames, which often wholly replace the name proper (compare Seltén 1965), presumably reflect the linguistic milieux in which their bearers moved and especially the relative liveliness and originality characterising the use of each language (compare Dauzat 1945: 180). Indeed, such nicknames are probably our only records of ordinary colloquial usage, of the language of street and market-place (compare Tengvik 1938: 23–7 and Reaney 1967: 223–9).

Only current nicknames, however, would truly reflect the milieu, not those already fossilised into hereditary family names. So caution is needed in so far as some of the nicknames here do seem to be inherited: *a me Baldewino Caluello . . . de patre meo Willelmo Caluello* VIII: about 1149; *Radulphus f. Eilwini Hearm* XI: before 1153 beside *Radulfum cognomento Hearm* A6: 1153–67; *Hamo Coppe f. Henrici Coppe* XXXIII: about 1200; *Hamo Cupere f. Roberti Cupere* SG 48: 1200–5; *Elgarus f. Joseph Copelose* SG 54: 1200–7 beside *Eilgaro Copelose* SG 57: before 1216; *Roberto Colle & Radulfo fr. eius* SG 54 beside *Radulfo Colle* SG 57; *Reginoldus (H)Oker f. Salomonis (H)Oker* SG 70 and 71: 1198–1213; *Johannes f. Johannis Chorbeile . . . Ricardum Chorbeile, avum meum* LXV: about 1205; *Ricardus Bonemfant . . . Willelmi fratris sui* B33: 1163–7 beside *Ricardi & Willelmi Bonemfant* B66; *Michael f. Brictwoldi Bonenfant* D11: about 1200 beside *Michael Bonenfant* F84: about 1206; *Johannes f. Thome Slupe* F420: about 1206 beside *Johannes Slupe* F417; *Johanne Turte, Radulfo fr. eius* LXIII: about 1200 beside *Radulpho Turte* LXX: about 1220; *Willelmo Brabacum & Radulfo fr. suo* SG 72: 1215–20 beside *Radulfo le brabacun* SG 154: about 1215. At first sight evidence for regular inheritance of nicknames or surnames looks convincing; but closer scrutiny shows a more complex picture. Terms of nationality like *Brabacun* and patronymics like *Colle*[ss] and probably *Coppe*[ss] would naturally be common to brothers; occupational terms like *Cupere*[ss] and probably *Chorbeile* and *Turte*[ss] and residential ones such as can be seen in *Slupe* (see below 193) and *Hoker*[ss] might apply literally to successive generations.[17] Usage, moreover, fluctuates – thus, in addition to instances already quoted, *Geruasius ampollarius* D144

---

[16] As elsewhere, certain simple epithets are often translated: *albus, blundus, diues, iuuenis, longus, ruf(f)us, anglicus, flandrensis, francigena, iudeus, scottus*, and so on. Other nicknames and toponymics are translated much more rarely: but *Willelmi bouis* B223 (compare *Willelmi le Bof* XLV) and *Walteri Bovys* AppA (compare *Waltero f. Bues* SG 43), *Johannis Rati* F393, *Roberti Angeli* XLII (compare *Robertus Angulus* BB 560) *Godwini freni* SG 36 'bridle', *Arnoldus de monte* D149 (compare *Godelief attehelle* F650), and *Liuiue ad fontem* F479 (compare *Elfsi Atparwelle* B47); for these latter forms see also below 200.

[17] The forms marked with a superscript [ss] are more fully discussed in my paper 'Some early Canterbury surnames', below 207–20.

beside *Geruasius f. Seuugel* F625 (entries referring to the same holding, see Urry 1967: 272, n.), or *Simon de Balneario f. Wulnothi de Pette* SG 72 – and some people seem so far to lack any surname of their own as to have to be specified by clumsy periphrases: *Martino nepote Germani monachi* XI: before 1153; *Jordanus qui habet filiam Reginaldi* B42: 1163–7; *Joseph fr. Roberti cognomento Angeli* XLII: late C12; *Sedegos & Scolastica f. Eluiue que fuit uxor Eadulfi et postea Brummani secretarii* XLIII: 1167–75. With practice so fluid, nicknames might well be personal and fresh more often than hereditary and out-of-date; but, for safety's sake, a few Norman names dating to Domesday Book and earlier, such as *Folet, Malet, Picot* and *Talebot,* as well as *Cauvel* (see above 186), will be left out of the reckoning.

Heredity is only the first of many problems. True nicknames are often hard to distinguish from place-names, from baptismal names used patronymically, or even from baptismal names proper. Many are etymologically obscure; some might indeed be plausibly referred to either vernacular. Moreover, as will later be considered more fully, scribes may have had a bias away from English towards French strong enough to inspire at least sporadic translation; with so few dual forms,[18] however, this cannot be more than surmised. Nevertheless, in spite of the uncertainties, comparison between the uses of the two main vernaculars may not be wholly futile.

The simplest nicknames – excluding, that is, occupational terms[19] – consist of adjectives and other straightforward epithets, often traditional and widely used. French nicknames of this type are:[20] *Hendrico le* AFAITE SG 7 'elegant'; *Rodbertus* etc. BASSET B167 etc. 'short-legged', a nickname current in Arras and common in England from DB on; BLANC(H)ARD standing alone C47 etc., and *Robertus* etc. (*le*) BLUND PR, D32 etc. 'blond', very common indeed both in England and in France and used here interchangeably with *Blundus/Albus* (compare below *se Wite*); *Rogeri* CAITEUEL B1 etc. 'feeble wretch' as in the title of Marie de France's lai, *Chaitivel:* *Willelmi* etc. COKIN D366 etc., SG 197 etc., BB 383 etc. (PR KOKAN) 'idle rascal', current in Eu, Arras and Calais; *Osberti* etc. CURTEIS SA, B74, BB 581 'courteous', current in Arras and Calais; probably *Arnoldus* FERRE[ss] PR, D121 etc., SG 42 etc., if meaning 'iron-clad'; *Galfridus le* FORT SG 16 'strong', current in Arras; probably *Henricus* GREDLE LV, if meaning 'pock-marked';[21] *Hugone le* LONGE AppA, alias *Longus* F183, 'tall', current in Arras and in general very common; *Willelmus le* NOBLE F268 etc., alias *Nobilis* SG 114 and 115, BB 166; *Iohanni* PELERUN BB 600 'pilgrim'; *Willelmus* PUNGNANT SA 'stabbing' or perhaps 'punching', found also in

---

18 In this respect practice here differs markedly from that of thirteenth-century Calais, where many individuals' surnames interchange between Flemish and French (Gysseling and Bougard 1963).

19 Some of the rarer occupational terms are discussed in my paper mentioned in note 17. See also below 199–200.

20 Again economy forbids documentation of each individual form. My authorities are: (a) the standard dictionaries – Bosworth-Toller; MED; NED; EDD; Godefroy; and Tobler-Lommatzsch; (b) Dauzat 1945; Dauzat and Morlet 1969; Ekwall 1947, 1963 and 1965; Feilitzen 1939, 1945 and 1968; Kristensson 1970; Löfvenberg 1942 and 1946; Reaney 1958 and 1967; Seltén 1965 and 1969; Smith 1934 and 1956a and b; Sundby 1963; Tengstrand 1949; and Tengvik 1938. The continental material used for comparison has been taken from: Arnould 1952 (Mons); Beauvillé 1953, 1954 and 1955; Berger 1963 and 1970 (Arras); Blottière 1973; Carrez 1937, 1938a and b, and 1947; Gessler 1931; Gysseling and Bougard 1963 (Calais); Morlet 1959 and 1960 (Eu); Poerck 1951a, b and c.

21 The standard interpretation, but compare *greidle* for *Graille* 'trumpet' in, for instance, Jordan Fantosme (Howlett 1886: lines 470, 1309); compare also *Henricus de Gredele* BB 242.

DB; *Maynero le* RICHE PR, E31, alias *Diuite* D255, compare SG 225; *Rogero* STURDI SG 40 'reckless', current in Arras; just possibly *Willelmi* STUTHE SG 61, if meaning 'bold' (but see below 193 and 194); and also *Aschetilli* BELLI F353 may render a French original rather than an English one, *le Beals* being a common epithet in BB. Some terms of nationality keep a continental form: *Radulfi/Willelmi* BRABACUN F78 etc., SG 72 etc.; *Willelmus* BRETUN SG 40; *Henrici* CAMPENES BB 337 'from Champagne'; *Lambinus* etc. FLAMENG/FLEMENG F299 etc., SG 205, alias *Fland-rensis* and *Frese*, a common form in BB; MANSEL standing alone C62 etc., possibly 'from Le Mans', but more probably a personal name; *Robertus li* SARACIN XVIII, current in Eu and Arras, presumably used metaphorically either for 'swarthy' or for 'traveller returned from the East', compare *Roberto Saladin* SG 66. Analogous forms apparently referring to English origins are: *Willelmus* NOREIS XXV 'Northerner', very common in BB; and *le* WALDEIS C29 etc., always with a form of *Æilmer*, 'from the Weald', compare *Dieringe le Waldisse* BB 500 for the English equivalent. English terms, that is, not only those of Old English origin but also established loans from Norse and from Latin, cover a similar, perhaps slightly wider range: *Elfegi* etc. BIGKE D382, SG 69; probably *Ainulfo* CAUAST LI, if meaning 'the boldest';[22] probably *Osbertus se* COCCHERE/COCKERE[ss] B2, B3, B45, and *Henricus* COKERE PR, if meaning 'brawler'; *Petri le* DEAF BB 177; *Rogeri se* DESIE D232 etc. 'silly', a Kentish form from OE *se dysiga*; *Eadmundo* DUMBE SG 47; *Lambinus* FRESE B79 etc., alias *Flemeng* or *Flandrensis* (see above 188); *Hukelot* etc. *se/le* FRODE C68 etc., SG 95, very common in BB, 'wise', compare from Calais *le Vroede* alternating with *le Sage*; *Lamberti* etc. (*se/le*) GODE B1 etc., SG 69, BB 47 'good', compare *Iohannes Buns* BB 336; *Rogeri* HOLEMAN F203 'dwelling in the dell'; *Godwini se* [IU]NGE B95, *Eadwardi se* [IU]NGGE B98[23] 'young', very common, also *Iuuenis*; *Osbertus se* LITHLE D265, *Winedei* LITEL F411, likewise *Stace* SMALE SG 211, both English terms being common in BB alongside *Parvus/le Petis*; *Elwine* MAN SG 60, a form also current in Calais; *Eilredi* etc. (*se*) PRUDE D252 etc., SG 77, BB 17 etc. 'proud', a pre-Conquest loanword; *Willelmi* etc. (*se*) STAMERE F87 etc., BB 165 'stammerer', compare *Emme Balbine* BB 601; *Elfwini se* WITE B18, for (*le*) *Blund, Blanchard, Albus* and *Blundus* see above 190 and compare the form *le Witte* current in Calais; probably *Henrici le* WODE LXX, if meaning 'mad'. A rare example of an epithet interchanging between the two vernaculars in *Goderus* PAUMIER LX (2x) beside *Godere (se/le)* PALMERE D244 etc., compare *Roberto* PALMERE SG 197.

Much trickier are the noun nicknames. Far more than with adjectives, it can even be uncertain to which language they belong – and hence statistics are impossible. And that is only one of the possible kinds of ambiguity. Take the form *pic*: both in Old English and in Old French this could mean 'pointed tool', with various secondary senses, and in Old French had several diminutive forms such as *picot* and *piquet*;[24] in Old English a similar spelling, but pronounced with final affricate, meant 'tar'. English nicknames in particular are often deeply obscure, as is shown by Tengvik's frequent recourse to

---

22 Compare, however, *Giles Canastus* and *Wit canast Sawales*, both current in Arras (Berger 1963–1970: 1: 24, 33), and Mod. Fr. *canast* 'basket'.

23 My own emendations for *se uinge, se uingge* (Urry 1967: 234); I am indebted to Miss Anne Oakley, the Canterbury Cathedral archivist, for verifying these and many other readings for me.

24 For English *pic* secondary senses, far from easy to date, include 'kind of fish' and 'pointed hill' (mainly northern, see Smith 1956b: 63); for the OFr. word they include 'woodpecker', 'suit of cards'.

comparative philology for their elucidation and, even more, by his occasional contra-dictory alternative interpretations (for instance, 1938: 36, under *Hagg*). In any case, even when etymology and dictionary meaning are clear, the full implications usually elude us: some nicknames mark trade, some residence; some comment on looks or character, either literally or metaphorically, perhaps with an ironical twist; and no hint normally survives what sense was meant, or indeed whether the name cryptically commemorates some long-forgotten farce or drama, or fossilises some catch-phrase. Such questions, even though unanswerable, are not irrelevant, for metaphor, and much more so irony, imply far greater vigour of mind and of tongue than does mere occupa-tional or residential labelling.

Noun nicknames – other than animal names, which will be treated later – apparently of French origin are: *Henricus* etc. BARAT(E)[ss] PR, F232 etc., SG 57 etc. 'fraud, strife', a form current in Eu, Arras and Calais; probably *Robin* (f.) BOISUN D256 etc., if meaning either 'beverage' or 'box-wood', and for the latter sense compare *Willelmus Box f. Alani Box* SG 225; *Johannes* etc. CALDERUN/CAUDRUN B73 etc., current in Eu, Mons and Arras, beside *caudronier* in Calais; *Hugo* COFFIN B61 etc. but COFINUS standing alone A9 etc. 'basket, box', compare from Arras the diminutive *Cofinel*; *Ricardi* etc. CORBEILLE F303 etc., SG 143 etc. 'basket', current also in Arras; *Robert* CUUENANT BB 584 etc. 'agreement'; probably *Henrico* GALLE LXIV, if meaning 'oak-gall, as an inferior black dye-stuff' (see Poerck 1951a: 190–2 and b: 246), the probable sense of the same form current in Calais;[25] *Lambert* GARE-GATE B71 etc., BB 338 'throat', current in Eu and Arras; *Willelmus* GERNUN F152 'moustache', current in Eu and Arras; *Reginaldi* etc. IOIE F47 etc., BB 338 etc. 'joy', current in Arras, Mons and Calais; just possibly *Æilwordi* PICH F236 etc. and twice PIC standing alone, if French rather than English (see above); *Willelmus* PIKACE F311 etc. 'pick-axe', current in Arras; just possibly *Johanne* PIKENET LX, although the form is hard to trace;[26] possibly *Rodbertus* PIN B9 etc., if French rather than English for 'pine-tree' (see also below); *Johanne* PINEL A2 etc. 'small pine-tree', current in Eu; *Johannes* ROSE D140, BB 598, current in France and sometimes taken as a metronymic, but compare *Iohannes Blosme* BB 160; *Azo* SCACHE[ss] B179 etc. 'wooden leg; crutch', current in Arras; *Willelmus* TIMPAN D213 'drum'; *Admero* TROTE XI 'trot', probably a name for a messenger; *Johanne/Radulfo* TURTE[ss] LXV etc., SG 81 etc. 'coarse round loaf'; *Johannes* (*le*) VOLT PR, D271 etc., SG 52 'face'; *Rodbertus* (*le*) WANTE B43 etc. 'glove', current in Arras, compare *Robertus glouere* F557. Nicknames which appear to be English, although admittedly a number of them are pretty obscure, include: *Staphano le* BREAC LI, if an un-Kentish form for either *brǣc* 'clearing' or *brǣc* 'brushwood' (Smith 1956a: 45, 46, 47), although the normal Kentish reflex for both words should be *brec*; *Wlnodo* BRI XI, probably OE *brēo*, Kentish *brio* 'broth'; *Nichellus* BROCH D137, probably *brōc* in the Kentish, and Flemish, sense 'water-meadow', and possibly distinct from the surname seen in *Robertus del Broc* D343, *Ricardo del Broc* SG 79, and as that of one of Becket's enemies (Stubbs 1879: 49, 221; compare Urry 1967: 182–3), as this latter may be manorial (Douglas 1944: 92); *Geru[a]sio* CHESE C42 'cheese', with which compare

[25] But in the Midlands especially there is a common topographical term *galle* 'barren ground' (Reaney 1935: 596; Gover, Mawer and Stenton 1940a: 263 and b: 282; Cameron 1959: 729).

[26] I can find no OFr. **picquenet* or similar form; perhaps the spelling here represents a corruption of OFr. *picavet* 'faggot', current as a nickname in Arras (Berger 1963: under the year 1224, etc.). Compare *Ricardus Pikenot* (Dodwell 1958 for 1956: 256).

the name *Case* current in Calais, and *Simonis* CRUDDE B114 'curd'; possibly *Simon* etc. (*de*) CHICH(E)ss PR, F178 etc., SG 133 etc., if this is the common noun *cicc* 'river-bend' rather than the proper place-name *Cicc*, Essex, now St Osyth; *Wluordi* CLUT G29 etc. 'rag, patch', compare *God' Clutessune* C48; *Henricus* COD PR, D170 etc. 'bag'; COLHOPPE standing alone XVI 'fried morsel'; just possibly *Hamo* COPPE *f. Henrici* COPPEss XXXIII etc., SG 50, if not a patronymic but meaning 'at the hill-top'; *Lifwinus* CRUC/CRUKE/CRUCHE B84 etc. 'at the cross'; *Eadwino* CRUME SG 69 'fragment, for instance, of land'; *Rodbertus* FELD SA 'field'; just possibly *Arnoldus* FERREss D121 etc., if meaning 'by the fir-tree' (but for a preferable interpretation see above, 190); perhaps *Henrico* GALLE LXIV, if meaning 'bitter humour' (but see above, 192); *Rodbert* GOGGE B73 etc., probably 'by the marsh'; *Eilwini* etc. H(E)ARM XI etc. 'danger' (see below, 195 for *Eilwini Kipeharm* BB 338); *Willelmus* HUNGERE PR 'famine', if not a patronymic; probably *Salomon* (*f.*) KIET/CHIET/KET/KETH/CHETss B15 etc., if from ME *ket*, a loan-word from Norse *kjǫt* 'flesh-meat'; *Elfegus* KING D187 and commonly in BB; *Alfredi* etc. PETE D147 etc., probably 'by the pit', compare *atte Pette* BB 42 etc.; probably *Æilwordi* PICH F236 etc., if English and meaning 'tool' rather than 'fish' (see above, 192); probably *Rodbertus* PIN B9 etc., perhaps as English rather than French for 'pine-tree' (see above), although in OE this is usually compounded as *pin-beam* or *pin-treow*, but more likely for OE *pinn* '(drinking-)peg', often found in nicknames (Feilitzen 1937: 344), compare also the twelfth-century London form *Drinkepin* (Ekwall 1947: 148); *Robertus* etc. POLRE D126 etc., SG 53 etc., BB 341 etc. 'marsh', but possibly a proper place-name, thus, *alter [mariscus] vocatur Polre* BB 419 – the term is in any case characteristically Kentish (Smith 1956b: 69; Ekwall 1963: 159); *Osbertus* PRET D186 etc., also common in BB, 'trick', an old nickname; *Johannes* SAULE F42 etc., probably OE *sāwol* 'soul' rather than the rarish OFr. *saule* 'willow'; *Henricus* SCRIP SG 54 etc. 'satchel'; *Willelmi* SCUTEL B105 'dish'; *Thome* etc. SLUPE D294 etc., probably 'slippery, muddy place';[27] SPANGE/SPONGE standing alone F255 etc., either 'brooch, buckle' (compare *Genesis B*, line 445: *spenn mid spangum* 'fastened with clasps') or more probably a derived topographical sense (Smith 1956b: 135); perhaps *Willelmi* SPROTss F58 etc., SG 64 etc., if not a patronymic, and if meaning 'twig, wood-chip, roofing-shingle' (but see also below, 194); probably *Willelmi* STUTHE SG 61, if meaning 'on the hillock' (but compare above, 191 and below, 194); *Euerardus* TOD B29 'bushy mass (of hair)', the other sense 'fox' being northern (Smith 1956b: 180–1); *Walterus* WIN PR 'wine', rather than OE *wynn* 'joy', Kentish *wen*; *Eadwini* etc. WINTER B21, BB 85, a similar form being current in Calais, compare also *Willelmus Sumer* BB 33. Allowing always for the uncertain cases on both sides, the English list seems slightly longer and richer, with, perhaps, fewer conventionalised forms. One significant difference is that, whereas many of the French forms clearly refer to merchandise, the probable toponyms are mainly English (but compare *Johanne* PINEL A2, 3 and *Rodbertus* PIN B9, etc. and see also below, 198–9).

The animal nicknames, even though many of these too must have been occupational rather than picturesque or imaginative, again suggest somewhat greater vitality on the English side. French names of this kind are: *Willelmi le* BOF XLV etc. alias *Boue* or

---

[27] Presumably cognate with the strong verb *slūpan* 'to slide'; for a similar form from Gloucestershire an OE etymon *slype* has been suggested (Kristensson 1970: 41–2; compare Smith 1956b: 129, 130), but that should give Kentish *slepe*.

Bouis, and *Walterus* (*f.*) BUES/BES PR, D9 etc., SG 43 etc. 'ox', a name current in Eu; *Tomas* BUTOR SA 'bittern'; perhaps *Helie* CATH F134, as the form was current in Eu and Arras (but compare below); *Willelmi* etc. CORBIN D42 etc. 'raven'; *Roberto* CUNING SG 53 'rabbit'; *Robertus* CURLIWE BB 336; *Henrico* (*le*) JAY/JAI XXXVII etc., SG I.7, BB 397 'jay', current in Arras; *Sigari* etc. KEUEREL B12 etc., that is, Norman *quevrel* 'kid', the base *Kievre* 'goat' being a current nickname in Eu and Arras; *Warini* KIEN/CHIEN C68 etc. 'dog', current in Eu, Arras and Calais, compare the mid-thirteenth-century *Hamo Doge* SG 198 etc.; *Godwinus* MUCHET/MUSCHET B106 etc. 'small fly' literally and hence secondarily 'small hawk, especially tiercel of kestrel or sparrow-hawk', a nickname current in Arras; *Godric* MUISSUN B123 'sparrow', current in Eu and Arras; *Willelmus* etc. PER-TRICH/PERDITC(H)/PARDIC(H) F91 etc. 'partridge', compare *Perdix* BB 202; *Henrici* PULEYN BB 344 'colt', current in Eu and Arras. The English examples, a little more numerous, are: *Arnoldus* BUCCE/BUCHE/BUCKE D115˙ etc., SG 49 etc., BB 167 etc. 'he-goat'; *Ordmeri se* CAT B127, with *se* implying an English form (compare above); *Wido* CRANE SA, either 'tall bird' or the secondary sense 'lifting gear', a similar nickname being current in Calais; *Brunman* etc. *se* DORE D236 etc., BB 36 'bumble-bee'; GOLDFING standing alone B170 'goldfinch' (compare below *Spinke*); *Sunwini* etc. HARE D355 etc., BB 177; *Willelmi* HERING[ss] D368 'herring' – an important local commodity, witness the rent of 40,000 herring paid annually to Christ Church by Sandwich (VCH Kent: 209), compare *Hagemunt Freteharing* (see 195); *Geruasius* HOG F72 etc., SG 66, and *Iohannis* SWIN D332 etc. 'pig'; *Wibertus* etc. KIDE/CHIDE B195 etc. 'kid' (compare above *Keuerel*); *Eadwardo* etc. (*le*) LAMB A21 etc., SG 85 etc., common in BB; *Winedei* OXE B91, compare *Osberni le Rether* BB 581 (also *le Bof* and variants above); *Vitalis* etc. PACOC F136 etc., BB 174 'peacock'; perhaps *Æilwordi* PICH F236, if the sense 'fish' was already current (compare 192 and 193); *Johanne* RAM SG 40; *Æilredi* SNAKE F260; *Osbertus* SPINKE D9 etc., SG 41 etc. 'finch', compare the form *Vinch* common in other sections of both SG and BB; probably *Willelmi* SPROT[ss] F58 etc., if not a patronymic and if meaning 'sprat' (compare above, 193); possibly *Willelmi* STUTHE SG 61, if meaning 'gnat' (but compare above, 191 and 193). *Lamberti* WRENNE/WERNE/WRAN A21 etc., probably OE *wrenna/werna* 'wren', not *wrǣne* 'wanton'.

   With compound epithets and phrase-names the dominance of English becomes more marked – we may note in passing that the rural material in the Black Book, here quoted only for comparison, is strikingly rich in such names. Some compounds offer straight-forward descriptions: *Henrici dicti quondam* CANDELCLERK BB 397 'acolyte', where, with *cler(e)c* a long-standing loanword in OE, there is no need to invoke OFr. *clerc*; *Robertus* GODIUERE C17 etc., SG 74 'good companion'; *Rogeri* SAMELES BB 166 'shameless'; *Mathei* STRANGMAN SG 143, BB 241. Another group consists of 'Bahuvrīhi adjectives', that is, adjectival formations in which the second element is a substantive, thus, *heardheort* 'hard-hearted': forms typical of Old English but hardly used in later English except for nicknames (see Tengstrand 1949: esp. 221–2), the same usage being found also in the Flemish of Calais. Nicknames of this kind include: *Godwinus* BRADHEFED F139 etc. 'broad-headed' – although some prefer to regard such forms as toponymic rather than personal (Kristensson 1970: 51); likewise RUCHHEUED standing alone F268 etc. 'rough-headed', and *Roberti* LANGHEUED BB 179 'long-headed', compare *Osberti Veyrheaued* BB 31; *Gleduse* FAIRHE(G)NE D202 etc. 'fine-eyed'; *Simone* LANGWAMBE LI 'long-bellied', compare *Langheued* above and *Thoma Langnase* BB 30; *Robertus* SCHORTHALS PR 'short-necked', compare the Calais form *Corthals*. A large and miscellaneous group records various associations – wares, residence, looks, attire, habits, and so on: ALEPOT standing alone D335, if *pot* can be taken as established English, analogous forms and senses being *Pot* BB47, *Birecop* BB 285, *Robertus Alegod* BB 312; *Godwine* etc. BERE(M)BREAD XVIII etc. BB 179 etc. 'barley bread', compare *Simon Witbrad* BB 17; *Winedei cognomento* BUTERCLUNCC XIX etc. 'mass of butter'; *Æduardi* CATTEBITE F277 etc. 'cat-bite'; *Humfridi* CRISTEMESSE BB 167; *Johannes* DODEKERE C3 etc., *tunc preposito Cantuarie* BB 393, showing *æcer* 'field' either with the name *Dodda* or else with the common noun *dod* meaning 'measure of corn, as rent',[28] and *Robertus* TOLEKERE F282, where *æcer* is compounded with *toll* 'rent', compare also the various other compounds of *-ekere* figuring as surnames in BB; HEGGESFOT standing alone F82, *Simon* HECCHEFOT D16 'at the foot of the hedge', with which compare *Iohannis ate Hegge* BB 250;[29] HERLOC standing alone F452 'lock of hair', compare *Elrich Witloc* BB 19 and the many other compounds in *-loc* common as nicknames from OE times on, *Brunloc, Gildeneloc, Harloc, Scirloc*; just possibly *Rogeri* PATFOT BB 170 etc., if the first element is *pat(te)* 'mud';[30] *Roberti* SEPESONKE BB 338 'sheep-shank'; *Æiluord* etc. SMALSPON F247, BB 32, where *spōn* probably means 'roofing-shingle'; *Wlfwardi* SWIRHOD D344 etc. 'neck-hood', compare for the sense *Willelmus Caperun* BB 68; WINDECLIUE standing alone BB 170 etc. 'wind-cliff'; *Walteri* etc. WITEPESE B71, SG 96, BB 17 etc. 'white pea', a staple of the monastic diet;[31] *Willelmus* EACTETENE F204 etc. 'eighteen' beside *William de setuit uel eachtene* Rental XI (Urry 1967: 171; compare Reaney 1967: 250). Liveliest of all are the verbal compounds, often of the 'Shakespeare' phrasal pattern: *Ricardus* BREKEPOT BB 342; *Godwinus* CRIPUP SA 'creep up'; perhaps *Willelmus* etc. DRAUET PR, F255, BB 337, if meaning 'drag feet'; *Siredus* DRINCHEDRESTE B141 etc. 'drink dregs', alias *Siredi scutellarii* D18, and *Walterus* DRINKENOZ BB 338 'drink enough'; *Elfwinus* EUERGA XII etc. 'always go'; *Johannes* FRETECOC D279 'eat a cock', and *Hagemunt* FRETEHARING PR 'eat a herring', where we may note that *fretan* often means 'devour, eat like a beast'; *Amfridi* HATEGOD BB 6, probably '(I) promise God', with *hātan* 'promise' plus *God* (compare *Hatecrist*, usually taken to indicate a blasphemer); *Eilwini* KIPEHARM BB 338 'watch for danger' (compare 193 *Eilwini Hearm*);[32] *Edit* MAKEPAD SA, probably

---

[28] The alternative sense for *dod*, 'round hill', is unlikely because mainly northern (Smith 1956a: 133). Monothematic names like *Dodda* are especially common in the south (Smart 1968: 271).

[29] Alternatively, but less probably, *Hecchefot* might represent a 'Shakespeare' compound with the verb *icchen* 'move briskly'.

[30] The most likely origin is Flemish *paddevoet* 'defect in weaving' (Poerck 1951a: 86 and c: 104). For *pat(te)* 'mud', see Löfvenberg 1942: 148 and Smith 1956b: 60. As for the verb *pat* (trans. and intrans.) and the adj. *pat* 'prompt' and its corresponding adv., of none of these do medieval records survive.

[31] See, for instance, BB 5: Item, prouisum est vt supra de pisis albis ad potagium conuentus quod firma plene, id est, lij summe soluatur ita quod grauiter puniature per cuius defectum contigerit quominus cotidie conuentus pisa habeat.

[32] Compare also the thirteenth-century nickname *Wecheharm* (Sundby 1963: 147). [[Cecily Clark later came to revise this interpretation of the name *Kipeharm*: 'Bosworth-Toller . . . cites, *s.v. cēpan*, several Ælfrician and other instances of an OE idiom *hearmes cēpan* "to intend injury (to someone)". Similar meanings of this verb continued into ME, but with such shifts of construction as were necessitated by the disuse of synthetic genitives as verbal objects (cf. T. Mustanoja, *A Middle English Syntax*, I [Helsinki, 1960], 87–8): therefore, *kepe harm*, instead of older *h(e)armes*. Being datable approximately to the early twelfth century, this syntactic change marks

meaning 'make cushion', although clear records of a noun *pad*, whether as 'cushion' or as 'heavy footfall', hardly date from before the sixteenth century (note that cushion- and mattress-makers are commonly women); perhaps *Mathei* PREKEPELSE B23 may be listed here, although the second element may be Flemish *pels* 'fleece' (Poerck 1951a: 31 and b: 105) rather than a Kentish form of OE *pylece* 'fur-cloak', the whole compound meaning 'pierce a fleece'; another dubious case concerns the names of several women who are tenants of shops, *Cristina* etc. SLAPEGRUT BB 591, in which *grout* 'malt liquor' is probably compounded with the verb *slop/slap* rather than with the adj. *slape* 'smooth, especially of ale', as the latter word, apt though it is, is mainly northern (see EDD); *Goduini* WENDEMALT F248 'turn malt'. French, on the other hand, offers a markedly narrower range of compound nicknames: *Iohannis* BELES-MAINS D251 etc., also the name of another Canterbury man who became archbishop of Lyon (Clay 1943: 11–19), and *Willelmo* MALEMEYN AppA; BONECHOSE stand-ing alone LI; *Ricardus* etc. BONEMFANT B33 etc. and *Willelmus* PETITFANT D159, with the latter showing the aphetic *-fa(u)nt* common in ME (see MED and Reaney 1958: col. 115a); *Ricardus* C(U)ER DE LEUN BB 343 etc., alias *Cor Leonis* BB 336; probably *Matheus* DURNEIS XXIII, if, as seems likely, a North-East OFr. form for 'hard nose';[33] GARBADOS standing alone IX and X 'sheaf on back'; *Osberti* GRASPOREE B118 'bacon and vegetable broth', similar forms with *Cras(s)e-* being current in Arras and Calais; apparently *Willelmi* MALBAN D31, perhaps with *ban* 'proclamation' and so meaning 'ill news' (this would be the French equivalent of the London nickname *Ilborde*, see Ekwall 1947: 155); *Willelmi* MALEMIE D103, SG 40 and 154, perhaps 'nasty bread', compare *Waltero Mala Mica* in a St Paul's charter of before 1127 (Gibbs 1939: 147); *Willelmi* MAUUEISIN D255 etc. 'bad neighbour', but for short plain *Veisin* D256, SG 42, BB 177; *Willelmo* PEDELEUERE LXX 'harefoot', a similar form being current in Arras; two Jews' names, DEUDUNE, DEULESAUT LI, respectively meaning 'God-given', 'God save him' (for *saut* as pres. subj. of *sauver*, see Pope 1934: 353; DEUSLESALT is also found as a Jew's name in London in 1130, see Pipe Roll Society 1929: 147); two all-French 'Shakespeare' compounds, *Johannes* BEIUIN A23 etc., BB 598 'drink wine', a nickname widely current both in France and in England, and *Radulfus* WASTECAR(N) II etc. 'spoil meat', a typical North-French form;[34] also one apparent French-English hybrid compound, PISSE-BOLLE standing alone XXV, with OE *bolla* 'bowl'. As well as being few, the French compounds are less original than the English ones, the monotonous reliance on *mal(e)* being especially noticeable. Moreover, the paucity of French 'Shakespeare' forms in particular strengthens recent doubts of the traditional view that English borrowed this

the by-names found in twelfth-century records as recent formations.

    This revised interpretation squares well with the Canterbury interchange, for the same name-bearer, between the simplex *H(e)arm* and the phrasal *Kipeharm*, that is, "injury" as short for "intend injury" (the *i-* spelling for OE *ē* found in the Black Book of St Augustine's is paralleled elsewhere in Kentish usage).'

    ("The Middle English nickname *Kepeharm*", *Nomina* 5 [1981], 94.)]]

[33] For this suggestion and for comments on *Malban* and *Malemie* I am indebted to Dr Peter Rickard of Emmanuel College, Cambridge. The form *durneis* would be analogous to the nickname of the mid-twelfth-century prior of Canterbury, Walter *Durdent*, and to forms such as *Dure teste* current in Arras; compare also the Calais nickname *a le neis* (Gysseling and Bougard 1963: 57).

[34] Compare the *sobriquet normand 'Gâtechair'* (Beauvillé 1955: 302 – suggested explanation to be ignored), also *Wastecarbon* Arras 1206 and *Waste-Bleit* Mons; *car(n)* is the normal NE OFr. word for 'meat'.

pattern from French (compare Tengvik 1938: 383–4; Reaney 1967: 280; Seltén 1969: 3, 19; also Dauzat 1945: 206–9), doubts further supported by the richness of all-English forms such as *cutwood, slay-horse*, in the rural material in the Black Book.

Yet, dominant though English may seem, some delicacy in the cultural balance is confirmed by the varied ways in which baptismal names and nicknames can be combined. With 'continental' personal names so widely used, as we have seen, by people of English stock, naturally these often combine with English nicknames, thus *Ærnoldus Bucke, Bartholomeus Berebred, Geruasius Hog, Hukelot se Frode, Simone Langwambe, Robertus Sepesonke*, and so on. More significantly, an old-fashioned insular name may be coupled with a French nickname, thus, *Brictwoldus Bonenfant, Sigarus Keuerel, Godric Muissun, Godwinus Mu(s)chet, Admerus Trote* – sometimes, as with *Muissun* 'sparrow', even when the French word involved was not destined for adoption into English. It might be suggested that some of these forms are due merely to scribal translation, and it cannot be conclusively proved that they are not; but the pattern of usage here could have been produced by such translation only if scribes had tempered capriciousness about whether to keep, say, English *Kide*, or to render it as *Keuerel*, both with a remarkable consistency in treating each individual case and also with a knack of choosing only such French forms as were current in France. In so far as these French nicknames were in fact current here they must imply fair knowledge of French vocabulary even among those English people conservative enough to retain insular baptismal names, thus offering a slight corrective to a recent assertion that, although "there were at least some townspeople who still [that is, in the later twelfth century] had . . . some knowledge of French", "there is no contemporary evidence to definitely prove this" (Berndt 1965: 155). For even allowing for some scribal bias, for the percolation of French loanwords like *baret, curlew, noble*, and so on into everyday English, and also for persistence of traditional French surnames among immigrant families – and in this context we may note to what degree the French nicknames here are drawn from the same reservoir as those, for instance, of Eu, Arras, and Calais, a topic to which I hope to return in a further article:[35] even allowing for all these complicating factors, the French element here still seems too strong to be wholly accounted for in this way. Both vernaculars, these nicknames seem to imply, were to be heard in the streets of Canterbury, although with English certainly having the edge for resource and inventiveness; we may compare Ekwall's comment on the similarly cosmopolitan nicknames of contemporary London as having "arisen in a thoroughly English milieu" (1947: 173).

This implication is not contradicted by the *Kentish Sermons*. True, the translating of these from the French of Maurice of Sully has earlier been cited as evidence of some inability to profit from the originals (above, 180). On the other hand, their language is heavily Gallicised, with hybrid adverbs such as *pardurableliche*, and with a host of well integrated verb forms such as *epierede, aresunede, ientred, moveth, ofserueth, signefieth, itravailed*, and so on, often interchanging with native synonyms, as with *sucuri* beside *helpe*. Of course, the translator's own vocabulary would not have been identical with that of his flock; but a preacher alive to his audience's needs would surely temper his own cosmopolitan eloquence and refrain from bewildering them with foreign jargon. Now, it is a commonplace that widespread borrowing from one language into

---

[35] [["Thoughts on the French connections of Middle-English nicknames", *Nomina* 2 (1978), 38–44.]]

another, 'lexical interference' as linguists call it, arises only when there are sizeable groups of bilingual speakers (Halliday, McIntosh and Strevens 1964: 66, 101–2; Haugen 1972: 60–1, 66–9 esp. 68, 78); and some add that linguistic exchanges are freest when relations between the groups speaking the different languages are friendly (for instance, Diebold 1962: 47). So, unless wholly out of keeping with the purpose of the work, the vocabulary of the *Kentish Sermons* implies that Kent had known at the least a fair degree of 'passive bilingualism'.

Nevertheless, French seems to have had only a limited currency in the streets of Canterbury, for the names of those streets, interesting in themselves because recorded so early, bear a somewhat different cast from those of their inhabitants. Topographical terms, although now and then Latinised, thus *in Merceria* commonly in all the sources, also *in uico Mercerie* LII (compare modern *Mercery Lane*), *prope scorcheriam* B83 etc. and *in macellario* B86 etc., *in corueseria* F295, normally appear in English and in clearly Kentish forms. The city gates and their associated wards are: *Burhgate* I, *Burgate* A23 etc. 'city gates' (Wallenberg 1931: 4, 349–50); *Cueningate* B61 etc., probably from OE *æt þam cwenan gatum* 'Queen's gates' (Wallenberg 1931: 46–7, also 350); *Ni(e)wengate* SG 53, B92 etc., probably from OE *æt þam niowum gatum* 'new gates' (Wallenberg 1934: 606); *Nordgate* A5 etc. 'north gates'; *Readingate(n)* I etc., SG 144 with some spelling variants, probably from OE *æt þam readum gatum* 'red gates' (Wallenberg 1934: 606); *Westgate* B52 etc.; *Weuergate* and variants[36] A19 etc., with which compare OE *Uueowera get* 'gate of the men of Wye' and the DB 'lathe'-name, *Wiwarlest* (Wallenberg 1931: 182–3); and *Andresgate* B208 etc., beside St Andrew's church. Other district-names are: *Baggeberi* B48 etc., possibly formed with OE *bagga 'badger' (Smith 1956a: 17–18); *Drutintuna* and variants B61, SG 51, also *Trutintune* D77, *Trutindune* F432, well evidenced but none the less obscure (Wallenberg 1931: 4, 5, for a form *Druting stræt*, and 1934; 606–7), the modern form being *Ruttington Lane*; *T(h)erne* A27 etc., SG 134, BB 156 etc., evidently 'turning' from the OE verb *tyrnan* borrowed from Latin *tornare*, indicating the crossroads where Watling Street meets Castle Street. There are three 'markets': *Retherchieape* D138, with OE *hryðer*, Kentish *(h)reðer* 'cattle'; *Timbercheppe* F638, with OE *timber* 'building-material'; and *Wenchiape* F26 etc., SG 52, probably with OE *wægn*, Kentish *we(g)n* 'waggon' (Wallenberg 1931: 5 and 1934: 608). Streets and lanes are: *Holestrate* D139, BB 393, with OE *holh* 'hollow'; *Niewestrete* D138, with OE *niwe*, *niowe* 'new'; *Griene-* or *Crienemelnelane* D332 etc., compare *Crienemelne* SG 14 etc. and *uiam de Crienemeldne* D362, with Kentish *melne* from OE *mylen* 'mill' and an obscure first element;[37] *Crocchereslane* D217, with OE *croccere 'potter'; *Sporiereslane* BB 346, with ME *sporyer* from OE *spora/spura* 'spur'; and *Webbenelane* (Urry 1967: 121), with OE *webba* 'weaver'; *Dudelane* B64 etc., probably with the name *Dud(d)a*, which belonged to, amongst others, a late tenth-century Canterbury moneyer (Smart 1968: 259–60), compare also *Dudindale* (Wallenberg 1934: 605); *Hallelane* F52, BB 338, perhaps with OE *heall* 'hall', or perhaps a variant for *Hellelane* D213, with Kentish

---

36 *Weuer-*, *Wiwer-*, *Wuwer-*, *Wuer-*, *Wuur-*, *Wure-*, *Wur-*, *Wer-*, *Wr-* (modern *Worthgate*).

37 The variation *Gr-/Cr-* is difficult: in the Rentals *Gr-* occurs 2x beside *Cr-* 5x; in SG *Cr-* occurs consistently 7x; consistent *Cr-* also appears in some contemporary papal documents (for instance, Holtzmann 1935: 371). With *Gr-* the first element could be the rare *grēon*, Kentish *grīon*, later *grien* 'grit', assumed by Ekwall in the place-name *Isle of Grain* (1963: 160; compare Ek 1972: 73). Another odd form which may, or may not, be related is the nickname *Crinwivel* SG 53, 68, where the second element is *weevil*.

hell for OE *hyll*; *Hethenestret* BB 35, with OE *hǣðen* 'pagan, Norseman', compare *uicum qui anglice appellatur Hethenmannelane* XLIX; *Horsmelnelane* D378 'horse-mill lane'; *Litlepettelane* F28, with Kentish *pett* for OE *pytt* 'pit'; *Loddereslane* F188, BB 177, with OE *loddere* 'beggar'; and, with leading residents' names, *Geroldeslane* D210, *Lambertes lane Wrenne* B104 etc., *Neeleslane* D386, *Semereslane* SG 46 etc., *Sunwineslane* F175 etc.; also *Unþancheswei* B32 etc., with OE *unþanc* 'annoyance, especially from squatters' (Smith 1956b: 227). Other landmarks include: *Eastbregge* SG 54, D308 etc., with Kentish *bregge* from OE *brycg* 'bridge'; *Salthelle* B91, F188 etc. 'salt hill'; *Halistane* F130, with OE *hālig* 'holy' and *stān* 'stone'; *Hottewelle* D247, presumably with OE *hāt* 'hot' and *wille, welle* 'spring', compare *Hottemed* D235 etc. a little way away; and, as well as the two mills already noted as giving names to lanes, *Hottemeldne* D231, hard by *Hottewelle*, and *Scepeschotesmelne* (Urry 1967: 123–4).[38] Churches have colloquial names coupled with their dedications: *sancte Marie Bredmanne*ss D269 (compare BB 343) 'church of the bread-merchants'; and *Fismannechereche*ss and variants D94 etc., BB 595, compare *ecclesia piscariorum* LII, 'church of the fish-merchants'; also *sancte Marie de Bredene cherche* D160, *ecclesie sancte Marie de Bredene* AppA 'the wooden church', with OE *breden* 'made of planks', compare *ecclesiam sancte Marie que quondam lignea fuit* F266. Earlier we remarked the strong native element in the toponymic nicknames (above, 193); here among the topographical proper names there is, apart from a few personal names, hardly one continental element to be found, as though this tradition were too strong for immigrant fashions to touch.

Our original focus of investigation was, however, not the town at large but the cathedral priory and its scriptorium, not the tenants of Christ Church so much as the scribes who entered their names in the Rentals. These Rentals and their scribes are indeed highly relevant to *Eadwine's Psalter* and its garbled English gloss; for, work-aday as they are, they belong to the same world as the *Psalter*, with the hand of Rental B (1163–7) closely resembling that of the *Psalter's* exegetical gloss (Urry 1967: 5).

Scribal practice, of course, does not so much directly reflect any linguistic milieu as represent a compromise between various constraints. In legal documents, with precision paramount, names of people and of places had to be recorded in recognisable, indeed unambiguous form: normally, therefore, as we have seen, in the vernacular.[39] With that reservation, the scribes' ideal, unrealised, would no doubt have been to render everything into Latin, at least of a kind; but in practice the Latin of the Rentals is unpedantic, even by the standards of the day, with one or other vernacular slipping in from time to time.

Most often occupational terms, for instance, are given in Latin, thus, consistently, *faber, pelliparius, pistor, textor* – we do not, in any event, even when vernacular terms are used, know whether such terms formed part of the current name or whether they were added for bureaucratic convenience. Now and then, however, vernacular terms are used, most often in the late Rental F (about 1206) but with no systematic increase over the years: *macun* interchanges with *cementarius*; *corueisier* and *cordewantuer* are

---

[38] Apparently contemporary with the documents printed; previously *sheepcot* seems not to have been noted before the fourteenth century (Löfvenberg 1946: 96).

[39] On the continent the early practice of Latinising nicknames and so on seems by the thirteenth century to have been abandoned in favour of keeping the vernacular forms, evidently for the sake of precision (Blottière 1973: 32).

commoner than *sutor*; English *uphealdere*[ss] A27 etc. 'repairer, second-hand dealer' seems untranslatable, so too *mederere*[ss] D138 etc. 'madderman', and also *baggere*[ss] B34, B40, either 'hawker' or 'bag-merchant' – unless perhaps *sacur*[ss] F112 may be a superficially Gallicised equivalent; equally untranslatable would seem to be the French *loremier* B103 'spurrier'. In the main the vernaculars seem evenly balanced in this sphere, except that in Rental F, with its high proportion of vernacular terms – nearly a quarter, as against an eighth to a tenth of instances in the earlier long Rentals B and D –, French instances predominate over English by about five to three. Of course, statistics so crudely stated are misleading, for by 1200 such terms as *macun* and *mercier* might well have been passing as 'English'; even so, however, they would remain evidence of recent close contact between the two languages.

Other vernacular elements too slip in from time to time as one language or the other comes readiest to the pen: *uersus nort(h)* is commoner than *uersus septentrionem*, and so with the other points of the compass; the already part-vernacular *ab east ad west* further varies with *del east al west*, likewise *uiam del suth* D354 etc., and so on. Perhaps these lapses into the vernaculars may help to gauge the scribes' own linguistic bias, as distinct from that of the community at large. With odd snatches statistics would again hardly be to the point; but observation suggests that French slips in at least as often as English, or rather more so. As well as Latinised French forms such as *grancia/grangia* F39 etc., *paiantur* AppA, or *saisiet* XI, unmodified ones also appear, thus, *uersus lest* D26, *uersus kemin* LIV, *ad gaiole* D106 beside *iuxta carcerem* D117, *uersus danjvn* D159,[40] *unum pleinpein* XLVII beside *duos planos panes* XXV, *fossam del bali* F233 beside *fossatum turris* XXV, *contra pillori* F308, *del braccin* F115 beside the commoner *de bracino* B153 etc. and *del parc* D163 beside *de parco* C40 etc., and occasionally *Terre est* F214 etc. for the formula *Terra est*. English terms occur most often in traditional Latinisations, such as *aldermannus* B92 etc., *in burgimoto* XXXIII, *coram hallimoto* A9 etc., *ad terram gilde* B112, *de burcgilde* D226, *ad gildehalle* C60, *smithchilde* D138, *bertuna* B33 etc., *haghas* XL, and so on; English terms slip in unmodified more rarely, thus *ælderman* XXV, *prope sandpet* B179, and also *spechhus* from an unprinted text of about 1230 (Urry 1967: 91).

A special case concerns the toponymic phrases such as later set into surnames like *Attwood* or *Atteridge* (Löfvenberg 1942: xxi–xxiii, xxix–xxxiv; Reaney 1967: 36, 48–52, over-simplifies when asserting that the 'earliest documents' show French or Latin prepositions). Sometimes these keep a purely English form, thus, *Elfsi Atþar-welle* and variants B47 etc., *Rogeri/Morin/Godelief atte(n) helle* F631 etc.: sometimes they are rendered into Latin, thus, *Elfsi de fonte* SA, *Liueue de fonte* F258/*ad fontem* F479, *Arnoldus de monte* D149, *Adam de cruce* F187, who lives opposite Newingate Cross, and *Osmundo de fraxino* XXXIII, XXXIV. Sometimes, more often in the associated charters than in the Rentals themselves, only preposition and article, the latter usually in 'feminine' form, are Gallicised – this being the commonest practice throughout the Middle English period: thus, *Godrici/Siredi de la helle* IX and X, near neighbours in the Dover Road suburb of *Rogerius de Helle* D145/*Rogeri attenhelle* F631 and of *Arnoldus de monte* (Urry 1967: map-sheets 1(b)7, 2(b)9), likewise *Godefrido de la Dene* LXIV, *Rogero de la Le* LXIV, *Simon de la Tune* F635. Similarly *le* occasionally replaces the English article *se* – nom. sing. masc. properly speaking, but in this usage

---

[40] The earliest record of the name, modern *Dane John* (Wallenberg 1934: 605).

quasi-indeclinable – with English epithets or occupational terms, thus *Hugonis le frode* D30, *Arnold le gode* XVIII, *Roberti le mederere* D151, *Eadpardo le Lamb* B218.

Such token Gallicisations remind us that to some extent the French element in documents of this kind must always be discounted; for French carried so much more official as well as social prestige than English that for some scribes and in some contexts it became 'a sort of ignoble substitute for Latin' (Legge 1941: 165). Therefore, lapsing from Latin into French rather than into English in no way proves French to be the scribe's dominant language, either as mother-tongue or as everyday medium, but only that he felt it to be more admissible in the context; not to labour the point that the resemblance between Latin and French might encourage involuntary switching between the languages, all the more so perhaps if both were imperfectly acquired, as is suggested by such a sequence as *de scorcheria* (common), *de scorcherie* D112, *de escorgeria* F359, *de lescorcherie* F216, or by the interchange of *de hosteleria* and *de hostelerie* in two parts of a chirograph (IX and X).

Given this scribal bias towards French, it is the strength of the English strain in the Rentals that is striking, and all the more convincing for the lack of any desire for prestige behind its use. It comes out in the very script. Most of the scribes use *æ*, and some of them, especially that of Rental B, the one resembling a glossing hand in the *Psalter*, also occasionally use *þ*, *ƿ*, and also *ȝ*. Naturally, the insular characters are mainly used in native names: *Ðettekera* A6, *Elfsi Atþar(e)ƿelle* B7 and B148, *Sunepini* B75, *Nipingate* B91 etc., *Godpini* B106, *de Ðellis* B109, *Ðinedei* and *Ðulnodus* B217, *Eadpardo* B218, *Egeldreþa* B108, *Brictiþa* B191, *Ælldeham* A3, *Ædieua* B120, *Ælfegi* C37, *Ædwardus* D148, *Ædmundi* D150, *Ælfwinus* F2, *Ædwini* F20, *Ætelburge* F97, *Æileue* F127, *Æilmeri* F231, *Æilwordi* F236, *Æilredi* F256, *Ædmeri* F311, and so on. An odd spelling several times repeated is *L(i)efwini Lunȝ* D19, F81, F413, F418, beside *Lifwini longi* B39, where the use of the insular ȝ seems at variance with a vowel more characteristic of Anglo-Norman (for instance, *Roland*, line 3374: *lung tens*) than of Middle English, for a sound-change *-ang> -ōng> -ung* is observed only sporadically and then mainly in western dialects (Serjeantson 1931). Now and then insular characters appear even in continental names and terms: *Baldepini* B51, *parini* B56, *Ðibertus* B218, *cordepantuer* B108, *Æliz* B124 etc., *Ærnold* F161, *Ærnoldi* F19, F169. For all the French fashions English traditions seem to be dying hard.

Moreover, as has already been noted from time to time, the English element here has a strong Kentish colouring, with *e* for OE *ă* in *-ekere* (OE *æcer*), *mederere* (from OE *mædere*), *Pret* (OE *prætt*), *Winedei* (OE *-dæg*), and so on, and especially with *e* for OE *ў* in *bregge, chereche, se Desie, helle, melne, pet* and with *ie* for OE *ēo* in *Liefwinus, Niewe-*, and so on. In the late twelfth century this might seem scarcely noteworthy, since throughout England the West-Saxon *Schriftsprache* was by then discarded in favour of local dialect. Yet is is noteworthy in so far as it contrasts with the Christ Church practice of the beginning of the century, in such texts as the BL MS. Cotton Domitian A VIII bilingual *Chronicle*, which among many 'late' forms shows few specifically Kentish ones; and in so far as it therefore serves to measure the shift away from the unified Old English culture towards the localised, fragmented vernacular cultures of Middle English times.

This does, furthermore, begin to explain the English gloss in *Eadwine's Psalter*, which shows, amongst other features, a thick Kentish overlay on a traditional text, and indeed to suggest in what way 'history of education' may be concerned here. French influence would, in the end of the day, seem to be relevant only indirectly. For, if we suppose that respect for the West-Saxon standard lingered on until the middle of the twelfth century – and the 'comet' note in the *Psalter* itself might support that supposition – and so outlived accurate command of its proper usages, then uncritical copying of an archaic original becomes comprehensible and at the same time compatible with frequent lapses into current dialectal forms. Even though the cases are not wholly analogous, since one is a matter of copying but the other evidently of original composition, we may perhaps compare the First Continuation (1122–31) of the *Peterborough Chronicle*, where a clear intention of writing in West-Saxon is frustrated by inability to suppress current local forms (Clark 1970: xlv, lii, lxi). In a sense, therefore, the English gloss in *Eadwine's Psalter* is at one and the same time a witness to continuing respect for Old English traditions and evidence of their final dissolution.

LITERATURE

Adigard des Gautries, J. 1954. Les noms de personnes scandinaves en Normandie de 911 à 1066. NG 11. Lund.

Adler, M. 1939. The Jews of medieval England. London.

Arngart, O. (ed.) 1942 and 1955. The proverbs of Alfred. 2 vols. Acta RSHLL 32. Lund.

Arnould, M.-A. 1952. Les plus anciens rôles d'impôt de la ville de Mons (Hainaut), 1281–99. In: Mélanges de philologie offerts à M. Karl Michaëlsson, 11–30. Göteborg.

Ballard, A. (ed.) 1920. An eleventh-century inquisition of St Augustine's, Canterbury. London.

Barlow, F. (ed. and tr.) 1962. The life of King Edward. London.

Beauvillé, G. de. 1953, 1954 and 1955. Les noms de famille de France tirés des noms de métiers, de charges et de dignités. RIO 5: 45–59, 139–55, 201–8, 295–306. RIO 6: 53–65, 137–42, 221–34, 301–13. RIO 7: 59–72, 147–59, 225–34, 289–303.

Bennett, J.A.W. and G.V. Smithers (eds) 1966. Early Middle English verse and prose. Oxford.

Berger, R. (ed.) 1963 and 1970. Le nécrologe de la confrérie des jongleurs et des bourgeois d'Arras (1194–1361). 2 vols continuously paginated. Mémoires de la commission départementale des monuments historiques du Pas-de-Calais 11/2 and 13/2. Arras.

Berndt, R. 1965. The linguistic situation in England from the Norman Conquest to the loss of Normandy. Philologica Pragensia 8: 145–63.

Bishop, T.A.M. and P. Chaplais (eds) 1957. Facsimiles of English royal writs to A.D. 1100 presented to V.H. Galbraith. Oxford.

Blaess, M. 1973. Les manuscrits français dans les monastères anglais au moyen âge. Romania 94: 321–58.

Blottière, J. 1973. Surnoms et patronymes du xie au xiiie siècle dans le Vexin français, le Pinserais et le Mantois. RIO 25: 31–44.

Bosworth, J. and T.N. Toller, also A. Campbell. 1898 and 1921; 1972. An Anglo-Saxon dictionary and supplement. 2 vols. Also Enlarged addenda and corrigenda. Oxford.

[Brewer, J.S. (ed.)] 1846. Chronicon monasterii de Bello. Anglia Christiana Society. London.

Brooke, G.C. 1916a and b. A catalogue of coins in the British Museum: the Norman kings. 2 vols. London.

Cameron, K. 1959. The place-names of Derbyshire. 3 vols. continuously paginated. EPNS 27, 28 and 29. Cambridge.

Campbell, A. 1959. An Old English grammar. Oxford.

Campbell, A.P. 1968. The richness of the Eadwine Psalter. Revue de l'Université d'Ottawa 38: 132–43 and plates.

Carrez, H. 1937. Particularités physiques et noms de personne dans la région dijonnaise du xiie au xve siècle. Annales de Bourgogne 9: 97–131.

Carrez, H. 1938a. Particularités du domicile et noms de personnes dans la région dijonnaise du xiie au xve siècle. Annales de Bourgogne 10: 7–46.

Carrez, H. 1938b. Le vocabulaire de l'alimentation et les noms de personnes dans la région dijonnaise du xiie au xve siècle. Annales de Bourgogne 10: 173–88.

Carrez, H. 1947. Surnoms évocant des infirmités portés dans la région dijonnaise du xiie au xve siècle. Onomastica 1: 41–51.

Chibnall, M. (ed. and tr.) 1969. The ecclesiastical history of Orderic Vitalis, 2. Oxford.

Clark, C. (ed.) 1970. The Peterborough chronicle 1070–1154. Second edition. Oxford.

Clay, C.T. 1943. The early treasurers of York. Yorkshire archaeological journal 25: 7–34.

Clover, V.H. (ed.) 1962. The correspondence of Archbishop Lanfranc: a critical edition. Unpublished Cambridge Ph.D. thesis no. 4201.

Crawford, S.J. 1923. The late Old English notes of MS. (British Museum) Cotton Claudius B IV. Anglia 47: 124–35.

Darby, H.C. 1952. The Domesday geography of eastern England. Cambridge.

Dauzat, A. 1945. Les noms de famille de France. Paris.

Dauzat, A. and M.-Th. Morlet. 1969. Dictionnaire étymologique des noms de famille et prénoms de France. Revised edition. Paris.

Derolez, R. 1974. Cross-Channel language ties. Anglo-Saxon England 3: 1–14.

Diebold, A.R. 1962. A laboratory for language contact. Anthropological linguistics 4/no. 1: 41–51.

Dodwell, B. (ed.) 1958 for 1956. Feet of fines for the county of Norfolk for the reign of King John 1201–1215; for the county of Suffolk for the reign of King John 1199–1214. Pipe Roll Society new series 32. London.

Dodwell, C.R. 1954. The Canterbury school of illumination 1066–1200. Cambridge.

Dodwell, C.R. and P. Clemoes (eds) 1974. The Old English illustrated Hexateuch. Early English manuscripts in facsimile 18. Copenhagen.

Douglas, D.C. (ed.) 1944. The Domesday monachorum of Christ Church, Canterbury. London.

Dufrenne, S. 1964. Les copies anglaises du psautier d'Utrecht. Scriptorium 18: 185–97.

Ek, K.-G. 1972. The development of OE $\bar{y}$ and $\breve{e}o$ in south-eastern Middle English. LSE 42. Lund.

Ekwall, E. 1947. Early London personal names. Acta RSHLL 43. Lund.

Ekwall, E. 1963. Selected papers. LSE 33. Lund.

Ekwall, E. 1965. Some early London bynames and surnames. ES 46: 113–18.

Emden, A.B. 1968. Donors of books to S. Augustine's abbey, Canterbury. Oxford Bibliographical Society: occasional publications 4. Oxford.

Feilitzen, O. von. 1937. The pre-Conquest personal names of Domesday Book. NG 3. Uppsala.

Feilitzen, O. von. 1939. Notes on Old English bynames. Namn och Bygd 27: 116–30.

Feilitzen, O. von. 1945. Some unrecorded Old and Middle English personal names. Namn och Bygd 33: 69–98.

Feilitzen, O. von. 1963. Some continental-Germanic personal names in England. In: Early English and Norse studies presented to Hugh Smith, 46–61. London.

Feilitzen, O. von. 1968. Some Old English uncompounded personal names and bynames. Studia neophilologica 40: 516.

Feilitzen, O. von and C. Blunt. 1971. Personal names on the coinage of Edgar. In: England before the Conquest: studies in primary sources presented to Dorothy Whitelock, 183–214. Cambridge.

Fernquist, C.-H. 1937. Study on the O.E. version of the Anglo-Saxon chronicle in Cott. Domitian A. VIII. SMS 13: 41–103.

Forssner, T. 1916. Continental-Germanic personal names in England in Old and Middle English times. Uppsala.

Gesler, J. (ed.) 1931. Le livre des mestiers de Bruges et ses dérivés. Bruges.

Gibbs, M. (ed.) 1939. Early charters of the cathedral church of St Paul, London. Camden third series 58. London.

Godefroy, F. 1881–1902. Dictionnaire de l'ancienne langue française et de tous ses dialectes du ixe au xve siècle. 10 vols. Paris.

Gover, J.E.B., A. Mawer and F.M. Stenton. 1940a. The place-names of Northamptonshire. EPNS 10. Cambridge.

Gover, J.E.B., A. Mawer and F.M. Stenton. 1940b. The place-names of Nottinghamshire. EPNS 17. Cambridge.

Gradon, P. (ed.) 1979. Dan Michel's Ayenbite of inwyt. Vol. 2. EETS OS 278. Oxford.

Gysseling, M. and P. Bougard. 1963. L'onomastique calaisienne à la fin du 13e siècle. Onomastica neerlandica: anthroponymica 13. Louvain.

Hall, J. (ed.) 1920a and b. Selections from early Middle English 1130–1250. 2 pts. continuously paginated. Oxford.

Halliday, M.A.K., A. McIntosh and P. Strevens. 1964. The linguistic sciences and language teaching. London.

Hargreaves, H. and C. Clark. 1965. An unpublished Old English psalter-gloss fragment. Notes and queries 210: 443–6.

Harsley, F. (ed.) 1889. Eadwine's Canterbury psalter. EETS OS 92. London.

Haugen, E. 1972. The ecology of language. Stanford. California.

Heimann, E. 1975. The last copy of the Utrecht psalter. In: The year 1200: a symposium, 313-38. New York.

Hill, B. 1977. The twelfth-century 'Conduct of life', formerly the 'Poema morale' or 'A moral ode'. Leeds studies in English NS 9: 97–144.

Holtzmann, W. (ed.) 1935. Papsturkunden in England, 2. Berlin.

Howlett, R. (ed.) 1886. Chronicles of the reigns of Stephen, etc., 3. RS. London.

James, M.R. (ed.) 1903. The ancient libraries of Canterbury and Dover. Cambridge.

James, M.R. (ed.) 1935. The Canterbury psalter. London.

Ker, N.R. 1936. MS. Cotton Galba A xix: the proverbs of Alfred. Medium ævum 5: 115–20.

Ker, N.R. 1957. Catalogue of manuscripts containing Anglo-Saxon. Oxford.

Ker, N.R. 1960. English manuscripts in the century after the Norman Conquest. Oxford.

Ker, N.R. 1964. Medieval libraries of Great Britain. Second edition. London.

Knoop, D. and G.P. Jones. 1967. The mediaeval mason. Third edition. Manchester.

Knowles, D. 1963. The monastic order in England. Second edition. Cambridge.

Knowles, D., and others. 1972. The heads of religious houses, England and Wales, 940–1216. Cambridge.

Kristensson, G. 1970. Studies on Middle English topographical terms. Acta Universitatis Lundensis, sectio 1: 13. Lund.

Kurath, H., S.M. Kuhn, and others. 1954– in progress. Middle English dictionary. Ann Arbor, Michigan.

Leclercq, Dom J. 1953. Ecrits spirituels d'Elmer de Cantorbéry. Analecta monastica, 2e série: Studia Anselmiana 31: 45–117. Roma.

Legge, M.D. 1941. Anglo-Norman and the historian. History n.s. 26: 163–75.

Legge, M.D. 1963. Anglo-Norman literature and its background. Oxford.

Liebermann, F. (ed.) 1879. Ungedruckte anglo-normannische Geschichtsquellen. Strasbourg.

Löfvenberg, M.T. 1942. Studies on Middle English local surnames. LSE 11. Lund.

Löfvenberg, M.T. 1946. Contributions to Middle English lexicography and etymology. Lunds Universitets Årsskrift n.s. 41, no. 8. Lund.

Meritt, H.D. (ed.) 1945. Old English glosses (a collection). New York.

Michel, F. (ed.) 1876. Le livre des psaumes. Paris.

Morlet, M.-Th. 1959 and 1960. Les noms de personne à Eu du xiiie au xve siècle. RIO 11: 131–48, 174–82. RIO 12: 62–70, 137–48, 205–19.

Morlet, M.-Th. 1968 and 1972. Les noms de personne sur le territoire de l'ancienne Gaule du vi^e au xiie siècle. 2 vols. Paris.

Morris, R. (ed.) 1876. Dan Michel's Ayenbite of inwyt. EETS OS 23. London.

Mozley, J.H. 1932. Nigel Wireker or Wetekre? Modern language review 27: 314–17.

Mozley, J.H. and R.H. Raymo (eds) 1960. Nigel de Longchamps: Speculum stultorum. Berkeley, California.

Murray, J.A.H., and others. 1884–1928 (1933). A new English dictionary on historical principles (The Oxford English dictionary). 13 vols. Oxford.

Page, W. (ed.) 1932. The Victoria history of the county of Kent, 3. London.

Pipe Roll Society 1929. The pipe roll of 31 Henry I: Michaelmas 1130. London.

Plummer, C. and J. Earle (eds) 1892. Two of the Saxon chronicles parallel, 1. Oxford.

Poerck, G. de, and others. 1951a, b and c. La draperie médiévale en Flandre et en Artois: technique et terminologie. 3 vols. Rijksuniversiteit te Gent: Werken uitgegeven door de Faculteit van Wijsbegeerte en Letteren 110, 111 and 112. Bruges.

Pope, M.K. 1934. From Latin to Modern French. Manchester.

Reaney, P.H. 1935. The place-names of Essex. EPNS 12. Cambridge.

Reaney, P.H. 1952. Pedigrees of villeins and freemen. Notes and queries 197: 222–5.

Reaney, P.H. 1953. Notes on the survival of Old English personal names in Middle English. SMS 18: 84–112.

Reaney, P.H. 1958. A dictionary of British surnames. London.

Redin, M. 1919. Studies on uncompounded personal names in Old English. Uppsala.

Richardson, H.G. 1960. The English Jewry under the Angevin kings. London.

Robertson, J.C. (ed.) 1875 and 1876. Materials for the history of Thomas Becket, 1 and 2. RS. London.

Robson, C.A. (ed.) 1952. Maurice of Sully and the medieval vernacular homily. Oxford.

Salzman, L.F. 1952. Building in England down to 1540. Oxford.

Samuels, M.L. 1971. Kent and the Low Countries: some linguistic evidence. In: Edinburgh studies in English and Scots, 3–19. London.

Sawyer, P. (ed.) 1957 and 1962. Textus Roffensis. Early English manuscripts in facsimile 7 and 11. Copenhagen.

Schmitt, F.S. (ed.) 1946. S. Anselmi Cantuariensis archiepiscopi opera omnia, 3. Edinburgh.

Searle, W.G. 1902. Christ Church, Canterbury. Cambridge Antiquarian Society: publications (8vo) 34. Cambridge.

Seltén, B. 1965. Some notes on Middle English by-names in independent use. ES 46: 165–81.

Seltén, B. 1969. Early East-Anglian nicknames: 'Shakespeare' names. RSHLL: Scripta minora 1968–9, pt. 3.

Seltén, B. 1972. The Anglo-Saxon heritage in Middle English personal names: East Anglia 1100–1399. LSE 43. Lund.

Serjeantson, M.S. 1931. Middle English *-ong* > *-ung*. Review of English studies 7: 450–2.

Sisam, C. and K. (eds) 1959. The Salisbury psalter. EETS OS 242. Oxford.

Smart, V.J. 1968. Moneyers of the late Anglo-Saxon coinage 973–1016. Kungl. vitterhets historie och antikvitets akademiens handlingar, antikvariska serien 19 (commentationes de nummis saeculorum ix–xi in Suecia repertis, pt. 2), 191–276. Stockholm.

Smith, A.H. 1934. Early northern nicknames and surnames. Saga-book of the Viking Society 9: 30–60.

Smith, A.H. 1956a and b. The elements of English place-names. 2 vols. EPNS 25 and 26. Cambridge.

Southern, R.W. 1958. The English origins of the 'Miracles of the Virgin'. Mediaeval and Renaissance studies 4: 176–216.

Southern, R.W. (ed. and tr.) 1962. The life of St Anselm. London.

Southern, R.W. 1963. St Anselm and his biographer. Cambridge.

Stenton, D.M. (ed.) 1932. The great roll of the Pipe: 10 Richard I. Pipe Roll Society n.s. 9. London.

Stubbs, W. (ed.) 1874. Memorials of St Dunstan. RS. London.

Stubbs, W. (ed.) 1879 and 1880. The historical works of Gervase of Canterbury. 2 vols. RS. London.

Sundby, B. 1963. Studies in the Middle English dialect material of Worcestershire records. Norwegian studies in English 10. Bergen.

Tengstrand, E. 1949. Three Middle English Bahuvrīhi adjectives. SMS 17: 210–26.

Tengvik, G. 1938. Old English bynames. NG 4. Uppsala.

Thompson, E.M. (ed.) 1902. Customary of the Benedictine monastery of St Augustine, Canterbury, 1. Henry Bradshaw Society 23. London.

Tobler, A. and E. Lommatzsch 1925– in progress. Altfranzösisches Wörterbuch. Berlin, later Wiesbaden.

Turner, G.J. and H.E. Salter (eds) 1915 and 1924. The register of St Augustine's abbey, Canterbury, commonly called the Black Book. 2 pts continuously paginated. London.

Urry, W. 1958. The Normans in Canterbury. Annales de Normandie 8: 119–38.

Urry, W. 1959. Saint Anselm and his cult at Canterbury. Spicilegium Beccense: 571–93. Le Bec-Hellouin.

Urry, W. 1967. Canterbury under the Angevin kings. London.

Walberg, E. (ed.) 1936. Guernes de Pont-Sainte-Maxence: la vie de saint Thomas Becket. Classiques français du moyen âge 77. Paris.

Wallenberg, J.K. 1923. The vocabulary of Dan Michel's Ayenbite of inwyt. Uppsala.

Wallenberg, J.K. 1931. Kentish place-names. Uppsala universitets årsskrift: filosofi, språk-vetenskap och historiska vetenskaper, 2. Uppsala.

Wallenberg, J.K. 1934. The place-names of Kent. Uppsala.

Webb, G. 1965. Architecture in Britain: the middle ages. Second edition. London.

Whitelock, D. 1940. Scandinavian personal names in the Liber Vitae of Thorney abbey. Saga-book of the Viking Society 12: 127–53.

Whitelock, D., and others (eds and trs) 1961. The Anglo-Saxon chronicle: a revised translation. London.

Woledge, B. and H.P. Clive. 1964. Répertoire des plus anciens textes en prose française depuis 842 jusqu'aux premières années du xiiie siècle. Publications romanes et françaises 79. Genève.

Woodcock, A.M. (ed.) 1956. Cartulary of the priory of St Gregory, Canterbury. Camden third series 88. London.

Wright, J. 1898–1905. The English dialect dictionary. 6 vols. Oxford.

Wright, T. (ed.) 1839. The political songs of England. Camden Society. London.

Wright, T. (ed.) 1872. The Anglo-Latin satirical poets and epigrammatists of the twelfth century, 1. RS. London.

15

Some Early Canterbury Surnames*

Early surnames, like early place-names, offer lexicographical treasures at every turn.[1] Equally, they can be deeply frustrating, owing to the difficulty of interpreting forms, often oddly spelt, which are devoid of limiting context. Moreover, just because unexpected finds are to be expected, temptations will be great for any worker whose imagination is uncurbed by prudence.

Recent explorations among some published Canterbury materials ranging in date from the mid-twelfth century to the early thirteenth[2] have brought to light some fine specimens of early surnames: some supplementing existing records; some affording a basis for alternative speculations; a few still awaiting elucidation.

I. *Occupational Terms*

The simplest of these Canterbury surnames offer supplementary records, mainly antedatings, of straightforward occupational terms.[3] Yet all is not wholly straightforward.

* I am deeply grateful to Professor Dorothy Whitelock, who very kindly read this article in draft and gave me the benefit of her expert criticism. See also my 'People and Languages in Post-Conquest Canterbury', above pp. 179–206.

[1] See A. Mawer, 'Some Unworked Sources for English Lexicography', in *A Grammatical Miscellany offered to Otto Jespersen* (Copenhagen and London, 1930), pp. 11–16; G. Tengvik, *Old English Bynames*, Nomina Germanica, IV (Uppsala, 1938), pp. 23–7; M.T. Löfvenberg, *Studies on Middle English Local Surnames*, Lund Studies in English, XI (1942), p. xviii; O. Arngart, 'Middle English Dialects', *Studier i modern Språkvetenskap*, XVII (1949), 17–19, esp. 28; B. Thuresson, *Middle English Occupational Terms*, Lund Studies in English, XIX (1950), p. 21; G. Kristensson, *Studies on Middle English Topographical Terms*, Acta Universitatis Lundensis: sectio I.13 (1970), p. 9.

[2] CC = W. Urry, *Canterbury Under the Angevin Kings*, 1 vol. and map-folder (London, 1967): Christ Church rentals and associated documents edited pp. 221–444 [cited by item no.].

SA = W. Urry, 'Saint Anselm and his Cult at Canterbury', *Spicilegium Beccense*, I (1959), 571–93: the list of 'votaries' printed p. 585.

PR = D.M. Stenton, ed., *The Great Roll of the Pipe: 10 Richard I*, Pipe Roll Society New Series, IX (1932): the list of citizens paying tallage printed pp. 207–9.

SG = A.M. Woodcock, ed., *Cartulary of the Priory of St Gregory, Canterbury*, Camden Third Series, LXXXIII (London, 1956) [cited by item no.].

Also BB = G.J. Turner and H.E. Salter, eds, *The Register of St Augustine's Abbey, Commonly Called the Black Book*, 2 pts continuously paginated (London, 1915–24): used only for occasional comparison, as, apart from the inadequate dating of the various sections, many of the forms are badly garbled [cited by p.].

[3] For occupational terms I have consulted, in addition to NED, MED, Godefroy, *Dictionnaire de l'ancienne langue française*, 9 vols and *Complément* (Paris, 1881–1902), and Tobler-Lommatzsch, *Altfranzösisches Wörterbuch* (Berlin, later Wiesbaden, 1925–, in progress): G. Fransson, *Middle English Surnames of Occupation 1100–1350*, Lund Studies in English, III (1935); Tengvik, *Bynames*; E. Ekwall, *Early London Personal Names*, Acta Regiae Societatis

To begin with, we cannot be sure whether the occupational terms used in administrative documents were in fact all current as surnames, that is, in daily use among neighbours, or whether some were supplied by the scribes as formal specifiers, just as occupations and addresses are in legal documents of the present day. Nor can we be sure in what form neighbours would have used such terms as they did. With those examples that are latinized – a proportion varying in the present material from three-quarters to nine-tenths – scribal intervention is patent, although sometimes reconstruction of the vernacular base seems easy (such forms, and other speculative cases, are cited in square brackets). With those given in a French form matters are more complex. On the one hand, scribes had a general bias away from English and towards French, as though the latter were, as has been said, 'a sort of ignoble substitute for Latin';[4] therefore, use of a French occupational term guarantees neither its currency in the English speech of the time nor, alternatively, any currency of French outside the scriptorium: in so far as such terms appear neither in literary sources nor as modern surnames MED is justified in excluding them. On the other hand, many 'French' terms were adopted into English very early; use of these would by no means imply currency of French as such, either in the community at large or in the scriptorium itself.

ampoller   Thuresson, p. 238: 1242; see also MED. The simplex *ampulla* 'phial' is
                    an OE borrowing from Latin.
— Petrus ampoller *SG 204: eC13*. [Geruasius ampollarius *CC D144, D155: c.1200*].
'Maker/seller of holy-water phials': an appropriate occupation in Canterbury with its pilgrim trade.[5]

baggere   Fransson, pp. 94–5: 1246, with the remark 'most common in Yorkshire
                    . . . not . . . found in southern counties'; MED: from midC15, but as
                    surname from midC13.

Humaniorum Litterarum Lundensis, XLIII (1947); *idem, Two Early London Subsidy Rolls*, Acta Regiae Societatis Humaniorum Litterarum Lundensis, XLVIII (1951), esp. pp. 354–9; and *idem*, 'Names of Trades in English Place-Names', in *Selected Papers*, Lund Studies in English, XXXIII (1963), pp. 68–79 (reprinted from *Tait Festschrift* [1933]); Thuresson, *Occupational Terms*; B. Sundby, 'Some Middle English Occupational Terms', *English Studies*, XXXIII (1952), 18–20; G. de Beauvillé, 'Les noms de famille de France tirés des noms de métiers, de charges et de dignités', *Revue internationale d'onomastique* [*RIO*], V (1953), 45–59, 139–55, 201–8, 295–306, VI (1954), 53–65, 137–42, 221–34, 301–13, VII (1955), 59–72, 147–59, 225–34, 389–403; A.H. Smith, *English Place-Name Elements*, EPNS XXV and XXVI (Cambridge, 1956); P.H. Reaney, *A Dictionary of British Surnames* (London, 1958); M.-Th. Morlet, 'Les noms de personne à Eu du xiiie au xve siècle', *Revue internationale d'onomastique*, XI (1959), 131–48, 174–82, XII (1960), 62–70, 137–48, 205–19 and *eadem, Etude d'anthroponymie picarde: les noms de personne en Haute Picardie aux XIIIe, XIVe, XVe siècles*, Collection de la Société de linguistique picarde VI (Amiens, 1967); M. Gysseling and P. Bougard, *L'Onomastique calaisienne à la fin du 13e siècle*, Onomastica Neerlandica: Anthroponymica, XIII (Louvain and Brussels, 1963); A.D. Mills, 'Some Middle English Occupational Terms', *Studia Neophilologica*, XL (1968), 35–48; R. Berger, ed., *Le nécrologe de la confrérie des jongleurs et des bourgeois d'Arras (1194–1361)*, 2 vols, Mémoires de la Commission Départementale des Monuments Historiques du Pas-de-Calais, XI/2 and XIII/2 (Arras, 1963–70).
4 M.D. Legge, 'Anglo-Norman and the Historian', *History* n.s., XXVI (1941), 165.
5 See E. Walberg, ed., *Guernes de Pont-Sainte-Maxence: La vie de Saint Thomas Becket*, Les Classiques français du Moyen Age, LXXVII (Paris, 1936), lines 5895, 5899–900, also E.-R. Laborde, 'Recherches sur les pèlerins dans l'Europe des XIe et XIIe siècles', *Cahiers de civilisation médiévale*, I (1958), 159–69, 339–47, esp. 344; and cf. E. Cohen, '*In haec signa*: Pilgrim-Badge Trade in Southern France', *Journal of Medieval History*, II (1976), 193–214.

— Raulfo bagger *CC XI: ante 1153*. Ælfegus se baggere *CC B34*, Æ. baggere *B40: 1163/7*.
Evidently from ME *bagge* 'sack', recorded by MED from eC13 (possibly of ON origin).
The meaning is doubtful: MED, although showing 'grain-retailer' quite unambiguously in
C15 contexts, suggests for the surname 'bag-maker' or 'hawker'; Fransson, also offering
all three senses, suggests that two distinct occupational terms, *bagger/badger*, may be in
question, and takes the main sense of the surname as 'bag-maker'. Cf. also below *sacker*.

batur	Fransson, p. 102 (cf. p. 134): 1199; see also MED and Mills, *SN*, p. 37: *battere* 1439.

— Robertus le batur *CC F364*, R. batur *F39: c.1206*. [cf. Richard Chiebatur *PR: 1198*;
Selida batar' *Winchester 1148*[6]].
The sense is doubtful: MED suggests '? a slaughterer', but Fransson 'fuller' or 'metal-
beater', apparently preferring the former. Presumably OFr. *batere(s)/bateur*, for which also
interpretations vary, including 'thresher' and 'wool-dresser'[7] as well as 'fuller' and 'metal-
beater'[8] (the sense 'metal-beater, especially of copper or brass' has been demonstrated by
Ekwall with quotations both in English and in French).[9]

Chiebatur I am so far at a loss to interpret, unless as a compound with OE *cæg* 'key'.

blakestre	MED and Fransson, p. 109: 1199.

— Cristine Blakiestre *CC LX: c.1200*.
'Dyer in black': although Fransson's examples show some masculine personal names, the
form is originally feminine, as here; survival in ME of the feminine force of *-estre* seems
characteristically southern.[10]

bredman	Not in MED, Fransson, or Thuresson.

Parochia sancte Marie Bredmanne *CC D269: c.1200, but evidently traditional*; cf.
ecclesiam sancte Marie de Bredmanne *BB p. 343*.
'Bread-merchant'; cf. below *fishman*.

bunetir	Not in MED, Fransson, or Thuresson. The simplex *bonet* 'cap' is recorded by MED from eC15, but as a surname by Reaney, *Dictionary*, from 1201; but cf. C. Clark, 'The Early Personal Names of King's Lynn: An Essay in Socio-Cultural History. Part II – By-Names', below pp. 258–79, at 263 and 273–4.

— Rogerus bunetir *SA: c.1166*.
'Cap-maker': OFr. *bonnetier*.

[*bureller*	MED and Thuresson, p. 209: 1277 (also: *burelman* 1311); see also Ekwall, *Subsidy Rolls*, p. 355. The simplex *burel* 'coarse cloth' is recorded by MED from lC13, and as surname by Reaney, *Dictionary*, from 1194.

— Blakemannus burarius *CC D195: c.1200*.

---

6   O. von Feilitzen, 'The Personal Names and Bynames of the Winton Domesday', in M. Biddle,
    ed., *Winchester in the Early Middle Ages: An Edition and Discussion of the Winton Domesday*,
    Winchester Studies, I (Oxford, 1976), pp. 143–239, at 87a and 200.
7   See G. de Poerck *et alii*, *La draperie médiévale en Flandre et en Artois: technique et termin-
    ologie*, 3 vols, Rijksuniversiteit te Gent. Werken uitgegeven door de Faculteit van Wijsbegeerte
    en Letteren 110, 111 and 112 (Bruges, 1951), i. 52–3, ii. 17.
8   As well as Godefroy (*Complément*) and Tobler-Lommatzsch, see de Beauvillé, *RIO* v. 145, vi. 56
    and vii. 63, and Morlet, *RIO* xii. 137 and *Haute Picardie*, p. 391, also pp. 152, 163.
9   Ekwall, *Subsidy Rolls*, p. 354.
10 See B. Sundby, *Studies in the Middle English Dialect Materials of Worcestershire Records*,
    Norwegian Studies in English, X (Bergen and Oslo, 1963), pp. 236–8.

'Merchant dealing in coarse cloth': OFr. *burellier*, from *burel*, current especially in Normandy and Picardy.][11]

cannere   MED and Fransson, p. 140: 1305.
— Godwini Cannere *SG 53: 1200/07*.
'Maker/seller of jars, etc.': from OE *canne*; but cf. 'reed-cutter', given as a sense for Med. Lat. *cannarius* (R.E. Latham, *Revised Medieval Latin Word-List from British and Irish Sources* [London, 1965], col. 67a).

cartere   MED: 1193 (*caretier*); Thuresson, pp. 92–3: 1200 (*caretier*) and 1243 (*cartere*); see also Reaney, *Dictionary*.
— Ricardus cartere *CC A35: 1153/67*, R. caretier *CC F638: c.1206*. Johannes caretier *CC C5: c.1180*.
'Waggoner, carrier': from OE *cræt* 'waggon' and ONFr. *caretier* (= *charetier*).

[*cockere*   MED, as surname: 1176 (cf. Thuresson, p. 39).
— Osbertus se cocchere *CC B2, B45*, O. se cockere *B3: 1163/7*.
Since 'haycock-maker', from *cokken* vb. (lC14), seems too seasonal and too unspecialised to afford a distinctive surname, the likeliest sense may be 'brawler', from *cokken* vb. 'to fight', noun and verb both being first noted from *The Proverbs of Alfred*. The existence of a contemporary *Osberto de coquina* CC XI: ante 1153 (cf. also *Osberti Grasporee* CC B118: 1163/7 'bacon and vegetable broth') raises the question whether *cocchere* might not mean 'cook': the verb 'to cook' seems, however, not to be recorded until lC14, nor is 'cooker' normally applied at any date to a person; moreover, the spelling here, in so far as it may be relied on, seems to imply a short root-vowel.]

cornmongere   MED and Fransson, p. 60: 1177.
— Godwini cornmangere *CC A36: 1153/67*. [cf. Godefridus cornem' *Winchester 1148* (von Feilitzen, 'Winton Domesday', pp. 85a, 201)].
'Corn-chandler': from OE *corn* 'grain' plus *mangere* from *mangian* 'to trade'.

crokere   MED: 1222; Mills, *N&Q*, p. 253: c.1230; see also Fransson, p. 185, Ekwall, *Selected Papers*, p. 76, and Smith, *Elements*, i. 112.
— Crocchereslane *CC D217: c.1200, but evidently traditional*.
'Potter': from OE *crocca* 'pot'.

cupere/cuppere   MED: (a) *coupere*, from MedLat *cuparius* 'barrel-maker': c.1176; (b) *cuppere*, from OE *cuppe* 'drinking vessel': lC13. Fransson, pp. 168–9.
— Hamo Cupere f. Roberti Cupere *SG 48: 1200/05*, R. Cupere *SG 50: 1200/05. In BB* (le) Cupere *is common*.
    Cuppere (*standing alone*) *CC D328: c.1200*.
MED distinguishes two words. Fransson takes all the forms and instances, dating from 1181, as probable variants of *coupere*, although admitting the analogy of ON *koppari* 'cup-maker' as support for a distinct *cuppere*; OFr. *coppier*, *coupier* 'goblet-maker'[12] might point the same way. (In Calais, where French and Flemish surnames may interchange for one individual, *cupere* varies with *le cuvelier*).[13]

---

[11] See de Beauvillé, *RIO* vi. 307, Morlet, *RIO* xii. 137, and Ekwall, *Subsidy Rolls*, p. 355; cf. de Poerck, *La draperie médiévale*, i. 207–9, ii. 30.
[12] De Beauvillé, *RIO* vi. 139.
[13] Gysseling and Bougard, *L'Onomastique calaisienne*, p. 7, 32. Certain other resemblances between the Canterbury corpus and the Calais one suggest that, for an investigator appropriately qualified, Flemish influences on Kentish names might offer a fruitful field (the C12 population included a fair contingent of *Flandrenses*).

[fagard   Not in standard reference books.
— Hugo Fagard *CC C37*: *c.1180, CC F203, F397*: *c.1206*. [cf. H. Flagard *CC D72*: *c.1200, F566*: *c.1206*].
Fagard is a current surname in NE France and Belgium; one interpretation suggested is as a pejorative term for 'faggot-maker'.][14]

feiner   MED and Thuresson, p. 194: 1271.
— Symonis le feiner *CC D112*: *c.1200*, S. fenier *CC F56 etc. (4x)*: *c.1206*.
'Hay-dealer': OFr. *fenier, feinier*.

fishman   MED: 1360; see also Thuresson, p. 88, and Mills, *SN*, p. 44.
— Fismannechirche *CC B71*: 1163/7, *but evidently traditional; occurs altogether 6x, with spelling variants*; cf. Fismannecherch' *BB p. 595*. [*Also* ecclesia piscariorum *CC LII*: *1187*].
'Fish-merchant': cf. above *bredman*.

[furbur   Reaney, *Dictionary*: 1180; see also Fransson, p. 151, and Ekwall, *Subsidy Rolls*, p. 356.
— Willelmi furbatoris *CC XXVI, XXVII*: 1177.
'Furbisher of arms': OFr. *fourbeur*, cf. *fourbisseur*.[15]]

glovere   MED and Fransson, p. 126: 1250.
— Helyas se glouere *CC D221*: *c.1200*. Willelmi Glouere *CC F237, F301*: *c.1206*. Robertus glouere *CC F557*: *c.1206*.
'Glove-maker/-seller': from OE *glōf*.

hokere   Not in MED; Tengvik, p. 254: midC10; see also Fransson, p. 198.
— Elrici Hoker *CC F608*, E. Oker *CC F178, F397, F642*: *c.1206*, Ailrici se ocher *CC D131*: *c.1200*, Ælrici soker *CC F21*: *c.1206*. Salomonis Hoker *SG 69, 70*: 1198/1213, S. Oker *SG 67*: *c.1215*, 68, 71: 1198/1213, S. Ocher *CC B145*: 1163/7. Reginoldus Hoker (filius S.H.) *SG 70*: 1198/1213, R. Oker (f. S.O.) *SG 71*: 1198/1213. [*Perhaps also* Henrici Seuchere *SG 47*: 1200/05, *beside* Henricus Hokiere *BB p. 30 and* Henricus Okier' *BB p. 17. Note also the odd forms* Henrico Juchgere *CC LXIV*: *c.1200*, Henrici Chuchere *CC D91, D92*: *c.1200*; cf. Leofnoð Huhere *Tengvik p. 390, from Hyde Liber Vitae c.1030*].
— Hokeresfeld(e) *SG 68, 69*: 1198/1213; Okeresland *SG 179*: ante 1226.
Presumably modern *Hooker*; and presumably from OE *hōc*. The earliest instance extant seems to be *Osmundo, cognomento Hócere* from midC10 material in the lC12 *Liber Eliensis*.[16] The meaning is disputed. Mawer suggested 'user of (agricultural) hook'.[17] Fransson gives a toponymic sense, 'dweller by some hook-shaped feature of landscape, especially a river-bend'; this interpretation, although rejected by Tengvik through a somewhat circular argument from anachronism, would be in keeping with the well-attested topographical use of the simplex *hoc*,[18] as in phrasal surnames such as *Iohannis Atenhoke* BB p. 277, *Iohannes Attioche* BB p. 34, also *Roberti del Brodhoc* BB p. 136. *Reginoldus Hoker* is also *parmenter SG* 67 and 68, so that, if originally occupational, the surname would at this point be purely hereditary.

limbrennere   MED: *c.1226*; see also Fransson, p. 183.
— Aluredus limburnere *SG 211*: 1238/42. [Symon limbernarius *SG 113, 114*: ante 1215].
'Lime-burner': OE *līm* plus an agent-noun from SVIII *birnan/beornan*.

14 See de Beauvillé, *RIO* v. 146; cf. *fagotter* (Thuresson, p. 74: 1279) and A. Carnoy, *Origines des noms de familles en Belgique* (Louvain, 1953), p. 188.
15 See Morlet, *Haute Picardie*, pp. 162–3, 403.
16 E.O. Blake, ed., *Liber Eliensis*, Camden Third Series, XCII (London, 1962), p. 91.
17 Mawer, 'Some Unworked Sources', p. 13; cf. Reaney, *Dictionary*.
18 See Löfvenberg, *Local Surnames*, pp. 101–2, Smith, *Elements*, i. 255, also MED, s.v. *Hok*.

macecrier   Fransson, p. 75: 1235.
— Rodberti le macecrier *CC B68, B202: 1163/7.*
'Butcher': OFr. *maçacrier*, described as characteristically Norman.[19]

madermongere   Fransson, p. 108: 1230.
— Godfridi Medermangere *CC F23: c.1206.*
'Dye-merchant': from OE *mædere*, Kentish **medere*.[20] Cf. above *cornmongere.*

madrer   Fransson, p. 108: 1333 (cf. Thuresson, p. 208: *maderman* 1293).
— Roberti le mederere *CC D151: c.1200, F278: c.1206, SG 139: ante 1233*, R. mederere
CC D138: c.1200.
'Dyer (using madder)': from OE *mædere.*

marlur   Fransson, p. 182: 1275.
— Stephano le marlur *SG 183: 1215/40.*
Usually taken as 'one who prepares marl', form OFr. *marle* 'limey clay'; but cf. also OFr.
marleor 'bell-ringer'.

mulner   Fransson, p. 56: 1275, noted as rare in south and west.
— Picot[21] le mulner *SA: c.1166.*
'Miller': from OE *mylen*, but *u* instead of Kentish *e* as the reflex of OE *y* might be due to
influence from OFr. *moulinier.*

parere/por(r)ere Fransson, p. 69: *porer* 1285.
— Ædwardus parere *CC D148: c.1200*, Edwardo Parere *BB p. 386*, Eadwardum Parere *BB
p. 387:* ? *c.1188.* Hamonis le Porere *BB p. 563*, H. Porere *BB p. 161 (2x)*, H. Porrer' *BB p.
157.* Iohannes (le) Porere *BB p. 157 etc. (18x in all)*, I. filius H. P. *BB p. 157.* Hugonis le
Porere *BB p. 563.*
Fransson derived *porer* from OFr. *porier* 'leek-seller, greengrocer'.[22] Here, however,
parere appears as an alternative (early) form: the St Augustine's document of 1188 which
names *Eadwardum Parere* in connection with land at *Stauerdinge* mentions a son *Hamo*
(BB pp. 386–7); and elsewhere in the Black Book we read 'apud Steuerlinge de tenementis
que fuerunt quondam Hamonis le Porere et Iohannis le Porere et Radulphi filii Hugonis le
Porere' (BB p. 563), cf. *pro Porere apud Steuerlinge* (BB p. 157): leaving aside the variant
spellings of the place-name,[23] this must be one family with an hereditary, perhaps occupational, surname. Etymology is difficult. OFr. has a form *parere(s)/pareur* 'finisher, of cloth
or leather';[24] but for OFr. *a* in an open syllable to be identified with OE *ā* and so develop to

---

[19] See de Beauvillé, *RIO* vi. 231–2, and Morlet, *Haute Picardie*, pp. 169, 407; IC13 Calais prefers
   the variant *macheclier*, see Gysseling and Bougard, *L'Onomastique calaisienne*, p. 51, and cf.
   Arras 1195 etc. *li Macecliers.*

[20] For this dye-stuff, see de Poerck, *La draperie médiévale*, i. 175–9, and cf. Arras 1195 etc. *de le
   Warance.*

[21] *Picot*, i.e. 'pick-axe', apparently originally an occupational nickname (see Morlet, *RIO* xii. 65),
   had already become current as a personal name by the time of Domesday Book, for instance, the
   Sheriff of Cambridge (see J. Morris, ed. and tr., *Domesday Book*, 38 vols [Chichester, 1975–92],
   vol. xviii: Cambridgeshire, section 30[32]). The form reappears thirty-five and forty years later
   as the surname, apparently patronymic, of another miller, *Goddardus molendinarius et frater
   eius CC F596* and *Godardus frater Willelmi Picot CC D201* (concerning the same holding)
   beside *Godard Picot CC F380* (cf. Urry, *Spicilegium Beccense*, 584; see Morris, *Domesday
   Book*, vol. iii: Surrey, section 19/20, 21, 22).

[22] See also de Beauvillé, *RIO* v. 152 (with feminine *La Poraière*); Morlet, *Haute Picardie*, p. 144.

[23] See J.K. Wallenberg, *The Place-Names of Kent* (Uppsala, 1934), p. 607.

[24] See de Beauvillé, *RIO* vi. 61, 307, and Morlet, *RIO* xii. 137, also de Poerck, *La draperie
   médiévale*, i. 190 *et seq.*, 226, ii. 143.

ME *ō* would be quite anomalous, no matter how early the borrowing took place (cf., for instance, *mason*). Perhaps the early *parere* shows 'inverted spelling': if the *a*-spelling were kept in native words after the OE sound had been raised and rounded to [ɔ], then conceivably *a* might sometimes have been used to render a similar [ɔ] in a word such as *porier*, *o* being replaced when the native sound became consistently so spelt.

peser   Thuresson, p. 155: 1222.
— Simon le Peser *PR*: *1198*.
Probably 'weigh-master': OFr. *peseur*.[25]

pindere   Reaney, *Dictionary*, and Thuresson, p. 108: 1219; see also Fransson, p.
                         200, and Ekwall, *Selected Papers*, p. 70.
— Willelmo Pendere *SG 67*: *1198/1213*.
Fransson suggests a toponymic, 'dwelling by the enclosure (OE **pynd*)', cf. *Robertus atte Pende* BB p. 31 beside *Gilebertus Pendere* BB p. 37, cf. 38; but Thuresson and Reaney prefer 'officer responsible for impounding strays', from OE *(ge)-pyndan* 'to pen up' (cf. also OFr. *pendere/pendeur* possibly 'hangman').[26]

pinnere   Fransson, p. 148: 1244.
— Will' Pinere *CC XLI*: *lC12*.
'Peg-maker': from OE *pinn*.

plaidur   Thuresson, p. 143: 1221.
— Godefridus le plaidur *SG 146*: *c.1213/14*.
'Advocate': OFr. *plaideur*.

sacker   Fransson, p. 94: 1225.
— Roberti le sacur *CC F465*, R. sacur *F112*: *c.1206*, *SG 72*: *1215/20*.
'Bag-/sack-merchant': referred by Fransson to OE *sacc*, Kentish *sæc*, but OFr. *sachier* might also be involved. Cf. above *baggere*.

sadelere   Fransson, pp. 123–4: 1288.
— Wlfwini sadelere *CC F55*: *c.1206*.
'Saddler': from OE *sadol*. Cf. below *selier*.

selier   Fransson, p. 124: 1227 (but cf. Reaney, *Dictionary*: *sellere* 1086).
— Reinberti le selier *CC B102*: *1163/7*. [Jordano sellario *CC XLVII*: *1175/7*]. Roberti le seleir *CC F501*: *c.1206*, [Roberti sellarii *CC F54*: *c.1206*].
'Saddler': OFr. *selier*.[27] Cf. above *sadelere*.

stablier
                         Thuresson, p. 91: 1196.
— Relicta Godwini stablier *CC D2*: *c.1200*, [relicta Goduini de stabulo *CC C22*: *c.1180*].
'Stable-lad' or possibly 'master of horse': OFr. *establier*.

thecchere
                         Fransson, p. 178: 1275 (also pp. 178–9: *thecker* 1199).
— Wiberto thecchere *CC XLVII*: *1175/7*.
'Roofer': from OE *þeccan*.

---

[25] See de Beauvillé, *RIO* vii. 151; also Morlet, *Haute Picardie*, pp. 177, 412.
[26] See Tobler-Lommatzsch, and cf. Arras 1206 etc. (*li*) *Pendere*; also Morlet, *Haute Picardie*, pp. 178, 412.
[27] But cf. Ekwall, *Subsidy Rolls*, p. 357.

upholdere   Fransson, p. 113: 1280; cf. Ekwall, *Early London Personal Names*, p. 43.[28]
— Godardus uphealdere *CC A27: 1153/67*, G. huphaldere *CC D263, also De terra Huphaldere D290: c.1200*, G. Huppeheldere *CC F618 etc.: c.1206 (7x in all)*.
'Repairer; second-hand dealer': cf. OE *upheald* 'maintenance'.

[?*ussher*   Thuresson, p. 150: 1243.
— Rodbertus urser *SA: c.1166*.
Probably an error for *usser* 'door-keeper': OFr. (*h*)*uissier* (cf. *Thoma le Vsser* BB p. 571). Although with so common a name it counts for little, *Robertus portarius/de porta* is commonly mentioned, e.g. CC C20, LV etc.].

van(n)ur   Cf. Thuresson, p. 42: *vanner* 1275.
— Edwordus le uaneur *SA: c.1166*. Æilweker le Uanur *CC XLV: post 1170*. Walterius le uannur *CC XXIII: 1175/7*. Cf. Simon le Vannere *BB p. 5*. Probably from OFr. *vanneur, vanier* 'wicker-worker';[29] whereas *vannere* is evidently a southern form from OE *fannian* vb. 'to winnow', from *fann* 'winnowing-device' (perhaps with some influence from OFr. *van* in the same sense). Cf., however, MedLat. *vannator* 'winnower', common in twelfth- and thirteenth-century Anglo-Latin.[30]

wolmongere   Fransson, p. 90: 1250.
— Reginaldi wlmangere *CC F307: c.1206*.
'Wool-merchant': from OE *wull*. Cf. above *cornmongere, madermongere*.

II. *Patronymics: Likely and Unlikely*

Further supplementary records concern forms which, either at first or at second glance, look like rarish personal names used patronymically.[31] Ambiguities are rife here,

---

[28] Cf. also Godwinus le pheliper *London c.1292*, reported by Ekwall, *Subsidy Rolls*, p. 204: 'The surname varies between *Pheliper* and *Upheldere*, both "fripperer", and *Hodere*.'

[29] See, in addition to the dictionaries, de Beauvillé, *RIO* vii. 66, and Morlet, *Haute Picarde*, p. 146.

[30] See T. Stapleton, ed., *Chronicon Petroburgense*, Camden First Series, XLVII (London, 1849), p. 167; W.H. Hart and P.A. Lyons, eds, *Cartularium monasterii de Rameseie*, 3 vols, Rolls Society [RS] 1884–93, i. 320, i. 351, etc.; A. Watkin, ed., *The Great Chartulary of Glastonbury*, 3 vols, Somerset Record Society, LIX, LXII, LXIV (Frome, 1947–56), ii. 268.

[31] For personal names I have consulted, in addition to works already listed: T. Forssner, *Continental-Germanic Personal Names in England in Old and Middle English Times* (Uppsala, 1916); M. Redin, *Studies in Uncompounded Personal Names in Old English* (Uppsala, 1919); O. v. Feilitzen, *Pre-Conquest Personal Names of Domesday Book*, Nomina Germanica, III (Uppsala, 1937); *idem*, 'Notes on Old English Bynames', *Namn och Bygd*, XXVII (1939), 116–30 (comments on Tengvik, *Bynames*); *idem*, 'Some Unrecorded Old and Middle English Personal Names', *Namn och Bygd*, XXXIII (1945), 69–98; *idem*, 'Some Continental-Germanic Personal Names in England', in A. Brown and P. Foote, eds, *Early English and Norse Studies presented to Hugh Smith* (London, 1963), pp. 46–61; *idem*, 'Some Old English Uncompounded Personal Names and Bynames', *Studia Neophilologica*, XL (1968), 5–16; O. v. Feilitzen and C. Blunt, 'Personal Names on the Coinage of Edgar', in P. Clemoes and K.W. Hughes, eds, *England before the Conquest: Studies in Primary Sources presented to Dorothy Whitelock* (Cambridge, 1971), pp. 183–214; P.H. Reaney, 'Notes on the Survival of Old English Personal Names in Middle English', *Studier i modern Språkvetenskap*, XVIII (1953), 84–112; J. Adigard des Gautries, *Les noms de personnes scandinaves en Normandie de 911 à 1066*, Nomina Germanica, XI (Uppsala, 1954); *idem*, 'Les noms de personnes d'origine scandinave dans les obituaires de Jumièges', in *Jumièges: Congrès scientifique du xiiie Centenaire*, 2 pts continuously paginated (Rouen, 1955), pp. 57–67; G. Fellows Jensen, *Scandinavian Personal Names in Lincolnshire and Yorkshire*

mainly involving confusion between personal names and common nouns:[32] any decisions ventured must depend on likelihood in each separate case. Inclusion of a form in this section by no means implies that the patronymic interpretation is preferred.

barat(e)

— Radulfo Barat *CC XL: 1179/1210.* Henrici Barat *CC F232: c.1206, SG 57, 115, 134: ante 1215/16;* H. Barath *CC F38 etc. (4x): c.1206, SG 112, 113, 114: ante 1215;* H. Barate *CC D200: c.1200, CC F589: c.1206, CC LXV: c.1205;* H. Baratte *CC LXIII: c.1200.* Galfridi Barat *SG 152: 1215/27.*

Patronymic use of the name *Baret/Bared* found in Domesday Book and probably derived from ON *Bárðr*[33] is unlikely here owing to its mainly northern distribution. OFr. *barat* 'fraud', which often occurs in continental nicknames,[34] is early borrowed into ME, but apparently with some contamination from *barate* 'agitation, ostentation', so that *baret* normally means 'strife' rather than 'fraud' and *baratour*, 'brawler' rather than 'swindler'. Since not only is *baret* current in ME from c.1230 on, but *le Baratur* occurs as a surname by 1156, the occurrence of *Barat(e)* here offers no problem.

burre

— Willelmus Burre *CC AppA33:* ?*c.1234.*

Probably from OE *Burra*[35] rather than from the common noun *burre* 'burdock; sticky seed-pod'. Monothematic OE names seem to have been especially common in the south.[36]

burri

— Einulfus Burri *SG 173: 1217/18.*

Either from *Burgric*[37] or, rather better, from a hypothetical **Burgwig.*[38]

cari

— Wlfwinus Cari *CC B189: 1163/7.*

From ON *Kári*, current also in Normandy.[39]

colle

— Roberto Colle, Radulfo Colle *SG 57: ante 1216, etc. (Ro. 10x; Ra. 3x);* Roberto Colo *SG 211: c.1238/42.* Cf. Radulfus Colekin *CC F542: c.1206.* Possibly from ON *Kol(l)i,*

[*SPLY*], Navnestudier udgivet af Institut for Navneforskning, VII (Copenhagen, 1968); M.-Th. Morlet, *Les noms de personne sur le territoire de l'ancienne Gaule du vi^e au xiie siècle*, 2 vols (Paris, 1968–72); B. Seltén, *The Anglo-Saxon Heritage in Middle English Personal Names: East Anglia 1100–1399*, Lund Studies in English, XLIII (1972).

32 See also above note 21.

33 Von Feilitzen, *Pre-Conquest Personal Names*, p. 192; cf. Tengvik, *Bynames*, p. 213, and Fellows Jensen, pp. 46–7.

34 See von Feilitzen, *Namn och Bygd*, XXVII, 126, also Morlet, *RIO* xii. 210, Gysseling and Bougard, *L'Onomastique calaisienne*, p. 14, and Berger, *Le nécrologe*, index, s.v.

35 Redin, *Uncompounded Personal Names*, p. 87, and von Feilitzen, *Pre-Conquest Personal Names*, p. 212.

36 See V.J. Smart, 'Moneyers of the Late Anglo-Saxon Coinage 973–1016', *Kungl. Vitterhets Historie och Antikvitets Akademiens Handlingar: Antikvariska Serien*, XIX (*Commentationes de nummis sæculorum ix–xi in Suecia repertis*, pt 2 [Stockholm, 1968]), 191–276, esp. 271.

37 Von Feilitzen, *Pre-Conquest Personal Names*, p. 212, and Seltén, *Anglo-Saxon Heritage*, p. 143.

38 See von Feilitzen, *ibid.*, pp. 211–12.

39 Von Feilitzen, *ibid.*, p. 301; Adigard des Gautries, *Les noms de personnes*, p. 116 and Fellows Jensen, *SPLY*, p. 161.

current in Normandy as well as in the Danelaw;[40] but more probably a hypocoristic form of *Nicolas*. The personal name *Cole* is found here: *Cole longus* CC A34: 1153/67, *Cole de balneario* CC XXI: 1167/75, *Heres Cole* CC F400: c.1206. Identification of *Radulfus Colle* with *Radulfus Colekin* may be supported by the fact that the brother *Robertus* has a son *Notekin* SG 57; perhaps the family, like many in Canterbury, had Flemish connections.

coppe
— Hamo Coppe filius Henrici Coppe *CC XXXIII: c.1200 etc.* (*Ha. 3x*; *He. 2x*), Hamone Coppe *SG 49, 50: c.1200/05*.
Probably from OE *Coppa*,[41] but cf. *coppe* 'spider', and (*æt þam*) *coppe* 'at the hill-top'.

cudie
— Egelwini Cudie *CC B183, B184: 1163/7*.
Possibly a patronymic use of a name in *Cuð-*, such as *Cuðwig*, or of a monothematic *Cud(d)i*;[42] either way the final *-e* seems anomalous.

hering
— Willelmi Hering *CC D368: c.1200*. [Radulfo Harang' *SG 88: 1223*]. *Also*: Hagemunt Freteharing *PR: 1198* (cf. Agemundus Fetharing *SG 46, 48, 49, 50: 1200/05*).
The surname *Hering* has been referred to a personal name from the root *here-* 'army'[43] rather than to OE *hæring* 'kind of fish'. On the other hand, the form *Freteharing* (and the evident error *Fetharing*) requires reference to the fish: an important local commodity, witness the annual rent of 40,000 herring paid to Christ Church by Sandwich[44] (the vowel in *haring* might be due either to OFr. *harenc* or to influence from Essex dialect). OFr. *Harenc* occurs as a suname in Calais and also (beside *le Harenguier*) in Eu and Arras, as well as in other parts of France.[45]

munin
— Simon Munin *CC F262, F477: c.1206*.
A spelling for *Monin*, a hypocoristic form of *Simon* (or possibly *Salomon*) current in Arras and Calais.[46]

norioth
— Ade f. Norioth *CC F178: c.1206*.
Norioth may represent the continental name *Nor(i)got, Norigaud*.[47]

---

40 Von Feilitzen, *ibid.*, p. 307; Fellows Jensen, pp. 176–7; Adigard des Gautries, *ibid.*, pp. 122–3; also Ekwall, *Early London Personal Names*, pp. 78–9.

41 Redin, *Uncompounded Personal Names*, p. 75.

42 *Ibid.*, p. 126, cf. pp. 16, 46, 62.

43 *Ibid.*, p. 172; but cf. Fellows Jensen, *SPLY*, pp. 147–8, for *hæringr* 'hoary old man'.

44 *VCH Kent*, iii. 209.

45 Gysseling and Bougard, *L'Onomastique calaisienne*, p. 42–3; Morlet, *RIO* xii. 144, and *Haute Picardie*, pp. 170, 377 and Berger, *Le nécrologe*, s.a. 1200, 1203, etc. (but J. Blottière, 'Surnoms et patronymes du xie au xiiie siècle dans le Vexin français, etc.', *RIO*, XXV [1973], pp. 31–44, esp. 37, prefers derivation from the Gmc. personal name). For 'fish' surnames in general, see P.H. Reaney, *The Origin of English Surnames* (London, 1967), p. 274; Flemish nicknames in Calais include *Cattevisch, Ghervisch, Witinc* (Gysseling and Bougard, *op. cit.*, pp. 25, 26, 85). Cf. also below *sprot*.

46 Gysseling and Bougard, *ibid.*, pp. 97, 99; Berger, *ibid.* pp. 89, 95.

47 See Forssner, *Continental-Germanic Personal Names*, p. 193, and Ekwall, *Early London Personal Names*, p. 114; cf. *Noryet de srede* BB p. 187, *Noriaht* BB p. 197, *Norwat de Reide* BB p. 206.

rabel
— Willelmus Rabel *CC D82: c.1200*. Ada Rabel *CC AppA: c.1234, SG 197: ante 1237*. Cf. Alexander Rabel *BB 9*.
From the Continental-Germanic personal name *Ratbellus*,[48] Domesday Book *Rabellus*, for instance, the minor tenant-in-chief *Rabellus carpentarius* or *artifex*.[49]

siluestre
— Willelmi Siluestre *CC D104, D106: c.1200, CC F217 etc. (5x): c.1206*. Thoma Siluestris *SG 104: 1194*.
As *Silvester* was a current personal name in C12 Canterbury, thus, *Magistro Siluestro* SG 16: 1185/90 and Silvester abbot of St Augustine's 1151–61,[50] these examples most probably show simple patronymics. *Siluester* could also, however, be a nickname for a man who inhabited or frequented woodlands, as in William of Canterbury's tale of the fowler whose hawk was healed by St Thomas: 'Miles est Robertus, Normanniae regionis indigena, sed et hujus quam inhabitamus accola. Qui si adhuc tibi minus notus est ex nomine, ex cognomine potest innotescere; Silvester enim cognominari dignoscitur'.[51]

sprot
— Willelmus Sprot *CC F58 etc. (4x): c.1206, SG 119, 120, 121: 1213/14, SG 64: 1215/27, SG 65: ante 1238*.
A common Canterbury surname, borne by, amongst others, the St Augustine's monk who wrote a lost history of his abbey extending to 1272.[52]
Probably a patronymic use of the monothematic OE or ON name *Sprot(t)*,[53] but *Radulfus Litesprot* BB p. 290 suggests that the simplex also may be a nickname, based on *sprot* either as 'twig' or, more probably, as 'tiny fish'.[54]

tretel
— Johannes Tretel *CC D160: c.1200, CC F377: c.1206*.
Possibly a metathesised Kentish reflex of the OE name *Tyrhtel*, a diminutive of *Torht* (unfortunately, the recorded instances are not only rare but all early).[55] Confusion with OFr. *cretel* 'battlement'[56] is unlikely, as the C12 form was *crestel*; nor are early forms of Fr. *tréteau* 'trestle' at all relevant.[57]

turte
— Salomon filius Turte *CC B8, B128, B138: 1163/7*; S. Turte *CC LXV: c.1205, CC F432: c.1206*. Johannes Turte (prepositus) *CC LXVIII: c.1209, etc. (8x in all), SG 81: 1227/31*,

---

[48] Morlet, *Les noms de personne*, i. 181.
[49] Morris, *Domesday Book*, vol. xxxiii: Norfolk (Part Two), section 55.
[50] D. Knowles *et alii*, *The Heads of Religious Houses, England and Wales, 940–1216* (Cambridge, 1972), p. 36.
[51] J.C. Robertson and J.B. Sheppard, eds, *Materials for the History of Thomas Becket*, 7 vols, RS 1875–85, i. 388. See also Tengvik, *Bynames*, p. 136.
[52] See, e.g., A.B. Emden, *Donors of Books to S. Augustine's Abbey, Canterbury*, Oxford Bibliographical Society: Occasional Publications, IV (Oxford, 1968), p. 16.
[53] Redin, *Uncompounded Personal Names*, p. 8; see also Ekwall, *Early London Personal Names*, pp. 64, 65, and Fellows Jensen, *SPLY*, p. 261.
[54] Cf. above *hering*, esp. note 45.
[55] Redin, *Uncompounded Personal Names*, p. 140. For the early eighth-century bishop of Hereford called *Tyrhtil*, see M. Gibbs, ed., *Early Charters of the Cathedral Church of St Paul, London*, Camden Third Series, LVIII (London, 1939), p. 3.
[56] Cf. Tengvik, *Bynames*, pp. 374–5.
[57] See C.H. Livingston, 'French *Tréteau*: English *Trestle*', *MPh*, XLIII (1945–6), 89–93. Cf., however, *Reginaldi monachi Dunelmensis libellus de admirandis Beati Cuthberti virtutibus*, Surtees Society, I (Durham, 1835), p. 24: *Cretel* 'quod carrum anglicè dicitur'.

etc. (*6x in all*); Radulfo Turte *CC LXX*: *c.1220*; Johanne Turte, Radulfo fratre suo alder-manno *CC XXXVII*: *c.1227*, *also CC LXIII*: *c.1200 and CC LXV*: *c.1205*. Augustino Turt' *SG I.8*: *1240/50*.

A prominent family. At first *filius Turte* suggests some rare personal name, perhaps a hypocoristic form of one of the Franco-Norse *Tur-* names current in Normandy.[58] More probably, however, OFr. *tourte* 'coarse round loaf' is used here, as often in France, as a nickname;[59] this word appears in English c.1300 in the occupational term *tourtebaker*[60] (in French *tourte* is also, however, applied to one of the stages in the preparation of woad[61]). A father's nickname was often used on its own to form a patronymic, e.g., *filius Caiteuel* CC B2 beside *filius Rogeri Caiteuel* CC B1;[62] cf. below *ket*.

III. *Some Difficult Forms*

chekerel
— Eadmerus/Ædmerus Checherelle *CC B16, B31, B32*: *1163/7*; E./Æ./ Chekerel *CC F363 etc.* (*4x*): *c.1206*; Chekerel (*standing alone*) *CC D32*: *c.1200*; Æ. Gekerel *CC F98*: *c.1206*. Not easy to parallel: perhaps a diminutive based on OFr. *eschequer* 'chess-board' (ME *cheker* seems so far unrecorded until c.1300).[63]

chich
— Ærnaldus de Chiche *CC LII*: *1187*; Arnoldo Chiche *SG 212*: *ante 1223*; A. Chic *CC D115*: *c.1200*; A. de Chigh *CC F165*: *c.1206*; A. Chigh *CC F550*: *c.1206*; A. Chig *CC D295*: *c.1200*; Æ. Chig *CC F169*: *c.1206*. Ailwinus Chiche *PR*: *1198*. Evdo de Chich *CC G21*: *c.1206*; E. Chich *CC LXVIII*: *c.1209, SG 133, 136, 146*: *1213/14, SG 176*: *ante 1226*. Johanne de Chich *SG I.7*: *1240*; J. Chich' *SG 197*: *ante 1237*; J. Chich tunc preposito *SG 184*: *1227/31*, cf. *SG 210*: *1227/41*. Simon Chiche *PR*: *1198*; S. Chich *CC F178 etc.* (*6 x*): *c.1206*; S. Chigh *CC F608*: *c.1206*; S. Chig *CC D128*: *c.1200*.

Another prominent family often enjoying civic office. The forms with *de*, even though in the minority and not especially early, seem to imply a toponymic (in any case, the range of spellings hardly fits the OFr. adj. *chiche* 'mean'): either general, with OE *cicc* 'river-bend',[64] or specific, with the Essex place-name *Cicc* (derived from the common noun).[65]

---

[58] Cf. *Turto, Turtin*, listed by von Feilitzen, *Pre-Conquest Personal Names*, pp. 391, 396; cf. Adigard des Gautries, *Les noms de personnes*, pp. 473–4, also 472.

[59] See H. Carrez, 'Le vocabulaire de l'alimentation et les noms de personnes dans la région dijonnaise du xiie au xve siècle', *Annales de Bourgogne*, X (1938), 174, 176–80; *Male tourte* is common in Arras, see Berger, *Le nécrologe*, s.a. 1222, and index s.v.

[60] Sundby, *ES*, XXXIII, 18–20; cf. OFr. *tourtier* (de Beauvillé, *RIO* vi. 227), fem. *tourtière* (Arras 1309). In England *turte* 'loaf' may also occur in the midC12 nickname *Butteturte* from Holme (J.R. West, ed., *St Benet of Holme 1020–1210*, 2 pts continuously paginated, Norfolk Record Society, II and III [London, 1932], p. 175), although the meaning of this is not clear (? a 'Shakespeare' compound, 'smite loaf'; ? or a slip for 'butter-loaf').

[61] An important dye-stuff, see de Poerck, *La draperie médiévale*, i. 154, ii. 206; also E.M. Carus-Wilson, 'La guède française en Angleterre: un grand commerce du Moyen Age', *Revue du Nord*, XXXV (1953), 89–105.

[62] For nicknames used on their own, see von Feilitzen, *Pre-Conquest Personal Names*, pp. 17–18, and B. Seltén, 'Some Notes on Middle English By-Names in Independent Use', *ES*, XLVI (1965), 165–81.

[63] Cf., tentatively, *Kikerel* Arras 1231 etc. (Berger offers no gloss or etymology). Note that diminu-tives in *-crel* are common among French occupational terms.

[64] Smith, *Elements*, i. 93.

[65] Now St Osyth: see P.H. Reaney, *The Place-Names of Essex*, EPNS, XII (Cambridge, 1935), pp. 347–8.

The latter possibility may be strengthened by the fact that William of Corbeil, archbishop of Canterbury 1123–36, had been a canon at *Cicc* just before his elevation.[66]

ferre

— Hernoldum Ferre:[67] *?1189*, Ernaldus Ferre *PR: 1198*, Arnoldus Ferre *CC D121: c.1200*, etc. *(8x)*, (prepositus) *SG 42: ante 1216 etc. (22x)*, Arnaldo Ferre *SG 43: ante 1216 etc. (3x)*, Ærnold Ferre *CC F375: c.1206*, Ernoldo Ferre *CC LXIII: c.1200*. Cf. Ærnulfo Ferre *CC LIV: lC12*.

As *Ærnulfo* looks like an error, this nickname (although to reappear in the 1240s as a surname[68]) could at this date be purely personal. It is far from easy to identify. Connection with the modern surname *Farr*, in so far as correctly derived from OE *fearr* 'bull',[69] seems ruled out by the consistent final *-e*; the form likewise tells against derivation from OE *fearh* 'piglet' (= *farrow*). One possible base might be (*æt þam*) *fyrre*, Kentish *ferre* 'by the fir-tree', from OE **fyrh*. Most likely perhaps is OFr. *ferré* meaning 'iron-clad' or, less probably, 'iron-grey' (= the common *ferrant*).

ket/kete

— Salomon filius Kiet *CC B15, B28*; S.f. Chiet *CC B11*; S. Kiet *CC B149, B155: 1163/7*; S. Ket *SG 73: 1200/20*; S. Keth *CC D60: c.1200, F108, F378: c.1206*; S. Chet *CC F75: c.1206*.

— . . . de Godwino Kete et Roberto Kete et de Alueua Kete et Godeleua Kete *SG 85: ante 1223*; Roberto filio Edwini Kete *SG 214: 1238*.

Evidently two distinct surnames. Formally *Kete* could be derived from OE *cȳta* 'bird of prey' (cf. *Ayenbite*: 'þe ilke byeþ propreliche glotounes þet al uorzuelȝeþ ase deþ þe kete of his sperringe'),[70] which has been identified in West-Midland nicknames.[71] More probably, however, it is a toponymic derived from OE **cyte* 'hut', cognate with *cot(e)* 'cottage', and often found in south-eastern forms such as *atte Kete*.[72]

On the other hand, *Kiet* (etc.), which among all the spelling variants never shows final *-e*, looks like a personal nickname used here patronymically (cf. above *turte*). The most likely etymon seems to be ON *kjǫt* 'meat', sometimes borrowed into ME as *ket*; although ON influence is not strong in Kentish, an unusual word might be apt as a nickname, perhaps for a man from the North-East.

scache

— Azo Scache *CC B179: 1163/7, CC D22: c.1200, CC F48: c.1206*; A. Scace *CC D23: c.1200*; A. Scage *CC F415, F419: c.1200*.

The likeliest base is OFr. *eschace*, Normanno-Picard *escache* (= modern *échasse*) 'stilt', 'wooden leg' or 'crutch', as in the Picard tale of *Witasse le Moine*: 'Wistasces se fist eschachier; Sa jambe ot lié a sa nace, Molt bien set aler a escache', 'Il n'a c'un pié et une escache';[73] in eC13 Arras *Escace, Eskache, Eschace*, is a common nickname.[74] In English *scatch* 'stilt' occurs by C16, but must have been borrowed much earlier, and from the ONorthFr. form in question here.

[66] *ASC* s.a. 1123.
[67] W. Stubbs, ed., *Epistolæ Cantuarienses*, RS 1865, p. 311.
[68] Urry, *Canterbury Under the Angevin Kings*, p. 137: John Ferre.
[69] Cf. Reaney, *Dictionary*, s.v.
[70] R. Morris, ed., *Dan Michel's Ayenbite of Inwyt*, EETS OS 23 (London, 1866), pp. 52–3.
[71] Sundby, *Worcestershire Records*, p. 110: *kute, kuyte*.
[72] See M.T. Löfvenberg, 'An Etymological Note', *Studia Neophilologica*, XVIII (1944), 259–64.
[73] D.J. Conlon, ed., *Li Romans de Witasse le Moine*, University of North Carolina Studies in the Romance Languages and Literatures 126 (Chapel Hill, 1972), lines 1423–5, 1463, also 1474.
[74] Arras 1236 shows *li Escaciers* as equivalent to *Lignipes*; some eC13 instances of (*a l'*) *Eschace, Escace, Eskace*, seem likely to carry the same sense, but Berger takes some C14 examples of *de*

IV. *Enigmatic Forms*

Some names here resist my own attempts at identifying them; I list them, in the hope that some investigator more inspired may throw light on them.

buþelibag
— Godwinus buþelibag *CC B146: 1163/7.*
The simplex *buthel* is current as a surname, e.g. *Henricus Buthel, Robertus Buthel* BB 41: possibly connected with OE *botl, boþl* 'dwelling'. Very tentatively one might suggest 'with a dwelling in "Bag" [i.e., *Baggeberi*]', as his holding is in the appropriate area;[75] on the other hand, without further evidence, proposing such a slang usage seems over-bold.

copelose
— Willelmi Copelose *SG 60: c.1200.* Johannis Copelose *SG 54: 1200/07.* Elgarus f. Joseph Copelose *SG 54: 1200/07*; Eilgaro Copelose *SG 58: c.1200, SG 57: ante 1216.*

furdenel
— Alberb Furdenel *CC XVIII: c.1167.*

nolohat
— Galfridus Nolohat *CC LXVI: c.1200*; cf. Ade Noloth' *Suffolk 1209.*[76]

scoca
— Goldwardo Scoca *CC IX: 1152*; G. Scoce *CC X: 1152*; G. Scoche *CC XVI: 1153/67, CC B126: 1163/7*; G. Scache *CC F117: c.1206.*
The form *Scache*, forty and more years later than the other example, may result from confusion with *Azo Scache* (see above). Possibly OE *scucca* 'demon'?

scrideman
— Eadwini/Æduini Scrideman *CC C57: c.1180, G58, G59: c.1206.*
Possibly an occupational term, from *scrydan*, in the sense 'prune'?

stethese
— Godwini Stethese *CC B106: 1163/7.*
The second element may be the Kentish form of *-hyse*, 'young warrior', often found in dithematic OE names. Is the first *stæþ* 'river-bank'?

wadecac
— Radulfus Wadecac *CC A27: 1153/67.*

watkeke
— Radulfus Watkeke *CC F619: c.1206.*

---

l'Escace, de l'Eskache, as residential, see *Le nécrologe*, ii. 175 (cf. index, s.vv., also s.a. 1201, 1213, etc.). Morlet, *Haute Picardie*, p. 179, suggests 'arme tranchante'.

[75] See Urry, *Canterbury Under the Angevin Kings*, Map 1 (b), large-scale, sheet 1. An apparent abbreviation *in Bagge* does occur B180 beside the more expected *in Bagg'* B182; cf. also *Bagguri* C18.

[76] B. Dodwell, ed., *Feet of Fines for the County of Norfolk for the Reign of King John 1201–1215; for the County of Suffolk for the Reign of King John 1199–1214*, Pipe Roll Society New Series, XXXII (London, 1958 for 1956), p. 254.

16

Battle c.1110: An Anthroponymist Looks at an Anglo-Norman New Town*

When, in her recent book on *English Medieval Towns*, Susan Reynolds raised the question of medieval townspeople, their origins, and their outlooks, she remarked that 'Medieval records are more or less inadequate to answer such questions . . .'[1] She did not leave the matter there; neither should we. How can we learn more about our earliest burgesses? At least we know some of their names, from such twelfth-century records as list the holders of individual burgess-plots. Of these the most imposing are the *Winton Domesday*, with its two surveys of c.1115 and of 1148, and the great series of Canterbury rentals published a dozen years ago; hardly less valuable is the 1177 taxation-list from Newark.[2] Less impressive perhaps, but with special claims on our attention, is the list, dating from c.1110, which records the names of nearly all the householders in Battle: some 110 names, arranged, as in the larger surveys, according to the lay-out of the town.[3] What can such lists be made to tell us?

The personal names alone will concern us here, not the lay-out of the town, still less the rents. To a limited extent such names already form an accepted source of historical evidence, occupational terms being scrutinized for light on economic activity and *noms d'origine* for population-shifts. Over the last half-dozen years, however, experience has suggested that, when evidence on social and cultural history is sparse,

* I have to acknowledge the help towards the cost of preparing and presenting this paper given by the British Academy Research Grant awarded to me in spring 1979.

1 Reynolds, Susan, *An introduction to the history of English medieval towns*, Oxford 1977, ch. 4, esp. 66. Cf. Beresford, Maurice, *New towns of the Middle Ages: town plantation in England, Wales and Gascony*, London 1967, ch. 7, esp. 191–8, 299.

2 Biddle, Martin, ed., *et al.*, *Winchester in the early Middle Ages: an edition and discussion of the Winton Domesday*, Winchester studies i. Oxford 1976, with text on 33–141 (for the date of the earlier survey, see 410) and anthroponymical analysis by Olof von Feilitzen on 143–229 (see also review in *Archives* xiii, autumn 1977, 84–9); Urry, William, *Canterbury under the Angevin kings*, London 1967, with text on 221–444; Barley, M.W., *et al.*, eds., *Documents relating to the Manor and Soke of Newark-on-Trent*, Thoroton Society Record Series xvi, Nottingham 1956, with text on 1–15 and comments by Kenneth Cameron on xi–xv.

3 See Appendix, below 234–40, for an annotated edition of these names, independently transcribed from BL Cotton ms. Domitian A II, fols 16r–18r; also printed by Searle, Eleanor, ed., *The Chronicle of Battle Abbey*, Oxford 1980, 52–8 (I am deeply grateful to Dr Searle for allowing me access to her text in advance of publication; the divergences between her version and mine are mainly due to differing editorial conventions), and in [Brewer, J.S., ed.] *Chronicon Monasterii de Bello*, London 1846, 12–16. For the date, see Searle, Eleanor, *Lordship and community: Battle Abbey and its banlieu 1066–1538*, Toronto 1974, 69–70; also *eadem, Chronicle*, 52–3 nn. The qualification 'nearly all' the householders is made because, with plots large and with certain tenants holding several, there must have been sub-tenants whose names went unrecorded.

these domains too can be illuminated by analysing the whole bodies of personal names used by the groups in question (merely comparing, for instance, the lists of personal names figuring in the place-name surveys of Wiltshire, of Nottinghamshire and of Westmorland gives a certain insight into cultural patterns). For twelfth-century England in particular this technique seems to bring out social patterns hardly perceptible by any other light.[4]

Before looking at the Battle document itself, we must consider the principles and methodology of personal-name study.[5] For the implicit purpose here, ultimately the more important one, is not so much to throw light on the early history of an Anglo-Norman new town but, even more, to invite discussion of an investigative technique so far still experimental.

With place-names, their use as historical clues – as evidence of migrations and settlements, of land-holding customs and of cultivation-patterns, even of prehistoric religions – is something with which we have all been familiar (corporately if not individually) for well over half a century. Often the most significant elements in the place-names thus exploited have been the personal names of early lords and land-holders, as Geoffrey Barrow showed last year in his fascinating paper on alien settlement in south-western Scotland.[6] On their own, however, personal names have far less often been treated as a source of historical evidence. Indeed, for all the striking use which certain scholars have made of them – most notably, each in his own way, David Douglas, Eilert Ekwall, and Sir Frank Stenton – their testimony seems widely underestimated. Necessarily, personal names present different problems from place-names; but, equally, they offer distinct advantages. Instead of remaining current for centuries, no individual personal name lasts for more than a single human life (hereditary family-names being for the moment left aside); so that a chronological succession of personal names can mirror changing patterns of cultural allegiance. Not being tied to specific locations, personal names may reflect, more promptly and more closely than place-names can, demographic shifts and other causes of cross-cultural influence. Above all, personal names are hundreds of times, often tens of thousands of times more numerous than the corresponding place-names, so that they can give a shaded, nuanced impression both of settlement-patterns and of cultural ones, representing minorities and repressed elements as well as the dominant ones stamping the place-names.

This numerousness invites analytical and comparative techniques of study. A pioneering work in this field has been Veronica Smart's paper on moneyers' names from late Anglo-Saxon England.[7] Mrs Smart has shown that analysing separately the names

---

4   See: 'People and languages in post-Conquest Canterbury', above 179–206; 'Women's names in post-Conquest England: observations and speculations', above 117–43; 'Thoughts on the French connections of Middle-English nicknames', *Nomina* ii, 1978, 38–44; 'L'Anthroponymie cantor-bérienne du XIIᵉ siècle: quelques exemples de l'influence normanno-picarde', *Nouvelle revue d'onomastique*, iii–iv, 1984, 157–66.

5   Cf. 'Clark's First Three Laws of Applied Anthroponymics', above 77–83 (extract from a paper read in April 1979 at the Nottingham Conference of the Council for Name Studies in Great Britain and Ireland).

6   Barrow, Geoffrey, 'The "Norman" settlement in Scotland', read at the first Battle Conference, but not printed in the *Proceedings*; the topic will be treated in his forthcoming Ford lectures [[*The Anglo-Norman era in Scottish history*, Oxford 1980, 30–60]].

7   Smart, V.J., 'Moneyers of the late Anglo-Saxon coinage, 973–1016', *Commentationes de nummis sæculorum ix–xi in Suecia repertis*, pt ii, Kungl. Vitterhets Historie och Antikvitets Akademiens Handlingar: Antikvariska Serien xix, Stockholm 1968, 191–276.

representing each locality and then comparing the analyses offers valuable pointers to cultural variations. Her own survey shows the frequencies of Scandinavian forms, among moneyers' names at least, to vary in close relationship with the presumable densities of the different Viking settlements. Such an approach I have been trying to apply more widely, taking less specialized samples of personal names and, until now, considering the Norman settlement in England rather than the Scandinavian one.

Unfortunately, study of personal names proves beset by problems grave enough to have persuaded some medieval anthroponymists, among them the great Karl Michaëlsson, that neither statistical analysis nor, *a fortiori*, comparison is at all feasible.[8] A major stumbling-block is the non-comparability of the extant materials. It might, indeed, be wise to compare only like with like – manorial extent with manorial extent, Assize Roll with Assize Roll, Feet of Fines with Feet of Fines. On the other hand, as work has proceeded, so often have similar patterns emerged from materials which, although of disparate types, roughly represent the same place, date and milieu, that faith in the representative value of all the types of record becomes partly restored. One precaution is, however, essential: to disregard the smaller apparent discrepancies – for instance, those of 5% or less. Any name-analysis citing percentages to several decimal places gives a misleading view of the precision even theoretically obtainable by even the best investigator. All the extant records contain random elements, none offering anything approaching a complete or systematic census-return: the Battle list, for instance, names rather less than one individual per holding, omitting all juvenile or otherwise subordinate members of households, showing less than 10% of women, and remaining silent about possible sub-tenants. Often, too, unsystematic repetitions make it impossible to calculate the exact total of individuals involved: does the Battle list contain two *Emmas* (46, 72), or one holding two burgage plots; three *Sevugels* (24, 56, 95), two of whom (24 and 56) each held two plots, or only two, one a sub-landlord exploiting four plots?[9] Moreover, not even the most learned investigator possible will ever succeed in definitively classifying every name-form under one category and one only, for ambiguities are rife.

The personal names of twelfth-century England fall into manifold categories.[10] Most obviously, they are divided into baptismal names and by-names; but even here an overlap occurs, because a by-name, instead of qualifying a baptismal name, might sometimes replace it, as here with 80 *Brembel* and 101 *Cocard*, and then perhaps be adopted by subsequent generations as a baptismal name in its own right.[11] The baptismal names proper stem either from the pre-Conquest or 'insular' stock or from the post-Conquest, 'continental' forms introduced by the Norman settlers. In turn, the insular stock falls into Old English names and the Scandinavian ones introduced by the Viking settlers in the Danelaw. The continental names likewise fall into several groups: those stemming from Continental Germanic but mostly brought to England in

---

8   See Michaëlsson, Karl, 'L'anthroponymie et la statistique', *Quatrième congrès international des sciences onomastiques*, Uppsala 1954, 380–94; also O. Brattö, *Notes d'anthroponymie messine*, Göteborgs Universitets Årsskrift lxii/4, Göteborg 1956, 24–9.

9   The numbers are those of the messuages concerned, see Appendix. The names, in the original all in the gen. because qualifying *mansura*, are normalized when quoted in the text.

10   For a working bibliography relevant to the present study, see the list of special abbreviations prefixed to the Appendix, below 235–6. Fuller references will be found in the notes to the articles listed in nn. 4 and 5.

11   See, for instance, B. Seltén, 'Some notes on Middle English by-names in independent use', *English Studies* xlvi, 1965, 168–81.

Gallicized forms – the conventional written forms being sometimes ambiguous, owing to the close links between Continental Germanic and Old English; the specifically 'Christian' names taken from saints and from Biblical characters – a category which, although available to the pre-Conquest English, had been little favoured by them; the Scandinavian names brought to Normandy by the Vikings – in written form often hard to tell from the corresponding Anglo-Scandinavian forms; and, lastly, certain minor categories, such as Breton names, and the Irish ones which the Dublin-based Vikings had brought to Normandy. By-names too fall into several categories, this time semantic as well as etymological. Necessarily, patronymics and metronymics belong to the same classes as baptismal names in general, although often differing in kind from the particular ones they qualify. Residential names may involve either place-names proper, whether English or continental, or farm-names, again either English or continental, such as may not survive on the modern map, or simple topographical forms of the 'Atwood' type. Terms of rank and occupation may occur in either of the two vernaculars or, more commonly, in Latin. As for the most fascinating and most perplexing category, personal and characteristic nicknames, most of those recorded in twelfth-century England are either English or French, although a few fossilized Scandinavian survivals also occur and a few stray specimens that look Flemish; especially when forms are obscure, it is wise to confirm them as far as possible by parallels and analogues – a process emphasizing that most French by-names seen in England echo forms current on the continent, in Normandy and Picardy especially.

Some of the ambiguities dogging name-classification have just been noted; and how rife these are can hardly be overstated. The criteria are of two kinds: distributional and linguistic. The latter are by far the safer: thus, all names beginning with *Ēad-* (by the twelfth century usually spelt *Æd-*) must be English in origin, because in Continental-Germanic dialects the corresponding element is *Aud-, Od-*. Too often, however, evidence comes from distribution alone, as for classing the specifically 'Christian' names as (for the present purpose) 'continental'. With many Germanic name-elements and name-compounds too their apparent distributions form the main grounds for labelling them as either 'English' or 'continental'; and, as not all the extant documents have yet been excerpted and as, even though they had, they could still not have been trusted to have recorded every name-form ever used, labelling based solely on distribution can never be certain, now or in the future. Sometimes distributional and phonological evidence converge, as with 11 *Legarda*: as no feminine second element corresponding to Continental-Germanic *-garda/-gardis* is certainly found in Old English names and as it would in any case have had an initial [j] such as would not have absorbed the final consonant of the preceding *Lēof-* (or the much rarer *Lēod-*), therefore *Legarda* cannot be other than continental. Sometimes the two kinds of evidence clash, as with 52 *Maðelgar*, 4 *Malgar*, and the patronymic 76 *Hunger*, showing different reflexes of the same second element, OE *-gār*/CG *-ger*. For *Hunger* the continental origin the form suggests is likely: the existence of an OE **Hūngār* is little more than conjectural, and the third possible etymon, Scandinavian *Hungeirr*, is very rare.[12] *Maðelgar/Malgar* presents, however, greater problems: Continental-Germanic *Madalger* and the OFr *Malger > Maugier* derived from it are common, whereas in Old English the element *Mæðel-* is one of the rarest and the compound **Mæðelgār* hardly occurs, being no more than tentatively identified in a place-name or two (the reduction to *Mal-*,

---

[12] I am grateful to John Insley for pointing this out.

although not impossible, would be anomalous); on the other hand, the second element of continental *Ma(da)lger* would not normally appear as *-gar* – perhaps it has here been remodelled by analogy with Old English names such as *Ordgār*.[13] Even a name seemingly as archetypically Old English as *Godwine* had its continental counterpart, often spelt *Godoinus*; and it may be the latter that appears here beside a possibly continental patronymic in 112 *Goduinus Gisard*.[14]

These difficulties inherent in the material are at present exacerbated by the inadequacy of the reference-books available. A comprehensive *Old English Onomasticon* had been planned by the late Olof von Feilitzen, but since his death in 1976 the project has lain fallow.[15] Meanwhile, Searle's *Onomasticon Anglo-Saxonicum* is so obsolete that every investigator must compile a personal working-list of pre-Conquest English names from a myriad miscellaneous sources, not least by casting a properly critical eye over every survey so far published by the English Place-Name Society.[16] At present a *Middle English Onomasticon* is hardly conceivable, so vast and so disorganized is the corpus of relevant material. As for Reaney's *Dictionary of British Surnames*, this remains, even in its second edition revised by Professor R.M. Wilson, an heroic but wholly premature essay, valuable mainly for its citations.[17] Likewise, the essential continental sources and analogues are only partly available in usable form; as most studies available happen to concern Picardy rather than Normandy, the continental parallels cited for forms found in England are probably unrepresentative. Thus the would-be anthroponymist must choose between devoting a lifetime merely to laying the foundations of adequate reference-books, in the hope that later generations may

---

[13] For a sceptical note about the currency of this name in England, see Smith, A.H., *The place-names of Gloucestershire*, 4 vols, E[nglish] P[lace-] N[ame] S[ociety] xxxviii–xli, Cambridge 1964–65, i. 222; cf. the even more dubious cases discussed in Mawer, A., and Stenton, F.M., *The place-names of Bedfordshire and Huntingdonshire*, EPNS iii, Cambridge 1926, 264–5, in Smith, A.H., *The place-names of the North Riding of Yorkshire*, EPNS v, Cambridge 1928, 166, and in Cameron, K., *The place-names of Derbyshire*, 3 vols continuously paginated, EPNS xxvii–xxix, Cambridge 1959, 284. For another possible occurrence of the rare name-element *Mæðel-*, see Gover, J.E.B., *et al.*, *The place-names of Wiltshire*, EPNS xvi, Cambridge 1939, 351 (*Mæðelhelm*); cf. also von Feilitzen, Olof, *The pre-Conquest personal names of Domesday Book*, Nomina Germanica iii, Uppsala 1937, *s.n. Madelgrim*.

[14] For *Godoinus*, see Morlet, M.-Th., *Les Noms de personne sur le territoire de l'ancienne Gaule du VIᵉ au XIIᵉ siècle*, 2 vols, Paris 1968–70, i: *Les Noms issus du germanique continental et les créations gallo-germaniques*, 113, and von Feilitzen, *Winton Domesday*, 159. The form *Gisard* offers some difficulty, as, although a Continental-Germanic *Gis-hard* could have existed, the nearest form recorded seems to be the *Gisoard* of the *Polyptyque d'Irminon* (Morlet, *Les Noms . . . gallo-germaniques*, 110); for the modern surname *Gizard*, see Dauzat, A., *Dictionnaire étymologique des noms de famille et prénoms de France*, 2nd edn rev. M.-Th. Morlet, Paris 1969, 294.

[15] See von Feilitzen, Olof, 'Planning a new *Old English Onomasticon*', in Voitl, Herbert, ed., *The study of the personal names of the British Isles: proceedings of a working conference at Erlangen*, Erlangen 1976, 16–39 and discussion 40–2; cf. Professor K. Cameron's obituary notice of Dr von Feilitzen in *The Times* for 27 July 1976.

[16] Cf., for instance, n. 13. See also Insley, John, 'Addenda to the survey of English place-names: personal names in field and minor names', *Journal of the English Place-Name Society* x, 1977–78, 41–72. For Searle's *Onomasticon*, see the paper by von Feilitzen cited in n. 15.

[17] Reaney, P.H., *A dictionary of British surnames* [*DBS*], 2nd edn rev. R.M. Wilson, London 1976. Cf. the comments by George Redmonds and Olof von Feilitzen in *Conference at Erlangen*, 78–80 and 83–4 respectively, and my own in Appendix, *passim*.

complete and then exploit them, or else making amateurish and approximate attempts to show how the discipline might develop if only circumstances were more propitious.

If the second choice is made, then the inevitability of being, in some respects, 'amateurish and approximate' must not entail any further abrogation of scholarly standards. The technique adopted must take full account of dialectal and orthographical problems. Spelling, fundamental to all studies in the vernaculars, is the thorniest aspect of all twelfth-century English documents. With name-material uncertainties are at their worst, because names lack the grammatical and semantic contexts usually allowing identification of words, however oddly spelt, used in connected verse or prose; moreover, the Latin contexts so common afford few clues to the writer's vernacular spelling-systems. Certainly twelfth-century England knew a plurality of such systems. As Old English literature, and the homiletic works especially, continued to be recopied well into the twelfth century, the 'standard' Anglo-Saxon orthographic patterns remained familiar, although now sometimes garbled and always presumably interpreted in terms of current pronunciation.[18] An example of specifically Old English spelling relevant to our present study concerns *c*, which in the vicinity of [i] and [e] usually indicated the assibilated [tʃ], as in *cild* [tʃiːld], modern *child*, so that for [k] before [i] or [e], whether in a foreign word or a native one, some other symbol was desirable. Even more, perhaps, all scribes of this time would have been familiar with the Latin, or rather Franco-Latin, 'powers of the letters' – best deduced not from the highly conventionalized Latin itself, but from some of the earliest Anglo-Norman manuscripts, such as the text of the *Vie de saint Alexis* preserved in the so-called 'St Albans' Psalter. A relevant spelling here is *ch*, which had several values, including [k], for which a number of other spellings also occurred.[19] So the first step in analysing any name-list must be to decode its spellings into conventional 'dictionary' forms; then dialectology takes over. For Sussex the spelling- and sound-systems of the medieval dialects have already been studied, mainly through the personal names and place-names found in documents such as the Lay Subsidy Rolls.[20] A dialect boundary, probably responding to the pattern of medieval woodland as well as to that of the original settlement, approximately coincides with the modern administrative boundary between East and West Sussex.[21] Not surprisingly, the East-Sussex dialect of the Rape of Hastings agreed in certain features, though by no means in all, with Kentish. As Battle itself, like the other Wealden settlements new in the eleventh century, could have

---

[18] See *The Peterborough Chronicle 1070–1154*, 2nd edn, Oxford 1970, esp. lxiii–lxv; also Strang, Barbara M.H., *A history of English*, London 1970, 284–9, 227–30 (the book is in reverse-chronological order).

[19] See: Storey, Christopher, ed., *La Vie de saint Alexis*, Geneva 1968, 46; Waters, E.G.R., ed., *The Anglo-Norman Voyage of St Brendan by Benedeit*, Oxford 1928, 171–2; Ekwall, Eilert, *Early London personal names*, Lund 1947, 195; and von Feilitzen, *Winton Domesday*, 225.

[20] See Rubin, S., *The phonology of the Middle English dialect of Sussex*, Lund Studies in English xxi, 1951. For certain caveats concerning evidence from the Lay Subsidy Rolls, see McClure, Peter, 'Lay Subsidy Rolls and Dialect Phonology', *Acta Bibliothecæ Regiæ Stockholmiensis* xvi (= *Otium et negotium: studies in onomatology and library science presented to Olof von Feilitzen*), 1973, 188–94.

[21] See Rubin, *Dialect*, 14, 224–7, and Mawer, A., and Stenton, F.M., *The place-names of Sussex*, 2 vols continuously paginated, EPNS vi–vii, Cambridge 1929–30, xxvii–xxix; also Ek, K.-G., *The development of OE* ў *and* ēo *in south-eastern Middle English*, Lund Studies in English xlii, 1972, map on 123 (ў < *e*).

had no native dialect of its own, the forms found here may throw light on the settlers' origins.

With all these caveats in mind, we may now turn to the document itself, the rental of c.1110 incorporated into the late-twelfth-century *Chronicle* of Battle Abbey, to see whether the personal names there may reveal anything of value. This is not the first time such an exercise has been tried. In 1967 Maurice Beresford glanced briefly at the occupational terms there.[22] Then, in 1974, Dr Searle, using criteria slightly different from mine, suggested that, whereas those holding outlying plots mostly bore names of insular types and pursued agricultural occupations, those living close beside the Abbey bore names of continental types or else by-names marking them as administrators or skilled craftsmen – a distribution squaring with the general impression that in early-twelfth-century England those enjoying high status either were of immigrant origin or at least followed continental fashions.[23] So far, then, the omens seem modestly favourable for further investigation along similar lines.

Historians complain of knowing too little about medieval townspeople, and especially about the first burgesses of new towns. For origin and status, the most obvious clues lie in by-names, such as some three-quarters of the subjects here display, of one kind or another. Not quite half the by-names are occupational: that is, we know the trades of only some third of the burgesses here (the rest need not all be supposed unskilled, for a man with another sort of by-name or a distinctive baptismal name would be adequately identified without mention of his trade). Mostly the terms are Latinized (*aurifaber, bovarius, bubulcus*, 95 *cannarius, carpentarius* 2x, *clericus, cocus* 3x, 6 *corduanarius, dapifer, dispensator, faber* 2x, *molendinarius, ortolanus*, probably 10 *pionius, pistor* 3x, *porcarius* 2x, *presbiter*, 16 *purgator, textor, secretarius* 2x, *sutor* 3x), but one or two occur in English (1 *Bedel*, and perhaps 77 *Cniht*) and two, towards the end, in French (109 *braceur*, 106 *corueiser*).[24] Incomplete though it is, this list shows Battle to have already been a true 'town', not only in its enjoyment of a quasi-burgage tenure, but also in living by craft and trade.[25] Mostly commonplace, the crafts include a few, such as 'goldsmith', 'bursar' and 'butler', and 'bell-founder' (38 *Ædric qui signa fundebat*), which recall that the town served the Abbey as well as boosting its revenues; and a few presage the importance the leather industry was later to have here.[26] As for the languages in which the terms are set down, these reflect the usages of the scribes rather than that of the townsfolk themselves.[27] For determining the geographical origins of the settlers, *noms d'origine* might have been hoped to provide useful clues, in spite of the suspicion with which some historians regard them; but they prove rare, unexpectedly so, by contrast with their profusion in such documents as the two Winchester surveys.[28] Three link their bearers with places in southern England, two within the *leuga* itself (2 *de Bece*, 104 *de Bodeherstegate*) and one on

---

22 Beresford, *New towns*, 194–5.

23 Searle, *Battle Abbey*, 71–6. Cf. the similar analysis in Biddle, *Winton Domesday*, 463–4, 474–6.

24 Several of the Latin terms (such as 6 *corduanarius* and 10 *pionius*) are French ones only lightly disguised, and may indeed provide useful datings for French lexicography.

25 On Battle's somewhat anomalous status, owing to its lack of a borough charter, see Searle, *Battle Abbey*, 79–88.

26 See Searle, *Battle Abbey*, 299–303.

27 Cf. 'Some early Canterbury surnames', above 207–20, esp. 208.

28 For a sceptical view of *noms d'origine*, see Beresford, *New towns*, 193–4. Richard McKinley has recently shown that some apparent *noms d'origine* must in fact have been mere nicknames (*The surnames of Oxfordshire*, London 1977, 203–6).

Battle's Kentish estates (35 *de Dengemar¹*); and one remains unidentified (18 *de Hauena*).[29] Only one links its bearer with the continent: 51 *de Cirisi*, which, ambiguous though it is, must refer to one of the several French places called Cerisy or Cérisy.[30] Such paucity of *noms d'origine* contrasts with their plentifulness among the overseas settlers here in the thirteenth century.[31] Another by-name, 34 *Gilebertus extraneus*, vaguely labelling its bearer as 'foreign', seems at the same time to imply that neither of the other Gilberts (9, 63) was such. Indeed, almost all by-names, if rightly examined, will throw some light on social background. Of the probable patronymics and metronymics, up to ten may be insular (5 *Dot*, 7 *Gotcild* – if not a nickname, 12 *Trewæ* – if not a nickname, 14 *filius Colsuein*, 28 *filius Siflet*, 31 *Hert* – if not a nickname, 62 *filius Fareman* – if not a nickname, 83 *Tipæ*, 103 *Hecæ*), whereas only two at most seem continental (108 *Ælfuine Turpin* and probably 112 *Godwine Gisard*), and they qualify what look like insular baptismal names.[32] A somewhat different cultural balance seems implied by the characteristic nicknames; for, beside the many English ones (7 *Gotcild* – if not a patronymic, 12 *Trewæ* – if not a patronymic, 27 *Grei*, perhaps 29 *Gris*, 31 *Hert* – if not a patronymic, 41 *Cild*, 53 *Stigerop*, 70 *Gest* – if not a patronymic, 77 *Cniht* – if not occupational, 80 *Brembel*, 93 *Abbat*, 94 *Crul*, 107 *Barhc*), there occur nearly as many French ones, mostly well paralleled in continental records (21 *Pinel*, 25 *Coche[t]*, perhaps 29 *Gris*, 43 *Franc enfant*, 81 *Barate*, 90 & 100 *Peche(t*, 101 *Cocard*, 105 & 111 *Genester*) and, again, as with the patronymics, sometimes qualifying insular-looking baptismal names. In so far as this evidence allows of any conclusion at all, it suggests a community predominantly English, yet with a tinge of bilingual cosmopolitanism.

Can the baptismal names help to clear the view? Notorious for capricious relationships with the nationalities of their bearers, they might be feared to offer the social historian testimony even less reliable than that of by-names. Yet, misleading as an isolated name often is about its bearer's 'race' or nationality, in the mass names cannot but reflect the cultural influences at work in the group concerned. Here, analysis of the just under a hundred men's names shows the dominant elements to be Old English and Continental Germanic; Scandinavian forms appear only in a patronymic or two (14 *Colsuein*, 62 *Fareman* – both among the most widespread of such forms, seen both at Winchester and in Devon place-names – and perhaps 70 *Gest*), forms identifiable as Normanno-Scandinavian being notably absent; the specifically 'Christian' names are only a little less sparsely represented.[33] The paucity of Scandinavian forms not only

29 For the surname *Haven*, *DBS* suggests derivation from the common noun; cf. the possibility mentioned below 232 that some settlers at Battle may have hailed from the ports of Pevensey, Hastings or Rye.

30 See *Dictionnaire des communes* (listing eight possibilities) and Dauzat, A., and Rostaing, Ch., *Dictionnaire étymologique des noms de lieux en France*, Paris 1963, 162. One possibility is Cerisy-la-Forêt (*dép.* Manche), as some early records show *Cirisiacus* beside the commoner *Cerisiacus* (see Adigard des Gautries, Jean, 'Les noms de lieux de la Manche attestés entre 911 et 1066', *Annales de Normandie* i, 1951, 9–44, esp. 21; also Fauroux, M., ed., *Recueil des actes des ducs de Normandie de 911 à 1066*, Caen 1961, 194).

31 Cf. Searle, *Battle Abbey*, 121, 272, 471.

32 For *Gisard*, see n. 14. For *Colsuein* and *Fareman*, see n. 33. For the other forms, see Appendix *ad locos*. One form, 102 Ælfuine *Hachet*, remains entirely dubious, see Appendix.

33 For *Colsuein* and *Fareman*, see von Feilitzen, *Winton Domesday*, 153, 157, and also, for instance, Gover, J.E.B., *et al.*, *The place-names of Devon*, 2 vols continuously paginated, EPNS viii–ix, Cambridge 1931–32, 687; cf. Fellows Jensen, G., *Scandinavian personal names in*

contrasts with the name-patterns of the old Danelaw, whether at Newark or even at Colchester, but even undercuts the 4% seen in the *TRE* tenants at Winchester; it agrees, however, with Mrs Smart's findings about Sussex moneyers' names of the pre-Cnutian period.[34] About Sussex this says little new; but about the English settlers at Battle it confirms the tentative deduction from the few *noms d'origine* that most of them were local men, southerners, rather than from the East Midlands or further afield. Dialect also bears on this question: an abbey founded in a district previously uninhabited would have needed models for its vernacular usage, whether its own English recruits or its new burgesses; the dialect here, south-eastern without being specifically Kentish, confirms the local origin of most settlers.[35] That the immigrants' own versions of their names were respected is implied by western 40 *Burnulf* alongside the commoner south-eastern forms such as 67 *Chebel* and 98 *Cheneward*; and this gives the latter's predominance added force. The paucity of 'Christian' forms, amounting to no more than some 7% of the 'continental' names here, agrees with the 6% or so in the earlier Winchester survey (perhaps a shade later than our Battle list).[36] As the twelfth century saw the ratio of 'Christian' forms steadily increasing, both on the Continent and in England (by 1148 the Winchester figure has risen to over 16%), the low figure at Battle confirms the early date which Dr Searle assigns to the rental.[37] The main interest must, however, lie in the balance between the two main categories, insular and continental. As far as the ambiguities allow us to judge, continental forms here account for almost 40% of men's names, whether reckoned by stock or by frequency of use – a figure whose significance can be gauged only by comparison. The earlier Winchester survey shows such forms constituting nearly 60% of the name-stock and accounting for between 65% and 70% of occurrences: great as the discrepancy seems between this distribution and the Battle one, it proves easily explicable, because the Battle list deals mainly with actual householders (the persistence of certain surnames among later burgesses modestly confirms that the names belong to residents, not to property middlemen), whereas many Winchester entries concern Norman magnates renting plots for investment.[38] Another survey approximately contemporaneous is 'Burton B', where continental forms constitute less than 20% of the men's names: this opposite discrepancy too may be at least partly explained by the status of those listed – at Burton

---

Lincolnshire and Yorkshire, Copenhagen 1968, 179–80, 79–80. Only one DB instance of *Gest* is noted, in Wiltshire.

[34] At Newark in the 1170s Scandinavian forms account for some 60% of occurrences of insular names, and among the king's burgesses at Colchester *TRW* for some 10% (*Domesday Book seu Liber Censualis Willelmi Primi Regis Angliae, &c.*, 4 vols, London 1783–1816, ii. 104r–106r). For pre-Cnutian Sussex, see Smart, 'Moneyers', 261 (no Scandinavian names at Hastings; one at Lewes).

[35] The most marked south-eastern trait is the appearance of *e* for OE *ȳ*, as in 67 *Chebel*, 98 *Cheneward*, and 104 *Bodeherste* (see Rubin, *Dialect*, 83–120, cf. von Feilitzen, *Winton Domesday*, 223–4). The almost regular *e* for OE *ēo* tells against south-western influence (10 *Dering*, 12 *Trewœ*, 31 *Hert*, 64 *Lefuine*, 69 *Leffelm*, 82 *Lefflet*, but 40 *Burnulf*); cf. von Feilitzen, *Winton Domesday*, 224. In the abbey itself south-eastern tendencies might have been reinforced by the drafting here in the 1090s of monks from Canterbury (see Searle, *Battle Abbey*, 28), but specifically Kentish spellings seem not to occur.

[36] See von Feilitzen, *Winton Domesday*, 185 (table 7), also 184 (table 6).

[37] For the dating, see n. 3. For the increasing popularity of 'Christian' names, see, for instance, Le Pesant, M., 'Les noms de personne à Evreux du XIIᵉ au XIVᵉ siècles', *Annales de Normandie* vi, 1956, 47–74, esp. 50–1.

[38] See von Feilitzen, *Winton Domesday*, 189.

peasants, not burgesses.[39] A like explanation may be proffered for the discrepancy between the almost 40% at Battle and the mere 5% found in the Bury St Edmunds survey datable no more than a dozen years earlier, if that.[40] The question needs pursuing, however; and so, as no other contemporaneous lists of names seem available, comparison will have to be risked with material from nearly two generations later, from the 1160s, that is. A Canterbury rental of that date shows continental forms accounting for some 75% of the occurrences of men's names, beside some 65% in the roughly contemporaneous list of Canterbury 'votaries of St Anselm' – the latter being perhaps on average older than the Christ Church tenants, or of more modest condition.[41] As all our mid-twelfth-century records show an accelerating shift from insular names to continental ones, does the almost 40% at Battle c.1110 seem high beside this average of some 70% at Canterbury about fifty years later, and that in one of the most cosmopolitan of cities? The question is more insistently raised by the 1166 Pipe Roll and its list of citizens of King's Lynn, amongst whose names continental forms amount to little more than 50% and whose patronymics and metronymics are predominantly insular.[42] Even though the men of Lynn were (as is suggested elsewhere) the senior merchants of the day, born in the 1120s or earlier, even then a difference of hardly more than 10% between the incidence of continental forms in their names and that two whole generations earlier at Battle seems puzzling, and all the more so because the Lynn patronymics and metronymics imply fashions of the 1120s notably less advanced than those of Battle c.1110. These discrepancies might be lightly dismissed by supposing each district to have had its own rate of change; but that seems facile. Perhaps the discrepancy between Battle and Lynn was, paradoxically, due to what the two had in common; for, as both were, in their different ways, late-eleventh-century new towns, with 'artificial' populations, the different name-patterns might reflect different sources of recruitment, Battle's settlers being more strongly tinged with continental influences.[43] Thus, the baptismal names, albeit so much more indirectly and indeed uncertainly, are pointing the same way as the by-names did: to a modest cosmopolitanism about the early days of Battle.

All the figures, it must be reiterated, refer to names, and all the deductions to cultural influences; neither refer to individual men or to their nationalities. And what such material can ever tell us is limited – perhaps no more than the stamps on incoming mail could tell about the professional, social, and familial relationships of a household. Of its nature, name-evidence cannot, except by some happy accident, answer the

---

[39] See Bridgeman, C.G.O., ed., 'The Burton Abbey twelfth-century surveys', *Collections for a History of Staffordshire edited by the William Salt Archaeological Society 1916*, London 1918, 209–310, esp. 212–47.

[40] See Douglas, D.C., ed., *Feudal Documents from the abbey of Bury St Edmunds*, London 1932, 25–44; for the date, see xlix, but cf. Galbraith, V.H., 'The making of Domesday Book', *EHR* lvii, 1942, 161–77, esp. 168 n. 1, where he suggests 'the early part of Henry I's reign'.

[41] Rental B in Urry, *Canterbury*; also Urry, W., 'Saint Anselm and his cult at Canterbury', *Spicilegium Beccense* i, 1959, 571–93, esp. 585.

[42] *The Great Roll of the Pipe for 12 Henry II, A.D. 1165–1166*, Pipe Roll Society ix, 1888, 21–9. Cf. my comments in 'First Three Laws', above 77–83.

[43] For Lynn, see Dorothy Owen, 'Bishop's Lynn: the first century of a new town?', *Proceedings of the Battle Conference on Anglo-Norman Studies* ii (1980 for 1979), 141–53 and 196–7, and, in due course, the introduction to her forthcoming edition of the town's early records [[*The making of King's Lynn: a documentary survey*, Records of Social and Economic History, New Series ix, London 1984, 1–65]] (superseding the brief remarks by Beresford, *New towns*, 467–8).

central question historians ask about recruits to medieval towns: what manner of men they were, whether craftsmen, or minor gentry, yeomen, or the younger sons of burgesses elsewhere, itinerant traders, or fugitive villeins. As with the stamps, all it can illuminate, and that dimly, are geographical origins. The Battle householders' names show most of them as English, native to East Sussex and speakers of its dialect. But there is also that admixture of continental forms: not only the common baptismal names, such as *William* and *Robert*, which in post-Conquest England spread so rapidly through all regions and classes, but also French sobriquets such as 43 *Franc enfant* and 101 *Cocard*. Continental baptismal names were, as the example of 28 *Rotbert filius Siflet* makes clear, already being adopted by English people; and Englishmen might equally have picked up and copied the sobriquets of French immigrants they met. Yet, whether or not borne here by Englishmen, such names imply some French presence, either in Battle itself or in the places from which the settlers had come; for, among populations in the main illiterate, names can have travelled only on people's backs. And, to judge by comparison with name-patterns elsewhere, for Battle the French presence in the background seems to have been substantial. Moreover, the occasional pairings of insular forms with continental ones, such as 10 *Dering pionius* and 108 *Ælfuine Turpin*, imply some eagerness to merge the two cultures.

A side issue remains for comment. So far only men's names have been studied, the eight or nine women's names being disregarded because observation elsewhere in twelfth-century England has shown that women's names follow fashions of their own.[44] In any case, the sample is not only too small to represent a female population of some three hundred individuals or more, but also too small for safe expression in percentages (thus, the solitary Scandinavian name – 39 *Gunnild*, one of the commonest – represents over 15% of the insular forms recorded, out of all keeping with the findings elsewhere of lower ratios of Scandinavian forms among women's names).[45] For what it is worth, the ratio of continental forms to insular ones amounts at most – that is, if the two *Emmas* are taken as separate individuals – to between 30% and 35%, against nearly 40% for the men's names. Some discrepancy between the names of the sexes is regular in twelfth-century England; the one here might, however, be slighter than usual and, moreover, the tiny stock of names includes not only the common *Emma* but the rarer 11 *Legarda*. Without dwelling too much on the dubious statistics, we may ask whether name-patterns at Battle might have shown some idiosyncrasy. Then as now, new towns must have begun with abnormal population-structures, for the settlers must have arrived in the early prime of their lives, unencumbered by elderly relatives. Even by 1110 Battle may still not have had a normal age-stratification, because the growth from a score of households in 1086 to over five score some twenty years later implies continuing new settlement. There is no foolproof way to investigate age-stratification through the names recorded, but the high proportion of continental names would be in keeping with a population young as well as subject to fair French influence. Furthermore, the original settlers must have arrived mainly as couples, for, in a community so new, lone men would have found few potential wives. In so far as the regular discrepancy

---

[44] See 'Women's names', *passim*.

[45] For Scandinavian forms among English women's names, see 'First Three Laws', above 82–3. The name *Gunnild*, borne by one of Harold Godwinesson's daughters, appears in Sussex *TRE* and is also one of the few Scandinavian personal names to have been identified in Sussex field-names (see von Feilitzen, *Pre-Conquest personal names*, 277, and Mawer and Stenton, *Sussex*, 564).

between the names of the sexes in twelfth-century England is attributable to a large surplus of men among the Norman incomers, settlements of a new town by couples might have warped the name-pattern by reducing that discrepancy. The sample is, however, inadequate to confirm whether such was the case here.

One metronym occurs: 28 *Rotbert filius Siflet*. At first sight unremarkable, this begins to raise a demographic question when set beside the profusion of such forms in the Pipe Roll list of Lynn burgesses (obvious metronyms there are *Alfled, Alfware* 2x, *Alswed, Ælveve, Edilde*, to which may be added the less clear short-forms, *Biffæ, Duvæ, Givæ, Godæ, Munnæ, Tettæ, Tittæ*). To suppose all bearers of metronyms to have been illegitimate would be naïve; yet some of them may have been so, especially if post-Conquest English society were somewhat unstable. The question these forms therefore raise is whether new towns may have attracted the illegitimate, who at home might have had to be content with inferior positions and prospects.

Speculation grows apace – can its validity be checked? The suggestion that at Battle most settlers had come from elsewhere in East Sussex chimes both with the general observation that recruits to medieval English towns often came from near at hand and with the specific one that Wealden assarters chiefly hailed from the coastal towns and villages of Sussex.[46] Indeed, 'burgess' stock for Battle might have come from the towns already existing on the coast, Pevensey, Hastings, and Rye.[47] Likewise, a French presence here would agree with the well-recorded pattern of post-Conquest French immigration into so many other English towns.[48]

Indeed, even though full background documentation will remain impossible until more of the surviving archives have been published, the tentative findings from our name-evidence are amply confirmed by the very *Chronicle* into which the rental was copied. Two contingents of founding monks, nine in all, had been brought from Marmoutier, near Tours; and even three-quarters of a century later the continental connections of the house were well enough remembered to be urged in an admittedly tendentious political speech.[49] During the building of the abbey cross-Channel commerce had been constant. Because at first the locality seemed to offer no suitable stone, the Conqueror himself gave funds for bringing supplies from Normandy and ships 'quibus a Cadomensi uico lapidum copia ad opus propositum transueheretur'.[50] For overseeing the work 'peritissimi . . . artifices' were assembled from far and wide and, although exactly whence is nowhere specified, Normandy and France might have been laid under contribution.[51] Given this background, it seems natural that the *Chronicle*

---

[46] For Wealden assarters, see Searle, *Battle Abbey*, 46–8, and cf. Darby, H.C., and Campbell, E.M.J., *The Domesday geography of South-East England*, Cambridge 1962, 420–1, 477 *et seq.*

[47] Cf. above n. 29, and see Darby and Campbell, *South-East England*, 438, 463, 469, 471–2, also Beresford, *New towns*, 494–6. For the general tendency of medieval towns to recruit from near at hand, see Reynolds, *English medieval towns*, 70, and cf. McKinley, *Surnames of Oxfordshire*, 105, and McClure, Peter, 'Patterns of migration in the late Middle Ages: the evidence of English place-name surnames', *Economic History Review*, 2nd ser. xxxii, 1979, 167–82.

[48] See *Domesday Book*, i. 52r, 56r, 179r, 189r, 252r, 298r, and ii. 118r; also [Stevenson, W.H., ed.] *Records of the borough of Nottingham, &c.*, i: *1155–1399*, London and Nottingham 1882, 116, 124–6 (*in burgo francisco*) and Platt, C., *Medieval Southampton*, London 1973, 7 (*French Street*). Cf. Le Patourel, John, *The Norman Empire*, Oxford 1976, 38–40; also 'French connections', 38–40.

[49] Searle, *Chronicle*, 178. Cf. *eadem, Battle Abbey*, 34–5.

[50] Searle, *Chronicle*, 44.

[51] Searle, *Chronicle*, 44.

notes 'overseas' (presumably, that is, French) elements both among the first farm-tenants and among the first burgesses:

> In uilla uero de Bello et per totam leugam . . . quamplurimi ex comprouincialibus, et nonnulli etiam ex transmarinis partibus asciti, . . . sibi mansiones iam parabant . . .[52]
>
> Igitur leuga circumiacente in predicti loci proprietatem hoc modo redacta, et iam ecclesie etiam proficiente fabrica, accitis hominibus quampluribus ex comprouin-tialibus quidem multis, ex transmarinis etiam partibus nonnullis, ceperunt fratres qui fabrice operam dabant circa ambitum eiusdem loci certis dimensionibus mansiones singulis distribuere . . .[53]

Exactly whence on the Continent the new burgesses 'from overseas' may have hailed is never stated, and the paucity of *noms d'origine* does nothing to assuage our curiosity.[54] The crucial point is that the *Chronicle* confirms our main deductions from the name-evidence: that there might have been a fair French presence here; and that the English majority had come mainly from districts near-by, 'ex comprouincialibus . . . partibus'. In the long run, for all the superficial eagerness to pick up fashionable French names, the latter strain proved dominant: in the later twelfth century, so the *Chronicle* notes, the accomplished Abbot Odo preached 'ad edificationem audientium nunc Latine nunc Gallico sermone, frequenter uero ad edificationem rudis uulgi lingua materna publice pronuntiabat' – and in this context the 'mother-tongue' Odo shared with the unculti-vated mob can only have been English.[55]

Nevertheless, our evidence, both from the personal names of all kinds and from the *Chronicle*, all points the same way: to a substantial, even influential French minority in Battle, among the burgesses as well as among the monks. What then of the local place-names? Do they show any unusual French element? If not, that will hardly undermine our argument, because place-names are so much less ready than personal names to reflect minor or short-lived influences; that very inflexibility will, of course, enhance the significance of any French place-names that may occur. The name *Battle* is itself purely French, recalling how a Norman king settled monks from Touraine here in thanksgiving for his victory over the English. Did French influence leave any further marks? Unfortunately, the English Place-Name Society's Sussex volumes, compiled though they were by two of its most distinguished scholars, date from its pioneering days, before the analytic schemes had been fully worked out, when prehistoric ele-ments attracted more attention than medieval accretions, and when farm- and field-names were treated less thoroughly than they are nowadays. Nonetheless, names collected from around Battle include some significant forms. From the mid-thirteenth century at least there has been a *Caldbec* Hill close by.[56] Apparently a Scandinavian

---

[52] Searle, *Battle Abbey*, 61 n. 51; *eadem, Chronicle*, 76.

[53] Searle, *Battle Abbey*, 69 n. 2; *eadem, Chronicle*, 50.

[54] Although the absence of Normanno-Scandinavian names raises the question whether the link with Marmoutier may have attracted settlers from the Loire Valley, no special similarities of name seem to support this (cf., for instance, Laurain, E., ed., *Cartulaire manceau de Marmou-tier*, 2 vols, Laval 1945).

[55] Searle, *Chronicle*, 306, 308.

[56] Mawer and Stenton, *PNSussex*, 496–7. For a Norman example, see Adigard des Gautries, J., 'Les noms de lieux de la Seine-Maritime attestés entre 911 et 1066', *Annales de Normandie* vi, 1956, 119–34 and 223–44, esp. 236.

form for 'cold stream' and as such inexplicable in Sussex except as an implantation from Normandy, where several such forms occur, this might have arisen in either of two ways: from the *nom d'origine* of some immigrant land-holder (the unpublished archives may one day show whether or not this is likely); or as a Normanno-Scandinavian name for the cold spring said to rise there. Not noted at all by the Place-Name Society is the field poetically named from the *Malfossed, Malfossé, Maufossé*.[57] Above all, there is the name *Mountjoy, Montjoie*, given to the little township's new suburb developed during the thirteenth century – even when its etymological complications are disregarded, a name of manifold evocations.[58] As a French war-cry, it seems to recall how a battle inspired the town's foundation. The site on which it was bestowed is hilly, and, whatever the true etymology, some contemporaries certainly understood the term as 'hill of rejoicing', 'Mons Gaudii', 'Mons Gaudis'. Moreover, the name reappears elsewhere among medieval new towns, for instance, in Gascony.[59] Although by no means the only place-names in Sussex to show Norman-French influence, these forms may nonetheless confirm the cultural influence we have surmised from the external history of town and abbey as well as from the personal names.

'Confirmation' has indeed been the key-note of this study, which cannot pretend to have brought to light much not deducible from other sources. At the outset, however, it was made clear that the underlying purpose was not so much to illuminate the early history of Battle as to test the technique; and with that in mind it was essential to take a topic on which ample independent evidence survived. In the event, findings from the purely onomastic study have proved wholly in keeping with those from the narrative sources; and to that extent the technique may be claimed to have vindicated itself. Whether or not it will ever be deemed reliable enough to use in contexts where such cross-checks from other evidence are not available remains to be seen. Meanwhile, testing it has for a while concentrated attention on one of the less-studied facets of the community at Battle: its cultural affiliations.

APPENDIX: HOUSEHOLDERS AT BATTLE c.1110

The list is transcribed as closely as possible from BL Cotton ms. Domitian A II, fols 16r–18r, but without note of erasures or of apparent changes of hand. Expansions are italicized. Emendations are kept for the commentary. Letter-variants other than *u/v* are not, however, reproduced; tagged ę is transcribed as *æ*, for which the lower-case form does not otherwise appear (of the OE letters only capital Æ is regularly used here; although ð occurs, often it is replaced by *d*).

[57] See: ms. Domitian A II, f. 10r; Searle, *Chronicle*, 15–16, 38; *eadem, Battle Abbey*, 131, 146, 147; *eadem* and Ross, B., eds, *The cellarers' rolls of Battle Abbey 1275–1513*, Sussex Record Society lxv, Lewes 1967, 48.
[58] See Mawer and Stenton, *PNSussex* 498; also Searle, *Battle Abbey*, 121–2, 152. For the meanings of the term and a bibliography, see Tobler, A., and Lommatzsch, E., *Altfranzösisches Wörterbuch*, Berlin and later Wiesbaden, 1925–, *s.v.* monjoie. See also Rohlfs, G., '*Munjoie, ço est l'enseigne Carlun* (querelles d'une étymologie)', *Revue de linguistique romane* xxxviii, 1974, 444–52.
[59] See Beresford, *New towns*, 634; cf. Dauzat and Rostaing, *Dictionnaire*, 466–7 (examples include one in Manche).

To keep the commentary within bounds, the commoner OE and CG names are not annotated and the following special abbreviations are used:

Amiens	Morlet, M.-Th., 'Les noms de personne à Amiens au XIVe siècle', *Bulletin philologique et historique 1960*, Paris 1961, 527–52.
Arras	Berger, R., ed., *Le Nécrologe de la confrérie des jongleurs et des bourgeois d'Arras (1194–1361)*, 2 vols, Arras 1963–70 [cited by year].
BAB	Searle, E., *Lordship and community: Battle Abbey and its banlieu, 1066–1538*, Toronto 1974.
Beauvais	Morlet, M.-Th., 'Les noms de personne à Beauvais au XIVe siècle', *Bulletin philologique et historique 1955 & 1956*, Paris 1957, 295–309.
BT (*Supp*)	Bosworth, J., and Toller, T.N., *An Anglo-Saxon dictionary*, with *Supplement*, 2 vols, Oxford 1898–1921.
Canterbury	'Some early Canterbury surnames', above 207–20.
CBA	Searle, E., ed., *The chronicle of Battle Abbey*, Oxford 1980.
CG	Continental Germanic.
DBS	Reaney, P.H., *A dictionary of British surnames*, 2nd edn rev. R.M. Wilson, London 1976.
Dialect	Rubin, S., *The phonology of the Middle English dialect of Sussex*, Lund Studies in English xxi, 1951.
Eu	Morlet, M.-Th., 'Les noms de personne à Eu du XIIIe au XVe siècle', *Revue internationale d'onomastique* xi, 1959, 131–48, 174–82, and xii, 1960, 62–70, 137–48, 205–19.
f.	feminine.
France I	Dauzat, A., *Les Noms de famille de France*, 3rd edn rev. M.-Th. Morlet, Paris 1977.
France II	Dauzat, A., *Dictionnaire étymologique des noms de famille et prénoms de France*, 2nd edn rev. M.-Th. Morlet, Paris 1969.
Gaule	Morlet, M.-Th., *Les Noms de personne sur le territoire de l'ancienne Gaule du VIe au XIIe siècle*, 2 vols, Paris 1968–72, i: *Les Noms issus du germanique continental et les créations gallo-germaniques*.
Haute Picardie	Morlet, M.-Th., *Les Noms de personne en Haute Picardie aux XIIIe, XIVe, XVe siècles*, Amiens 1967.
L	Latin (usually of 'Christian' name).
London	Ekwall, E., *Early London personal names*, Lund 1947.
Lynn	(With Dorothy Owen) 'Lexicographical notes from King's Lynn', *Norfolk Archaeology* xxxvii, 1978, 56–69.
m.	metronymic.
masc.	masculine.
ME	Middle English.
MED	Kurath, H., *et alii*, *Middle English dictionary*, Ann Arbor 1954– .
n.	nickname.
NOB	von Feilitzen, Olof, 'Some unrecorded Old and Middle English personal names', *Namn och Bygd* xxxiii, 1945, 68–98.
o.	occupational term.
OE	Old English (= Anglo-Saxon).
OEB	Tengvik, G., *Old English Bynames*, Nomina Germanica iv, Uppsala 1938.
OFr	Old French.
p.	patronymic.
PN[*County*]	Publications of the English Place-Name Society.

PNDB   von Feilitzen, Olof, *The pre-Conquest personal names of Domesday Book*, Nomina Germanica iii, Uppsala 1937.

S   Scandinavian.

SN   von Feilitzen, Olof, 'Some Old English uncompounded personal names and by-names', *Studia Neophilologica* xl, 1968, 5–16.

SPLY   Fellows Jensen, G., *Scandinavian personal names in Lincolnshire and Yorkshire*, Copenhagen 1968.

SSR   Hudson, W., ed., *The three earliest Subsidies for the county of Sussex in the years 1296, 1327, 1332*, Sussex Record Society x, 1910.

t.   toponymic.

TL   Tobler, A., and Lommatzsch, E., *Altfranzösisches Wörterbuch*, Berlin, later Wiesbaden 1925– .

UCPN   Redin, M., *Studies on uncompounded personal names in Old English*, Diss. Uppsala 1919.

Winchester   von Feilitzen, Olof, 'The personal names and bynames of the Winton Domesday', in Biddle, M., ed., *Winchester in the early Middle Ages*, Oxford 1976, 143–229.

*   hypothetical form.

fol. 16r

1. Brihtwini [OE *Beorhtwine*] . . . Bedel [o.]
    Bedel: Probably the Kentish and ESussex reflex of OE *bȳdel* (BT *Supp s.v.*; cf. *MED s.v. bidel*, also *DBS s.n. Beadel*), with the characteristic *e* < [y] (see *Dialect*, 83–120, also above 226 n. 21 and 229 n. 35), rather than OFr *bedel* (TL *s.v.*; also *France II* 35).

2. Rei*n*berti [CG] de Bece
    Bece: a farm within the *leuga* (*BAB* 60, 62–3; *PNSussex* 501). The family remained dominant throughout C13 (*BAB* 115, 185–6, 267 n. 2; *SSR* 18).

3. Wulm*e*ri [OE *Wulfmǣr*]

4. Malgari [? CG/OE] fabri
    Cf. 52 *Maðelgari* and see above 224 and 225 n. 13.

5. Ælurici [OE *Ælfrīc*] Dot [p.; OE *Dodd* – see *PNDB* 224–5, cf. *DBS s.n. Dod*; but *PNDB* 226 suggests a genuine form *Dot*]
    Dot: for *-t* instead of *-d*, see *Winchester* 225, and cf. 28 *Siflet*, 82 *Lefflet* < OE *-flǣd*.

6. Will*e*lmi [CG] corduanarii [o.; see *OEB* 248, *Winchester* 201, and *MED s.v. cordewaner*]
    corduanarii: the surname *Cordewaner* found here later (*BAB* 118 n. 37) need not belong to the same family, because leather-workers abounded in Battle (*BAB* 268, 299–303).

7. Æduardi [OE *Ēadweard*] Gotcild [n. or p.; OE *Gŏdcild* – cf. *DBS s.n. Goodchild*]

8. Rad*u*lfi [CG] Dvcgi
    Dvcgi: perhaps miscopied from a Latinization of ME *dwergh* 'dwarf' (*MED s.v.*) as *Duergus*, *Du^lgus*. Cf., however, *DBS s.n. Dodge*.

9. Gileb*e*rti [CG] textoris
    textoris: the surname *Webbe* occurs in 1296 (*SSR* 17).

10. Deringi [OE *Dēoring*] pionii [o.; OFr/L]
    pionii: Latinization of the OFr by-name *Pion* (*Haute Picardie* 140, cf. *France II* 486; cf. TL *s.v. pëon* 'foot-soldier').

11. Legardæ [CG *Liutgard* f. – *Gaule* 159, *Winchester* 164; see above 224]

12. Ælfuini [OE *Ælfwine*] Trewæ [n. or, more probably, p.; OE *Trēowa* – UCPN 79, *Winchester* 174, cf. *DBS s.n. True*]
    Trewæ: the surname persists (*BAB* 114 n. 25, 141 n. 29).

13. Godieue [OE *Gōdg(i)efu* f.]
14. Goduini [OE *Gōdwine*] filii Colsuein [p.; S *Kolsveinn* – *SPLY* 179–80, see also *London* 79 and above 228 and 228–9 n. 33]
15. Goduini [OE] coci
16. Ædvardi [OE] purgatoris
    purgatoris: sense uncertain, see *CBA* 53 n. 5.
17. Rotb*erti* [CG] Molendinarii
18. Rotb*erti* [CG] de Hauena [t.; see above 228 and n. 29]
19. Selaf [OE *Sǣlāf*] bovarii
20. Wulurici [OE *Wulfrīc*] Aurifabri
    Aurifabri: the surname *Goldsmyth* appears here later (*SSR* 205, 317).
21. Wille*lm*i [CG] Pinel [n. or t.; OFr *pinel* 'small pine-tree']
    Pinel: an OFr by-name very common in England (see *OEB* 369); opinion seems divided as to whether it refers to residence (*Haute Picardie* 69) or stature (*DBS s.n. Pinnell*).
22. La*mb*erti [CG] sutoris
23. Ordrici [OE *Ordrīc*] porcarii
24. Sevugel [OE *Sǣfugol* – *Winchester* 171] cochec
    cochec: probably a mistake for *cochet* (TL *s.v.*), a diminutive of *coq* and a common OFr by-name (*Amiens* 551, *Eu* xii 216, *Haute Picardie* 215, cf. *France I* 198–9 and *France II* 145). As Sevugel held at least two plots (24 and 25), possibly four (also 56 and 57), the sense 'coq de village' might fit. (The suggestions in *DBS s.n. Cockin* are to be disregarded.)

fol. 16v
26. Blachem*anni* [OE *Blǣcmann*] bubulci
27. Wille*lm*i [CG] grei [n.; OE *grǣg* 'grey-coloured']
    grei: the exact sense is uncertain, as OE *grǣg* has two secondary senses: (a) 'badger', a possible nickname, as with OFr *taisson*; and (b) 'grey fur', applicable either to a furrier or to an ostentatious dresser (see *MED s.vv. grei* adj., n. (1) and n. (2)).
28. Rotb*erti* [CG] filii Siflet [m.; OE *Sigeflǣd* f.]
29. Sewardi [OE *Sǣweard*] Gris [n.; ?]
    Gris: ambiguous (see *DBS s.n. Grice*), involving either: (a) the ME loan from S *gris* 'pig(let)' (see *MED s.v. grīs* n. (1)); or (b) OFr *gris* 'grey' (see *France I* 186, *France II* 308).
30. Ælurici [OE] dispensatoris
31. Wulfuini [OE *Wulfwine*] hert [n. or, more probably, p.; OE *Heort* – *SN* 8, cf. *PNSussex* 555]
33. Lefui [OE *Lēofwīg*] Nvc
    Nvc: so far unexplained; perhaps for *Not* < OE *hnott* 'bald' (see *NOB* 83), or for *nute* < OE *hnutu* 'nut' (cf. *DBS s.n. Nutt*).
34. Gileb*erti* [CG] ext*r*anei
35. Ælvrici [OE] Dengemar^l
    Dengemar^l: Dengemarsh, Kent, in Battle's manor of Wye (*BAB* 23 &c.)
36. Benedicti [L] Dapiferi
37. Mauricii [L]
38. Ædrici [OE *Ēadrīc*] *qui* signa fundebat
    fundebat: on the tense, see *CBS* 55 n. 6.
39. Gunnild [S *Gunnildr* f. – *SPLY* 114–16, see also above 231 n. 45]
40. Burnulfi [OE *Beornwulf*] carpentarii
    Burn-: a rare example, for this list, of western *u* for 'standard' OE *eo* by breaking (see *Dialect*, 192, 198–204).

41. Æilrici [OE *Æðelrīc*] cild [n.; OE *cild* – see *London* 144–5, *Winchester* 209, and *DBS s.n. Child*]
42. Æilnodi [OE *Æðelnōð*] sutoris
43. Francenfant [n.; OFr *franc* + *enfant*]

    Although no exact continental parallel has yet been noted, cf. *Franc homme* (*Eu* xii 214, *Haute Picardie* 192, cf. *France II* 266) and *Bo(i)n enfant* (*Arras* 1347, cf. 1276); also the English *Freebairn* (*DBS s.n.*)
44. Ælduini [OE *Ealdwine*] coci
46. Emmæ [CG *Emma* f.]
47. Ælstrildis [OE *Ēastorhild* f. – *NOB* 78–9] nonnæ

    Ælstr-: read *Æstr-*, the *-l-* being either repeated from 44 *Æl-* or anticipated from the next syllable.

    nonnæ: n. rather than o. (in spite of *DBS s.n. Nunn*), or perhaps more probably a mistaken Latinization of a p. *Nunne* < OE *Nunna* masc. (*UCPN* 68; common in place-names, e.g., *PNSussex* 556).
48. Petri [L] pistoris

fol. 17r

49. Sewini [OE *Sǣwine*]
51. Rotberti [CG] de Cirisi [t.; see above 228 and n. 30]
52. Maðelgari [? OE/CG; see above 224–5 and n. 13] Ruffi
53. Siwardi [OE *Sigeweard*] Stigerop [n.; OE *stigrāp* 'stirrup']
54. Golduini [OE *Goldwine*]
55. Æduini [OE *Ēadwine*] fabri
56. Sevugel [OE]

    Cf. 24.
58. Gotselmi [CG – *Gaule* 105, cf. *France II* 299, *s.n. Gossart*, and 346, *s.n. Josse*]
59. Russelli [n.; OFr *Roussel* – *Winchester* 215]

    In C13 *Russel* occurs here as a surname (*BAB* 125 n. 21).
60. Lamberti [CG]

    Cf. 22.
61. Ailrici [OE] pistoris
62. Æilnodi [OE] filii fareman [p.; S *Farmaðr* – *SPLY* 79–80, see also above 228 and 228–9 n. 33]
63. Gileberti [CG] clerici
64. Lefuini [OE *Lēofwine*] pistoris
65. Herod[l] [? L]

    As the Biblical name is hardly suitable for baptismal use, this and similar forms from elsewhere in C12 England (e.g., Davis, R.H.C., ed., *Kalendar of Abbot Samson*, London 1954, 37) and from France (*Haute Picardie*, 223, cf. Michaëlsson, K., *Etudes sur les noms de personne français*, i, Uppsala 1927, 89, 97) may be nicknames, possibly so-called 'pageant names'. Perhaps (in spite of *DBS s.n. Harold*) the origin of modern *Harrod*.
66. Orgari [OE *Ordgār*]
67. Chebel [OE **Cybbel* – see *Winchester* 209 n. 5, and cf. *DBS s.n. Keeble*]

    Commonish in place-names, including a C14 Sussex field-name (*PNSussex* 563). This example shows Kentish and ESussex *e* < [y] (cf. 1 *Bedel*) and the Anglo-Norman spelling *ch* for [k] (cf. 98 *Chene-* < *Cyne-*, and see above 226 and n. 19)
68. Deringi [OE]

    Cf. 10.
69. Leffelmi [OE *Lēofhelm*]

70. Benwoldi [OE *Beornweald*] Gest [n. or p.; OE *gæst* 'stranger' – *OEB* 219, *DBS s.n. Guest*, cf. *MED s.n. gest*; or S *Gestr* – *PNDB* 260]
   Ben-: as there is no such name-element, read *Bern-* < *Beorn-* (but cf. 40 *Burnulfi*).
71. Wulfrici [OE] porcarii
72. Emmæ [CG]
   Cf. 46.
73. Slote [?]
   DBS refers *Slot(t* to ME *s(c)lott* 'mire', so this may be a topographical nickname; less probably a characteristic one.
74. Gosfr*idi* [CG] coci
75. Godefr*idi* [CG]
76. Lefuini [OE] hunger [p.; ? CG – see above 224]
77. Ædvini [OE] Cniht [n. or o.; OE *cniht* – cf. *DBS s.n. Knight*]
   Cniht: the surname *Knyst* = *Knight* occurs in 1296 (*SSR* 17).
78. Goldstani [OE *Goldstān*]
79. Wulbaldi [OE *Wulfbeald*] Winnoc [p.; OE *Winuc* – *UCPN* 152]
80. Brembel [n. or t.; OE *brǣmel, brēmel* 'bramble']
   The surname *Brembel* occurs here later (*BAB* 364, *SSR* 317). Note also the place-names *Bremblegh* (*BAB* 72 n. 10, 73 – apparently for the district where *Brembel* lived), *Bremlisferd, -fricht* in late C12, and *Brembelshulle* c.1240 (*PNSussex* 496).
81. Rotb*erti* [CG] Barate [n.; OFr *barat, barate* – *Winchester* 207, *Canterbury* 303]
82. Lefflet [OE *Lēofflǣd* f.] loungæ [n.; ? OE Latinized]
83. Edildæ [OE *Ēadhild* f.] tipæ [p.; OE *Tippa* masc.]
   tipæ: the masc. OE *Tippa* here assumed is well evidenced in place-names, including one in Sussex (*PNSussex* 214–15, also *PNDevon* 606, *PNEssex* 66, 307, and *PNHerts* 149). Ignore the comments in *DBS s.n. Tipp*, but cf. *s.n. Tipping*.
84. Goldingi [OE *Golding*]
86. Ælurici [OE] Curlebasse [? n.; so far unexplained]

fol. 17v
87. Wulfuini [OE] Scot [p.; OE *Scot* – *Winchester* 171 n. 8]
88. Hvgon*is* [CG] Secretarii
89. Hunfr*idi* [CG] presbiteri
   Cf. 111.
90. Pagani [L] Peche [n.; ? OFr]
   See 100 *Pechet*.
91. Durand*i* [L/CG – *Winchester* 155]
92. Jvliot [OFr dimin < L *Julianus*] lupi [n.; cf. OFr *le Leu* – e.g., *Amiens* 551; see also *Winchester* 213]
93. Ælfuini [OE] abbat [n.; ME *abbot* – *London* 177, also *DBS s.n. Abbatt*]
94. Siwardi [OE] Crulli [n.; ME *crul* 'curly-haired' Latinized – *Winchester* 210, *DBS s.n. Curl*]
95. Sevugel [OE] cannarii
   cannarii 'reed-cutter', according to Latham; but, as the surname *le Cannere* appears here later (*BAB* 125), perhaps a Latinization of ME *cannere* 'potter' (see *Canterbury* [above 210], *DBS s.n. Canner*, and *MED s.v.*).
96. Brictr*ici* [OE *Beorhtrīc*] ortolani
   ortolani: the surname *Gardener* occurs in 1296 (*SSR* 17).
97. Ælwini [OE *Ælfwine*] secretarii
98. Chenewardi [OE *Cyneweard*]
   Cf. 67 *Chebel*.

99. Balduini [CG] svtoris
100. Os*berti* [CG] pechet [n.; ? OFr]
    pechet: possibly identical with the name, Latinized as *Peccatum*, borne by the
    well-known *Peachey* family, including an early C12 bishop of Coventry (see *OEB*
    353, also *Complete Peerage s.n.*); TL classes this spelling under *pechié* 'sin'. The
    question remains open whether 90 *Peche* represents the same name with loss of -*t*
    (in which case it would be dissyllabic) or OFr *pesche* 'fishing'. *DBS s.nn. Peckett,
    Petch* &c., fails to go into the matter deeply enough.
101. Cocardi [n.; OFr *cocart*, pej. < *coq* – *Eu* xii 216, *Haute Picardie* 215, cf. *Lynn* 59]
102. Ælfuini [OE] Hachet
    Hachet: current on the Continent (e.g., Fauroux, *Recueil des actes*, 366, and
    Gysseling, M., and Bougard, P., *L'Onomastique calaisienne*, Louvain 1963, 41) as
    well as in C12 England (see *SPLY* 123–4); needs fuller study.
103. Æilnoð [OE] Hecæ [p.; OE *Heca* masc. – *UCPN* 97]
    Hecæ: the bearers of OE *Heca* included a mid C11 bishop of Selsey.
104. Blachemann*i* [OE] de Bodeherstegate
    Bodeherste-: Bathurst, within the *leuga* (*PNSussex* 496). This surname appears
    in 1296 (*SSR* 17). Note the ESussex *herst* < OE *hyrst* (= WSussex *hurst*).
105. Re*i*nberti [CG] Genestær [n. or t.; OFr *genestier* 'broom-bush' – *France II* 286]
106. Ælurici [OE] Corueiser [o.; OFr – *Winchester* 201, also *MED s.v.*]
107. Brict*r*ici [OE] barhc [n.; OE *bearg* 'pig' – see *MED s.v. barow*]
108. Ælfuini [OE] Tvrpin [p.; OFr *Turpin* – e.g., *Beauvais* 298, cf. *Winchester* 175]
109. Rogeri [CG] braceur [o.; OFr]
110. Walt*eri* [CG] ruffi
111. Hunf*ridi* [CG] Genester
    See 105.
    Either this man or 89 *Hunfridus presbiter* might be the ancestor of the *Umfray*
    family found here later (*SSR* 17, 317).
112. Goduini [? OE/CG] Gisard [p.; ? OFr]
    See above 225 n. 14.
113. Siwardi Crulli
    See 94.
114. Brunieve [OE *Brūng(i)efu* f.]

fol. 18r
115. Wulfuini [OE] Carpentarii
    Carpentarii: cf. 40; the surname *Carpentar'* occurs in 1296 (*SSR* 17).

17

The Early Personal Names of King's Lynn: An Essay in Socio-Cultural History*

Part I – Baptismal Names

Despite the advocacy and the examples, dating back at least sixty years, of Sir Frank Stenton and of other distinguished scholars,[1] personal names found until recently little favour as historical source-material.[2] But now their evidence, although not yet exploited for such purposes as often as that of place-names, is at last gaining more general recognition, in ways that suggest it may in time prove to have a certain edge over its better-established rival.[3]

* Originally, this essay was to have appeared as an appendix to the collection of King's Lynn materials being edited by Dorothy Owen and to be published in the British Academy's series of Records of Social and Economic History [[*The making of King's Lynn: a documentary survey*, Records of Social and Economic History new ser. IX (London, 1984)]]; but, for reasons of economy, that plan has had to be abandoned. My heartiest thanks are therefore due to Peter McClure – to whom I was already indebted for having read the work in draft and gently corrected many shortcomings – for having stepped into the breach and agreed to publish it in *Nomina*. Because *Nomina* VI will in the event be going to press sooner than the British Academy volume, certain intended cross-references are no longer possible; I hope that readers will appreciate the problem and take on trust the assertions now apparently unsupported. To Dorothy Owen herself, with whom I had constantly discussed the project as it evolved over more than five years, my debts are pervasive and unquantifiable.

For a research grant, awarded in March 1979, which assisted with my working expenses during the later stages of this study, I must express my gratitude to the British Academy.

1 See, for instance: F.M. [Sir Frank] Stenton, ed., *Documents illustrative of the social and economic history of the Danelaw, &c.* (Oxford, 1920), esp. xix, xcviii, cii, cxi–cxviii; *idem*, ed., *The free peasantry of the Northern Danelaw* (Oxford, 1969; repr. from *Bulletin de la Société royale des Lettres de Lund*, 1925–26), esp. 17 and n.; and *idem*, 'The Danes in England', *Proceedings of the British Academy* [*PBA*] XIII (1927), 203–46, esp. 207–8, 227–33; D.C. Douglas, *The social structure of medieval East Anglia* (Oxford, 1927), 215; E. Ekwall, 'The proportion of Scandinavian settlers in the Danelaw', *Saga-Book of the Viking Society* XII (1937–45), 19–34, esp. 20–1; and O. Arngart, 'Some aspects of the relation between the English and the Danish elements in the Danelaw', *Studia Neophilologica* XX (1947–48), 73–87, esp. 77–80.

2 See, for instance: R.H.C. Davis, 'East Anglia and the Danelaw', *Transactions of the Royal Historical Society*, 5th ser. V (1955), 23–39, esp. 20–30; P.H. Sawyer, 'The density of the Danish settlement in England', *University of Birmingham Historical Journal* VI (1957–58), 1–17, esp. 13–14; and *idem*, *The age of the Vikings*, 2nd edn (London, 1971), 157–8.

3 See, for instance, 'Clark's First Three Laws of Applied Anthroponymics', above 77–83, and 'Battle c.1110: an anthroponymist looks at an Anglo-Norman New Town', above 221–40. Rapprochements are also proceeding from the historians' side, see: A. Everitt's preface to R.A. McKinley, *Norfolk and Suffolk surnames in the Middle Ages* (London and Chichester, 1975), ix–xiii; and G.S. Barrow, *The Anglo-Norman era in Scottish history*, Ford Lectures 1977 (Oxford, 1980), passim.

For, whereas a place is represented by a single name, its scores, hundreds, even thousands of early inhabitants all bore baptismal names chosen by parents or godparents, and many also bore nicknames, patronyms and other by-names recognized and often created by the community at large. And, whereas place-names are, like language itself, communal and slow to change,[4] each personal name not only recorded an individual and conscious response to custom and to the models available but died with its bearer. So, being datable and individually chosen as well as multitudinous, personal names reflected social composition and social attitudes, in their contemporaneous variety and in their evolution, far more sensitively than place-names ever could. They can thus reveal the balance between several competing cultures, not in black and white, nor once for all, but in a gradation shaded through time and space. They allow balances between cultures to be struck – admittedly, at only the most superficial level – for different places, or for different dates, and then compared.

Superficial the evidence and the conclusions will necessarily remain, because adoption of foreign names need imply no deep cultural allegiance. Some cultural contact it must, however, imply. Enthusiasm of response to an influence will be measured more easily than the latter's volume, because multiple instances of a single form (like *William* in twelfth-century England) may, or may not, all be traceable to a single celebrated bearer of it.[5] Yet even evidence so ambiguous and so superficial may be valuable for times and areas otherwise sparsely documented: had nothing survived from eleventh- and twelfth-century England but lists of names, those would by themselves have allowed the Norman Conquest and settlement to be deduced and approximately dated.[6] In many ways, indeed, twelfth-century England affords an ideal 'laboratory' for testing personal names as a source for social and cultural history; and, both as one of the 'new' towns of this period and as a port with wide and well-documented foreign contacts. Lynn offers special scope to the investigator.[7] Because by c.1300 the main patterns of naming seem provisionally established, that date has, somewhat arbitrarily, been taken as the later terminus of the present study.

Baptismal names current in twelfth-century England fell into several categories.[8] The older name-stock, conveniently called 'insular' and comprising Old-English names[9]

---

4   F.T. Wainwright, *Archaeology and place-names and history: an essay on problems of co-ordination* (London, 1962), 46–7; cf. A. Dauzat, *Les noms de personnes* (Paris, 1925; repr. 1944), 4–6.

5   Thus, in Flanders the foreign names of several countesses were widely imitated (see J. Lindemans, 'Over de infloed van enige vorstinnennamen op de naamgeving in de Middeleeuwen', *Verslagen en Mededelingen der Koninklijke Academie voor Taal- en Letterkunde*, 1950, 99–106) and in Normandy the names most favoured were those associated with the ducal house (see M. Le Pesant, 'Les noms de personne à Evreux du xiie au xive siècle', *Annales de Normandie* IV (1956), 47–74, esp. 55).

6   In the admissions lists of Hyde Abbey, for instance, continental names start to appear regularly, especially for 'pueri', from about the 1070s on, see W. de Gray Birch, ed., *Liber vitae: register and martyrology of New Minster and Hyde Abbey, Winchester*, Hampshire Record Society (London, 1892), esp. 36–7.

7   Cf. 'Battle', passim.

8   Cf. 'Women's names in post-Conquest England: observations and speculations', above 117–43, esp. 126–8, and 'Battle', above 223–5.

9   For this element the main works of reference are: W.G. Searle, *Onomasticon Anglo-Saxonicum* (Cambridge, 1897) (for some shortcomings of which, see O. von Feilitzen, in H. Voitl *et alii*, eds, *The study of the personal names of the British Isles: proceedings of a working conference at Erlangen, 21–24 September 1975* (Erlangen, 1976), 16–18); M. Redin, *Studies on*

plus Anglo-Scandinavian ones,[10] was during the century and a half following the Conquest gradually being discarded in favour of 'continental' forms such as the new aristocracy bore.[11] These latter names themselves fell into three main groups (certain minor ones, such as Breton and Normanno-Irish, being for the moment disregarded): Continental-Germanic names, in everyday use mostly Gallicized but in documents normally represented by archaic Latinized forms;[12] Franco-Scandinavian

uncompounded personal names in Old English (Uppsala, 1919); M. Boehler, *Die altenglischen Frauennamen*, Germanische Studien XCVIII (Berlin, 1930); O. von Feilitzen, *The pre-Conquest personal names of Domesday Book*, Nomina Germanica III (Uppsala, 1937) [*PNDB*]; *idem*, 'Some unrecorded Old and Middle English personal names', *Namn och Bygd*, XXXIII (1945), 68–98; *idem*, 'Some Old English uncompounded personal names and by-names', *Studia Neophilologica* XL (1968), 5–16; *idem*, 'Personal names', in M. Biddle *et alii*, eds and trss, *Winchester in the early Middle Ages: an edition and discussion of the Winton Domesday*, Winchester Studies I (Oxford, 1976) [*PNWD*], 143–229; *idem* and C. Blunt, 'Personal names on the coinage of Edgar', in P. Clemoes and K. Hughes, eds, *England before the Conquest: studies in primary sources presented to Dorothy Whitelock* (Cambridge, 1971), 183–214; also V. Smart, *Cumulative index of volumes 1–20*, Sylloge of Coins of the British Isles XXVIII (London, 1981).

10 This term here denotes Scandinavian names current in England, not hybrid formations (for which, see n. 51 below). For this element, already touched on in several works listed in n. 9, see especially: E. Björkman, *Nordische Personennamen in England in alt- und frühmittelenglischer Zeit*, Studien zur englischen Philologie [StEP] XXXVII (Halle, 1910) and *idem*, *Zur englischen Namenkunde*, StEP XLVII (Halle, 1912), plus the review article by R.E. Zachrisson in *Studier i Modern Språkvetenskap* VI (1917), 269–98 (still useful, although dated); D. Whitelock, 'Scandinavian personal names in the Liber Vitae of Thorney Abbey', *Saga-Book* XII (1937–45), 127–53; O. von Feilitzen, *PNDB*, 18–20, and *idem*, 'Notes on some Scandinavian personal names in English twelfth-century records', in *Personnamnstudier 1964 tillägnade minnet av Ivar Modéer (1904–1960)*, Anthroponymica Suecana VI (Stockholm 1965), 52–68; G. Fellows Jensen, *Scandinavian personal names in Lincolnshire and Yorkshire* (Copenhagen, 1968) [*SPLY*] (cf. the author's own comments in *The Study of the Personal Names of the British Isles*, ed. H. Voitl (Erlangen, 1976), 43 *et seq.*); J. Insley, 'Regional variation in Scandinavian personal nomenclature in England', *Nomina* III (1979), 52–60 (it is to be hoped that Dr Insley's 1980 Nottingham thesis on *Scandinavian personal names in Norfolk* – see *Nomina* IV (1980), 13 – will soon appear in print). [[J. Insley, *Scandinavian Personal Names in Norfolk: A Survey Based on Medieval Records and Place-Names*, Acta Academiae Regiae Gustavi Adolphi LXII (Uppsala, 1994).]]

11 See: E. Ekwall, *Early London personal names*, Acta Regiae Societatis Humaniorum Litterarum Lundensis XLIII (Lund, 1947); P.H. Reaney, 'Pedigrees of villeins and freemen', *Notes and Queries*, May 1952, 222–5; *idem*, 'Notes on the survival of Old English personal names in Middle English', *Studier i Modern Språkvetenskap* XVIII (1953), 84–112; also *idem*, *The origin of English surnames* (London, 1967), 129–52; B. Seltén, *The Anglo-Saxon heritage in Middle English personal names: East Anglia 1100–1399*, Part I: Lund Studies in English [LSE] XLIII (Lund, 1972) and Part II: Acta Regiae Societatis Humaniorum Litterarum Lundensis LXXIII (Lund, 1979) (see reviews in *English Studies* LIX (1978), 257–60, and LXII (1981), 473); G. Fellows Jensen, 'The names of the Lincolnshire tenants of the Bishop of Lincoln', in F. Sandgren, ed., *Otium et negotium: studies in onomatology and library science presented to Olof von Feilitzen* = Acta Bibliothecae Regiae Stockholmiensis XVI (1973), 86–95.

12 For Germanic name-traditions in general, see: E. Förstemann, *Altdeutsches Namenbuch*, rev. edn, 3 vols (Bonn, 1900–16), I: *Personennamen*, plus H. Kaufmann, *Ergänzungsband* (Munich, 1968); H.B. Woolf, *The Old Germanic principles of name-giving* (Baltimore, 1939); W. Schlaug, *Studien zu den altsächsischen Personennamen des 11. und 12. Jahrhunderts*, Lunder Germanistische Forschungen [LGF] XXX (Lund, 1955) [I], and *idem*, *Die altsächsischen Personennamen vor dem Jahre 1000*, LGF XXXVI (Lund, 1962) [II]. For further references, see nn. 14 and 60–3 below.

For the impact of this tradition on England, see: T. Forssner, *Continental-Germanic personal names in England in Old and Middle English times* (Uppsala, 1916); O. von Feilitzen, *PNDB*, 26–9, and *idem*, 'Some Continental-Germanic personal names in England', in A. Brown and P.

names;[13] and also the classical and Biblical names, mainly 'Christian' in association,[14] such as on the Continent itself were at this date gaining popularity at the expense of the Germanic ones.[15] At Lynn the Norman-French influences being felt throughout England were supplemented and complicated by other, more localized foreign contacts arising through the town's trade with the Low Countries and with what were later to become the Hanseatic ports;[16] and here therefore direct Low-German and even Baltic influences might also have been at work.

Analysis of any medieval name-sample is hampered by manifold difficulties, not least by the inadequacy of the reference-books currently available.[17] Chronology can seldom, because of the life-long currency of every name, be more than approximate. Then, either because of the document's specialized purpose or through too limited a range, a sample may fail to represent the community fairly. How many individuals were indicated by repetitions of the same form often proves impossible to determine. For the name-stocks current in medieval England, moreover, the Germanic tradition shared by several of the categories makes many specimens etymologicaly ambiguous, at all events in their documentary forms: *Wimundus*, for instance, might with equal plausibility be referred to Old-English, Scandinavian or Norman origins;[18] many Scandinavian names might indeed, with exactly opposite cultural implications, be classed either as proper to the Danelaw or as imported from Normandy.[19] Spelling and dialect pose constant problems. Manifold uncertainties must therefore be borne in mind; and so only gross statistical discrepancies can be held significant.[20]

Above all, the 'national' origins of names, whether Continental-Germanic or Scandinavian, must never be confused with those of their bearers. Names reflect cultural influences only, not 'racial' origins; and, although in times of scanty written communication cultural influence implies human contact and therefore some population-movement, the evidence which names give of such movements can be only indirect. What they do reflect are social attitudes.

Foote, eds, *Early English and Norse studies presented to Hugh Smith* (London, 1963), 46–61; plus several further works already cited in nn. 9 and 11.

13 See J. Adigard des Gautries, *Les noms de personnes scandinaves en Normandie de 911 à 1066*, Nomina Germanica XI (Lund, 1954).

14 See, for instance, M.-Th. Morlet, *Les noms de personne sur le territoire de l'ancienne Gaule du vi^e au xiie siècle*, 2 vols (Paris, 1968–72), II: *Les noms latins ou transmis par le latin*. Some studies listed in nn. 9 and 11 above and 60, 62 and 63 below include names of this type.

15 A topic touched on in most studies of medieval French and Flemish naming cited here: see in particular P. Aebischer, 'L'anthroponymie wallonne d'après quelques anciens cartulaires', *Bulletin du dictionnaire wallon* XIII (1924), 73–168, esp. 80, 112–16, 118–20, 123, 161–2; also O. Leys, 'La substitution des noms chrétiens aux noms pré-chrétiens en Flandre occidentale avant 1225', in *Actes et mémoires du Ve Congrès international de toponymie et d'anthroponymie = Acta Salmanticensia (Filosofía y Letras)* XI (1958), 2 pts, I. 403–12, and G.T. Beech, 'Les noms de personne poitevins du ixe au xiie siècles', *Revue internationale d'onomastique [RIO]* XXVI (1974), 81–100.

16 This topic will be fully treated by Dorothy Owen in her British Academy volume [[41–7]].

17 Cf. 'Battle', above 225–6.

18 See, for instance, Seltén, *Heritage*, II. 167 and references there given.

19 Cf., for instance, *SPLY*, xxiv, lix–lxi; also *PNWD*, 191.

20 See 'Battle', above 223; cf. K. Michaëlsson, 'L'anthroponymie et la statistique', in *IVe Congrès des sciences onomastiques* (Uppsala, 1954), 380–94; O. Brattö, *Notes d'anthroponymie messine*, Göteborgs Universitets Årsskrift LXII/4, 1956, 22–9; also A. Ellegård, 'Notes on the use of statistical methods in the study of name-vocabularies', *Studia Neophilologica* XXX (1958), 214–31 (somewhat over-mathematical).

(i)   Pre-Conquest Elements

The Old-English names current in twelfth-century Lynn were in themselves hardly noteworthy.[21] What invites study is the balance between these and the Anglo-Scandinavian ones stemming from the Viking settlement of over two centuries earlier.

Traditionally, clues to that settlement have been sought in place-names, especially those showing Scandinavian personal names compounded either with Scandinavian topographical terms or with English ones. From these a succession of scholars – among the most notable being in an earlier generation Eilert Ekwall and Sir Frank Stenton, and more recently Kenneth Cameron – have set out to map the Viking settlements according to relative dates and densities.[22] But for East Anglia no adequately-published corpus of place-names is yet available.[23] Meanwhile, the density of Viking settlement here has excited some controversy, turning mainly on tenurial

---

[21] A provisional list of the Old-English names for men deducible from the present material, patronyms included, offers the following dithematic forms, here given in standardized West-Saxon spelling: perhaps *Āchere*; *Ælfgār*, *Ælfhere*, *Ælfmǣr*, *Ælfnōð*, *Ælfrǣd*, *Ælfrīc*, *Ælfsige*, *Ælfstān*, *Ælfweard*, *Ælfwine* (*Al-* may sometimes, however, have represented not *Ælf-* but *Æðel-*, *Eald-* or *Ealh-*); *Æðelmǣr*, *Æðelrīc*, *Æðelweald*, *Æðelweard*, *Æðelwīg*, *Æðelwine*; *Beorhtmǣr*, *Beorhtrīc*, *Beorhtsige*; *Blǣcmann*; *Brūnsunu*; *Burgrīc* or *Burgwīg*; perhaps *Cūðfrið* (see Seltén, *Heritage*, II. 56); *Cynegār*, *Cynemann*; *Ēadmund*, *Ēadrīc*, *Ēadstān*, *Ēadweard*; perhaps *Ealdrǣd* (if *Arled* is a slip for *Alred*); (a rare *Forðwine* has been identified in Norfolk records – see Seltén, *Heritage*, II. 83 – but cannot be represented in the late forms like *Fordewan*, *Fordewayne*); *Gōdhere*, *Gōdlamb*, *Gōdmann*, *Gōdrīc*, *Gōdwine*; perhaps *Goldrīc* (rather than *Cūðfrið* as above); *Hereweard*; *Hūnstān*, *Hūnwine*; *Lēofgēat*, *Lēofmann*, *Lēofmǣr*, *Lēofrīc*, *Lēofwine*; *Ordrīc*; *Ōsfrið*; *Sǣlida*, *Sǣmann*, *Sǣweard*; *Selemann*, *Selewine*; *Sigebeald*, probably *Sigerīc*; perhaps *Spilemann* (but see 262 below); *Stānheard*; *Swētmann*; perhaps *Wīgmund* (cf. n. 18 above); *Wulffrið*, *Wulfhere*, *Wulfmǣr*, *Wulfnōð*, *Wulfrīc*, *Wulfsige*, *Wulfwine*; *Wynfrið*.

Several *-ing*-forms such as became increasingly popular in the Late-Old-English period (see Smart, *Index*, xiv) occur here: *Brūning*, *Cypping*, *Dunning*, *Golding*, (but for *Goding* here, see 252 and n. 61 below).

Among single-element names, always hard to classify, the following seem likely to be masculine, and English (cf. n. 74 below): *Beorht*, *B(r)ord(a)*, perhaps *Cola*, *Ecca*, *Lēof*, *Scott*, *Swift*.

[22] See the studies cited in nn. 1 and 2 above, and also: E. Ekwall, 'The Scandinavian element', in A. Mawer and F.M. Stenton, eds, *Introduction to the Survey of English place-names*, EPNS I, pt. i (Cambridge, 1924), 55–92, and *idem*, 'The Scandinavian settlement', in H.C. Darby, ed., *An historical geography of England before A.D. 1800* (Cambridge, 1936), 133–64; F.M. Stenton, 'Personal names and place-names', 'The historical bearing of place-name studies: the Danish settlement of Eastern England', and 'The Scandinavian colonies in England and Normandy' – all reprinted in D.M. Stenton, ed., *Preparatory to Anglo-Saxon England* (Oxford, 1970); K. Cameron, 'The significance of English place-names', *PBA* LXII (1976), 135–55, and *idem*, ed., *Place-name evidence for the Anglo-Saxon invasion and Scandinavian settlements* (Nottingham, 1977).

[23] Unhappily, my one-time colleague, O.K. Schram, who had for many years been collecting Norfolk place-names, died before completing his work; responsibility for this county has now been transferred to Dr K.I. Sandred. [[K.I. Sandred and B. Lindström, *The place-names of Norfolk*, pt. i, EPNS LXI (Nottingham, 1989).]] See, however, Schram's short papers in *Norwich and its region*, British Association for the Advancement of Science (Norwich, 1961), 141–9, and in Sir Cyril Fox and B. Dickins, eds, *The early cultures of North-West Europe (H.M. Chadwick memorial volume)* (Cambridge, 1950), 429–41; and cf. Ekwall, 'The Scandinavian element', 76–7, 81–3, and *idem*, 'The Scandinavian settlement', 151–3, together with comments by Insley in *Conference at Erlangen*, 55. See also [Ordnance Survey,] *Britain before the Norman Conquest* (Southampton, 1973), 11–12 and map.

evidence.[24] Such brief studies of major Norfolk place-names as have appeared show Scandinavian forms scattered thinly, except for a batch of -by-forms around Yarmouth. Towards the west, in Lynn's own hinterland, overtly Scandinavian place-names are rare, except for some -thorpes, usually interpreted as small secondary settlements.[25] In the main, therefore, Viking settlers in Norfolk may be supposed to have merged into the existing population rather than have remained in enclaves (for what such comparisons are worth, the Lincolnshire shores of the Wash likewise show fewer Scandinavian place-names than do other parts of that county, and are likewise believed to have seen the Vikings blending into the native population).[26] About the likely density of the ninth-century settlement this tells us little.

Elsewhere in the Danelaw minor toponyms, and field-names in particular, have sometimes allowed Scandinavian influence to be assessed more precisely than through the corresponding major place-names.[27] On Norfolk little work has so far been done, but what has appeared suggests that here too minor names may show more such influence than do major ones.[28] Another potential source of evidence about linguistic and cultural patterns might have been early dialect, had it but been adequately recorded; but it is not.[29]

Failing these sorts of evidence, perhaps personal names, which elsewhere have sometimes revealed Scandinavian influences where even well-studied place-names partly conceal it,[30] may help out. Admittedly, their evidence too has its limitations.

---

[24] See the papers by Arngart, Ekwall, Davis and Sawyer cited in nn. 1 and 2 above.

[25] See K. Cameron, 'Scandinavian settlement in the territory of the Five Boroughs: the place-name evidence – II: Place-names in *thorp*', *Medieval Scandinavia* III (1970), 35–49 (repr. in *Place-name evidence*, 139–56).

[26] See H.E. Hallam, *The new lands of Elloe*, University [College] of Leicester Department of English Local History: Occasional Papers VI (Leicester, 1954), 6–8.

[27] See especially K.I. Sandred, 'Scandinavian place-names and appellatives in Norfolk: a study of the medieval field-names of Flitcham', *Namn och Bygd* LXVII (1979), 98–122; cf. K. Cameron, 'Early field-names in an English-named Lincolnshire village', in *Otium et negotium*, 38–43, idem, 'The minor names and field-names of the Holland division of Lincolnshire', in T. Andersson and K.I. Sandred, eds, *The Vikings* (Uppsala, 1978), 81–8, and G. Fellows Jensen, 'English field-names and the Danish settlement', in *Festschrift til Kristian Hald* (Copenhagen, 1974), 46–55; also J. Insley, 'Addenda to the Survey of English Place-Names: personal names in field- and minor names', *Journal of the English Place-Name Society* X (1977–78), 41–72.

[28] See especially K.I. Sandred, 'Ortnamns- och ordstudier i Englands Fenland', *Ortnamnssäll-skapets i Uppsala Årsskrift 1972*, 41–52 (English summary 51–2).

[29] Although from c.1375 onwards vernacular materials from Lynn itself are ample (see S.B. Meech and H.E. Allen, eds, *The Book of Margery Kempe*, Early English Text Society: Original Series 212 (Oxford, 1940), x–xi, xxxii; cf. A. McIntosh, 'The language of the extant versions of *Havelok the Dane*', *Medium Ævum* XLV (1976), 36–49), for earlier periods reliable dialect records from any part of Norfolk are scarce: for instance, the mid-thirteenth-century *Genesis and Exodus* cannot without circularity be used to exemplify Norfolk dialect, in so far as its localization depends wholly on linguistic argument (see O.S. Arngart, ed., LSE XXVI (Lund, 1968), 43, 45–7). Fifteenth-century usages, for what they are worth, tell somewhat against heavy Scandinavian influence, showing, for instance, h- rather than th- forms for 'them' and 'their', and this at a date when the latter were gaining popularity. As yet, comparative incidences of lexical loanwords have not been fully studied, but see A. Rynell, *The rivalry of Scandinavian and native synonyms in Middle English*, LSE XIII (Lund, 1948), 357 et seqq.; cf., more generally, A. McIntosh, 'Middle English word-geography: its potential rôle in the study of the long-term impact of the Scandinavian settlements upon English', in *The Vikings*, 124–30.

[30] See, for instance, Ekwall, 'The Scandinavian element', 72–4; also idem, 'Proportion', 20–1, and Arngart, 'Aspects', 79–81. The main document concerned is BCS 1130, a late-tenth-century

Twelfth-century names, the earliest extant from most parts of the Danelaw in adequate numbers, cannot speak directly about a ninth-century settlement, nor even about the Cnutian hegemony, but only about the survival of certain superficial effects of these events. In such circumstances, varied name-forms will mean more than would great frequency of a few. Because in isolation the mere number of Scandinavian forms, and even their ratio to other elements, would have limited significance, an assessment may best be arrived at by comparison with contemporaneous materials from other areas. That being so, then, although the date allows of little discrimination between the effects of the ninth-century settlement and those of Cnut's enfeoffments of his followers,[31] perhaps the latter, in so far as more or less common to the whole country, may not in the event confuse the pattern too gravely.[32]

A specific limitation of personal-name evidence concerns the balance between the several Scandinavian 'nations'.[33] At Lynn, as normally in Eastern England, a good few names belong to the East-Scandinavian (that is, Danish and Swedish) stocks, for instance, *Áki*, *Auti*, *Þeinn*, and perhaps *Flikkr*.[34] Exclusively West-Scandinavian currency of particular items is, on the other hand, always hard to prove, because Norwegian and Icelandic names happen to be more amply recorded than the Eastern ones; and this, in the context of Lynn's flourishing Norwegian trade, is disappointing. Even with those few forms, such as *Steingrímr*, which are identifiable as West-Scandinavian, it is hard to tell whether they stemmed from the original settlement or were brought in by later trade. Against the latter origin seems to argue the general failure of such items to survive the normal late-twelfth-century abandonment of the old 'insular' name-stock.

Thus, the basically Danish cast of Lynn's Scandinavian names seemingly shows this rapidly-growing town conforming with the surrounding area. How close this conformity was must be a main question.[35] Veronica Smart's notable survey of Æthelredian moneyers' names has shown that – at least among this special group – Scandinavian

---

Northamptonshire memorandum (conveniently printed in A.J. Robertson, ed. and tr., *Anglo-Saxon charters* (Cambridge, 1939), 74–82).

31 An aspect of the Cnutian conquest usually passed over, with most accounts assuming that, generous though the new king was in rewarding his followers with estates, no settlement occurred at this time comparable with that of the late ninth century: thus H.R. Loyn, *Anglo-Saxon England and the Norman Conquest* (London, 1962), 62: 'There was no migration on the scale of the late ninth and early tenth centuries. Canute's triumph was essentially political'; cf. Sir Frank Stenton, *Anglo-Saxon England*, 3rd edn (Oxford, 1971), 413–4. See also n. 32 below.

32 Dr V.J. Smart, in her as-yet unpublished 1981 Nottingham Ph.D. thesis, *Moneyers of the late Anglo-Saxon coinage 1016–1042*, which follows on from her study of the Æthelredian moneyers' names cited in n. 36 below, shows that, for this special group at least, neither Cnut's reign nor those of his two sons saw any significant shifts in naming-patterns (I am grateful to her for allowing me to refer to these findings). [[See now V.J. Smart, 'Moneyers of the late Anglo-Saxon coinage: the Danish dynasty 1017–42', *Anglo-Saxon England* XVI (1987), 233–308, esp. 304–05.]] But, given the time-lags often intervening before changes in name-fashion become visible in records, definitive assessment of the Scandinavian hegemony's cultural effects must wait upon full analysis of the moneyers' and other personal names surviving from the Confessor's reign.

33 Cf. Insley, 'Regional variation', passim.

34 See von Feilitzen, *PNDB*, 21–3, also in *Personnamnstudier*, 61–2; cf. *SPLY*, xxvi–xxviii.

35 In his Ph.D. thesis [n. 10 above] Insley describes as on the high side the incidence of Scandinavian personal names found in Lynn and its hinterland (I am grateful to him for allowing me to refer to this work). [[See now Insley, *Scandinavian Personal Names in Norfolk*, p. xxxviii.]]

influence was lighter in Norfolk than in mid-Lincolnshire, with only 15% to 20% of names Scandinavian here, beside some 40% at Lincoln;[36] but, as the pre-Conquest incidence among them of Continental-Germanic names shows,[37] moneyers were not wholly typical of the places for which they struck. It would not, therefore, be surprising to find Lynn's name-patterns differing from those of the Norfolk moneyers. The balance between English and Scandinavian forms here can, in any case, be determined only approximately. Several obstacles to precise analysis have already been cited. In particular, scribal conventions make it hard to tell Anglo-Scandinavian names from Franco-Scandinavian ones; still, rather as with Cnutian influences, an interference affecting the whole country may perhaps not falsify regional comparisons too greatly. Nor is the documentation available for Lynn as compact as that for some other towns. Figures must, therefore, remain somewhat rough.

In the event, the early Lynn materials fairly consistently show Scandinavian forms accounting for some 40% of the instances of insular names for men. As for the name-stocks, the English one has only a slight advantage, with just over 70 items beside some 65 Scandinavian ones (about 53%).[38] Beside the figures just quoted for Æthelredian moneyers' names, these Lynn ones at first look high – even with allowances made for some increase due both to Cnutian and to Norman influences; they prove in fact to agree fairly well with those for other post-Conquest Norfolk records. Thus, the cartulary of St Benet of Holme (midway between Norwich and Yarmouth) shows Scandinavian forms accounting for over a third of insular name-occurrences, with the two stocks almost evenly balanced, at just under 35 Scandinavian items to just over 35 English ones.[39] Again, the insular names (some admittedly belonging to citizens of Lynn) appearing in the twelfth-century charters of Norwich Cathedral Priory represent a stock of some 40 items, likewise fairly evenly divided between the two elements.[40] The Norfolk Feet of Fines from 1198 to 1215 offer a masculine insular

---

[36] V.J. Smart, 'Moneyers of the late Anglo-Saxon coinage, 973–1016', in *Commentationes de nummis saeculorum ix–xi in Suecia repertis II*, Kungl. Vitterhets Historie och Antikvitets Akademiens Handlingar: Antikvariska serien XIX (Stockholm, 1968), 191–276, esp. 242–4; cf. *eadem*, 'A note on the moneyers of the mint of Lincoln', in H.R. Mossop *et alii*, *The Lincoln mint c.890–1279* (Newcastle-upon-Tyne, 1970), 20–9.

[37] See Smart, 'Moneyers 973–1016', passim, and esp. von Feilitzen and Blunt, 'Coinage of Edgar', 208–9; also C.E. Blunt, 'The St Edmund memorial coinage', *Proceedings of the Suffolk Institute of Archæology* XXXI (1967–69), 234–55, esp. 242.

[38] A provisional list of the Scandinavian names for men deducible from the present material, patronyms included, offers the following items, given in normalized spelling and with no attempt to distinguish forms showing possible Norman influence: *Aggi, Áki, Arnketill, Ásbjǫrn, Ásgautr, Ásketill (-kell), Áslákr, Auti, Beli, Bolli, Bóndi, Brúni, Feggi* or *Feigr*, perhaps *Fenkell, Finnr*, probably *Flikkr, Gamall*, probably *Gauki, Gauti, Gunni*, perhaps *Hagni, Hákr, Halfdan, Hámundr, Hávarðr*, probably *Horn, Hrólfr, Húskarl, Illhugi*, perhaps *Jarl, Kappi, Ketilbjǫrn*, perhaps *Kol(l)i*, perhaps *Kollingr, Lurkr*, perhaps *Milla, Oddi* or *Oddr, Oggi, Oðinn, Sæfugl, Sighvatr*, perhaps *Sígríkr, Skalli, Skarfr, Skjǫtr, Sprakaleggr*, perhaps *Sprækr, Steingrímr, Steinn, Sumarliði, Sunnulfr, Svartgeirr, Sveinn, Tóki, Tóli, Þóraldr, Þórketill, Þórmóðr, Þórsteinn, Ulfr, Ulfketill, Úspákr*, perhaps *Vígmundr, Viðarr, Víðr, Vrangr, Ǫnundr*. For English names, cf. n. 21 above.

[39] J.R. West, ed., *St Benet of Holme 1020–1210*, 2 vols continuously paginated, Norfolk Record Society II and III (n.p., 1932), esp. II. 258–60 (some name-classifications there need adjustment).

[40] B. Dodwell, ed., *The charters of Norwich Cathedral Priory*, pt. I, Pipe Roll Society [PRS]: new ser. XL (London, 1974).

name-stock of some 135 items (partly, it is true, featuring there only as patronyms), of which about 60 are Scandinavian.[41] So far, then, the name-patterns of the early citizens of Lynn look roughly compatible with those elsewhere in Norfolk.

These patterns must now be viewed in a wider perspective. Despite possible Cnutian reinforcement, incidence of Scandinavian names generally remained light outside the old Danelaw, so that in the *Winton Domesday*, for instance, they constitute only 8% of the insular name-stock characteristic of landholders *TRE*, providing a mere 4% of occurrences; and among the insular names surviving in the Canterbury 'Rental B', datable to the 1160s, show even lower ratios.[42] With such figures those from the Northern Danelaw offer a marked contrast. Some late-twelfth- and early-thirteenth-century charters from Holland and Kesteven, not the most heavily Scandinavianized parts of Lincolnshire, show Scandinavian forms providing about 65% of the insular name-stock for men;[43] the Lincolnshire Feet of Fines from 1199 to 1216 likewise show about 65%, and the Lincolnshire Assize Rolls from 1202 to 1209 about 60%, with a Scandinavian name-vocabulary of some 80 items (in both, admittedly, some items are represented only by patronyms, which tend to favour the rarer names).[44] At Newark, in the heartland of the Five Boroughs, Scandinavian forms provided in 1177 nearly 60% of the insular names for men.[45] As for regions south of Lynn, the male peasants' names in the late-twelfth-century Ramsey survey, when analyzed according to the counties where the manors lay, agree roughly with the other records in showing for Norfolk an insular name-stock featuring some 40% of Scandinavian items, beside just under 30% for Huntingdonshire, about 25% for Cambridgeshire (agreeing with the ratio for the pre-Cnutian parts of *Liber Eliensis*[46]) and 20% for Bedfordshire.[47] For Suffolk, Abbot Samson's survey shows about 45 Scandinavian items accounting for just over 30% of the masculine insular name-stock;[48] and similarly in the small insular name-stock of the Suffolk Feet of Fines from 1199 to 1214 some 16 Scandinavian items represent between 30% and 35% of the men's names.[49]

41 B. Dodwell, ed., *Feet of Fines for the country of Norfolk for . . . 1198–1199 and . . . 1199–1202, &c.*, PRS: new ser. XXVII (London, 1952), and comments xxviii–xxxi; and *eadem*, ed., *Feet of Fines for the county of Norfolk . . . 1201–1215; for the county of Suffolk . . . 1199–1214 &c.* [*FFSuffolk*], PRS: new ser. XXXII (London, 1958), and comments xxx–xxxi.

42 See *PNWD*, 184–5, and W. Urry, *Canterbury under the Angevin kings* (London, 1967), 226–43. Because von Feilitzen's statistics lump men's names together with women's more old-fashioned ones (see 256 below), the strictly-comparable Winchester figures should be even lower.

43 K. Major, ed., *The Registrum Antiquissimum of the Cathedral Church of Lincoln*, VII, Lincoln Record Society [LRS] XLVI (Hereford, 1953). Insular names occur here mainly among peasant occupiers, those of witnesses being predominantly 'continental'.

44 M.S. Walker, ed., *Feet of Fines for the county of Lincoln for . . . 1199–1216*, PRS: new ser. XXIX (London, 1954); D.M. Stenton, ed., *The earliest Lincolnshire Assize Rolls, A.D. 1202–1209*, LRS XXII (n.p., 1926).

45 M.W. Barley *et alii*, eds, *Documents concerning the manor and soke of Newark-on-Trent*, Thoroton Society Record Series XVI (Nottingham, 1956), 1–4, and notes by K. Cameron, xi–xv, 5–15.

46 E.O. Blake, ed., *Liber Eliensis*, Camden Third Series XCII (London, 1962), 72–142 (studied in my paper, 'On dating *The Battle of Maldon*: certain evidence reviewed', above 20–36).

47 W.A. Hart and P.A. Lyons, eds, *Cartularium monasterii de Rameseia*, 3 vols, Rolls Series (London, 1884–93), III. 218–315.

48 R.H.C. Davis, ed., *The kalendar of Abbot Samson of Bury St Edmunds, &c.*, Camden Third Series LXXXIV (London, 1954), 3–77.

49 *FFSuffolk* [see n. 41].

True, the sources just quoted have not been strictly comparable with one another either in date or in scope; but, even so, certain outlines of name-distribution appear with fair consistency. Among the insular names for men the incidence of Scandinavian items forms a shaded pattern, with ratios varying from 60% to 65% in the Northern Danelaw down to half that in Suffolk and less still in Bedfordshire. Norfolk, with about 40% to 45% or more, is statistically as well as geographically intermediate. Such a pattern, in reasonable keeping with other (admittedly, sometimes controversial) evidence about the varying densities of Scandinavian settlement, is not in fact, despite the higher figures involved, altogether inconsistent with the profile derived from the pre-Cnutian moneyers' names. Such general consistency suggests that personal-name distributions are here reflecting real variations in cultural pattern. If so, then two main conclusions can be drawn: (a) that Viking influence in Norfolk, although less preponderant than in Lincolnshire and Nottinghamshire, left a fair legacy; and (b) that the cultural patterns of Lynn, like those of another post-Conquest town previously investigated,[50] followed those of the surrounding region.

Too much should not be read into these findings. A 40% to 45% element in a name-stock by no means implies other cultural influences in like proportion. How dominant English speech-patterns remained here is emphasized by the frequent Anglicizations such as *Swan* for *Swein*, *Stangrim* for *Steingrim*, and *Suartgar* for *Svartgeirr*, as well as by the hybrid formations like *Brunswein*.[51] So, although dominant enough to impose their own name-fashions, the Viking settlers in Norfolk cannot have been so numerous as profoundly to affect local speech-habits. And, although this name-survey may have suggested answers to certain questions, it ends by posing new ones. What, for instance, had been the social standing of Scandinavian names in pre-Conquest Eastern England? Was it just by accident that certain families prominent in twelfth-century Lynn favoured them?

(ii)   *Continental Influences*

Throughout twelfth-century England the ratio of continental names to insular ones was, as already noted, rising rapidly enough to make dating crucial to a far greater degree than with the Scandinavian element.

For Lynn one dated, and in a sense homogeneous, sample is the list of certain of its citizens entered in the Pipe Roll for 1166. Here, if dubious forms and the Scandinavian ones probably of Norman origin are left aside, then insular names account for nearly 50% of occurrences; if all Scandinavian forms showing French spelling-influence were reckoned as 'continental' (and, given the likely orthographical bias of royal clerks, that might be unwise), then insular forms would still amount to 45%. The name-stock shows about 40 insular items alongside some 32 continental ones (5 ambiguous Scandinavian ones being left out of the reckoning), with the former therefore amounting to around 55%. As for patronyms and metronyms, these, apart from not necessarily being truly representative of the name-stock, here qualify hardly more than a third of the individuals, and on both counts need treating with caution. For what they are worth, only three at most are not arguably insular: the abbreviated *Ern'*, the ambivalent *Oger*,

---

50 See 'Battle', above, esp. 229, 231.
51 Such formations are discussed by von Feilitzen in *Personnamnstudier*, 63–4; cf. Arngart, 'Aspects', 78–9.

and the doubtful *Amabil'*.[52] These patterns all square with the conclusion just drawn from analyzing the Scandinavian element here: that Lynn's early population was predominantly local in origin, rather than exotic.

That is by no means all. Such name-patterns seem to lag oddly behind the current fashion. Admittedly, the point is delicate, because records exactly comparable in date and scope are not easily come by. Perhaps Canterbury, for which in the 1160s 'Rental B' shows insular men's names accounting for only 25% of occurrences and 35% of the stock, may be thought too cosmopolitan to be fairly compared with Lynn, and Winchester, with even lower figures already by 1148, even more so.[53] But Newark should be comparable with Lynn, and there only ten years later no more than 20% of men's names remained insular.[54] For Norfolk in general one estimate has suggested that by the late twelfth century only a quarter of current names (women's more traditional ones included[55]) usually remained insular;[56] and certainly the abundant patronyms in the Feet of Fines from 1198 to 1202, presumably representing a generation flourishing in the late 1160s to 1170s, show only 30% to 35% of insular forms.[57] So, insular names running at nearly 50% make the Lynn burgesses listed in 1166 look somewhat old-fashioned. Sometimes a low ratio of continental names may be explained by humble status, in so far as the peasantry, although also coming to favour continental names, may have been rather slower in doing so than burgesses were; but citizens figuring in a Pipe Roll must have been prominent. Moreover, the burgesses of a 'new' town may be thought especially unlikely to have been uncommonly attached to traditional ways (indeed, as early as 1096 one Lynn notable was called 'William son of Stangrim'[58]), and those of an active port least likely of all, given their constant exposure to foreign ways. All in all, the most acceptable explanation for this old-fashioned name-distribution may in the event be chronological: that is, whereas surveys like those from Canterbury and Newark included all householders of whatsoever age, the Pipe Roll may have been concerned only with certain senior burgesses, born about or before 1120 rather than in the 1130s or 1140s. This would explain also their predomi-

---

[52] *Ern'*: comparison of *Siṁ.fil.Ern'*. with the later *Seman fil. Ernisii* in the same document suggests that the suspension may represent, not an OE name in *Earn-* (see *PNDB*, 243–4, and Seltén, *Heritage*, II. 78–9), but *Erneis*, a specifically French reflex of CG *Arnegis* (see *PNDB*, 248, and *PNWD*, 156).

Oger: either Scandinavian *Auðgeirr* or CG *Otger* (see *SPLY*, 203); in a Pipe Roll the 'continental' spelling may not be significant, especially as the son's name, *Turchetil*, may favour the former etymology.

Amabil': either a Latinized nickname or, and perhaps more probably, a metronymic use of *Amabilia* (*Mabille* occurred as a by-name in fourteenth-century Beauvais, see M.-Th. Morlet, 'Les noms de personne à Beauvais au xive siècle', *Bulletin philologique et historique (jusqu'à 1715) du Comité des Travaux historiques et scientifiques 1955 et 1956 [Bulletin]* (Paris, 1957), 295–309, esp. 297).

Several etymologically-ambiguous short-forms, such as *Biffe* and *Tette/Titte*, seem on balance probably native and feminine (see further n. 74 below).

[53] See n. 42 above. Note that the caveat concerning the Winchester figures again applies.

[54] See n. 45 above.

[55] See 256 below.

[56] See Seltén, *Heritage*, I. 43 (the basis of calculation may differ from that used here).

[57] See n. 41 above.

[58] *Norwich Cathedral Priory*, 57–8. The case of the later Bartholomew of Farne, born *Tosti* but dubbed *William* by trendy playmates, shows that social pressure could cause replacement of old-fashioned names by more current ones.

nantly insular patronyms and metronyms, as going back to the generation born in the late eleventh century, before the new fashions had taken great hold. Such an identification of this Pipe Roll group as consisting mainly of seniors is partly confirmed by the appearance of many of them as witnesses to a Norwich charter of *ante* 1150.[59]

Thus far, 'continental' names have been treated without regional distinction, as though all had alike reached England in the wake of the Norman Conquest. But, as has already been suggested, for this North Sea port no such assumption can be left untested. Trade was bringing Lynn foreign contacts far wider than the Conquest alone would have afforded, ranging from Picardy all along the Flemish and North German seaboards to the Baltic; and, in consequence, many different areas east of the North Sea were sending immigrants to settle here.

Checking what effects such trade-links and consequent settlements may have had on name-fashions will not, however, be easy. The personal names favoured in the Low Countries and in northern Germany differed little – in their documentary forms, that is – from French ones, so that, for instance, names like the *Folcardus* and *Gerardus* here qualified as *Estrenses* could otherwise – with conventional spellings muffling their true pronunciations – just as well have been assigned to Flemish or even French provenances. Nor, indeed, are 'continental' names always readily distinguishable from native English ones, because the basic Germanic stocks partly overlapped and, although with some elements the English and the Low-German reflexes had diverged markedly (*Ēad-*, later *Æd-*, beside *Od-*, for example), with others the documentary forms coincided: thus, *Goding Flandrensis* had a wife, *Geri[t]rud*, whose name, phonologically continental as well as being widespread throughout Germany and the Low Countries, was specifically that of the patron saint of Nivelles,[60] but without the by-name his own could equally well have been native English,[61] the same being true of many other Continental-Germanic [CG] forms. 'Christian' names too, like the *Iohannes* and the *Thomas* also qualified here as *Estrenses*, were common throughout Western Europe, and from the twelfth century on were being increasingly favoured by the English themselves. Some forms can nonetheless be tentatively assigned to particular provenances, the criteria being of two kinds, distributional and linguistic. For the latter, the present material, with its zealous Latinization, offers only limited scope: thus, as well as a few phonological divergences like that between English *Ēad-* and CG *Od-* and also some specially French sound-changes, certain modes of formation too, hypocoristic ones in particular, can be noted as typical of certain areas – *Bo(i)dekyn*, for instance, being a hypocoristic for *Baldwin* of a type found mainly in Flanders (which includes Calais);[62] but too few such pet-forms have reached the present records. As for distributions, although the wide currency of most name-forms seldom allows of

[59] *Norwich Cathedral Priory*, 70.

[60] See, for instance, C. Tavernier-Vereecken, *Gentse Naamkunde van ca.1000 tot 1252: een bijdrage tot de kennis van het oudste Middelnederlands* (Tongeren, 1968), 125; also Schlaug I. 98.

[61] See *PNDB*, 265. In Flanders the commoner form was *Godinus*: see, for instance, C. Marynissen, *Hypokoristische suffixen in oudnederlandse persoonsnamen, inz. de -z- en -l-suffixen*, 2 vols continuously paginated (Diss. Leuven, 1971), 206 (I am grateful to Dr Folke Sandgren, of the Royal Library, Stockholm, who, as Olof von Feilitzen's academic executor, procured me a copy of this dissertation); also other relevant works listed in n. 63.

[62] See: M. Gysseling and P. Bougard, *L'onomastique calaisienne à la fin du xiiᵉ siècle*, Onomastica Neerlandica: Anthroponymica XIII (Leuven, 1963), 18; W. Beele, *Studie van de ieperse per-*

pinning any item to a narrow area, some likely provenances can be approximately defined by consulting individual name-repertories luckily available for a chain of localities stretching from Normandy and Picardy through Flanders, Frisia and Saxony to the Baltic coast.[63]

Mainly on linguistic grounds, a few forms here are, not unexpectedly, identifiable as French, or sometimes Franco-Flemish.[64] These include: *Anger*, a Gallicized form either of Scandinavian *Ásgeirr* or of Frankish *Ansger*, and common in Normandy but not, apparently, farther east; *Bertin*, a short-form of names in *Bert-* or *-bert* (equalling

---

soonsnamen uit de stads- en baljuwsrekeningen 1250–1400, 2 vols (Handzame, 1975), II. 73; and Tavernier-Vereecken, *Gentse Naamkunde*, 49.

[63] The regional monographs and other studies consulted are, in roughly west-to-east order: M.-Th. Morlet, *Gaule* [see n. 14], esp. I: *Les noms issus du germanique continental et les créations gallo-germaniques* (for some limitations of this work, see the review by C. Wells in *Medium Ævum* XXXIX (1970), 358–64); *eadem*, 'Les noms de personne à Eu du xiiie au xve siècle', *RIO* XI (1959), 131–48, 174–84, and XII (1960), 62–70, 137–48, and 205–19; *eadem*, 'Beauvais' [n. 52]; *eadem*, 'Les noms de personne à Amiens au xive siècle', *Bulletin 1960* (Paris, 1961), 527–52; *eadem*, 'Les noms de personne à Corbie au xive siècle', *Bulletin 1967* (Paris, 1969), 739–78; *eadem*, *Etude d'anthroponymie picarde: les noms de personne en Haute Picardie aux xiiie, xive, xve siècles* (Amiens, 1967); Le Pesant, 'Evreux' [n. 5]; P. Bougard and M. Gysseling, *L'impôt royal en Artois (1295–1302)*, Anthroponymica XVIII (Leuven, 1970); R. Berger, ed., *Le nécrologe de la confrérie des jongleurs et des bourgeois d'Arras (1194–1361)*, 2 vols (Arras, 1963–70); *idem*, 'Les anciens noms de famille d'Arras: anthroponymie et lexicologie', *Annales de la Fédération historique et archéologique de Belgique: 35e congrès, 1953*, 107–21; H. Jacobsson, *Etudes d'anthroponymie lorraine: les bans de tréfonds de Metz (1267–1298)* (Göteborg, 1955) (cf. Brattö, *Notes d'anthroponymie messine* [n. 20]); E. Hlawitschka *et alii*, eds, *Liber memorialis von Remiremont*, 2 pts, Monumenta Germaniae Historica (Zürich and Dublin, 1970); Aebischer, 'L'anthroponymie wallonne' [n. 15]; Marynissen, *Hypokoristische suffixen* [n. 61]; Gysseling and Bougard, *L'onomastique calaisienne* [n. 62]; F. Debrabandere, *Persoonsnamen in het Kortrijkse (1300–1350)*, Anthroponymica XIX (Leuven, 1971); Beele, *De ieperse persoonsnamen* [n. 62]; O. Leys, 'De anthroponymie van een 14[e]-eeuws Renteboek uit Maritiem-Vlaanderen', *Mededelingen van de Vereniging voor Naamkunde te Leuven, &c.* [*Naamkunde I*] XXIX (1953), 125–46; *idem*, 'De bijen beroepsnamen van Germaanse oorsprong in de Westvlaamse oorkonden tot 1225', *Naamkunde I* XXXIII (1957), 105–25, XXXIV (1958), 147–58, and XXXV (1959), 83–98, and 139–57; Tavernier-Vereecken, *Gentse Naamkunde* [n. 60]; J. Lindemans, *Brabantse persoonsnamen in de xiii[e] en de xiv[e] eeuw*, Anthroponymica I (Leuven, 1947); M. Gysseling, *Overzieht over de noordnederlandse persoonsnamen tot 1225*, Anthroponymica XVI (Leuven, 1966); S. Hagström, *Kölner Beinamen des 12. und 13. Jahrhunderts*, Nomina Germanica VIII (Uppsala, 1949); F. Wagner, *Studien über die Namengebung in Köln im zwölften Jahrhundert*, I: *Die Rufnamen* (Diss. Göttingen, 1913); Schlaug I and II [n. 12]; K. Carstens, *Beiträge zur Geschichte der bremischen Familiennamen* (Diss. Marburg; Bremen, 1906); G. Mahnken, *Die hamburgischen niederdeutschen Personennamen des 13. Jahrhunderts*, Hamburgische Texte und Untersuchungen zur deutschen Philologie II/4 (Dortmund, 1925); A. Reimpell, *Die lübecker Personennamen unter besonderer Berücksichtigung der Familiennamenbildung bis zur Mitte des 14. Jahrhunderts* (Diss. Hamburg, 1928); H. Brockmüller, *Die rostocker Personennamen bis 1304* (Diss. Rostock, 1933).

Because these works are mostly alphabetically arranged and/or well-indexed, full references will only exceptionally be given.

[64] French forms were early borrowed into Flemish areas: as well as relevant works listed in n. 63, see O. Leys, 'Romaanse leenwoorden in de Westvlaamse naamgeving tot 1225', *Naamkunde I* XXX (1954), 149–69. Although not pretending to offer any medieval documentation, A. Carnoy, *Origines des noms de familles en Belgique* (Louvain, 1953) not only gives helpful insights into name-patterns in these linguistic border-areas but also offers many forms analogous to those found in Lynn. For some further spread of French influence, see Hagström, *Kölner Beinamen*, 478–82.

OE *Beorht-/Byrht-/Briht-*) and current at least from Evreux to Ieper (Ypres); *Deuduneth* (*Deodatus*), a French form often, but not exclusively, figuring among those used by Jews to render their Hebrew names, in this case *Nathaniel* or *Jonathan*;[65] perhaps *Doeð*, which looks like a variant of the Old French *Doön* from CG *Dodo/Dudo*;[66] *Ernis*, a specifically French reflex of CG *Arnegis*; *Firmyn*, found thus at Eu, but in Picardy and farther east usually represented by *Fremin*; *Race* (*Raceus*; here a vintner's name), which resembles the *Rase* found at Calais and likewise, albeit to a lesser degree, the *Raisse* found at Eu and at Arras for CG *Razo*, a hypocoristic of names in *Rad-/Rat-*; *Terri*, the specifically French reflex of CG *Theodric*; and *Wybelot*, a diminutive for *Wigbald* or *Wigbert* found, for instance, at Arras (cf. *Wibelet* at Eu and in Picardy).

For documentary forms offering no clue to their everyday counterparts, possible provenances are deducible only from distributions. With most 'Christian' forms these are, as noted, too wide to serve great purpose: true, the frequent appearance at Lynn of names such as *Clemens*, *Jacobus*, *Lambertus*, *Laurentius*, *Nicholas* and *Simon* would square with influence from the Low Countries, but, in the absence of any typically Flemish forms, it proves nothing. Some Continental-Germanic names found here can, however, be traced through the name-repertories to various localities from Flanders to the Baltic. Among these are: *Cunrod*, for *Conrad*, favoured in Ieper, Ghent, Cologne, Bremen, Hamburg, Lübeck, and Rostock (but in northern France usually represented by the hypocoristic *Conon*); *Godebald* (*-bold*), found, for instance, in Ghent and in Saxony, and *Godebert*, found in Arras and Ghent and also in Saxony (the specifically French forms being *Gobaut* and *Gobert/Gubert* respectively); *Godescalc*, current in Arras as well as in Calais, Ieper and Ghent and in all five German ports; *Haðebrand*, rarer, but found in Saxony,[67] and *Herdeger* likewise;[68] *Hermannus*, common from Ieper to Rostock, but found also in Evreux and in Metz; *Hildebrand*, current from Ieper to Rostock; *Hungar*, which, despite its Anglicized second element,[69] probably represented the CG *Hunger* common from Cologne to Rostock; *Ricolf*, an ambiguous form attributable either to Scandinavian *Ríkulfr* or, and here perhaps more probably, to the CG *Ricolf* common from Ieper to Rostock; and *Tidemannus*, here qualified as *le Ger'*, amply paralleled in all five German ports. Although distributions so widespread (and, at that, by no means complete) do nothing to pin any of the Lynn forms to a specific provenance, they are far from irrelevant. Except as surnames, few forms in

---

[65] Although it is a commonplace that medieval Jews in England often used French equivalents of their Hebrew names, no systematic study of the equations favoured seems yet available: see, however, C. Roth, *A history of the Jews in England*, 3rd edn (Oxford, 1964), 93–4, and cf. *idem*, ed., *The Jews of medieval Oxford*, Oxford Historical Society n.s. IX (Oxford, 1951), 5 n. 4 and 113 n. 5; also the indexes of Jewish names in H.G. Richardson, *The English Jewry under Angevin kings* (London, 1960) and in V.D. Lipman, *The Jews of medieval Norwich* (London, 1967).

[66] See E. Langlois, *Table des noms propres de toute nature compris dans les chansons de geste imprimées* (Paris, 1904), *s.n. Doon de Maience*; also W. Kalbow, *Die germanischen Personennamen des altfranzösischen Heldenepos und ihre lautliche Entwicklung* (Halle, 1913), 55, 65.

[67] The son's name in the *Hildebrandslied*, but rare in real-life records: see Forssner, *Continental-Germanic personal names*, Schlaug I. 103, and Morlet, *Gaule*, I. 119a (although apparently noted from 'Gaul' only at early dates, perhaps it underlies the French surname *Habrand*, see A. Dauzat, *Dictionnaire étymologique des noms de famille et prénoms de France*, 2nd edn rev. M.-Th. Morlet (Paris, 1969), 614, and cf. Carnoy, *Origines*, 295).

[68] See Schlaug I. 105, also II. 99; but cf. Seltén, *Heritage*, II. 95, for the possibility of native origin.

[69] See 'Battle', above 224, also 239.

this group seem to have been common in France proper after c.1000, although in Lorraine and in Wallonia they kept their popularity somewhat longer; and in a twelfth-century English context that itself is interesting. At Lynn, when set against the known trading-patterns, such predominantly Low-German distributions, imprecise and incomplete though they are, suggest that, on this level at least, cultural influences from Flanders, Frisia and the North-German and Baltic ports were hardly less strong than those from France.

For a few names no convincing sources or parallels have yet been found. These difficult cases include that of *Heneg*[or *Heuk-*]*wald* the tanner – a citizen prominent enough to have given his name to a fleet (creek), *Henk*[or *Heuk-*]*waldsflet*, as well as to an alley, *Enq*[or *Euk-*]*ualdislane*. If it is right to prefer, from among the not only varied but even mutually contradictory spellings of this name, the forms in *Hen-*, these could perhaps represent a reflex of CG *Ingwald* or else of Scandinavian *Ingivaldr*.[70]

(iii) *Women's Names*

So far statistics and commentary have referred only to men's names. Partly this has been because the Lynn materials, like most medieval records other than *libri vitae*, fail to include women's names in anything like due proportion to men's: outside the Gaywood Bede-Roll, women's names are rare except as metronyms, and the Pipe Roll and the Trinity Gild Bede-Roll, of their natures, offer none apart from metronyms.[71] What dictates separate treatment is not so much, however, this paucity as the general tendency of women's names to follow fashions of their own, either because in some cultures principles of name-choice vary according to sex or else because at times the models for men's names and for women's differ in type. In twelfth-century England such contrasts in name-fashion were in fact marked.

One difference between women's names and men's, far from being local, or even typically English, was shared by most of Western Europe. When the Gaywood Roll shows 'Christian' forms amounting to half the total stock of women's names but to less than a third of men's, it reflects a pattern common at this time in, for instance, France and Flanders.[72] Apart from the names of saints and of Biblical characters, such as had counterparts among men's names, women's names also included an element with no masculine equivalent: the abstract terms like *Constancia, Leticia, Sapientia*. If names encapsulate sponsors' wishes for their godchildren, the greater popularity for girls of 'Christian' names and of virtue-names implies conscious distinction between the qualities admired in women and in men – an attitude sharply contrasting with the older common Germanic tradition, where semantic distinctions between the names of the

---

[70] The problem here arises from the frequent *-u-* spellings, which produce a form hardly possible to 'etymologize'. The temptation is, therefore, to prefer the *-n-* forms, which at least allow of tentative attribution either to the CG *Ingwald* (*Ingoald*) noted in, for instance, Morlet, *Gaule*, I. 145a, and *Remiremont*, 258, or else to the Scandinavian *Ingvaldr/Ingivaldr*, for which see G. Knudsen and M. Kristensen, *Danmarks gamle Personnavne*, I – *Fornavne*, 2 vols (Copenhagen, 1936–38), col. 639 (but for *Ingold* as its usual ME reflex, see *SPLY*, 151–2).

[71] For these two bede-rolls, see C. Clark and D. Owen, 'Lexicographical notes from King's Lynn', *Norfolk Archaeology* XXXVII (1978), 56–69, esp. 56 and nn. on 66.

Metronyms will be further considered in 'Part II – By-Names' below, esp. 265.

[72] See, for instance: Le Pesant, 'Evreux', 51, 63; Morlet, *Haute Picardie*, 23; Berger, *Nécrologe*, 306; and Leys, 'Substitution', 411.

sexes had been minimal (the first elements of dithematic names were wholly shared, and the second ones, although distinguished by grammatical gender, were not so by sense, with feminine -*gyð* and -*hild* both meaning 'battle' and masculine *frið*, 'peace'). Contrasting attitudes (in scribal minds at least) may also underlie the somewhat freer admission to the records of colloquial diminutives for women's names, like *Anote* and *Mariote*, than of the corresponding forms for men's.

Other findings, however, at first suggest less rather than more innovation in the naming of girls. Throughout twelfth-century England women's names normally appear as about a generation more 'old-fashioned' – less 'continental', that is – than the corresponding men's: a time-lag elsewhere tentatively explained as reflecting a low proportion of women among the Norman settlers.[73] Norfolk records in general illustrate this clearly, with the current women's names in the Feet of Fines 1198–1215 showing about 25% of insular forms, in contrast with the mere 7% characterizing the men's. For Lynn itself relevant forms are too scarce to mean much; such as do occur suggest no departure from the general pattern. It may be added that, much as with men's names, the range of women's names found here would be compatible with – but by no means proves – some influence from the Low Countries.

What women's names from Lynn do show clearly is an incidence of Scandinavian forms lower than among men's: by contrast with the 40% to 45% of Scandinavian items in the masculine insular name-stock, the feminine stock (admittedly much smaller, and so less representative) shows only some 7 Scandinavian forms beside about two dozen dithematic English ones plus an uncertain number of English short-forms[74] – well under half the masculine ratio, that is. By itself so small a sample would certainly have been dismissed as unrepresentative, did not other records show similar discrepancies: thus, the Norfolk Feet of Fines 1198–1215, with almost 45% of Scandinavian forms in the masculine insular name-stock, show only just over 20% for the feminine one, and the Lincolnshire Feet of Fines 1199–1216, with some 60% in the masculine stock, only about 40% for the feminine one; the Thorney *Liber vitae*, representing a 'catchment area' stretching from Holland to Bedfordshire, shows nearly

---

[73] See 'Women's names in post-Conquest England' [n. 8], passim.

[74] Provisional lists of the insular women's names deducible from the present material, metronyms included, offer the following forms, again in standardized spelling: Old English – *Ælfflæd*, *Ælfgifu*, *Ælfswyð*, *Ælfwaru*, *Æðelgyð*, *Æðelðrȳð* (as with men's names, the true etymologies of ME forms in *Al-* are often uncertain, see n. 21 above), *Beorhtgifu*, *Burgwynn*, *Cūðwynn*, *Dēorlēofu* or -*lufu*, *Ēadgyð*, *Ēadhild*, *Ēadwīf*, *Ēadwynn* (for these four items, cf. the short-forms *Ede*, *Edus*), *Ealdgyð*, *Ēastorhild*, *Gōdgifu*, *Hild*(e)*gyð*, *Hūnburg* (alternatively, but here less probably, CG), *Lēofcwēn*, *Lēofdæg*, *Lēofgifu*, *Lēofrūn*, *Lēofðrȳð* (for these five items, cf. the short-form *Lufe*), *Rǣdgyð*, *Sǣgifu*, *Sǣlēofu* or -*lufu*, *Wulfgifu*; Scandinavian – *Gufa*, *Gunnhildr*, *Hrafnhildr*, *Ingiríðr*, *Ke*(*ti*)*llog* (for which, see 'Part II', n. 24), *Langlíf*, *Sigríðr*; the original by-name *Dufe* could be of either origin.

Several short-forms, mainly found in Pipe Roll 1166 as metronyms and therefore probably garbed as Latin genitives, are uncertain in etymology, in so far as analogues are better recorded in CG materials than in English ones (see, for instance, Marynissen, *Hypokoristische suffixen*, *s.nn.*). Given the notorious underrecording of OE lower-class women's names, whether this lack of documentation is significant must be a matter of opinion. At all events, most such forms can easily be explained as possible childish contractions of common OE dithematic names: *Biffe* (perhaps from *Beorhtflæd* or *Beorhtgifu*), *Gevel/Give* (if pronounced with initial [j]) and *Gode* (cf. *PNDB*, 260, 263), *Lelle* (perhaps from *Lēofflæd*; current also in the Northern Danelaw, see Stenton, *Free peasantry*, 92, 110–11). Well-authenticated OE names of this type found here include *Tette*, St Guthlac's mother's name.

50% of Scandinavian forms among insular names for men, but only some 25% among those for women; and Abbot Samson's Bury survey, with over 30% among insular men's names, has under 20% among women's. Recognized for at least a quarter of a century (and perhaps for twice that time),[75] this regular discrepancy has been variously interpreted. Sir Frank Stenton (like Steenstrup before him) argued that the occurrence of any women's names at all implied a 'genuine migration'; but on that Arngart cast doubt, pointing out how often 'women' accompanying Viking hordes seem to have been classed along with 'plunder'. The question will not be easily resolved. Archaeology cannot help, because goods in a woman's grave prove nothing about her own origins or cultural affinities. And name-evidence involves its own uncertainties. Certainly, in themselves Scandinavian names for women carry little weight, because a Viking with daughters by an English wife might well have named some of them according to his own family-traditions. On the other hand, perhaps the comparative paucity of such forms may, by an argument analogous to that already deployed concerning the Norman-French settlement, be thought to imply a low proportion of women among the Viking settlers too.[76]

---

[75] See Arngart, 'Aspects', passim, esp. 73–6 and references there given; cf. Stenton, 'The Danes in England', 231–2. The same references are noted, with little comment, by P.T.H. Unwin, 'The Anglo-Saxon and Scandinavian occupation of Nottinghamshire and Derbyshire', *Journal EP-NS* XIV (1981–82), 1–31, esp. 16.

[76] Cf. 'First Three Laws', above 82–3. The likelihood of widespread intermarriage is accepted by, for instance, Sawyer, 'Density', 8, and *Age of the Vikings*, 253 n. 60. Norman materials show in this respect an even more marked discrepancy between the names of the sexes, see Adigard, *Les noms de personnes*, 251–3.

Part II – By-Names

At pp. 241–57 above, a study of the baptismal names recorded in certain documents concerning the King's (or rather, Bishop's) Lynn of the twelfth and thirteenth centuries argued that the relative incidences there of the various types of name reflected the young town's mercantile, social and cultural history. Baptismal names reveal, however, only half the story; by-names too have their tales to tell, from their own multiple as well as complementary points of view.

Fortunately, the same partly-unpublished materials drawn upon for the previous article offer also a splendid range of by-names. All these materials have been collected by Mrs Dorothy Owen for her forthcoming volume in the British Academy's series of records of Social and Economic History,[1] and most generously communicated to me in advance of publication; I should like again to thank her for her unfailing readiness to help with whatever problems have arisen in the course of my work upon them.

This further study devoted to by-names will concentrate on those of people flourishing before c.1300. Because these items will require treating individually, rather than in terms of stocks and vocabularies, additional details must now be given of the major sources used. The list of burgesses' names found in the 1166 Pipe Roll, and previously exploited for its baptismal names, also offers by-names of all types.[2] The main chronological emphasis of this present study will, however, fall later than did that of the work on baptismal names, the richest stocks of which dated from the twelfth century. Now a principal source will be the first section, extant in a late-thirteenth-century hand, of the Trinity Gild Roll (King's Lynn Borough Archives GD 44), where no baptismal name is without a qualifier of some kind. The Gild was founded c.1205, and cross-checks with other records show men listed in this section of its Roll as having flourished at dates ranging from the 1190s up to c.1300; the marshalling of their names in the Roll, although partly chronological, is by no means strictly so.[3] A still richer source of early by-names is the unpublished bede-roll of the Hospital of St Mary Magdalene at Gaywood (Norfolk Record Office: Bradfer-Lawrence MS IX b); its opening section

---

[1] Because the British Academy volume includes a full *Index nominum* (460–505), only summary references will be given here.

[2] *The Great Roll of the Pipe for 12 Henry II, A.D. 1165–1166*, Pipe Roll Society IX (1888), 21–9. Cf. Part I, above 250–2.

[3] Previously edited, not entirely accurately but with some suggested identifications and datings, by R. Howlett in Walter Rye's rare *Norfolk Antiquarian Miscellany*, 2nd ser., part III (Norwich, 1908), 45–79. See also C. Clark and D. Owen, 'Lexicographical notes from King's Lynn', *Norfolk Archaeology* XXXVII (1978), 56–69, esp. 56 and n. 5 on 66.

was likewise compiled c.1300. Here are brought together – seemingly with scant regard for chronological, or other, order – names dating from every period since the Hospital's foundation (allegedly, c.1135); if attempting to date this material from purely onomastic evidence were less perilously circular, predominantly thirteenth-century origins might be suggested for it, on the grounds that few of the baptismal names involved, mostly belonging to people apparently of modest condition, are of the Insular types which Part I of this study has shown to have remained in frequent use here until late in the twelfth century. In contrast with the wide chronological spread of these Rolls, the unpublished Newland Survey (King's Lynn Borough Records BC 1), dealing with the town's northern sector, is datable to the 1270s, probably to 1279; but this is, unfortunately, extant only in a fifteenth-century copy whose orthographical detail is suspect.[4] Apart from the intrinsic value of its entries, the Survey also affords cross-references that assist with the dating of entries in other documents.

Even so, many of the forms to be cited, although safely placed '*ante* c.1300', cannot at present be dated precisely; but, except for those taken from the 1166 Pipe Roll and from a few individual charters, not many seem likely to date back far into the twelfth century. None of the records has the authority of a full census; not even the Survey, because (apart from being confined to one sector of the town) it deals only with major burgess-tenants, not with occupiers to whom they might have sub-let some of their holdings, and is *a fortiori* unconcerned with subsidiary members of families. Nevertheless, the representativeness of the by-name corpus assembled from these disparate sources may be thought to be modestly confirmed by the reappearance of many forms from it in, for instance, some early-fourteenth-century Norfolk Gaol Delivery Rolls recently published.[5]

To annotate each form individually would be impossible here; some indeed remain, at least in the current state of knowledge, impenetrable.[6] The chief interest of such a corpus, firmly localized even though for the most part only approximately datable, lies in any event in the governing principles it may reveal and in whatever cultural bearings these may have.

(i) *Family-Groups and their By-Names*

The first question, how far twelfth- and thirteenth-century Lynn by-names represented transmissible family-names, allows of no simple answer. In Norfolk, just as elsewhere in medieval England, the surnames of different families were being provisionally stabilized at differing dates between the twelfth and the fifteenth centuries, with those of the gentry as a rule the earliest to be passed from generation to generation and others following suit.[7]

---

4 See E. and P. Rutledge, 'King's Lynn and Great Yarmouth: two thirteenth-century surveys', *Norfolk Archaeology* XXXVII (1978), 92–114, esp. 92–110.
5 See, for instance, B. Hanawalt, ed., *Crime in East Anglia in the fourteenth century: Norfolk Gaol Delivery Rolls, 1307–1316*, Norfolk Record Society XLIV (n.p., 1976), esp. Index.
6 For some tentative treatments of individual names, see 'Lexicographical notes', passim, noting that some suggestions there have since been modified (cf. below nn. 46, 89, 91, 96 and 98).
7 See R.A. McKinley, *Norfolk and Suffolk surnames in the Middle Ages*, English Surname Series [ESS] II (London and Chichester, 1975), 3–22; cf. *idem, The surnames of Oxfordshire*, ESS III (London, 1977), 7–30, and also G. Fellows Jensen, 'The surnames of the tenants of the Bishop of Lincoln in nine English counties', in T. Andersson, ed., *NORNA-Rapporter VIII: Binamn och Släktnamn, avgränsning och ursprung* (Uppsala, 1975), 39–60.

The present materials prove not entirely helpful on this score. Apart from the frequent vaguenesses of dating, the Trinity Roll lists only men, entering each individually; the Gaywood Roll, although often marshalling its entries in apparent family-groups, specifies only sporadically the relationships concerned. Furthermore, styles and usages at first sight differ markedly from document to document. Partly, this seems attributable to differences in purpose and consequently in standards of identification. The Newland survey, being a business document, aimed at clear specification, with some pretence to system. The Gaywood Roll, dealing at a more spiritual level, in prayers instead of rents, could on the other hand afford not only to veer between full descriptions like ('Pray for the soul of') *Sabine uxoris Willelmi Le Kervile de Tilneye*[8] and bare mentions like those of *Matildis et Ascili* and of others left innocent of any kind of by-name, but even to allow entries to trail away in the generous inclusivity of *et liberorum, et fratrum et amicorum*; such inconsistencies might have seemed attributable to its having been compiled from miscellaneous older records, were it not that the different styles, far from occurring in compact blocks, are scattered throughout, as though at random. The Newland Survey too falls well short of consistency, even in referring to single individuals; and also has, as already noted, the more serious defect (from our point of view) of rarely naming more than one member of any family.

In any case, by no means all the patronymic, occupational and, especially, residential qualifiers found in this material seem to have represented forms in regular, everyday currency. Some bear signs of having been devised *ad hoc* by the scribe, constituting descriptions, potted biographies even, rather than 'names' as ordinarily understood: thus, beside the Gaywood Roll's already-quoted phrase identifying 'Sabine . . . of Tilney' may be set the Newland Survey's *Elena uxore Radulphi de Suthmer apud Wigehal manente*, varying with *Helena que fuit uxor Radulphi de Suthmer* – the individual concerned being a burgess-widow of fair standing. Such periphrases are not, of course, unrelated to probable colloquial usages ('Helen, Ralph Southmere's widow, the one that lives over at Wiggenhall') and could be said to represent an embryonic stage in by-naming, before the distinguishing traits have been selected and given set expression. Locative phrases (which term will here be used to denote those involving proper place-names) may, when tacked on after the first, or 'primary' by-name, as often in the Gaywood Roll and sporadically elsewhere, have represented 'addresses' rather than alternative or supplementary names. When such a locative is added after a *filius*-formula, as with the survey's *Ricardus filius Ade de Wigehal* and countless other instances there and elsewhere, its reference is ambiguous, and may sometimes have been appropriately so. But instances abound of such phrases supplementing by-names of every other kind: with appositional ('asyndetic') patronymics, as in, amongst others, the Survey's *Petro Safrey de Wtton* and the Gaywood Roll's *Cecilie Kineman de Dersingham, Gocelini Hildebrand de Tyringtone, Walteri Swein de Munding, Willelmi Haldeyn de Gedeneye*, and so on; with occupational by-names, as in the Gaywood Roll's *Thome Pistoris de Geywude, Thome Le Taliur de Wlfretone, Willelmi Fabri de Grimestune, Willelmi Le Tronur de Lenna*, and so on; with nickname-forms of all kinds, as in the Survey's *Agnete Kid de Lenna* and the Gaywood Roll's *Alexandri Pipe de Mintlinge, Anne Le Bret de Dunham, Hawise Avenant de Northwicton, Iohannis Kide de Parva Dunham, Ricardi Sparwe de Estweniz, Rogeri Hotes de Brunham Sancti Clementis, Willelmi Woderoue de Geywude*, and so on; and, most significantly, even

---

8   All names in the Gaywood Roll are in the genitive, after *Pro anima*.

after topographical by-names, vernacular or Latinized, as in the Survey's *Iohannis de Vallibus de Westacre* and the Gaywood Roll's *Burdy atte Phorche de Tyringtone, Claricie atte Delhus de Walpol, Davidi de Dune de Snetisham, Henrici in Wode de Bodeham, Isabelle Wude de Bauseye, Ricardi filii Johannis de Foro de Snetesham, Ricardi ad Pontem de Hechem,* and so on. The sporadic occurrence of added locatives in the Newland Survey of c.1279 shows that these were not necessarily, by the present criteria, an 'early' feature; their infrequency in the Survey as well as in the Trinity Roll may be linked partly with the fair incidence in both of primary locative by-names and partly with the pointlessness, in these contexts, of adding *de Lenna.* Yet, although locative phrases in documents may often have been functioning mainly as 'addresses', the widespread recourse to such aids to identification may help to explain the frequency with which those who moved from village to town succeeded in adopting a socially more distinguished by-name of such type.[9]

The pervasive inconsistencies assist the study of family-naming practices. As to the hereditariness of by-names (best investigated through men's names), evidence foreseeably conflicts. On the one hand, the repeated, indeed regular reappearances, across several generations, of certain unusual forms like *Kelloc*[10] (found at least from the mid-twelfth century until the late-thirteenth), imply that well before the end of the twelfth century some men's by-names were being conventionalized and carried over to later generations. On the other hand, mid- to late-thirteenth-century records often show true patronyms, sometimes elaborately phrased, as with the Newland Survey's *Iohanne filio et herede Thome Galien,* and sometimes even double forms like the Trinity Roll's *Galf. fil. Will. fil. Mile* and *Thom. fil. Will. fil. Mile,* based on the *Will. fil. Milonis* entered near the Roll's early-thirteenth-century beginning. Such forms suggest some continuing lack of acknowledged family-names, even among such prosperous burgesses as appear in both records. Other entries in the Trinity Roll confirm this impression: several, mainly but not exclusively near the beginning of it, specify a man in a way that had been common in the 1166 Pipe Roll, simply as *frater* of another, usually of the immediately preceding member (straightforward when the earlier is given a patronymic or a locative by-name, less so when he is *Henricus Parvus*); a good few even show a man just as *serviens* or *socius* of another; others again use periphrases like *Goscelin nepos W. de Hale, Will. nepos Sim. del Both* and, vaguest of all, *Hardeger cum Sim. de Botha.* As for the Gaywood Roll, this – partly because it may include entries going back to the twelfth century but also partly perhaps because of the *liber vitae* tradition of relying on divine omniscience for the precise identification of those for whom prayers were offered – includes some groups of which no member at all bears a by-name, as well as others where only one is so distinguished, sometimes the first, as with *Benedicti de Swafham at Ayliez et Agnetis,* and sometimes the last, as with *Wlsi et Radulphi et Willelmi de Penteneye*; and such a locative phrase may, as already suggested, sometimes represent an 'address' rather than a by-name in daily use. Yet, despite this Roll's frequent silence about relationships, some groupings of individuals bearing identical by-names strongly suggest shared family-names, as, for instance, with *Willelmi Woderoue de Geywode et Yngrie uxoris Johannis Woderoue* (John having probably been William's father, or perhaps his brother). The Survey, datable and tempering its inconsistencies with clarity, offers some enlightening examples: *Thomas filius Nicholai* involves a true patronym, the father being *Nicholas de Brecham*; so

---

[9] See below nn. 28 and 34.
[10] See Part I, n. 74, *s.n. Ke(ti)llog.*

apparently does *Willelmus filius Angeri Spitelman*, subsequently abbreviated to *Willelmo filio Angeri*; on the other hand, the evidently patronymic *Ricardus filius Nicolai Ode* gives place to the hereditary form *Ricardus Ode*, the same by-name being borne by several other individuals here; as for *Robertus frater dicti Johannis*, it specifies unambiguously, and according to accepted convention, but without recourse to any set form.

A special aspect of family-naming concerns transference of men's by-names to their wives. This, as Richard McKinley has shown, became the regular custom in England only after c.1400.[11] So, with thirteenth-century attitudes to family-naming as unsettled as has just been shown, little consistency is, *a fortiori*, to be expected from women's by-names. Several instances of elaborate periphrasis have already been quoted; but women equally appear under more compact designations, such as the Survey's *Agnete Culling*, *Agnes de Wirham*, *Christina Ode*, *Constantia de Cibeceya*, *Juliana Champeneys*, *Katerina de Berneya*, *Katerina filia Brice*, *Katerina Dod*, *Mabilia Le Marchal*, *Margeria Derlyng*, *Matildis Wiz*, *Sibilla Banyard*, and other similar forms. As to the relative frequencies of the various styles, the present material by no means lends itself to statistics; and seldom shows whether women's by-names were personal, inherited, or marital. Some women – like some men – apparently had no recognized by-name, being specified solely by a family-relationship, as with the Gaywood Roll's *Agnetis sororis Geruasii de Tyringtone*. The relationship most often invoked is marriage (or widowhood), with the husband sometimes figuring in the same record in his own right, as with the Gaywood Roll's *Iohannis de Frenge et Alicie uxoris eius*, but sometimes not, as with an early-thirteenth-century charter's *Agnes que fuit uxor Willelmi f. Willelmi de Wigehale* and the Survey's *Helena . . . de Suthmer*. In contrast, other women had their own recognized by-names, which the Gaywood Roll shows them as keeping after marriage: *Godman Le Chapman de Holcham et Agnetis Walet uxoris eius*, *Willelmi Le Glowere de Walsokne . . . Cecilie Colet uxoris eius*, and *Ricardi Osbern de Holkam . . . Heluyse le Meyre uxoris eius*. How common such a practice was cannot be gauged, because often when masculine and feminine names are paired the Roll leaves the relationship unspecified: one such pair is *Elene Kede et Radulphi Cheuere* – seemingly, an Anglo-Scandinavian 'kid' with a French '(nanny-)goat'. Exceptionally, a wife might appear with a by-name but her husband apparently without, as with the Gaywood Roll's *Alexandri. et Margarete Godsaule uxoris eius*. Other women, however, are shown as sharing their husbands' by-names: the Newland Survey of c.1279 refers to the same person either as *Matildis que fuit uxor Reginaldi Wiz* or simply as *Matilda Wiz*. Evidence is likewise insufficient to allow the frequency of this usage to be estimated. Certainly, both the Gaywood Roll and the Survey show women bearing by-names either masculine in form or referring to trades or offices unlikely to have been their own – thus, *Alicie Wisman* and *Felicie Wysman*, *Agnetis Dispenser*, *Alicia Aurifaber/Le Orfeuer*, *Emme Barbur*, *Juliane Ledbetere*, *Mabilia Le Marchal*, *Matildis le Meyre*, also *Mirielis Spileman* (though this is more probably a simple patronym), and others; such forms must in some sort represent family-names, but it is seldom clear whether they had been inherited from the paternal line or transferred from husbands.

---

[11] See McKinley, *Oxfordshire*, 181–91.

(ii)   *Identifying and Interpreting By-Names*

Taking analysis of by-names beyond mere distribution requires 'etymologizing' the forms concerned. That, as must time and again appear, is seldom simple: first, because by-names are less predictable than baptismal ones; and, secondly, because they lack the semantic contexts which ease recognition and interpretation of common vocabulary. Dictionaries are of limited help. A name may exemplify a term far earlier than does any extant 'literary' text and so supplement the usual reference-books rather than be explained by them:[12] thus, *(Le) Mellow* appears in the Gaywood Roll at least a century and a half before its first 'dictionary' record (interestingly, in the mid-fifteenth-century Latin dictionary from Lynn known as *Promptorium Parvulorum*[13]).

Lack of context aggravates the ambiguities of spelling always bedevilling attempts to get to grips with a medieval vernacular. To add to the universal problems with minim-letters, here *u/v* often interchanges with *w*: a tendency probably connected with Norfolk-dialect pronunciation.[14] One or two forms in the Gaywood Roll seem, more-over, best explicable in terms of earlier spellings with *wynn*.[15] With much of the material resulting from recopying, orthographical vagaries of these and other kinds – for instance, especially in the Survey, use of *z* (ʒ) for *þ* – and associated blunders (such as a misleading *Selowd* found, in a late-fourteenth-century copy of a thirteenth-century charter, for *[filius] Seloue*) may well have compounded any older corruptions due to oral transmission. A proportion of obscure forms is, therefore, to be expected.

Even when spellings are clear and consistent, etymology and/or meaning can often be in doubt: the Gaywood Roll's *Bonet*, for instance, although at first glance possibly a nickname for someone who either made caps or wore a remarkable one, more probably shows patronymic use of the (saint's) name *Bonitus* current throughout France;[16] again, the surname *Bakun* found in the Trinity and Gaywood Rolls, although at first sug-gesting 'cured pork', probably represents patronymic use of CG *Bac(c)o*.[17] For forms interpretable either as nicknames or as patronyms, statistical probability (for what that is worth) must favour the latter. When, however, two or more nickname-meanings conflict, principles to guide choice are less easily discoverable: the already-cited Alexander *Pipe's* by-name, for instance, although very likely referring to a musical

---

[12] Cf. 'Lexicographical notes', passim, esp. references given on 65–6; also various instances below.

[13] A.L. Mayhew, ed., *The Promptorium Parvulorum: the first English-Latin Dictionary, &c.*, Early English Text Society [EETS]: Extra Series 102 (London, 1908), col. 284; cf. 'Lexicographical notes', 61.

[14] Cf. B. Sundby, 'Middle English overlapping of *v* and *w* and its phonemic significance', *Anglia* LXXXIV (1956), 438–44, and B. Seltén, *The Anglo-Saxon heritage in Middle English personal names, East Anglia 1100–1399*, Part I: Lund Studies in English [LSE] XLIII (Lund, 1972), 167–8.

[15] See 'Lexicographical notes', 66 n. 9.

[16] See, for instance, A. Vallet, *Les noms de personne du Forez . . . aux xiiᵉ, xiiiᵉ et xivᵉ siècles*, Publications de l'Institut de linguistique romane de Lyon XVIII (Paris, 1961), 70, also 87. Cf. below 273–4.

[17] For *Bac(c)o*, see W. Schlaug, *Die altsächsischen Personennamen vor dem Jahre 1000*, Lunder Germanistische Forschungen [LGF] XXXVI (Lund, 1962), 56, and M.-Th. Morlet, *Les noms de personne sur le territoire de l'ancienne Gaule du viᵉ au xiiᵉ siècle*, 2 vols (Paris, 1968–1972), i.50a. As the surname of (amongst others) a feudal family, this was in any case probably imported rather than created on English soil: see L.C. Loyd *et alii*, *The origins of some Anglo-Norman families*, Harleian Society CIII (Leeds, 1951), 10–11.

instrument, might, alternatively, have been derived from a conduit, or a wine-measure, or a bobbin; at present there seems no way of knowing which.[18]

Even with the 'dictionary' meaning clear, the true sense of a nickname often remains in doubt. The Gaywood Roll lists, separately, a John *Ioie* and an Alan *Ioie*: should one suppose the bearer of such a name, or the ancestor from whom he took it, to have been an uncommonly merry fellow, or a worry-guts and killjoy whose doleful countenance excited mockery? Study of modern nicknaming brings out the critical, often cruel, tone characterizing the genre; nor is there reason to suppose our medieval ancestors more mealy-mouthed. Hence, names like the Pipe Roll's *Bonpain* and *Godchep* and the Gaywood Roll's *Trouthe* are scarcely to be taken at face-value: most likely, they perpetuate ironical plays by neighbours (not to say, colleagues, competitors, and customers) on their bearers' habitual self-advertisement.[19] Much, admittedly, remains speculative; but it will be wise to bear in mind how harsh demotic wit can be.[20]

Amid such manifold uncertainties, nickname-interpretation hangs between the twin perils of fantasy and over-literalness. Special traps include unrecognized minor place-names such as, if no preposition is present, may look to the unwary like phrase-nicknames.[21] 'Meanings' proposed can seldom be more than guesses; and all the following comments are to be read in the shadow of that warning.

Once provisionally identified and interpreted, by-names may then, no less provisionally, be classified in various ways: semantically, for instance, or geographically.

(iii)   *The Meanings of Some By-Names*

The meanings of by-names fall into four general categories: family relationships; place either of present domicile or of familial origins; occupation or rank; and miscellaneous characterizations. Each of these categories can, to some degree, be further subdivided.

Family relationships allow of limited variation. As already-quoted periphrases have shown, an individual might on occasion be defined as 'brother' or 'sister' of another or as someone's 'grandson/nephew' (*nepos* being ambiguous); but such designations seldom evolved into set name-forms. Exceptionally, the 1166 Pipe Roll offers the compound *Lellesmai* 'Lelle's kinsman' (*Lelle* being probably a feminine short-form, perhaps from *Lēofflǣd*[22] – in this dialect the -*s*-genitive would by this date have been

---

[18] A by-name *Pipe* was current not only in England but also in Franco-Flemish areas (cf. below 277): French meanings offered by Godefroy and by Tobler-Lommatzsch include 'tube', 'whistle', and 'fluid-measure'; for 'bobbin' as a Flemish meaning, see G. de Poerck, *La draperie médiévale en Flandre et en Artois: technique et terminologie*, 3 vols (Bruges, 1951), i.69 and iii.108. Cf. also *MED*, *s.vv.*

[19] For fuller discussion of nicknaming-modes, see P. McClure, 'Nicknames and petnames', *Nomina* V (1981), 63–76, together with his two reviews, *ibidem*, 95–104 and 121–3; also my own review of J. Jönsjö, *Studies on Middle English nicknames, Part I: Compounds*, LSE LV (Lund, 1979), in *English Studies* LXIII (1982), 168–70.

[20] A point repeatedly made over the last half-century by Dauzat (see, for instance, *Les noms de personnes* [Paris, 1925], 75–6, 96–7, 165) and by his disciples, but by others too often unheeded (cf. n. 19 above).

[21] Gillian Fellows Jensen made this point in her review of Jönsjö, *Nicknames*, published in *Namn och Bygd* LXVIII (1980), 102–15.

[22] See Part I, n. 74.

generalized); but when the Trinity Roll later shows the simplex *Lelle* figuring as a by-name, there is no way to tell whether the same family is involved.

For men the standard vernacular form of family-specification shows a simple apposition of the baptismal name of the father or some earlier male ancestor (or, less often, of the mother), with no -*s* or -*son* suffix.[23] The scribes, however, more usually render such by-names in Latin using the *filius*-formula, though only occasionally do the records oblige with an exemplificatory parallel: thus the 1166 Pipe Roll offers *Rob. Tein* apparently interchanging with *Rob. fil. Thein*. Whether the by-name appears only in the vernacular form (instances range from the 1166 Pipe Roll's *Ric. Chelloc* to numerous ones throughout all the thirteenth-century records), or whether it occurs only in the *filius*-form, there is rarely sufficient evidence to demonstrate if a particular name is a true patronymic, denoting actual parentage (as must very frequently have been the case), or had, as with the already-cited *Ricardus Ode* (alias *filius Nicolai Ode*), become hereditary.

For women, the commonest designation is as *uxor*, although *filia* and *soror* (but not, in the material excerpted, *neptia*) also occur. Again it remains uncertain how far the Latin formulas corresponded to everyday usage. Women, like men, also appear with apparent appositional patronyms, as with the Gaywood Roll's *Beatricis Guntard*, *Cecilie Kineman*, *Marie Lambert*, *Olive Dawe*, and others. Whether such forms were true patronyms, inherited family-names, or husbands' by-names transferred is, without fuller evidence, impossible to tell.

Among the men listed in the 1166 Pipe Roll, a good few bear metronyms: clear cases are those involving *Alfled*, *Ælueue* (2x), *Alswed*, *Alfware* (2x), the appositional *Chelloc*,[24] *Edilde* and *Leftred*; to these should probably be added the ambiguous *Amabil'*,[25] and some at least of the short-forms *Biffe*, *Duve*, *Give*, *Gode*, *Tette* (locally famous as the name of St Guthlac's mother) and *Titte*, all of which look like Latinized (genitive) feminines.[26] The Gaywood Roll also offers several true metronyms, such as *Iohannis filii Ysabelle* and *Radulphi filii Mariote*, together with a fair number of appositional metronymic by-names, such as *Godfridi Langlif*, *Reginaldi Sirith*, *Ricardi Hymeyn*, *Rogeri Hodierne*, *Willelmi Leverun*, and others. Although no standard can be adduced for comparison, such an incidence of metronyms is certainly not low. Perhaps, as suggested elsewhere,[27] forms like this hint at one source for the peopling of new or expanding towns, in so far as the illegitimate (unlikely to succeed to land, but possibly compensated with cash) and the sons of widows might have been especially eager to try their luck there.

---

23 Exceptionally, the Gaywood Roll offers *Alicie Cakardes* (cf. 'Lexicographical notes', 59) and also *Rogeri Hotes*; alternatively, these might represent a sporadic scribal over-zealousness in putting names into the genitive.
   The normal usage here is compatible with McKinley's findings that suffixal forms appear later than appositional ones: see his *Norfolk and Suffolk*, 3, 129–38, and *Oxfordshire*, 216–35, also Fellows Jensen, 'Surnames', 54.

24 The name, in Anglo-French versions of the Havelok story, of one of the fisherman Grim's daughters: see A. Bell, ed., *Le lai d'Haveloc* (Manchester, 1925), 264. For non-fictional instances, see E. Björkman, *Nordische Personennamen in England*, Studien zur englischen Philologie [StEP] XXXVII (Halle, 1910), 181, and *idem*, *Zur englischen Namenkunde*, StEP XLVII (Halle, 1912), 53. A surname *Kellock* still occurs in East Anglia.

25 See Part I, n. 52.

26 See Part I, n. 74.

27 See 'Battle c.1110: an anthroponymist looks at an Anglo-Norman new town', above 221–40, esp. 232.

The two, contrasting types of geographical by-name have already been noted in passing: 'locative', based on proper place-names; and 'topographical', based on common nouns denoting elements of rural or urban landscape. The two categories are distinct. Already it has been noted how locatives can freely be added, as secondary qualifiers, to primary by-names of all other types, topographical ones included; but the latter are never so used.

Furthermore, when primary by-names alone are considered, the two types can be seen to characterize different sorts of records. Of the present range of materials, the Gaywood Roll most often shows topographical forms, which in the Pipe Roll, the Trinity Roll and the Survey are relatively rarer; the latter, by contrast, show higher incidences of primary locatives. These distributions correlate with what can be deduced about the 'catchment areas' of the documents: as the citations of secondary locatives have already made clear, the Gaywood Roll, to a far greater extent than the Trinity Roll and by definition unlike the Newland Survey, lists not only residents in the town of Lynn but also, indeed more often, people from the villages of its hinterland. That is, topographical names are characteristic of people, mainly of modest condition, living in small settlements and on what were probably ancestral holdings, whereas locatives mark out those who have migrated from villages and small towns to larger centres. The 'meaning' of both sorts of by-name may be thus as much social as geographical.[28]

At these dates, most topographical phrases probably still indicated their bearers' present homes. Examples, dating unless otherwise noted from the thirteenth century, include: the 1166 Pipe Roll's *atte Bal*, although this in fact probably involves a minor place-name;[29] *atte Delhus*, meaning either 'at the house in the hollow' or, alternatively, 'at the wooden house' (*deal* 'plank' – possibly also found on its own among the by-names here – being a Low-German loanword into Middle English); *atte Gap*, with a common Scandinavian loanword, and likewise *atte Ling* 'beside the heather'; *atte Lode* 'beside the watercourse'; *atte Phorche*, possibly meaning 'beside the gallows';[30] *atte Pinfolde*; *atte Sloye* 'beside the slough'; the Pipe Roll's *atte Was* 'beside the Wash', again probably with the proper place-name; *atte Wellehus*; *atte Wode* and *in Wode*; *over the Watere* and *be west half the Watere*, that is, 'from West Lynn'. Often scribes wholly or partly Gallicized such phrases: *del Both* and *de la Bothe* 'of the booth or hut', again with a Scandinavian loanword; *de la Castel*; *de (la) Corner* 'from (North) Hurn'; *del Hil*; *de la Launde*; *de la Verte Place*; *de la Winde* 'of the twisty path'.[31] Sometimes they thoroughly Latinized them: *ad Aquam*, *ad Capud Pontis*, *ad Crucem*, *ad Ecclesiam*, *ad Pontem*, *de Angulo*, *de Ecclesia*, *de Foro*, *de Marisco*, *de Monasterio*, *de Puteo*, *de*

---

[28] See McKinley, *Oxfordshire*, 41–4, 65, 68, 199–207; cf. below n. 34.

[29] For topographical terms in general, see M.T. Löfvenberg, *Studies on Middle English local surnames*, LSE XI (Lund, 1942), and G. Kristensson, *Studies on Middle English topographical terms*, Acta Universitatis Lundensis Sect. I: 13 (Lund, 1970); also A.H. Smith, *The elements of English place-names*, 2 vols, English Place-Name Society XXV and XXVI (Cambridge, 1956), plus each of the county volumes. For several terms found here, see also McKinley, *Norfolk and Suffolk*, 109–16.

For the term *bal*, see Löfvenberg, *Local surnames*, 56, and cf. *MED*, *s.v.* Here (as also with *atte Was* 'beside the Wash') a proper place-name seems involved, that of the *Bal(le)* or open space at Cold Hurn in South Lynn.

[30] See 'Lexicographical notes', 62.

[31] See Löfvenberg, *Local surnames*, 232.

Vallibus, (de) ultra Aquam (the Trinity Roll's *de Botha* and the Gaywood Roll's *de Fenne* have only superficially been given the right look). Less often, residence might be shown by a simple appositional ('asyndetic') form, as apparently with *Hovel, Kot, Wude*. Alternatively, descriptive compounds were used, such as *Daleman, le Border* 'cottager' and *(le) Hokere*; but no *-wine*-formations based on topographical terms have been noted here.[32]

By-names formed with place-names proper occur in all the materials. Usually they show Latinized *de*, and then the only problem is to identify the place concerned. A few, like the Trinity Roll's *Will. Matelaske*, are, however, asyndetic, in this probably reflecting colloquial usage; these, as already observed, can prove misleading. Some locative names denote domicile; those of the gentry often referred to a principal estate. With burgesses, on the other hand, and with some families of gentry as well, they functioned mainly as *noms d'origine*, personal or familial; locatives of this sort offer vital evidence about population-movements.[33] As already noted, this type of by-name, so frequent in Lynn's specifically urban records, seems to have been especially common among men who were mobile socially as well as geographically.[34]

Occupational by-names, like locative ones, appear in either primary or secondary position. Instances of the latter – always, presumably, indicating the actual trade practised – include the Gaywood Roll's *Ricardi Hymeyn, calwere* 'R.H., calf-herd (or -dealer)'[35] and the Trinity Roll's *Alex. de Morle, tanour, Herveus de Geyton, fenur, Johannes de Acra, laner, Johannes de Tilneye, aurifaber, Radulphus de Riveshale, clericus*, and so on. (As with other secondary by-names, those added after *filius*-formulas are ambiguous, and again often no doubt appropriately so.) Double forms are, however, rare in the present materials.

Occupational by-names standing in primary place are never to be uncritically accepted at face-value. Latinized ones fall – equally with *filius*-formulas and with some locative phrases – under suspicion of being scribal contributions: in which case their evidence is excellent for economic activities, less so for colloquial name-usage. Of course, because scribes simply systematized current attitudes and habits, all such forms must have reflected, generally when not specifically, colloquial modes of identification (as amply illustrated by modern family-names). With a vernacular form, less likely to have been scribally devised, the question is whether it recorded the bearer's own trade or that of a relative: some women have been noted as bearing occupational by-names that cannot have been their own, and with men's names too the possibility of inheritance is, although less obvious, ever-present. For individuals this question can seldom be answered. On the other hand, the fluidity evident in all the by-naming here encourages an assumption that most of the occupational terms found, whether or not

---

[32] For *hokere*, see 'Some early Canterbury surnames', above 211. For formations in *-er* and in *-man*, cf. McKinley, *Norfolk and Suffolk*, 119; for *-wine*-compounds see Seltén, *Heritage*, I, 20–2.

[33] For the methodology involved in interpreting evidence of this kind, see P. McClure, 'Surnames from English place-names as evidence for mobility in the Middle Ages', *Local Historian* XIII (1978), 80–6, and *idem*, 'Patterns of migration in the late Middle Ages: the evidence of English place-name surnames', *Economic History Review*, 2nd ser. XXXII (1979), 167–82.

[34] See McKinley, *Norfolk and Suffolk*, 141–9, and *idem*, 'Social class and the origin of surnames', *Genealogists' Magazine* XX (1980), 52–6, esp. 53–4; cf. above, n. 28.

[35] See 'Lexicographical notes', 58.

accurately describing all their actual bearers, did represent trades currently – or, at worst, recently – practised in this locality. Certain foreign terms must, however, for reasons to be explained,[36] be treated with caution.

Basic and universal trade-terms – like 'baker', 'hay-merchant', 'smith' and 'tailor' – need little comment. Other thirteenth-century forms – some antedating the present 'dictionary' record – more specifically reflect local patterns of life. *Anger Le Spitelman*, for instance, who flourished in the century's earlier half, must have been warden of one of the several hospitals here, probably of St John's in Damgate. Especially apposite, as the Gaywood bidding prayer *pro nautis maris* underlines, are the by-names *Schipmen* and *(Le) Steresman*. Another local trade appears in *Salter*, Gallicized as *Le Sauner*. Lynn's role as port, wool-staple, and general market, together with the consequent importance of revenues derived from the various sorts of toll, explain the frequency of by-names like *Coliur* 'tax-collector' (to be distinguished from *coliere* 'charcoal-burner'), *Le Cuner* 'market-inspector' (cf. *ale-conner*), *Le Cuntur* probably 'auditor',[37] and the very common *(Le) Tronur/Tronator* 'weigh-master' (*tronage* being among the most productive of the dues levied here). A minor trade-name found in the survey, *Oylman* (the present record of c.1279 being among the earliest known[38]), links up with the known existence here of oil-mills. Local relevance also characterizes another compound – apparently hitherto unrecorded – *Kirmetre* 'fen-surveyor' (from the Scandinavian loanword *ker* 'swampy scrubland') found in the same Survey.[39]

By contrast, the cloth-trades so prominent in Lynn's economic life are sparsely represented among the twelfth- and thirteenth-century by-names, and even then partly by Latinized ones: *Le Chalunher*, *Le Comber*, *Fulere/Fullo*, *Laner*, *(Le) Lindraper*, *Le Teler/Telarius/Le Tistor/Textor*. Perhaps the very frequency of these trades deprived the associated terms of great distinguishing power. The vigorous trade in dyestuffs is represented by *Le Weyder*, by the metonymic by-name *Madyr*, and probably by the apparent 'Shakespeare' compound *Rouleweyd*, which could refer to the rolling of woad-paste into balls.[40] The related industry, from which a whole street, *Litisterisgate* alias *Vicus Tinctorum*, took its thirteenth-century name,[41] produced not only the by-name *Le Litestere* but also *Le Blekestere* 'bleacher', both being based on Scandinavian loanwords.

---

36 See below 275–8.

37 See *MED*, *s.v. cǒuntǒur* n. (1), sense 1.(a); also B. Thuresson, *Middle English occupational terms*, LSE XIX (Lund, 1950), 140. An alternative sense is 'pleader in law-court' (*MED*, sense 1.(c); cf. also J. Mann, *Chaucer and medieval estates satire* [Cambridge, 1973], 158-9 and 280-1, followed by N. Saul, in *Medium Ævum* LII [1983], 10–26, esp. 19).

38 G. Fransson, *Middle English surnames of occupation, 1100–1350*, LSE III (Lund, 1935), 70, cites his earliest example from c.1275. Cf. below n.43.

39 For *ker* (cf. the modern surname *Carr*), see especially McKinley, *Norfolk and Suffolk*, 110; also *MED*, *s.v.* The spelling *kir* might have resulted from confusion of its *e*, derived from Viking Norse (equivalent to later *ja*), with the reflex of OE *y*, which in Norfolk varied between *e* and *i*, but with *i*-forms usually dominant (see Seltén, *Heritage* I, 113–16; also S.B. Meech and H.E. Allen, eds, *The Book of Margery Kempe*, EETS: Original Series 212 [London, 1940], xvii–xxi). The Survey spelling interestingly finds a later parallel in the *aldyrkyr* in *Promptorium Parvulorum*, 9.

40 No English or continental parallel has yet come to light. For the probably relevant process in the manufacture of woad-paste, see de Poerck, *La draperie médiévale*, i. 152–3.

41 See E. and P. Rutledge, 'Two surveys', 104–5, where they note that few of the named landholders in this area are, however, described as dyers.

Among the then luxury trades, rabbit-breeding is denoted by *Le Warner*;[42] others include *Habertasker* (= *-dasher*) – the instance found here in the Survey being among the earliest known[43] – and also *Le Orfevere/Aurifaber*, *Le Peyntour/Pictor*, and *Vinetarius*. Professional aid seems promised by the Trinity Roll's *Le Parlur* 'pleader';[44] and also, more crucially, by *Apothecarius* and *Le Leche/Medicus*. The town's need to cater for visiting seafarers is reflected by the frequency of *(Le) Tavern(i)er*, one of the few trade-terms which the thirteenth-century records show in secondary as well as primary position, as in the Survey's *Eadmundi de Sutton, taverner/tabernarii* (the Gaywood bidding prayer specifically requests supplications *pro omnibus pandaxatoribus Lenne*). The same context explains the *Joculator* of the 1166 Pipe Roll; but *Gliuman*, found there in a *filius*-formula, and *Spileman*, found later as a by-name, although they had etymologically the same sense, were at these dates probably functioning simply as personal names.[45] The likeliest interpretation of the Trinity Roll's *Vilour/Le Viliur* is 'fiddler', these instances again being amongst the earliest so far noted.[46]

As well as reflecting Lynn's considerable import-trade in wax, the previously-unnoted term *Candelwif* found in the Gaywood Roll (cf. the masculine *Kandeler* also found there) supplements the tiny corpus of specifically feminine Middle-English trade-terms.[47] Another form apparently so far uncollected is the *Chesewoman* found in a court-roll of 1301 (cf. the Gaywood Roll's *Cheseman*). It is, as explained, often hard to tell whether occupational by-names attributed to women were their own or transferred from father or husband; given the family basis of much early 'industry', the distinction may be partly irrelevant.

The comparative paucity of occupational names proper may to some extent have been counterbalanced by use of metonymic 'nicknames' – like *Candel* and like the *Madyr* already cited – referring to characteristic tools or wares.[48] The feminine *Le Koyfe* found in the Gaywood Roll, rather than alluding to its bearer's own attire, probably reflected the existence in Lynn of a coifmakers' gild.[49] Such forms are, however, too uncertain of interpretation to have great value for economic and social history: thus, the Pipe Roll's *Baril* (a French form) might have denoted a tubby man rather than one who made casks or shipped his wares in them, and the Gaywood Roll's *Peper*, a hot-tempered man rather than either a spicer or someone who paid or collected 'peppercorn rents'; the Survey's *Portehors* 'breviary' (*portiforium*) and *Primer* might have denoted either dealers in religious texts or people of ostentatious piety.

---

[42] Cf. E.M. Veale, 'The rabbit in England', *Agricultural History Review* V (1957), 85–90.

[43] The earliest instance cited by *MED*, *s.v. haberdasher*, is dated 1280; Thuresson, *Occupational terms*, 212, had offered none from earlier than the fifteenth century. Other early instances of tradenames – not especially significant in meaning – include those of Survey's *Mustardman*, of the Gaywood Roll's *Feccher*, not in Thuresson and not noted by *MED* until the fifteenth century, and of the *Fetherman* in the Tallage Roll of c.1290.

[44] Absent from *MED* and apparently not a term of common vocabulary but a scribal Gallicism; not listed by Thuresson, *Occupational terms*.

[45] *Spilemann* (but not **Glēowmann*) is classed as a personal name by B. Seltén, *Heritage*, Part II: Acta Regiae Societatis Humaniorum Litterarum Lundensis LXXIII (Lund, 1979), 149.

[46] See Thuresson, *Occupational terms*, 186 ('Lexicographical notes', 65, is therefore now superseded).

[47] See 'Lexicographical notes', 58.

[48] Cf., for instance, P.H. Reaney, *The origin of English surnames* (London, 1967), 176, 245–8 and 274.

[49] Cf. 'Lexicographical notes', 59.

Several by-names refer to seafaring matters or to fish, as with the Gaywood Roll's *Schip* and perhaps with its *Slingge*, if correctly interpreted as 'lifting-gear',[50] and likewise in the same Roll as well as in the Survey, with *Codling*[51] (with which name the *Codlingelane* figuring in a 1577 list of streets may, or may not, be linked), with *Haddoc*, frequent in the Trinity Roll, and also with the *Herryng* borne in the late fourteenth century by a man paying dues *pro iure unius naviculi*. Some phrase-names too may have been occupational: *Rouleweyd* has already been mentioned; another is the Survey's *Wendut(h)* 'fare out', an apt name for a seafarer and indeed given in *Havelok the Dane* to one of the hero's fishermen foster-brothers.[52] Other by-names suiting a mercantile community include some taken, like the Trinity Roll's *Besaunt* and *Schyllyng*, from coinage.

True nicknames, characterizing the bearer personally rather than by trade, by residence or by origin, constitute the most varied range of all, in form as well as in meaning, varying as they do from simple epithets (often Latinized in the records, thus, *Juvenis*, *Parvus*) to complex phrases. As previously observed, this category not only merges confusingly into the occupational one but is, of its own nature, beset with obscurities and ironies of all kinds.

Epithets like the Gaywood Roll's *Freman* and (*Le*) *Neuman* are scarcely noteworthy. The same might be supposed of commonplace physical descriptions, like the *Blak*, *Blund*, *Brun*, *Crul*, *Le Longe*, *Le Rede*, *Le Rus*, *Le Wyte/Albus*, found throughout our thirteenth-century records, but especially characteristic of the Gaywood Roll. On the other hand, experience suggests the likelihood of crude ironies (here unverifiable) like calling a bald man *Curly* or a huge one *Tiny*.

As soon as character is in question, irony must constantly be suspected: the Gaywood Roll's *Joie* has been discussed, and the Trinity Roll's *Blithe*, *Swift* and *Scherewynd* are analogous. A crucial aspect of nicknaming – admittedly impossible to treat with any exactitude in a non-contemporary context – is its use to express, and so obliquely to enforce, standards of behaviour.[53] One vice constantly harped on in medieval naming is stinginess, here alluded to by the 1166 Pipe Roll's *Locheburs* 'lock purse' and probably also by its *Pilecat* 'skin a cat'. From another point of view, the latter and several other forms, like the *Milnemus* 'mill-mouse' (the opposite of 'church-mouse') found in two charters datable to the first quarter of the thirteenth century, can be seen as encapsulating popular sayings.[54]

As yet, such interpretations are too uncertain, as well as too few, to afford usable evidence about our ancestors' attitudes and beliefs, or even about their colloquial usages.[55] In time, however, medieval nicknames will undoubtedly have a great deal to

---

[50] See 'Lexicographical notes', 63.

[51] A conjectural etymology of *cod(fish)* is proposed by W.B. Lockwood, in *Zeitschrift für Anglistik und Amerikanistik* XVII (1969), 252–3. For *Codfish* and for *Codling*, by-names afford the earliest attestations known.

[52] A common nickname: cf. (ignoring the interpretation suggested) Jönsjö, *Nicknames*, 186.

[53] Cf. J. Morgan *et alii*, *Nicknames: their origins and social consequences* (London, 1979) – reviewed by P. McClure in *Nomina* V, 121–3.

[54] See 'Lexicographical notes', 61, also 57.

[55] A line whose exploration has often been mooted – for instance, by G. Tengvik, *Old English by-names*, Nomina Germanica IV (Uppsala, 1938), 23–7; Reaney, *Origin*, 223–9; and O. von Feilitzen, 'The personal names and bynames of the Winton Domesday', in M. Biddle *et alii*, eds

tell about such matters, not least through such allusions and collocational puns as seem embalmed in the Trinity Roll's *Simon Magus*, for a man whose original by-name seems to have been *Mager*, and the Gaywood Roll's *Philippi Makebeus*.

(iv) *The Provenances of Certain By-Names*

In an historical context special interest attaches to the geographical analysis applicable, in varying degrees, to all except topographical by-names. For Lynn, the outside contacts and the consequent immigration – from overseas as well as from other parts of England – which the town experienced are well documented; and already the baptismal names found here have been argued partly to reflect them.[56] So it seems worthwhile to investigate whether by-names can likewise be make to throw light on the social and cultural repercussions of these foreign contacts.

The most obvious material for geographical analysis consists of the *noms d'origine* so dominant in the specifically urban records like the Trinity Roll and the Newland Survey; these by-names have already been noted as typical of people socially as well as physically mobile. Some locative names – especially in the Gaywood Roll's secondary additions – refer to Lynn itself and to places near-by: these may indicate current residence. Many, on the other hand, refer to places much farther afield, from Lindsey to Lübeck; and these must point to sources of the growing town's population.

About the English *noms d'origine* recognizable in these records little will be said here. Mrs Owen herself has made a study of this material and its implications, and hopes to publish it in due course.[57]

The epithets and *noms d'origine* referring to continental localities are, by contrast, central to a main present purpose: that of exploring the possible range of foreign influences impinging upon such a port as Lynn. These items will therefore be considered as pointers to potential sources for other sorts of apparently foreign by-name found here.

Various epithets found throughout the thirteenth-century records imply French extraction, often but not invariably from the north and north-east quarters: (*Le*) *Fraunceis* and *Frankis*, perhaps *Le Bret* if meaning 'Breton' rather than 'Welsh', (*Le*) *Burguliun*, *Champeneis, Picard, Poer* (that is, probably *Po(i)hier* 'from Poix, near Amiens'[58]). Many *noms d'origine* found here, in the Trinity Roll especially, point the same way: *de Amiens, de Bavent* (*dép.* Calvados), *de Bek, de Beauveys/de Belvaco* (the name of a

---

and trss, *Winchester in the early Middle Ages*, Winchester Studies I (Oxford, 1976) [*PNWD*], 143–229, esp. 229.

56 See Part I, above 241–57, *passim*.

57 [[See the remarks in D.M. Owen, 'Bishop's Lynn: the first century of a new town?', *Proceedings of the Battle Conference on Anglo-Norman Studies*, II (1979), 141–53 and 196–7, esp. 152, and *eadem, King's Lynn*, 41.]]

58 P.H. Reaney, *A Dictionary of British Surnames*, 2nd edn (London, 1976) [*DBS*], *s.n. Poor* (&c.), gives simply 'Picard'. For the narrower sense, 'from Poix and, by extension, from Ponthieu', see F. Godefroy, *Dictionnaire de l'ancienne langue française* (Paris, 1881–1902), *s.v. pohier* (cf. Mod. Fr. *poyais*), followed by M.-Th. Morlet, 'Les noms de personne à Eu du xiiie au xve siècle (suite)', *Revue internationale d'onomastique* [*RIO*] XI (1959), 174–82, esp. 177, and by M. Gysseling and P. Bougard, *L'Onomastique calaisienne à la fin du xiiie siècle*, Anthroponymica XIII (Leuven, 1963). On the other hand, A. Dauzat and M.-Th. Morlet, *Dictionnaire étymologique des noms de famille et prénoms de France* (Paris, 1969), give *Poher* 'breton'.

principal merchant dynasty here), *de Berneye, de Creci*, probably *Cundi* (if represent-ing the *Condé* common in Normandy and in NE France), probably the so-far-unidentified *de Gailencourt*,[59] *de Hauvile* (perhaps *Hauville, dép.* Eure), *de Ispania* (if correctly identified as *Epaignes, dép.* Eure),[60] *de Lanvale* (compare, perhaps, *Lanval-lay, dép.* Côtes-du-Nord), *de Lysewys* (*Lisieux*), *de Paris*, probably *Robeis* (if repre-senting *Roubaix*),[61] *de Saint Lo, de S. Omero*, the unexpected *de Runcival* (perhaps reflecting Gascon trade in wine and in salt), and *de Viane* (alluding probably to one of several northern *Viennes* rather than to the ancient city on the Rhône).[62] The repeated references to places in Picardy and thereabouts recall the brisk commerce between Lynn and Amiens, then the centre of the woad-trade;[63] they can be set against the resemblances already noted between some baptismal names found in Lynn records and forms characteristic of north-eastern France.[64]

Lynn also had a vigorous trade along the Dutch and North German coasts, and with the future Hanseatic ports in particular. This too is sometimes reflected in thirteenth-century geographical by-names, both epithets and *noms d'origine*: *Flandrensis/(Le) Flemyng, de Flandria, de Alos(t), de Stavere* (*Stavoren* in Friesland), also *Caron de Suris* (if rightly taken as 'Wainwright from Surice, near Namur'); *Aleman, Estrich/Es-treis/Estrensis* (another surname belonging to a leading merchant dynasty),[65] *le Ger', de Almayne/de Almania, de Coloigne/de Colonia, de Lubyk*. And, be it noted, just as in the early fifteenth century a son of Margery Kempe's was to marry in Dantzig, so at least one thirteenth-century 'Easterling' in Lynn married into a prominent local family: the Trinity Roll's *Folcardus Estrensis qui duxit in uxorem fil. Roberti de Cybeceye*.

Lynn's equally flourishing Norwegian trade has left disappointingly few recogniz-able traces among extant thirteenth-century names. The most remarkable character, Siglan Susse of Gotland, who first appears as an alien fallen foul of the law and later as a 'king's merchant', belongs to the early fourteenth century.[66] The *Thur(u)ndeyn* dynasty, one of whose members appears in the Trinity Roll, is believed to have taken its name from *Trondheim*; and probably the by-name *Le Noreys* found several times in the Trinity Roll meant here, as it sometimes did elsewhere in Middle English, 'Norwegian' rather than 'northerner' in a more general sense.[67]

Geographical analysis applies also, although more impressionistically, to patronyms, whose distributions naturally follow those of baptismal names,[68] but with some twists. Being less subject than baptismal names to Latinization and thus oftener recorded in

[59] No exact parallel for this name has so far been found; but a place-name element *Gaillon-* occurs in NE France, and fourteenth-century Beauvais offers an apparently unidentified *de Gallencourt* (M.-Th. Morlet, 'Les noms de personne à Beauvais au xive siècle', *Bulletin philologique et historique . . . 1955 et 1956* [Paris, 1957], 295–309, esp. 300).

[60] See Loyd, *Origins*, 51–2; such a name need not indicate immigration directly into Lynn.

[61] See 'Lexicographical notes', 65.

[62] See 'Lexicographical notes', 67 n. 17.

[63] See E.M. Carus-Wilson, 'La guède française en Angleterre: un grand commerce du Moyen Age', *Revue du Nord* XXXV (1953), 89–105, esp. 98–9.

[64] See Part I, above 253–4.

[65] See 'Lexicographical notes', 60.

[66] See *Calendar of the Close Rolls* (PRO, 1892–), *1307*, 514, and *Calendar of the Patent Rolls* (PRO, 1891–), *1315*, 260 and 280, and *1320*, 431.

[67] See *MED, s.v. norreis*.

[68] See Part I, passim, and esp. 250–5.

their true shape, patronyms are more readily referred to their likely provenances. With certain Lynn by-names of continental form, corresponding baptismal ones seem rare not just locally but in Middle English usage generally. True, the lack of any comprehensive Middle English onomasticon precludes dogmatism on such matters; but, on present evidence, foreign forms recorded in England mainly as 'patronyms' may reasonably be supposed often to have been imported as established surnames. In individual cases, verification is seldom possible; but the probabilities can to some extent be assessed through comparison with known usages in the appropriate areas of the Continent. At the moment such comparisons can, unfortunately, be no more than approximate, because for certain of the areas the only secondary studies as yet available deal with periods somewhat later than those of the present Lynn materials.[69]

Predictably, many patronyms found in these Lynn materials show characteristically French linguistic forms, backed by French, or Franco-Flemish, distributions. Mostly, however, these involve baptismal names common also throughout medieval England, such as *Andru*, *Austin*, *Davi*, *Drewe*, *Hunfrey*, and so on. But all the records, and not least the Gaywood Roll, despite its more rural 'catchment area', equally offer 'patronyms' for which corresponding baptismal forms are, if not totally absent from English records, at all events rare. These potentially more significant forms include: *Aubin* (cf. the Trinity Roll's *fil. Albini*), which represents either the saint's name *Albinus* or else a hypocoristic of *Albert* or of *Aubrey* – in either case showing a characteristically French vocalization of preconsonantal [ł] – and which was current in Evreux, Eu, Beauvais, Corbie, Arras and Artois; *Bon(n)et*, probably, as noted, representing *Bonitus* and

---

[69] The secondary studies consulted for French and Franco-Flemish usages are, in roughly west-to-east order: M. Le Pesant, 'Les noms de personne à Evreux du xiie au xive siècle', *Annales de Normandie* VI (1956), 47–74; Morlet, 'Eu', *RIO* XI (1959), 131–48, 174–84, and XII (1960), 62–70, 137–48, and 205–19; *eadem*, 'Beauvais'; *eadem*, *Etude d'anthroponymie picarde* (Amiens, 1967); *eadem*, 'Les noms de personne à Corbie au xive siècle', *Bulletin philologique et historique . . . 1967* (Paris, 1969), 739–78; P. Bougard and M. Gysseling, *L'Impôt royal en Artois (1295–1302)*, Anthroponymica XVIII (Leuven, 1970); R. Berger, ed., *Le nécrologe de la confrérie des jongleurs et des bourgeois d'Arras (1194–1361)*, 2 vols (Arras, 1963–70); H. Jacobsson, *Etudes d'anthroponymie lorraine* (Göteborg, 1955); Gysseling and Bougard, *L'Onomastique calaisienne*.

Secondary studies consulted for Dutch and German usages are: C. Marynissen, *Hypokoristische suffixen in oudnederlandse persoonsnamen*, 2 vols (Diss. Leuven, 1971); F. Debrabandere, *Persoonsnamen in het Kortrijkse (1300–1350)*, Anthroponymica XIX (Leuven, 1971), and *idem*, *Kortrijkse Naamkunden 1200–1300*, Anthroponymica XXII (Leuven, 1980); W. Beele, *Studie van de ieperse persoonsnamen uit de stads- en baljuwsrekeningen 1250–1400*, 2 vols (Handzame, 1975); C. Tavernier-Vereecken, *Gentse Naamkunde van ca.1000 tot 1252* (Tongeren, 1968); J. Lindemans, *Brabantse persoonsnamen in de xiiie en de xive eeuw*, Anthroponymica I (Leuven, 1947); M. Gysseling, *Overzieht over de noordnederlandse persoonsnamen tot 1225*, Anthroponymica XVI (Leuven, 1966); S. Hagström, *Kölner Beinamen des 12. und 13. Jahrhunderts*, Nomina Germanica VIII (Uppsala, 1949); F. Wagner, *Studien über die Namengebung in Köln im zwölften Jahrhundert*, I: *Die Rufnamen* (Diss. Göttingen, 1913); W. Schlaug, *Studien zu den altsächsischen Personennamen des 11. und 12. Jahrhunderts*, LGF XXX (Lund, 1955) [cf. n. 17]; K. Carstens, *Beiträge zur Geschichte der bremischen Familiennamen* (Diss. Marburg; Bremen, 1906); G. Mahnken, *Die hamburgischen niederdeutschen Personennamen des 13. Jahrhunderts* (Dortmund, 1925); A. Reimpell, *Die lübecker Personennamen unter besonderer Berücksichtigung der Familiennamenbildung bis zur Mitte des 14. Jahrhunderts* (Diss. Hamburg, 1928); H. Brockmüller, *Die rostocker Personennamen bis 1304* (Diss. Rostock, 1933).

Cf. Part I, n. 63. Because these studies are mostly alphabetically arranged and/or well indexed, detailed references will not be given.

recorded, for instance, in Eu and in Picardy, as well as in the Arras by-name *Bonete*; *Boselin*, a double-diminutive, current in Flanders as well as in France, of the CG short-form *Boso*, of which *Buzun* shows the French reflex;[70] *Fubert*, resembling the *Foubert* noted in Artois, and elsewhere, as a French reflex of CG *Folcber(h)t*; *Galien/Galiun* (also *fil. Galione*), found as a baptismal name as well as a by-name in many parts of France including Arras,[71] and also in Calais and Ieper; *Gubilliun*, probably a French double-diminutive of *Gobaut* or *Gobert* (from CG *Gode-*);[72] perhaps *Howardyn*, if representing a double-diminutive of CG *Hugo*; *Hulin*, which seems to correspond either to the double-diminutive *Hugelinus* noted in Artois and also, as *Huelin*, in Eu and in Arras, or else to the Picard *Heulin* conjecturally attributed to an etymon in *Hilde-*;[73] *Moyse*,[74] comparable with the *Mois* found, for instance, at Calais; *Polard*, a derivative of *Pol* (*Paul*) seen at Eu, for instance, as *Polart*, and likewise *Poligrand* (also *Porigrand*, with assimilation of *-l-* to *-r-*), which latter evidently shows patronymic use of the compound *Pol li grand* 'Tall Paul', thus incorporating one of the commonest French nicknames;[75] *Ruffin*, from *Rufinus*, found as a baptismal name in Picardy and in other French-speaking areas as well as being current as a by-name in Corbie, Arras and Ieper; *Turpin*,[76] found in Picardy, and especially at Beauvais, Corbie and Arras; *Yvori*, perhaps a metronym based on *Yvoria*, as noted at Calais, rather than a nickname-use of the common noun. One difficult form is the Trinity Roll's *Sykard*: on the one hand, *Sicardus* was a typically southern form,[77] but, on the other, *Siquart* was also proper to Picardy and Flanders. None of the quoted distributions pretends to completeness; and, as already stated, for some localities the evidence available post-dates the present records by a century or so (a shortcoming which may be partly counterbalanced by the often-distinctive linguistic forms involved). No more is claimed than the establishment of some general parallels, in keeping with what is known of Lynn's trading contacts.

Identifiably Low German patronyms seem less plentiful in our thirteenth-century Lynn records than do French ones. Forms such as *Vertekin* apparently show the characteristically Flemish form of diminutive.[78] Other items seemingly linked with that area include: *Damet*, found as a baptismal name in the Low Countries and in Saxony;[79] *Gerberge*, a metronym involving a phonologically-continental name current, for instance, in Ghent; *Guntard*, found in Ghent and also, as a by-name, in Picardy and in

---

[70] See Marynissen, *Hypokoristische suffixen*, 132–4 (cf. *Bozo*, 129–30).

[71] As well as the studies of naming in NE France, see also Vallet, *Le Forez*, 87.

[72] See Jacobsson, *Anthroponymie lorraine*, 33, 175.

[73] See Morlet, *Etude*, 96.

[74] Current as personal name and as by-name in Suffolk also: see McKinley, *Norfolk and Suffolk*, 129.

[75] See 'Lexicographical notes', 64.

[76] See, for instance, *PNWD*, 175; cf. 'Battle', above 240.

[77] The citations in Morlet, *Gaule*, i.198a, show no clear geographical pattern; but for the currency of *Sicardus* in SW France, see, for instance, F. Michel and C. Bémont, eds, *Rôles gascons*, 3 vols (Paris, 1885–1906), index-entries on i.185 and iii.763, and Ch. Samaran and Ch. Higounet, eds, *Recueil des actes de l'abbaye cistercienne de Bonnefont-en-Comminges* (Paris, 1970), 321.

[78] Cf. Part I, above 252.

[79] See Marynissen, *Hypokoristische suffixen*, 142, for a feminine *Dameta* noted at Cambrai; also Schlaug, *Personennamen des 11. und 12. Jahrhunderts*, 185. In England similar forms have been noted, as it happens, among Jews: see V.D. Lipman, *The Jews of medieval Norwich* (London, 1967), index.

Wallonia; and *Her(e)brand*, current in Kortrijk (Courtrai), Ghent, Cologne, Saxony and Lübeck.

Even though the provenances cited are not only incomplete but also possibly unrepresentative (depending as they do on the availability of reference-books: apart from gaps in the record, several of the studies consulted were, unhappily, loaned too briefly to be fully exploited), they join with those already noted, under similar cautions, for baptismal names, to reflect some of the social and cultural influences which Lynn assimilated from its multifarious trading contacts fanning out across the North Sea from Picardy to the Baltic.

Extending the geographical perspective reveals some occupational terms and nick-names as likewise apparently traceable – no less than *noms d'origine*, baptismal names and patronyms – to Lynn's varied continental contacts. Nicknames might have been especially responsive to any mingling of vernaculars in the market-places. But, the further the topic is explored, the more complex the problems appear. Of these, the progressive stabilization of family-names throughout most of Western Europe is among the least, in so far as it bears only on chronology and thus freshness of coinage. The crucial questions concern provenances and their cultural implications.

As for Scandinavian forms, although by-names of such etymology have been noted elsewhere in Norfolk,[80] the twelfth-and thirteenth-century Lynn records offer only a few common loanwords, distributed throughout the name-categories: the occupational *Blekestere* 'bleacher'; *del Both* 'stall, hut'; *atte Gap*; the nickname (occupational or characteristic) *Galt* 'boar'; perhaps *Gris* if here it means 'pig';[81] the frequent *Kide*; the occupational *Kirmet(e)re* with *ker* 'scrubby marshland'; *atte Ling*; *Litestere*; and perhaps the adverb *taite* 'briskly' (unless *Pistaite* is a meaningless corruption of the Flemish by-name *Pasteit* 'pie'; if, however, it were a humorous deformation, the evidence for the adverb would be as good as from a native coinage).

By-names of obviously French form – superficially far more distinct than Low German ones from the native English – are frequent. At first they may seem straight-forward; but they are in fact by no means so. Descriptions like *Le Iuuene* and *Le Vius* were usually scribal alternatives for *Iuvenis* and *Senex*; *de la Verte Place* renders *atte Grene*. By-names based on terms early adopted into Middle English, like *Curteis* and *Large*, have no necessary bearing either on the presence of French immigrants in Lynn or on the currency of French speech here. Uncertainties crystallize with occupational terms found as by-names in France itself as well as being adopted into the general Middle English vocabulary. Each case needs individual assessment: *(Le) Tavern(i)er*, for instance, already noted as sometimes found here in secondary position, must be a living, 'English', occupational term, not a fossilized imported surname; but the status of other foreign forms, and especially of those, like *Le Weyder*, connected with French trade, remains uncertain. On the other hand, here as in other bodies of medieval

---

[80] See B. Seltén, *Early East-Anglian nicknames: 'Shakespeare' names*, Scripta Minora Regiae Societatis Humaniorum Litterarum Lundensis [Scripta Minora] 1968–69/iii (Lund, 1969), 20, and *idem*, *Early East-Anglian nicknames: bahuvrihi names*, Scripta Minora 1974–75/iii (Lund, 1975), 46. Cf. K.I. Sandred's notes on the currency in Norfolk of a good few topographical terms of Scandinavian origin: 'Scandinavian place-names and appellatives in Norfolk: a study of the medieval field-names of Flitcham', *Namn och Bygd* LXVII (1979), 98–122.

[81] Cf. 'Battle', above 237.

English by-names,[82] some French forms occur that never figured in the general Middle English vocabulary: *Blanchard, Boivin, Durdent, Hurel, Morel,* and so on. By-names like these, abounding in parts of France with which other evidence links the Lynn name-stock, presumably had been imported as ready-made surnames: the Trinity Roll's *Mal(h)erbe,* for instance, was the name of a thirteenth-century woad-merchant hailing from Amiens.[83] Yet not all bearers of such names seem to have been of purely French extraction: when the 1166 Pipe Roll shows French by-names qualifying Insular first names – *Sum[erli]da Cusin, Staingrim Bonpain, Saman Passelewe* (this last oddly tautologous, as well as seeming to prefigure the later by-names like *de ultra Aquam*) – the questions are whether the Westminster scribe had Gallicized native forms, whether native Englishmen had adopted fashionable French by-names even while keeping their Insular baptismal ones, or whether these name-bearers had perhaps been born of mixed marriages. Although similar hybrid combinations are recorded elsewhere, and in records free of 'central' taint,[84] they do not as yet enable those questions to be answered. So, frequent though they are, the 'French' by-names here offer little clue as to how current that language was in the Lynn of the twelfth and thirteenth centuries. Some scribes were equal to simple translation; others stuck at *del Both* and *del Hil.* One form seemingly based on a characteristically French relative-clause by-name, the Trinity Roll's *Quipvait,* would, if its interpretation as *Qui puait* 'who used to stink' is correct, imply a scribe nimble enough among the tenses to respond to the obituary context with an ironical imperfect.[85] On the other hand, the treatment of the phrase-name *Poligrand,*[86] already in the thirteenth century sometimes garbled to *Porigrand,* suggests general unawareness of, and indifference to, its structure.

In any event, not all names French in form need have been either direct imports or Middle English coinages. Not only England but also the Low Countries and even Northern Germany, with all of which areas Lynn's commerical ties were at least as strong as with Normandy and Picardy, had likewise been touched by French name-fashions; therefore some 'French' by-names might have arrived *viâ* Flanders or Cologne, their exact provenance remaining open. Again the varying dates of the comparative materials available do nothing to reduce the tentativeness of the findings; it seemed nevertheless a pity to omit fourteenth-century parallels when for certain localities these happened to be the only ones so far published. Among these 'international' French forms are: *Argent,* current as a baptismal name in twelfth-and thirteenth-century Cologne; *Bayhard,* for *Baiard,*[87] current in Ghent before the

---

[82] Cf. 'Thoughts on the French connections of Middle English nicknames', *Nomina* II (1978), 38–40; also 'Lexicographical notes', 57–8, and my article, 'Quelques exemples de l'influence normanno-picarde sur l'anthroponymie cantorbérienne du xiie siècle', *Nouvelle revue d'onomastique* III–IV (1984), 157–66.

[83] See Carus-Wilson, 'La guède', 98–9.

[84] See 'People and languages in post-Conquest Canterbury', above 179–206, esp. 196.

[85] Cf. 'Lexicographical notes', 64–5 (no **Qui pue* has yet been found in any source consulted).

[86] See n. 75.

[87] Originally, one of the many medieval names for horses derived from colour-terms. As a human by-name too it has often, in French and English contexts alike, been taken to refer to colouring; but, unless *bai/bay* (now 'reddish-brown of body, with black mane, tail and legs') has undergone substantial semantic change, that seems unlikely. More probably, it alludes to the temperamental characteristics, rashness especially, associated with the horse-name: see the literary discussions (i) by J.D. Burnley in *Notes and Queries*, April 1976, 148–52, and (ii) by A. Renoir in *Orbis Litterarum* XXXVI (1981), 116–40; cf. also A. Carnoy, *Origines des noms de familles en Belgique* (Louvain, 1953), 388, and *DBS s.n. Bayard.*

mid-thirteenth century and in Ieper from at least the later thirteenth century on; the 1166 Pipe Roll's *Cusin*, as recorded somewhat later in Ieper, North Holland and Cologne; *Joie*, current in Ieper and in Ghent, and perhaps to be compared with Cologne's *Makejoie*; (*Le*) *Meyre*, current in Ghent as well as in thirteenth-century Kortrijk (Courtrai) and in the Artois of c.1300; *Morel*, current in Ieper, Kortrijk and Ghent; *Pipe*, current by 1300 in Kortrijk; *Purdeu*, probably comparable with the *Pardiu* seen in Ieper and Ghent; and *Saphir*, current in Ghent and in Cologne.

Such pervasive affinities, time and again appearing between Lynn by-names and those of north-eastern France and of the Franco-Flemish area, encourage an attempt at further, even more tentative rapprochements. One or two of the obscurer forms found in thirteenth-century Lynn teasingly resemble by-names found, for instance, in Artois and in some of the Flemish towns: the Gaywood Roll's *Burghet* seemingly parallels the Artois forms of c.1300, *Burget* and *dou Bourghet*; the Trinity Roll's *Pugeis* – although possibly representing *pujois* 'from (one of the various places called) *Le Puy*', also current as the name of a proverbially worthless small coin – might more convincingly be compared with the Artois by-name *de Pugieus*, taken as 'from Puisieux';[88] *Pugeman* and *Picemain* could be boss-shots at a by-name resembling Ghentish *Pucemain* (from *puteus magnus*) or the Kortrijk *Putsemeyn*; and *Struyere* strongly suggests the thirteenth-century Calais by-name *Stroiere* 'thatcher'.[89] Less convincingly, the Gaywood Roll's *Begeney* partly resembles the Artois form (*de*) *Beghenes*, taken by some modern scholars to refer to *Bientques* (*dép.* Pas-de-Calais).[90] The Trinity Roll's *Caylleweit*, instead of being taken to represent a place-name such as *Caillouet*, might instead be compared with forms like the *Calewart/Kaellewart* found in Kortrijk, Ieper and Ghent.[91] Although none of the instances in this paragraph (the last two least of all) allows of establishing any firm etymology, the repeated resemblances may be thought to suggest lines for future English surname-study.

These resemblances between Lynn's by-names and French and Franco-Flemish ones suggest that links at least as strong ought to appear between Lynn names and those of the Low German areas with which trading ties were so close. Difficulties, however, intervene. Although occupational terms and nicknames might *a priori* have been expected to reflect Lynn's German contacts at least as amply as its French ones, in practice the shared Germanic background which at times blurs the provenance of other name-forms[92] here proves an especial handicap. Apart from the similarities persisting between Middle English and Middle Low German, imported names seeming outlandish, but recognizable, to English ears might well have been normalized by English tongues, in particular by those of any local people – wives, virtuous apprentices, sons-in-law, and the like – who borrowed the incomers' names. (Recent studies stress a need, when tracing name-histories, to allow for folk-etymologizing of unfamiliar forms.)[93] However that may have been, few forms here can in the event be singled out

---

[88] See Bougard and Gysseling, *Artois*, 261; but for the modern surname *Putseys*, Carnoy, *Origines*, 118, suggests a different place-name origin.

[89] This suggestion supersedes that in 'Lexicographical notes', 61.

[90] See Bougard and Gysseling, *Artois*, 173.

[91] Cf. 'Lexicographical notes', 63.

[92] See Part I, above 252, 254.

[93] Cf. G. Ruckdeschel, 'Secondary motivation in English family-names' [abstract of thesis], *Nomina* IV (1980), 64–6 (but for serious methodological shortcomings in this study, see the review by J. Insley, *ibidem*, V [1981], 117–20).

as incontrovertibly Flemish or Low German. Teasing resemblances, on the other hand, again appear. One probable case is that of *Timberman*, the by-name of the thirteenth-century holder of the plot where the Steelyard now stands; for, whereas from Calais to Rostock this word (or its variant in *Timmer-*) was throughout the Middle Ages the regular term and by-name for 'carpenter', its English counterpart seems not to have become current until much later. The Newland Survey's *Berdekyn* looks like the Brabant *Berdeken*.[94] For the *Gir(re)* frequent in the Gaywood Roll, no compelling native etymology presents itself (depending upon pronunciation, the best candidate might be *gire*, later *jeer*, 'item of ship's tackle'; but so far that seems unnoted until the fifteenth century); but it does resemble the by-name *Gir*, meaning either 'rapacity' or 'vulture', borne by a family prominent in thirteenth-century Cologne, and current also in Lübeck and in Rostock (a similar form, *Le Ghier*, appears also in Ieper).[95] Another possibly Low German form seems to be the Gaywood Roll's *Scele*, which might be compared with *Sc(h)ele* 'squinting', a name current from Cologne to Rostock (altern-atively, it might perhaps represent an aphetic derivative of *Askell*).

So much for some apparently un-English forms. Even more perplexing are the apparently native ones which nevertheless find abundant Low German analogues. (With the 'meanings' of by-names so seldom verifiable, even for contemporaries, 'parallelism' will here, just as with some examples already cited, be limited to form.) Whereas with French by-names, linguistic form establishes the direction (although not necessarily the mode) of borrowing, with the English/Low German ones nothing can be relied on: Germans frequented Lynn, Lynn men travelled overseas, so that, in theory at least, influence might have gone either way. Equally, similar forms might have been independently evolved in each community. Some of these ambiguous forms are none-theless worth citing; the most telling parallels will be with Calais, for which the material available dates from the late thirteenth century, with Ghent, for which it antedates 1252, with Cologne, for which it dates from the twelfth and thirteenth centuries, and with Hamburg and with Rostock, for both of which it dates from the thirteenth century or before. Such by-names – found in all the Lynn materials, the partly rural Gaywood Roll included – include: *Blome*, paralleled in Kortrijk, Ieper, Ghent, Hamburg, Lübeck and Rostock, and perhaps comparable with Cologne's *Blume*; *Brun*, current at least from Kortrijk to Rostock; *Crul*, found also in Lübeck; *Dingel*, exactly paralleled in Brabant;[96] *Flicke*, possibly an Anglo-Scandinavian patro-nym but alternatively, and especially because here coupled with *Hermannus*, to be linked with *Flikken* from Cologne and *Vlicke* from Lübeck; *Hengest*, possibly an English nickname or even patronym (for an *Engistus* is named in a late-twelfth-century Norfolk record[97]) but alternatively to be linked with the Flemish by-name *Hincst* and the Cologne *Henxt*; *Hot*, paralleled in Calais and in Rostock; *Kempe*, universally common from Calais to Rostock; *(de) Krane*, likewise paralleled from Calais to Rostock; *Mast*, similar to forms found in Calais, Ieper and Lübeck; *Pape*, another form current from Calais to Rostock; *Peper*, current in Kortrijk, Lübeck and Rostock; *Rust*, found in Cologne and in Lübeck; *Schyllyng*, current in Cologne and in Rostock; perhaps the Pipe Roll's *Tripel*, if allowed to be comparable with the Rostock form

[94] See Lindemans, *Brabantse persoonsnamen*, 54.

[95] See especially Hagström, *Kölner Beinamen*, 101; cf. 'Lexicographical notes', 64.

[96] See Lindemans, *Brabantse persoonsnamen*, 53; this supersedes the suggestion in 'Lexicograph-ical notes', 59.

[97] Quoted in Seltén, *Heritage*, II, 106.

Tribel.[98] It is constantly difficult to know how far the undeniable analogies have resulted from influence (whether in one direction or the other) and how far from common habits of mind. This is especially so with the compound forms, like the Trinity Roll's *Bendedevel*, with its similarities to Ieper's *Bauduinus die den dievel bant* and Cologne's *Bunzzeduvil*, and also the Gaywood Roll's *Swetmuth*,[99] paralleled in sense although not in form by Ieper's *Zoutemond*. These scrappy notes on possible Low German analogues (rather than sources) for some of Lynn's thirteenth-century by-names cannot therefore pretend to disentangle direct influences from the pervasive legacy of common tradition; most emphatically, they by no means assert continental origins for every form discussed. What is argued is that in a busy, cosmopolitan port like Lynn not all apparently English-looking forms can safely be taken as purely native in inspiration. Some at least might have represented Low German names which, just because so easily adjusted to English usage, survived their bearers' settlement in England: a probability reinforced by the clearer findings about French forms. That being so, the pervasive affinities between Lynn's name-patterns and those of places at least as far east as Rostock (for practical reasons the limit of the present survey; there is no saying whether or not an expert on Balto-Slavonic dialects and names might find anything of interest here) suggest something about the social and cultural openness of this East-Coast port. In particular, they may explain the adoption at Lynn of the Middle Dutch loan *lufcop* 'toll',[100] and also perhaps the Low German loanwords found not only in Lynn's own fifteenth-century *Promptorium Parvulorum* but also in the thirteenth-century *Genesis and Exodus* provisionally localized in Norfolk.[101] They chime in too with the traditions of intellectual and spiritual, as well as mercantile, commerce with Germany later to be implied throughout the early-fifteenth-century *Book of Margery Kempe*.

*   *   *

This exercise in name-study, far from being carried out blind, has endeavoured constantly to take account of available findings in other spheres, those in commerical history especially. Some might therefore feel that using its results to throw light back on social history smacks of circularity. Apart, however, from certain Low German analogues no more than tentatively proposed, the linguistic findings prove strong enough to stand without external support. They testify that Lynn's trade was carried on in an atmosphere of cultural openness and receptivity, with marked lack of xenophobia.

Perhaps, however, the sharpest lesson here concerns name-study itself and its methodology. Viewing the recorded forms, not in isolation, but in relation to the place that produced them and to its known circumstances and activities has enabled etymological questions to be put into a fresh, and truer, perspective. Names, and above all nicknames, ought never to be studied without reference to the social and economic life of the communities which use them.

---

[98] A suggestion now preferred to that in 'Lexicographical notes', 65.

[99] For further instances of *Swetemouth*, see Jönsjö, *Nicknames*, 174.

[100] See D. Owen, 'Bishop's Lynn', esp. 149. *MED* cites *lŏve-cŏp* 'tax or toll' first in 1299, and chiefly from Lynn records.

[101] See O.S. Arngart, ed., *Genesis and Exodus* (Lund, 1968), 43. More generally, see also M.S. Serjeantson, *A history of foreign words in English* (London, 1935), 170–5, and, with special reference to *Promptorium Parvulorum*, 173–5; and E.C. Llewellyn, *The influence of Low Dutch on the English vocabulary*, Publications of the Philological Society XII (Oxford, 1936), ch. iii.

18

*Willelmus rex? vel alius Willelmus?**

Post-Conquest English personal-name fashions have scarcely had their due. Between the late eleventh century and the mid thirteenth, the baptismal-name stock was almost wholly renewed, forms like *Ælfgifu, Godwine, Gunnild, Lēofðrȳð, Ōscytel* and *Wulfstān* being discarded in favour of ones still current today, such as (to give their modern forms) *Alice, John, Margery, Robert, Susan* and *William*.[1] Little close study has, however, been made of this process, let alone of its social context. Unannotated data-bases of restricted availability apart, there is, for instance, as yet no onomasticon for the 1086 stratum of Domesday Book.[2] It is as though historians and philologists alike were – with some honourable exceptions[3] – taking it as natural and inevitable for true-born Englishmen to be called *Alan, Geoffrey, Henry, Richard, Simon, Thomas, Walter*, and so on: too natural and inevitable to need investigation. This disregard contrasts with the enthusiasm as well as learning lavished upon pre-Conquest name-styles and their brief post-Conquest survival.[4]

The shift of fashion was swift, comprehensive, and quasi-permanent. Even among the peasantry, names of post-Conquest types appear in, for instance, a Bury St Edmunds estate-survey datable possibly as early as c.1100:[5] a date which, if accepted,

---

* This is a revised version of the paper delivered on 26 March 1987 at the XIXth Annual Conference of the Council for Name Studies in Great Britain and Ireland, held at the University of Nottingham.

1   The earlier name-stock, comprising Anglo-Scand as well as native OE items, will be termed 'pre-Conquest' and the later, consisting chiefly of CG items and ones with Christian associations (both types often Gallicized), either 'post-Conquest' or 'Continental', according to context.

2   The lists in H. Ellis, *A General Introduction to Domesday Book*, 2 vols (London, 1833), retain only limited value; but Professor J.McN. Dodgson's projected *Index* to the Phillimore edition of DB, expected shortly, should go some way towards remedying the lack of an onomasticon for the 1086 stratum. [[J. McN. Dodgson and J.J.N. Palmer, *Index of Persons*, Domesday Book, XXXVII (Chichester, 1992).]] For data-bases, see, for instance, J. Palmer, 'Domesday Book and the computer', in P. Sawyer, ed., *Domesday Book: A Reassessment* (London, 1985), 164–74, and R. Fleming, 'Domesday Book and the tenurial revolution', *Anglo-Norman Studies IX: Proceedings of the Battle Conference 1986* (Woodbridge, 1987), 87–102, esp. 87–8.

3   E.g.: *ELPN*, 91–100; *PNWD*; J.McN. Dodgson, 'Some Domesday personal-names, mainly post-Conquest', *Nomina* IX (1985), 41–51. Forssner, although treating relevant material, approached it from a different point of view.

4   E.g., the works by Redin, Ström, Reaney and Seltén listed below under *Abbreviations*, together with several of those by von Feilitzen.

5   *FDB*, 24–44 (checked against CUL MS. Mm.iv.19, fos 134v–143v). For the dating, see: *FDB*, pp. xlvi–xlix, lvii–lxvii (*ante* 1098); V.H. Galbraith, 'The making of Domesday Book', *English Historical Review* LVII (1942), 161–77, esp. 168 n. 1, and R. Lennard, *Rural England 1086–1135* (Oxford, 1959), 359 n. 1 ('the early part of Henry I's reign' and *ante* 1119, respectively, but neither sets out evidence); Davis, *KS*, p. xxxviii and n. 4 (1098 × 1119); A. Gransden, 'Baldwin, abbot of Bury St Edmunds, 1065–1097', *Proceedings of the Battle Conference on Anglo-*

implies – unless we postulate post-baptismal renaming – christenings *ante* 1080. Renaming could occur: thus, in perhaps the early 1130s, the future St Bartholomew of Farne, a Northumbrian boy baptized by the Anglo-Scandinavian name of *Tōsti*, was constrained by his playmates' mockery to adopt the more up-to-date one of *William*.[6] Yet, even if renaming were conceded to play some part, the chronology based on the extant records would need adjusting only by a dozen or so years; and, more importantly, the renaming would itself testify to the dominance of the new fashions. These spread apace, so that by c.1200 names of pre-Conquest types had become rare except among the peasantry, and were within two further generations virtually extinct.[7] A few, notably *Edmund* and *Edward*, did survive into the later Middle Ages and beyond, but these were mostly ones tacitly reclassified as 'saints' names', and especially royal saints' names popularized through readoption by later royalty.

Received wisdom concerning this change seems to be that it reflects 'fashion': a banal aping by the lower orders of the customs of their betters.[8] True enough, no doubt; but matters cannot rest there. Which of their betters were twelfth-century English people aping? Why, in the aftermath of a conquest followed by widespread expropriations, were they moved to imitate their new masters at all, let alone as early and as eagerly as they did? In any detail, 'Why?' must be unanswerable; but 'Whom did post-Conquest English people imitate?' may not be beyond all conjecture. Among the peasantry, acquaintance with the styles characteristic of the foreign settlers must have come from two main sources: from the lords of their own and of neighbouring vills; and from rumours of magnates further afield.

The greatest magnate was the king, and for the first thirty-five years after the Conquest the two successive kings were called *William*. That name soon became favoured in post-Conquest England, among all classes, being by the 1130s, as noted, commonplace enough for the future Bartholomew of Farne to adopt it as protective colouring. Other instances from *Vitae* of its adoption in non-aristocratic English milieux involve St William of Norwich, the apprentice furrier supposedly martyred in 1144, and, two generations earlier, St Godric of Finchale's brother, probably baptized in the 1080s.[9] In thirteenth-century estate-surveys, *William* regularly figures among the

---

Norman Studies IV: 1981 (Woodbridge, 1982), 65–76 and 187–95, esp. 68 (consonant with Baldwin's known policies). Although no onomastic analysis of this document has appeared, forms from it have often been discussed (cf. below, nn. 26, 27, 31); for some provisional comments on the name-patterns to be examined, see C. Clark, 'Women's names in post-Conquest England: observations and speculations', above 117–43, esp. 131–3 and n. 80.

6 T. Arnold, ed., *Symeonis monachi opera omnia*, 2 vols (London, 1882–5), I, 296. For *William* (*Willelm*) and other names discussed here, see the Onomastic Appendix below. (I am happy to acknowledge the help towards compiling it that I have derived from the von Feilitzen papers in my care.)

7 See, e.g., C. Clark, 'The early personal names of King's Lynn – I', above 241–57, esp. 250–2; *ELPN*, 87; Seltén I, 38–46; cf. also the articles cited in n. 10 below. A popular account, now dated, appears in P.H. Reaney, *The Origin of English Surnames* (London, 1967), 101–7, 128–49; that given by E.G. Withycombe, *Oxford Dictionary of English Christian Names*, 3rd edn (Oxford, 1977), pp. xxv–xxviii, is unreliable.

8 E.g., 'It became fashionable for Englishmen to give their children French names . . . But what those new names were, and for how long they were fashionable, these are problems which have never been satisfactorily discussed': Reaney, *Origin*, 102, 129–30.

9 A. Jessop and M.R. James, eds, *The Life and Miracles of St William of Norwich* (Cambridge, 1896); [J. Stevenson, ed.,] *Libellus de vita et miraculis S. Godrici*, Surtees Society XX (London and Edinburgh, 1845), 23.

most frequent names.[10] Was it then mainly royalty whom humbler people were aping?[11] A seeming parallel might be adduced with Normandy itself, where names associated with the ducal house enjoyed a great vogue and *Guillaume* alone accounted for some 12% of the men's names recorded during the twelfth and thirteenth centuries in, for instance, Évreux.[12] For neither country can one, however, be sure what models and motivations underlay recorded usages. The Conqueror and Rufus were merely the most prestigious of many Williams to be found in late eleventh-century England. Only a little less prominent were the tenants-in-chief of that name, including several bishops; lower down the scale, but far from inconspicuous in their own neighbourhoods, there were many under-tenants so named,[13] and that is without counting lesser clergy or foreign merchants. When evidence does survive of the inspiration behind a christening, the model may prove to have been near at hand: thus, the half-French boy who grew up to be the chronicler Orderic Vitalis received his Old English name of *Ordrīc* in compliment to the priest who baptized him.[14] That instance, dating from 1075, admittedly goes against the tide, but it by no means follows that its social, human motivation was atypical. The Bury list of (?)c.1100 offers only a single instance of *Willelm*, beside two each of *Raulf* and of *Salomon* and over half-a-dozen of *Ro(d)bert*: this hardly suggests royalty as the chief influence. Nor are any pre-Conquest kings' names much favoured there: *Alfred* occurs once, *Edgar* and *Edward* twice each, *Edmund* three times, *Cnut* and *Harold* not at all.[15] Nor, in later times, did *Henry* become more than moderately frequent, despite having been borne by two twelfth-century kings and an early thirteenth-century one who were all effective and respected rulers.[16] These observations likewise point to models near at hand rather than far afield in distant courts.

Determining the dominant name-models for any particular district will not be easy. As at Orderic Vitalis's christening, such a model might have been a parish priest or other person of merely local prestige and of whom no record need therefore survive (for women, under-recording affects even the nobility). Motivation is more speculative still. A name like *Robertus filius Siflet*, showing a man as bearing a post-Conquest name even though his mother had had the purely Old English one of *Sigeflæd*, might

---

[10] See, e.g., G. Fellows Jensen, 'The names of the Lincolnshire tenants of the bishop of Lincoln c.1225', in F. Sandgren, ed., *Otium et Negotium*, Acta Bibliothecae Universitatis Stockholmiensis XVI (Stockholm, 1973), 85–95, esp. 87, where *William* is said to account for 14% of name-occurrences; and J. Insley, 'The names of the tenants of the bishop of Ely in 1251', *Ortnamnssällskapets i Uppsala Årsskrift* 1985, 58–78, esp. 75–6.

[11] Cf. 'A fact of . . . significance is that "William" became and remained the single most common recorded name in the twelfth century, which suggests that William the Conqueror and William Rufus were not as unpopular as the Anglo-Saxon Chronicle made out': M.T. Clanchy, *England and its Rulers 1066–1272* (London, 1983), 57.

[12] M. Le Pesant, 'Les noms de personne à Évreux du xiie au xive siècle', *Annales de Normandie* VI (1956), 47–74, esp. 55. The fashions go back well into the eleventh century: e.g., Fauroux offers almost five columns of *Willelmus* and four of *Robertus*, beside single entries for many other names.

[13] For DB tenants, see Ellis, *Index*, I, 510–12, and II, 411–14; for bishops, see D.C. Douglas and G.W. Greenaway, eds, *English Historical Documents 1042–1189*, 2nd edn (London, 1981), 1070–5 (four of the name appointed *ante* 1100).

[14] M. Chibnall, ed., *The Ecclesiastical History of Orderic Vitalis*, 6 vols (Oxford, 1969–80), III, 6.

[15] For the names in fact disproportionately favoured here, see below 284.

[16] See, e.g., E. Ekwall, ed., *Two Early London Subsidy Rolls*, Acta Regiae Societatis Humaniorum Litterarum Lundensis XLVIII (Lund, 1951), 35 (1292: *Henry* 33x, *John* 143x, *William* 117x) and 36 (1319: *Henry* 61x, *John* 431x, *William* 246x). Note that *KS* and other documents show the popularity of *John*, a saint's name before it was a king's, as beginning well before 1199.

inspire a guess as to his possibly being the illegitimate son of an immigrant after whom he had been named:[17] plausible perhaps, but unverifiable. Even less verifiable is another possibility: that sometimes a peasant woman might have named a child of her own after an aristocratic one that she had nursed.

The best to be hoped for is documentary evidence suggesting links between early instances of Continental-type names in use among the native English, the peasantry especially, and styles current among local nobility, gentry and clergy. Demonstration can never be exact, partly because no early medieval records offer more than partial and, onomastically speaking, random samples of the population, and also because little can be said about transmission of the overwhelmingly frequent names like *Robert* and *William*. If, however, sporadic and imperfect correspondences between peasants' names and those of local gentry have any value for socio-onomastic history, some can be exhibited.

The Bury St Edmunds survey of (?)c.1100 preserves the names not only of the *feudati homines* holding by knight-service (all but a few corresponding with those listed in Little Domesday Book) but also of over 600 peasant landholders (free, paying rent, holding parcels of land ranging from a quarter of an acre to more than eighty acres, and some also following other occupations besides farming). This latter schedule covers, however, only three out of the eight and a half hundreds over which the abbey had special rights, and so, given the variation in name-choice from vill to vill, offers an incomplete view of current usages. Interpretation of it also presents problems. The only surviving text, preserved in Cambridge University Library MS. Mm.iv.19, fos 134v–143v, postdates compilation by about a century.[18] Its vernacular orthography is – as often at such a date – capricious and ambivalent: the only Anglo-Saxon letter retained is *æ*; *d* represents [ð] as well as [d], and *t* represents [θ] as well as [t]; *u* stands for [v] and for [w] as well as for [u]. Some confusion occurs between reflexes of OE *Æðel-*, which regularly gave late OE *Æil-* or *Æl-*, and those of OE *Ælf-*, which before a deuterotheme beginning with a consonant could sometimes give *Æl-*.[19] Certain originally Scandinavian items might in theory be classed either as Norman imports or as naturalized into late Old English (the low incidence here of unambiguously post-Conquest items, which account for only some 8% of the stock, suggests that most belong in the latter category). Other items are classifiable alternatively as native (or naturalized) Old English or as adopted from Continental Germanic.[20] Uncertainties arise also from the structure of the survey: some peasants held more than one plot, sometimes in more than one vill, as is on occasion signalled by use of *item* to introduce a supplementary entry or else of a toponymic by-name that identifies a landholder as domiciled in a different vill; but how systematically such signalling was carried through is not clear. Precise figures are thus out of the question; and such statistics as

---

[17] C. Clark, 'Battle c.1110: an anthroponymist looks at an Anglo-Norman new town', above 221–40, esp. 231.

[18] R.M. Thomson, *The Archives of the Abbey of Bury St Edmunds*, Suffolk Record Society XXI (Woodbridge, 1980), item 1277, 119–21, dates the extant copy *post* 1207. (I am grateful to Miss Jayne Ringrose of Cambridge University Library for her advice concerning the manuscript.)

[19] See *PNDB*, 142, sub *Al-*; also F. Colman, 'The name-element *Æðel-* and related problems', *Notes and Queries* CCVI (1981), 195–201.

[20] See below 287–8.

are offered below will intentionally be couched in terms so vague as to engender no illusions about the exactitude attainable.[21]

The shortcomings of the Bury document are all the more frustrating because of its precision in other respects. As well as being poised upon the cusp of a major shift in name-fashions, this is one of the earliest known English estate-surveys to be compiled upon a territorial plan, vill by vill; and thus furnishes some of our earliest insights into name-distributions as perceived in everyday life. The familiar assertion, based mainly upon attestations to royal diplomas, of a late Old English loss of variety from personal-naming has never been claimed as more than a half-truth, uncertainly applicable to the peasantry.[22] Here, such loss of variety as appears is specific and limited. The pre-Conquest name-styles represented consist – apart from some extraneous items to be discussed below – of a mixture of Old English forms and Scandinavian ones, with the latter accounting for some 18% of the stock. Between 160 and 165 masculine name-forms are distributed among about 600 men: although falling short of the 'one name – one person' principle generally supposed by modern scholars to have been the old Germanic ideal, such a level of variety might – on the assumption that it was com-plemented by a comparable range of feminine forms[23] – seem ample for any group numbering up to some 350 souls all told, i.e., for a village of fifty to seventy house-holds. Onomastic behaviour here was, however, neither systematic nor wholly tradi-tional. Observance of the Germanic tradition in its supposed original form would have entailed generating enough additional names to obviate repetition within any local group. Systematic deployment of 165 names among 600 men would have meant bestowing them in rotation, at maximum geographical as well as chronological spac-ings, and thus using each three or four times. In fact, *Godwine* occurs in the Bury lists over forty times, *Godrīc* over thirty times, and *Ælfrīc*, *Ælfwine* and *Wulfrīc* between twenty-five and thirty times each. Conversely, about half the names in the stock occur only once each, and a further 15% only twice each. Popular names and rare ones alike tend, besides, to occur in local clusters, thus further reducing the variety experienced in practice.[24]

The inconveniences of this habit of repetition were mitigated – in this document, at all events – by using by-names to aid identification of almost half those listed: at Hinderclay, for instance, four out of the eleven men were called *Godrīc* and were

---

[21] See further my paper, 'Historical linguistics – linguistic archaeology', above 92–9.

[22] See F.M. Stenton, 'Personal names in place-names', in A. Mawer and F.M. Stenton, eds, *Intro-duction to the Survey of English Place-Names*, EPNS I/i (Cambridge, 1924), 165–89, esp. 176–9; cf. the comments by G. Fellows Jensen and O. von Feilitzen in H. Voitl *et alii*, eds, *The Study of the Personal Names of the British Isles* (Erlangen, 1976), 48–9, 57–8.

    Little is known about OE peasant fashions: the relevant names given in the late-10th-cent. will of Æthelgifu (ed. D. Whitelock, Roxburghe Club [Oxford, 1968]), those of serfs associated c.1000 with Hatfield, Herts, and, even more, those of the mid-11th-cent. ones at Wouldham, Kent, all show dithematic forms predominating: see D.A.E. Pelteret, 'Two Old English lists of serfs', *Mediaeval Studies* XLVIII (1986), 470–513, cf. A.R. Rumble, *Nomina* VIII (1984), 50–1.

[23] Feminine names (including metronyms) found here represent between 30 and 35 forms (five of which, about 15%, are probably of Scand origin), accounting for 50 to 55 occurrences. The most frequent are: *Ælfflǣd* 5x, *Ælfgifu* 4x, *Beorhtflǣd* 3x, *Beorhtgifu* 3x, *Godgifu* 4x and *Wulfgifu* 3x. There are none of post-Conquest types.

[24] Both instances of *Spearhafoc* occur in Troston, and clusters of names in *-cetel* appear in Honington and in Coney Weston; for the frequency of *Godrīc* in the Hinderclay list, see the following paragraph.

distinguished by patronymic and occupational by-names.[25] Of the by-names found, about half are of familial kinds, mainly patronymic; and the baptismal names involved set the current stock in some perspective. As recorded here, the current names are mainly dithematic; of the rare single-element forms, about half look Anglo-Scandinavian.[26] Among the smaller corpus of patronyms, single-element forms are relatively more frequent and include a higher proportion of Old English ones:[27] a

[25] *FDB* 40–1.

[26] The current short and single-element names found here are: *Achy* (Scand *Áki*: *SPLY*, 3–5), *Ællic* (*PNDB*, 182), *Æuic* (Redin, 150–1; *PNDB*, 172), *Boio* (*PNDB*, 205 and n. 1; F&B, 189–91; cf. Schlaug I, 179, II, 63–4), *Bondo* (Scand *Bóndi*: *SPLY*, 60–1; *PNDB*, 206), *Brother* (*SPLY*, 65; cf. *PNDB*, 208), *Brun* 2x (Redin, 11–12; *PNDB*, 209; cf. *SPLY*, 66), *Bruning* (Redin, 165; *PNDB*, 210; *SMS*, 86–7; *PNWD*, 152; *ELPN*, 22–3), *Challi* (Scand *Kalli*: *AS*, 57–8), *Chetel* 3x (Scand *Ketill*: *SPLY*, 166–70), *Cole* (OE *Cola*: *PNDB*, 217–8; or Scand *Kol(l)i*: *SPLY*, 176–7), *Fader* (*SPLY*, 79; cf. *PNDB*, 250), *Goding* (*PNDB*, 265), *Hagene* 3x (Scand *Hagni*: *SPLY*, 122; *PNDB*, 282; *ELPN*, 77), *Hune* (OE *Hūna*: Redin, 67; *PNDB*, 295; *ELPN*, 49; and cf. *DBS*, s.n. *Hunn*; or Scand *Húni*: *SPLY*, 145–6; *PNWD*, 162), *Hunting* (*NoB* XXXIII, 84), *Labbe* (Scand *Labbi*: *AS*, 58), *Lotene* (Scand *Loðinn*: *NPE*, 92–3; *SPLY*, 190; *PNDB*, 321), *Lunting* (*SN*, 9), *Lut(t)ing* 2x (Redin, 174; *PNDB*, 322; cf. Scand *Lúti*, *Lútr*: *AS*, 58; *SPLY*, 191), *Manne* (OE *Manna*: Redin, 52; *PNDB*, 324; or Scand *Manni*: *SPLY*, 194–5), *Neue* (? OE *nefa* or Scand *nefi* 'nephew'; cf. *DBS*, s.n. *Neave*), *Oppe* (cf. *KS*, 14; *SN*, 10), *Tate* (OE *Tāta* masc., *Tāte* fem.: Redin, 114; *SN*, 11, s.n. *Tætig*; cf. Scand *Teitr*: *PNDB*, 382), *Tuuida* (SN, 12), *Suarche* (also *KS*, 47; ? short for Scand *Svartkollr*: *PNDB*, 379; *SPLY*, 276; cf. n. 31 below), *Ulf* (Scand *Ulfr*: *SPLY*, 321–4; or OE *Wulf*: Redin, 10). For some further Scand forms, see n. 27 below. Names from the survey by no means exhaust the local stock of Scand short-forms: e.g., *Threm* (*FDB*, 138, 147–8; *KS*, 50, also 49, where *Thoem* is a misprint) represents Scand *Þrymr* (*NPE*, 154).

[27] Distinguishing between postposed nicknames and asyndetic patronyms is not easy. The short and single-element names best taken as patronyms are: *Ade sune* (OE *Ad[d]a*: Redin, 81–2), *Ædesdohter* (cf. LDB *Ædi*: *PNDB*, 171–2; cf. also OE *Ædda*, *Æddi*: Redin, 82, 131), *Ællice sune* (n. 26), *Becce f[ilius]* 2x (OE *Beocca*: Redin, 84; Tengvik, 173; *DBS*, s.n. *Beck*; cf. Anglo-Scand *Bekki*: *SPLY*, 51), *Boie f.* (n. 26), *Brune f.* 2x/*Brune sune*/*Brune stepsune* (Scand *Brúni*: *SPLY*, 66; *PNWD*, 152; cf. OE *Brún*: n. 26), *Bruningi f.* (n. 26; cf. *DBS*, s.n. *Browning*), *Celing* (Tengvik, 301; cf. OE *Cēol[l]a*: Redin, 46), *Chebbel* (Tengvik, 301; *PNWD*, 209 n. 5; cf. *DBS*, s.n. *Keeble*), *Ceteli f.* (n. 26), *Chipingi f.* (OE *Cypping*: Redin, 173; *PNDB*, 221–2; *PNWD*, 153), *Cobbe* (cf. LDB, 7/36: ? OE *Cobba*, or short for *Colbein*, as at *FDB*, 39; cf. Tengvik, 305–6, and *DBS*, s.n. *Cobb*), *Cocce sune* (? OE *Cocc[a]*: Tengvik, 153; cf. *DBS*, s.n. *Cock*), *Cole sune* (n. 26), *Crauue f.* 2x (OE *Crāwa*: *PNDB*, 219 – Suffolk; or OE *Crāwe* fem.: Redin, 115; cf. *DBS*, s.n. *Crow*), *Crite* (cf. OE *Cretta*: Redin, 90; Tengvik, 308), *Dages* (? Scand *Dagr*: cf. *NPE*, 31, and Tengvik, 208), *Dere f.* (OE *Dēora*: Redin, 47; *PNWD*, 154), *Dod*/*Dode*/*Doddes* (OE *Dodd*, *Dodda*: Redin, 16, 62; *PNDB*, 223–5; cf. Tengvik, 154, 179, 208, 310–11), *Frost* (Tengvik, 376; *NoB* XXXIII, 80; *PNWD*, 157, s.n. *Forst*; *DBS*, s.n.; cf. Scand *Frosti*: *SPLY*, 87–8), *Gode f.* (OE *Gōda*: Redin, 49, cf. 114; *PNDB*, 263; *DBS*, s.n. *Good*), *Gott* (? Scand *Gautr*: *SPLY*, 98; *PNWD*, 160; cf. *DBS*, s.n.), *Grelling* (Redin, 166–7; Tengvik, 143–4), *Hert* (OE *Heort*: *SN*, 8), *Hune f.* 2x (n. 26), *Hunte sune* (OE *Hunta*, or the underlying occupational term: Redin, 87; *PNDB*, 296; cf. *DBS*, s.n. *Hunt*), *Letig* (? OE *lytig* 'sly': Tengvik, 348; but cf. Scand *Leði*: *PNDB*, 319, *Leiðr*: *PNDB*, 309, and *Liótr*: *PNDB*, 320, and *SPLY*, 190), *Lute f.* (cf. *Lut[t]ing*: n. 26), *Moce sun* (OE *Mocca*, *Mucca*: Redin, 100–1; cf. Scand *Mukki*: *SPLY*, 198), *Pape* (Tengvik, 262–3), *Paue f.* (OE *pāwa* 'peacock': Tengvik, 194; *DBS*, s.n. *Paw*), *Puse sune* (OE *Pusa*: Redin, 78; cf. Scand *Pósi*: *SPLY*, 209), *Scule f.* (Scand *Skúli*: *PNDB*, 366; *SPLY*, 254); *Suete f.* (OE *Swēta*: Redin, 54; *PNDB*, 381; *PNWD*, 173), *Tates* (n. 26), *Thede f.* (see n. 32 below), *Torce* (? Anglo-Scand *Turke*: *AS*, 66), *Trege* (cf. *Trehes* [gen.]: *KS*, 15, in same vill; Scand *Tryggr*: *ZEN*, 84; *SPLY*, 292), *Uere f.* (? OE *Wæra*: Tengvik, 203–4). Note that citation of a reference does not necessarily imply endorsement of any opinion expressed.

Alongside the prevailing *filius*-formulas, all three vernacular patronymic strategies occur: asyndetic apposition; gen. phrases in *dohtor*/*sunu*; simple gen. of the parental name.

contrast, as it happens, in keeping with common, but inadequately tested, assumptions about non-aristocratic Old English name-styles.[28] Such a seeming shift of fashion raises the question whether, between the christenings of the present tenants' fathers and their own,[29] the Bury peasantry had come partly to eschew short-forms; if so, the shift might be taken as a delayed reflection of the similar one alleged to have affected aristocratic usages c.900. That is not, however, the only explanation possible: patronyms might have been recorded in more colloquial a style than were current baptismal names – a practice not unknown in later Middle English times; and this view is supported, albeit shakily, by a brief list of Bury peasants' names from (probably early in) the Conqueror's reign.[30] However that may be, no great statistical weight should be laid upon patronyms, which often provide only small samples (that here being hardly more than a fifth the size of the current stock) and are likely to be biased towards the rarer, more distinctive forms. This caveat lends an ambivalence to the observation that, already among the patronyms, *Ælfwine, Godrīc* and *Godwine* were, at five instances each, disproportionately frequent (and not one of these, be it noted, had ever been a characteristically royal name).

The development of disproportionate frequencies was, at all events, what had given the current name-stock its monotonous look. The currency here of a good few rare forms, and especially of Anglo-Scandinavian hybrids, implies little loss of ability to create fresh forms or of willingness to accept them from outside.[31] Nor had element-permutation been abandoned, for in some two dozen instances a man's name echoes an element from a relative's, usually his father's.[32] Probably this latter practice was indeed what produced disproportionate frequencies, because within any familial or local group the element-range must generally have been so limited as to put expressions of onomastic piety at constant risk of repetitiousness. Whatever its causation, repetitiousness was no purely English problem, but manifested itself throughout the old Germanic area, and already characterized the styles which the Norman Conquest was about to

28 Redin, 184–9; cf. n. 22 above.
29 On the assumptions (a) of a date c.1100 for the survey and (b) of a life-span of up to 65 years, the current tenants might be supposed to have been baptized at dates ranging from c.1035 to c.1080, and their fathers at ones ranging from c.970 to c.1060 (c.1055–c.1100 and c.990–c.1080 respectively, if the document be assigned to its latest possible date of 1119).
30 *FDB*, 151–2 (a notification of enfeoffment, datable 1066 × 1087, 'probably early' in that period), offers a list of peasants' names containing nine OE dithematic masc. forms, four Scand and two ambivalent ones, plus *Brother* (also one CG dithematic masc. form, three OE dithematic fem. ones, the apparently fem. OE monothematic *Lufe* and two blundered forms).
31 Unusual names here include: *Achulf* (also *FDB*, 151 [cf. n. 30 above]: *PNDB*, 140, from Norfolk and Suffolk), *Gangulf* (patronym: *AS*, 55), *Glauard* (patronym, also *KS*, 19: *SMS*, 93), *Godhuge* (*DBS*, s.n. Goodhew; cf. *AS*, 57), *Goldrauen* (*NoB* XXXIII, 82; cf. the moneyers' names *Goldcyta, Goldhavoc*), *Hafcuuine* (*NoB* XXXIII, 82), *Lefchetel* (*PNDB*, 313; *SPLY*, 186), *Lefthein* (*SMS*, 97), *Litemode* (patronym or metronym: *NoB* XXXIII, 85), *Mantat* (*SMS*, 97–8; *Will of Æthelgifu*, 6), *Meruin* 2x (? OE **Mærwine* or *Merewine*: *PNDB*, 327), *Moregrim* (also, as patronym, *KS*, 13: *PNDB*, 329), *Morstan* (*NoB* XXXIII, 86), *Mundingus* (*PNDB*, 330), *Sedemode* (patronym or metronym: *NoB* XXXIII, 88), *Sibman* (*NoB* XXXIII, 88), *Spileman* (*PNWD*, 173), *Strangman* (*NoB* XXXIII, 89), *Stubhard* (*PNDB*, 376–7; *SMS*, 103), *Suacheil* (? for Scand *Svartkollr* or **Svartke[ti]ll*; cf. *Suarche* in n. 26 above), *Winterhard* (CG: Forssner, 258), *Udelac* (patronym: *SMS*, 106).
32 E.g., *Æluric Ælflede f.*, 28, 29; *Æluricus Sistrici f.*, 43; *Goduin Aluini f.*, 25; *Goding Goduuini f.*, 25; *Lemmer Brihtmer*, 29; *Ordric Uuihtrici nepos*, 26; *Stanard Lefstani f.*, 29. For 12th-cent. East-Anglian instances of permutation, see Seltén I, 24–5.

introduce into England.[33] Repetition of whole names had, in short, come to oust permutation as the chief means of marking familial links.

Such was, in outline, the late-eleventh-century Suffolk name-system upon which this Bury survey shows post-Conquest fashions as having, probably by c.1080, begun to impinge. In practice, detecting new adoptions is less straightforward than the summary may have made it sound; for several strata of non-native (or uncertainly native) forms have to be dissected out.

Some names shown by phonology or distribution (or both) to be of Continental-Germanic origin had by 1066 been known in England for up to a century. *Fulcard* had in the mid to late tenth century appeared in East Anglia as a moneyer's name and also that of a landholder associated with Ely Abbey. The naturalization of *Grimbald* is underlined by its appearing here in patronymics that qualify classic Old English names and date probably *ante* 1060 (at latest, *ante* 1080), possibly even as early as c.970. *Sebode* represents the CG *Sigibodo* seen in the name of Æthelred II's moneyer Siboda (the same unEnglish *-bodo* figures also in the rare *Titebud*, apparently a reflex of CG *Theodbodo*). *Ærcebriht*, although in late Old English usage apparently an import, is Anglicized in a way implying naturalization. A further name that for practical purposes belongs in this category is the originally OIr *Col(e)man*, adopted into German usage and known in England from at least the early eleventh century.

Against that background, certain other forms look explicable, often almost indifferently, as either Continental or native (which latter category embraces, in this context, Anglo-Scandinavian forms as well as purely Old English ones). Formally, the parental *Thede* is ambiguous in gender as well as in etymology.[34] *Harduin* could represent either CG/OFr *Harduin(us)*, or an OE **Heardwine*: the latter seems supported by the occurrence in the same vill of the analogous *Hardman*, the former by that of a *Hardwynus* among the otherwise Continental-named followers of a pre-DB Bury under-tenant called Peter. *Ulbern* might, in the orthography of this document, represent CG *Wulfbern*, or Anglo-Scand *Ulfbeorn < Ulfbjǫrn*, or else a fresh compound between OE *Wulf-* and Anglo-Scand *-beorn*. For *Frebern*, here denoting at least two, possibly three, individuals and found several times in other post-Conquest materials, the etymologies suggested involve either an OE **Frēobeorn* or a Gallicized reflex (*sc.* with the intervocalic dental effaced) of CG *Fridebern/Fredebern*: against the former are alleged both the rarity of OE *Frēo-* and the uncertainly native standing of *-beorn*; in favour of the latter stands the occurrence in Suffolk TRE, not only of *Fridebern*, but also of its supposed OFr reflex *Friebern*, given as the name of an Edwardian king's-thegn (LDB, 25/28, 32/6). A French form need not be incongruous in the latter context (the Confessor's earl of Norfolk, to look no further, bore the CG/OFr name of *Raulf*); nor would its reappearance among the Bury peasantry conflict with the present thesis of name-transmission through local gentry. Yet native origins cannot be ruled out, for the Scandinavian-influenced Bury name-stock certainly included *-beorn*, and for Suffolk TRE OE *Frēo-* seems attested by the form *Freowinus* (LDB, 7/121). There is also a middle road: re-creation in native terms of the CG/OFr *Friebern*. As for *Osbern*,

---

[33] For some Continental usages, see, for instance, P. Aebischer, 'L'anthroponymie wallonne d'après quelques anciens cartulaires', *Bulletin du dictionnaire wallon* XIII (1924), 73–168, and G.T. Beech, 'Les noms de personne poitevins du IXᵉ au XIIᵉ siècle', *Revue internationale d'onomastique*, XXVI (1974), 81–100.

[34] Almost certainly masc., like most other gen. forms in *-e* found here (either < OE weak *-an* or else due to fusion of gen. *-s* with the initial of following *-sune*).

formally explicable as Anglo-Scandinavian, as Norman, or as Old Saxon, it may, or may not, be relevant to its appearance five times in the Bury survey that already in the Confessor's reign (although not, it seems, specifically in East Anglia) it had become associated with immigrant nobles and churchmen.

An etymological decision (if to be taken at all) may thus depend upon weighing probabilities, sometimes upon accepting some convergence of influences. The masculines *Godlef*, found twice here and several times elsewhere, and **Redlef*, deducible from a patronym here, are commonly ascribed to Low-German origins, on the grounds that, although *Lēof-* is among the most frequent of OE protothemes, no corresponding masculine deuterotheme is securely attested; yet, with the *-le(o)f* compounds recorded in England numbering over half a dozen, that argument itself could be deemed insecure. *Giulf*, explicable variously as a Gallicized spelling (*sc.* with *G-* for *W-*) of Anglo-Scand *Wi(g)ulf < Vigolfr*, or else as an OFr reflex either of the Normanno-Scand equivalent or of CG *Wigulf*, might perhaps be taken as French, in so far as *G-* for *W-* does not otherwise occur in the list of free peasants (though it does in that of the Bury knights), not even in certainly Continental names; this interpretation would, if accepted, bear upon that of the *Guiolfus* found, in addition to *Wicolfus*, in Suffolk *TRE* (LDB, 8/56). *Odin*, found five times here, could represent either CG *Odin(us)* or ODanish *Øthin < Auðunn*; the frequency in Abbot Samson's late-twelfth-century *Kalendar* of an apparent OFr reflex of the former, to wit, *Ohin(us)*, might support assigning the present examples also to an Old-French etymology.

That, then, is the already variegated background against which must be studied the names that the free peasants of Bury shared with the abbey's *feudati homines*: *Durand, Fulcher, Hubert, Ralph, Reeri, Richard, Robert, Walter, Warin, William*, and perhaps *Fredo*; as well as the famous late-eleventh-century abbot's own name of *Baldwin*. Although accounting for only 8% of the recorded stock and a yet smaller proportion of occurrences, these are the crucial names both for later developments in English personal-naming and for the present investigation into possible lines of transmission. Again interpretations prove less straightforward than at first sight they might have seemed.

Not all these names were post-Conquest novelties. *Baldwin* and *Durand* had both appeared sporadically in post-Conquest England, as names of minor landholders as well as of moneyers. *Durand* – seemingly current *TRE* mainly in East Anglia[35] – perhaps ranked among naturalized imports; in post-Conquest Suffolk it looks to be more commonly found among the more modest class of landholder.

Many of the shared names fall, besides, among those too frequent, in Normandy as well as in England, to have traceable transmission-patterns. *William*, some two dozen bearers of which figure in the Suffolk Domesday material, is a prime instance of this, despite the neatness of its appearing once among the Bury knights and once among the peasants. So too with the post-Conquest name most frequent among the latter: *Robert*, the nine instances of which denoted probably six or seven individuals. As well as figuring in England as a tenth-century moneyer's name, this had, during the Confessor's reign, been borne by the quasi-national figure, Robert (Champart) of Jumièges, bishop of London from 1044 and archbishop of Canterbury 1051–52, and also by the Suffolk landholder Robert fitzWymarc, a supposed kinsman of the king and probably

---

[35] Not too much should be read into contrasts in name-distribution between LDB and GDB, because these may reflect only the former's wider social coverage.

sheriff of Essex.[36] Post-Conquest Suffolk magnates of the name included Robert Corbucion, Robert Gernon, Robert Malet, Robert of Mortain, Robert of Tosny, Robert of Verly and, in particular, Robert Blund, not only a major tenant-in-chief, but also one of the abbey's *feudati homines*. *Raulf* (so spelt in the Bury survey, just as in the contemporary *ASC* annals), the three instances of which here denoted two individuals, had also long been familiar in pre-Conquest East Anglia, partly through the Confessor's Breton earl, Ralph the Staller, and then through the latter's son, Ralph of Gaël, banished for treason in 1075;[37] for Suffolk *TRW* it appears as the name of some half-dozen tenants-in-chief as well as of the abbey's under-tenant, *Radulfus Crassus*, and of a good few others of similar rank. *Walter*, not apparently known in pre-Conquest Suffolk (the *TRE* instances in Domesday Book all concern the Lotharingian bishop of Hereford), had by 1086 well over a dozen bearers recorded there, ranging from the magnate Walter Giffard to an indeterminate number of under-tenants, among them Bury's '*nepos* of Peter the clerk'. Thus, in late-eleventh-century England, names like *Ralph* and *Robert* were simply in the air, trailing clouds of prestige, and scarcely traceable to specific models. Often their adoption by English people may have been of multiple inspiration: *Hugo*, for instance, appears twice among our free peasants, although not at all among the relevant *feudati homines*; Domesday Book shows it as borne *TRW* by Suffolk magnates like Hugh of Avranches, Hugh of Grandmesnil and Hugh of Montfort, as well as by some half-dozen under-tenants throughout the county.

Surprisingly, *Richard* does not, in the present context, exhibit a like degree of over-frequency: in the *TRE* stratum of Domesday Book it refers mainly to the *protégé* whom the Confessor settled in the Welsh Marches; and, even for 1086, the Suffolk record offers only the magnate Richard fitzGilbert of Clare and a few under-tenants, among them Bury's *Ricardus Calvus* and Richard *Houerel/Hoverel*. For certain other names, still sparser distributions – at all events, as far as the records go – suggest some possibly significant connections. *Fulcher* (or, given the ambivalence of the -*ch*- spelling here, *Fulker*) appears twice among the Bury peasants; Suffolk Domesday offers only two bearers of the name, Fulcher the Breton and Fulcher of Mesnières, both under-tenants of the abbey. For *Hubert*, found once among the free peasants and once for a post-Conquest knight of Bury, the only Suffolk bearer recorded in Domesday Book is a minor tenant-in-chief, Hubert of Mont-Canisy. For *Warin*, also found once among the peasants and once among the Bury knights, the only Suffolk bearers in Domesday Book are two or three under-tenants, the abbey's man among them.

The problems of frequency pale beside those of rarity. Names attributed to Bury peasants include *Fredo* and *Reeri*: both reappear, applied to others, in Abbot Samson's *Kalendar*. Each presents a cryptic similarity with an anomalous variant of an under-tenant's name: *Fredo* appears in Domesday Book as a variant, or error, for *Frodo*, the name of Abbot Baldwin's brother, a major East-Anglian landholder as well as an under-tenant of the abbey (LDB, 14/65); *Rerius* occurs in the abbey's own schedule of under-tenants as a variant, or error, for the name elsewhere Latinized as *Roricus* (possibly, but not certainly, an OFr reflex of CG *Hrodricus*). The problem seems each time to be one that is too often glossed over: the discrepancy between spoken name-

---

[36] For Robert of Jumièges, see *DNB*, XVI, 1244–5, and F. Barlow, *Edward the Confessor* (London, 1970), passim and esp. 50, 79, 104–8, 114–16, 124–6. For Robert *fitzWymarc* 'the Staller', see *DNB*, XVI, 1245, and Barlow, *op. cit.*, esp. 94, 165.

[37] Ralph the Staller is discussed in *DNB*, VIII, 757, under his son Ralph Guader (= 'of Gaël'); see also *Complete Peerage*, IX, 568–71, and Barlow, *Confessor*, 165, 191.

forms and their conventional Latinizations, *Raulf/Radulfus* being a classic instance. *Fredo* is, in itself, an authentic form, a shortening of CG dithematic names in *Fride-/ Frede-*, like the *Fredebern* already cited. The questions are, first, why an LDB scribe on just one occasion substituted it for an otherwise regular *Frodo* and, second, how the form *Fredo* came to be ascribed to several Bury peasants. The former seems scarcely answerable. The latter could perhaps be met by supposing documentary *Fredo* here to represent an Anglicized reflex of Scand *Friði*. *Reeri* remains enigmatic.

For three non-Germanic names of post-Conquest types, problems lie not with etymology but with transmission. The two entries of *Salomon* in the survey have an uncertain relationship with the mentions in Bury documents datable 1121 × 1148 and 1148 × 1156 of a *Salomon* (*clericus*). The specifically OFr *Russel* (etymologically a nickname, 'small man with red hair') was familiar elsewhere in late-eleventh-century England, including Colchester. Then there is *Crispin*, given as the patronym of a man with the unambiguously Old English name of *Stānmǣr*. For such a saint's name to have been borne by an English peasant baptized probably before 1060 – and, at that, one apparently without clerical connections – would be unexpected; even more so would be occurrence here of the Old French nickname 'curly' (the by-name *Crispin* given to a witness of a Bury document datable 1186 × 1198 can have no bearing on the form in the survey). Provisionally, a scribal explanation might be proposed: later 'improvement' of a less exotic Latinized *Crispi filius*, as seen elsewhere in the survey.

That does not exhaust the problems. A major flaw in the evidential pattern is that only a minority of the early knights' names reappear among the free peasants of (?)c.1100. Given the selectivity of the record, such negative evidence is not to be pressed. Indeed, later Bury records fill some of the gaps, showing further knightly names, including *Anselm*, *Berard*, *Burchard*, *Elias* and *Peter*, appearing among people of English stock. Even so, the thesis of name-transmission through local gentry looks less cogent than it did when tentatively put forward a dozen years ago. Coincidences of the sort exhibited bear little weight, because ones no less close can be found almost at random: late-eleventh-century records from, for instance, the Norman town of Sées, offer parallels for the peasants' names *Baldwin*, *Durand*, *Fulcher*, *Harduin*, *Hubert*, *Hugo*, *Osbern*, *Ralph*, *Richard*, *Robert*, *Walter* and *William*[38] – but no-one claims any special relationship between Bury and Sées. Failure to substantiate the thesis by no means, however, discredits localized studies of the present kind. For, if fuller understanding is to be achieved of historical socio-onomastic processes, it must surely come from focusing upon local (or, perhaps, professional) groups, rather than, as in the pioneering days of anthroponymics, upon particular categories of name.[39] Signs are that continuities of name-choice may be traceable within individual vills.[40]

---

[38] See J. Adigard des Gautries, 'Les noms de personnes attestés à Sées de 1055 environ à 1108', *Bulletin de la Société historique et archéologique de l'Orne* LXXXII (1964), 17–27.

[39] Cf., for instance, J. Insley, 'Some aspects of regional variation in Early Middle English personal nomenclature', in *Studies in Honour of Kenneth Cameron = Leeds Studies in English*, n.s. XVIII (1987), 183–99.

[40] References to the same individuals apart, less frequent names reappearing in the same localities include: *Coleman* (*FDB*, 35: Rushbrooke: *KS*, 21, 22); *Hagene/Hahene* (*FDB*, 42: Hopton: *KS*, 51, 52); *Odin/Ohin* (*FDB*, 40 2x: Hepworth: *KS*, 45; cf. below and also 288 above); also the apparently patronymic by-name *Glauard* (*FDB*, 28: Rougham: *KS*, 19); but the occupational *croperer/croppars* may be descriptive rather than onomastic (*FDB*, 28, with second *-er* probably dittographic: Rougham; *KS*, 18, where the whole name is in gen.; cf. *MED*, s.v. *cropper*[*e*]).

Continuities in name-stock help to confirm emendations: e.g., *Thurferði* for (*f.*) *Hurefdi* is

In the broader sense, too, focusing upon name-fashions of the immediate post-Conquest period is salutary. At this time, as a mainstream historian has recently acknowledged, name-usage constitutes 'a better indicator of attitudes to foreign rule than are isolated statements in chronicles'.[41] True, we cannot uncover the motivations behind eleventh- and twelfth-century English christenings; we cannot find out whether the English followers of imported name-fashions were moved by simple snobbery, by desire to curry favour, by the charm of novelty, or by genuine admiration for the name-bearers whom they copied. What we can observe among these Suffolk peasants is what Ekwall observed forty years ago among the contemporaneous bourgeoisie of London: apparent absence of any nationalistic or xenophobic reaction against the cultural patterns associated with the new rulers and settlers.[42]

ONOMASTIC APPENDIX

N.B. The manuscript of the Bury survey of (?)c.1100 in general capitalizes the initial of the first item only in any group. In transcribing, capitalization has been extended to all regular names, recognizable patronyms included. [[Abbreviations are expanded at 297–8 below.]]

Terra Aelun, KS, 69 (Melford).
Possibly OE *Æðelhūn* (so Seltén II, 30; cf. *OEPN*, 156, and *PNDB*, 154, s.n. *Alun*); but in *KS* OE *Æðel-* usually appears as *Ail-* or *Eil-*. In LDB an apparent OFr *cas-sujet* form *Aelons* corresponds with the unusual *Adelund* used elsewhere of the same Bury u-t (14/32, 36, 58, 98) and with *Adelo* in *FDB* (21; for this as hypocoristic of CG names in *Adel-*, see Schlaug I, 169, Marynissen, 50–1, and Morlet I, 19a).

Godric anger, FDB, 36 (Timworth, 4 acres); *Lefuine anger, FDB,* 41 (Barningham, 4 acres).
The by-name *anger* could represent either a nickname based upon the Scand loanword meaning 'distress, wrath' (von Feilitzen in *NoB* XXVII, 126; cf. *MED,* s.v.) or an asyndetic patronym; but, although LDB has *Angarus* (32/4, 66/100) varying with *Ansgarus* and *Esgarus* for the name of Esgar the Staller, an Anglo-Dane who was a major *TRE* landholder in East Anglia and elsewhere (*PNDB,* 166–7; cf. below s.n. *Æfger*), colloquial currency of Norman *An-* < Scand *Ans-* (> *Ás-*) may seem unlikely in pre-Conquest England.

Anselmi (gen.). *FDB* 148 (son of Osward; *fl.* at Thurston a generation *ante* 1156 × 1180); *Anselmus colt, KS,* 12.
CG *Anshelm* (Schlaug I, 71; Morlet I, 39a), borne not only by the abbot of Bury 1121–48 but also by the abbey's 1086 u-t, *Anselmus homo Frodonis* (LDB, 14/139; cf. *FDB,* 10). (*Osw[e]ard,* not uncommon in the Bury vills, is either OE or Anglo-Scand [*PNDB,* 340–1; *SPLY,* 35–6; Seltén II, 129] rather than OSaxon [as Schlaug II, 140].)

---

backed by the *Turuerdi* (*f.*) in the earlier list for the same vill (*KS,* 46: Wattisfield: *FDB,* 39), plus the *Hurketel* for *Thurketel* found elsewhere in *KS* itself (15).

[41] Clanchy, *England and its Rulers,* 56–7.

[42] 'There is no trace in London of such an opposition [*sc.* to the Normans] or of English national consciousness in the history of personal nomenclature': *ELPN,* 91–6, 98–100.

Æfger, FDB, 31 2x. Read: *Æsger.*
    Æsger/Esger, an 11th-cent. Danish reflex of Scand *Ásgeirr*; introduced into England under the Cnutian hegemony (*PNBD*, 166–7; *SPLY*, 22–4; J. Insley, 'Some Scandinavian personal names from south-west England', *NoB* LXX (1982), 77–93, esp. 82; cf. above s.n. *anger*).

Æilgild, FDB, 33. Read: *Æilgid.*
    Therefore cancel note at *EENS*, 48.

Ærcebriht, FDB, 41 (Hinderclay, 1 acre).
    Whereas OE *Eorconbeorht* seems confined to the early period (*OEPN*, 166; not in *PNDB*), CG *Ercanbert* is widely, though not heavily, attested (Schlaug II, 79; TV, 69; Morlet I, 80a; for pre-Conquest English occurrences of other CG names in *Ercan-*, see: Forssner, 75–7, *PNDB*, 247, Smart, '973–1016', 243, and *Index*, 35).

Balduin, FDB, 25 (Barton, 3 acres); cf. *Folcardus f. Baldewini, KS*, 94 (former landholder in Barton; *ante* 1182 × 1200).
    CG *Baldwin* (Schlaug I, 73; TV, 40; Morlet I, 50b; Fauroux, 479–80), found sporadically in England from mid 10th cent. on, mainly as a moneyer's name (Forssner, 41–2; *PNDB*, 191; F&B, 188; Smart, *Index*, 16). For Baldwin, abbot of Bury 1065–98, a former monk of Saint-Denis and prominent at the Confessor's court, see Gransden, 'Baldwin' (n. 5 above).

Berardo (dat.) *f. Aldstani, FDB*, 116 (kinsman *Wlurici Aquenesune*; 1121 × 1148), 126–7 (1134 × 1148); *Berardus nepos* [of *Leomerus de Berningeham*], 115 (witness; 1121 × 1138).
    CG *Berhard* (Morlet I, 52a; cf. Forssner, 282), borne by a 1086 u-t of the abbey (LDB, 14/16; cf. *FDB*, 20). (*Āccwēn* or *Ācwynn* fem., *Ealdstān, Lēofmǣr* and *Wulfrīc* are all typical OE forms [*PNDB*, 242, 313, 423–4; *SMS*, 85].)

Goduine blurf, FDB, 27 (Pakenham, 3 acres).
    The by-name *blurf* may be a blundered asyndetic patronym, perhaps OE **Brūnwulf* (deduced from place-names: *NoB* XXXIII, 76) *via* a spelling **brũulf* (*Brūn* appears in the same vill and also, together with related compounds, elsewhere in the survey: cf. nn. 26, 27 above).

Brihtled, FDB, 26 (Rougham, 1 acre); *Brihtled et Siuuard*, 34 (Whelnetham, 30 acres).
    Brihtled, found also elsewhere, represents OE *Beorhtflǣd fem. (so FDB*, index, 199a) with the consonant-group at the element-junction simplified (analogy with *Ælf[f]lǣd* and *Lēof[f]lǣd* might have aided acceptance of *-led* as a second element); so cancel note at *SMS*, 86.

Burchardus, FDB, 111 (brother of *Lemmerus*; witness, 1114 × 1119).
    Either OE *Burgh(e)ard* (*PNDB*, 211–12; Seltén II, 51–2) or CG *Burghard* (Schlaug I, 76–9, II, 67; Morlet I, 62ab; cf. Forssner, 53–4). A *Burchardus/Bucardus*, said to have a brother Peter, was the abbey's 1086 u-t in Bardwell, Barningham and Hunston (LDB, 14/81, 82, 95; cf. 14/17 and *FDB*, 19). (The witness's brother *Lemmerus* [OE *Lēofmǣr*] might have been the one at Barningham with a *nepos* called *Berardus* [q.v. above].)

Coleman, FDB, 35 (Rushbrooke, 1 acre).
    Ultimately < OIr *Columbanus* (*LHEB*, 509) but adopted in Germany, perhaps in memory of the saint martyred at Würzburg c.689; found in England from mid 10th cent., mainly as a moneyer's name and with a distribution including EAnglia (Forssner, 55–6; *PNDB*, 28; *ELPN*, 24; Smart, '973–1016', 256, and *Index*, 24). Borne also by a minor 1086 u-t of the abbey and by a monk of Bury witnessing in 1112, it reappears in Rushbrooke in the later 12th cent. (LDB, 14/24; *FDB*, 154, cf. 128; *KS*, 21–2).

Stanmer crispini f., *FDB*, 42 (Hopton, 4 acres).

A patronym involving the saint's name *Crispin* (Morlet II, 37) would be unexpected at this date and social level, especially with an OE baptismal name like *Stānmǣr*; so, equally, would be nickname use of the OFr adj. *crispin* 'curly-haired', the explanation given by the family itself for the Norman family-name *Crispin* (J. Armitage Robinson, *Gilbert Crispin, Abbot of Westminster* [Cambridge, 1911], 13–18; cf. von Feilitzen in *NoB* XXVII, 127). Perhaps the form here represents scribal 'improvement' of a patronym like that of *Odin crispi f.* (see below), that is, a re-Latinization of the OE by-name based on the Latin loanword *crips/cyrps* 'curly-haired' (Tengvik, 179; *PNWD*, 210).

Alduine duluert, *FDB*, 27 (Rougham, 15 acres).

The by-name could represent miscopying of *chiluert*, a frequent spelling for Anglo-Scand **Ketilfrøðr* (*NPE*, 81; *ZEN*, 54; *PNDB*, 215; *SPLY*, 171; but Tengvik, 217, suggests *Þórfrøðr*).

Durand Æilmari f., *FDB*, 38 (Langham, 9 acres).

Romance-based *Durand* (Morlet II, 43; cf. I, 76b; Fauroux, 494), found in England from mid-10th cent., mainly as a moneyer's name, with a distribution including Suffolk (Forssner, 62; *PNDB*, 229; *PNWD*, 155 and n. 3; F&B, 193–4; Smart, '973–1016', 223, and *Index*, 28). The abbey's 1086 u-ts included a *Durandus clericus* (LDB, 14/119; cf. *FDB*, 11, 24). (The patronym is OE *Æðelmǣr* [*PNDB*, 184–5].)

Elyas f. Lefwini, *KS*, 133 (minor landholder; *ante* 1182 × 1200).

The Biblical name (Morlet II, 45b). An Helias *de Bolonia* witnessed a Bury charter of 1121 × 1148, and an Helias *de Pressenni* (? Presigny, *dép.* Seine-Maritime), who held by knight-service, witnessed one of 1156 × 1178 (*FDB*, 125, 169 n. 9). The diminutive *Elyot* also occurs among late-12th-cent. Bury peasants (*KS*, 4, 13). (The patronym is OE *Lēofwine* [*PNDB*, 317–19].)

Ermand, *FDB*, 29 (Rougham, 18 acres).

Perhaps representing CG *Ermeno* or CG *Her(e)man* (Morlet I, 83b, 126ab; Forssner, 80).

Stanard Euengiue f., *FDB*, 29 (Rougham, 16 acres). Read: *cuengiue*.

So cancel note at *NoB* XXXIII, 79. OE *Cwēngifu* fem. (*PNDB*, 220; *SMS*, 87; Seltén II, 57) was borne by a *TRE* tenant of the abbey, and evidently underlay the late-12th-cent. entry for *Reri* (gen.) *f. q̄uheue* (LDB, 14/117; cf. *FDB*, 16; *KS*, 4; see further *sub Reeri* below).

Fanri, *FDB*, 33 (Woolpit, 1½ acres). Read: *Tanri*.

John Insley, who has independently established this reading, suggests that it may represent OSax *Thankric* (Schlaug I, 82, II, 159).

Frebern, *FDB*, 31 (Hessett, 16 acres); 35 (Timworth, 60 acres); *Frebern presbiter*, 43 (*Huntefelde*, 5 acres).

For a possible LE **Frēobeorn*, see *SMS*, 92, also s.n. *Frēowine*, and Seltén II, 83. For CG *Fridebern* and its appearances in England, see Schlaug I, 94, II, 87 (the name is not in Morlet or Fauroux) and *PNDB*, 253–4, esp. 254 n. 2.

Fredo et fratres sui, *FDB*, 27 (Pakenham, 19 acres jointly).

This name reappears in the late 12th cent., denoting several individuals, one of them at Pakenham (*KS*, 4, 9, 10, 18, 19, 20, 21, 52). Although there was a CG *Fredo*, short for names in *Frid-/-fridus* (Marynissen, 118; Morlet I, 94a), here this form might represent a reflex of Scand *Friði* (*SPLY*, 87; *ELPN*, 76; Adigard, 204–6, classes it as ambivalently Scand/Frankish).

Fulcard, *FDB*, 26 (Barton, 15 acres); *Folcardus presbiter* (*de Bertonia*), 125, 133 n. 10, 135 (witness; 1121 × 1148, 1148 × 1156, 1156 × 1160); cf. *Osberto* (dat.) *f. Folcardi de Bertona*, *KS*, 94 (grantee; 1182 × 1200); see also above *sub Balduin*.

    CG *Folcard*, *Fulcard* (Schlaug I, 93, II, 84–5; TV, 43; Morlet I, 95a), found in England, mainly as a moneyer's name, from mid 10th cent. on (Forssner, 98; *PNDB*, 256 and n. 2 – all from Suffolk; F&B, 195–6; Smart, '973–1016', 234 – Norwich, 244 – Thetford, and *Index*, 36).

Fulcher, *FDB*, 38 (Honington, 2 acres); 41 (Hopton, 6 acres); *Fulcherius frater Godrici*, 111; cf. *Fulcherius frater Edrici*, 110 n. 9 (witnesses, in lists otherwise similar; 1114 × 1119; *FDB* records an Ædric and a Godric for Honington and a Godric for Hopton); cf. *Godwinus f. Folcheri*, *KS*, 51 (Hopton).

    CG *Folchere* (Schlaug I, 93, II, 85; TV, 62; Morlet I, 95a), seemingly hardly known in pre-Conquest England (not in Forssner; *PNDB*, 256 and n. 6; cf. *PNWD*, 157, and *ELPN*, 112–13); borne by two of the abbey's 1086 u-ts (LDB, 14/11, 78, 80 [Hopton], 89, 90, 99, cf. *FDB*, 17–18; LDB, 14/22, cf. *FDB*, 21).

Giulf cum fratribus, *FDB*, 43 (*Huntefelde*, 30 acres jointly).

    A Gallicized spelling either of the 10th-cent. 'English' *Wiulf*, probably < the rare Scand *Vígúlfr* (not in *NPN*, *SPLY* or Adigard; see *PNDB*, 404–5 and n., with instances all from EAnglia), or of CG *Wigulf* (Morlet I, 223b).

Godlef crepunder hwitel, *FDB*, 28 (Barton, ¾ acre); *Godlef equarius*, 32 (Woolpit, 4 acres); cf. *Ulmer Redleui f.*, 39 (Wattisfield, 1½ acres).

    God(e)le(o)f, found in England as a moneyer's name from late 10th cent. (Smart, '973–1016', 237, and *Index*, 38–9 – Stamford, Huntingdon, Thetford, London), is usually attributed, along with other masc. names in -*le(o)f*, to CG origins (*EENS*, 49, 55, 56, 57, 58; but cf. *SMS*, 93, 99, and esp. Seltén II, 156, 185; whether Scand -*leifr* might be implicated seems unexplored).

Grimbold Ulurici f., *FDB*, 28 (Rougham, 5 acres); *Godui Grimboldi f.*, 25 (Barton, 7 acres); *Lefuine Grimboldi f.*, 28 (Rougham, 20 acres); cf. *Grimbaldus presbiter*, 151 (1066 × 1087).

    CG *Grimbald* (Schlaug II, 97; Morlet I, 115a), known in England from the early 10th cent. (Forssner, 130–1; *PNDB*, 275; *PNWD*, 160).

Harduin, *FDB*, 25 (Barton, 4 acres).

    Either CG *Hardwin* (Schlaug I, 106, II, 99; TV, 17; Morlet I, 124ab; cf. Forssner, 143, and *PNDB*, 186–7, with instances all from EAnglia) or OE *Heardwine* (Seltén II, 95–6; in *FDB*, *Hardman* occurs in the same list). A *Hardwynus* figures 1066 × 1087 among witnesses, otherwise all with Continental names, to a document for an u-t of the abbey called Peter (*FDB*, 152).

Hared, *FDB*, 37 (Troston, 5 acres).

    PNDB, 287 and n. 1, refers *Haret*, also from Suffolk, either to OE *Hererǣd* or to OE *H(e)aðurǣd*; other possible etyma include OE *Heardrǣd* (*ELPN*, 47), with assimilation and simplification of medial [rdr], and OE *Hēahrǣd*.

Hubert faber, *FDB*, 32 (Woolpit, 2 acres).

    CG *Hugbert* (Schlaug I, 115, II, 116; TV, 77; Morlet I, 140a), probably unknown in pre-Conquest England (not in *PNDB*; cf. Forssner, 156, and *PNWD*, 162), was borne by a *post*-DB u-t of the abbey (*FDB*, 22; no corresponding entry in LDB).

Hugo, *FDB*, 39 (Wattisfield, 3 acres); *Hugo Ælurici f.*, 44 (Littlechurch, 15 acres); cf. *Hugo f. Alstani*, 157 (witness; 1154).

    Either CG *Hugo* (Schlaug I, 205, II, 117; TV, 124; Morlet I, 140a; cf. Forssner, 157–8,

PNDB, 294, and *PNWD*, 162) or for EScand *Hughi* (cf. *AS*, 57). (The patronyms here represent respectively OE *Ælfrīc* and either OE *Ælfstān* or OE *Æðelstān.)*

Odin, FDB, 40 (Hepworth, 9 acres); 41 (Hopton, 4 acres); *Ælfuine cum Odino*, 41 (Coney Weston, 7 acres jointly); *Odin crispi f.*, 40 (Hepworth, 1½ acres); *Odin Mum*, 42 (Hopton, 1 acre); cf. *Ædwardus f. Odin'*, 120 (witness; 1121 × 1148).

Either the CG diminutive *Odino/Odinus* (not in Marynissen; Morlet I, 45; Fauroux, 523) or the ODan *Øthin* < *Auðunn* found, e.g., as a York moneyer's name (*NPE*, 100–3; *ZEN*, 66–7; *PNDB*, 170; Smart, *Index*, 16), the latter origin seeming consonant with its appearance as patronym to OE *Ēadw(e)ard*. Yet, *Ohin(us)*, apparently the former's Gallicized reflex, later enjoys localized currencies including some of the same vills (*KS*, 45: Hepworth 2x, 47–8: Wattisfield, 3 or 4x [for *Ohina* here, read *Ohinus*]; cf. *PNWD*, 166–7 and nn. 9, 1–2).

Odric Tederi, FDB, 26 (Barton, 3 acres).

Either OE *Ordrīc* (*PNDB*, 366–7), with the first *r* lost by scribal error or by dissimilation, or else CG *Odric* < *Audric* (Schlaug II, 137; Morlet I, 44b; cf. *EENS*, 55, and *PNWD*, 167, s.n. *Oricus*). The by-name, if taken to represent an early OFr reflex of CG *Theodric* (see below; but Tengvik, 209, proposes OE *Þeodhere*), would support the latter; but a by-name is, in this text, normally used only with a baptismal name duplicated in the same vill, and an *Ordric Uuihtrici nepos* occurs a few entries earlier.

Osbernus, FDB, 28 (Rougham, 5 acres); *Osbern*, 35 (Timworth, 7½ acres); *Osbern cum fratre*, 42 (Hopton, 6 acres); *Osbern rufus*, 38 (Langham, 9 acres); *Osbern cattesnese*, 38 (Langham, 3 acres).

A classic case of multiple ambivalence – Anglo-Scand, Normanno-Scand, or OSaxon: see J. Insley, in *NoB* LXX (1982), 77–93, esp. 79–81 and references there given. Here Anglo-Scand origins seem most likely.

Petrus f. Hugenild', KS, 11 (Thurston).

The Biblical name (Morlet II, 90a), borne by three of the abbey's *feudati homines*: the steward, the brother of Burchard (q.v.), and the magnat Peter of Valognes (*FDB*, 18, 19, 23). (*Hugenild* may represent miscopying, not uncommon in *KS*, of *Hagenild* fem.)

Raulf, FDB, 36 (Livermere, 7½ acres); *Raulfus de Liuremere*, 36 (Timworth, 4 acres); *Raulfus clericus*, 35 (Rushbrooke, 2 acres).

Raðulf < CG *Radulf* (Schlaug I, 138, II, 143; Morlet I, 182b; Fauroux, 529–30) was found in England as a mid-10th-cent. moneyer's name (F&B, 189; Smart, *Index*, 62); its OFr reflex *Raulf*, borne by the Confessor's EAnglian staller (n. 37 above) and by a 1086 u-t of the abbey, was generally current in the district (LDB, 14/3, 35, 53; cf. *FDB*, 18, 24, also index, 226; *PNDB*, 345, *PNWD*, 169, and *ELPN*, 91–2).

Reeri, FDB, 30 (Hessett, 48 acres); *Rerius*, 110 (witness; 1114 × 1119); *Reri de Walnetham, Fulco f. Reri*, 119 (witnesses; 1121 × 1148); *Symon f. Reri*, 147 (tenant in Hessett ante 1156 × 1180; cf. *KS*, 13 n. 3), *Willelmo* (dat.) *f. Rery de Hegesete, KS*, 99 (grantee; 1182 × 1188), *Reri* (gen.) *f. q̃uheue*, 4 (Hessett), and *Reri* (gen.) *f. Brictheue*, 4 (Hessett).

This name, well-attested though it is, has so far no established etymology. Cf. 'Ad Bradefelde tenet Rerius' (*FDB*, 18), where LDB (14/59, also 79) has *Roricus*, a recognized reflex of CG *Hrodricus* (Marynissen, 218; Morlet I, 138a, also 191a; cf. Forssner, 219). (Of the metronyms, *q̃uheue*, with an abbreviation-mark over the first element, represents OE *Cwēngifu* [see above] and *Brictheue*, OE *Beorhtgifu* [*PNDB*, 194].)

Ricardus Vlfui f., FDB, 43 (*Huntefelde*, 60 acres).

CG/OFr *Ric(h)ard* (TV, 34; Morlet I, 188b–189a; Fauroux, 532), sparsely attested in pre-Conquest England (Forssner, 213–14; *PNDB*, 349), was borne by two of the abbey's 1086 u-ts (LDB, 14/54, 151; cf. *FDB*, 10, 24). (The patronym represents OE *Wulfwīg*.)

Robertus, *FDB*, 26 (Barton, 19 acres); *Rotbert*, 28, *Item Rotbert*, 30 2x (Rougham, 3, 1, 60 acres); *Robert*, 31 (Hessett, 25 acres); *Leueh cum Rotberto*, 30 (Hessett, 40 acres jointly); *Robert et Ælric*, 35 (Rushbrooke, 16 acres jointly); *Rotbert et Vlstan*, 39 (Walsham, 3 acres jointly); *Rotbert*, 44 (Littlechurch, 10 acres).

CG *Hrodbert* and its OFr reflex (TV, 77; Morlet I, 136a; Fauroux, 533–5) had been known in England as a moneyer's name since the mid-10th cent. (F&B, 204; Smart, '973–1016', 236, and *Index*, 64; Forssner, 216–17); all DB instances *TRE* refer, however, to Robert son of Wymarc (*PNDB*, 349–50). For Robert Blund as u-t of the abbey, see LDB, 14/92 (cf. *FDB*, 21–2).

Russel, *FDB*, 43 (*Huntefelde*, 1 acre).

An OFr name based on the adj. *ro(u)ssel*, diminutive of *ro(u)s* 'red-haired'; seemingly unknown in pre-Conquest England, but attested by 1086 (LDB Essex, B3 [Colchester]; cf. *PNWD*, 215, referring to a tenant in Winchester *ante* 1110).

Salomon, *FDB*, 28 (Rougham, 7½ acres); 43 (Littlechurch, 6 acres); *Salomon*, 119, and *Salomon clericus*, 121 (witnesses; 1121 × 1148); *Salomonis* (gen.) *clerici . . . de Rucham*, 131, and *Salomonis* (gen.), 132 (uncle of Herbert son of Robert, kinsman of Abbot Ording of Bury; 1148 × 1156; cf. *KS*, 18 n. 2).

The Biblical name (Morlet II, 101b; Fauroux, 538), found only once in DB *TRE* (*PNDB*, 351; cf. *ELPN*, 94).

Æilmer et Sebode, *FDB*, 39 (Walsham, 1 acre jointly).

CG *Sigibodo* > *Seibodo* (Schlaug I, 148, II, 151; Morlet I, 197b), found in England in the early 11th cent. as the moneyer's name *Siboda* (Forssner, 225; Smart, '973–1016', 270, and *Index*, 67; see further *ELPN*, 61).

Tedricus Paue f., *FDB*, 43 (Cosford, 5 acres); cf. perhaps, as above, *Odric Tederi*, 26 (Barton, 3 acres).

Although a native OE *Þeodrīc* is possible (*ELPN*, 66, cf. 2; Seltén II, 160), the widespread CG *Theodric* may seem more likely here (Schlaug I, 85, II, 163; TV, 116; Morlet I, 69b–70a; Fauroux, 549; cf. Forssner, 231–3, Smart, *Index*, 71, *PNDB*, 383–4, and *PNWD*, 174). (For the patronymic *Paue*, see n. 27 above.)

Goduine Thede f., *FDB*, 25 (Barton, 10 acres).

The patronym probably represents an OE short-form **Þēoda* (*NoB* XXXIII, 90; also F&B, 204 n. 1; an OE **Þēode* fem. is formally possible, but see n. 34 above; for the well-attested CG *Theudo/Thiedo* and corresponding fem. forms, see Schlaug I, 187, II, 164, Marynissen, 93–4, TV, 139, and Morlet I, 71a).

Titebud, *FDB*, 35 (Rushbrooke, 1 acre).

CG *Theodbodo/Teutbodus* (Morlet I, 67b, showing also variants in *Tï(e)t-* for other *Theod-* compounds; cf. *Titbertus*: TV, 78).

Ulbern, *FDB*, 38 (Honington, ¼ acre).

Because four of the eleven Honington names are Scand, and because, as a moneyer's name, *Wulfbern/Ulfbeorn* seems peculiar to Lincoln, the rare ODan *Ulfbjǫrn* (*SPLY*, 324–5, followed by Smart, *Index*, 74) seems the likeliest etymon (for the better-attested CG *Wulfbern*, see Schlaug I, 166, and cf. *EENS*, 54).

Walter, *FDB*, 37 (Troston, ½ acre).

CG *Waldhere* (Schlaug I, 153, II, 168; Morlet I, 213ab; Fauroux, 556–7), little known in pre-Conquest England (Forssner, 243–4; *PNDB*, 409; *PNWD*, 167), was borne by a 1086 u-t of the abbey (LDB, 14/23, 87; cf. *FDB*, 20).

Warin, FDB, 31 (Hessett, 2 acres).
    CG/OFr *Warin* (Marynissen, 234–5; TV, 26; Morlet I, 219b; Fauroux, 505), found in England as a mid-10th-cent. moneyer's name (Smart, *Index*, 76) but not in DB *TRE* (cf. Forssner, 246–7, and *PNWD*, 176), was borne by a 1086 u-t of the abbey (LDB, 14/15, 66; cf. *FDB*, 19).

Willelmus cum fratre suo Ælfuine, FDB, 38 (Langham, 5½ acres jointly); *Willelmus f. Ailboldi*, 109 &c. (witness; 1112–48 × 1153; and grantee; 1135 × 1148).
    CG *Wilhelm* (Schlaug I, 163–4, II, 179; TV, 80; Morlet I, 225a; Fauroux, 558–60), little known in pre-Conquest England (*PNDB*, 415), soon spread rapidly (Forssner, 255–7; *PNWD*, 177; cf. above 281–2 and nn. 9–11). (For the patronym < OE *Æðelb[e]ald*, see Seltén II, 25–6.)

Abbreviations

AS	O. von Feilitzen, 'Notes on some Scandinavian personal names in English 12th-century records', in *Personnamnsstudier 1964*, Anthroponymica Suecana VI (Stockholm, 1964), 52–68.
DNB	L. Stephen and S. Lee, eds, *The Dictionary of National Biography*, 22 vols (repr. Oxford, 1921–22).
EENS	O. von Feilitzen, 'Some Continental-Germanic personal names in England', in A. Brown and P. Foote, eds, *Early English and Norse Studies presented to Hugh Smith* (London, 1963), 46–61.
ELPN	E. Ekwall, *Early London Personal Names*, Acta Regiae Societatis Humaniorum Litterarum Lundensis XLIII (Lund, 1947).
F&B	O. von Feilitzen and C. Blunt, 'Personal names on the coinage of Edgar', in P. Clemoes and K. Hughes, eds, *England before the Conquest* (Cambridge, 1971), 183–214.
Fauroux	M. Fauroux, ed., *Recueil des actes des ducs de Normandie (911–1066)* (Caen, 1961), esp. index.
FDB	D.C. Douglas, ed., *Feudal Documents from the Abbey of Bury St Edmunds* (London, 1932).
Forssner	Th. Forssner, *Continental-Germanic Personal Names in England* (Uppsala, 1916).
KS	R.H.C. Davis, ed., *The Kalendar of Abbot Samson of Bury St Edmunds*, Camden Third Series LXXXIV (London, 1954).
LDB	A.R. Rumble, ed., *Domesday Book*, XXXIV: *Suffolk*, 2 pts (Chichester, 1986).
Marynissen	C. Marynissen, *Hypokoristische Suffixen in oudnederlandse Persoonsnamen, inz. de -z- en -l-Suffixen* (Ghent, 1986).
MED	H. Kurath, S.M. Kuhn *et alii*, eds, *Middle English Dictionary* (Ann Arbor, 1952–).
Morlet I, II	M.-Th. Morlet, *Les Noms de personne sur le territoire de l'ancienne Gaule du VIe au XIIe siècle* (Paris, 1968–72): I = *Les Noms issus du germanique continental*; II = *Les Noms latins ou transmis par le latin*.
NoB XXXIII	O. von Feilitzen, 'Some unrecorded Old and Middle English personal names', *Namn och Bygd* XXXIII (1945), 69–98.
NPE	E. Björkman, *Nordische Personennamen in England*, Studien zur englischen Philologie XXXVIII (Halle, 1910).
OEPN	H. Ström, *Old English Personal Names in Bede's History*, Lund Studies in English VIII (Lund, 1939).
PNWD	O. von Feilitzen, 'The personal names and bynames of the Winton Domesday', in M. Biddle *et alii*, eds, *Winchester in the Early Middle Ages* (Oxford, 1976), 143–229.
Redin	M. Redin, *Studies on Uncompounded Personal Names in Old English* (Uppsala, 1919).

Words, Names and History

Schlaug I, II   W. Schlaug: I = *Studien zu den altsächsischen Personennamen des 11. und 12. Jahrhunderts*, Lunder Germanistische Forschungen XXX (Lund, 1955); II = *Die altsächsischen Personennamen vor dem Jahre 1000*, LGF XXXVI (Lund, 1962).

Seltén I, II   B. Seltén, *The Anglo-Saxon Heritage in Middle English Personal Names: East Anglia 1100–1399*: I = Lund Studies in English XLIII (Lund, 1972); II = Acta Regiae Societatis Humaniorum Litterarum Lundensis LXXII (Lund, 1979).

Smart, *Index*   V. Smart, *Cumulative Index of Volumes 1–20*, Sylloge of Coins of the British Isles XXVIII (London, 1981).

Smart,   V. Smart, 'Moneyers of the late Anglo-Saxon coinage, 973–1016', in *Commenta-*
'973–1016'   *tiones de nummis saeculorum IX–XI in Suecia repertis* II, Kungl. Vitterhets Historie och Antikvitets Akademiens Handlingar: Antikvariska Serien XIX (Stockholm, 1968), 191–276.

SMS   P.H. Reaney, 'Notes on the survival of Old English personal names in Middle English', *Studier i Modern Språkvetenskap* XVIII (1953), 84–112.

SN   O. von Feilitzen, 'Some Old English uncompounded personal names and bynames', *Studia Neophilologica* XL (1968), 5–16.

SPLY   G. Fellows Jensen, *Scandinavian Personal Names in Lincolnshire and Yorkshire* (Copenhagen, 1968).

Tengvik   G. Tengvik, *Old English Bynames*, Nomina Germanica IV (Uppsala, 1938).

TRE   *Tempore Regis Edwardi*, before 1066.

TRW   *Tempore Regis Willelmi*, after 1066.

TV   C. Tavernier-Vereecken, *Gentse Naamkunde van ca.1100 tot 1252* (Tongeren, 1968).

ZEN   E. Björkman, *Zur englischen Namenkunde*, Studien zur englischen Philologie XLVII (Halle, 1912).

THE *LIBER VITAE* OF THORNEY ABBEY

19

British Library Additional MS. 40,000, ff. 1v–12r

Nomina quæ iniuncta fuerant mihi ut a me in hoc scriberentur libro sed ob incautelam inertiae oblivionis meæ dimissa tibi, Christe, et genetrici tuae omnique celesti commendo virtuti ut hic et in aeterna vita eorum beatitudinis celebretur memoria.[1]

The manuscript known as BL Additional MS. 40,000 is a gospel-book written in an early-tenth-century hand which experts assign to the low Countries or Northern France.[2] It contains eighty-seven folios, whose quiring is hidden by a tight eighteenth-century binding; the gospel-text begins on f. 13r and breaks off with St John's Gospel incomplete. Upon the twelve preliminary leaves assorted items have been entered: f. 1r is blank; the top third of f. 1v carried name-lists, the rest remaining blank; ff. 2r–v and 3r–v are wholly filled with name-lists; f. 4r carries miscellaneous entries, a few name-lists included; from f. 4v to halfway across f. 9v are entered the Eusebian canon-tables forming an index to the gospel-texts, with the remaining vertical half-page on f. 9v filled by name-lists; ff. 10r–v are wholly filled by name-lists; f. 11r has three name-entries in its top left-hand corner, being otherwise occupied by a fifteenth-century table of abbots; f. 11v carries a Latin schedule, in a hand datable c.1100, of the saints' relics reposing at Thorney Abbey; f. 12r has name-entries only in its top left-hand corner, the rest remaining blank. It is the name-lists, amounting *in toto* to some 2,300 items, that give this manuscript its interest; although well-known, they are still unpublished and have as yet been little discussed.[3]

As to the volume's provenance, little seems discoverable beyond a tentative

---

[1] *Das Verbrüderungsbuch der Abtei Reichenau*, ed. J. Autenrieth *et alii*, MGH: Libri Memoriales et Necrologia, nova ser. i, Hanover 1979, 229.

[2] *British Museum Catalogue of Additions to the Manuscripts 1916–1920*, London 1933, 276–9, and N.R. Ker, *Catalogue of Manuscripts containing Anglo-Saxon*, Oxford 1957, 163 (item 131); also below nn. 4, 12, 30. I owe the late Neil Ker an immense debt for his generous and patient help with the problems which this manuscript presents. In particular, the division of the name-lists into 'blocks' demarcated by change of hand and/or ink depends almost entirely on his expert eye, and I hope that I have not in any way misrepresented or misused the information which he so kindly gave me.

[3] At his death in 1976 Olof von Feilitzen left an all-but-completed onomasticon based upon these name-lists and comparable in style and in scope of documentation with the Winton Domesday one (*Winchester in the Early Middle Ages*, ed. M. Biddle *et alii*, Oxford 1976, 143–229). This monograph his literary executor invited me to complete and see through the press; its still remaining unpublished is mainly attributable to the fact that the task of compiling the necessary Introduction has proved more demanding than was foreseen. Whatever value this present paper may possess is largely derived from von Feilitzen's close documentation of the names and of their bearers' careers.

attribution to the Low Countries, Northern France or perhaps Brittany of the hand that wrote the gospel-text and its associated canon-tables. In the context of the name-lists that provenance may, however, be of small moment, in so far as these need have no connection with the original compilation. Palaeographical examination reveals them as added by various hands dating from c.1100 to c.1175; many of these show unmistakably English features, including sporadic use of *æ*, *þ* and *ð*, *ȝ*, and *ƿ*. The presence of later English materials in a tenth-century book of Flemish or North-French origin offers little problem, because the Benedictine Revival saw many continental texts imported into this country.[4] This particular book may in fact have arrived before that movement was fully under way: not only did an English hand datable to the late tenth or early eleventh century add marginal lectionary notes throughout the gospel-text, but one datable before the middle of the tenth copied Latin verses onto the lower margin of f. 30r and a similar one interlineated fifty-odd scratched glosses in Old English here and there on ff. 30–32 and 48.[5] Gratifying though it would be to learn the volume's exact provenance and, even more so, by what agency it reached this country, the crucial point is clear: by the mid-tenth century it was being used and annotated in England, exactly where remaining unknown.

Where the book was when the name-lists were being entered on its preliminary folios is implied by the other items found alongside them. The schedule on f. 11v of the saints' relics preserved at Thorney Abbey is, like the earliest of the name-lists, datable roughly to the early twelfth century.[6] The fifteenth-century abbatial table entered on f. 11r as *huius monasterii* proves to be prefaced by an account of the same abbey's foundation in 973.[7] The name-lists may therefore be surmised also to emanate from Thorney, as indeed a glance at them confirms, because in the first column on f. 10r a sequence of names each labelled as an abbot's agrees, for the period it covers, with the list on f. 11r.

Upon inspection, the order and structure of these Thorney name-lists appear as far from straightforward, their palaeographical chronology being at variance with the foliation. There figure on f. 2v several 'business-hands' such as came into use only from the mid-twelfth century on, whereas on f. 10r and part of f. 10v the main hand is datable c.1100. On f. 4r the first of the miscellaneous entries – the 'goldsmiths' entry', quoted below – is in passable Late Old English and seems datable to the 1060s or 1070s. These and similar observations suggest for these lists the following order: first, the 'goldsmiths' entry' on f. 4r; next, f. 10r, followed by ff. 10v and 9v, evidently in that order; after that, ff. 3r–v, followed by ff. 2r–v; in no precise order, but latish in the sequence, the few entries found on the mainly blank ff. 11r and 12r, together with some added material on f. 4r; last of all, the entries on the partly blank f. 1v.

---

4   See F. Rella, 'Continental manuscripts acquired for English centers in the tenth and early eleventh centuries – a preliminary check-list', *Anglia*, xcviii, 1980, 107–16 (our manuscript is omitted, apparently because the author regards as inconclusive the evidence of glossing hands); cf. H. Gneuss, 'A preliminary list of manuscripts written or owned in England up to 1100', *Anglo-Saxon England*, ix, 1981, 1–60, esp. 21 (a Breton provenance is suggested).

5   These glosses are printed by H.D. Meritt, 'Old English glosses in Latin manuscripts', *American Philosophical Society: Yearbook 1959*, Philadelphia 1960, 541–4, esp. 542.

6   It is printed in *English Benedictine Kalendars after A.D. 1100*, ed. F. Wormald, 2 vols, Henry Bradshaw Society lxxvii and lxxxi, London, 1939–46, i, 129–30.

7   For Thorney Abbey, see: W. Dugdale, *Monasticon Anglicanum*, ed. J. Caley *et alii*, 6 vols, London, 1817–30, ii, 593–613; D. Knowles and R.N. Hadcock, *Medieval Religious Houses: England and Wales*, rev. ed., London 1971, 78; D. Knowles *et alii*, *The Heads of Religious Houses: England and Wales 940–1216*, Cambridge 1972, 73–5.

Odd though such an order seems, it proves to be confirmed by the patterns into which the lists' other features fall. A sporadic use of Anglo-Saxon characters has already been noted. By itself their distribution would have little chronological bearing, because in post-Conquest England use or avoidance of these characters was partly governed by factors other than passage of time.[8] Here, however, their incidence, in names of continental type especially, does seem to fall into a chronological pattern. The hand identifiable as earliest – if, that is, the 'goldsmith's entry' on f. 4r is disregarded – is the main one of f. 10r and of the first section on the verso; for native names this hand normally uses fairly traditional Old English spellings, and it frequently spells continental ones with Anglo-Saxon characters, *yogh* and *wynn* included: *Liȝerd/Liȝarda, Drœpe, Bœrta, Albreðe, Roȝer* (4x)/*Rodȝerius, Huȝo* (3x), *Byȝod, ȝrantamaȝni, Aȝnes, Sœȝar,*[9] *Malfœȝð,*[10] *Gosfrið.* Some later hands on f. 10v occasionally offer spellings like *Roȝerius, Haðeuuis, Albreiða* (2x); others, by contrast, even in native names prefer caroline g to *yogh* and graphics such as *uu* to *wynn*. The main hand of f. 9v, identifiable as among the earlier ones, nevertheless consistently prefers caroline g and, although sporadically using ð and *wynn* in continental names (*Ðalter, Aðelasc, Tereðe, Albreiða*), also shows, by correcting to *w* the *wynn* originally used in *Hathawis*, a conscious effort to eschew Anglicised spelling. The presumed next stratum, on f. 3r, continues to show sporadic use of Anglo-Saxon characters in continental names: *Albereða/Albreþa* (3x)/*Albreiðe, Æðelic/Æþeliza, Mecœriel, Mabiliœ, Rorȝeis, Ærnoldus, Raȝemer, Ædpida/Aþepis, Æþelina, Haþeuuis* (2x)/*Haþapis/Haþepis, Ærnichu[n], Freþesenda, Baldepinus;* f. 3v similarly offers: *Ædelina, Haðepis/Haðeuuis, Ærnulfus, Ærnis, Helepis, Aðelais/Ædeliza, Ærnoldus, Æmma, Roœis.* From such a variety of hands as appears here, no consistent usage is to be expected; but progressive disuse of *yogh* is evident, together with a tendency – out of step with the wider history of the language – to prefer ð to þ. Among these Anglicised forms women's names, although *in toto* less numerous here than men's, predominate markedly, in a way that suggests weaker traditions of conventional spelling. On f. 2r the only Anglo-Saxon characters still appearing in continental names are ð and capital Æ (everywhere retained longer than its 'lower-case' equivalent[11]), only two instances being found: *Ærnaldus, Ærmentruða;* likewise on the verso the only relevant forms – apart from two instances within a single 'block' of *Ædpid* with *wynn* so ill-shapen as to resemble *thorn* – are *Ærnoldus, Heðewisa, Æðelina.* Entries on the unfilled ff. 1v, 11r and 12r and additional ones on f. 4r – material already surmised to represent late strata of compilation – show no such forms at all. Thus, spelling-practices, which over the three-quarters of a century in question saw Anglo-Saxon characters partly discarded, fall into a pattern compatible with the chronology suggested by palaeographical observations.

---

8 See C. Clark, 'L'Angleterre anglo-normande et ses ambivalences socio-culturelles', in *Actes du IVᵉ Colloque international anselmien (1982)*, ed. R. Foreville and C. Viola, Paris 1984, 99–110.

9 Because its bearer can be identifed as 'Sigar', brother of Gunfrid de Chocques (see W. Farrer, *Honours and Knights' Fees*, 3 vols, London 1923–25, i, 20–30), this name-form cannot represent Old English *Sægar* but must be an Anglicisation of Continental Germanic *Sigher* = Old French *Seiher* (see von Feilitzen, *Winchester*, 171, *s.n.*).

10 See 'L'Angleterre anglo-normande', 109 n. 47: this form may represent either Old French *mal(e) fei* (*Malefoi*) or OFr *malfait*; either way, the Anglicised spelling carries the same general implication.

11 See E. Ekwall, *Early London Personal Names*, Acta Regiae Societatis Humaniorum Litterarum Lundensis xliii, Lund 1947, 192.

A similarly compatible pattern is formed by the lay-outs adopted on the various folios. On f. 10r the earliest stratum of the register has accordingly been disposed in five neat and narrow columns, with frequent hyphenated breaks to keep their right-hand margins straight. But soon other lay-outs were tried, and, if the folios are studied according to the chronology proposed, there appears a general, though not wholly systematic, evolution from the first awkwardly-narrow columns to the long lines characterising the presumed final strata. Already on f. 10v later hands show command so much less sure than the first scribe had had of the columnar structure that entries towards its right-hand side are fitted together jigsaw-wise with no pretence at regular lay-out. F. 3r was begun – by hands closely resembling the dominant ones of f. 10 – with a three-column structure, but this was soon disrupted by subdivision as well as by overlaps; it was continued in two uneven as well as unequal columns until near its foot, where these were abandoned in favour of long lines. On f. 3v long lines were adopted from the outset and maintained until two-thirds the way down entries were once more divided into two unequal and untidy columns. Both sides of f. 2 consistently show long lines, the choice also on the uncompleted ff. 1v and 4r, but the few entries made on the other uncompleted pages, ff. 11r and 12r, look as though intended to inaugurate two-column lay-outs.

So all the signs seem alike to indicate a formal beginning on ff. 10r–v, followed by use first of f. 9v, then ff. 3r–v, 2r–v and 1v in that order, with also some sporadic entries on ff. 4r, 11r and 12r. Why the lists which by all criteria so far invoked can be identified as the later ones should now be placed earlier in the group remains a question. At present the make-up of the volume is, as noted, masked by a tight binding. Two signatures are found: on f. 20v, for the end of *A*, and on f. 21r, for the start of *B*. With quiring in eights, *A* would begin with f. 13, the one upon which St Matthew's Gospel in fact opens. That seems to put in doubt the status of all twelve preliminary leaves. But ff. 4–9 must have formed part of the original scheme because they carry canon-tables contemporaneous with the gospel-text and set in framing tinted with pigments like those used in the gospel initials. The status of ff. 1–3 and 10–12 is less obvious; but, even though not all these leaves need have belonged to the original scheme, it cannot well be doubted that the name-lists they carry represent a single twelfth-century enterprise and that this enterprise was from the outset meant to be intimately associated with the gospel-book. For one thing, although the first scribe of the name-lists began on a wholly blank leaf, another early hand entered similar material on the vertical half-page left vacant on f. 9v. Moreover, the 'goldsmiths' entry' which, as we shall see, seems anticipatory of the main name-register, had previously been made on f. 4r. Besides, whatever the detailed structure of the group of twelve leaves, off-sets between ff. 1v and 2r and between ff. 3v and 4r prove that at the time when the name-lists were being entered on them these pairs of facing pages were already established in their present relationship to each other.[12] To explain the present order of the name-lists in terms of *ad hoc* procedure may thus be justifiable. That the compilers had no great sense of system is, after all, evident not only from the existence of four folios begun but left mainly blank but also from the many cramped entries made in margins despite availability of ample blank space elsewhere. Especially revealing is the

---

[12] F. 3v carried off-sets from the forms *palmerarius* and *Adelicia* on f. 4r, together with other corresponding blots and smears, and the left-hand margin of f. 2r carries one from an instance of *filius* written on f. 1v. For discussion of the codicological problems, see the Appendix kindly contributed by Dr Elisabeth van Houts, below, 317–19.

occasional duplication of entries and, even more so, a fair number of apparent omissions.[13]

With order of compilation established and provisionally explained, the next desideratum might seem to be more precise dating, not so much of the texts as of the individuals whose names they record. That seems, however, best left until certain general questions have been settled: in particular, the nature and purpose of these lists.

Various reasons existed for a medieval religious house to compile a register of names. Here any purely administrative one can be ruled out because hardly any of the entries is annotated, and none of the sparse notes that do occur concerns holdings, rents or services. That makes the purpose likely to be in some way commemorative. The style is not that of a 'benefactors' book', which by definition specified for what gifts the community's gratitude is due. Nor are the records in the calendar-form usual, indeed necessary, when obits and other anniversaries are to be celebrated. So presumably these lists constitute either a necrology or a confraternity-book, a main distinction being that the former records only the dead, the latter mainly the living.[14] Annotations seem at first ambiguous. One entry on f. 2r takes an apparently *post-mortem* form: *Godwini pro anima & pro anima Wataburg .ii.*, where the figure may indicate the number of Masses to be said (rather than the amount of a money offering); five previous entries in the same 'block' also include the figures .i. or .ii., but without the clarifying phrase *pro anima*.[15] A later entry on the same folio proclaims the individual enrolled, a Hugh de Beauchamp,[16] as still alive, citing the provision: *qui si monachus effici uoluerit, hic fiat.*[17] Other notes point the same way. On f. 3v a financial arrangement is noted with a priest called Rainger: *In quantum hic moraturus, duos denarios annuatim persoluet; in decessione autem, duodecim.* An occasional inclusive phrase also refers unambiguously to the living, as with the enrolment on f. 3v of Emma, mother of Alan de Percy, together with *omnes qui cum illa fuerunt* [corrected from *uenerunt*] and that on f. 2v of *Simon comes & omnes qui cum eo uenerunt.* Living

---

13 See below, 310, 311, 316.
14 Among the voluminous literature on these topics, see, for instance: Dom U. Berlière, 'Les confraternités monastiques au Moyen Age', *Revue liturgique et monastique*, xi, 1926, 134–42; K. Schmid, 'Probleme der Erforschung frühmittelalterliche Gedenkbücher', *Frühmittelalterliche Studien [FMS]*, i, 1967, 366–89; Dom N. Huyghebaert, *Les Documents nécrologiques*, Typologie des sources du Moyen Age occidental iv, Turnhout 1972; O.G. Oexle, 'Memoria und Memorial-überlieferung im früheren Mittelalter', *FMS*, x, 1976, 70–95; J. Wollasch, 'Les obituaires, témoins de la vie clunisienne', *Cahiers de civilisation médiévale* xxii, 1979, 139–49 (many of these articles have extensive bibliographical notes). Older materials still of value include E. Bishop, 'Some ancient Benedictine confraternity-books', in his *Liturgica Historica*, Oxford 1918, 349–61. For contemporary English practices, see C. Harper-Bill, 'The piety of the Anglo-Norman knightly class', *Proceedings of the Battle Conference on Anglo-Norman Studies*, ii, 1979, 63–77 and 173–6, esp. 64–5, 67, 74; cf. S. Wood, *English Monasteries and their Patrons in the Thirteenth Century*, Oxford, 1955, 30, 122, 127, 129, 131, 133.
15 The term 'block' is used here to indicate a group of entries demarcated from neighbouring ones by changes of hand and/or ink; see above, n. 2.
16 For chronological reasons (see below, 311), the most likely bearer of this name may be the lord of Eaton Socon who died on crusade in 1187 (see I.J. Sanders, *English Baronies*, Oxford 1960, 40, and also G.H. Fowler, 'The Beauchamps, barons of Eaton', *Publications of the Bedfordshire Historical Records Society [PBHRS]*, ii, 1914, 61–91, esp. 68–71; also S. Raban, *The Estates of Thorney and Crowland*, Cambridge 1977, 35, where she notes that land in Eaton was donated to Thorney by a Hugh son of Oliver de Beauchamp).
17 Transcriptions are given with modernised punctuation and capitalisation.

enrolment is equally implied by inclusion of extended family-groups, a category that includes a crucial block on f. 2r:

> Main pater Willelmi de Albinico. Adeleisa, Hunfredus de Buun auunculus eius. Hos colligimus in anniuersario quem facimus pro animabus patrum & matrum nostrarum. UUillelmus de Albinico. Cecilia uxor eius. Filii eius UUillelmus, Rogerius. Matildis filia eius. Istis concedimus fraternitatem loci.[18]

Such entries primarily record admission of laypeople to 'confraternity' with the abbey, but with posthumous privileges extended also to their dead. That this was the purpose of the register as a whole is confirmed by the heading on f. 10r, the one surmised to carry the earliest of the systematised name-lists: *Hæc sunt nomina fratrum istius loci.* The names belonged, then, to 'brothers' of the house, and this cannot mean 'monks' because many of those enrolled were, as in the block quoted, unquestionably laymen and laywomen; indeed, the entries immediately under this heading name *Rex Cnut. Rex Harold. Rex Hardecnut. Imma Regina. & Ælfgifu.* For these lists to represent a 'confraternity-book' or *liber vitae*[19] chimes in with the already-quoted provision for Hugh de Beauchamp, that he should have, should he so wish, the right to take the cowl at the abbey. It agrees also with the mention of 'brotherhood' in the earliest entry of all, on f. 4r:

> Ælfric & Þulfƿine, Eadȝife ȝoldsmiðes, ȝeafen to broþerrædenne tƿeȝen orn peȝhenes ȝoldes, þæt is on þis ilce boc herforuten ȝepired.

Our document thus finds itself in a small and distinguished company. From English houses only two earlier *libri vitae* survive: that of Durham Cathedral Priory (now BL Cotton MS. Domitian A VII) and that of Hyde Abbey (now BL MS. Stowe 944).[20] Continental records of this kind – currently enjoying much attention, both prosopographical and anthroponymical – are more ample, among the best-known *libri* being those of St Gall, Reichenau, Pfäfers, Salzburg and Remiremont.[21] As the several published facsimiles show, structures and modes of compilation resemble those of the Thorney lists, with blocks of sparsely-annotated names entered by divers hands that

---

[18] For the family concerned, see Sanders, 12, under *Belvoir*.

[19] This was the contemporary term: see Schmid, 'Probleme', 367.

[20] *Liber Vitae Ecclesiae Dunelmensis: a Collotype Facsimile*, ed. A. Hamilton Thompson, Surtees Society cxxxvi, Durham and London 1923; *Liber Vitae: Register and Martyrology of New Minster and Hyde Abbey, Winchester*, ed. W. de Gray Birch, Winchester Record Society, London 1892.

[21] *Libri Confraternitatum Sancti Galli Augiensis Fabariensis*, ed. P. Piper, *MGH*, Berlin 1884 (see also: J. Autenrieth, 'Das St Galler Verbrüderungsbuch: Möglichkeiten und Grenzen paläographischer Bestimmung', *FMS*, ix, 1975, 215–25; *Reichenau*, ed. Autenrieth, and its extensive bibliography; D. Geuenich, 'Die ältere Geschichte von Pfäfers im Spiegel der Mönchslisten des Liber Viventium Fabariensis', *FMS*, ix, 1975, 226–32); *Dioecesis Salisburgensis*, ed. S. Hertzberg-Fränkel, *MGH*: Necrologia Germaniae ii, Berlin 1904 (see also *idem*, 'Über das älteste Verbrüderungsbuch von St Peter in Salzburg', *Neues Archiv der Gesellschaft für ältere deutsche Geschichtskunde* xii, 1886, 53–107); *Liber memorialis von Remiremont*, ed. E. Hlawitschka *et alii*, 2 pts, *MGH*: Libri Memoriales i, Dublin and Zürich 1970 (see also G. Tellenbach, 'Uno dei più singolari libri del mondo: il manoscritto 10 della Biblioteca Angelica in Roma (Liber memorialis di Remiremont)', *Archivio della Società romana di Storia patria*, 3rd ser., xxii, 1968, 29–43, and G. Constable, 'The *Liber memorialis* of Remiremont' [review article], *Speculum* xlvii, 1972, 261–77). See also above, n. 14, and below, nn. 22 and 23.

sometimes range over several centuries.[22] Those of Pfäfers and of Cividale are, like the Thorney lists, entered in gospel-books.[23] This, although far from being universal practice, was logical. For in ceremonial admission of laypeople to confraternity a gospel-book was instrumental: Lanfranc's *Monastic Constitutions*, for instance, lay down that, whereas a monk of another house receives from the abbot as token of his admission a copy of the Rule, a layperson is admitted *per textum evangelii*.[24] Such was certainly the usage at Thorney, because a record preserved in the abbey's fourteenth-century cartulary, the Red Book, describes how, during Abbot Gunter's day (1085–1112), an Ingelramn who on the occasion of being received into confraternity was also ceding certain lands to the abbey,

> ipse textum euangelii super quem beneficium suscepit super altare detulit et semetipsum cum illo obtulit donum et cultellum suum in vadimonium super altare posuit.[25]

Almost certainly, the 'gospel-book' referred to there, and in a similar record of a Henry of March's admission to confraternity at the same time as he quitclaimed an advowson [RB, ff. 150v, 421r], was the one under scrutiny.[26] Admission ceremonies apart, a *liber vitae* had a regular liturgical rôle to play, of a kind making crucial the inscribing there of a brother's or sister's name. The proem to the Hyde book describes earthly enrolment as figuring that *in cælestis libri . . . pagina* and explains how each day at Mass the sub-deacon presents the register before the high altar, reciting from it as many entries as time permits, and then, to symbolise the participation in the Office of all enrolled there, lays it beside the sacred vessels; a briefer but similar account occurs in the Salzburg *liber vitae*.[27] Daily ceremonial use may be the reason why in our manuscript the folios that carry the name-lists are grubbier and more crumpled than those of the gospel-text itself.

As for the sorts of people admitted into confraternity with Thorney Abbey, one customary type of enrolment seems missing here. At most houses major contingents among those admitted consisted of members of other houses, enrolled *en bloc* by

---

22 For a facsimile of the Reichenau book, see above, n. 1; for the Durham book, n. 20; and for the Remiremont book, n. 21. Others include *Liber Viventium Fabariensis: Faksimile-Edition*, Basle 1973, and *Das Verbrüderungsbuch von St Peter in Salzburg*, ed. K. Forstner, Graz 1974.

23 See: *Liber Viventium*, also Geuenich, 'Pfäfers', 229–30; C.L. Bethmann, 'Die Evangelienhandschrift zu Cividale', *Neues Archiv*, ii, 1877, 112–28, and R. Bergmann, 'Die germanischen Namen im Evangeliar von Cividale', *Beiträge zur Namenforschung*, new ser. vi, 1971, 111–29, with full bibliographical notes.

24 *The Monastic Constitutions of Lanfranc*, ed. and tr. D. Knowles, London 1951, 114–15.

25 Cambridge University Library Additional MSS. 3020/3021 (continuously foliated), ff. 414v–415r [subsequent references will be inserted in the text, using the abbreviation 'RB']. This cartulary has been neither published nor calendared, and only brief extracts from it have appeared in print; but it was studied by Sandra Raban in her Cambridge Ph.D. thesis of 1974, 'The property of Thorney and Crowland abbeys: a study in purchase and patronage', cf. her book, *The Estates of Thorney and Crowland*.

26 'Texts' and 'gospel-books' were regularly used as tokens of secular transactions, a local example being Robert of Yaxley's renunciation of his claims to Thorney's estates at Sibson (see, in general, M.T. Clanchy, *From Memory to Written Record*, London 1979, 20, 204–5, 229, 232, and, in particular, D.M. Stenton, *English Justice between the Norman Conquest and the Great Charter 1066–1215*, London 1965, 140–7, where she prints relevant documents from the Red Book).

27 Birch, 11–12, and *Dioecesis Salisburgensis*, 6, 42. See also Oexle, 'Memoria'.

mutual agreement; but nowhere do the Thorney lists even hint at such a practice. Any unlabelled block containing names all of the same gender might perhaps represent a monastery or nunnery, but without explicit indication no more can be said; and in any case single-sex groups of any size are rare here. Monastic enrolments, if made at Thorney, might have been kept in a separate register, possibly one associated (as the St Gall *liber vitae* is) with a copy of the Rule.[28]

Various laypeople enrolled here have been mentioned in passing: not only post-Conquest landholders of various ranks, from William d'Aubigné of Belvoir to the obscure Ingelramn, but also King Cnut, with his sons and his wives. The inner chronology of the lists thus proves complex; for, instead of dating, as in the present copy, from the twelfth century, they go back in part to the 1030s, perhaps to the 1020s or before. In the first column of f. 10r, headed by the entries for Cnut and his family, enrolments are organised primarily by ranks and categories and only secondarily by date; they bring together individuals with heydays ranging from the late tenth century (the period of the abbey's foundation) to the first decade of the twelfth. Churchmen listed include – not consecutively, but in this order – Archbishop Æthelnoth of Canterbury (in office 1020–38), Bishop Remigius of Lincoln (*ob.*1092), Bishop Herbert of Norwich (appointed 1091), Abbot Godeman of Thorney itself (*ob.*1013), and Bishop Rannulf Passeflambard of Durham (appointed 1099).[29] Furthermore, as Dorothy Whitelock pointed out forty years ago, the third column opens by listing Cnut's principal jarls and continues with a group of names, all masculine and all of Scandinavian type, that she conjectured to represent the bodyguard of one of these early-eleventh-century jarls.[30] The 'catchment period' of the *liber vitae* thus goes back at least to the beginning of the eleventh century, whose earlier half is well represented. As for the earliest section of the present text, the listing of Passeflambard as bishop puts it after c.1100, and the enrolment out of order and by a different hand of the abbey's own Abbot Robert seems to show the original text as antedating his appointment in 1113. It evidently dates from late in the abbacy of his immediate predecessor Gunter, a former monk of Battle, appointed to Thorney in 1085.[31]

Whether subsequent enrolments, made by divers hands over more than half a century, were normally contemporaneous with admissions can be checked only, and then incompletely, by surveying the careers of those named. Identification and dating thus become twin aspects of a single process. Although only a few of those enrolled can be identified, some of those few are richly documented. Dating from an individual's career is, however, frustratingly vague, because a healthy and prudent magnate might enjoy an active, that is, 'documentary', life of forty years or more.[32] When family-members from different generations are enrolled together, there may, besides, be doubt

---

[28] See J. Autenrieth, 'Das St Galler Verbrüderungsbuch', also 'Der Codex Sangallensis 915', *Festschrift für Otto Herding*, ed. K. Elm *et alii*, Stuttgart 1977, 42–55.

[29] *DNB*, under *Ethelnoth*; D.E. Greenway, *John Le Neve: Fasti Ecclesiae Anglicanae 1066–1300*, III: *Lincoln*, London 1977, 1, and II: *Monastic Cathedrals*, London 1971, 55, 29.

[30] D. Whitelock, 'Scandinavian personal names in the Liber Vitae of Thorney Abbey', *Saga-Book of the Viking Society*, xii, 1937–45, 127–53, esp. 132–40; cf. E. Jørgensen, 'Bidrag til ældre nordisk kirke- og litteraturhistorie', *Nordisk Tidskrift för Bok- och Biblioteksväsen*, xx, 1933, 186–91.

[31] See *The Ecclesiastical History of Orderic Vitalis*, ed. M. Chibnall, 6 vols, Oxford, 1969–80, vi, 150–2, and *The Chronicle of Battle Abbey*, ed. E. Searle, Oxford, 1980, 82; also Knowles, *Heads*, 74. Gunter organised the rebuilding of the abbey church and of much of the conventual complex: cf. RB, f. 414v.

[32] Cf. Clanchy, 39.

as to the prime mover; nor is precision well served by the custom of repeating the same personal names over many generations.[33] This is not only inconvenient but dangerous, offering as it does a temptation to choose whichever individual best suits a pre-conceived time-scheme. Even a clear identification seldom provides more than a rough indication not actually in conflict with that arrived at on other grounds. In a few cases – that of Ingelramn is one in point – a record survives, usually in the abbey's own cartulary, of that individual's admission to confraternity;[34] but all too often this proves datable only to an abbacy, and several of Thorney's twelfth-century abbots were long-lived. The present survey is further handicapped by constraints on space that forbid discussion of more than a few of the datable individuals; choice will partly focus on those whose enrolments occur at significant points on the page.

Despite its shortcomings, such a method has enabled the opening section of the *liber vitae* to be dated to the first decade of the twelfth century, but with a 'catchment period' stretching back over at least a century. The first hand stops work partway through f. 10v, the exact point seeming a matter of judgment. One name that it enrols on the verso is that of Almoth the archdeacon, in dispute with Thorney Abbey until c.1112.[35] Subsequent additions were made, for the most part less neatly, by various hands. Were the enrolments that these represent new ones? In the margin of f. 10v, and so apparently as one of the later entries there, stands an enrolment for Thurstan of Stamford, *monitarius* – presumably the moneyer at work from late in Æthelred II's time until the Confessor's;[36] if so, this must represent rescue of an early admission omitted by the first scribe, the neatness of whose hand is no guarantee of efficiency as a compiler. But usually chronology seems less capricious. Near the foot of the second column – evidently as an early addition – is a block of enrolments for the Trelly (*de Traili*) family, headed by a *Gosfridus* identifiable as the Bedfordshire landholder of 1086 whose confraternity-agreement dates from Gunter's time [RB, f. 414v, cf. f. 297v].[37] Near the head of the third column are enrolled, separately, Robert of Rouen (*Rodbertus capellanus de Rotomago*), probably the royal clerk at work until c.1114,[38] and Robert of Yaxley (*de Iekesle*), Gunter's favoured nephew, installed on abbey lands well before his uncle's death in 1112 and later embroiled in disputes over them.[39] In the bottom right-hand corner stands an entry for a Roger d'Ivry (*de Iuri*), probably not the baron of 1086 but rather his son believed to have survived until c.1112.[40] Several lines

---

33 Plain from the briefest glance at, say, the index to Sanders, *Baronies*; cf. Emma Mason's comments in *The Beauchamp Cartulary: Charters 1100–1268*, Publications of the Pipe Roll Society, ns xliii, London 1980, p. xxiv.

34 For such records in general, see W.G. Clark-Maxwell, 'Some letters of confraternity', *Archaeologia*, 2nd ser. xxv, 1926, 19–60, esp. 23–6; also *idem*, 'Some further letters of fraternity', *ibid.* xxix, 1929, 179–216.

35 See R.C. van Caenegem, *Royal Writs in England from the Conquest to Glanvill*, Selden Society lxxvii, London 1959, 430 (no. 37); also Raban, *Estates*, 24, and RB, f. 419r.

36 See V.J. Smart, 'Moneyers of the late Anglo-Saxon coinage 973–1016', *Commentationes de nummis saeculorum IX–XI in Suecia repertis*, ii, Kungl. Vitterhets Historie och Antikvitets Akademiens Handlingar: Antikvariska Ser. xix, Stockholm 1968, 191–276, esp. 238, and *eadem*, *Cumulative Index of Volumes 1–20*, Sylloge of Coins of the British Isles xxviii, London 1981, 73.

37 See W. Farrer, 'The Honour of Old Wardon', *PBHRS*, xi, 1927, 1–46, esp. 35–41, with chart-pedigree; also Sanders, 134.

38 *Regesta Regum Anglo-Normannorum, 1066–1154*, ed. H.W.C. Davis *et alii*, 4 vols, Oxford 1913–69, ii, p. xi.

39 Stenton, *Justice*, 24–5, 140–7.

40 See Sanders, 9, under *Beckley*.

above that entry stands, however, one for a Hugh *de Prun'* and if, as is likely, the place-name abbreviated is *Prunereto*, that of Abbot Robert's native place, then this enrolment would presumably postdate his appointment in 1113.[41] Chronological hiccups notwithstanding, it looks as though not only the first hand of the *liber vitae* but also the additional entries on this folio belong mainly towards the end of Gunter's abbacy.

F. 9v offers, in contrast, no clearly identifiable individuals. What it does show are complex name-patterns, upon which a hypothetical dating might be based; but that would be another story.

The next major stratum of compilation has been deduced to appear on f. 3r. An early block, entered in a hand resembling some on f. 10v, concerns the Craon (*de Crehun*) family of Lincolnshire, here headed by Alan, son of the Domesday baron Guy (dead by 1118) and active into the 1140s.[42] Near the head of the central column, and in a similar hand, is a block duplicating and supplementing the Trelly one on f. 10v; the reasons for duplication seem here, as elsewhere in this *liber vitae*, obscure. Midway down the left side a block enrolling the Longueville family of Huntingdonshire includes the *Rorgeis* (*Rorgkes, Rorghes*) for whom there survives a confraternity-agreement made during Robert's abbacy [RB, f. 318r] and who in 1127 witnessed a pact between Robert of Yaxley and Abbot Robert [RB, ff. 145r–v]. Several other witnesses to this pact are separately enrolled on this folio, including Sihtric of *Dudintune*,[43] Gumer of Stanton, and Roger *de Gisnei*. The Longueville block is immediately followed by one enrolling the families of the Domesday landholder Thurkill of Arden and of his son Siward; the latter, who made grants to Thorney in Robert's time as well as Gunter's [RB, f. 416r], figures in the 1130 Pipe Roll, and with him are listed here several other men flourishing into the 1130s, including Reiner of Bath, sheriff of Lincolnshire 1128–30.[44] An entry in the top margin names a Maud de Beauchamp, perhaps the one appearing in documents of the late 1120s.[45] Entries on this folio thus seem compatible with use of it mainly during that decade.

F. 3v offers fewer identifiable individuals, those that there are having often had careers either vague or else inconveniently long. In slight compensation, a lay-out mainly in long lines makes stratification far plainer here than on earlier folios. The first name enrolled is that of a Robert of Huntingdon, probably the one who, at some point during Robert's four-decade abbacy (1113–51), made Thorney a grant on the occasion of his son's taking the cowl there [RB, f. 419r]. A Hugh *le Bigot* entered a quarter the way down may be the royal *dapifer*, later earl of Norfolk, active from the 1120s to the

---

[41] For Robert *Pruneriensis*, see Orderic, vi, 150.

[42] See Sanders, 47, under *Frieston*, and Raban, *Estates*, 34–5; also E.M. Poynton, 'The Fee of Creon', *Genealogist*, ns xviii, 1902, 162–6 and 219–25, and *Early Yorkshire Charters*, ed. W. Farrer and C.T. Clay, 12 vols, Edinburgh etc. 1914–65, ix, 72–3.

[43] A frequent form of place-name: in the Huntingdonshire context the likeliest identification may be with the north Cambridgeshire Doddington, just south of March (P.H. Reaney, *The Place-Names of Cambridgeshire and the Isle of Ely*, English Place-Name Society [EPNS] xix, Cambridge 1943, 251–2; for some possible alternatives, see J.E.B. Gover *et alii*, *The Place-Names of Northamptonshire*, EPNS x, Cambridge 1933, 201, also 138, 146). [[But cf. 328 below.]]

[44] *Magnus Rotulus Scaccarii . . . anno tricesimo-primo regni Henrici Primi*, ed. J. Hunter, London 1833, 6, 108; Orderic, vi, 16 (early years of Rufus's reign), and *Regesta*, ii, 1133, 1640, 1652.

[45] See C.G. Chambers and G.H. Fowler, 'The Beauchamps, barons of Bedford', *PBHRS*, i, 1913, 1–24, esp. 3–4.

1170s.[46] An enrolment of a William *Peurel* might concern the elder, 'of Dover', who died c.1133.[47] The most difficult entry, made well down the page, names *Emma, mater Alain de Perci*: the mother of Alan son of William had been widowed before 1100 and there seems no record of her survival into the 1130s, but Alan's wife too was an Emma and he had, by an unnamed mother, an illegitimate son also called Alan.[48] Perhaps this entry is best taken as another belated rescue. Other apparent contradictions are more readily resolved. The *Yuo Tallebois* enrolled near the bottom right-hand corner is identifiable, not with Rufus's *dapifer* and sheriff of Lincolnshire (*ob*.1093), but as the namesake who between 1144 and 1156 attested, alongside a Robert *de Broi* (from another family figuring in the *liber vitae*), a charter in Thorney's favour [RB, f. 295r]; he might also be identified as, or as a son of, the *Talgebosch* witnessing the 1127 pact between Robert of Yaxley and Abbot Robert. The Hugh d'Elbeuf (*de Uldebobo*) entered just beneath this Yvo may be the one making Thorney several grants datable between 1144 and 1166.[49] Entries here thus seem to run roughly from c.1130 up to the 1140s. The Roger *de Mungubun* whose name is entered near the top of the left-hand margin must be the *Munbegun* figuring, with a similar family-group, late on f. 2r.

On both sides of f. 2 long-line lay-outs make stratification clear. On the recto two blocks entered by different hands (the earlier already quoted above) centre upon William d'Aubigné of Belvoir, the second naming additional children; no confraternity-agreement for William seems to survive, but before c.1133 he made Thorney a grant of lands in Northamptonshire [RB, f. 205r]. Other fairly early entries here concern William the Fleming of Thornhaugh (*de Tornehaga*), named in the 1130 Pipe Roll,[50] and Tovi of Lowick (*de Lufwico*), dead by the late 1130s, when a grant of his to Thorney was posthumously confirmed [RB, f. 229r, cf. the confraternity-agreement ff. 419r–v].[51] A group entered a third the way down is headed by Gilbert of Folksworth, another witness to the pact of 1127; his confraternity-agreement likewise dates from Robert's abbacy [RB, f. 419v]. Towards the foot of the page comes a block listing members of the Clare family, including Earl Gilbert of Hertford (*de Hereford*), who enjoyed that rank only from 1136 to 1152;[52] this is a complex block, centring probably on Gilbert's grandmother, Alice de Clermont, for it lists not only several people – *Rodbertus capellanus*, *Rodbertus de Bertuna*, *Mabilia filia Gaufridi de Cotes*, *Rodbertus dapifer*, *Adericus Hefede* – who witnessed a grant of hers to Thorney datable c.1140 [RB, f. 206v] but also her long-dead brother-in-law, Earl Hugh of Chester (*ob*.1101).[53] Entries here, apparently running from the 1130s to the 1140s, seem to overlap chronologically with those on f. 3v.

46 GEC, *Complete Peerage of England, Scotland, Ireland, Great Britain and the United Kingdom*, 13 vols in 14, London 1910–59 [GEC], ix, 579–86.

47 Identification is delicate: William Peverel (I) 'of Dover' died c.1133 and his nephew William Peverel (II) 'of Bourn' inherited his honour (Sanders, 19, and 151, under *Wrinstead*) and may then have adopted his uncle's style, cf. below, n. 54.

48 Farrer and Clay, xi, 1–2; GEC, x, 437–40; also Sanders, 148, under *Topcliffe*.

49 *Monasticon*, ii, 601, 602, 605.

50 *Magnus Rotulus*, ed. Hunter, 83–4.

51 See also *Facsimiles of Early Charters from Northamptonshire Collections*, ed. F.M. Stenton, Northamptonshire Record Society iv, Lincoln and London 1930, 52–4, where the confirmation is dated 1136–38.

52 GEC, vi, 498–9, also ii, 244. For *Hereford* as a spelling for *Hertford*, see J.E.B. Gover *et alii*, *The Place-Names of Hertfordshire*, EPNS xv, Cambridge 1938, 1, 225.

53 GEC, iii, 243, also 164–5. For the Clares as benefactors of Thorney, see Raban, *Estates*, 30–2,

On f. 2v what seems the earliest block enrols a group of men several of whom are associated with a charter, datable c.1140, of William Peverel (II) – 'of Bourn', later also 'of Dover': the grantor himself, the grantee Hamo Pichard, and the witnesses William de La Mouche (*de La Musce*) and Eustace of Madingley (*de Mediggele*).[54] It also includes Hugh of Lisores (*Lusuriarum*), whose known grant to Thorney was confirmed by William Peverel 'of Dover' [RB, ff. 82r, 127r].[55] Others enrolled here include Bishop Nigel of Ely (in office 1133–69), who before 1151 granted Thorney the former hermitage at Throkenholt [RB, ff. 189r–190r], and John d'Etoutteville (*de Stuteuilla*), whose confraternity-agreement dates from the early 1150s [RB, f. 232 r–v].[56] Well down the page is enrolled another group of men linked by a charter, this time in Thorney's favour and datable between 1148 and 1161 [RB, f. 206r]: the grantor Ralph *Cheneduit* and his witnesses Warin de Blacqueville, Richard of Farndon, Roger son of William of Braybrooke and Leofric of Charwelton, the link being made explicit by a note after Warin's name: *qui testis est de nostra carta de lxᵗᵃ acris de Cherwolto-nia* (again implying living enrolment). The next block lists members of the Oiry or D'Oyry (*Deuri*) family of Lincolnshire, apparently centring on the matriarch Emechin who seems to have survived into the 1160s.[57] Two entries, which may be either first on this folio or else late additions in the top margin, concern a Eustace and a Robert son of Stephen of *La Leie*, the father being presumably the Stephen *de Leghia* who in the late 1130s witnessed a grant in Thorney's favour [RB, f. 229r];[58] these entries may be compared with that at the top of f. 11r for a Eustace son of Stephen.

Predictably, entries on the folios left uncompleted seem among the latest made in this *liber vitae*. The Herlewin of Raunds enrolled on f. 12r can be dated to the late twelfth century.[59] For f. 1v a *terminus post quem* is given by the entry near its head of *Ricardus frater abbatis Salomonis*, because Salomon was appointed in 1176. Such a date seems consonant with other enrolments there; of Robert *Disci* and of Robert de Brouay (*de Broi*), both linked with Thorney during Salomon's time [RB, ff. 296v, 297r]; of Geoffrey of *La Leie*, if he is the *Galfridus de Lega* named in several Pipe Rolls of the 1190s;[60] and of Robert of Stanton, still active after the turn of the century.[61] One of the latest entries of all concerns Richard of Fleet, whose links with Thorney went back to the 1160s [RB, f. 250r–v] but who likewise remained active into the 1190s.[62]

34, 36; their most substantial gift was Baldwin son of Gilbert's foundation c.1139 of a dependent priory at Deeping (cf. Wormald, *Kalendars*, i, 129–44). For some minor identifications, see below, 314.

[54] F.M. Stenton, *The First Century of English Feudalism 1066–1166*, 2nd edn, Oxford 1961, 275, cf. 156; the grantor is styled *de Duure*.

[55] Cf. above, n. 47.

[56] Greenway, *Fasti*, ii, 45; Farrer and Clay, ix, 2–4, 23–7, 132–3.

[57] See K. Major, *The D'Oyrys of South Lincolnshire, Norfolk, and Holderness 1130–1275*, Lincoln 1984, 1–5; I am grateful to Dr Major for a gift to me of a copy of this work.

[58] *Charters*, ed. Stenton, 52. La Leie might be identifiable as Thurleigh (see A. Mawer and F.M. Stenton, *The Place-Names of Bedfordshire and Huntingdonshire*, EPNS iii, Cambridge 1926, 47–8), but the form is so common that without fuller evidence no more can be said.

[59] *Great Roll of the Pipe for 22 Henry II (1175–1176)*, London 1904, 51.

[60] *Great Rolls of the Pipe of 3 & 4 Richard I (1191–1192)*, London 1926, 111, 203; *Chancellor's Roll for 8 Richard I (1196)*, London 1930, 154; cf. n. 58.

[61] *Curia Regis Rolls Richard I – 2 John*, London 1922, 124, under *Huntend'* (*anno 1200*); *CRR 5–7 John*, London 1926, 224–5 (*anno 1204*).

[62] See H.E. Hallam, *Settlement and Society*, Cambridge 1965, 23, where he is dated 1160–95.

Despite the prevailing imprecision, it is clear that, as each folio is taken in the chronological order hypothesised, so the average range of likely dates consistently falls later. Equally, it seems wise to allow for some concurrent use of different folios.

The survey aimed at dating the various strata of this *liber vitae* has focussed on certain identifiable individuals enrolled there. People who are thus identifiable form, it must be emphasised, a tiny minority because the typical block of entries is a string of single names, of both genders and of manifold types and etymologies, with no by-name at all to help place any of them, thus: *Ærnis, Helepis, Blacwina, Ealuiue, Radulfus, Ricardus, Orm, Ealuiue, Rodbertus* [f. 3v]. Only in the rarest cases can people so imprecisely named be identified.

For those few who are clearly identifiable, the sorts of relationship which they had with the abbey – and, more urgently, hoped to have with it in time to come – have sometimes been expressed in confraternity-agreements preserved in the Red Book of Thorney. That made by Geoffrey de Trelly (enrolled in near-duplicate on ff. 10v and 3r) is at once typical and comprehensive, first specifying a gift to the abbey and then continuing:

> Quo pacto, si quandoque, inspirante diuina clementia, monachari uoluero, cum parte substantie mee inibi monachandus suscipiar. Si uero in laico habitu – quod absit – nature satisfecero, illuc a meis humandus deferar. Si autem ex patriam obiero, et ad eos certus uenerit nuntius de obitu meo, omne obsequium anime mihi fideliter persoluerint uti pro monacho. Deinde, quot annis redeunte obitus mei anniuersario, fiet a fratribus meis anime mee commemoratio. Similiter, uxor mea, si uite uale-fecerit laica, illuc, allata secum portione substancie sue, humanda deferretur. Si uero in qualibet abbatia sanctimonialis effecta obierit, et ad fratres de eius obitu breue uel nuntius uenerit, uti pro sua sorore pro ea omne officium explebunt anime. Preterea, post uite exitum omnis mea soboles in cimiteri tumulabitur fratrum . . . [RB, f. 414v].

What those admitted to confraternity expected from their association with the monks were services assisting towards the salvation of their souls.

Our present subject is, however, not theology but history with a prosopographical bias. Documents preserved in the Red Book have regularly been invoked for the light they shed on enrolments in the *liber vitae*; and links between the two are not coincidental. Most confraternity-agreements extant – those of Geoffrey de Trelly and of Ingelramn being typical of their kind – doubled as land-conveyances and thus found places as of right among the abbey muniments.[63] Some *libri vitae* indeed combine both functions within the same covers: that from Remiremont, for instance, preserves along-side its name-lists some seven hundred business records. Nor was the overlap purely administrative, because between benefactions and spiritual benefits there existed a reciprocity that may most tactfully be attributed to mutual gratitude. Characteristically, bidding-prayers prefixed to *libri vitae* stress the house's gratitude for the benefactions it has received: Salzburg singles out those *qui elymosinis suis se commendaverunt*, Remiremont those *qui hunc locum per amore Dei ad usus monacharum de rebus suis ditauerunt uel suas largiti sunt cælemosinas*, and Hyde those *quorum beneficiis elemo-sinarum cotidie hæc ipsa familia, Christe largiente, pascitur.*[64] The Thorney book contains no prayer, but the same principle, indeed a gratitude spilling over from grantor

---

63 Cf. Raban, *Estates*, 41: 'Gifts which had been made in return for spiritual privileges tended to be more secure because the donor had a vested interest in their continuance'.

64 *Dioecesis Salisburgensis*, 6; *Remiremont*, i, 1 (f. 1v); Birch, 11–12.

to witnesses, seems implicit in the note identifying Warin de Blacqueville as witness to the Charwelton charter. The Red Book, for its part, regularly records people as having been received into confraternity 'when giving' (*dans*) or 'through giving' (*dando*) lands or monies [e.g., RB, ff. 189r, 419v]. In particular, a grant of confraternity might symbolise settlement of a dispute. This was so with Henry of March, whose admission coincided with his surrender of an advowson to which he had once laid claim [RB, f. 150v], and with Ralph son of Segbold of Lowick, who had 'invaded' two holdings [RB, f. 420r]. At other times a veiled business-transaction seems implied. Rorgeis of Orton Longueville and his wife, making a grant *pro animabus suis et pro fraternitate*, received also thirty shillings *de caritate Sancti* [RB, f. 418r]. When Odo Revel, pleading embarrassment because of mortgages unwisely taken on, made certain lands over to the abbey, *partim pro fraternitate loci, partim pro caritate Sancti*, the relief afforded him in his 'necessity' amounted to sixty shillings and a palfrey which Hugh de Vatierville had donated to the abbey [RB, f. 419v, cf. ff. 77r–v, 415r].

Whether or not benefaction was directly involved, business records and spiritual ones constantly interlocked. This too was natural. Usually, it may be supposed, a 'block' of confraternity-entries marked off by change of hand and/or ink represented a group of people – relatives, friends, neighbours, feudal associates – jointly admitted. Often, as we have seen, kinship is made clear. When a magnate is concerned, a blanket extension of privilege may cover all in his or her train (*omnes qui cum eo uenerunt, omnes qui cum illa fuerunt*); and that train, or household, included the *capellani, clerici* and *milites* who, together with an occasional cook or other artisan, witnessed their lord's or lady's charters. People associated in the one context are likely to be so also in the other. Regular overlaps often allow more precise identification of those figuring in either type of record. As already implied, the *Guarinus miles* and the *Rogerus filius Willelmi* witnessing the Charwelton quitclaim [RB, f. 206r] can be firmly identified with the Warin de Blacqueville (*de Blacheuilla*) and the Roger son of William of Braybrooke (*de Braibroc*) both enrolled on f. 2v in the confraternity-block headed by the grantor Ralph Cheneduit. On f. 2r an Ordric whose name, together with those of a William son of Sliki and a Robert, seems to have been inserted out of order to fill a spare half-line can similarly be identified as the *Ordricus uinitor* who witnesses the same quitclaim alongside a Robert son of Sliki; and at the same time William and Robert are revealed as brothers. The already-quoted mention, as dependant of Alice de Clermont and together with Robert the chaplain, Robert of Barton, Robert the steward and Æthelric 'Head', of a Mabel daughter of Geoffrey of Coton furnishes a family background for the *Mabilia puella mea* who, with the same three Roberts and *Aderiz heued*, witnesses a confirmation granted by her mistress [RB, f. 206v]. In the next block but one (entered in a strongly contrasting hand) an Albert whose entry immediately follows that of William *de Dena* can likewise be identified as the *Albertus magister puerorum* witnessing for the Lady Alice beside the same William [RB, f. 206r]; and by the same token it must have been in her household that the Hugh *dapifer domine* enrolled alongside William and Albert was steward.

Sometimes a bold guess, impossible to substantiate, may nevertheless be ventured. A block entered about a third of the way down f. 3v reads: *Adam, Agustinus, Gunnilda, Emma, Cecilia, et uxor archidiaconi*. Who was this 'archdeacon's wife' or 'widow' enrolled just before William *Peurel* and so perhaps c.1130? Who was indeed the married archdeacon? To be specified by office alone he must have been well-known at Thorney. Two likely candidates present themselves: the historian Henry of Huntingdon, not only an official but also a local landholder, at Stukeley; or, alternatively, his father

Nicholas (*ob.*1110), who had preceded him in the archdeaconry.[65] Both men were well-known at the abbey, in whose business they were often involved [e.g., RB, ff. 114r, 145v, 166r, 166v, etc.]. Given Henry's partisanship of clerical marriage, to find his wife or his mother admitted to confraternity with this most austere of abbeys would be piquant;[66] and there are encouraging clues. A Thorney memorandum issued by Archdeacon Nicholas was witnessed by an Adam of Stukeley (*de Stiuecle*) [RB, f. 114r]; and Stukeley was, as noted, where the family holdings lay.[67] Henry's own son, Nicholas's grandson, was also to be an Adam [RB, f. 421v]. Therefore, the presence of an Adam in the same block as the unnamed archdeacon's unnamed wife or widow seems to encourage her identification as a member of the Stukeley family (*Augustine* too is a name they might have favoured, seeing that a later scion of this stock was to be an Aristotle).[68]

Whether or not any identification is defensible, that entry, made about 1130, of an 'archdeacon's wife' illustrates the continuing respectability, well into the twelfth century, of clerical 'marriage'. Because Thorney was, according to William of Malmesbury, among the most austere of houses, exploiting its geographical isolation so as to keep the world, and women in particular, at bay, its confraternity-book might seem hardly likely to condone irregularities of life. Yet throughout its earlier strata there appear married priests, together with their 'wives' and their children: on f. 10r we find *Sumerlede p[resbiter], & Ðulfled uxor eius, & filia eius Æluiue*, also *Gunni pr[esbiter], & uxor eius Ispara, Merȝet filius eius*, and *Inȝolf p[resbiter], & uxor eius Speterun*; on f. 9v we find *Wfpi sacerdos & filius eius Ægelpine*, followed later by a separate entry for *Godgifu uxor Ðulpi p[resbiteri]*. Admittedly, these entries, found in the book's earliest strata and all referring to people with Insular names, cannot be dated precisely and might well go back to times before the Gregorian reforms had taken effect. However that may be, their recopying after 1100 seems to imply for that date no sense that such relationships put the participants beyond the pale. The entry for the 'archdeacon's wife' or 'widow' seems, as we have seen, to date – at all events in its present form – from c.1130. Similar hints continue indeed into the mid century. Often clerical marriage had – as with Ailred of Rievaulx's family – had as its concomitant heredity of benefice; and this may be implied by successive entries found in a small block made midway down f. 2v and headed by Bishop Nigel of Ely, because here an entry for *Wluricus presbiter de Titt* is immediately followed by another for *Lefsius presbit[er], pater eius*, although admittedly without its being made clear whether the same benefice was involved. Such entries counterpoint the rôle played by a priest of Tydd's *nefandissima concubina* – perhaps a member of this very family – in an episode of the *Life*, copied into the Red Book, of the hermit Godric of Throkenholt, who had been born in Wisbech before the Conquest [RB, ff. 190r–196r]. Just when Godric's penitential hauberk had almost rusted away, as a sign that his sins were forgiven him, a visit to his hermitage by the person in question effected its instant restoration. Yet the

---

65 Greenway, *Fasti*, iii, 27.
66 Huntingdon, 234, 245–6, 250–1; cf. *De gestis pontificum*, 326–9, esp. 327: '*Femina ibi, si visitur, monstro habetur* . . .'
67 For the place-name, see *PN Beds. and Hunts.*, 224.
68 See C. Clay, 'Master Aristotle', *EHR* lxxvi, 1961, 303–8. On married archdeacons, cf. C. Harper-Bill, 'Bishop William Turbe and the diocese of Norwich, 1146–74', *Anglo-Norman Studies*, vii, 1984 (= *Proceedings of the Battle Conference 1984*), 142–60, esp. 149, also 157–9.

confraternity-entries imply such women to have been respectable enough to be made 'sisters' of the abbey.

There are, in conclusion, two puzzles on which to reflect: one perhaps a mere administrative matter; the other involving the whole question of popular piety and of the forms it took. Both puzzles alike concern not what is in the *liber vitae* but what is missing from it.

The Red Book of Thorney and the *liber vitae* have thus far been exhibited as throwing light on each other; but in fact correspondence between them is notably imperfect. Agreements could, of course, hardly be expected to have survived for more than a small minority of enrolments: scribes compiling a fourteenth-century cartulary would have been interested only in those that doubled as land-conveyances and would therefore not have copied out any based on other kinds of reciprocity. What is unexpected is that by no means all the extant agreements find corresponding entries in the *liber vitae*. No one is more amply represented by confraternity-records than the Huntingdonshire landholder Odo Revel, whose wife and son Andrew were also received into confraternity with Thorney [RB, ff. 77r–v, 415r, 419v], but whether he figures anywhere in the *liber vitae* is uncertain: nowhere does the by-name *Revel(lus)* occur; men called Odo are few, and none occurs in proximity to an *Andreas*. As for Ingelramn, he is quite certainly not enrolled in the extant *liber vitae*: the only occurrence of the name is in an entry fairly late on f. 2v for *Arturus pater Ingelranni*, where reference may be to the *Ingelrannus camerarius* often witnessing abbey charters [e.g., RB, f. 150v]. Some omissions may be due simply to scribal negligence – a risk of which one Reichenau scribe was only too well aware[69] – as, for instance, when Rorgeis of Longueville is enrolled amid his family-group but without the wife Genovefa for whose admission his agreement with the abbey explicitly provides [RB, f. 418r]. An alternative explanation might be based on hypothesising use of loose folios, some of which have been lost.

A more fundamental mystery – and one on which opinions would be welcomed from historians of theology and liturgy – is why the *liber vitae* should have fallen into disuse during the last quarter of the twelfth century, and that despite ample blank space on four of its folios. It had been reorganised during the opening decade of that century, with a bringing-together of materials dating back over at least a century. It was then kept up for sixty or seventy years, only to be abandoned before the century was out. One thing that makes this odd from a practical point of view is the achievement of a clear and manageable style of lay-out; there would seem to have been no need to abandon this recension in order to recopy everything and start afresh. It would be good to have some expert opinions on popular piety at the turn of the twelfth and thirteenth centuries, and on how the forms that it subsequently took might have affected lay-people's admission to confraternity.

---

[69] See above, 301 and n. 1.

APPENDIX

THE GENESIS OF BRITISH LIBRARY ADDITIONAL MS. 40,000, ff. 1–12

Elisabeth M.C. van Houts

Although the binding of the Thorney manuscript is tight, an attempt can be made to reconstruct the genesis of the first twelve folia. The diagrams on p. 318 show successive phases of the growth of the name-list and its integration beside the gospel canon-tables. From the outset the names were meant to be an integral part of the preliminary matter of the gospel-book. It seems likely, however, that at first this part of the codex existed independently of the gospel-book, or, at the most, was only provisionally attached to it. The fact that most names occur on leaves that were originally separate suggests that the order of the folia might have changed. The diagrams show the folia in their present position.

I.   In the beginning the preliminary section of the codex consisted of three bifolia (ff. 5–10) and a single leaf (f. 4), which might be the surviving half of another bifolium. The Eusebian canon-tables for the gospels begin on f. 4v and end on f. 9v (left half of the page). F. 4r as well as the right half of f. 9v were blank at this stage. Ff. 4–9 show ruling designed for the canon-tables, but no pricking. F. 10, however, has prickings for forty-one lines and no ruling. The writing of the name-list, which, judging by the rubric, began on f. 10r, follows a five column lay-out. The excellent quality of the parchment of the two bifolia 6–9 and 7–8 is comparable to that of the gospel-text; the parchment of the bifolium 5–10 is inferior. On f. 4r the goldsmiths' entry followed by various early materials was written c.1060–70.

II.   After the goldsmiths' entry the names were written on ff. 10r, 10v and 9v (right half of the page). By c.1115/20 all available blank space was filled and additional folia were required to continue the name-list.

A codicological description of ff. 1, 2, 3, 11 and 12 is necessary before we can proceed with an account of the reconstruction. F. 1 is a single leaf of inferior brownish parchment. There is no sign of ruling or pricking. The quality of the other four leaves is equally poor. Ff. 2, 3, 11 and 12 are also separate sheets. Differences in colour and especially in the sorts of parchment preclude the conclusion that these four folia once formed two bifolia. They seem to have been prepared for writing all at once, for they show similar pricking and dry-point ruling meant for a lay-out of five columns each of forty-one lines. The pricking is different from that of f. 10.

III.   F. 3 was written upon in the period c.1115–40 and was added during that time.

IV.   Another leaf, f. 2, containing names from c.1130 to c.1160, joined the previous one.

V.   F. 11, containing an early-twelfth-century list of saints' relics on the verso, was added most probably in the early 1160s. The blank recto was used for a few names written c.1160. This entry makes it likely that f. 11 was inserted at this stage and not earlier when the relic-list was composed. It is, however, conceivable that this leaf was reversed in the 1160s after originally having been added before f. 3. If so, why then was the blank space not used for the names which now occur on f. 3?

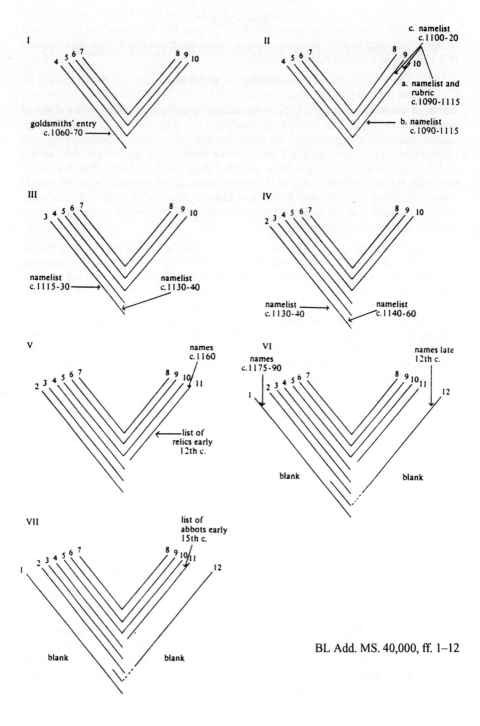

I

4 5 6 7   8 9 10

goldsmiths' entry
c.1060-70 ——→

II

4 5 6 7   8 9

c. namelist
c.1100-20

10

a. namelist and
rubric
c.1090-1115

b. namelist
c.1090-1115

III

3 4 5 6 7   8 9 10

namelist
c.1115-30——→

namelist
c.1130-40

IV

2 3 4 5 6 7   8 9 10

namelist ——→
c.1130-40

namelist
c.1140-60

V

2 3 4 5 6 7   8 9 10 11

names
c.1160

←— list of
relics early
12th c.

VI

names
c.1175-90

1 2 3 4 5 6 7   8 9 10 11

names late
12th c.

12

blank   blank

VII

1 2 3 4 5 6 7   8 9 10 11

list of
abbots early
15th c.

12

blank   blank

BL Add. MS. 40,000, ff. 1–12

VI.   As a finishing touch two leaves, ff. 1 and 12, were bound on the outside of this group of folia. The inner surfaces of both, ff. 1v and 12r, were used for a few more names, while their outside provided a cover which remained blank. The stub between ff. 1 and 2 most probably belongs to f. 12.

VII.   The final stage was the entering of the fifteenth-century list of abbots on f. 11r below the entry of the names written in the 1160s. As is said above, it remains a matter of conjecture when ff. 1–12 were definitively bound together with the actual gospel-book.

20

The *Liber Vitae* of Thorney Abbey and its 'Catchment Area'*

Gaudete et exultate quia nomina vestra scripta sunt in celis.[1]

During the twelfth century there were entered on preliminary leaves associated with the gospel-book now known as British Library Add. MS. 40,000[2] name-lists which, although as yet unpublished, have long been recognized as constituting a confraternity-list, or *liber vitae*, of Thorney Abbey.[3]

Assigning these name-lists to Thorney Abbey is only a first step towards their effective localization. The abbey stood, and its truncated remains still stand, on the north-western borders of Cambridgeshire, where that county marches with Huntingdonshire, Northamptonshire and Lincolnshire.[4] In the twelfth century there was at Thorney no 'community' apart from the abbey itself: contemporary witness agrees in emphasizing the absence of any native, self-renewing lay settlement.[5] So, until some way can be found of localizing, not the book, nor the many scribes of the lists, but the several thousand people whose names those lists record, little of import can be said about name-patterns found here, least of all about the marked Scandinavian element.[6]

---

* This is a revised version of the paper given on 23 March 1985 at the XVIIth Annual Conference of the Council for Name Studies held at Christ's College, Cambridge.

1 W. de Gray Birch, ed., *Liber Vitae: Register and Martyrology of New Minster and Hyde Abbey, Winchester* (London, 1892), 13.

2 See: *British Museum Catalogue of Additions to the Manuscripts 1916–20* (London, 1933), 276–9; N.R. Ker, *Catalogue of Manuscripts containing Anglo-Saxon* (Oxford, 1957), 163, item 131; E.M.C. van Houts, 'The genesis of British Library Additional MS. 40,000, ff. 1–12', above 317–19.

3 See D. Whitelock, 'Scandinavian personal names in the *Liber Vitae* of Thorney Abbey', *Saga-Book of the Viking Society* XII (1937–45), 127–53, and C. Clark, 'British Library Additional MS. 40,000, ff. 1v–12r', above 301–16.
For *liber vitae* as a current medieval term, see K. Schmid, 'Probleme der Erforschung frühmittelalterliche Gedenkbücher', *Frühmittelalterliche Studien* I (1967), 366–89, esp. 367; cf. also J.-L. Lemaître, *Répertoire des documents nécrologiques français*, 2 parts continuously paginated (Paris, 1980), 5–11.

4 Throughout this paper references to counties assume the pre-1974 system.

5 See: N.E.S.A. Hamilton, ed., *Willelmi Malmesbiriensis monachi de gestis pontificum Anglorum libri quinque* (London, 1870), 326–7; W.T. Mellows, ed., *The Chronicle of Hugh Candidus* (Oxford, 1949), 42–3; M. Chibnall, ed. and tr., *The Ecclesiastical History of Orderic Vitalis*, 6 vols (Oxford, 1969–80), VI, 150–2, *ab omni semotum est secularium cohabitatione*.

6 For Whitelock's pioneer work on this topic, see n. 3 above. It is hoped to publish separately the discussion of Scandinavian naming that formed the second part of the paper as delivered. [[This discussion remained unpublished; but see the remarks in 'A witness to post-Conquest English cultural patterns: the *Liber Vitae* of Thorney Abbey', below 339–47, esp. 343.]]

Devising a technique for such a localization poses problems. The name-lists have no necessary unity outside their common association with Thorney Abbey. Entered in 'blocks' of widely-varying sizes by a multiplicity of hands working over the best part of a century – that is, from 1100×1112 to *post*-1176 – upon inspection they prove in part to date back at least to the early eleventh century.[7] Many of these blocks distinguishable by changes of hand and of ink are, besides, made up solely of unqualified single names impossible to link with specific people or specific localities.

If this confraternity-book were to represent a wholly random harvesting of pious intentions, its onomastic value would be limited. *A priori*, however, that seems unlikely. A candidate for confraternity normally attended an admission ceremony, usually held at the abbey itself;[8] and, with twelfth-century travel as it was, many people, it may be surmised, would have sought their spiritual benefits fairly near at hand.

Such an assumption, optimistic though it is, hardly forwards the investigation. An accepted method for determining the territorial affinities of a medieval community – that is, of the individuals composing it – is to analyze whatever toponymical by-names appear in use among them. Here, unfortunately, by-names of all kinds, even Latinized patronymics, are far scarcer than in administrative records of like date[9] (because a confraternity-book was primarily an *aide-mémoire* for the deity, not for fallible humanity, imprecision was not unusual[10]). By-names are not, however, totally lacking; and one must do the best one can with what one finds.[11]

Such toponymical by-names as do occur in these lists belong mainly to nobility and gentry. They fall into two main groups: those referring to continental places, and those referring to English ones. Self-evidently, the latter afford more straightforward evidence of territorial affinities within England, the point of most immediate concern to an anthroponymist.

Distribution of these English toponymical by-names proves far from random. A few forms – among them *Bertuna* (Barton), *Dudintune* (Doddington or Duddington) and *Houctune* (Houghton) – are admittedly too commonplace to be definitively identified in default of fuller evidence.[12] But, even with an ambiguous name-form, evidence from witness-lists and the like as to the name-bearer's associations will sometimes allow of

7 See Clark, 'BL. Add. MS. 40,000', above 308; cf. Whitelock, 'Scandinavian personal names', 131–42.

8 See Clark, 'BL. Add. MS. 40,000', above 307.

9 Cf., for instance, the Bury St Edmunds survey datable c.1100 [D.C. Douglas, ed., *Feudal Documents from the Abbey of Bury St Edmunds* (London, 1932), 25–44].

10 Reliance upon divine omniscience is elsewhere made explicit in phrases such as: *ceterorum omnium quorum nomina Deus scit, nomina uicinorum omnium . . . quorum nomina Deus scit, nomina . . . ob incautelam inertiae oblivionis meæ dimissa* [J. Autenrieth *et alii*, eds, *Das Verbrüderungsbuch der Abtei Reichenau*, MGH: Libri memoriales et necrologia, nova ser. I (Hanover, 1979), 229]; and the repeated *quorum numerum et nomina tu scis, Domine*, of Remiremont [E. Hlawitschka *et alii*, eds, *Liber memorialis von Remiremont*, 2 parts, MGH: Libri memoriales I (Dublin and Zurich, 1970), I, 1, 3].

11 Identifications of places and of people will mainly be based upon documentation taken from Olof von Feilitzen's posthumous papers, entrusted to me by his academic executor, Dr Folke Sandgren, to whom I wish to express my gratitude. Von Feilitzen is not, of course, to be held responsible for any unwise use to which his material may have been put.

12 See, for instance, E. Ekwall, *The Concise Oxford Dictionary of English Place-Names*, 4th edn (Oxford, 1960), s.nn. *Barton, Dodington, Duddington, Houghton*.

tentative assignment to a particular one among possible localities.[13] Analysis of such toponymical by-names as can, one way or another, be with fair confidence assigned to specific places shows certain counties as strongly predominant. In rough order of dominance, these are:

Northamptonshire: Braybrooke (*Braibroc*), Castor (*Castra*), Charwelton (*Cherwoltonia*), Farndon 2x (*Ferendonia, Ferenduna*), Lilford (*Lilef'*), Lowick (*Lufuico*), Raunds (*Rand'*), Singlesole (*Senglesolt*), Thornhaugh (*Tornehaga*), Woodcroft (*Wdecroft*), and, by inference, also Deene (*Dena*), Milton Park (*Milituna*), Peterborough (*Burh*) and Northampton (*Hamtune*).

Lincolnshire: Bicker (*Biker'*), Fleet 3x (*Flet, Fleth*), Lincoln (*Nicol'*), Stamford 2x (*Stanforde, Stamford*), Swaton (*Suauetun*), Tydd St Mary (*Titt*), Wigtoft (*Wiketot*).

Cambridgeshire: Coton (*Cotes*), Ely 5x (*Eli, Heli*), Madingley (*Mediggele*), Milton (*Middeltuna*), Witchford (*Wicheford*), and, by inference, perhaps Longstanton (*Stantun*).

Huntingdonshire: Folksworth (*Fulchesuurðe*), Glatton (*Glattun'*), Huntingdon 2x (*Huntedona, Huntedune*), Ramsey (*Ramesia*), Yaxley (*Iekesle*), and probably Fen Stanton (*Stant'*).

Not unexpectedly, the area most amply represented is that surrounding Thorney: the northern part of its own county of Cambs. and, clockwise, Hunts., whose border lies five or so miles to the south, Nthants, whose border lies two or three miles to the west, and the southern division of Lincs., whose border lies three or four miles to the north. An outer area is also represented, but more sparsely:

Norfolk: Diss (*Disce*), Narford (*Nereford, Nereforde*), Thetford (*Tetford*), Walsoken (*Walsoc*).

Suffolk: Mendham (*Mendam*), Rumburgh (*Romburc*).

Rutland: Empingham (*Empi[n]gham*).

Bedfordshire: Goldington (*Golditun*), Thurleigh (*la Leie*).

Hertfordshire: Pelham (*Peleam*), St Albans (*de Sancto Albano*).

Buckinghamshire: Desborough (*Dusberge*).

Middlesex: London 3x (*Lundonia*).

Warwickshire: Arden (*Ardene*), Warwick (*Wareuic*), and possibly Ratley (*Rotel'*).

This preliminary survey, based only on English toponymical by-names, produces a geographical pattern featuring a core made up of Nthants, south Lincs., north Cambs., and Hunts., this being fringed on its east, south and west by areas more sparsely represented, to wit, Norfolk and north Suffolk, Rutland, Beds., Herts., Bucks., Middx. and Warks. This is hardly a random distribution; nor, on the other hand, is the pattern simply centred upon the abbey.

The next step must therefore be to try to explain the shape and extent of this area – from now on to be called the *Liber Vitae*'s 'catchment area' – or, if not fully to explain it, at least to explore the concept. The other major document surviving from Thorney Abbey, more explicit about the abbey's relationships with the lay world, is the

---

[13] See below Appendix A, where relevant names (listed alphabetically by by-name) are discussed; cf. Clark, 'BL. Add. MS. 40,000', above 313–15.

early-fourteenth-century cartulary commonly known as the Red Book (Cambridge University Library Add. MSS. 3020/3021 = RB).[14] The briefest glance at this sets off ideas about the catchment area just postulated. In it documents are organized under county headings, and the counties concerned are, in order: Hunts. (where the bulk of the abbey's original endowment lay[15]), Cambs., Nthants, Rutland, Warks., Lincs., Beds. (in which is intercalated material relating to Norfolk), and Middx. Thus, the area represented by the abbey's territorial interests, although not wholly coinciding with that deduced from the English toponymical by-names figuring in the *Liber Vitae*, tallies with it fairly well.[16] Candidates for confraternity might perhaps, then, be supposed to have hailed mainly from districts where the abbey held land. There was, however, no easy equation between feudal ties and confraternity: men enrolled in the *Liber Vitae* include, for instance, knights of Peterborough Abbey. Furthermore, one reason why the abbey held land in districts from which it drew candidates for confraternity was that the latter, in gratitude for the spiritual privileges extended to them, not uncommonly made donations to it of parcels of land.[17] These ambivalences notwithstanding, the cartulary's evidence is compatible with Thorney Abbey's possession of a sort of catchment area, partly economic, partly social and spiritual, stretching some way north, a small way east and a good way south and west. Full study of this area would demand comparison between it and the spheres of interest centred upon each of the neighbouring abbeys, and so cannot here be attempted.

The pattern is not perfect: not every English toponymical by-name in the *Liber Vitae* falls neatly within the area postulated. Several clerics have by-names apparently linking them with Oxon. (Cold Norton Priory), Somerset (Muchelney Abbey), even Devon (if *Emmestun* is correctly identified as Hempston). But this need not raise too great difficulties: the name of the monk of Muchelney, given in a Latinized ablative and grouped with four similar forms, might have been taken from some unknown witness-list; the other names might have belonged, say, to travellers made graciously free of a house where they lodged – all, that is, being possibly special cases with little bearing upon normal practice in regard to lay people. More perplexingly, two laymen – entered on f. 12r alongside the Raunds and *Traili* families, both localizable well within the area postulated – have by-names difficult to interpret otherwise than as referring to Syde, Glos. Other apparent discrepancies turn out less serious than at first sight might have appeared. Reiner 'of Bath' was sheriff of Lincs. and also married to a daughter of the pre-Conquest Lincs. landholder Archilbar/Erkelbern. An Odo 'of Beverley' in all likelihood belonged not to Yorks., but to a Hunts. family of that name.

A by-name's bearing upon possibilities of localizing an individual or a family may sometimes therefore be independent of whatever immediate reference the name-form possesses. This prompts investigation, upon such broader lines, of other sorts of by-name occurring in the *Liber Vitae*: continental *noms d'origine*, that is, and nicknames

---

[14] This cartulary has not as yet been even calendared; excerpts have, however, been printed in various places, especially in *Monasticon Anglicanum*, II, 598–613. See also S.G. Raban, 'The property of Thorney and Crowland Abbeys: a Study in Purchase and Patronage', Cambridge PhD 1972, 6–7; I am grateful to Dr Raban for permission to refer to her unpublished work.

[15] See Raban, 'Property', 20–7; cf. *eadem*, *The Estates of Thorney and Crowland: a Study in Medieval Monastic Land Tenure* (Cambridge, 1977), 8.

[16] Cf. Raban, 'Property', tables on 345–7 and map on 354; also *Estates*, tables on 92, 94–5, and map on 27.

[17] Cf. Clark, 'BL. Add. MS. 40,000', above 313–14, also 307.

of various sorts. Upon examination, such by-names (whether or not intelligible or identifiable in themselves[18]) often reveal their bearers as holders of specific English lands. Admittedly, many families' holdings were, from the present point of view, inconveniently widespread. The Red Book usually makes clear which estates underlay the Thorney connection (often ones peripheral to the donors' principal holdings[19]); but, in so far as the Red Book's testimony has already been taken into account, this cannot constitute fresh evidence for demarcating the catchment area. It none the less underlines how closely the abbey's spiritual relationships with the lay world were bound up with its temporal and economic ones. Fortunately, there also exists for many individuals and families independent evidence linking them firmly either with appropriate districts or, less conclusively, with other people so linked.[20]

Some bearers of by-names remain, at least for the present, unidentifiable.[21] Among those whose territorial background can be established, nearly all prove in some degree linked with districts within the postulated catchment area. Exceptions are few: one involves the *Cheuurchurt* (Quièvrecourt) family, whose known connections seem limited to Notts. and Leics. The main groupings echo those of the English toponymical by-names (and are given here in the same order):

Northamptonshire:	*de Albinico* with *de Buun*; ? *de Barnauilla*; *Cheneduit* with *de Blakeuilla*; *de Claromonte* with *de Ierborai* and *de Muntmorenci*; *de Coc'* with *de Gorram*; *Engaine*; *de E[n]uermo*; *de Grantamagni*; *Hefede*; *de La Musce*; *Oliuard*; *Ridel*; *de Walteruile*.
Lincolnshire:	*de Crehun* with *Barri* and *de Pissi*; *de Buru[n]*; *de Coc'*; *de Greli*; *de La Haie*; *de Munbegun*; *de Normanuilla*; *de Nouauilla*; *de Ouile*; *Picot*; *de Ros*; *de Uri*.
Cambridgeshire:	? *de Ard'*; ? *Corbof*; *de Furnels*; *Kebbe*; ? *de la Mare*; *Oliuard*; *Peuerel* ? with *le Chenteis*; ? *de Perci*; *Pichard*; *Picot*.
Huntingdonshire:	*Disci*; *de Gisnei*; *de Iuri*; *de Longauilla* with *de Alfai*; *Lusuriarum*; *de La Mare*; *Meilleme*; *Pichard*.
Norfolk:	*Bigot*; ? *Corbof*; *de Gisnei*; *de Greli*.
Suffolk:	*Bigot* with *de Todeneie*; *Corbof*; *de Gisnei*; *de Greli*.
Rutland:	*de Stuteuilla*.
Bedfordshire:	? *de Ard'*; *de Belcamp*; *Brito*; *de Broi*; *de Coc'*; *Engaine*; *Faucillun*; ? *Fortin*; ? *de Furnels*; *Tallebois*; *de Traili* with *de Belcesne*; *de UUeldebuef* with *Canu*.
Hertfordshire:	*de Broi*; *Cheneduit*; *de Coc'*; ? *Faucillun*.
Middlesex:	*VIII Denarii*.

Demonstration is necessarily less clear than with English toponymical by-names. Several families held, as shown, in more than one part of the *Liber Vitae*'s catchment area. Some had their main holdings outside that area (therefore not noted above) and only minor ones within it. That is to say, the evidence of these other sorts of by-name

---

[18] In order to confine this paper within reasonable bounds, no attempt is here made to etymologize or otherwise explain by-names in these categories; cf. below 332.

[19] Raban remarks on magnates' tendencies to grant away their own outlying estates with only scant regard for the recipients' convenience ['Property', 87–91, 94–5, 99].

[20] See below Appendix B.

[21] See below Appendix C.

proves in general compatible with postulation of a catchment area such as has been delineated above but could by no means be used on its own to argue for it.

Once the geographical pattern is accepted, certain other groups of entries can be seen as partly conforming to it. The earliest section of all, in the first column of f. 10r,[22] includes ecclesiastical dignitaries of various dates from the late tenth century onwards. Apart from archbishops of Canterbury and of York and the great Bishop Wulfstan of Worcester, these seem to be mainly regional.[23] There may be here a risk of evidence-bending, so that it would be safest to say only that the names listed are capable of regional interpretation. The name *Remigius* can hardly belong to any bishop other than the one of Dorchester-on-Thames/Lincoln 1067–92, and so the name immediately following, *Rodbertus*, presumably indicates Remigius's successor, in office 1094–1123. By the same token, the entry *Æðericus episcopus* probably denotes the bishop of Dorchester in office 1016–34. The name *Herebertus* denotes the bishop of Thetford/Norwich in office 1091–1119. Among the abbots listed at the foot of this column, *Balduuinus* ruled Bury 1066–97, *Ægelsi* ruled Ramsey 1080–87, and *Toroldus* ruled Peterborough 1069–98; *Gosbertus* was abbot of Battle 1076–95, and that was the house from which in the mid-1080s Gunter had come to be abbot of Thorney. *Agelricus episcopus* and *Randulfus 'passeflambardus' episcopus*, although bishops of Durham 1042–56 and 1099–1128 respectively, both had local connections, Ægelric having retired to Peterborough and Ranulf possessing family connections in Huntingdon.[24]

How far delineation of this catchment area[25] will further anthroponymical investigation remains to be seen. It ought, at all events, to enable such work to be more intelligently pursued.

---

22 See Clark, 'BL. Add. MS. 40,000', above 308, and references there given.

23 Cf. Whitelock, 'Scandinavian personal names', 131–2.

24 See C. Clark, *The Peterborough Chronicle 1070–1154*, 2nd edn (Oxford, 1970), 64–5, and R.W. Southern, *Medieval Humanism* (Oxford, 1970), 186, 191.

25 Between preparation of the original paper and that of the present version, my attention was drawn to a new French work embodying conclusions which, although based on types of evidence different from mine, are similar to my own put forward here. A late-thirteenth-century anniversary-list from the abbey of Saint-Pierre at Solignac (near Limoges) records grants made towards commemorations as coming mainly from within a Limoges-Châlus-Sussac triangle and being proportionately most numerous from the abbey's near vicinity; lay people commemorated there consisted almost entirely of local gentry [see Jean-Loup Lemaître, ed., *Les Documents nécrologiques de l'abbaye Saint-Pierre de Solignac*, Recueil des historiens de la France: Obituaires – série in-8°, I (Paris, 1984), 381–94, 567–610].

My warmest thanks go, first, to Professor Giles Constable (Institute for Advanced Study, Princeton) for his reassuring comments on the original version of this paper as well as for referring me to Lemaître's work and also to M. Lemaître himself for generously arranging for me to receive a copy of his book.

APPENDICES OF BY-NAME EVIDENCE

Abbreviations

CP	G.E. C[okayne] *et alii*, *The Complete Peerage*, 13 vols in 14 (London, 1910–59).
DEPN	Ekwall, *Dictionary of English Place-Names* (see above n. 12).
FCambs.	W. Farrer, *Feudal Cambridgeshire* (Cambridge, 1920).
Fees	*Liber Feodorum: The Book of Fees*, 2 vols in 3, HMSO (London, 1920–31).
GDB, LDB	Great and Little Domesday Book respectively, cited by folio.
HKF	W. Farrer, *Honors and Knights' Fees*, 3 vols (London, 1923–25).
Houses	D. Knowles and R.N. Hadcock, *Medieval Religious Houses: England and Wales* (London, 1971).
King	E. King, *Peterborough Abbey 1086–1310: a Study in the Land Market* (Cambridge, 1973).
LDB	see GDB, LDB
LV	The *Liber Vitae* of Thorney Abbey (BL., Add. MS. 40,000).
Morris	W.A. Morris, *The Medieval English Sheriff to 1300* (Manchester, 1927).
PN+	County survey in EPNS series, with usual abbreviation of county-name.
PR	Pipe Roll, cited by year (of the completed account) and p.-reference to PR Society edition.
RB	The Red Book of Thorney (CUL, Add. MSS. 3020/3021, continuously foliated).
RBE	H. Hall (ed.), *The Red Book of the Exchequer*, 3 parts continuously paginated, Rolls Series (London, 1896).
Regesta	H.W.C. Davis *et alii* (edd.), *Regesta Regum Anglo-Normannorum 1066–1154*, 4 vols (Oxford, 1913–69), cited by vol. and item no.
Sanders	I.J. Sanders, *English Baronies* (Oxford, 1960).
Seals	L.C. Loyd and D.M. Stenton (edd.), *Sir Christopher Hatton's Book of Seals*, Northamptonshire Record Society XV (1950), cited by item no.
Stenton, *First Century*	F.M. Stenton, *The First Century of English Feudalism*, 2nd edn (Oxford, 1961).
t-i-c	tenant-in-chief.
TRE	*tempore regis Edwardi.*
VCH	Victoria County History.
u-t	under-tenant.

Dating

Entries were made in the *Liber Vitae* in the following approximate order: f. 10r = 1100 × 1112; f. 10v = c.1112–13; f. 9v = ?1100 × 1112; f. 3r = c.1115–c.1130; f. 3v = c.1130–*post* 1145; f. 2r = *ante* 1135–c.1140; f. 2v = c.1140–c.1155; ff. 4r and 11r = ?midC12; ff. 1v and 12r = *post* 1176 [see Clark, 'BL. Add. MS. 40,000', above 308–13]. These dates concern only entry in the present version of the LV.

Transcription

The OE characters Æ/æ, ð and þ are reproduced; *wynn* and insular minuscule g (ʒ) are represented by w and g respectively. Abbreviated forms of first-names and of *presbiter* are silently expanded. Capitalization follows, as far as is feasible, that of the MS. Spacing is normalized. Superscript insertions are enclosed between raised strokes. Emendation and conjectural expansion are shown by enclosing the relevant letters in square brackets.

Appendix A: English Toponymical By-Names

Turkill de *ardene* f. 3r   Arden, Warks. [*PNWa*, 11–12]

> In 1086 a t-i-c in Warks.; sheriff in Staffs [GDB, ff. 240v–241v; Morris, 43 n. 16]; also Thorney Abbey's u-t in Sawbridge, Warks. [GDB, f. 222v]. His son and heir Siward granted the abbey lands in *Fleckenho* (Flecknoe) and *Rugentunie* (Ryton-on-Dunsmore), Warks.; another son, Peter, took the cowl there [RB, ff. 238r, 416r; *PNWa*, 150, 178–9].

Reinerus de *bathe* f. 3r   Bath, Somerset [*DEPN*, s.n.]

> Sheriff of Lincs. c.1128–30 [Morris, 85 n. 94, 86 n. 95; *Orderic Vitalis* [see n. 5], VI, 16–7; 1130 PR, 109]. LV shows him as married to a daughter of the *TRE* Lincs. landholder Archilbar/Erkelbern [GDB, f. 352v, as antecessor of Roger Poitevin].

Rodbertus de *bertuna* f. 2r   Place uncertain [cf. *DEPN* s.n. *Barton*]

> Evidently the R. *miles* . . . *de Bertonia* witnessing (at Melchbourne, Beds.) Alice de Clermont's confirmation to Thorney Abbey of land in Raunds, Nthants [RB, f. 206v]. The *Barton* involved may be the apparently-unidentified one from which Alice, in a deed witnessed by a Robert *de berth.*, surrendered rents to Thorney Abbey [RB, ff. 206v–207r; RB puts the deed under Nthants, but *FCambs.*, 241, associates Robert with Barton, Cambs.].

Odo 'de *beuerlic'* f. 3v   Beverley, ER Yorks. [*PNYE*, 192–4]

> A family of this name associated with Thorney Abbey held in Stanground, Hunts. [RB, ff. 85r, 92v–93r, 108r, etc.].

Æilricus presbiter de *biker'* f. 3v   Bicker, Lincs. [*DEPN*, s.n.]

Roger filius Willelmi de *braibroc* f. 2v   Braybrooke, Nthants [*PNNth*, 110–11]

> Entered beside the *Cheneduit* family [AppxB], whose quitclaim to Thorney Abbey of land in Charwelton, Nthants, he witnessed [RB, f. 206r].

Leuiue de *burh* f. 10v   ? Peterborough, Nthants [*PNNth*, 224]

Toroldus 'de *castra'* f. 3r   Castor, Nthants [*PNNth*, 232; *VCH Nthants*, II, 472–8]

> He held the manor from Peterborough Abbey by knight-service [King, 25, 35].

Hugo comes de *cestria* f. 2r   Chester [*CP*, III, 164–5; cf. *PNCh*, V (I:i), 2–7]

> Hugh (Lupus) d'Avranches, *ob.*1101, but posthumously entered in LV as kinsman of the de Clermont family [AppxB, s.n. *Claromonte*].

Lefricus de *Cherwoltonia* f. 2v   Charwelton, Nthants [*PNNth*, 17–18]

> Witness to the *Cheneduit* family's Charwelton quitclaim [RB, f. 206r].

Mabilia filia Gaufridi de *cotes* f. 2r   Coton, Cambs. [*PNC*, 74–5]

> Entered in LV beside Alice de Clermont, whose *puella* she was [RB, f. 206v]. Geoffrey, a bastard son of Eustace de Boulogne and a son-in-law of Geoffrey I de Mandeville, held Coton from his father [J.H. Round, 'Faramus of Boulogne', *Genealogist*, n.s. XII (1895–6), 145–51].

Willelmus de *dena* f. 2r   ? Deene, Nthants [*PNNth*, 163]

> Witness in 1143 to Alice de Clermont's confirmation to Thorney Abbey of land in

Raunds, Nthants [RB, f. 206r]. In Abbot Salomon's time (*post* 1176) a Simon son of Ralph *de Den* confirmed his father's grant to the abbey of land in Weng, Rutland [RB, ff. 233r–v].

Wlketelus presbiter de *disce* f. 3v   Diss, Norfolk [*DEPN*, s.n.]

Sistricus de *dudintune* f. 3r   Place uncertain [cf. *DEPN* s.nn.
                                                    Dodington, Duddington]

Witness to the 1127 agreement made at Huntingdon between the abbot of Thorney and Robert of Yaxley [RB, ff. 145r–v; below, s.n. *Iekesle*]. A suggestion of Doddington, near March, Cambs., ought probably to be withdrawn because Ely Abbey held that manor in demesne [Clark, 'BL. Add. MS. 40,000', above 310 n. 43; cf. *FCambs.*, 274].

Radulfus musket de *dusberge* f. 3r   Desborough, Bucks. [*PNBk*, 174, 267]

Witness, as R. *de Dust.*, to Alice de Clermont's confirmation to Thorney Abbey of land in Raunds, Nthants [RB, f. 207v]. The Bucks. localization may be confirmed by a mid-13th cent.-reference to R. Muschet's heirs as holding in *Edelesbur'* [*Fees*, 876; cf. *PNBk*, 92–4, s.n. *Edlesborough*].

Æleminus 'de *eli'* f. 3r; Al 'f'wine de *ely*   Ely, Cambs. [*PNC*, 213–14]
f. 3r; Askillus frater domini hugonis de
Hely f. 3v; Geruasius capellanus *heliensis*
f. 2v; Obsernus de *heli* f. 3r

Vmfredus *Emmestun'* clericus f. 11r   ? Broadhempston or Little Hempston,
                                                    Devon [*PND*, 509, 514]

Wulfricus presbiter de *empi*[*n*]*gham* f. 3r   Empingham, Rutland [*DEPN*, s.n.]

Ricardus de *ferendonia* f. 2v; Rodbertus de   Farndon, Nthants [*PNNth*, 37, 113]
ferenduna f. 2v

Richard *de F.* witnessed the *Cheneduit* family's Charwelton quitclaim [RB, f. 206r].

Fulco de *flet* f. 2v; Goce de *flet* f. 2v;   Fleet, Lincs. [*DEPN*, s.n.]
Ricardus de *fleth* f. 1v

G. de F., with sons F. and R. as witnesses, granted Thorney Abbey lands in Tydd St Mary, Lincs., at the same time craving prayers for Roger *de Munbegum* [AppxB] and William de Ros [AppxB]; as *Josce* de F., he himself witnessed a grant concerning Tydd by W. de Ros [RB, ff. 244r, 247r]. R. de F., when admitted to confraternity, granted the abbey lands in *Chukroft* and *Neulond*, Lincs. [RB, f. 250r].

Gilebertus de *fulchesuurðe* f. 2r   Folksworth, Hunts. [*PNBdHu*, 186–7;
                                                    VCH Hunts., III, 173–6]

Witness to the 1127 agreement made at Huntingdon between Thorney Abbey and Robert of Yaxley [RB, ff. 145r–v]. On being admitted to confraternity, he granted Thorney Abbey land in Folksworth [RB, f. 419v]. Later, he took the cowl at Crowland [Raban, *Estates* (see n. 15), 41].

Swanus presbiter de *glattun'* f. 3v   Glatton, Hunts. [*PNBdHu*, 187; *VCH
                                                    Hunts.*, III, 177–82]

Hugo de *golditun* f. 2v   Goldington, Beds. [*PNBdHu*, 59–60]

Hugo de *hamtune* f. 2v   ? Northampton [*PNNth*, 6; cf. *DEPN*,
                                                    s.n. *Hampton*]

Gilebertus comes de *hereford* f. 2r

Hertford, Herts. [*CP*, VI, 498–9; cf. III, 242–4, and also M. Altschul, *A Baronial Family* (Baltimore, 1965), 17–24; *PNHrt*, 225]

Gilbert, who succeeded to the earldom in 1136 × 1138 and died in 1152, is entered beside other members of the Clare family; he confirms a *Traili* [AppxB] grant to Thorney Abbey in *Giuelden* (Yelden), Beds. [RB, ff. 298v–299r].

Osbernus capellanus de *hereford* f. 10v

Hertford or Hereford?

The same block includes Reinald of Huntingdon and his chaplain Osbern.

Adam de *houctune* f. 4r

Place uncertain [cf. *DEPN*, s.n. *Houghton*]

A William *de Hochtun* witnessed a Thorney deed of *ante* 1112 concerning Charwelton, Nthants; in 1124 × 1129 a royal chamberlain of that name held in Houghton Parva, Nthants [RB, f. 414v; *HKF*, II, 308, 387]. A Roger brother of W. *de Hochton* witnessed the 1127 agreement made at Huntingdon between Thorney Abbey and Robert of Yaxley [RB, ff. 145r–v].

Reinaldus de *huntedune* f. 10v; Rodbertus de *huntedona* f. 3v

Huntingdon, Hunts. [*PNBdHu*, 261]

Robert de H., on the occasion 1113 × 1151 of his son Henry's taking the cowl at Thorney Abbey, granted the monks two houses in the town [RB, f. 419r].

Rodbertus dapifer de *iekesle* f. 10v

Yaxley, Hunts. [*PNBdHu*, 201–2; *VCH Nthants*, 241–3]

Yaxley formed part of Thorney Abbey's original endowment. R., a nephew of abbot Gunter (1085–1112), figures in many abbey transactions [e.g., RB, ff. 145r–v, 417r–418r, etc.; cf. D.M. Stenton, *English Justice between the Norman Conquest and the Great Charter 1066–1215* (London, 1965), 24–5, 140–7].

Gaufridus de *la lei* f. 1v; Rodbertus filius Stephani de *la leie* f. 2v

Thurleigh, Beds. [*PNBdHu*, 47; cf. *VCH Beds.*, III, 104–7]

Stephen *de Leghia* witnessed Alice de Clermont's confirmation of Tovi of Lowick's [below] grant to Thorney Abbey of lands in Lowick and in Raunds, Nthants [RB, f. 229r]; probably the landholder of that name who c.1150 founded Canons Ashby Priory [*HKF*, I, 69; *Houses*, 152; *VCH Northants*, I, 372]. G. de L. is entered in LV beside the Beds. landholder Robert *de Broi* [AppxB]; the name *Geoffrey* occurs in the Thurleigh family [*HKF*, I, 70; PR 1191, 111, etc.].

Radulfus de *lilef'* f. 10v

Lilford, Nthants [*PNNth*, 185]

Probably a dependant of the Olifards [AppxB], who held Lilford as u-ts of Earl Simon de Saint-Liz [*HKF*, II, 354–5; *VCH Nthants*, III, 227–8].

Touius de *lufuico* f. 2r

Lowick, Nthants [*PNNth*, 185–6; *VCH Nthants*, III, 235–40]

Tovi granted Thorney Abbey *pro fraternitate* lands in Lowick and in Raunds, Nthants [RB, ff. 229r, 419r–v].

Cozelin 'de *lundonia'* f. 3r; Galterius de *lundonia* f. 3r; Willelmus de *lundonia* f. 3r

London, Middx [*DEPN*, s.n.]

Eustachius de *mediggele* f. 2v

Madingley, Cambs. [*PNC*, 181]

Entered in LV apparently among associates of William Peverel [AppxB] of Bourn,

Cambs. Because Madingley was held in 1086 by Sheriff Picot [GDB, ff. 190r, 201r], E. de M. might be the same as E. *Picot* [AppxB; *FCambs.*, 182–3].

Osgodus 'de *mendam'* f. 3v.   Mendham, Suffolk [*DEPN*, s.n.]

An Osgod is named in a mid-12th-cent. deed concerning Mendham Priory [*Seals*, 355]. Mendham was then held by William son of Roger, a kinsman of the *Crehun* family [AppxB], evidently the man of that name entered with them on f. 3r of LV.

Æfrico monacho de *michelenei* f. 2r   Muchelney, Somerset [*DEPN*, s.n.; *Houses*, 478]

The name figures in a group of ablatives, as though copied from a witness-list.

Euerard de *middeltuna* f. 2v   Milton, Cambs. [*PNC*, 182]

Entered in LV among William Peverel [AppxB] of Bourn's associates. Otherwise known as E. *de Beche* [i.e., Waterbeach, Cambs.: see *PNC*, 184–5, cf. 179], he was sheriff of Cambs. and Hunts. in 1168–77, and his may be the name commemorated in the Cambs. place-name *Papworth Everard* [*FCambs.*, 8, 97, 195; *PNC*, 171; for the Peverel connection, see also Stenton, *First Century*, 275].

Radulfus 'de *milituna'* f. 10v   ? Milton Park, Nthants (a hamlet of Castor) [*PNNth*, 233; cf. King, 45]

Ricardus de *nereford* / *nereforde* f. 2v (2x) Narford, Norfolk [*DEPN*, s.n. *Narborough*]

Willelmus de *nicol'* f. 1v   Lincoln [*PNL*, 1–3]

Haroldus canonicus prior de *nortuna* f. 2v   Probably Cold Norton, Oxon. [*Houses*, 155, and *VCH Oxon.*, II, 95–9; *PNO*, 396]

Hugo de *peleam* f. 3r   Pelham, Herts. [*PNHrt*, 184–5]

Herluinus de *Rand'* f. 12r   Raunds, Nthants [*PNNth*, 194; *VCH Nthants*, IV, 29–31; also G. Cadman and G. Foard, 'Raunds', in M.L. Faull, ed., *Studies in Late Anglo-Saxon Settlement* (Oxford, 1984), 81–100]

Rodbertus de *rocolunda* f. 10v   ? Ruckland, Lincs., or one of several Rocklands in Norfolk [*DEPN*, s.nn.]

Alueredus 'de *romburc'* f. 3r   Rumburgh, Suffolk [*DEPN*, s.n. *Rumbridge*]

Albreðe de *rotel'* f. 10r   ? Ratley, Warks. [*PNWa*, 272–3]

In 1086 *Rotelei* (Ratley) was held by Thurkill of Arden [GDB, f. 241v; above].

Rogerus 'filius comitis de *salesberi'* f. 2v.   Salisbury, Wilts. [*CP*, XI, 375–7; *PNW*, 18–19]

Entered in a block otherwise consisting of unidentifiable individuals.

Iohannes de *Sancto Albano* f. 10v   St Albans, Herts. [*PNHrt*, 86–7]

Rogerus de *senglesolt* f. 2v   Singlesole, Nthants [*PNNth*, 235]

Ascelinus de *sid'* f. 12r; Henri de *siða[m]*   ? Syde, Glos. [*PNGl*, I, 162]
f. 12r

> Entered beside members of the Raunds family [above] of Nthants and of the *Traili*
> one [AppxB] of Beds.

Petrus presbiter de *stamford* f. 2v;   Stamford, Lincs. [*DEPN*, s.n.]
Turstanus de *stanforde* monitarius f. 10v

Gumer de *stantun* f. 3r; Rodbertus de
stant' f. 1v

> G. de S. witnessed the 1127 agreement made at Huntingdon between Thorney
> Abbey and Robert of Yaxley; in 1185 two elderly daughters of his lived in Papworth,
> Cambs. [RB, ff. 145r–v; *FCambs.*, 97]; this seems to leave identification of the
> place open as between Fen Stanton, Hunts., and Longstanton, Cambs. [*PNBdHu*,
> 267; *PNC*, 183–4]. The later R. de S. may be the landholder of the name in Fen
> Stanton [*VCH Hunts.*, II, 285].

Henricus de *stif'* f. 1v   ? Stukeley, Hunts. [*PNBdHu*, 224], or
                                Stiffkey, Norfolk, or Stifford, Essex
                                [*DEPN*, s.nn.]

Æilmær p[re]st of *Suauetun* f. 3v   Swaton, Lincs. [*DEPN*, s.n.]

Magister Rannulfus decanus de *tetford'*   Thetford, Norfolk [*DEPN*, s.n.]
f. 2v

> In a deed of 1113 × 1151 Thorney Abbey granted St George's Church, Thetford, to
> Thetford Priory [RB, f. 324v (witness-list omitted)].

Wluricus presbiter de *titt* f. 2v   Tydd St Mary, Lincs. [*DEPN*, s.n. *Tydd*]

> Land-grants to Thorney Abbey in Tydd were witnessed by W. and by Fulco, priests
> of *Tid* [RB, f. 244r].

Guillelmus flandrensis de *tornehaga* f. 2r   Thornhaugh, Nthants [*PNNth*, 243;
                                                  VCH Nthants, III, 528–31]

Godefridus de *Walsoc* f. 2v   Walsoken, Norfolk [*DEPN*, s.n.]

> A Master Gilbert of Walsoken later witnessed a Lincs. deed executed by a successor
> of William de Ros [AppxB] in Thorney Abbey's favour [RB, f. 244v].

Rodbertus de *Warewic* f. 3r   Warwick, Warks. [*PNWa*, 259–60]

> Entered in LV beside the *Crehun* family [AppxB] of Lincs. An R. *miles de Warwike*
> witnesses Thomas of Arden's confirmation of his family's grants to Thorney Abbey
> [RB, f. 238v].

Rogerus de *Wdecroft* f. 11r   Woodcroft, Nthants [*PNNth*, 234]

> Woodcroft was one of the lesser fees of Peterborough Abbey [King, 27].

Magister Willelmus de *Wicheford* f. 2v   Witchford, Cambs. [*PNC*, 245–6]

Hugo de *Wiketot* f. 12r   Wigtoft, Lincs. [*DEPN*, s.n.]

> *Hugo miles filius Roberti de Wiketoft* granted Thorney Abbey lands in Lincs. [RB,
> ff. 251r–252r]; he is entered in LV beside Albert *de greli* (AppxB). Various other
> bearers of the by-name also figure in the abbey's transactions [RB, ff. 250v–251v].

Appendix B: Other By-Names

For reasons of space, no attempt is here made to etymologize by-names or to identify places concerned (cf. above n. 18). Such matters are to be fully treated in the projected edition of Olof von Feilitzen's onomasticon to the LV. Meanwhile, especially for *noms d'origine*, provisional reference may be made to G. Tengvik, *Old English Bynames*, Nomina Germanica IV (Uppsala, 1938) and to L.C. Loyd *et alii*, *The Origins of some Anglo-Norman Familes*, Harleian Society CIII (Leeds, 1951), and also, even though the two corpora do not greatly overlap, to von Feilitzen's own onomasticon to the *Liber Wintoniensis*, in M. Biddle *et alii*, eds, *Winchester in the Early Middle Ages* (Oxford, 1976), 192–221.

Willelmus de *Albinico* f. 2r (2x)

> Lord of Belvoir, Leics., through his wife Cecily, daughter of Roger Bigod [Sanders, 12; also below], and sheriff of Rutland. In 1086 his father Main(o) Brito, entered beside him in LV, was a t-i-c in Herts., Nthants, and elsewhere [GDB, ff. 142r, 151v–152r, 228r, 236r]. W. granted Thorney Abbey lands in Pipewell and in Stoke Albany, Nthants [RB, ff. 205r–v; cf. *PNNth*, 171–2, 175–6].

Bernardus de *Alfai* f. 3r

> Entered in LV beside the Longueville family [below] of Orton, Hunts. [*Ouertun*: *PNBdHu*, 193–4]; probably the B. witnessing, as Rorges of Orton's man, the 1127 agreement made at Huntingdon between Thorney Abbey and Robert of Yaxley [RB, ff. 145r–v].

Gosfridus de *Ard'* f. 12r

> Entered in LV beside the Raunds family [AppxB]; perhaps linked with the Ernulf *de Arde/Arda* who as u-t of Count Eustace in 1086 held Trumpington, Cambs. and several manors in Beds. [GDB, ff. 196r, 211r; *FCambs.*, 219].

Ærnoldus de *barnauilla* f. 3v

> Families of the name held in Nthants, Lincs. and elsewhere [*RBE*, 332, 517].

Radulfus *barri* f. 3r

> Entered in LV beside the *Crehun* family [below] of Lincs.

Hugo de *bellocampo* f. 2r; Mahalt de *belcamp* f. 3r; Meæriel de *belcamp* f. 3r

> H. de B., son of Oliver de B., granted Thorney Abbey land in *Etone* [RB, f. 295v]; this identifies him as lord of Eaton Socon, Beds. [Sanders, 40]. A Maud was mother of Simon I de B. of Bedford [Sanders, 10]. Muriel de B., listed with the *Crehun* family [below], may have been Alan de C.'s wife [probably the M. de B. mentioned under Leics. in 1130 PR, 89].

Rodbertus de *belcesne* f. 3r

> Entered in LV beside the *Traili* family [below] of Beds.; probably the R. *de Belcusne* witnessing *ante* 1112 a charter of theirs in Thorney Abbey's favour [RB, f. 414v].

Hvgo *le bigot* f. 3v; Roger *le bygod* f. 10v; Rotbertus *bigot* f. 10v

> Roger le B. held in Framlingham, Suffolk, in 1071 and later was sheriff of Norfolk and Suffolk [Sanders, 46–7; Morris, 47 n. 47]; he was present when c.1098 the Thorney Abbey saints' relics were translated to the new church [Cyril Hart, 'The

Ramsey "computus" ', *English Historical Review* LXXXV (1970), 29–44, at 44].
His son H. was created earl of Norfolk c.1140 [*CP*, IX, 575–86].

Hugo de *blakeuilla/blacheuilla* f. 2v; Radulfus de *blacheuilla* f. 2v; Ricardus de
blacheuilla f. 2v; Warinus de *blacheuilla* f. 2v; Willelmus de *blacheuilla* f. 2v

> Warin de B. is the *Guarinus miles* attesting the *Cheneduit* family's [below] quit-
> claim to Thorney Abbey of land in Charwelton, Nthants [RB, f. 206r].

Goscelinus *brito* f. 3v; Nigellus *brito* f. 2r

> In 1086 G.B. was a t-i-c in Bucks. and Beds. [GDB, ff. 152r, 217r]. N.B. is entered
> in LV beside the *UUeldebuef* family [below] of Beds.

Rodbertus de *broi* f. 1v

> He confirmed *post* 1176 his father Walter's grant to Thorney Abbey of land in
> *Chelse* (Chelsing), Herts., and of tithes from *Derhannewelle* in *la Leie*; he wit-
> nessed others of the abbey's Beds. deeds [RB, ff. 296v–297r, also 295r; cf. *PNHrt*,
> 216, and AppxA, s.n. *la lei(e)*]. His grandfather, also Robert, witnessed the agree-
> ment made at Huntingdon in 1127 between Thorney Abbey and Robert of Yaxley
> [RB, ff. 145r–v, cf. 421r].

Roger de *buru*[*n*] f. 10v

> In 1086 members of a *Burun* family were t-i-cs in Lincs. and elsewhere [GDB, ff.
> 362r–v, 375r–v].

Hunfredus de *buun* f. 2r

> Entered in LV as *avunculus* of William *de Albinico* [above].

Willelmus '*canu*' f. 2r.

> Entered in LV as *nepos* of Ralph *de UUeldebuef* [below].

Radulfus *Cheneduit* f. 2v; Roger *Chehneduit* f. 2v; Simon *Cheneduit* f. 2v;
Willelmus *Cheneduit* f. 2v

> Landholders in Herts. and in Nthants [*VCH Herts.*, II, 240, 265; cf. *PNHrt*, 46, and
> *PNNth*, 55]. In the mid-12th cent. Ralph C. quitclaimed to Thorney Abbey land in
> Charwelton, Nthants [RB, f. 206r].

Willelmus *le chenteis* f. 2v

> Entered in LV apparently among associates of William Peverel [below] of Bourn
> (there seems little call to link him with a W. *Centensis/Centeis* occurring in Suffolk
> records [Douglas, ed., *Feudal Documents*, 157, 172]).

Radulfus de *cheuurchurt* f. 3r

> Entered in LV beside the Longueville family [below] of Hunts.; but his own nearest
> links seem to be with Leics. and Notts. [*Fees*, 33, 517, etc.].

Hugo comes de *claromonte* f. 2r

> Entered in LV beside his daughter Alice, who confirmed to Thorney Abbey various
> estates in Northants [RB, ff. 206r–207r, 229r].

Gunfridus de *coc'* f. 10v; Sægar de *c'* f. 10v

> In 1086 the brothers Gunfrid and Sigar de Chocques were t-i-cs in Herts., Beds.,
> Nthants, Lincs. and elsewhere [GDB, ff. 142r, 216r, 227v–228r, 366v, etc.; *HKF*, I,
> 20–53].

Reinaldus *corbof* f. 10v

> Families of the name occur in Norfolk, Suffolk and Cambs. [*Fees*, 127, 138, 280, 282, 346, 390, 403; *FCambs.*, 58; see also B. Seltén, *Early East-Anglian Nicknames: Bahuvrihi Names* (Lund, 1975), 20].

Aleinus de *crehun* f. 3r

> A major landholder in Lincs. and elsewhere [Sanders, 47; for his father Guy's holdings, see GDB, ff. 367r–368r; see further E.M. Poynton, 'The Fee of Creon', *Genealogist*, n.s. XVIII (1901–2), 162–6, 219–25].

Rodbertus *Disci* f. 1v

> A landholder in Folksworth, Hunts., and benefactor of Thorney Abbey [RB, ff. 44v–46r, also 5r, 78v, 195r, 422r; cf. *VCH Hunts.*, III, 175].

Radulfus *engaine* f. 2v

> In the 1130s witness, together with his brother Vitalis, to Tovi of Lowick's [AppxA] confraternity-agreement [RB, f. 419v]. The Engaine family held of Peterborough Abbey by knight-service [King, 24–5; cf. *CP*, V, 71–3, with chart-pedigree]. There was an R.E. holding land in Beds. in 1166 [*RBE*, 322].

Hugo de *e[n]uermo* f. 10v

> He held of Peterborough Abbey by knight-service [King, 24].

Albericus *faucill[un]* f. 2v; Gilebertus *faucill[un]* f. 2v; Helta *faucill[un]* f. 2v; Hugo *faucill[un]* f. 2v; Rodbertus *faucillun/falceliun* f. 2v; Roger *faucillun* f. 2v

> Robert F. made Thorney Abbey a grant, confirmed by Countess Rohais (daughter of Alice de Clermont and wife of Payn Peverel, earl of Essex, and herself entered in LV on f. 2v), of land in Herts. [RB, f. 297r].

Rogerius *Fortin* f. 10v

> A William F. granted Thorney Abbey for his father's soul a small parcel of land, possibly in Beds. [RB, f. 295r].

Galterius de *furnels* f. 3r

> Families of the name held in Barham and Fulbourn, Cambs., and in Raunds and Twywell, Nthants [*FCambs*, 59, 75; *VCH Nthants*, III, 248–50, and IV, 31–2; also Cadman and Foard, 'Raunds', 94–5]; but Walter is entered in LV beside the *Traili* family [below] of Beds., with whom a Furnels family was later connected [*VCH Nthants*, IV, 31].

Rogerus de *gisnei* f. 3r

> The family held land, in part as u-ts of the Clares, in Norfolk, Suffolk and Hunts. [Stenton, *First Century*, 92; *VCH Hunts.*, III, 31, 123]. R. de G. witnessed the 1127 agreement made at Huntingdon between Thorney Abbey and Robert of Yaxley [RB, ff. 145r–v, also 415v].

Willelmus magister de *Gorram* f. 3r

> By c.1200 a family of the name were holding, as u-ts of the Chocques family [above], land in Floore, Nthants [*HKF*, I, 45–7, 49].

Rodbertus de *grantamagni* f. 10v

> Probably a son of Hugh de Grandmesnil, sheriff of Leics. and in 1086 a t-i-c in Herts., Nthants, Warks., Suffolk and elsewhere [GDB, ff. 138v, 224v, 242r; LDB, f. 432r; Morris, 49 n. 58].

Albertus de *greli* f. 12r

A landholder in Lincs. and elsewhere [*HKF*, II, 193–4; cf. *VCH Lancs.*, I, 326–34]. Entered in LV beside Hugh of Wigtoft [AppxA], he figures in that family's grants to Thorney Abbey of lands in Lincs. as sharer in spiritual benefits [RB, ff. 251r–v].

Ricardus de la *haie* f. 2v

Hereditary constable of Lincoln [Sanders, 109]; entered in LV beside associates of William Peverel of Bourn [below].

Adericus *hefede* f. 2r

Witness, as *Aderiz heued*, to Alice de Clermont's confirmation to Thorney Abbey of lands in Nthants [RB, f. 206v]. In the 13th cent. a Head-Hoved family held land at Comberton, Cambs. [*FCambs.*, 226].

Margareta de *ierborai* f. 2r

Entered in LV as sister of Alice de Clermont, Thorney's benefactor.

Roger de *iuri* f. 10v

In 1086 a R. de I. was t-i-c in Hunts., Warks. and elsewhere; this entry in LV may refer either to him or to his son and namesake [GDB, ff. 151v, 205v, 242r; Sanders, 9].

Sæm[an] *kebbe* f. 2r

Witness, as *Seman cheb*, to Hervey le Moyne's grant to Thorney Abbey, on his admission to confraternity, of rights in *Welle* (Upwell), Cambs. [RB, f. 194v; cf. *PNC*, 288; but the extant version of LV contains no identifiable reference to H. le M.].

Ingoldus de *longauilla* f. 2r; Rainaldus de *lonuilla* f. 2r

Lords of Orton Longueville, Hunts. [*VCH Hunts.*, III, 190–3, to which the LV entries provide a supplement; *PNBdHu*, 193–4]. R. and his son Henry witnessed a grant to Thorney Abbey of land in Hunts.; another son, Rorges, made with the abbey a confraternity-agreement embodying a grant of land in Stanton, Hunts. [RB, ff. 78r, 418r].

Hugo *lusuriarum* f. 2v

Entered in LV beside William Peverel of Bourn [below]. His grant to Thorney Abbey *pro fraternitate* of lands in Botolphbridge and *Coppedethorn*, Hunts., was confirmed either by this William or by the latter's uncle and namesake 'of Dover' [RB, ff. 82r, 127r]. The Fulk (son of William) *de Lisures* mentioned elsewhere in RB may be a kinsman, perhaps identifiable with the F. who was a royal forester and/or the one who in 1166 held from Ramsey Abbey land in Quy-cum-Stow, Cambs. [RB, ff. 229r, 420r–v; *FCambs.*, 124; King, 81; *VCH Nthants*, III, 77, and IV, 66].

Willelmus *malfægð* f. 10v

Chaplain of Richard *filius comitis* (probably Richard of Clare, *ob.* c.1090). A possibly similar by-name *Malfyt* is borne by a witness to Geoffrey *de Traili*'s [below] confraternity-agreement [RB, f. 414v].

Willelmus de la *mare* f. 1v

A family of the name were hereditary constables of Peterborough Abbey; the same or another held land in Wood Ditton, Cambs. [King, 24, 32, 34; *FCambs.*, 41–4]. A Ralph de la M. witnessed the 1127 agreement made at Huntingdon between

Thorney Abbey and Robert of Yaxley and figured in another Hunts. transaction [RB, ff. 145r–v, 417r].

Hugo *meilleme* f. 2r

Entered in LV as brother of Gilbert of Folksworth [AppxA].

Roger de *munbegun* f. 2r (de mungubun f. 3v)

Uncle of William de Ros [below], whose land-grant to Thorney Abbey he witnessed [RB, f. 244r]; a landholder in Lincs. and elsewhere [*VCH Lancs.*, I, 319–26; also *Seals*, 149].

Burchardus de *muntmorenci* f. 2r

Entered in LV as second husband of Thorney's benefactor, Alice de Clermont.

Willelmus de la *musce* f. 2v

A landholder in Northants, he figures in LV and elsewhere among associates of William Peverel [below] of Bourn [Stenton, *First Century*, 275].

Reginaldus de *normanuilla* f. 2v

By 1160 a family of the name held in Lincs. [*HKF*, II, 176].

Gilebertus de *noua uilla* f. 2v; Goifridus de *nouauilla* f. 10v; Iohannes de *noua uilla* f. 2v

Gilbert and J. are entered in LV beside the Fleet family [AppxA] of Lincs. Branches of the Neville family held of Peterborough Abbey as well as in Lincs. [*CP*, IX, 478; King, 24].

Osbernus *viii d[enarii]* f. 3r (2x)

A leading member of the London patriciate [see S. Reynolds, 'The rulers of London in the twelfth century', *History* LVII (1972), 337–57, at 354 and n. 17].

Roger *oliuard* f. 10v; Walter *oliuard* f. 10v

In 1086 R.O. held land in Cambs. and W. in Nthants; the family also held from Peterborough Abbey by knight-service [GDB, ff. 202r, 229r; King, 25]. Various men of the name witnessed Thorney Abbey documents [RB, ff. 145r–v, 419v, etc.].

Hugo de *ou[ile]* f. 1v; Simon de *ouile* f. 1v

S. *de Ouuilla* granted Thorney Abbey rents in *Widridele*, apparently in Nthants [RB, ff. 205v–206r]. Both H. and S. also had Lincs. connections [e.g., PR 1174–5, 149; PR 1180–1, 60].

Emma mater Alain de *perci* f. 3v

A daughter of Hugh de Port, the 1086 holder of Isleham and Snailwell, Cambs., manors held in 1166 by Alan de Percy [GDB, ff. 199r–v; *FCambs.*, 140, 150–2].

W[i]llelmus *peurel* f. 3v; Wilelmus *peuerel* f. 2v

Respectively: William Peverel 'of Dover'; and his nephew, heir and namesake, 'of Bourn', who granted Thorney Abbey lands in Wilden, Beds. [RB, f. 297r, also ff. 82r, 127r; Sanders, 19, 151; *FCambs.*, 160–1, 182; cf. above s.n. *Lusariarum*].

Hamo *pichard* f. 2v

A landholder in Cambs. and in Hunts., he appears in LV and elsewhere among associates of William Peverel [above] of Bourn [Stenton, *First Century*, 275; 1168–9 PR, 147, etc.].

Eustachius *picot* f. 3r; Roger *picot* f. 3r

An R.P. occurs under Cambs. and Lincs. in 1130 [PR, 45, 112; *FCambs.*, 124–5]. An E.P., probably descended from P. the 1086 sheriff of Cambs., in 1166 held land in Rampton, Cambs. [*FCambs.*, 3, 192; *RBE*, I, 368; cf. AppxA, s.n. *Mediggele*].

Rogerus de *pissi* f. 3r

He figures in LV and elsewhere as an associate of the *Crehun* family [above] of Lincs. ['The Fee of Creon', 163].

Matildis de *port* f. 2v

Entered in LV as wife of Ralph *Cheneduit* [above].

G. *ridel* f. 10v

Probably Geoffrey R. (*ob.*1120), the justiciar [*DNB*, s.n. *Ridel*].

Asketinus de *ros* f. 2r; Willelmus de *ros* f. 2r (2x)

W. de R., a nephew of Roger *de Munbegun* [above], when receiving spiritual benefits from Thorney Abbey, granted the monks land in Tydd St Mary, Lincs., witnesses to this including R. de M. and Josce of Fleet [AppxA] [RB, f. 244r]. William himself figures as witness elsewhere [RB, f. 233v].

Iohannes de *Stuteuilla* f. 2v

A major landholder in Nthants and other Midland counties, he confirmed to Thorney Abbey *pro fraternitate loci* land in Weng, Rutland [RB, ff. 232r–v].

Yuo *tallebois* f. 3v

Witness to a mid-12th-cent. confirmation to Thorney Abbey of lands in Beds.; probably a son of the *Talabois* enrolled on f. 10r of the LV, and either son of or the same as the *Talgebosch* witnessing the 1127 agreement made at Huntingdon between the abbey and Robert of Yaxley [RB, ff. 295r, 145r–v].

Rodbertus de *tiuile* f. 2r

Entered in LV beside the *UUeldebuef* family [below] of Beds. *Tiville* families held land in Beds., Hunts. and Norfolk [*HKF*, III, 180–1, 265].

Willelmus de *todeneie* f. 10v

Father-in-law of Roger Bigot of Framlingham [above], whose group of entries immediately precedes his. In 1086 the Tosny family were major t-i-cs in Herts., Norfolk and elsewhere, the *caput* of the honour being at Flamstead, Herts. [GDB, ff. 62v, 138r, 168r, 176r, 183r–v; LDB, 91r, 235r–236r; *CP*, XII/i 753–75].

Gesfridus de *traili* f. 3r; Gosfridus de *traili* f. 10v; Ala uxor Josfridi de *traili* f. 2r; Walter de *t*[*ra*]*ile* f. 12r; Willelmus de *t*[*ra*]*ili* f. 12r

Landholders in Beds. [W. Farrer, 'The Honour of Old Wardon', *Publications of the Bedfordshire Historical Records Society* XI (1927), 1–46]. *Ante* 1112 Geoffrey de T., whose confraternity-agreement survives, granted Thorney Abbey land and tithes in Yelden, Beds. [RB, ff. 297v, 414v].

Hugo de *uldebobo* f. 3v; Radulfus de *uueldebuef* f. 2r

As u-ts of the Beauchamps, the family (otherwise *de Oildebof*) held land in Beds., where they granted Thorney Abbey lands in Colmworth and in Sandy [RB, ff. 295r, and 295v, 303r–v, 313v, 318v].

Balduinus de *uri* f. 2v; Waleram de *uri* f. 2v

> The D'Oyry family of South Lincs. were benefactors of Thorney Abbey and figure several times in RB [ff. 247v–248r, 255r, 259r; see further K. Major, *The D'Oyrys of South Lincolnshire, Norfolk and Holderness* (Lincoln, 1984)].

Atselinus de *walteruile* f. 10v

> He witnessed a deed *ante* 1112 concerning Thorney Abbey's rights in Charwelton, Nthants [RB, f. 414v, also f. 415v]. The family, whose name is preserved in *Orton Waterville*, Hunts., were hereditary stewards of Peterborough Abbey [King, 24, 32–3; *VCH Hunts.*, III, 198–200].

Appendix C: Unidentifiable Individuals

As yet no firm territorial links in England have been established for: Geffridus de *angoio* f. 3r; Petrus de *aretin* f. 10v; Robertus de *caho* f. 2v; Rodbertus de *ierusalem* f. 10v; Willelmus de *luer* f. 3r; Hugo del *mund* f. 9v; Rogerus de *ornign'* f. 1v; Iohannes de *rotomago* f. 3r; Rodbertus *capellanus* de *rotomago* f. 10v; Randulfus de *war'* f. 10v; Alanus de *uesd'* f. 1v; Lemmerus cognomento *aleim* f. 10v; Leofwinus *architectus* f. 10v; Simon *bened'* f. 10v; Ærnichu[n] *li blunt* f. 3r; Radulfus *buche* f. 12r; Hugo/Willelmus *burnel* f. 2v; Leofricus *carpentarius* f. 10v; Godgiue uxor petri *cementarii* f. 3r; Adam *constabularius* f. 2v; Galterius *coterel* f. 2r; Willelmus *craspes* f. 1v; Leofric *duua* f. 9v; Albertus *le engles* f. 3v; Ælfwine/Lefuuinus *faber* ff. 9v, 2v; Harold *frisun* f. 9v; Siual *God'* f. 1v; Iohannes *gurdan* f. 1v; Leouuinus *heort* f. 3v; Atsere *hofő* f. 10r [but cf. AppxB, s.n. *hefede*]; Willelmus *keuerol* f. 9v; Walter *laceru*[n] f. 9v; Rodbertus *langeuin* f. 2v; Alfhelm *lithewar* f. 2v; Rodbertus *mutus* f. 3r; Almer *nummularius* f. 9v; Langliue `*nunn'* f. 10v; Æluricus *palmarius* f. 2r, Iohannes *palmerarius* f. 4r, Rainulfus *le palmer* f. 9v; Ælfricus *piscator* f. 3r; Brien/Ricardus/Ringolfus *pistor* ff. 3v, 3r; Ricardus `*Rid'* f. 10v; Willelmus *scot* f. 10v; Alman *tinctor* f. 9v; Vuluuine *tobbe* f. 10v; Alanus *Valt*[rari]*us* f. 3r; Iuo *uenator* f. 2v; Ælmer *wort* f. 3r; Azo *ybrieu* f. 3v.

N.B. Not all occupational by-names have been included in the above list: ecclesiastical titles are excluded, and instances of *cocus, dapifer*, etc., have been disregarded when context implies the individuals concerned to have been dependants of a particular magnate.

A Witness to Post-Conquest English Cultural Patterns: The *Liber Vitae* of Thorney Abbey[1]

No scholar concerned with post-Conquest England could remain unmoved at the idea of a twelfth-century document hitherto almost unexploited. The one in question is the confraternity-book – in medieval parlance, *liber vitae* – of Thorney Abbey. Not in the physical sense a 'book', it consists of name-lists entered, during roughly the first three-quarters of the century, on preliminary leaves associated with the gospel-book now preserved as British Library Additional MS. 40,000 (Clark 1985a: above 301–2; van Houts 1985). Although the existence of this *liber vitae* has long been known, little commentary on it has so far been published (Jørgenson 1933; Whitelock 1937–45). The Swedish anthroponymist, Olof von Feilitzen had, however, at the time of his death in 1976 all but completed an onomasticon based upon the name-material that it contains. His drafts, together with the related notebooks, have been entrusted by his academic executor, Dr Folke Sandgren, to the present writer. Their preparation for publication has sadly been delayed by various problems, so that only recently has work become far enough advanced to permit of publicly tackling some of the questions that the *Liber Vitae* raises. One such concerns English cultural patterns and their post-Conquest survival. In so far as the record consists of names and little else, its testimony is limited; but that is no reason to refrain from interrogating it on its own terms.

Like every confraternity-book, the Thorney one has a dual aspect, from one view-point reflecting the abbey and its monks, from the other reflecting those – in this case, mainly laypeople – whom the monks admitted to confraternity with them. For reasons of space, the present paper will focus on the abbey itself, leaving for other occasions investigation into cultural patterns manifested in the name-register as a whole.

Thorney Abbey lay in the north-western corner of Cambridgeshire, with Peter-borough Abbey some seven miles to its west across the Northamptonshire border, and Crowland Abbey less than five miles to its north, across the Lincolnshire one. Now a neat village accessible dryshod, in the twelfth century and for long after Thorney stood, as its name *þorn-ēg* implies, on an island surrounded by fens (Reaney 1943: 280, also p. lx): a situation allowing the monks to maintain an austere isolation (Hardy 1862–71: I, 373–4n; Hamilton 1870: 326–7; Mellows 1949: 4–5, 43; Chibnall 1969–80: VI, 150–2). No lay settlement then existed there. In so far as it lacked a native, self-renewing lay community, Thorney might seem to possess only a questionable right to a place on any Old or Middle English dialect or cultural map. Yet intellectually and

[1] I am grateful for this opportunity to acknowledge the pervasive debt that this study owes to the unpublished papers of Olof von Feilitzen mentioned in the first paragraph. I wish also to thank Dr A.R. Rumble (University of Manchester) for kindly reading this paper in draft and advising me on matters of palaeography; whatsoever errors or oversights may remain are the author's sole responsibility.

culturally an abbey must be at least as effectively self-renewing as any biological community. A main question therefore concerns the sorts of tradition, linguistic and other, that Thorney Abbey transmitted to the novices who, in order to take the cowl there, forsook homes and families.

As to how and where the abbey recruited its monks, little evidence survives. Perhaps an initial approach to the problem may be made through analogy. Elsewhere I argue for localizing the *Liber Vitae* in a 'catchment area' extending from Holland and Kesteven south towards London and south-west into Warwickshire, evidence for this being drawn from English toponymical by-names applied to some of those enrolled, from territorial interests that they and others are known to have had, and from the pattern of the abbey's own holdings of land (Clark 1985c). It seems possible that the abbey's relationships, both economic and spiritual, with the lay world mostly fell within this area. If so, then monastic recruitment might also have come from there; but getting beyond surmise is difficult.

One small, uncertain piece of evidence exists. On f. 10r of the *Liber Vitae*, its earliest stratum, set down during the first decade of the twelfth century but partly incorporating older material (Clark 1985a: above 308), includes a section in col. I labelled *monachi* and consisting of 43 names:[2]

> Ælfricus. Tur3odus. Burmundus. Godþinus. A3amundus. Guðmundus. Grimketelus. Ædþi. Wulfricus. Wulfricus. Ædricus. Remigius. Hermerius. Willelmus. Erenbaldus. Alfþoldus. Spartin3. Godricus. Godricus. Vitalis. Landbertus. Odo. Petrus. Wido. Rodbertus. Osbernus. Petrus. Benedictus. Paulinus. Radulfus. Hugo 'f.' Walterius. Ordricus. Andreas. Leofricus. Vitalis. Ilbertus. Martinus. Alexander. Hugo 'cild.' Walterius. Hugo 'c.' Ansfredus.

Being immediately preceded by a list of Thorney's own abbots, this list too might be guessed to represent the abbey itself; but evidence to corroborate this is sparse. Confraternal abbeys listed in the Hyde and Durham *Libri Vitae* do not include Thorney; the Thorney *titulus* in the *Vitalis Roll* of 1122–3 fails to name any monks (Birch 1892; Thompson 1923; Delisle 1909: plate XLVI, *titulus* 194).

A few contemporary references to monks of Thorney can nevertheless be adduced; and, for what they are worth, these tend to confirm that the monks whom this list records were indeed the abbey's own. The *Liber Vitae* itself enrols in the first column of f. 3r, in an entry probably made *ante* 1120, the parents and brothers *domni Benedicti monachi*; and the name *Benedict* occurs in twenty-eighth place of the list. Thorney Easter-table notes in British Library Cotton MS. Nero C. VII, f. 81v, mention an early-twelfth-century monk *Gualterius* who, together with five abbey servants (the later all bearing names of 'pre-Conquest' types[3]), was involved in a shipwreck; in the *Liber Vitae* list two Walters appear, in thirty-second place and in forty-first. The richest

---

2 In transcribing extracts from the two manuscripts, standard abbreviations (including *mo* = *monachus*) have been silently expanded. Superscript additions are enclosed within raised strokes. When successive entries are quoted, points followed by '7' are omitted. Æ, æ, Ð, ð, þ, *wynn* and the insular form of 'g' are reproduced; but, for practical reasons, no attempt is made to distinguish typographically between the two forms of *f*, four of *r*, and three of *s* (cf. below 345). Column-numbering always starts from the formal left-hand margin, entries left of the line being regarded as marginal additions.

3 The servants' names are, in normalized form: Old English *Lēofwīg*, **Selewīg* and *Wihtgār*; Anglo-Scandinavian *Ingulf* and *Sæfari*.

source of possible parallels is the abbey's only surviving cartulary, the early-fourteenth-century *Red Book* (Cambridge University Library Additional MSS. 3020/3021, continuously foliated = RB). Among witnesses to two deeds executed in the abbey's favour by Siward of Arden, son of the Warwickshire landholder Thurkill, there figures Siward's own brother: *Petrus eiusdem loci monachus meusque frater germanus, Petrus frater meus eiusdem ecclesie monachus* (RB, ff. 238r, 416r); and in the *Liber Vitae* list the name *Petrus* occurs twice, in twenty-third and twenty-seventh places. Of these two witness-lists, the former, of uncertain date, also names a *Wido monachus*, possibly the one enrolled in twenty-fourth place. The latter, datable *ante* 1112 and thus not far in date from the *Liber Vitae* entries, names immediately after *Petrus*, but without specifying those concerned as monks, not only *Vuido* but also *Osbernus, Reinbaldus, Galterius, Lambertus, Paulinus*. The names *Reinbaldus* and *Osbernus* likewise occur side by side in the witness-list to Geoffrey de Trelly's confraternity-agreement, also datable *ante* 1112, and are there marked as those of monks (RB, f. 414v). Apart from *Reinbaldus*, these names all appear in the *Liber Vitae* list, in twenty-sixth, thirty-second and forty-first, twenty-first, and twenty-ninth places respectively. The confraternity-agreement of Ralph son of Segbold of Lowick, datable *post* 1113, names three monks, *Radulfus, Rogerius* and *Vitalis* (RB, f. 416v); the name *Radulfus* appears in thirtieth place of the *Liber Vitae* list and *Vitalis* appears there twice, in twentieth and thirty-sixth places, but *Rogerius*, like *Reinbaldus*, is absent from it. The agreement made in 1127 between the abbot of Thorney and Robert of Yaxley was also witnessed by *Radulfus*, together, as before, with *Rogerius* and with another monk likewise absent from the *Liber Vitae* list, *Gilbertus*[4] (RB, ff. 145r–v). The dates of these last two documents make the discrepancies unimportant without detracting from the value of the parallels. Another deed, datable to the time of 'Earl David' (*sc.* of Huntingdon) – that is, 1113×1124[5] – names *Hugo monachus* and *alius Hugo monachus* (RB, f. 417r); and the name *Hugo* occurs in the list in thirty-first, fortieth and forty-second places (but the last two entries, for *Hugo 'cild'* and *Hugo 'c'*, might conceivably be dittographic). Because the cartulary has not as yet been even calendared, further relevant mentions of monks might have escaped notice. At all events, names corresponding to those of monks active in abbey business during the early twelfth century often figure in the *Liber Vitae* list, but only in its latter part. Occurrence by c.1112 also of names not figuring in the list suggests that this may date from c.1100 rather than from later in the decade.

The next question is whether this list of monks goes back, like that of Thorney's own abbots, to the house's foundation in the 970s. Some chronological stratification seems likely, because 'pre-Conquest' name-forms – ones, that is, of Old English or Anglo-Scandinavian etymology – dominate its earlier part but then fall off sharply in numbers, accounting for fifteen of the first nineteen names but for only two or three of the remaining twenty-four, the ambiguous form being the already-cited *Osbernus* (for which, see von Feilitzen 1937: 165, 338–9, and Fellows Jensen 1968: 18–19). Moreover, the entry of *Hugo 'cild'*, with a by-name probably meaning 'boy-monk, oblate' (Bäck 1934: 46–8), is one of the latest made. Yet the proportions hardly square with over ninety pre-Conquest years followed by less than half as many post-Conquest ones.

---

[4] Perhaps the *Gilebertus monachus* entered beside *Rodbertus nepos abbatis* in the top margin of f. 3r of the *Liber Vitae*.

[5] For Earl David of Huntingdon, who in 1124 succeeded to the Scottish throne, see Cokayne 1910–59: VI, 641.

The list might represent the abbey's strength c.1100, consisting of monks recruited over the previous forty or more years and enrolled in order of seniority; that would, however, involve supposing no seniors to take any part in early-twelfth-century abbey business. A likelier interpretation might therefore be that the list was indeed cumulative, but begun only in, say, 1050, thus preserving names only of the more recent among former brethren.

As to local and social backgrounds from which monks might be drawn, hints are sparse. It is uncertain what may be betokened by the names of 'post-Conquest' types – that is, Continental-Germanic in etymology or possessing Christian associations – dominating the latter part of the list. Some monastic recruits bearing such names did come from families of recent settlers: at Thorney a case is that of the kinsman (*propinquus*) Robert (possibly the monk listed here in twenty-fifth place) on whose behalf *Albericus Camerarius Regis* – that is, Aubrey II de Vere – in an undatable transaction made over to the abbey certain tithes in Twywell, Northamptonshire (RB, f. 416v).[6] Among men holding land in England Continental-Germanic names had, on the other hand, been appearing well before the Conquest (von Feilitzen 1937: 26–9), and subsequently they soon spread among all classes of the native English. Their 'racial' and cultural implications are therefore ambivalent. There is a further complication. The proportion here of names drawn from Christian tradition – ten instances out of twenty-five or twenty-six post-Conquest forms – is almost five times as high as among laymen enrolled in corresponding strata of the *Liber Vitae*,[7] so perhaps implying some at least of the monks' names to be ones taken in religion. This might, for instance, have been the case with the above-mentioned Peter, once 'of Arden', descended from a pre-Conquest line whose heir bore the pre-Conquest name *Siward*, representing Old English *Sigeweard* probably reinforced by Scandinavian *Sigvarðr* (von Feilitzen 1937: 361–3, 364; Fellows Jensen 1968: 236–9).

The same example modestly bears out the hypothesis of monastic recruitment drawn at least partly from the same families, and therefore districts, as furnished candidates for confraternity. On f. 3r the *Liber Vitae* enrols in col. I, perhaps *ante* 1120, Peter's father Thurkill of Arden, his brother Siward and the latter's wife, together with various of their train. A similar linkage appears in the enrolment on f. 10v, a third the way down col. III, of *Toui frater Petri prioris*. With the list of monks including two Peters, it cannot be assumed that Siward's brother and Tovi's were one and the same; but both alike came from families continuing to favour Anglo-Scandinavian names (*Tófi* is far more characteristic of English usage than of Norman, see Fellows Jensen 1968: 285–6 and Adigard des Gautries 1954: 147–8). Enrolment on f. 3r of the parents and brothers of a monk Benedict has already been noted; this time the relevant block of entries shows names as all of post-Conquest types, the father's being the Christian one *Laurentius*. Another clear linkage involves the Robert of Huntingdon enrolled in the *Liber*

---

[6] For Aubrey II de Vere (*ob.*1141) and his connection with Twywell, see: RB, ff. 19, 227v–228r; Cokayne 1910–59: X, 193–9; *VCH Northants* 1930: 249. An entry made for *Albri & uxor eius & filii eius* in col. II of f. 10v of the *Liber Vitae* and datable probably to the first decade of the twelfth century could conceivably concern this Aubrey, but there seems no evidence that it does.

[7] If as 'corresponding' strata we take the material on f. 10r written by the original hand plus the first column and a half on f. 10v, then among names apparently belonging to laymen we find 73 instances of post-Conquest forms (representing a stock of 43 items), of which 6 (4) are Christian: all but one of the latter occur, as it happens, in a group of entries apparently linked with 'Earl Simon' (*sc.* of Huntingdon, *ob.*c.1111; f. 10v, col. I, foot).

Vitae at the top of f. 3v, in an entry difficult to date but perhaps of c.1130; at some time between 1113 and 1141 he granted to Thorney Abbey, on the occasion of his son Henry's taking the cowl there, two houses in his own town (RB, f. 419r). Evidence remains thin, and that even though the nature of our documents favours links between monks and *confratres*, leaving in obscurity the backgrounds of monks not so connected.

Such few identifications apart,[8] the name-list has only oblique evidence to offer. As noted, seventeen or eighteen names, mostly in its earlier part, are of pre-Conquest types. The stock represented consists of fifteen or sixteen items, five or six of which are Scandinavian by etymology: *Agamund, Grimketel, Guðmund, Swarting, Thurgod*, and perhaps *Osbern* (von Feilitzen 1937: 141, 275, 279, 381, 393; Fellows Jensen 1968: 2–3, 107–8, 110–11, 304–5). At roughly 30%, this proportion of Scandinavian forms would be compatible with recruitment mainly drawn from the 'catchment area' postulated, with its East-Midland core (Clark 1985c; cf. Clark 1982: above 246–50).

Whatever the backgrounds of its monks, at the highest levels Thorney Abbey was at this time certainly experiencing continental influence. About the heads of the house, especially those presiding over the earlier stages of the *Liber Vitae's* compilation, fair information survives (Knowles *et alii* 1972: 73–5). Foreign rule began just after the Conquest, with the arrival of the Fleming Fulcard, a prolific hagiographer, who, although never consecrated abbot, governed the house for some twenty years (cf. Clark 1979: 45, 50 n. 7). The next two abbots were French. Gunter of Le Mans, previously a monk of Battle, ruled Thorney from c.1085 until 1112, introducing there the customs of Marmoutier (Chibnall 1969–80: VI, 150–2; Searle 1980: 82); it was towards the end of his abbacy that the extant version of the *Liber Vitae* was inaugurated (Clark 1985a: above 308). Gunter was succeeded by Robert *Pruneriensis, de Prunereto* ('of Prunelai'), a former monk of Saint-Evroul, whose abbacy lasted nearly thirty years, that is, until 1141 (Chibnall 1969–80: VI, 152). All three were cultivated as well as active men, likely to have interested themselves in the abbey scriptorium. Their presence thus raises again, more specifically, the question of how far English traditions were holding their own against Franco-Latin ones.

The *Liber Vitae's* linguistic testimony is limited. Name-lists can never afford great insight into most aspects of language; and here fairly consistent Latinization further restricts informativeness.

A few English scraps did escape scribal vigilance, almost all in the earlier strata: those, that is, copied 1100 × 1112. On f. 10r three names entered by the first hand include patronymics in English form: in col. III, the consecutive entries *Asbern haces sunu. Đorð clapes sunu 7 his pif*; in col. IV, *Turȝysle hameles sune*. A few further vernacular expressions of relationship appear in col. III, in *Eȝlaf comes 7 his broðer Vlf* and in *Ælfȝifu osȝotes pif*, together with a further instance of *7 his pif* (by contrast with the normal *7 uxor eius*). Nearly all occur in or soon after the section that Dorothy Whitelock identified as dating from the reign of Cnut (1937–45: 132–40). Apart from the Old English feminine *Ælfgifu*, the names involved are Scandinavian by etymology (von Feilitzen 1937: 165, 165–6, 246, 393, 396–7, 400–1; Fellows Jensen 1968: 18–19,

---

8   Several further entries of 'monks' in the *Liber Vitae* leave house unspecified: *Hugo monachus, Odo monachus* (f. 3v, halfway down left margin); *Ricardus monachus* (f. 2r, halfway down); *Willelmus monachus* (f. 10v, far right, a third the way down, in a block also including *Iohannes de Sancto Albano*); cf. n. 4 above. The picture is complicated by the existence in the neighbourhood of a Le Moyne family.

20–2, 74–5, 123, 130, 173, 302, 305–6, 321–4). On f. 9v, where dates of individuals enrolled are uncertain but names of seemingly post-Conquest types occasionally appear, a sequence of entries near the foot of the page is likewise in vernacular terms: *Rinȝolf Tummes sunu, Leofcpen [h]is pif. Iol 7 his pif Scelduuere* (for the latter couple, see Whitelock 1937–45: 141). As before, names are of pre-Conquest types and again, apart from the Old English feminine *Leofcwen* and the ambivalent masculine *Ringolf*, predominantly Scandinavian by etymology (von Feilitzen 1937: 293, 300, 311, 365, 388; Fellows Jensen 1968: 157, 219, 250, 293); at the same time as making those concerned difficult to date with respect to the Norman settlement, this suggests East-Midland connections. As to the date, there is one, uncertain, clue: for by the early twelfth century, when our extant text was set down, the spelling *sunu* may have been obsolescent, in so far as annals copied, seemingly carefully, at Peterborough c.1121 from originals drafted during the preceding thirty-five years show the nom. sing. of the common noun, less likely to be obscured, sometimes spelt *sune* (e.g., *his sune* 1087/line 163, *Edward his sune* 1093/24 – Clark 1970: 14, 20). So probably these *Liber Vitae* entries represent accurate copying of older notes, anomalous scraps reproduced *tels quels*, neither Latinized nor modernized. Among later strata, an entry about halfway down f. 3v, datable perhaps to the 1130s, reads: *Æilmær p̄st of Suauetun*, with *p̄st* probably representing *pre(o)st*, not *presbiter*.

English is the only vernacular whose common vocabulary figures in the *Liber Vitae*. This chimes in with the only by-name in the list of monks' names: *cild*, which, if rightly taken as 'oblate' (above 341), must have been bestowed on Hugh by his fellow-monks, thus implying the community's preferred vernacular to be English (cf. Richter 1979: 90–4, also 83, 85–6).

Certainly, French by-names appear in the *Liber Vitae*. But when attributed to gentry of Norman extraction otherwise known to have used them regularly, these may be assumed to have been set down by the abbey scribes as given. Even with names of unknown people a like assumption may be tenable for forms corresponding to later family-names (cf. Clark 1985b). This leaves hardly any instances where scribal translation might be suspected: perhaps *Harold frisun* (f. 9v) may indicate a man unlikely to have named himself in French; but the name of *Willelmus le chenteis* (f. 2v, top) figures apparently among those of the Peverel family's associates, and that of *Albertus le engles* (f. 3v, two-thirds the way down, far right) is entered in the same hand as and immediately following that of *Willelmus de corsolt* (*sc.* Corseul, *dép.* Côtes-du-Nord).

Demonstration that the Thorney *Liber Vitae* emanated from a predominantly English milieu does not, in the event, depend on lexical evidence. Spheres in which a religious house's traditions manifest themselves include handwriting and spelling. Here both prove significant.

Numerous and disparate as are the hands contributing to the *Liber Vitae*, many continue native traditions more faithfully than the nature of the document required. This is in principle a Latin record: the heading on f. 10r reads: *Hec sunt nomina fratrum istius loci*, the sparse annotations are in Latin (Clark 1985a: above 305–6), and most names are at least perfunctorily Latinized. So, given that by the late Old English period Latin tended to be written in caroline rather than insular script, the former might be expected to predominate here (cf., for instance, the discussion in Whitelock 1954: 14–18 of the main hand of Bodleian Library MS. Laud Misc. 636). Usage, largely independent of the names, linguistic or social affinities, is too complex to be treated here otherwise than summarily (see also Clark 1985a: above 303). As excerpts have shown, the first hand, datable 1100 × 1112, often uses *æ* and *Æ*, also *ð* (seldom *þ*) and

Ð, but *wynn* and the insular form of *g* only in lower case, with capitals represented by *W* and *G*; as in *Reȝina* (col. I, line 6), the insular form of *g* in fact constitutes a simple alternative to the caroline form also used. Other insular letter-forms used here alongside their caroline equivalents include triangular *a* and the low forms of *f, r* and *s*. Despite availability of two alphabets, little attempt seems made to distinguish graphically between languages. Continuators' usages also vary, although in the main tending towards gradual disuse of insular forms. Occasionally in additions on f. 10v and regularly on f. 9v, caroline *g* is preferred even for rendering native spirants, as in *Ægelpine, Godgiue*. That apart, however, the main hand of f. 9v regularly used *æ* and *Æ, ð* and *þ*, together with capital as well as small *wynn* and an occasional low *f*. Early in its stint this hand subpuncts a *wynn* written in the post-Conquest name *Hathawis* and relaces it by *w*, but halfway down the page it employs capital *wynn* for an instance of *Walter* accompanied by the French by-name *lacerun*. On f. 3r, dating perhaps from c.1115 to c.1130, some hands still sometimes use insular characters. By f. 2v, datable from c.1140 to c.1155, *ð* and *wynn*, although current, have become rare, whereas *Æ* still appears fairly often. The dominant trait throughout seems to be lack of apparent desire for consistency. Yet even such unsystematic conservatism as this may imply some conscious adherence to native traditions, because already by c.1100 ageing eyes and arthritic fingers must have hindered from their craft most surviving pre-Conquest scribes.

Script cannot be divorced from spelling. Here as in the *Peterborough Chronicle* – in original and copied annals alike – Englishness shows itself most plainly in imposition of native orthography on foreign names (Clark 1984: 103–5). Unsettled though French vernacular spelling long remained, Latin documentary styles were by this time fairly well established (see, for instance, Fauroux 1961: passim and index, cited below as F) and could hardly have been unknown to a house with a succession of continental heads. Nor were they: witness, for instance, the *Liber Vitae*'s *de rotomago* (f. 10v, col. III; f. 3r, far right) in contrast with the *Chronicle*'s *Roðem* as appropriate to a vernacular context (PC 1124/line 14), not to dwell upon the former's countless conventional Latinizations of personal names. Yet in the *Liber Vitae*'s earlier strata the Englishness of some scribes asserts itself in their spelling quite unmistakably. Sometimes insular letter-forms appear in names of post-Conquest types, as with *Baldewinus* spelt with *wynn* (f. 3r, midway down, far right), and even in ones of known Anglo-Normans, notably the insular forms of 'g' seen in those of the sheriff *Roȝer le byȝod* and of the nobleman *Rodbertus de ȝrantamaȝni* (f. 10v, col. I) – a type of spelling regular in the contemporary English annals. Documentary usages are at times disregarded in favour of quasi-phonetic rendering in insular terms. Examples of this include: *aðelasc, Æðelic, Æþeliza* (ff. 9v, 3r; cf. PC *Æðelic* 1127/line 5, but F *Adelaidis, Adeliz, Adelis)*; *Dræpe* (f. 10r, col. IV; cf. *Dreus* f. 10v, col. II, and *driw* f. 3v, but F *Drogo)*; *Freþesenda* (f. 3r, col. III, top; cf. F *Frede-)*; *Gosfrið* (f. 10v, col. I, foot; cf. PC *Gosfrið* 1088/line 6, *Gosfreið* 1125/30 and 1127/10, but F *Gosfridus/-fredus)*. *Haþapis, Haþepis, Haðewis* (ff. 3r, 3v; cf. F *Hadvis)*. Spellings of this kind seem especially frequent with women's names, perhaps because documentary traditions were there at their weakest. In particular, we find forms such as *Albreiða, Albreþa*, for the name of Geoffrey de Trelly's wife (ff. 10v, 3r; cf. F *Albreda)* and *Ærmentruða* for that of Earl Hugh of Chester's (f. 2r; cf. F *Ermentrudis)*.

Evidence has admittedly been selected from a particular viewpoint, and to that extent might be held to misrepresent the situation. A straight count of conventional Franco-Latin spellings on the one hand and of Anglicized ones on the other would unquestionably give victory to the former. What may, however, justify the emphasis chosen is the enhanced significance of whatever is unfashionable, whether paraded or inadvertently revealed. Here, though to a lesser degree than in the *Chronicle*, there is revealed a measure of self-confidence in early-twelfth-century English attitudes to foreign name-material; and this chimes in with the other evidence of a predominantly English community at Thorney. Internationalization of culture there undoubtedly was, but it may not, one suspects, have gone very deep.

REFERENCES

Adigard des Gautries, J. (1954): *Les noms de personnes scandinaves en Normandie de 911 à 1066*. Nomina Germanica 11. Lund: Carl Bloms Boktryckeri A.-B.

Bäck, H. (1934): *The Synomyms for 'Child', 'Boy', 'Girl' in Old English: An Etymological-Semasiological Investigation*. Lund Studies in English 2. Lund: C.W.K. Gleerups Forlag.

Birch, W. de Gray, ed. (1892): *Liber Vitae: Register and Martyrology of New Minster and Hyde Abbey, Winchester*. Hampshire Record Society. London: Simpkin and Co.

Chibnall, M., ed. and tr. (1969–80): *The Ecclesiastical History of Orderic Vitalis*. 6 vols. Oxford: Clarendon Press.

Clark, C., ed. (1970): *The Peterborough Chronicle 1070–1154*. 2nd edn. Oxford: Clarendon Press.

Clark, C. (1979): Notes on a *Life* of three Thorney saints: Thancred, Thorhtred and Tova. *Proceedings of the Cambridge Antiquarian Society* 69: 45–52.

Clark, C. (1982): The early personal names of King's Lynn: Part I – Baptismal names. Above, 241–57.

Clark, C. (1984): L'Angleterre anglo-normande et ses ambivalences socio-culturelles: un coup d'oeil de philologue. In *Les Mutations socio-culturelles au tournant des XIe–XIIe siècles*, ed. R. Foreville. Paris: Editions du Centre National de la Recherche Scientifique, pp. 99–110.

Clark, C. (1985a): British Library Additional MS. 40,000, ff. 1v–12r. Above, 301–16.

Clark, C. (1985b): Certains éléments français de l'anthroponymie anglaise du Moyen Age: essai méthodologique. Above, 84–91.

Clark, C. (1985c): The *Liber Vitae* of Thorney Abbey and its 'catchment area'. Above, 320–38.

C[okayne], G.E., *et alii* (1910–59): *The Complete Peerage*. 13 vols in 14. London: St Catherine Press.

Delisle, L., ed. (1909): *Rouleau mortuaire du B. Vital, abbé de Savigni*. Paris: H. Champion.

Fauroux, M., ed. (1961): *Recueil des actes des ducs de Normandie (911–1066)*. Mémoires de la Société des Antiquaires de Normandie 36. Caen: Caron et cie.

Feilitzen, O. von (1937): *The Pre-Conquest Personal Names of Domesday Book*. Nomina Germanica 3. Uppsala: Almqvist and Wiksells Boktryckeri A.-B.

Fellows Jensen, G. (1968): *Scandinavian Personal Names in Lincolnshire and Yorkshire*. Navnestudier 7. Copenhagen: Akademisk forlag.

Hamilton, N.E.S.A., ed. (1870): *Willelmi Malmesbiriensis monachi de Gestis pontificum Anglorum libri quinque*. Rolls Series. London: Longman and Co., etc.

Hardy, T.D. (1862–71): *Descriptive Catalogue of Materials relating to the History of Great Britain and Ireland*. 3 vols in 4. Rolls Series. London: Longman and Co., etc.

Houts, E.M.C. van (1985): The genesis of British Library Additional MS. 40,000, ff. 1–12. Above, 317–19.

Jørgensen, E. (1933): Bidrag til ældre kirke- og litteraturhistorie. *Nordisk Tidskrift för Bok-och Bibliotheksväsen* 20: 186–91.

Knowles, D., *et alii* (1972): *The Heads of Religious Houses: England and Wales 940–1216.* Cambridge University Press.

Mellows, W.T., ed. (1949): *The Chronicle of Hugh Candidus.* Oxford University Press.

Reaney, P.H. (1943): *The Place-Names of Cambridgeshire and the Isle of Ely.* English Place-Name Society 19. Cambridge: Cambridge University Press.

Richter, M. (1979): *Sprache und Gesellschaft im Mittelalter.* Monographien zur Geschichte des Mittelalters 18. Stuttgart: Anton Hiersemann.

Searle, E., ed. (1980): *The Chronicle of Battle Abbey.* Oxford: Clarendon Press.

Thompson, A.H., ed. (1923): *Liber Vitae Ecclesiae Dunelmensis.* Surtees Society 136. Durham: Andrews and Co.

Victoria History of the County of Northampton, vol. III. 1930. London: St Catherine Press.

Whitelock, D. (1937–45): Scandinavian personal names in the *Liber Vitae* of Thorney Abbey. *Saga-Book of the Viking Society* 12: 127–53.

Whitelock, D., ed. (1954): *The Peterborough Chronicle (the Bodleian Manuscript Laud Misc. 636).* Early English Manuscripts in Facsimile 4. Copenhagen: Rosenkilde and Bagger.

DIVERSIONS AND REVIEWS

———————————

22

Nickname-Creation: Some Sources of Evidence, 'Naive' Memoirs Especially

Les surnoms villageois . . . sont précieux à étudier, car ils reflètent encore, à très peu près, la même mentalité qui, au moyen âge, forma les ancêtres des noms de famille, et ils servent, plus d'une fois, par comparaison, à éclairer l'histoire de ceux-ci.[1]

From an historical hardly less than from a philological point of view, a tricky aspect of early surname-creation involves such forms as apparently sprang from nicknames. These, from the outset bedevilled by confusions with asyndetic uses of minor place-names[2] as well as with patronymic uses of baptismal names,[3] too often remain obscure even after those confusions have been provisionally resolved (and in neither case would it often be wise to claim more than provisional solution); and so remain they must until scholars can imaginatively recreate the habits of mind and the social attitudes underlying their medieval origins.

Now and then medieval writers themselves proffer comments or explanatory anecdotes. For instance, the twelfth-century *Chronicle of Battle Abbey* tells how a monk of gentle birth had got the nickname *Faber*:

. . . a monk of Marmoutier, one William, named 'the Smith'. He had picked up this name when he was a servitor of the Duke in former times, for once when he was hunting with some companions they ran out of arrows, and the smith they went to happened to be unfamiliar with work of that sort. William immediately took up the man's hammers, and improvising cleverly he fashioned an arrow. Some time afterwards he changed course and made profession at Marmoutier . . .[4]

Such enlightening comments are, however, all too rare; and the great bulk of medieval names occur in official contexts only, often in bare lists like the Subsidy Rolls.

* * *

Failing direct, medieval evidence, the would-be nickname-interpreter is driven to oblique, analogical approaches. Two of the most stimulating papers presented at the conference of the Council for Name Studies at Hull in 1981 treated of present-day

1 A. Dauzat, *Les noms de personnes* (Paris, 1925; repr. 1944), 172; cf. 105, also *idem, Les noms de famille de France* (Paris, 1945; repr. 1977), 180.
2 See the review article by Gillian Fellows Jensen based on J. Jönsjö, *Studies on Middle English Nickames: I – Compounds*, Lund Studies in English LV (Lund, 1979), and published in *Namn och Bygd* LXVIII (1980), 102–15, esp. 111–12.
3 See my own review of Jönsjö, *Studies, English Studies* LXIII (1982), 168–70.
4 E. Searle, ed. and tr., *The Chronicle of Battle Abbey* (Oxford, 1980), 36–7.

name-creation: that by Alan Binns on fishermen's names for seamarks and, especially relevant here, Peter McClure's on some sociological aspects of nicknaming.[5] Perhaps, as scholars like Dauzat long since asserted, present-day nicknaming might yield analogies, or contrasts, such as would cast at least a flickering light on medieval practices.

Assembling an authentically annotated corpus of modern nicknames will not be easy. Some surveys already attempted have been methodologically flawed. Certain types of flaw scholars can repair for themselves, as Peter McClure demonstrated by imposing order on the schoolchildren's nicknames assembled pell-mell by Morgan *et alii*; but others may be more fundamental, as, in that case, the invitation to fantasize implicit in questionnaires distributed to schoolchildren. Moreover, although nicknaming still thrives, its accurate and systematic study might seem to require acceptance in appropriate small, closed communities – not an option open to every philologist or socio-linguist. True, an outsider may sometimes encourage individuals belonging to such groups to reminisce: by this means I have learnt that half a century or more ago in the Cambridgeshire village (now suburb) of Chesterton the many Taylor families were distinguished partly by the men's occupations, thus, *Boatman Taylor* and *Policeman Taylor*, and partly by physical or other characteristics, thus, *Bandy Taylor*, *Long Nell Taylor*, and the now-inexplicable *Buttons Taylor*. Too often, however, appeals to adult informants run aground (as we had occasion to note at Hull) on reticence.

Written sources may perhaps help to fill the breach. Many sporting and other public personalities are widely known by nicknames: some seem self-explanatory, others from time to time are annotated by the press. In this category specimens recently collected include:

Frenchie Nicholson . . . had been apprenticed in France, for his father worked over there, and that is how he got his nickname. [*Observer*, 10. viii. 80, 21]

David Nicholson [son of *Frenchie*], known as *The Duke* to his friends because of his immaculate appearance. [*Field*, 23. i. 80, 150]

To his friends [Prince Philip] was known as *Flop*, a nickname derived with prep.-school logic from his real name (*Philip* . . . *Flip* . . . *Flop*). [*Telegraph Sunday Magazine*, 7. vi. 81, 29]

Harry (*Scrubber*) Dale . . . got the nickname of *Scrubber* by accident. A sports paper used to publish pictures of schoolboy stars. Dale was known as *Squibber* at school because of his lack of inches, but in the picture-caption . . . he was called *Scrubber Dale* by mistake and the name stuck. [*Hull Star*, 24. x. 80, 20: supplied by courtesy of Peter McClure]

"When you were young, your nickname was *Dutch*. Why Dutch?" "When I was a small boy, there was a hairstyle some mothers favoured for their sons called a 'Dutch bob', and my father used to refer to me as *the Dutchman*. It got shortened to *Dutch*. Nothing to do with nationality, no Dutch in me at all. I'm a mixture of Irish, English and Scots." [*Observer*, 26. x. 80, 25; interview with President Reagan]

Mr William Rees-Davies, Q.C., Conservative M.P., . . . who is known as *Count Dracula* because of the black cloak he wears, . . . said he was used to the nickname. [*The Times*, 11. iii. 80, 3]

---

[5] [[Printed on pp. 20–7 and pp. 63–76 of *Nomina* V (1981).]]

. . . a piercing-eyed naval chaplain (retired) known in clerical circles as *Mr Never-on-Sundays*. . . . Because it's a City guild church, there are no services on Sundays – hence the rector's sobriquet. [*Sunday Times*, 8. iii. 81, 4]

The last example, particularly, raises the question whether sometimes in such material a journalistic enrichment of reality may intervene. Besides, such references rarely make clear the status of the nickname: whether it is current in second or even first person, or only in third; and, if the last, how widely and in what contexts it is used. Apart from that, such items are rare enough to make assembling a worthwhile corpus slow and unpredictable. That goes, too, for the sporadic raising of such topics in the correspondence-columns of newspapers and magazines. We need more consistent seams to mine.

If fantasy must be eschewed, then fictional nicknames – for instance, those abounding in P.G. Wodehouse's novels – cannot be used. A safer source might perhaps be the sort of local history that deals in 'characters'. For instance, a booklet called *Essex Eccentrics* purports to 'etymologize' several names:[6]

Marmalade Emma (so called because of her great fondness for this preserve) . . . [10]

A solitary tramp . . . was William Foster, better known as *Torp-Torp*. Attired in full hunting regalia he would walk along muttering to himself and occasionally shouting out, 'Torp torp torpee', hence the nickname. . . . Another lone tramp was *Ardleigh Ben*, who originated from the village whose name he bore. [12]

A solitary highwayman who frequented the Epping district in the 1770s was John Rann, otherwise known as *Sixteen-String Jack*. He was a flamboyant coxcomb whose clothes were always outlandishly original. . . . And his nickname came about because of the sixteen coloured ribbons that generally fluttered from the knees of his breeches. [25]

But here, as the mention of the eighteenth-century highwayman implies and the bibliography confirms, the material is second-hand, having been assembled from earlier, primary memoirs.

Rather closer to the original sources may be George Ewart Evans's 'oral histories' of East Anglia, based on living testimony; some of these afford a modest harvest of nicknames:[7]

The business of making whitening for decorating rooms, . . . and so on, was carried on only by one family in Stonham Aspal – the Berry family. . . . Later it went to one of the daughters who married a Stonham man called George Race. . . . George soon acquired the distinctive name of *Whitening-Maker Race*. [*WBW*, 54]

Near us was a farmer who was known throughout this district as *Slap-arse Wharton*. If a boy had done something wrong on his farm he'd take down his trousers and tan him. [*WBW*, 100]

A drover would go out with, perhaps, a 1,000 sheep. . . . *Drover Green* was one of these. [*WBW*, 113]

---

[6] A. Barnes, *Essex Eccentrics* (Ipswich, 1975). Note that on all quotations from this and other sources a standard 'style' has been imposed.

[7] George Ewart Evans, *Where Beards Wag All: the Relevance of the Oral Tradition* (London, 1970; pb 1977)[*WBW*]; not all this author's works are equally rich in name-material.

James Moore . . . is one of the local cattle-drovers. . . . "I'm known as *Pinny Moore* –
that's what I go by. My father who was a cattle-drover too went by the same name".
[*WBW*, 134]

My grandfather was John Edwards, *Owd England*. . . . I reckon *Owd England* was
born around about 1830. [*WBW*, 208]

Tiny Crane . . . was a Lifeguardsman, and . . . we hadn't got a shoe to fit him. . . .
They made his boots special for him; and Bass's have still got the last pair that wasn't
issued ᴊ him. And that's a size fourteen! . . . He used to say that when he got back
home he'd sit on one side of the table and two of his children would sit opposite on
each big toe. [*WBW*, 272]

Already that little corpus parallels some regular features of medieval nicknaming: the
prominence of occupational terms and the hereditary tendencies, as well as the use of
anecdotal 'Shakespeare names'. Still, however, the material is second-hand. Perhaps
greater authenticity should be sought, not in compilations of this kind, but in whatever
individual memoirs might be available of people comparable with Evans's informants.

*   *   *

One autobiography through which a fine gathering of nicknamed eccentrics stalk and
caper their way is Laurie Lee's *Cider with Rosie*:[8]

Cabbage-Stump Charlie was our local bruiser. . . . He would set out each evening,
armed with his cabbage-stalk, ready to strike down the first man he saw. . . . And he
would take up his stand outside the pub, swing his great stump round his head, . . .
and challenge all comers to battle. . . . *Albert the Devil* was another alarmer – a
deaf-mute beggar with a black-beetle's body, short legs, and a mouth like a puppet's.
He had soft-boiled eyes of unusual power which filled every soul with disquiet. It
was said he could ruin a girl with a glance and take the manhood away from a man, or
scramble your brains. . . . *Percy-from-Painswick*, on the other hand, was a clown and a
ragged dandy, who used to come over the hill, dressed in frock-coat and leggings,
looking for local girls. Harmless, half-witted, he wooed only with his tongue. . . .
Then there was *Willy the Fish*, who came round on Fridays, mongering from door to
door, with baskets of mackerel of such antiquity that not even my family could eat
them. . . . *The Prospect Smiler* . . . was a manic farmer. Few men, I think, can have
been as unfortunate as he; for on the one hand he was a melancholic with a loathing
for mankind, on the other, some paralysis had twisted his mouth into a permanent and
radiant smile. So everyone he met, being warmed by this smile, would shout him a
happy greeting. And beaming upon them with his sunny face he would curse them all
to hell. [35–6]

The Head Teacher . . . was a bunched and punitive little body and the school had
christened her *Crabby*; she had a sour yellow look, lank hair coiled in earphones, and
the skin and voice of a turkey. [49]

But the cultivated originality of diction here (the man is a poet) warns that the line
dividing autobiography from fiction may be somewhat overstepped. Less 'literary'
memoirs might better, more safely, serve the turn.

Of course, no truly unsophisticated book or writer has ever existed; for, as William

---

8   Laurie Lee, *Cider with Rosie* (London, 1959; Penguin, 1962).

Matthews observed *à propos* of dialect-writings, 'a pen gives whoever holds it a sense of style and, therefore, modifies his native colloquialism'.[9] Nevertheless, if at some risk of taking a street-lamp for a will o' the wisp, perhaps the search for authenticity may be pursued through certain 'naive' memoirs – written, that is, by people with little pretension other than to record the traditions of their own communities.[10] Thus, Bob Copper, in his *Early to Rise: a Sussex Boyhood*, specifies nicknaming as a characteristic practice of the village lads:[11]

> Nicknames, often handed down from one generation to the next, were almost universally used for boys and it was usually a sign of affection or at least acceptance into a gang. My cousin Charles was known as *Chaulker*, which he had inherited from our uncle Charles. Cousin Ron was first *Marzi*, a contraction of *marzipan*, and later *Wigan*. My first nickname was *Agony* which was my reward for parodying a popular song of the time into *The Sheik of Agony* (*Araby*), but afterwards, because of my well-covered frame, I became known as *Plumpy*. Later still as the puppy fat diminished this was modified to *Plunky*. [65]

Disappointingly, not many further nicknames are cited here, partly because the writer (a one-time barber's assistant) tends to refer to his elders and betters by official names, with handles; a few good explanations are, however, given:

> . . . the *Penny Lady* who offered many of the miscellany of items she carried in her basket for that modest sum. [18–19]

> "How did ol' Steady get his nickname?" I asked. . . . "Wal, one night 'e 'as a tidy ol' wet, . . . an' when 'twas time t' go 'ome 'e was all over the road. . . . Next mornin' . . . they arsts 'im 'ow 'e got on goin' 'ome the night before. 'Oh', 'e says, 'instead o' goin' round th' road, I takes th' ol' gal down Smuggler's Track –' " the precipitous side-hill which . . . was far too steep for wheeled traffic . . . " 'That put a tidy ol' strain on the breechin's, I can tell ye', he says, 'But I lays well back an' kips sayin' t' th' ol' mare, "Steady! Steady! Steady, ol' gal, steady!" ' An' ol' Charlie's been *Steady* ever since". [107–8]

> Mr Adkins, the boss, as his nickname *Porky* implied, was in appearance inclined towards the porcine. [176]

> *Buck* Alce . . . was an old farm hand and had been a bit of a reprobate in days gone by. [195–6]

Another 'etymology' or two can be gleaned from *The Decline of an English Village* by Robin Page, son of a Cambridgeshire farmer:[12]

> One man, with a red face, was called *Happy*. Another, older man, with a wooden leg, looked like a pirate, and when out of earshot we called him *Peg Leg*. [22]

> All his life Mr Holben had been a keen sportsman; when in the army he had ridden horses and become an expert in lancing pegs while at full gallop. For this feat he was called *Pegger*, a nickname that stayed with him all his life. [40]

---

9 William Matthews, *Cockney Past and Present* (London, 1938), 1–2.
10 Cf. my earlier paper, 'Some early-twentieth-century Aberdeen nicknames', *Aberdeen University Review* XLVIII (1978–9), 195–9.
11 Bob Copper, *Early to Rise: a Sussex Boyhood* (London, 1976).
12 R. Page, *The Decline of an English Village* (London, 1974; Corgi, 1975).

An especially rich crop of annotated nicknames comes, not from one of these rural milieux, but from the urban one depicted in the serial memoirs of F.T. Unwin[13] – himself a Cambridge character, selling his neat paperbacks door-to-door from a shopping-trolley and signing them with a flourish. Like many who people his pages, he had himself as an orphan boy had a nickname which his foster-father gave him and he himself soon invested with a ramifying symbolism:

> "You remind me of a lovable circus clown I once knew; he had red hair, thin legs, and dimples, *Pimbo*, that was his name, and that's what I'll call you, my boy – *Pimbo*". . . . Besides, thought Bob, was it not the fashion to give a foster-child a nickname? It saved a lot of questions – and was kinder to the boy. [*P*, 9]

> Pimbo, surprised at hearing his real name, paused for a second. Since Bob Freestone had dubbed him *Pimbo*, everyone thought he had no other name. . . . Pimbo wondered whether the nickname meant that perhaps he oughtn't to be alive – it might be just a name to get him by. Then again he liked the name . . . [*P*, 12]

> "Why does my foster-father call me *Pimbo*? . . . He says I remind him of a clown". . . . "Pimbo was a wonderful clown, he brought laughter and tears to the world. The public knew him only as *Pimbo*, no-one wanted to know his real name". [*P*, 20]

> Somehow from the moment Miss Bragg had called him *Pimbo*, [his foster-mother] felt things were going to be all right. [*P*, 37]

> [The foster-father speaking] "I guess I've stopped kids calling you *Ginger*. Maude tells me *Pimbo* has stuck since the first day". [*P*, 59–60]

> Pimbo, whose nickname had stuck with him since a small child, . . . [*DF*, 7]

> It was then and there that Pimbo lost his identification. He was now Student Nurse J. Freestone, the nickname *Pimbo* no longer existed. It was amazing how the name had caught on at Fulbourn Hospital, he supposed it was easy around the tongue. [*DF*, 54]

But here again reality may be partly overlaid by fiction: for instance, not only is *J. Freestone* substituted for *F.T. Unwin*, but dialogue is freely invented, often with a didactic cast, and the chronology of the series shows inconsistencies. The preoccupation with nicknames itself recurs so often as almost to kindle suspicions of artifice. On the other hand, the undoubted ulterior purpose seems to be social and humanitarian rather than literary. What in itself may speak for the authenticity of the name-record here is that attempts to engage the author in anthroponymical discourse have so far foundered on his strong identification of names with their bearers. The critical standing of these books is of some moment because, if reliable, they constitute a nickname-treasury. Apart from a Dickensian *Golden Dustman* [*P*, 90–1] and an occasional rarity (thus, 'the well-known barber shop of *Chatty* Collins . . . [so-called] because of his regular use of dirty towels' [*P*, 14], where the 'etymon' is *chatt* 'louse'),[14] the name-glosses here seem to offer straightforward insights into the popular mind:

---

[13] F.T. Unwin, *Pimbo* (Ilfracombe, 1976) [*P*]; *idem, Dew on my Feet* (Ilfracombe, 1976) [*DF*]; *idem, Pimbo and Jenny in Old Cambridge* (Cambridge, 1978) [*OC*]; *idem, Knock on any Door with Pimbo and Jenny* (Cambridge, 1979) [*KD*] (the other volumes so far published in this series happen to be less rich in nicknames).

[14] See E. Partridge, *A Dictionary of Slang and Unconventional English*, 3rd edn (London, 1949), 142, *s.v.* (I owe this interpretation to Mr G. Stannard of the University Library, Cambridge).

[*Banger* Day, a policeman, speaking] "Can you tell me why he [*Dollar* Smith, a young thief]'s called *Dollar?*" . . . Nicknames seemed to be very common after all, [Pimbo] thought. Bobby had once told him that *Banger* was nicknamed as such because of his threat to bang naughty boys' heads together. . . . "It's because he's always betting people. In an argument he says, 'I'll bet you a dollar I'm right' ". [*P*, 57]

"Why do they call you *Old Jack?*" . . . "*Old Jack*, don't seem much of a name. I reckon that goes for the lot of us – just a symbol of all drunks", replied the tramp. [*P*, 95, cf. 63–4]

Harry the Beast was a popular figure on the Market Square, here he peddled, earned enough to keep himself. . . . *Harry, the Beast* was Harry's own brain-wave. . . . [He] chose a name like that because it was the exact opposite to his real personality. . . . The heading in the local paper, *Harry the Beast Found Dead*, was right up Harry's alley – that was the way he wanted to go. [*DF*, 112 and 114]

. . . *Irish Molly*. Her pub had a very bad name among the local residents. Known as the "George the Fourth"; it boarded Irish labourers, and Molly needed nerves of steel to keep in order the drunken, brawling Irishmen. [*OC*, 17]

The Salvation Army allowed David on all their marches, and very proud indeed was David to be seen walking alongside the flag. It was a pity, thought Pimbo, that boys teased him and called him *Jug-of-Water*. [*OC*, 18–19]

Lightning the newsvendor . . . was very astute at picking peak times for selling. He would charge from one cinema queue to another, frequent seasonal festivities, and was not afraid of hard work. [*OC*, 23–4]

. . . a workman known as *Slipper*; his daily footwear was a pair of white slippers. . . . Boys told of Slipper's relentless chasing; at the first call of his nickname he would chase a boy from one end of the town to the other. [*OC*, 70–1]

Paul Bootlace, whose nickname *Bootlace* was a derivative from *Boutilier*. Paul was a product of a fleeting romance during the days of the war, after which, having lost his father, the boy was left with a name of French origin, hence the ready-made nick-name of *Bootlace*. [*OC*, 104]

Hokie lived in York Terrace, . . . a man of very slow movement, with a slight slobb-ering round his mouth. Children used him as ready bait, and cried out, "Hokey, pokey, penny a lump – the more you have the more you jump." . . . "I tried everything to get a living. Then it came to selling ice-cream. . . . So they called me *Hokey-pokey, penny a lump* – and they've called me *Hokie* ever since". [*OC*, 116 and 121]

Mr Haynes, . . . affectionately known as *Hummer Haynes*, as throughout his entire serving procedure he would be intently humming a current song theme. [*OC*, 126; cf. 15, 'Mr Haynes, the humming grocer']

Whoop Gurner. . . . [His mother speaking] "My George's a good boy, like his Dad – not afraid of work. Me husband was called *Whoop* because he became excited at the idea of any kind of challenge – a funny little noise he'd make – like a whoop, I suppose". [*KD*, 27]

. . . a thin, tallish, witch-like woman. . . . Wearing a black, wide-brimmed hat, with black dress, stockings and shoes to match, she presented the kind of character portrayed by a Dracula thriller. "Who's she?" asked Pimbo. "Known as *Black Sally*, some call her *Black Bess*. . . . The mistress here lets her in once a week – reckon they get up to a little bit of black magic!" [*KD*, 96–7]

Those are just the best-annotated among the nicknames abounding in these recollections of working-class Cambridge life in the 1930s.

These memoirs illustrating nickname-usages have all represented similar backgrounds, that is, close-knit communities, urban no less than rural, and especially one near the heart of cosmopolitan Cambridge. In London, too, such quasi-villages lie embedded, and there, too, nicknaming has thriven. A recent popular booklet brings this out, suggesting that

> A number of Cockney practices and sayings have country origins – for example, nicknaming: old people in East Anglian villages recall the time when everybody around them had a nickname, and in East London (with more varied material to hand) the habit has persisted.[15]

Perhaps life in Poplar (East London) has not differed too greatly from that in Barnwell (East Cambridge).

Again the writers' varied purposes pose some problems of source-criticism. Jo Anderson, for instance, who records in her *Anchor and Hope* the vanished life of London's Dockland, telling of characters 'whose nicknames filtered through Grandad's front-parlour door of a Sunday tea when old times were discussed',[16] also takes local social history far further back than living memory could reach (she would not thank me for classing her as 'naive'). Such widened scope need not, on the other hand, be incompatible with an accurate recording of gossip and folk-memory. This is a serious book, and if not all the nicknames quoted are as fully 'etymologized' as could be wished, that might in itself bear witness to a scrupulosity forbidding invented explanations. In the event, the material here is richer in communal traditions than in individual fancies:

> ... the little "cocks", fast-scudding boats operated by the Robinson clan of Bankside (which is why the Robinsons are known as *Cockies* to this day). [31; cf. 60]

> The up-river lightermen belonged to a tight-knit community – often tracing their ancestry back to the most distant recorded time, and within the community families are still known by early nicknames: the Robinsons are *Cockies* still; the Blyths *Nellies*; the Hopkins *Pollys*; and the Marshes are variously *Stackys*, *Stiltys*, *Rum* or *Pegs*. [60]

> ... Bankside characters going by the robust names of *Podge*, *Willow-Eye*, *Wiggy*, *Titchy* (who was 6ft 2in.), *Mad Brady*, *Moaner*, *Whisper Rivers*, and *Wooden Heights*, who supplied coal by lighter and whose speciality was swinging heavy sacks of the stuff as if they were bags of feathers. [61]

> *Big Nibby* – he was a mountain of flesh, fat everywhere, which made the eyes appear small; he was very nimble of foot considering his bulk. [65]

> ... the "casuals" ... Many of them were without boots, so they bound their feet in rags, hence their nickname of *Toe-rag*. [72]

> *Loopy Thomas*, ... who used to run along Riverside in a white sheet trying to scare courting couples till one night someone tripped him over; mad as a hatter he was. [136]

---

[15] R. Barltrop and J. Wolveridge, *The Muvver Tongue* (London, 1980), 94; but the few specimens quoted p. 90 are disappointingly conventional.

[16] Jo Anderson, *Anchor and Hope* (London, 1980).

Poor old *Mother No-Nose* had a grey porcelain nose tied on with tape round the back of her head. [136]

Mrs Richards, *the Sweet*; she used to make her own toffee. [137]

. . . the local copper, his name was Warby, *Bluebottle* we called him. [137]

Nitty Nora searching everybody's hair with the same comb. [139]

All the more valuable for being less wide-ranging are the more personal Dockland memoirs offered by Grace Foakes in *My Part of the River*,[17] where every nickname cited belongs within the writer's own experience:

My brother William, having very fair hair, used to look bald when he had his hair cut this way, shaved close, and much to his disgust the other children used to call him *Claudie Whitehead*. [19]

The gym slip was meant to reach the knees but my father insisted on it being longer and larger, so that I could grow into it. When I put it on it nearly reached my ankles, but I had to wear it and I felt awful. . . . I was laughed at by the other children. . . . I was named *Polly Long Frock*. [46–7]

Now I had heard of a place . . . where unwanted cats could be taken, so each time I could entice a cat into our house I would put it in a large bag and carry it until I reached this place. . . . The neighbours found out and called me *Queen of the Cats*. [50]

. . . one policeman, . . . a very large man with big feet and a big nose. I don't remember his proper name, but we could always give a name to anybody and we called him *Bootnose*. [59]

. . . a short, fat man . . . His nose was very red, with a large growth on either side giving the impression that he really had three noses stuck together. With the cold logic of children, we named him *Old Three Noses*. [59]

One poor woman who was a widow . . . was nearly always partly intoxicated. . . . Each time we children saw her we would shout at her; we called her *Old Mother Born-Drunk*. [59–60]

. . . a surly, grumpy man. He was a cripple and walked with a limp. . . . We knew he could not run, so we stood at a safe distance and shouted "*Grumpy* Lloyd", and by this name he became known. [60]

There was a searchlight operated by a local man affectionately known as *Searchlight Charlie*. [72]

Finally she returned home from hospital and was a hunchback for the rest of her life. We all knew her as *Little Edie*, for she never grew taller than a five-year-old. [180]

* * *

The books just excerpted are merely a random few out of the scores published; neither geographically representative, nor selected on any principle. The *florilegium* could be, perhaps will be, indefinitely extended. Meanwhile, it is time to take stock, asking

---

[17] Grace Foakes, *Between High Walls* (London, 1972) and *My Part of the River* (London, 1974), combined under the latter title in a Futura paperback (London, 1976).

whether such a modern nickname-corpus offers anything beyond a folkloric interest; whether it would provide medievalists with any useful analogies.

In one respect at least this will not be so: modern nicknames, forming part of a system where the family-name dominates over the individual name, necessarily have a 'syntax' totally different from the medieval one. Nowadays sobriquets of all kinds, when not used independently, are commonly prefixed to surnames, so that, far from qualifying 'individual' names, as in the medieval mode, they usurp their place: thus, *Squibber* (*Scrubber*), *Dale*, *Hummer Haynes*, *Grumpy Lloyd*, *Frenchie Nicholson*, *Bandy Taylor*, as well as *Cocky Robinson* and its like. When a nickname does qualify a 'first' name, then still, whatever its own structure, it is prefixed, adjective-like, more often than suffixed: thus, *Little Edie*, *Marmalade Emma*, *Nitty Nora*, *Searchlight Charlie*, and *Sixteen-String Jack*, beside *Polly Long Frock* and *Claudie Whitehead*.

In certain instances, moreover, the naming-structure is less straightforward than at first appears in so far as the bearers' official 'first' names have been displaced by conventional ones that have evolved halfway towards common nouns: *Polly Long Frock*'s real name was *Grace*, and *Claudie Whitehead*'s, *William*. Similar usages under-lie Laurie Lee's *Percy-from-Painswick*, and probably also *Nitty Nora* and some at least of the several *Charlies*. 'Christian names' used like this belong to the nickname-vocabulary no less than do conventional epithets like *Dusty* (*Miller*) and *Lofty* – and for that reason may become less favoured for official christenings. What analogous shifts may have taken place in medieval times would prove hard to check in the sorts of record extant; but, if ascertainable, they might help to explain some losses of popularity.

Semantic analogies may be more apt than structural ones. Admittedly, the sharpest lesson for medievalists comes from those anecdotal names, like *Agony*, *Dollar*, *Pegger* and *Steady*, whose genesis, if not recorded, could hardly have been guessed;[18] to how many of our early forms this may apply we shall never know. But not all hints are so negative. For instance, when the many medieval nicknames based on terms for food[19] find an apparent parallel in *Marmalade Emma*, it may, or may not, be relevant that this marks its bearer as eating the delicacy to excess, and perhaps constantly talking of it, rather than as making or selling it. More generally, the range of interpretations accept-able for any date must allow for the cruelty frequent here and never sparing the half-witted or the deformed: *Bootnose*, *Mother No Nose*, *Old Three Noses*, *Old Mother Born-Drunk*. Even names fairly innocuous on paper, like *Claudie Whitehead*, could be hurtfully meant; and Grace Foakes in particular stresses the harshness, the 'cold logic', not only of the nicknames other children gave her but equally of those she joined in giving to others. Some victims of taunting nicknames – *Grumpy Lloyd*, *Peg Leg*, *Slipper* – were even roused to physical retaliation.

Such reactions raise, in its acutest form, the question already mooted of nickname-status: whether given forms are strictly third-person (the classic case being children's names for their teachers), with the only possible second-person applications hostile ones; or whether they are acceptable in the second-person, and perhaps adopted in the first (like *Pimbo*). Even with contemporary nicknames this can rarely be resolved for

---

18 The point is not new: cf., for instance, P.H. Reaney, *The Origin of English Surnames* (London, 1967), 219–23, and Dauzat, *Les noms de famille*, 180–1, also *Les noms de personnes*, 97–100.

19 Cf., for instance, H. Carrez, 'Le vocabulaire de l'alimentation et les noms de personnes dans la région dijonnaise du xiie au xve siècle', *Annales de Bourgogne* X (1938), 173–88; also Reaney, *Origin*, 183–4.

forms not current in the observer's own circle. But, again, the matter may be germane to the genesis of transmissible family-names.

Surprisingly perhaps, these modern names do, as already remarked, sporadically exemplify an hereditary principle, as with *Whoop Gurner* and *Pinny Moore*, as well as all the fixed clan-epithets like *Cocky Robinson*. This implies a turn of mind comparable with that underlying the medieval creation of family-names.

Another link with medieval practices occurs in the way all the memoirs consulted show publicly-recognized nicknames as distinctively masculine; Bob Copper specifically connects them with boys' gangs. Feminine examples found here have never referred to 'respectable' women but only to raffish characters and aged grotesques – *Irish Molly, Black Sally, Mother No-Nose, Old Mother Born-Drunk*; and this is so whether the memorialists themselves are men or women. The feminine seclusion this implies shows indeed at its strongest in Winifred Foley's two volumes, *A Child in the Forest* and *No Pipe-Dreams for Father*, depicting the women's side of life in a Forest of Dean mining-village, for these record hardly any of the nicknames *a priori* to be expected in so small and isolated a community.[20] This agrees with the general impression from records of all types, dates and origins that women's naming and men's are governed by partly differing social conditions and conventions.

This present study is simply a pilot one putting forward such material as has randomly come to hand. Apart from any entertainment value, it at least illustrates social and onomastic attitudes in communities of sorts now fast vanishing. How far such recent usages will offer helpful analogies to medievalists remains to be seen. Certainly, any such are likely to concern individual interpretations rather than systems. Moreover, as already remarked, some 'etymologies' cited here inspire, more than anything, great scepticism towards academic efforts in this line, showing up for the thin stuff it is the mere dictionary-work with which some nickname-students have been contenting themselves.[21] Were that the only lesson, surveying these sources would have been worthwhile.

[20] Winifred Foley, *A Child in the Forest* (London, 1974; Futura, 1977) and *No Pipe-Dreams for Father* (1977; Futura, 1978).

[21] Cf. above n. 3.

23

The *Codretum* (Whatever That May Be) at Little Roborough*

> The boundary . . . starts from the rivulet which flows into the Tamar on the
> north side of the port. Then, moving inland, it goes . . . to the corner of the
> hedge made by Walter Merchant, and along the hedge to the corner of the
> *codretum* (whatever that may be) at Little Roborough. . . . From Little
> Roborough the boundary runs to a boundary-mark under a forked oak; after
> which it moves eastward, the remaining points mentioned being: . . . the old
> road from the port; the *codrum* at the higher end of the houses; the eastern
> corner of a ditch . . .

Because it is no part of my present purpose to pillory any individual, living or dead, I
refrain from giving an exact reference either for this, my main text, or for any other
specimen held in the tongs. The excerpt comes from a commentary – first published in
1945 and then reprinted, *tel quel*, in 1952 and 1969 – on a grant, datable 1235–40,
concerning Morwellham, a small port just north of Plymouth, on the Devon side of the
Tamar. The extant document, a fourteenth-century copy, there described as forming
part of the Duke of Bedford's muniments, has since been deposited in Devon Record
Office.[1]

Two unexplained terms are involved, related ones, it would seem: *codrum* or *codrus*;
and a presumably derived *codretum*.[2] Both must have been at one remove, possibly
two, from spoken usage. The range of possible meanings is limited by context: both
terms denote landmarks, that is, outdoor features which, whether natural or artificial,
are at once substantial and quasi-permanent. To anyone already knowing – never mind
how – what these terms mean, the writer's throwing-up of hands seems naive, and its
cavalier manner scarcely forgivable. Yet, before indulging the urge to mock, anyone
less than wholly confident of omniscience ought first to ask what excuse the writer, a
respected scholar now beyond self-defence, may have had for ignorance so unashamed.

Some excuse there was, because the main Latin-English dictionaries were then
silent on the point, and partly remain so. Under *codr-* Lewis and Short lists nothing
remotely relevant; nor does the *Oxford Latin Dictionary*, in any case not available until

---

* For his kindness in criticizing a first draft of this paper and offering many valuable suggestions I
  wish most warmly to thank Peter McClure (University of Hull).

[1] Now W1258M / Bundle D 39/5. I am grateful to Mrs M.M. Rowe and the staff of Devon Record
Office for locating this document and arranging for me to receive a photocopy of it. I should also
like to thank the Curator of Woburn Abbey, Miss Lavinia Wellicome, and the Archivist of the
Bedford Estates, Mrs M.P.G. Draper, for their courteous replies to my enquiries.

[2] The readings are: *ad angulu(m) codreti*; *ad codru(m)*.

1968.[3] Souter's *Glossary of Later Latin* has nothing to offer.[4] Latham's *Revised Medieval Latin Word-List*, published in 1965, offers in that alphabetical position nothing at all helpful, nor does his *Dictionary of Medieval Latin from British Sources*, of which the relevant fascicule appeared in 1981.[5] Niermeyer's *Mediae Latinitatis Lexicon Minus*, published in 1976, is equally uninformative.[6] Thus far, then, our commentator might have been throwing up his hands in fair company, and not only that of his own time. As for Du Cange, we shall come to that later.

Was throwing up the hands in fact the only possible course? Dictionaries are but products of philologists much like the rest except for a certain specialization; to cry off the hunt whenever their assistance fails is pusillanimous. The main, perhaps the only advantage that lexicographers enjoy lies in having to hand a representative, if not always comprehensive, collection of quotations. That apart, any competent medievalist ought to feel equal to essaying elucidation of an unusual word. Common sense, combined with a modicum of general experience, modern as well as medieval, and perhaps with a smattering of comparative philology, ought amply to compensate for lack of card-indexed quotations. Before tackling our main text, we may observe in action upon other cruces some possible modes of approach.

In 1975 an editor of *The Boke of St Albans* glossed as ' "pressed mutton"?' a phrase occurring among recommendations for dosing a hawk afflicted with internal parasites: *pressure made of a lombe that was borne in vntyme*. Even apart from confusion of two ages of sheep, this interpretation is, as the editor's own question-mark acknowledges, unconvincing. OED is, however, silent as to alternative meanings for *pressure*, nor does its *Supplement* even now afford help; MED had not then reached *pre-*.[7] Is there, then, an impasse?

Although conclusive evidence can come only from medieval sources, intermediate clues may legitimately be seized upon from anywhere whatsoever. The point has been made by Arthur Owen in his study of the topographical term *Hafdic*, where he says: 'I recalled . . . (from a visit to Denmark and a little study of its language many years previously) that *hav* in modern Danish means "sea" '.[8] In the present case too, what inspired an alternative interpretation of the therapeutic *pressure* was a term encountered during foreign travels: the legend *lait présuré*, to wit, 'junket', observed on cartons in the chill-cabinet and subsequently on the family table. Modern French *présure* means indeed 'rennet', i.e. a digestive enzyme found in a ruminant's fourth stomach and used by human beings in cheese-making and other processes.

Whether this clue would lead anywhere relevant remained to be seen. Certainly, Medieval French *presure/prisure*, like Medieval Latin *pre(n)sura*, also meant 'rennet'.[9]

---

[3] C.T. Lewis and C. Short, *A Latin Dictionary* (Oxford, 1900); *Oxford Latin Dictionary*, 2 vols (Oxford, 1968–76).

[4] A. Souter, *A Glossary of Later Latin to 600 A.D.* (Oxford, 1949).

[5] R.E. Latham, *Revised Medieval Latin Word-List from British and Irish Sources* (London, 1965); idem, *Dictionary of Medieval Latin from British Sources* (London, 1975– ; in progress).

[6] J.F. Niermeyer, *Mediae Latinitatis Lexicon Minus* (Leiden, 1976).

[7] *Middle English Dictionary*, ed. Hans Kurath, Sherman M. Kuhn *et alii* (Ann Arbor, 1954– ; in progress). Fasc. P6, copyrighted 1983, gives under *pressūre* n. (2) 'rennet' only this quotation from *The Boke of St Albans*.

[8] A.E.B. Owen, '*Hafdic*: a Lindsey name and its implications', *Journal of the English Place-Name Society* 7 (1974–75), pp. 45–56, esp. 49–50.

[9] F. Godefroy, *Dictionnaire de l'ancienne langue française*, 10 vols (Paris, 1881–1902), X

In the event, search among medieval cynegetica soon unearthed a French hunting-treatise that specified, also as a medicine, *la presure ou caillon d'un jeune cerf tué dedans le ventre de la biche*.[10] Although not exact, the parallel seems close enough, with its reference to another sort of young animal stillborn, to justify our assuming that the Middle English *pressure* to be obtained from a lamb was likewise *caillon*, that is, 'rennet'.[11]

Inspiration for our second gloss has been less autobiographical. A calendar, published in 1961, of thirteenth-century coroners' rolls from Bedfordshire offers under 1276 the following entry:

> About midnight on 12 Aug., when John Clarice was lying near his wife Joan daughter of Richard le Freman, as was his custom, in his bed in the chamber of his house at Houghton Regis in the liberty of Eaton Bray, madness took possession of him, and Joan, thinking that he was seized by death, took a small scythe (*falxsiculum*) and cut his throat. She also took a weapon called 'vonge' (*sc.* a bill-hook) and struck him on the right side of the head, so that his brain flowed forth . . .

Without the Latin text no comment can be ventured on inconsequentialities in the main plot. But here too the editor himself betrays unease, by bracketing the term translated as 'scythe'. To share that unease one hardly needs to be a medievalist, let alone a philologist; simply to visualize the scene. At close quarters the implement called in Modern English a 'scythe', with a handle as tall as a man, would make an unwieldy weapon.[12] A medieval bedchamber that doubled as tool-shed to the extent of offering one ready to the hand would surely have furnished also something more compact.

A scythe may no longer be an everyday object; but a medievalist whose life has been so sheltered or so over-mechanized as never to have afforded sight of one in action might be expected to have enjoyed, in compensation, some familiarity with the Labours of the Months. These regularly depict, as an element in the hay-making scene characterizing (according to the cycle's geographical affinities) June or July, the size, shape and lawful *modus operandi* of a scythe: the best-known illustration may be that for June in *Les Très Riches Heures du Duc de Berry*, but this is only one among scores of such scenes.[13] Even those to whom medieval art remains a closed book might recollect the size and shape of the emblematic implement that Old Father Time bears over his shoulder. Speaking in Modern English of 'a *small* scythe' comes close to being a contradiction in terms.

(*Complément*), s.v. *presure*; A. Tobler and E. Lommatzsch, *Altfranzösisches Wörterbuch* (Berlin &c., 1925– ; in progress), s.v. *presure*. Cf. Latham, *Word-List*, s.v. *presura*.

[10] Jacques du Fouilloux, *La Vénerie et l'Adolescence*, ed. G. Tilander, Cynegetica 16 (Karlshamn, 1967), p. 44, and gloss p. 201.

[11] See further C. Clark, review of *English Hawking and Hunting in 'The Boke of St Albans'*, ed. R. Hands (Oxford, 1975), *Review of English Studies* new ser. 28 (1977), pp. 201–02, esp. 202.

[12] *Encyclopaedia Britannica: Micropaedia*, IX (London, 1974) offers on p. 1 a nineteenth-century photograph of a scythe in use.

[13] J.C. Webster, *The Labors of the Months in Antique and Medieval Art to the End of the Twelfth Century*, North-Western University Studies in the Humanities 4 (Evanston and Chicago, 1938), pp. 37–8, 43–5, 55, 70, and plates 33b, 50, 72, 94, 95, &c. Also: F. Wormald, *The Winchester Psalter* (London, 1973), plate 112; L.F. Sandler, *The Peterborough Psalter in Brussels and other Fenland Manuscripts* (London, 1974), plate 11; J. Longnon *et alii*, *Les Très Riches Heures du Duc de Berry* (London, 1969), plate 7.

True, Latin *falxsiculum* (to retain the spelling cited) represents, morphologically speaking, a diminutive of *falx*, one meaning of which is 'scythe'; but, apart from the fact that etymology is an unreliable guide to meaning, the simplex term itself (of dubious origin) shows a wider range of meaning than does English *scythe*, being rendered in the *Oxford Latin Dictionary* as 'an agricultural implement with a curved blade, hook, bill, scythe, sickle'.

As with *pre(s)ure*, an initial approach may be tried through modern usage. Latin *falx* gives Modern French *faux*, nowadays certainly indicating the same sort of long-handled tool for cutting grass as is depicted in the hay-making scenes in Books of Hours – a 'scythe', that is (as with junket, I have in real life marked word and thing together); modern encyclopaedias show design and *modus operandi* as scarcely changed since medieval times.[14] As for the several Modern French diminutive forms, none means simply 'small *faux*'.

The term *faucille* denotes a tool that is – or, rather, was – used, not for mowing grass, but for reaping corn; illustrated encyclopaedias show it as not just far smaller than a *faux* but as distinctively shaped, with a short handle set at a different angle.[15] In Modern English this is called a *sickle*; a schematic depiction of it is familiar in the Soviet emblem. Medieval use of a similar tool is amply confirmed by reaping-scenes representing the Labour for July or August.[16] The form *faucille* already existed, with the same meaning, in Old French;[17] and, give or take grammatical gender, this might be thought to correspond passably well with Latin *falxsiculum*. Yet, though handier by far than a scythe, a sickle still does not seem the ideal throat-cutter.

The Modern French double-diminutive *faucillon* denotes, not 'a small *faucille*', but another distinct kind of tool, to wit, 'a pruning-knife'.[18] Again the term was already current in Old French, evidently with the same sense.[19] Pruning, although recognized as one of the Labours for March, was less consistently chosen for illustration than were mowing and reaping; some Books of Hours, *Les Très Riches Heures* among them, do none the less show vines or other bushes being trimmed by means of a short, stout curved blade such as might be effectively wielded in confined space, even by a feminine hand.[20] Although the vocabulary of medieval agriculture is not easy to investigate, such a pruning-knife is probably what medieval French-speakers denoted by the terms *faucillon* and *fauchoun*.[21]

---

[14] See, for instance, *Larousse du XXᵉ siècle*, III (Paris, 1930), p. 425, and *Grand Larousse encyclopédique*, IV (Paris, 1961), p. 932. Cf. nn. 12 and 13 above.

[15] *Larousse du XXᵉ siècle*, III, p. 420; *Grand Larousse*, IV, p. 922.

[16] Webster, *Labors*, pp. 38, 44, 70, and plates 50, 62, 72, 92, 93, 94, 95; *Winchester Psalter*, plate 113; *Peterborough Psalter*, plate 12; *Les Très Riches Heures*, plate 8.

[17] Godefroy, s.v.; Tobler-Lommatzsch, s.v.

[18] *Larousse du XXᵉ siècle*, III, p. 420; *Grand Larousse*, IV, p. 922.

[19] Godefroy, s.v.; Tobler-Lommatzsch, s.v., where one quotation shows as evidently interchangeable 'ou sarpe [= Modern French *serpe*] ou faucillon'; also s.v. *sarpe*, where quotations make use for trimming bushes clear. See further n. 21 below.

[20] Webster, *Labors*, pp. 70, 89, 175–8, and plates 50, 62, 97; *Les Très Riches Heures*, plate 4. Another good illustration occurs in the Bedford Book of Hours (British Library Additional MS 18850, French, c.1423), f. 3r; this also has clear depictions of scythe and of sickle.

[21] As noted above (n. 19), French *sarpe/serpe* seems more or less synonymous with *faucillon*, and *Larousse du XXᵉ siècle*, VI, p. 313, offers s.v. *serpe* illustrations of pruning-knives with varying degrees of curvature, some of which resemble those in the medieval depictions cited.

Of the Old French terms cited, only *fauchoun* seems to have been borrowed into Middle English, and then mostly to denote a weapon of war.[22] A few late-fifteenth- and sixteenth-century instances, on the other hand, show not only agricultural context ('plowemen . . . with their staues and fauchons' – Caxton) but also specific use for cutting wood ('Let thy bright fauchion lend me cypresse boughes' – Drayton).[23] The tool in question, presumably similar to those shown in pruning-scenes in Books of Hours, seems, however, more often to have been called in English a *bill* or *bill-hook*.[24] What thirteenth-century Bedfordshire peasants did indeed call their pruning-knives and hedging-bills may be at present unascertainable;[25] but it seems safe to assume that they had such tools, and used them as need arose. In the case in question the coroner's clerk, we may surmise, found himself called upon to Latinize a term for 'pruning-knife'. If that term were *fauchoun*, choice of *falxsiculum* might be natural. If it were some native Middle English one, such as *bil*, one sense of which was 'pruning-hook', perhaps he first rendered it mentally as *fauchoun* or *faucillon*, then cast about for a Latin equivalent (few can have named agricultural implements directly in Latin). At all events, visualization of the crime has gained in verisimilitude, with a compact pruning-knife replacing the supposed 'small scythe'. (In case any should wish to know the outcome of the case, Joan was sentenced to abjure the realm, *viâ* the Dover road.)

As to the terms from which this essay began, one surely unassailable assumption has been made: that *codretum* is derived from *codrus/codrum*. The rôle of the suffix *-ētum* might, from its occurrence in 'English' words like *arboretum*, be guessed even by someone with little Latin, let alone by a student of charters. It is, as the *Oxford Latin Dictionary* says, added 'to names of plants to denote the place where they grow'. That makes *codrus/codrum* a plant-name; and, in so far as a single specimen can serve as a landmark, the type of plant must be a tree.

A détour through modern usage, although feasible, can on this occasion be dispensed with, because medieval studies alone readily furnish all the clues we need. Marie de France uses for naming the twin sister of her heroine Le Fresne, herself named from the ash-tree under which she had been found, the form *La Co(u)dre*.[26] Those seeking to persuade Le Fresne's lover to discard her and marry La Codre pun on the names in a way implying that the latter too is a tree-name:

> Pur le freisne que vus larrez
> En eschange le codre avrez;
> En la codre ad noiz e deduiz,
> Li freisne ne porte unke fruiz!   (337–40)

(In exchange for the ash-tree that you will leave, you shall have the *codre*; from the *codre* come nuts and delights, but the ash-tree bears no fruits at all!)

---

[22] MED, s.v. *fauchoun*.

[23] OED, s.v. *falchion*, sense 2.

[24] See MED, s.v. *bil*, and OED, s.vv. *bill* sb.[1], sense 4, and *bill-hook*. The editor in fact supplies the term *bill-hook* in the passage quoted, but as a gloss for Latin *vanga*, normally rendered 'spade' or 'mattock' (Lewis and Short; Souter; Latham, *Word-List*); for the purpose in question a spade would have been the more appropriate tool.

[25] For modern Bedfordshire dialect, H. Orton *et alii*, *Survey of English Dialects (B) The Basic Material*, III, ii (Leeds, 1970), p. 441, gives only *bill*.

[26] *Les Lais de Marie de France*, ed. Jean Rychner, Les Classiques français du Moyen Age 93 (Paris, 1966), p. 54, line 335.

Marie's use of a corresponding common noun confirms this interpretation. In *Laüstic*, when traps are being set for the nightingale,

> N'i ot codre ne chastainier
> U il ne mettent laz u glu. (98–9)

> (There is no *codre* or chestnut-tree where they fail to lay a snare or some bird-lime.)

In *Chievrefoil* it is a *codre* from which Tristram cuts a wand on which to carve a message (line 51), and the same species of tree that in his message serves as symbol of a true lover:

> D'euls deus fu il tut autresi
> Cume del chievrefoil esteit
> Ki a la codre si perneit:
> Quant il s'i est laciez e pris
> E tut entur le fust s'est mis,
> Ensemble poënt bien durer;
> Mes ki puis les voelt desevrer,
> Li codres muert hastivement
> Et le chievrefoilz ensement.
> 'Bele amie, si est du nus:
> Ni vus sanz mei, ne jeo sanz vus'. (68–78)

> (It was for the two of them just as for a honeysuckle clinging to a *codre*: once it has entwined and fixed itself there and coiled itself all about the trunk, thus united both may thrive; but, should anyone try to part them, the *codre* will straightway die, and the honeysuckle too. 'Fair sweetheart, so it is with us: you cannot live without me, nor I without you'.)

A late-thirteenth-century English gloss to the term *co(u)dre* occurs in Walter of Bibbesworth's manual for teaching Anglo-Norman, where it is rendered 'hasil'.[27]

Once the trail has been followed thus far, dictionaries afford ample confirmation of the findings; some at least of them would have done so already in 1945. True, the necessary fascicule of the *Anglo-Norman Dictionary* appeared only in 1977.[28] But Godefroy in his second volume (1883) listed as collectives the forms *coudreel*, *coudrete* (more probably a diminutive) and *coudriere*; in his ninth (1898; *Complément*) he gave in fact *coldre* 'coudrier, noisetier' and its derivative *coldraie*. Tobler-Lommatzsch, the relevant volume of which appeared in 1936, likewise gave *coudre* 'Haselstrauch', together with the diminutives *coudrele* and *coudrete* and the collective *coudroie* 'Haselgebüsch'. Dictionaries of Modern French, such as the *Dictionnaire Robert*, also give *coudre* 'noisetier' alongside the more usual *coudrier* and the collective *coudraie*. With Old French *co(u)dre* thus established as meaning 'hazel-bush', little remains but to pursue it to its lair.

Easier said than done. Even for the Romanist, Old French *coldre*/*couldre*/*coudre*/*codre* proves an awkward customer. A Frankish etymology can

---

[27] *Le Traité de Walter de Bibbesworth sur la langue française*, ed. A. Owen (Paris, 1929), p. 69, line 250, where *coudre croule* is glossed 'hasil quakes' (cf. MED, s.v. *hāsel*).

[28] L.W. Stone *et alii*, *Anglo-Norman Dictionary* (London, 1977– ; in progress) s.vv. *coudre*, *coudrei*.

instantly be ruled out, because (as the German glosses just cited imply) the relevant Common Germanic root is the same *hasl-* as underlies our English term.[29] The Latin cognate is (as a nurseryman's catalogue might suggest) *corўlus*, with a collective *corўlētum*: near enough to *coldre* to raise hopes of finding some link, distant enough to make such endeavour a daunting one. Reflexes of *corўlus* prove in the event fairly scarce, apparently because over much of the Romance area this term was soon discarded in favour of neologisms spread by medieval marketing-men.[30] Such reflexes of it as are attested mostly imply an intermediate stage showing metathesis, probably to **colŭrus*. Whether or not to attribute such metathesis to contamination by the Gaulish cognate, probably **coll-* < **cosl-*, seems a matter of opinion.[31] After metathesis, development from Common Romance to Old French followed a normal path, with the unstressed medial vowel syncopated, a dental glide generated between [l] and [r], and then the now-preconsonantal [l] velarized and finally vocalized to [u]: **colŭr-* > **colr-* > *coldr-* > *coudr-*.[32] The derivative *corўlētum* 'hazel-copse' followed a parallel path, giving Old French *couldraie* (and variants).

Thus, our *codretum* represents use, in place of the classical *corўlētum*, of a relatinization of its Old French reflex *co(u)draie*. Now, when we scarcely need them, Latin dictionaries begin to serve us better. True, neither Lewis and Short nor the *Oxford Latin Dictionary* appears to have any truck with such latter-day corruptions; nor has Souter's *Glossary*. But, under *corўlus*, Latham's *Revised Word-List* – admittedly published rather late in the day for our original commentator – gives both a simplex form *coudra*, referred to Old French *coudre*, and a derivative *coudreium*; his *Dictionary* lists both *coudra* and *coudreicum* independently. One authority not so late in the day was, however, Du Cange; under *Codra* he had all along, albeit cryptically, given the essential clue:

> Interpres Gallicus *Codra* reddit per *Codres*, vocem mihi non magis notam, nisi forte sit item quod Gallis *Coudre* vel *Coudrier*, Corylus[33]

– all in a nutshell.

The same conclusion might have been reached by another route that would at the same time have shown Old French *coudraie* figuring on English soil in contexts other than those of courtly romance. There is in Sussex (as polo-fans in particular will recall) a place called *Cowdray Park*, likewise a *Cowdry Farm*.[34] These place-names represent

---

29 J. Pokorny, *Indogermanisches etymologisches Wörterbuch*, 2 vols (Bern and Munich, 1959–69), I, p. 616, s.r. *kos(e)lo-*; F. Kluge, *Etymologisches Wörterbuch der deutschen Sprache*, 20th edn rev. W. Mitzke (Berlin, 1967), s.v. *Hasel*; F. Holthausen, *Altenglisches etymologisches Wörterbuch* (Heidelberg, 1939), s.v. *hæsel*.

30 V. Bertoldi, 'Una voce moritura: ricerche sulla vitalità di *corylus* (> **colurus*)', *Revue de linguistique romane* 1 (1925), pp. 237–61. Cf. the review article by M[atteo] B[artoli] in *Archivio glottologico italiano* 20 (1926), sezione neolatina, pp. 172–80. Cf. W. von Wartburg, *Französisches etymologisches Wörterbuch* (Bonn, 1928– ; in progress), II, ii, p. 1240–2 (Basel, 1946), s.v. *corylus*.

31 Bertoldi, pp. 240–1; but cf. B[artoli], p. 175.

32 See M.K. Pope, *From Latin to Modern French*, 2nd edn (Manchester, 1952), §§250, 370, 382.2, 385, 387, 389–90.

33 Charles Du Cange, *Glossarium Mediae et Infimae Latinitatis*, 10 vols (Niort and London, 1884–87).

34 A. Mawer *et alii*, *The Place-Names of Sussex*, 2 vols continuously paginated, EPNS 6 and 7

Old French *coudraie*, regularly used in France itself for forming toponyms.[35] There seems, however, no evidence for any Middle English borrowing of **cowdray* as a common noun. So, when similar forms appear outside Sussex seemingly as topographical by-names,[36] the question becomes delicate. As Reaney pointed out, some at least of these medieval by-names probably referred back to continental localities so named; and modern family-names like *Cowdr(a)y* may thus go back either to continental origins or to the places in Sussex.[37] On the other hand, a Staffordshire occurrence c.1300 of a by-name *de la Coudrey/del Coudray*[38] might represent scribal translation of a native English *Hazelgrove, Hazelwood* or *Hazlett*; but without further documentation no more can be said. For all the uncertainties, there seems, however, little reason to doubt that among literate English people of the mid-thirteenth century Old French *co(u)dre* and *co(u)draie* could have been familiar enough to have sprung to the mind of a dog-Latinist improvising terms for landmarks.

It would have been gratifying, especially for this non-toponymist, to have rounded off this survey by reporting that maps of the Morwellham district offered a **Cowdray*, a **Hazlett* or a **Nutley* in just the right place. Alas, that is not so. Despite the most patient and generous help from the staff of the Map Room at Cambridge University Library, no map, at any scale, has been found that vouchsafes any even remotely appropriate microtoponym.[39] Woodlands still abound, but to the cartographer mostly remain nameless.

(Cambridge, 1929–30), pp. 17, 81. Cf. A.H. Smith, *English Place-Name Elements*, 2 vols, EPNS 25 and 26 (Cambridge, 1956), I, p. 110, s.v. *coudraie*.

[35] A. Dauzat, *Dictionnaire étymologique des noms de lieux en France*, 2nd edn rev. Ch. Rostaing (Paris, 1978), s.n. *Colroy*; also Charles de Beaurepaire, *Dictionnaire topographique du département de Seine-Maritime*, ed. Dom Jean Laporte, 2 vols continuously paginated (Paris, 1982–84), pp. 271–3.

[36] G. Kristensson, 'Studies in Middle English local surnames containing elements of French origin', *English Studies* 50 (1969), pp. 465–86, esp. 473.

[37] P.H. Reaney, *A Dictionary of British Surnames*, 2nd edn rev. R.M. Wilson (London, 1976), s.n. *Cowdray*.

[38] See n. 36 above.

[39] *A fortiori*, nothing relevant is to be found in J.E.B. Gover *et alii*, *The Place-Names of Devon*, 2 vols continuously paginated, EPNS 8 and 9 (Cambridge, 1931–32).

24

Review

P.H. REANEY, *The Origin of English Surnames*, London: Routledge and Kegan Paul, first published 1967; paperback re-issue 1980, xix + 415 pp.

With name-studies currently making vast strides, this unaugmented, indeed uncorrected, bargain-price re-issue of a book now nearly fifteen years old raises the question what popularization should mean.

Inevitably, some points here now need annotation. Some tentative observations have since been confirmed, as with 'OE women's names show a stronger tendency to persist than those of men' (p. 106; cf. above 117–43) and likewise with the note that the King's Lynn names in the 1166 Pipe Roll show a more old-fashioned distribution than those of the 1148 Winchester survey (p. 102; cf. *Nomina* III, 13–14, and see also pp. 370–1 below). Reaney's own wish to see the various 'national' name-vocabularies elucidated by further basic research (see, for instance, pp. 99, 118 and 130) is gradually being fulfilled, for instance, by Bo Seltén with his work on East-Anglian materials and especially by Gillian Fellows Jensen and by John Insley with theirs on the Scandinavian element in English. Likewise, the chronology of surname-fixing, the appearance of forms in *-s* and in *-son*, the nickname-use of terms of rank and occupation, and women's surnames could all now be treated more precisely in the light of the thriving English Surname Series, and especially Richard McKinley's contributions, which are also beginning to reveal local naming-variations.

Less happily, some material that passed muster in 1967 no longer does so. Continental background studies newly available, Flemish as well as French, are putting post-Conquest English naming into clearer perspective. Admittedly, some blurring of focus had arisen from notions such as 'Until well into the thirteenth century, at least, French was the language of all educated people, whilst the lower classes spoke English' (p. 178). But the main blanks concerned the dependence, now so much easier to trace, of English naming-patterns on continental ones: thus, the way that the once-dominant Continental-Germanic forms lost favour, especially for women's names, to 'Christian' ones was duly noted but nowhere linked with French and Flemish patterns; and the *-l-*, *-n-* and *-t-* diminutives were treated on the same footing as the characteristically English abbreviations like *Dawe*, *Gibbe* and *Hobbe*, with only stray notes acknowledging the former as imported and sometimes specifically Picard in form (e.g., pp. 153/n. 4, 155/n. 1). Newly available English material includes the twelfth-century Canterbury rent-rolls published by William Urry in 1967; these have disproved several assertions, such as that in *Atwell*-surnames the 'earliest' documents show 'French or Latin' prepositions (p. 49) and that the 'earliest' records of Middle English occupational terms and nicknames show 'French' definite articles (p. 34). Most importantly, Olof von Feilitzen's Winchester onomasticon published in 1976 now provides more accurate statistics of the landholders' names *TRE*, c.1115 and in 1148: whereas here the occurrences of Old English/Scandinavian/'French' forms were estimated as: *TRE* – 173/6/20, c.1115 – 85/18/167, and 1148 – 147/79/596 (p. 107), von Feilitzen, who subdivides the categories more subtly, gives figures equivalent to: *TRE* – 265/11/35, c.1115 – 68/11/149, and 1148 – 182/67/663 (*Winton Domesday*, p. 185). Likewise for King's Lynn 1166 and for Newark 1177 the corresponding statistics, here given respectively as: 81/50/83 and 64/43/167, might be amended to: 47/29/60 and 49/42/267 (for the latter, and for the Winton Domesday, more sensitive analyses would separate out the women's names, which show the usual Old English bias already mentioned). Of course, in judging as in compiling all such statistics some leeway must be allowed for ambiguous forms; but the discrepancies here seem too great to be thus explained away.

Calculation was indeed nowhere this book's strong point, as further appeared in the attempts to measure medieval population-movements by means of toponymic surnames. All such attempts, as Peter McClure has recently shown, must face the problems created by the non-uniqueness of some 60% of place-name forms (see *Economic History Review* XXXII, 167–82, esp. 169–70, and also *Local Historian* XIII, 80–6). Even though himself originally a toponymist rather than an anthroponymist, Reaney here fell into a dubious methodology, which deprived of full weight his comments on medieval immigration into Norwich and into London. In this sphere too McKinley's work and that of George Redmonds have been contributing towards more accurate understanding.

On a human level much must be forgiven a writer who died in the very year of publication, especially one grappling with such a plethora of often ambiguous detail; but compassion cannot cure the prematurity of a book embarked upon not only in awareness of how much basic research remained to be done but also with imperfect command of the data accessible. Points are laboured which no sensible reader would contest. Alternative etymologies are sometimes proposed without cross-reference, as for *Barker* (see pp. 177 and 209) and for *Furzer* (see pp. 190 and 201), and for *Brock* even within a single paragraph (see pp. 263–4). Some material might have been better arranged, with trades, for instance, grouped according to sense rather than to suffix (incidentally, although other obsolete by-names are often listed, the -*wife*-compounds parallel to those in -*man* seem to be omitted) and with nicknames marshalled in closer accord with their chapter-headings. Time and again the lost control betrayed itself syntactically, often in confusions of *signifiant* with *signifié* such as '*William* is the most popular name . . . until the end of the thirteenth century when he gives place to *John*' (p. 131) and 'the conspicuous exception of the dog and the horse, though these, too, were once nicknames' (p. 262), as well as a reference to 'intermarriage between men of English and Danish descent' (p. 329).

These flaws run together and merge with the major one carried over from the earlier *Dictionary of British Surnames* (for criticism of which by Redmonds and by von Feilitzen, see *Conference at Erlangen*, ed. Voitl, pp. 78–9 and 83–4), where the method had been baldly to cite, without pretence of proving any linkage, various medieval forms supposed to underlie present-day surnames. This book therefore abounds in unsupported assertions, such as 'The accusative *Faucon* [from the CG name *Falco*] may sometimes be the origin of *Falcon*, though this is usually from the name of the bird' (p. 139; cf. the similar misuses of 'obviously', 'usually', 'invariably' in comments like those on *Harkus* – p. 3, *Stirrup* – p. 43, *Drewes* – p. 138, and so on), with no indication of any basis of assessment. Hardest to forgive is the authoritative tone in which the uncertainties are propounded.

Methodology was further undermined by flaws more basic still. Sources were inadequately criticized, with little note taken either of the orthographical characteristics or of the social limitations presented by certain classes of document. Indeed, spelling and pronunciation often got slapdash treatment. Name-study being a branch of philology, orthographical and phonetic checks are bypassed only at peril; yet here, perhaps to propitiate the 'general' reader, phonetic notation was eschewed and spelling treated cavalierly (an occasional *yogh* pops up unannotated; *ye* is several times blandly printed for *þe*; *-wereste* is cited without explanation as a form of *-wright* – p. 207; and 'OE *y*', together with its assorted reflexes, is mentioned casually, with no definition attempted – p. 30). That 'general' reader must often have been reduced to chanting *credo quia impossibile est*; but, worse, the lack of rigour often ensnared its author. Time and again disparate forms were collocated without a hint of how the modern one might have evolved, in defiance of regular phonological and substitutional patterns, from the medieval: thus, ME *bouker* 'flax-dresser' is suggested as an alternative etymon for *Booker* (p. 197; admittedly, *MED* encourages confusion); *Bunney* is attributed to OFr. *bugne* (pp. 11 and 242), *Cowle(s)* to (*Ni*)*Col* rather than to 'hood' (p. 154), *Estridge* directly to OFr. *estreis* (p. 50; but cf. *Norfolk Archaeology* XXXVI, 60), *Rook* to *oak* (p. 50; but, pronunciation apart, cf. Fr. *Corneille* from the same avian group), *Soanes* to *son* (p. 81), and so on. Laxity is compounded by inconsistency: some unco-ordinated alternative etymologies have already been quoted, and others include that of *Jekyll*, which on p. 148 is attributed to Old Breton *Judhael* but on p. 149 to *Judicael*. Similar vagueness vitiates some attempts to link apparently toponymic surnames with specific places, a process tricky enough even when phonology is respected (see, for instance, pp. 45–6). It must all bewilder any tyro anthroponymist. Yet, before digging this pit for himself as well as for his readers, Reaney had most admirably explained how, for all surnames except those of a few privileged families, oral transmission had been the rule and that its laws must therefore be respected.

So carping a review may have given an impression that this is a useless book. Far from it: for a critical reader qualified and willing to make independent checks it offers inspiring hints (see the second paragraph above) as well as good principles and often-illuminating detail; and at least one recent monograph would have been the better of more diligent attention to it. In its endeavours to link naming-practices with social history it is salutary as well as admirable. What it is not is a safe guide for that 'general' public for name-studies whose existence is attested by the queries and theories so often canvassed in letters and notes published in magazines. Of course popularization must not be delayed until a subject be codified to full scholarly satisfaction (if indeed that ever happens): workers in related fields such as genealogy and local history must know both what we can tell them and, more urgently, what we need them to tell us. That is the point: wisdom lies in not trying to devise 'answers' when none as yet exist but in admitting ignorance and going on to define it. Had they been served up plain, as 'Contributions Towards' surname-history, the collections used here and in Reaney's *Dictionary of British Surnames* would have been invaluable; each time the error lay in aspiring to an unjustifiable degree of codification.

25

Review

ADRIAN ROOM, *Naming Names: Stories of Pseudonyms and Name Changes, with a Who's Who*, London and Henley: Routledge and Kegan Paul, 1981, x + 349 pp.

IDEM, *Dictionary of Trade Name Origins*, London, Boston [USA] and Henley: Routledge and Kegan Paul, 1982, vi + 217 pp.

These are both bedside books, gossipy and dippable, dealing in whimsicalities rather than systems or principles. Nevertheless, a claim on our daytime, indeed professional, attention has been staked by their display at our Bangor Conference, and fully registered by their arrival on our Reviews Editor's desk. The topics, at least, are rich in socio-onomastic implication.

In *Pseudonyms*, Mr Room chats about names which people have (mainly) picked for themselves rather than having had thrust upon them: from *Anna Akhmatova, Muhammad Ali* (*olim* Cassius Clay), *Irving Berlin, Lewis Carroll, George Eliot, Margot Fonteyn, William Hickey* and *Ho Chi Minh* to *Saint Paul, Edith Piaf, Rasputin, Saki, Tintoretto*, and so on. A seventy-page introduction precedes the main *catalogue raisonné*. Forty supplementary lists follow it, classified by the form or the motivation of change. Next stands a Who's Who-cum-index. Five appendices list: the 173 pseudonyms used by Voltaire and the 198 used by Defoe; selected lovers' pet-names culled from *The Times*'s Valentine-columns of 1978 ('From *Chublet* to *Booger-Face*' – presumably of different genders, but which is which?); some wrestlers' ring-names (*Gorilla Monsoon, Whiskers Savage*); and, lastly, four pagefuls of supposedly improbable 'real' names ('. . . after all, there could be no pseudonyms or name changes without an original name to start with' [p. 339]). How much of human life is here! And all is great, good, clean fun; inconsequent enough, too, not to dispel a courted drowsiness.

Naively pedagogic – disabusing us of the notion that *surname* derives from *sir(e*, translating each foreign tag, instructing us how to sound the French alphabet – this book hardly, notwithstanding the invitation to review it, aims at *Nomina*-readers, as indeed its show-bizzy bibliography confirms. In Chapter I surname-creation and genealogy are greatly over-simplified. Throughout, the world-view reflects an innocent Anglo-Americano-centricity: noting how immigrants into America had their names Anglicized wholesale, 'Would people', asks the author semi-rhetorically, 'ever change their English names to foreign ones?' [p. 8] – only if they were low enough cads to go on the stage, is the answer implied.

Life itself keeps slipping askew. For criminals, it is suggested, 'to have no name at all would be an excellent idea, since then the murderer would stand a good chance of escaping undetected' [p. 11]. A plagiarist is said to 'undergo a name change' when substituting his own name for the true author's [p. 19]. 'Our surname', we are assured, 'will probably continue to be borne by our children' [p. 1] – not, surely, if 'we' are respectable Englishwomen.

The forebodings thus aroused are swiftly fulfilled. Nowhere is the basic premiss stated that the concept of a 'real' name is already elastic, because convention allows, perhaps expects, not only varied hypocoristic play upon first names but also, even more, surname-changes consequent upon adoption, step-relationships, inheritance, marriage, and ennoblement. Hence few – foreign anthropologists apart – might find noteworthy those changes (unnoted indeed here) experienced by, say, Margaret Thatcher, *née* Roberts, and by Lord Dacre of Glanton, *né* Trevor-Roper. Yet, apart from symbolizing social structures (wherefore rebels against naming-customs are far from being so silly as they sometimes sound), these accepted changes should form the yardstick for measuring the more extravagant ones. Not so here. For women, surname-change upon marriage is, even in the 1980s, taken for granted; other familial name-customs get hit-or-miss treatment. Ennoblement (not to speak of the reverse process favoured by the one-time Lord Stansgate) is ignored.

This failure of definition lets in items barely ranking as 'change' at all: for instance, the Victorian *Mrs Beeton*; *Confucius*, a straight Latinization of the philosopher's Chinese name; *Desi Arnaz*, using the main elements of the actor's 'full' name; and (*Don*) *Ameche*, a 'phonetic' respelling of Italian *Amici*. Among genuine changes listed a good few are conventional rather than pseudonymous: *Julie Andrews* denotes a *Julia* whose stepfather was called *Andrews*; Richard, *né* Jenkins, adopted *Burton* from the benefactor whose legal ward he became; and Mozart's librettist took *Lorenzo da Ponti* from the bishop officiating at his adult baptism. As for the Americanizations of (Fred) *Astaire* from *Austerlitz* and (Maria) *Callas* from *Kalogeropoulos*, these were not effected by the celebrities listed but by their parents. Under all these heads one could, but for fear of alienating our Reviews Editor, go on down the alphabet . . .

Focussing (if that be the *mot juste*) on showy, not to say show-biz, pseudonyms partly blurs the view of name-change as rejection, or assertion, of group-membership. Yet even flamboyant fantasies obey social imperatives, and much folk-wisdom is therefore (give or take the howlers) garnered here for the winnowing. As Mr Room himself remarks, so closely do name and identity merge that name-change commonly forms part of a *rite de passage* and only in extreme cases, such as elevation to the Papacy, is the break clean. Time and again, as he shows, a new name, be it cartoonist's pseudonym or refugee's permanent identification, covertly asserts its bearer's 'real' identity by encoding – abbreviating, translating, anagrammatizing, or otherwise playing on – the original form (the modes acceptable for temporary pseudonyms should have been more sharply distinguished from those preferred for serious re-naming). Alternatively, people seeking a new surname often take their mother's, or their maternal grandmother's: a practice here acknowledged, but without note of how it reveals patriarchy as less deeply engrained in the folk-consciousness than official usage would pretend.

Well before setting eyes on *Trade Names*, I had noted the warm welcome it enjoyed from the media: from *The Times*'s 'Diary' [28. iv. 82, p. 14], Miles Kington's review in *The Sunday Times* [9. v. 82, p. 43], and Radio 4's 'Stop the Week' [15. v. 82] – to mention only such items as casually caught my eye or ear. Still, I had also perused *Pseudonyms*, and perhaps that nipped any budding *parti-pris*.

The books indeed show similar approaches. Here too the basic premisses are inadequately defined: it must be at least a moot point whether a full dictionary entry ought, unless justified by striking anecdote, to be allotted to any name consisting simply of the original trader's or inventor's own (e.g., *Addis, Bally, Bata, Bendix, Cessna, Chrysler*, and so on [cf. pp. 3, 12, 14] or that of the original place of manufacture (*Bournville, Longines*); for such items simple listing would amply have sufficed. Inconsistencies abound: thus, *Dry Sack* − surely a tautology based on the Shakespearean (*sherris*) *sacke*, apparently from Fr. *sec* [see *NED*], the scrap of hessian sometimes figuring as a marketing gimmick being just a rebus − is relegated to an appendix of 'unexplained' names [p. 206], whereas full entries grace not just the equally unexplained *Tio Pepe* but also scores of other such, from *Adamsez* to *Zubes* (the latter perhaps representing, at my guess, 'jujubes for the tubes').

Predictably, from one who finds *Mars bar* 'alliterative' [p. 116], the formal side of naming gets short shrift − markedly shorter, indeed, than in *Pseudonyms*. Whereas prefixed qualifiers are treated in the Introduction [pp. 4–5], suffixes are relegated to an appendix [pp. 196–202]. The 'erratic' spellings repeatedly noted [pp. 4, 8, 16, etc.] are but weakly linked with the legal embargo on registering common generics [cf. p. 8]. Despite insistence on the recurrence of certain letters, notably *o* and *x* [pp. 193–6], nothing is said of the usefulness, for services often sought in the Yellow Pages, of an initial early in the alphabet. The mention of *Dúnlop* (tyres) disregards the shifted stress peculiar to this context [p. 3; cf. *Dunlóp* cheese, distinct in other ways too]; and the entry for *Maclean*[ing one's teeth], the mispronunciation involved. Interactions between trade-names and current usage get skimped. The everyday verbs generated by some over-successful product-names (*to hoover* [why not the logical back-formation **to hoove?*], *to xerox*) are legalistically censured. Unremarked is the occasional adoption-back by household-name traders of colloquial diminutives such as *Woolies* and *Marks and Sparks* (*vide* the latter's cord jeans).

Again the readership envisaged combines magpie curiosity with minimal general knowledge. *Avon* is defined as 'a river', the *Dolomites* as 'a mountain group' [p. 13]. No foreign term escapes a gloss: not *Allegro, beau* [p. 5], *Corniche, Corona, Gauloises* (with a third-form history lesson, the like of which also encumbers *Drambuie*), *rex* [pp. 5, 198], nor *Vespa*. Among pet-food names *Felix* is singled out as unusually opaque [p. 12, cf. 76]; my own favourite, the French *Canigou*, is far too exotic for this company. The reader is not credited even with *gumption* [glossed p. 87], let alone the wit to etymologize *Brillo, Mirro, Mobiloil, Sifta, Aero* (chocolate) or *Smarties*. 'Saints' names', it is explained, 'are usually prefixed by "St" ' [p. 5]. The implications of qualifiers like *Express* and *Sovereign* are spelt out [p. 5].

Ventures into connotation veer between the over-literal and the surreal. A shoe-factory's name is linked with the local bishop's style [p. 128]. Any link between *Maltesers* and 'Maltese' is gravely discounted. Supposed, and supposedly helpful, free associations include 'jaguar' with *Jaeger* (but it's [jeɪgə], surely), and the 'Oxbridge' (*rectè*: principally Oxford) sense of *viva* [vaɪvə] with the car-name (surely [viːvə], as with *España*). Helpful? If these did work, they would *per contra*, and especially the former with its threat of a wildcat loose in the most correct of ladies' outfitters, send your Oxonian lady-reviewer to cower beneath the desk. But it is the supposed unhelpful associations that really reveal a knack of finding noon at 2.00 p.m. Of *Typhoo* it is remarked, almost with puzzlement, that 'the suggestion of "typhoid" ' seems not to have harmed the product's popularity; any 'viral' undertones in *Virol* are, upon consideration, rejected. Nor, it seems, has the name '*Omo, . . .* with its "threat-face" appearance . . . and suggestion of "homosexual" ' at all queered that marketing pitch [p. 14, cf. 130]. Although *Fairy Liquid* and *Snow* get only passing mention [p. 31, *s.n. Ariel*], their qualifier is listed among the signally wholesome [p. 4]; the underworld sense of 'cocaine' for *snow* seemingly goes unnoted.

Various gaps may surprise us. *Galaxy*, with its pun on *lac*(*tic*), is missing from the *Mars* constellation [but cf. p. 9]; missing too are the myriad TV, pop and space-age names for confectionery, ice-creams and savoury nibbles. The note on *Dyane* fails to observe the 'goddess'-theme characterizing Citroën names; *Avenger* and some other over-*macho* vehicle-names are ignored. Cosmetic- and shampoo-names are under-represented: no *Amami*(-night), despite its (Italian) etymological possibilities; no *Camay* soap, with its cameo-motif (cf. the identical French soap, *Camée*). Although the puzzlingly culinary *Persil* is almost explained, where are *Daz*, *Rinso*, *Tide* and *Surf* (the latter, through its rhymes with 'scurf' and 'the Turf', perhaps suggesting a bookie with dandruff)? Where is the *Falstaff* cigar, a heftier stable-mate of the *Hamlet* [p. 89]?

Even more than with *Pseudonyms*, this book's weakness lies partly in detachment from everyday life, in this case from the educative power of ITV 'break' and super-market shelf. No training in applied psychology, just normal self-awareness, is needed to tell one (as Mr Room does not) that it is with luxury items that brand-name magic is, for profit or loss, most potent: thus, although with its present name a much-advertised chocolate biscuit is not for me, yet renamed as, say, *Newmarket* the same confection might rapidly become my staple, my vice. Detergent, on the other hand, sells by supposed cost-effectiveness rather than by image, and hence perhaps better as an 'own' brand (a topic here neglected; but see, for instance, *The Times*, 26. i. 82, p. 16) than under a fancy name. There remain, in mass as well as individual psychology, mysteries which Mr Room, with his blanket categories of '(un)favourable' and '(un)helpful', never attempts to plumb.

For all its shortcomings, this book can, however, inform and chasten: never, to my shame, had it dawned on me that *Thames and Hudson* represented the fluvial rather than the human face of publishing. And, of course, like its twin, it is fun, stuffed with titbits such as strategies for selling writing-paper to the illiterate [p. 110], the rural inspiration behind *Turtle Wax*, the naming of *Milton* antiseptic after the poet, that of the *Liberty* bodice form the store (and the store from its founder) rather than – as folklore had it – from alleged comfort in wear, and the presence behind *Berlei* corsetry of a Mr *Burley*.

Certain incidental felicities like 'concentrated essence of beef and manufacturer' [p. 44] bring us back to the main charge against both these books: of a pervasive – worse, patronizing – sloppiness that 'popular' intent [*Trade Name Origins*, p. 3] in no way excuses. If I have seemed to be taking an axe to crack monkey-nuts, dismembering on the desk what was meant only to beguile on the pillow, I am unrepentant. Certainly both books represent feats of compilation from scattered sources, many of them in their own way rare and obscure; and for bringing the materials together and to public notice Mr Room deserves our congratulations as well as our thanks. Yet, whereas the themes promised comedy of manners, even satire, the treatments hardly get beyond slapstick, if that. Too often, a labouring literalness defeats even the books' primary object: an entertainment needs more, not less, crispness of style than an academic monograph, more wit and ironical edge, more complicity with the reader. Just as 'The Last Night of the Proms' presupposes the performers' confident professionalism, so ought literary fun to rest on accuracy, logic, stylistic skill, and some philosophical consistency. Still, as the French proverb points out (albeit with an unacceptable sex-ism), we are foolish if we expect of anyone more than (s)he has to give.

26

Review

G.W. LASKER, with A.J. BOYCE, G. BRUSH and C.G.N. MASCIE-TAYLOR, *Surnames and Genetic Structure*, Cambridge Studies in Biological Anthropology I, Cambridge: Cambridge University Press, 1985, viii + 148 pp.

Being neither a geneticist nor a statistician, the present reviewer can offer only a lopsided critique of this adventurous book. There is probably, however, no scholar alive who could do it all-round justice.

Its subject is only incidentally onomastic, the underlying purpose being to explore possible source-material for historical genetics. The thesis – ultimately attributable to a son of Darwin's but independently, it seems, taken up by statistical geneticists about a quarter-century ago – is that analysis of surname-distributions within a given population can throw light on levels of inbreeding there (given that each human being now alive had, in theory, some 4,000,000,000 ancestors living c.1200 A.D., a fair measure of inbreeding goes without saying). Over the past fifteen or so years this notion has excited international enthusiasm: references are made here to genetically-orientated surname-studies carried out on communities – mostly small and isolated ones – in Brazil, the French West Indies, Hawaii, Israel, the Italian and the Swiss Alps, Japan, Mexico, Newfoundland, North India, Peru, Pitcairn Island, the Pyrenees, Sardinia, Taiwan, Tasmania, and various parts of the United States (a good few of the relevant papers appear together in a symposium represented in *Human Biology* for May 1983). Of the twelve chapters, Great Britain gets four, these being supported by an appendix of maps and graphs showing the distributions of one hundred surnames chosen from among those of people whose marriages were registered in England and Wales during the first quarter of 1975; the present review will address only this British material.

For a non-mathematician to venture to criticize so heavily statistical a work is rash, because analytical techniques might well have compensated for what look like inappropriate selections of material – and, if so, I apologize unreservedly for what follows. Yet choice and assessment of raw material are at least as important as mode of analysis, which they ought partly to govern; and there are signs that care expended on the former has failed to match that devoted to the latter. Indeed, the nature of naming is imperfectly understood: saying that 'Smith was already recorded in Anglo-Saxon times' (p. 68) reveals confusion between name and descriptive term. Further confusion seems to have been fundamental to the methodology:

> In using a surname model to study its effects [*viz.*, those of migration], . . . one is concerned with migration from a single angle as the mechanism that redistributes genes geographically (p. 73, cf. p. 3).

What names indicate is partly, however, cultural rather than physical inheritance, and explanations here leave it uncertain how far analysis has allowed for this. At times truth hovers nearer, as in this comment on a name-survey of the Reading area:

> ... differences between coefficients are more likely to depend on random variations in the frequency of common surnames such as Smith than on such meaningful events such as the concentration of (generally rare) surnames of immigrants in selected cities. . . . The possibility of such findings being based on the history of surnames rather than on the genetic structure of the populations must be borne in mind (pp. 64–5).

But the insight comes late in the day.

Suspicions of too little attention having been given to 'the history of surnames' are confirmed by the eight-page bibliography: this lists Reaney's *Dictionary of British Surnames* [*DBS*] but not his *Origin of English Surnames*, one article of Peter McClure's and one of Richard McKinley's, but not a single volume of the English Surnames Series – an omission especially odd in view of the latter's specific and consistent concern with migration-patterns, the major preoccupation of the work under review. These and other failures of documentation prevent any creation of an historical perspective. The account of Scottish, Irish and Welsh history and naming-customs is markedly over-simplified (p. 50). In the event, the main point of historical reference has been *Homes of Family Names in Great Britain*, published in 1890 by H.B. Guppy (a surgeon by training and a naturalist by persuasion) and based upon a survey of yeoman farmers.

The reader's nascent unease is not allayed by details of presentation. References to 'the city of Kidlington' (near Otmoor) are puzzling (pp. 56, 63; but in *Annals of Human Biology* V [1978] Lasker said 'town'). A note under the distribution-map for *Marshall* comments that this name is 'usually considered to derive from "mare-schalks" (horse-groom or farrier) rather than from the French "marechal" '. The note on *Kelly* reads:

> Seated in the Devonshire parish of Kelly near the Cornish border since the twelfth century and frequent in these two south-western counties when Guppy wrote. However, the present distribution of *Kelly* is marked by its association in the same districts as recently introduced Irish surnames.

A couple of glances at *DBS* would have recalled, to any in need of a reminder, that the distinction made over the etymology of *Marshall* is one without a difference and that in most of England *Kelly* is indeed of predominantly Irish (and Manx) origins.

In the book's own context, the latter type of confusion is the more crippling, and it is pervasive. Among 'principal assumptions', it is laid down that normally 'surnames are monophyletic [*viz.*, each originating from a single family] and sharing a surname means sharing an ancestor from whom it was derived'; when once the 'extent of deviation' from this and other assumptions has been assessed, then, it is suggested, 'estimates of inbreeding from marital isonymy [*viz.*, the sharing of a surname by marriage-partners] can be improved' (pp. 21–2). This premiss is a mirror-image of what anthroponymists believe, which is that English surnames are almost all 'poly-phyletic', ones that stem from single ancestors being the exceptions; even toponymic surnames, the classic raw-material for study of migration-patterns, are deemed seldom to carry clear implications of common ancestry. Lasker himself, as noted, does become disquieted at the dominance of some findings by the frequent and immensely poly-phyletic names like *Smith*; and, from all points of view, this is the central problem of the project. Inability to follow the mathematics admittedly leaves the reviewer uncertain how far statistical techniques may have succeeded in palliating the inconvenience, for geneticists, that it is not the same Richard's genes that have shaped everyone called *Richardson*. In discussion, certainly, the question of 'polyphyly', although acknowledged in the passing here and also elsewhere in articles by the same team (e.g., pp. 4, 18; cf. *Annals of Human Biology* XII [1985], 397–401), is not faced fair and square; despite recognizing rare surnames as more likely to be localizable and even sometimes identifiable as probably monophyletic (e.g., pp. 24, 57–8), the authors persist in concentrating on ones frequent enough to provide substantial statistical samples. So the hundred surnames whose distributions are plotted include not only *Kelly* and *Marshall* but also *Baker, Brown, Carter, Cook, Green, Hill, Martin, Miller, Mills, Palmer, Parker, Short* (with a note alleging a sixteenth-century special link with Bideford; but cf. *DBS*), *Smith, Taylor, White, Wood, Wright* and *Young*. To a non-statistician's eye, some of the maps reveal little more than predictable clustering around London, Birmingham, the Liverpool-Manchester area, and, to a lesser extent, Newcastle-upon-Tyne.

No more remarkable are some of the other findings, such as that, in England, Irish surnames and Indian ones tend each to be found in clusters (p. 70). The discovery that in small traditional English communities close kin often dwell side by side (p. 59) might – if needing verification – have been reached more efficiently through a questionnaire-survey, which, unlike surname-analysis, would not have slighted the distaff side sometimes dominating such arrangements. As for cousin-marriage, central to the genetic theme, surname-based estimates of its incidence are admitted often to exceed, on occasion by as much as ten times, ones derived from pedigrees or from ecclesiastical dispensations (see, for instance, the studies of Eriskay and of the Orkneys reported in *Human Biology* for May 1983, by A.P. Robinson and by D.F. and M.J. Roberts respectively).

The present criticisms are not meant to imply the basic concept behind such work to be invalid. If determining general migration-patterns within England over the last eight or so centuries would benefit historical geneticists, this could certainly – as the English Surnames Series is beginning to demonstrate – be achieved through judicious exploitation of surname-evidence. Material would have, however, to be selected on principles different from those adopted here. In the context of the English 'breeding population', *Kaur, Mistry*, and *Patel* must be discarded as representing, in Lasker's own terminology, 'religious isolates'. *Edwards, Jones* and *Williams* must not be classed as 'Welsh' in the same sense as *Evans, Griffith(s), Morgan* and *Price* are (in mapping the hundred chosen surnames it was in any case ill-advised to treat 'England and Wales' as a unity). *Jones*, although extemely frequent and by no means exclusively Welsh in origin, cannot, being an *-s* patronymic, be treated as geographically neutral in the way that, say, *Smith* is. Apart from toponymic surnames referring to uniquely-named places, relevant categories of name include: (a) formations of specifically Welsh, Scottish and Irish types; (b) patronymics and metronymics based on medieval personal-names of geographically restricted currency, especially Welsh and Anglo-Scandinavian ones; (c) names involving dialectal lexis, phonology, orthography, or morphology, preferably taken in comparison with differently localized counterparts (e.g., ones like *Holmes*, or like the synonymous sets *Barker/Tanner, Dyer/Lister, Fuller/Tucker/Walker*; patronymics in *-s* and in *-son* contrasted with each other and with endingless ones; doublets like *Auld(s)/Old(s), La(i)ng/Long, Rae/Roe, Read(e)/Reid*, and so on; topographical formations in *-er*, such as *Hiller* and *Waterer*, compared with the synonymous *Hill(s)*, *Atwater*, and so on). The mapping of widespread names like *Smith* is (as Lasker and Mascie-Taylor acknowledged in *Journal of Biosocial Science* XVI [1984], 301–08) of value mainly for providing normal distributions against which to assess the regionally-skewed ones.

Not only differently chosen material but also a more complex and more rigorous scheme of historical comparison is required, with a longer time-scale. Present-day distribution maps must be superimposed, in the first instance, upon corresponding ones based upon thirteenth- and fourteenth-century materials such as estate surveys, manor-court rolls, Hundred Rolls, Lay Subsidy Rolls, and so on; and the process must be repeated for each intervening century. As far as data allow, note should be taken of social class, because this is partly definable in terms of interbreeding taboos, and also, for post-Reformation periods, of religion. Full attention must be paid to economic and social background. Such a project would require the enlistment of archivists, historians and philologists as well as of statisticians; but only by working on such a scale and with such a wide range of expertise can valid conclusions – whether genetically, socio-economically, or culturally framed – be reached about the nature of English population-movements.

27

Review

RICHARD McKINLEY, *The Surnames of Sussex*, English Surnames
Series V, Oxford: Leopard's Head Press, 1988, xiv + 483 pp.

This latest volume in the English Surnames Series opens up the unbroached area south
of the Thames, linking Sussex styles with those of the contiguous counties of Kent,
Surrey and Hampshire, and at the same time setting them in the wider context of
medieval English ones as a whole. Format and approach follow the established pattern.
    Geography and history combined to make medieval Sussex idiosyncratic. Unlike
most counties previously surveyed – with the partial exception, that is, of Oxfordshire
– it was all but free of Scandinavian influences. Its long Channel coastline did, on the
other hand, lay it open to Continental ones, Flemish as well as French, that stemmed as
much from mercantile contacts as from post-Conquest settlement. Inland, by contrast,
the Weald kept it isolated until well into modern times; toponymical by-names found
here seldom therefore originate from other counties. As for emigration out of Sussex,
the present remit has allowed no more than a glance at the by-name evidence; but in
medieval London, at all events, Sussex toponymics were notably scarcer than ones
from the neighbouring counties (see, e.g., E. Ekwall, *Studies on the Population of
Medieval London* [Lund, 1958], p. lx).
    Among regional onomastic markers, modes of patronymic formation have long been
recognized. In Sussex, the asyndetic mode characterizing twelfth-century usages
remained dominant, so that forms in *-e* were rare until after 1500 and ones in *-son*
hardly seen except as imports; the three contiguous counties show usages partly
related. A less-recognized form of regional variation involves skewed distribution of
standard terms for universal occupations: *smith*, for instance, proves relatively scarce
here – evidently, as McKinley indicates, because in Sussex ironworking skills were so
widespread as to lose identificatory value (pp. 228–9; this would, besides, have limited
call for full-time practitioners). Minor local quirks include an unexplained tendency
for by-names usually ending in ME unstressed *-e* to acquire a *-y*, e.g., *Leggy* beside
Legge.
    From the outset, the strength of this series has lain in its socio-onomastic approach;
and here too socially-based patterns are brought to the fore. Perhaps because isolation
meant stability, Sussex usages exemplify with particular clarity the general constras-
tive distribution between – to use the reviewer's terminology rather than the author's –
the two sorts of locative by-name. Toponymical formations, no matter whether the
place-names concerned were native ones or exotics, were characteristic, first, of landholders and, later, also of burgesses; among bondmen they were rare. Conversely, it
was mainly the humbler countryfolk, serfs and smallholders, who were labelled by
topographical phrases in *-atte*; that this is more marked in Sussex than in any county
previously surveyed seems due to local preference for this mode over the patronymic
one favoured among some peasantries elsewhere (did this preference, in turn, reflect

richer small-scale variation in the landscape?). Within the general pattern, local idio-syncrasy further asserts itself in interchanges, for the same individuals, between phrasal styles and synonymous compound terms in -*er* and in -*man*, so that, e.g., *atte bridge* varies with *bridger* and/or *bridgeman*; both latter styles, as well as sharing the same social distribution as the phrasal one, seem virtually confined to the more southerly counties. As for what may have underlain the formal variation, that remains unexplained.

Readiness to admit perplexity serves the author particularly well over nicknaming, in so far as it precludes the sort of mechanical etymologizing that mars much recent work in this field. Nor does a resultant tentativeness at all detract from the truth of the perspective:

> It is especially difficult to be sure of the significance of some compound surnames which occur independently in different parts of the country and which seem, there-fore, to be derived from phrases which were in general use over a large area, and which presumably had some generally understood meaning or implication. . . . For example, the rare name Strokehose. . . . It must be suspected that 'strokehose' was a phrase in general use in south-east England, that it conveyed to contemporaries some fairly precise impression of an individual so nicknamed, and that the surname was not merely a soubriquet bestowed on someone who had a habit of stroking his lower garments (p. 362).

The relevant fascicule of the *Middle English Dictionary*, when subsequently published, failed to afford any enlightenment on this point. Meanwhile, the socio-linguistic per-spective adopted here gets nearer to the motivation behind the naming than any purely lexical one ever could.

Sadly, the weak point is again philology (cf. John Insley's comments in *Nomina*, VI [1982], 96–7; also the present reviewer's, *ibid.*, III [1979], 113). Treatment of pronunci-ation, the basis of all linguistic analysis, is hamstrung by refusal to adopt the Inter-national Phonetic Alphabet; in all future volumes in the series, this system, which a single-page key makes accessible to all, must be used throughout. Awareness of pro-nunciation would enable phonological probabilities, and with them likely etymologies, to be better assessed than at present they are. Especially often confused are reflexes of the Old English voiced palatal and velar spirants. Thus, *Fagger/Vagger* is guessed to be a variant of *fayre* (p. 266): etymologizing this admittedly difficult name depends upon whether <-gg-> represented /g/ or /dʒ/, and in the latter event might involve the *fadger* 'flatterer' here virtually dimissed. Again, *Judwin* is claimed, regardless of the difficulty posed not just by substitution of /dʒ/ for the /g/ expected before a back vowel but indeed by initial /dʒ/ in any form supposedly of Old English origin, to be a variant reflex of OE *Goldwine*. Examples could be multiplied. Nor is the principle observed of interpreting spellings in the light of usages in the particular documents concerned. So an obeisance towards dialectology predictably collapses (pp. 15–19), leaving any neo-phyte likely to suppose vowels free to interchange at random. Much in need of annota-tion are the various reflexes of OE /y(:)/, as in, e.g., developments from OE *bydel* (pp. 261–2). If, as may be surmised, these reticences arise partly from fear of putting 'the general reader' off, they are self-defeating; for only by recourse to all technicalities can the points at issue be clarified and the uninitiated reader be assisted. In future, there-fore, the introductory chapters to volumes in this series must deal with orthographical and phonological history as well as with dialect.

Analogous bowdlerization obscures the surname-forming rôle of Old English personal names. Sometimes a potentially relevant name is seemingly overlooked, as when the surname *Elmer* is considered without mention of OE *Ælfmǣr* and such realizations of it as *Elfmær*, *Elmær*, *Elmer* (p. 162; for *El*-forms in the Domesday texts, found in Sussex as well as in Kent, Surrey and Hampshire, see O. von Feilitzen, *The pre-Conquest Personal Names of Domesday Book*, Nomina Germanica III [Uppsala, 1937], 148–9). Such mention of these names as is made is often circumlocutory to the point of euphemism: thus, 'It has been held that the surnames Lemmer and Lemm are both derived from an Old English personal name . . .' (p. 165, OE *Lēofmǣr* being left unspecified); and so almost consistently. Not only are Old English names seldom cited but, when they are, often they masquerade under nonce-spellings, sometimes Latinized ones, sometimes not: e.g., 'The personal name Brithmer or Bricmar' (p. 311; OE *Beorhtmǣr*) or 'the personal names Aluuinus, Goduinus, Vluuardus and Aluuardus' (p. 301; OE *Ælfwine* or, perhaps less probably, *Æðelwine*, *Ealdwine* or *Ealhwine*; *Godwine*; *Wulfweard*; *Ælfweard*). Why standardized citation-forms are avoided, and indeed why the customary italicization of specimen forms is eschewed, is left unexplained. Introductory chapters ought in future to include – in addition to the matters already requested – a digest of the principles and history of Germanic, and therefore Old English, personal-naming; for, once the reader may be assumed conversant with the concept of 'name-themes', then items like *Ælf*-, *Beorht-/-beorht*, *-mǣr*, *-wine*, and so on may confidently be introduced.

In one uncharacteristic lapse, prosopographical as much as etymological, a Continental-Germanic name borne by a recent immigrant is mistaken for a native one:

> The personal name Saefrith (or Seffrid) was that of two bishops of Chichester in the 12th century. . . . In this case the use by two bishops of a rare Old English name . . . (pp. 312–13).

But Bishop Seffrid I (1125–45), previously abbot of Glastonbury, was a brother of the archbishop of Canterbury Ralph d'Escures (see D. Knowles *et alii*, *The Heads of Religious Houses* [Cambridge, 1972], 51) and his name, taken from his own father's, is thus a reflex of CG *Sigefrid*, *Seifrid*.

In several other ways too, presentation might be improved. An additional index, of topics treated, would greatly help those readers more concerned with general principles than with particular names. In addition to the various matters already suggested, the introductory chapter needs to include analysis and criticism of the source-materials available and an exposition of how their character governs methodology; better still, a companion handbook might be provided for the whole series (an encounter with some amateur surname-enthusiasts has convinced the reviewer not only of the need for such a researcher's manual but also of the likelihood of its finding, if appropriately marketed, a ready sale). That is by no means to imply that either source-criticism or methodology is disregarded here: problems of both sorts are judiciously aired, but piecemeal, as occasion arises, instead of being the subject of systematic prolegomena – and, without an index of topics treated, there is little way of tracking the mentions down. So anyone not already knowing what a 'subsidy roll' is, let alone that it is by definition a dog-Latin document, might well sometimes get befogged, especially when expected spontaneously to recognize which forms cited were current vernacular ones and which documentary constructs. Again the lack of precision seems due to fear of being over-technical, and again it is misguided, because the less experienced the reader envisaged, the greater the need to give explicit descriptions and to use terms compatible with those found in standard reference-works. Not only, therefore, ought name-forms always to be precisely specified but place-names ought to be referred to the historical – and EPNS – counties rather than being trendily described as, e.g., 'Bellingham (Greater London)' (p. 17; *rectè* 'Kent': see J.K. Wallenberg, *Place-Names of Kent* [Uppsala, 1934], 6–7, and M. Gelling, *Place-Names in the Landscape* [London, 1984], 48–9). If only findings were given in all their full-blooded technicality, these surveys would at one and the same time strengthen our discipline and implant understanding of it in the public mind.

Any shortcomings noted here are nevertheless – and this must be emphasized – incidental and venial ones such as might be obviated by enlisting collaborators or advisers to supply any specialized skills needed. The great merit of the English Surnames Series, and of this addition to it, stands: in contrast with other recent works based on similar source-materials, these studies never lose sight of the special nature of naming, as distinct from common vocabulary, and so proceed consistently in terms of social status, of domicile and landholding, of migration-patterns, of economic activity, of gender and familial relationships, of types of milieu, and of ramification of individual clans. Etymology is not the core of the matter; still less so phonology. What is central is onomastic history; and that is honourably served.

Onomastic Index

This index is intended, not as a list of every name found in the book, but simply as an aid to finding any personal name or place-name, medieval or modern, that is cited in the text for its *onomastic* interest, rather than for the historical interest of its bearer. This limited aim, together with various difficulties and inconsistencies which the process of indexing uncovered in the studies reprinted here, has necessitated various editorial decisions and compromises which ought to be stated. First, Cecily Clark's own methods of citation sometimes vary. Usually she gives an entire name exactly as it stands in the document under discussion ('Willelmi Hering', 'Iohannis Swin'); occasionally baptismal names are given on their own and modernized ('Edith', 'Mary'); sometimes a hybrid form is given, where a modernized baptismal name is combined with an unmodernized by-name ('Robert de Iekesle', 'Geoffrey of La Leie'). Rather than impose on this edition a uniformity that the author herself obviously thought unnecessary, I have indexed each name in the form cited in the book; the only attempt at standardization has been to change to the nominative Latinized forms originally given in the genitive or dative. In particular, the reader should be warned that forms beginning with I and J, and those beginning with UU and W, are indexed separately. Secondly, the author sometimes (not always) provides 'normalized' forms for personal names (typically Old English, Old Norse or Continental Germanic) in addition to the documentary forms actually recorded; in the index these are listed in the main sequence prefixed by a dagger (†). Thirdly, in the original articles variant forms are sometimes grouped together under lemmata, but sometimes not, and here, after some hesitation, I have decided to index each such form separately. The vast majority of variant forms are to be found near each other in the index as it stands, or are easily accessible elsewhere (for example, variants of names beginning with Æ will be found under A and E); moreover, in most cases, the reader who locates one or two forms will very easily be guided to the full citation of variants in the main text. Cross-references have, however, been supplied for the indexes of modern personal names and of place-names, partly because the variants or referents are not always so easy to locate, at least in the former case.

Other editorial conventions are straightforward. Minor spelling variants within individual names, and queries, are supplied in round brackets, square brackets being reserved for expansions of abbreviated forms. Names beginning with Æ are listed within the A-sequence, but those beginning with 3 follow G, with Q or Ø follow O, with Đ or Þ follow T, and with Ƿ follow W. The erratic capitalization follows the practice of the original articles and reviews. Finally, I have not thought it necessary to index the various trade-names discussed in the review on pages 374–6.

Osbertus Curteis 190
Osbertus de coquina 210
Osbertus Grasporee 196, 210
Osbertus pechet 240
Osbertus Pret 193
Osbertus se Cocchere 191, 210
Osbertus se Cockere 191, 210
Osbertus se Lithle 191
Osbertus Spinke 194
Osbertus Veyrheaued 194
Oscitelus 27
Oscitellus son of Saxferð 30
†Õscytel 280
Oscytel 29, 29 n. 86, 30
Osebernus . . . of Soham 28
†Õsfrið 245 n. 21
Osgodus de mendam 330
Os3gote . . . his wife 343
†Õslāc 28 n. 77
Oslac son of Appe 28
Oslac kinsman of Hawardus 28
Oslac comes 30
Oslacus 28
Oslacus comes . . . his son 27, 27 n. 65
†Õsmund 28 n. 75
Osmundus 28, 188
Osmundus, cognomento Hócere 211
Osmundus de fraxino 200
†Osulf 120 n. 17
Osulf . . . his son 28
Osulfus 28
Osuui brother of Ulf 30
Osuuoldus 28
Oswald 29, 29 n. 86, 30
Osward 186
Osward . . . his son 291
†Õsw(e)ald 28 n. 75, 29 n. 86
Osw(e)ard 291
Oswi brother of Uvi 30
†Õswīg 27 n. 48
†Õswulf 28 n. 76
†Otger 251 n. 52
Otho, aurifaber 121, 140
Othulf of Exning 27
†Oðinn 248 n. 38
Oðon 34
Ouile, de 324
ou[ile], Hugo de 336
ouile, Simon de 336
Ouuilla, Simon de 336
Oxe, Windei 194
Oylman 268

†Qnundr 248 n. 38

†Øthin 288, 295

Pacoc, Vitalis 194
Paganus Peche 239, 240
palmarius, Æluricus 338
Palmarius, Ricardus 138
palmer, Rainulfus le 338
palmerarius 304 n. 12
palmerarius, Iohannes 338
Palmere, Godere le 191
Palmere, Godere se 191
Palmere, Robertus 191
Pape 278, 285 n. 27
Pardic(h), Willelmus 194
Pardiu 277
parere, Ædwardus 212
Parere, Eadwardus 212 . . . his son 212
Parere, Edwardus 212
Parere, Hamo, son of Eadwardus 212
Paris, de 272
Parlur, Le 269
(parmenter), Reginoldus Hoker, filius
    Salomonis Hoker 189, 211
Parva Dunham, Iohannes Kide de 260
Parvus 191, 270
Parvus, Henricus 261
'passeflambardus', Randulfus, episcopus 325
Passelewe, Saman 276
Pasteit 275
pater Ingelranni, Arturus 316
pater Willelmi de Albinico, Main 306
Patfot, Rogerus 195
Paue 296
Paue . . . his son 285 n. 27, 296
†Paul 274
Paulinus 340, 341
Paumier, Goderus 191
Peachey (family) 240
Peccatum 163, 240
Pecceþ 163
Peche, Paganus 239, 240
Peche(t) 88, 228, 239
pechet, Osbertus 240
Pedeleuere, Willelmus 196
peleam, Hugo de 330
Pelerun, Iohannis 190
pelliparius 199
Pende, Robertus atte 213
Pendere (li) 213 n. 26
Pendere, Gilebertus 213
Pendere, Willelmus 213
Penteneye, Willelmus de 261
Peper 269, 278
Perci, de 324

PERSONAL NAMES: MODERN

PLACE-NAMES

Index of Words and Phrases

This index lists all words and phrases discussed or mentioned in the text for their linguistic interest, excluding stems, prefixes and suffixes. Latinized word-forms in the vernacular, and phrases blending two or more languages, are indexed under both the languages concerned. Middle English words cited by the author in modernized spelling are indexed as Middle English items where the context makes it clear that it is the medieval use that is relevant.

1. OLD ENGLISH

æ 34
æcer 195, 201
æsc(here) 33
æt ðam niōwum gatum 198
æt ðam reādum gatum 198
æt ðam cwēnan gatum 198
ampulla 208
*bagga 198
barow 240
bearg 211
beornan 240
birnan 211
bolla 196
bonda 34
botl 220
boþl 220
bræc 192
brǣc 192
brǣmel 239
brec 192
brēden 199
bregge 199
brēmel 239
brēo 192
brio 192
brōc 192
brycg 199
(in) burgimoto 200
bydel 236, 382
cǣg 209
cald 33
(se) calewa 186 n. 11
calu 186 n. 11
canne 210
ceallian 33
cēpan 195 n. 32
cicc 193, 218
cild 226, 238
cler(e)c 194
cniht 34

coppe 216
(æt þam) coppe 216
corn 210
cot(e) 219
cræt 210
crips 293
crocca 210
*croccere 198
croperer 290 n. 40
croppars 290 n. 40
cropper(e) 290 n. 40
cuppe 210
cyrps 293
cȳta 219
*cyte 219
dīc 149
dod 195, 195 n. 28
dreng 33
(se) dysiga 191
ealdormann 34
eofor 93
eorl 20, 21, 21 n. 9, 25, 28, 31, 33, 34, 35, 36
fann 214
fannian 214
fearh 219
fearr 219
fesan 34
folclagu 34
forwegen 33
fretan 195
fyrh 219
gæst 239
gafol 33
glōf 211
God 195
grǣg 237
greidle 190 n. 21
grēon 198 n. 37
grīon 198 n. 37

grið 32, 34, 35, 36
griðian 34
griðleas 34
hālig 199
hardheort 194
hæring 216
hæsel 368 n. 29
hāt 199
hātan 195
hǣðen 199
heall 198
h(e)armes 195–6 n. 32
hearmes cēpan 195 n. 32
hell 199
heregeatu 33
heretoga 21
hlǣfdige 34
hlāford 34
hlāw 149 n. 9
hnott 237
hnutu 237
hōc 211
hold(as) 25, 195
holh 198
(h)reðer 198
hryðer 198
hyll 199
hyrst 240
icchen 195 n. 29
lagu 34, 35, 36
līm 211
loc 195
loddere 199
lytig 285 n. 27
mǣdere 201, 212
mangian 210
*medere 212
melne 198
mylen 198, 212
niowe 198

2. MIDDLE ENGLISH

3. MODERN ENGLISH

arboretum 366
bill 366, 366 nn. 24, 25
bill-hook 366, 366 n. 24
chatt 356
child 226
cod(fish) 270 n. 51
courteous 85
falchion 366 n. 23
farrow 219
February 151

*(to) hoove 375
(to) hoover 375
lac(tic) 376
pad 196
pat (vb) 195 n. 30
pat (adj.) 195 n. 30
peppery 111
scatch 219
secretary 151
sheepcot 199 n. 38

(sherris) sacke 375
sickle 365
snow 376
spicy 111
surname 373
veterinary 151
viva 375
(to) xerox 375

4. OLD FRENCH

barat(e) 215, 239
baret 197
bai 276 n. 87
batere(s) 209
bateur 209
bay 276 n. 87
beau lieu 149 n. 9
bedel 236
bonnetier 209
braceur 227
bugne 372
burel 210
burellier 210
caillon 364
calvellus 186
calz 149, 149 n. 10
car(n) 196 n. 34
caretier 210
chald 149, 149 n. 10
charetier 210
chiche 210
clerc 194
cocart 240
cochet 237
coldraie 367, 368
conte 34
coppier 210
coq 240
cordewantuer 199
corueis(i)er 199, 227
coudraie 369 n. 34, 367,
  368, 369
co(u)dre 367, 367 n. 28,
  368, 369
coudre croule 367 n. 27
coudreel 367
coudrei 367 n. 28
coudrele 367

coudrete 367
coudriere 367
coudroie 367
co(u)ldre 367, 368
coupier 210
crestel 217
cretel 217
crispin 293
curlew 197
(uersus) danjvn 200
de 173
(fossam) del bali 200
del braccin 200
del east al west 200
del parc 200
(uiam) del suth 200
enfant 238
escache 219
eschace 219
eschequer 218
(de) escorgeria 201
establier 213
estreis 372
fagard 211
fauchoun 365, 366, 366 n. 22
faucille 365
faucillon 365, 365 nn. 19,
  21, 366
feinier 211
fenier 211
ferr'ant 219
ferré 219
fourbeur 211
fourbisseur 211
franc 238
(ad) gaiole 200
genestier 240
grancia 200

grangia 200
gris 237
greidle 190 n. 28
harenc 216
(de) hostelerie 201
(h)uissier 214
(uersus) kemin 200
le 200
(de) lescorcherie 201
(uersus) lest 200
loremier 200
louet 113
lung tens 201
maçacrier 212
macheclier 212 n. 19
macun 199, 200
mal(e) 196
mal(e) fai 303 n. 10
malfait 303 n. 10
mansois 136 n. 101
marechal 378
marle 212
marleor 212
mercier 200
monjoie 234 n. 58
moulinier 212
noble 197
paiantur 200
pardurableliche 197
parere(s) 212
pareur 212
pechié 240
peivere 111 n. 46
peivre 111
pendere 213
pendeur 213
pëon 236
pesche 240

5. MODERN FRENCH

6. FLEMISH

7. MIDDLE DUTCH

8. MODERN GERMAN

9. MODERN DANISH

10. OLD NORSE

11. CONTINENTAL GERMANIC

12. LATIN

Index of Manuscripts